CREDITS FILMS ON OFFER 1993

Compiler / Editor
Siobhan Rowe

Production Manager
Tom Brownlie

Assistance
Christina Berry
Peter Cargin
Jim Dempster
Vanessa Maddox
Ainé O'Halloran
Juliet Roberts
Linda Woods

Special thanks to
James Brown (FB)
Markku Salmi
Pat Toomey (GB)
Tise Vahamagi
Andrew Youdell

Publication Design
Siobhan Rowe

Cover Design
Juliet Roberts

Disc Conversion
Comtech

Printer
Warwick Printers

British Library Cataloguing in Publication Data
FILMS ON OFFER. – 1993
1. MOVING PICTURES - CATALOGS
1. BRITISH FILM INSTITUTE

ISBN 0 - 85170 - 379 - 8

Copyright ©
British Film Institute

Published 1992 by
British Film Institute
21 Stephen Street
London W1P 1PL
Tel: 071 255 1444
Fax: 071 436 7950

CONTENTS

Over the years, Films On Offer has come to act as a barometer for Film Distribution in the UK. Recent editions of the publication have noted the decreasing role 16mm has been playing in the distribution cycle: cinema release, non-theatrical release, video then broadcast. More recently, the video release has eclipsed the non-theatrical release, creeping ever closer to the commercial opening, with satellite intercepting the first broadcast before tertiary delivery.

From the above, it may come as a surprise that Films On Offer continues to be published. But this is a sign of the fact that 16mm non-theatrical releases continue to have a role to play in exhibition throughout the UK. In 1991, of the 220 commercial cinema releases 134 found their way to 16mm. The obstacle is not so much lack of demand but cost. Unless distributors are able to buy good quality prints from the negative they are forced to make reversals - often costing more and of an inferior quality. This, in turn, puts off an audience who are seeking ever improving standards of presentation.

This edition of Films On Offer has been tailored to meet the changing needs of today's film exhibitor. In addition to the standard listings of feature films we have incorporated additional information:

a) 35mm Distributor

For the first time we have endeavoured to include the original 35mm distributor of the feature. You will see from glancing at the listings that this is not exhaustive. This is due to limitations, however, our policy has been to include the information from 1990 onwards (unless the 16mm distributor has given the name of the supplier) in addition to a number of key films which will always be in demand.

b) Shorts

The listing of short films returns after an absence of two editions. Again this is not complete. We have included a wide variety of material and a list of specialised libraries where the exhibitor will be able to take any further enquiries.

c) Video

As in the last edition of Films On Offer the availability of the title on video is identified by marking the entry in bold. Placed alongside the 1990 - 1991 edition of this catalogue, one can see roughly how video has expanded since then.

Cyrano de Bergerac, voted Film of the Year 1992 by the British Federation of Film Societies.

Finally, we hope that the new improved design of Films On Offer will make the publication more attractive and accessible. Siobhan Rowe is to be congratulated for the time and effort which has gone into the compilation. This has been built on the foundations laid out by Sarah Woods, Therese Cochrane and Ian Gilchrist - all previous compilers of Films On Offer. We would also like to thank all those individuals listed whose assistance has been invaluable in compiling this edition.

Tom Brownlie
Head of Film Society Unit

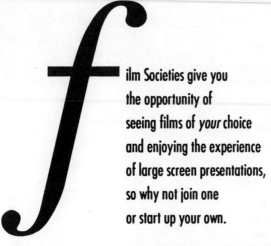

*f*ilm Societies give you
the opportunity of
seeing films of *your* choice
and enjoying the experience
of large screen presentations,
so why not join one
or start up your own.

**BFFS
21 STEPHEN STREET
LONDON W1P 1PL
TEL: 071 255 1444**

**The BFFS is a
Registered Company in England
No.1391200.
Limited by
Guarantee.
Registered Charity
No.276633**

The **British Federation of Film Societies** has over 60 years of experience in advising, campaigning and offering their services to film societies. So drop us a line or call us at the address above.

The **BFFS** is internationally recognised as the representative body of the Film Societies of Great Britain. When you become a member of the BFFS you are entitled to:

A copy of the Film Society Handbook
Bi-monthly copies of the BFFS journal FILM
Two annual film brochures
Information supplements
Invitation to BFFS Viewing Sessions
Opportunity to attend training events
Publicity materials for your society
Updates on film availability
Daily access to advice and support
Network of local support
News from the International Federation of Film Societies

----

please photocopy

Please send me:

Details of the British Federation of Film Societies	(free) ☐
The address of my nearest film society	(free) ☐
A copy of the *Film Society Book* which gives all the information needed to set up and run a film society.
I enclose a cheque/postal order in favour of the BFFS.	£11.50 ☐

Name

Address

Date

DISTRIBUTORS

The following is a list of Distributors referred to in the publication with their appropriate abbreviation. Please note that some distributors have their material handled by other agents. The listings provide the contact of where the print of the relevant gauge is available from.

AC
Arts Council Film Department
14 Great Peter Street
London SW1P 3NQ
Tel: 071 333 0100
Fax: 071 973 6590

AE
Artificial Eye
211 Camden High Street
London NW1 7BT
Tel: 071 267 6036
Fax: 071 267 6499

AMBER
Amber Films
9 Side
Newcastle upon Tyne NE1 3JE
Tel: 091 232 2000
Fax: 091 230 3217

APO
Apollo Film Distributors
14 Ensbury Park Road
Bournemouth
Dorset BH9 2SJ
Tel: 0202 520962

ARROW
Premier House
77 Oxford Street
London W1R 1RB
Tel: 071 437 4415

BAFC
Black Audio Film Collective
89 Ridley Rd
London E8 2NH
Tel: 071 254 9527

BFI
BFI Film + Video Distribution
British Film Institute
21 Stephen Street
London W1P 1PL
Tel: 071 255 1444
Fax: 071 436 7950

BD
Blue Dolphin Films
15/17 Old Compton Street
London W1V 7FS
Tel: 071 439 9511
Fax: 071 287 0370

CHC
Canadian High Commission
Film and Video Library
Canada House
Trafalgar Square
London SW1Y 5BJ
Tel: 071 629 9492
Fax: 071 321 0025

CEDDO
Ceddo Film and Video Ltd
South Tottenham Education Centre
Braemar Road
London N15 5EU
Tel: 081 802 9034
Fax: 081 800 6949

CFL
CFL Vision
Distribution Centre
PO Box 35
Wetherby
Yorkshire LS23 7EX
Tel: 0937 541010
Fax: 0937 541083

CN
Cine Nova
113 Roman Road
London NW3 3NR
Tel: 081 981 6828
Fax: 081983 4441

CA
Cinema Action
27 Winchester Road
London NW3 3NR
Tel: 071 586 2762
Fax: 071 722 5781

COL
Columbia Tri-Star Films (UK)
19 - 23 Wells Street
London W1P 3FP
Tel: 071 580 2090
Fax: 071 528 8990

CONC
Concord Video and Film Council
201 Felixstowe Road
Ipswich
Suffolk IP3 9BJ
Tel: 0473 726012

CONT
Contemporary Films
24 Southwood Lawn Road
Highgate
London N6 5SF
Tel: 081 340 5715
Fax: 081 348 1238

CZN
(see MAYFAIR)

DISNEY
(see WARNER)

ELEC
Electric Pictures
15 Percy Street
London W1
Tel: 071 636 1231

ENT
Entertainment Film Distributors
27 Soho Square
London W1V 5FL
Tel: 071 439 1606
Fax: 071 734 2483

ETV
Educational and Television Films
247a Upper Street
London N1 1RU
Tel: 071 226 2298

F
Twentieth Century Fox
20th Century House
31 - 32 Soho Square
London W1V 6AP
Tel: 071 437 7766
Fax: 071 437 1625
Fax: 071 381 2405

FB
Filmbank Distributors
Grayton House
498 - 504 Fulham Road
London SW6 5NH
Tel: 071 386 9909
Fax: 071 381 2405

FF
Feature Film Co,
60 - 70 Wardour Street
London W1V 3HP
Tel: 071 734 2266

FI
First Independent Films
69 New Oxford Street
London WC1A 1DG
Tel: 071 379 0406

FOP
Films of Poland
34 Poland Place
London W1N 4HQ
Tel: 071 636 6032

GA
Gala Films
26 Danbury Street, Islington
London N1 8JU
Tel: 071 226 5085

GB
Glenbuck Films
21 Stephen Street
London W1P 1PL
Tel: 071 957 8938

Haven't a clue where/else to look for information on films and videos?

Don't worry! The <u>British National Film & Video Catalogue</u> has the answers.

For details contact: Maureen Brown, Editor
BNFVC, 21 Stephen Street, London W1P 1PL
Telephone: 071-255 1444

BRITISH FILM INSTITUTE
bfi

Films  Offer

GFL
German Film Library
(see GLENBUCK)

GU
Guild Film Distribution
Kent House
14 - 17 Market Place
Great Titchfield Street
London W1N 8AR
Tel: 071 323 5151
Fax: 071 631 3568

GSV
Guild Sound and Vision
6 Royce Road
Peterborough PE1 5YB
Tel: 0733 315315
Fax: 0733 315395

IAC
IAC Film & Video Library
24c West Street
Epsom
Surrey KT18 7RJ
Tel: 0372 739672

ICA
ICA Projects
12 Carlton House Terrace
London SW1Y 5AH
Tel: 071 930 0493
Fax: 071 873 0051

JB
Jane Balfour Films Ltd
Burghley House
35 Fortress Road
London NW5 1AD
Tel: 071 267 5392
Fax: 071 267 4241

LAW
Leeds Animation Workshop
45 Bayswater Row
Leeds
West Yorkshire LS8 5LF
Tel: 0532 484997

LFMC
London Film Makers Co-op
42 Gloucester Avenue
London NW1 8JD
Tel: 071 586 4806

MAIN
Mainline Pictures
37 Museum Street
London WC1A 1LP
Tel: 071 242 5523
Fax: 071 430 0170

MAY
Mayfair Entertainment
9 St Martin's Court
London WC2N 4AJ
Tel: 071 895 0328
Fax: 071 895 0329

MP
Metro Pictures
79 Wardour Street
London W1V 3TH
Tel: 071 734 8508
Fax: 071 287 2112

NFS
National Film and Television School
Beaconsfield Studios
Beaconsfield
Bucks HP9 1LG
Tel: 0494 671234
Fax: 0494 674042

OA
Oasis (UK) Films
66 - 68 Margaret Street
London W1N 7FL
Tel: 071 734 7477
Fax: 071 734 7470

PO
The Post Office
Film and Video Library
PO Box 145
Sittingbourne
Kent ME10 1NH

PREMIER
(see ARROW)

R
Rank Film Distributors
127 Wardour Street
London W1V 4AD
Tel: 071 437 9020
Fax: 071 434 3689

RESP
Respectable Films
Silver Place
(off Beak Street)
London W1
Tel: 071 437 8562

RSPB
RSPB Film & Video Library
15 Beaconsfield Road
London NW10 2LE
Tel: 081 451 1127

SAN
Sankofa
Unit K
32 - 34 Gordon House Road
London NW5 1LP
Tel: 071 485 0848
Fax: 071 485 2869

SCFL
Scottish Central Film Library
74 Victoria Crescent Road
Dowanhill
Glasgow G12 9JN
Tel: 041 334 9314
Fax: 041 334 6519

SG
Sheila Graber Animation
50 Meldon Avenue
South Shields
Tyne and Wear NE34 0EL
Tel / Fax: 091 455 4985

SQUIRREL
119 Rotherhithe Street
London SE16 4NF
Tel: 071 231 2209
Fax: 071 231 2119

TCM
Twentieth Century Movies
120 Queen Margaret Drive
Glasgow G20 8N7
Tel: 041 946 1121

UIP
Mortimer House
37 - 41 Mortimer Street
London W1A 2JL
Tel: 071 636 1655
Fax: 071 636 4118

VIS
Viscom Ltd
Film & Video Communications
Park Hall Road Trading Estate
London SE21 8EL
Tel: 081 761 3035
Fax: 081 761 2876

W
Warner Brothers Distributors
135 Wardour Street
London W1V 4AP
Tel: 071 734 8400
Fax: 071 437 5521

WFA
Workers Film Association
9 Lucy Street
Manchester M15 4BX
Tel: 061 848 9782

FILMBANK
PRESENTS

Tim Burton's
BATMAN RETURNS

Lawrence Kasdan's
GRAND CANYON

Randa Haine's
THE DOCTOR

John Mackenzie's
RUBY

Ron Howard's
FAR AND AWAY

COMING SOON...

Roland Joffe's
CITY OF JOY

Francis Ford Coppola's
DRACULA

**FILMBANK
DISTRIBUTORS
LIMITED**

CATALOGUE AVAILABLE AT £10, RING THE BOOKINGS DEPT FOR DETAILS ON (071) 386 5411.
FILMBANK DISTRIBUTORS LTD, GRAYTON HOUSE, 498-504 FULHAM ROAD, LONDON SW6 5NH.

Genesis.

EXPLANATORY NOTES

The following notes clarify the terms used in the listings. Please read them carefully to as the exact title you are looking for and enable you to get the most out of this publication.

Feature Film Listings
A 'feature film', for the purposes of Films On Offer is defined as a film of 60 mins running time or over. The listing is predominantly geared towards fiction although one or two regularly requested non-fiction titles (over 60 mins) are included.

Titles
The following guidelines have been adopted, not as a rigid system, but to direct users to the information required.

British Titles of American Films
The film is listed under its British release title rather than the American title (eg *The Mean Machine* rather than *The Longest Yard*) unless the British title has fallen into disuse (eg *Damn Yankees* as opposed to *What Lola Wants*). If there are two titles still current, there is a cross reference back to the original title (eg *Build My Gallows High* see *Out Of The Past*).

Foreign Language Titles
The main reference is to the original language title unless the film is rarely referred to in that form (eg *Battleship Potemkin* is not cross-referenced to *Bronenosets Potemkin*). Conversely, if a film is usually referred to according to its foreign title and never according to its English title (eg *Les Biches* has no entry under *The Does*). Where both foreign and English titles have currency, both titles are listed and the English titles cross-referred to the original (eg *The Wanderer* see *Le Grand Meaulnes*).

Video Availability
Feature films which are available on video for group viewing are indicated by bold typeface entries in the Features listings (NB Video availability is not recorded in the Shorts Section). Video rental fees will be less than that listed for the 16mm hire and in the majority of cases will be available from the same source as the 16mm print. Since video operates at 25 frames per second the running time will be marginally shorter than the print, which screens at 24 fps. While titles may not be in bold it does not mean that they are unavailable for purchase for home use.

Country of Production
The country of production of any title depends on the registered nationality of the production companies involved and not on the location of production, where the film was first released nor the present name of such countries. The abbreviations used are:

ALB	Albania
ALG	Algeria
AN	Angola
ARG	Argentina
AUST	Austria
AUSTR	Australia
BEL	Belgium
BER	Bermuda
BF	Bukino Faso
BOL	Bolivia
BRAZ	Brazil
BULG	Bulgaria
CAN	Canada
CB	Cuba
CE	Ceylon
CH	Chile
CHI	China
COL	Colombia
CR	Costa Rica
CYP	Cyprus
CZ	Czechoslovakia
DEN	Denmark
EGY	Egypt
EIR	Ireland
EL SAL	El Salvador
ERI	Eritrea
FIN	Finland
FR	France
GB	Great Britain
GER	Germany
GR	Greece
GUY	Guyana
HK	Hong Kong
HOLL	Holland
HUNG	Hungary
ICE	Iceland
IND	India
IR	Iran
IS	Israel
IT	Italy
JAM	Jamaica
JAP	Japan
KEN	Kenya
LEB	Lebanon
LIECH	Liechtenstein
MART	Martinique
MEX	Mexico
MON	Monaco
MOR	Morocco
MOZ	Mozambique
NAM	Namibia
NETH	Netherlands
NGA	Nigeria
NIC	Nicaragua
NOR	Norway
NZ	New Zealand
PAK	Pakistan
PAL	Palestine
PAN	Panama
PER	Peru
PHIL	Philippines
POL	Poland
PORT	Portugal
RUM	Romania
S. AFR	South Africa
SEN	Senegal
SP	Spain
SWE	Sweden
SWITZ	Switzerland
SYR	Syria
TAI	Taiwan
TAN	Tanzania
THAI	Thailand
TUN	Tunisia
TUR	Turkey
UAR	United Arab Republic
UN	United Nations
URU	Uruguay
USA	United States of America
W. AFR	West Africa
W. GER	West Germany
YUGO	Yugoslavia

Year of Production

A self-explanatory entry indicating the year of completion of each film - not necessarily the year of release in Britain or its country of origin.

Running Time

The running time in this column is the running time of the original British release. Where this differs significantly from the version offered for hire, the 'Version' column will provide the relevant information .

Version

The information in this column will assist the exhibitor in selecting the most appropriate print for their screening. The following abbreviations are used:

sc	scope
std	standard
est	English subtitles
gst	German subtitles
eng	English version
fr dia	French dialogue
bw	black and white
t	tinted
col	colour
sd	sound
st	silent
dub	dubbed
nar	narrated
mag	magnetic sound track
ws	wide screen

The joint abbreviation **sc/std** means that both versions are available.

Black and White - **bw** indicates that, although the film was shot in colour, only monochrome copies are available for hire. You may otherwise assume that the prints on offer are colour or black and white depending on the original version.

Crocodile Dundee with subtitles for the hearing impaired.

16mm Distributor

The listed distributor is the company you should contact for the hire of the 16mm print - all addresses, phone and fax numbers are listed in the introduction section.

Catalogue Rate

The hire fee listed is the Renter's published rate for a single non-

Scope - scope prints require an anamorphic lens in order to project the print from you projector. BFFS members are able to hire such lenses by contacting their regional group or head office.

Standard - this indicates that although the film was shot in an anamorphic ratio, standard ratio prints are available. This may mean that some of the image has been cropped or has been electronically scanned, thereby altering the composition of the shot.

Wide screen - like standard, does not require an anamorphic lens. It will mean 'bands' at the top and the bottom of your picture - but this, which can be masked is preferable to cropping and scanning.

Sound and Silent - for films made before the arrival of sound, the entry in the version column will show either **sd** or **st**. If a music or effects track has been added, this is denoted by **sd**. If the print is mute, this is denoted by **st**.

Magnetic Sound - a very small number of prints are offered with a magnetic soundtrack (as opposed to optical). Such prints require projectors which can play sound from a magnetic stripe. Check your projector before hiring such prints.

35mm Distributor

This column lists the original 35mm distributor of the film in Britain. This is new to the publication and is limited to recent releases and selected 'classics'.

theatrical screening of the 16mm print. It should be noted when budgeting that this price is exclusive of carriage and VAT. Most distributors will be happy to negotiate discounts for block bookings.

PLEASE NOTE
The information in this book is provided by the Distributors and the BFI takes no responsibility for inaccuracies of rights holders etc. While every care has been taken to ensure that entries are correct we welcome any notes on misprints or suggestions from you, the user, to assist in further editions of the publication.

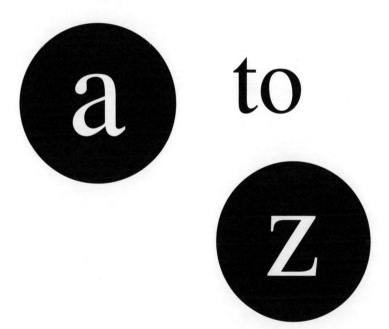

a	COUNTRY OF PRODUCTION	YEAR	DIRECTOR	RUNNING TIME	VERSION	35mm	16mm	16mm RENTAL FEE
A Propos de Nice	FR	1930	Jean Vigo	26			GB	15
A bout de Souffle	FR	1959	Jean-Luc Godard	90	st	OA	GB	40
ABBA - The Movie	SWE/AU	1977	Lasse Hallström	95	sc		FB	33
Abbott & Costello Meet Captain Kidd	USA	1952	Charles Lamont	79			GB	20
Abbott and Costello Go to Mars	USA	1953	Charles Lamont	77			FB	15
Abbott and Costello in Hollywood	USA	1945	S. Sylvan Simon	83			FB	15
Abbott and Costello in the Foreign Legion	USA	1950	Charles Lamont	78			FB	15
Abbott and Costello Meet the Keystone Kops	USA	1955	Charles Lamont	79			FB	15
Abdication, The	GB	1974	Anthony Harvey	103			FB	18
Abel Gance - The Charm of Dynamite	GB	1968	Kevin Brownlow	50			CONC	12
Abilene Town	USA	1946	Edwin L. Marin	89			GB	25
Abominable Dr Phibes,The	GB	1971	Robert Fuest	94			FB	18
About Mrs. Leslie	USA	1954	Daniel Mann	104			FB	15
About Last Night	USA	1986	Edward Zwick	113			FB	50
Above Us the Earth	GB	1977	Karl Francis	85			BFI/CONC	30
Above Us the Waves	GB	1955	Ralph Thomas	99			FB	15
Abraham Lincoln	USA	1930	D.W. Griffith	93			BFI	25
Absence of Malice	USA	1981	Sydney Pollack	116			FB	43
Absent Minded Professor, The	USA	1961	Robert Stevenson	96			FB	22
Absolute Beginners	GB	1986	Julien Temple	109	sc/std		GB	60
Abused Love Letters, The	W.GER	1969	Hans Dieter Schwarze	91	est		GFL	0
Accused, The	USA	1988	Jonathan Kaplan	110			FB	60
Ace of Aces	USA	1933	J. Walter Ruben	75			GB	15
Aces High	GB/FR	1976	Jack Gold	114			FB	22
Acre of Seats in a Garden of Dreams, An	GB	1973	Cinema Architecture	56			GB	20
Across 110th Street	USA	1972	Barry Shear	99			FB	18
Across the Great Divide	USA	1977	Stewart Raffill	89			GB	35
Across the Pacific	USA	1942	John Huston	97			FB	22
Across the Wide Missouri	USA	1951	William A. Wellman	77	bw		FB	15
Act of Murder, An	USA	1948	Michael Gordon	91			FB	15
Act of Violence	USA	1948	Fred Zinnemann	82			FB	15
Action by the Arsenal	POL	1978	Jan Lomnicki	100	est		FOP	0
Action in Arabia	USA	1944	Leonide Moguy	76			GB	15
Action in the North Atlantic	USA	1943	Lloyd Bacon	128			FB	22
Actor's Revenge, An	JAP	1963	Kon Ichikawa	113	sc/est	BFI	BFI	30
Actress, The	USA	1953	George Cukor	90			FB	15
Ada	USA	1961	Daniel Mann	108	std		FB	18
Adam's Rib	USA	1949	George Cukor	101			FB	15
Adieu Philippine	IT/FR	1962	Jacques Rozier	110	est		GB	25
Adolf Hitler - My Part In His Downfall	GB	1972	Norman Cohen	102			FB	22
Adventure Girl	US	1934	Herbert C. Raymaker	76			GB	15
Adventure in Baltimore	USA	1949	Richard Wallace	89			GB	15
Adventures of a Brown Man in Search of Civilisation	GB	1971	James Ivory	56			GB	20
Adventures of a Brown Man in Search of Civilisation	GB	1971	James Ivory	52			CONT	10
Adventures of a Rookie	USA	1943	Leslie Goodwins	67			GB	33
Adventures of Artyomka, The	USSR	1956	A. Apsolon	70	est		ETV	10
Adventures of Barry MacKenzie, The	AUSTR	1972	Bruce Beresford	114			FB	18
Adventures of Goopy and Bagha, The	INDIA	1968	Satyajit Ray	117	est		GB	25
Adventures of Hal 5	GB	1982	Don Sharp	59			GB	15
Adventures of Hercules II	USA	1984	Lewis Coates	99			FB	35
Adventures of Huckleberry Finn, The	USA	1960	Michael Curtiz	107	sc/std		FB	22
Adventures of Ichabod and Mr. Toad, The	USA	1949	Jack Kinney/Clyde Geronimi/ James Algar	68			FB	27
Adventures of Mark Twain, The	USA	1944	Irving Rapper	130			FB	15
Adventures of Prince Achmed, The	GER	1926	Lotte Reiniger	65	col/sd		GB	25
					bw/sd		GB	20
Adventures of Robin Hood, The	USA	1938	Michaell Curtiz/ William Keighley	111		UIP	FB	22
Adventure of Sherlock Holmes' Smarter Brother, The	USA	1975	Gene Wilder	90			FB	25
Adventures of the Wilderness Family, The	USA	1975	Stewart Raffill	95			GB	35

	COUNTRY OF PRODUCTION	YEAR	DIRECTOR	RUNNING TIME	VERSION	35mm	16mm	16mm RENTAL FEE
Adventures of Tom Sawyer, The	USA	1938	Norman Taurog	93		GB	GB	20
Adversary, The	INDIA	1970	Satyajit Ray	112	est		GB	25
Aelita	USSR	1924	Yakov Protazanov	90	bw		BFI	55
Affair to Remember, An	USA	1957	Leo McCarey	115	std		FB	18
Affair With a Stranger	USA	1953	Roy Rowland	87			GB	15
Affair, The	USA	1973	Gilbert Cates	92			GB	18
Affairs of Dobie Gillis, The	USA	1953	Don Weis	72			FB	15
African Lion, The	USA	1955	James Algar	67			FB	27
African Queen, The	GB	1951	John Huston	103			GB	50
After Hours	USA	1985	Martin Scorsese	97			FB	50
After the Fox	IT/USA	1966	Vittorio De Sica	103	sc		FB	18
After Tonight	USA	1933	George Archainbaud	71			GB	15
Against All	CZ	1957	Otakar Vavra	120	est		ETV	12
Against All Flags	USA	1952	George Sherman	82			FB	18
Against All Odds	USA	1984	Taylor Hackford	121			FB	45
Against the Grain	GB	1983	Margaret Dickinson	52			AC	15
Agatha	USA	1978	Michael Apted	98			FB	33
Age d'Or, L'	FR/SP	1930	Luis Buñuel	63	est		CONC	40
Age of Consent	USA	1932	Gregory La Cava	65			GB	15
Age of Consent	AUSTR	1969	Michael Powell	98			FB	18
Age of Innocence	CAN/GB	1977	Alan Bridges	100			FB	27
Agent for H.A.R.M.	USA	1966	Gerd Oswald	83	bw		FB	15
Aggie Appleby, Maker of Men	USA	1933	Mark Sandrich	73			GB	15
Agnes of God	USA	1985	Norman Jewison	98			FB	40
Agony and the Ecstasy, The	USA/IT	1965	Carol Reed	139	sc/std		FB	18
Aguirre, The Wrath of God	W.GER	1972	Werner Herzog	95	est		GB	35
Ai No Corrida (see, In The Realm of the Senses)								
Air America	US	1990	Roger Spottiswoode	112			GU	80
Air Force	USA	1943	Howard Hawks	124			FB	15
Airplane!	USA	1980	Jim Abrahams/David Zucker/Jerry Zucker	89			FB	48
Airplane II - The Sequel	USA	1982	Ken Finkleman	84			FB	48
Airport	USA	1970	George Seaton	136	std		FB	33
Airport 1975	USA	1974	Jack Smight	107	std		FB	38
Airport '77	USA	1977	Jerry Jameson	114	sc/std		FB	43
Airport '80: The Concorde	USA	1979	David Lowell Rich	114			FB	48
Akira	JAP	1988	Katsuhiro Otomo	124	st	BD	GB	70
Akira Kurosawa's Dreams	USA	1990	Akira Kurosawa	119		W	FB	60
Aladdin and His Magic Lamp	FR	1969	Jean Image	70			GB	25
Alan Quatermain and the Lost City of Gold	USA	1986	Gary Nelson	100			FB	45
Alex and the Gypsy	USA	1976	John Korty	99			FB	18
Alexander Nevsky	USSR	1938	Sergei Eisenstein/D. Vasiliev	112	est/dub	CONT	GB	25
Alf Garnett Saga, The	GB	1972	Bob Kellett	93			FB	18
Alfie	GB	1966	Lewis Gilbert	114	std		FB	18
Alfie Darling	GB	1975	Ken Hughes	102			FB	22
Alfred the Great	GB	1969	Clive Donner	122	sc/std		FB	24
Ali Baba and the Forty Thieves	USA	1944	Arthur Lubin	86	bw		FB	15
Alias a Gentleman	USA	1948	Harry Beaumont	76			FB	15
Alias French Gertie	USA	1930	George Archainbaud	71			GB	15
Alias Nick Beal	USA	1949	John Farrow	93			FB	15
Alias Will James	CAN	1988	Jacques Godbout	83			CHC	0
Alibi is Not Everything, An	CZ	1961	Vladimir Cech	94	est		ETV	10
Alice	USA	1991	Woody Allen	105		R	FB	75
Alice	SWITZ	1988	Jan Svankmajer	84	eng	ICA	BFI	50
Alice Adams	USA	1935	George Stevens	100			GB	15
Alice Doesn't Live Here Anymore	USA	1974	Martin Scorsese	112			FB	18
Alice in the Cities	W.GER	1974	Wim Wenders	110	est	BFI	BFI	45
Alice in Wonderland	USA	1951	Clyde Geronimi/Hamilton Luske/ Wilfred Jackson	75			FB	35
Alice's Restaurant	USA	1969	Arthur Penn	110			FB	22

a

	COUNTRY OF PRODUCTION	YEAR	DIRECTOR	RUNNING TIME	VERSION	35mm	16mm	16mm RENTAL FEE
Alien	GB	1979	Ridley Scott	116	sc/std		FB	45
Alien³	USA	1992	David Fincher	114	F		FB	75
Aliens	USA	1986	James Cameron	137			FB	50
Alive and Kicking	GB	1958	Cyril Frankel	94			FB	15
All at Sea	GB	1969	Ken Fairbairn	60			GB	25
All Coppers are...	GB	1971	Sidney Hayers	87			FB	18
All Creatures Great and Small	GB	1974	Claude Whatham	92			FB	27
All Dogs Go to Heaven	EIRE	1989	Don Bluth	85	R		FB	55
All Fall Down	USA	1962	John Frankenheimer	110			FB	15
All For Mary	GB	1955	Wendy Toye	79	bw		FB	15
All I Desire	USA	1953	Douglas Sirk	79			FB	22
All Mine to Give	USA	1957	Allen Reisner	102			GB	18
All Neat in Black Stockings	GB	1969	Christopher Morahan	99			FB	18
All Night Long	USA	1981	Jean-Claude Tramont	88			FB	43
All of Me	USA	1984	Carl Reiner	91			FB	40
All Quiet on the Western Front	USA	1930	Lewis Milestone	103		UIP	FB	22
All Quiet on the Western Front	USA	1979	Delbert Mann	129			GB	43
All That Heaven Allows	USA	1955	Douglas Sirk	89	bw		FB	15
All That Jazz	USA	1979	Bob Fosse	123			FR	43
All the Brothers Were Valiant	USA	1953	Richard Thorpe	94			FB	15
All the Fine Young Cannibals	USA	1960	Michael Anderson	122	std		FB	18
All the King's Men	USA	1949	Robert Rossen	109			FB	15
All the President's Men	USA	1976	Alan J. Pakula	138			FB	27
All the Way Up	GB	1970	James MacTaggart	97			FB	18
All This and World War II	USA	1976	Susan Winslow	99			FB	17
All Through the Night	USA	1942	Vincent Sherman	107			FB	22
All-Round Reduced Personality, The	W.GER	1977	Helke Sander	98	est		MP	46
Allegheny Uprising	USA	1939	William A. Seiter	82			GB	15
Alligator Named Daisy, An	GB	1955	J. Lee Thompson	88	bw		FB	15
Almonds and Raisins	GB/USA	1983	Russ Karel	90			GB	40
Almost a Gentleman	USA	1939	Leslie Goodwins	75			GB	20
Almost An Angel	USA	1990	John Cornell	95		UIP	FB	60
Almost Summer	USA	1977	Martin Davidson	89			FB	33
Almost There	GB	1984	Jayne Parker	103			CIRC	40
Aloha, Bobby and Rose	USA	1975	Floyd Mutrux	90			FB	18
Along Lenin's Road	USSR	1968		80			ETV	10
Along the Rio Grande	USA	1941	Edward Killy	64			GB	15
Alphabet Murders, The	GB	1965	Frank Tashlin	90			FB	15
Alphaville	FR/IT	1965	Jean-Luc Godard	98	est		GB	35
Altered States	USA	1980	Ken Russell	102			FB	48
Alvarez Kelly	USA	1966	Edward Dmytryk	109	sc		FB	18
Alvin Purple	AUSTR	1973	Tim Burstall	97			FB	18
Always	USA	1989	Steven Spielberg	123		UIP	FB	65
Always for Pleasure	USA	1978	Les Blank	58			GB	20
Amants, Les	FR	1958	Louis Malle	86	est/std		GB	25
Amarcord	IT/FR	1973	Federico Fellini	123	est		FB	33
Amateur, The	USA	1981	Charles Jarrott	112			FB	40
Amazing Howard Hughes, The	USA	1977	William A. Graham	123			FB	27
Amazing Captain Nemo, The	USA	1978	Alex March	102			FB	27
Amazing Mr. Blunden, The	GB	1972	Lionel Jeffries	99			GB	22
Ambassador, The	USA	1984	J. Lee Thompson	95			FB	40
Ambushers, The	USA	1967	Henry Levin	107			FB	18
America - From Hitler to M X	USA	1982	Joan Harvey	90			MP	46
American Boy: A Profile of Steven Prince	USA	1978	Martin Scorsese	54			BFI	30
American Dreamer	USA	1984	Rick Rosenthal	105			FB	40
American Dreamer, The	USA	1971	Lawrence Schiller/ L.M. Kit Carson	80			GB	22
American Friend, The	FR/ W.GER	1977	Wim Wenders	123	est	BFI	BFI	50
American Friends	GB	1991	Tristram Powell	95		FFC	GB	70

	COUNTRY OF PRODUCTION	YEAR	DIRECTOR	RUNNING TIME	VERSION	35mm	16mm	16mm RENTAL FEE
American Gigolo	USA	1980	Paul Schrader	117			FB	43
American Graffiti	USA	1973	George Lucas	110	std		FB	33
American Hot Wax	USA	1977	Floyd Mutrux	92			FB	27
American in Paris, An	USA	1951	Vincente Minnelli	113			FB	26
American Ninja	USA	1985	Sam Firstenberg	95			FB	40
American Ninja 2: The Confrontation	USA	1987	Sam Firstenberg	89			FB	40
American Tale II: Fieval Goes West, An	USA	1991	Phil Nibbelink/Simon Wells	75	C		FB	65
American Tragedy, An	USA	1931	Josef von Sternberg	100			FB	15
Amiche, Le	IT	1955	Michelangelo Antonioni	104	est		GB	25
Amityville Horror II: The Possession	USA	1982	Damiano Damiani	105			FB	40
Among the Living	USA	1941	Stuart Heisler	72			FB	15
Amore	W.GER	1977	Klaus Lemke	73	est		GFL	0
Amore in Città	IT	1953	Dino Risi/MichelangeloAntonioni/ FedericoFellini/Francesco Maselli/ Cesare Zavattini/ Alberto Lattuada	91	est		BFI	25
Amore, L' (A Human Voice and The Miracle)	IT	1948	Roberto Rossellini	79	est		BFI	25
Amorous Adventures of Moll Flanders, The	GB	1965	Terence Young	123	sc/std		FB	18
Amorous Milkman, The	GB	1974	Derren Nesbitt	94			FB	33
Amorous Prawn, The	GB	1962	Anthony Kimmins	89			FB	15
Amour Par Terre, L'	FR	1984	Jacques Rivette	127	est		FB	70
Ampersand	GB	1978	Stuart Pound	70			LFC	30
Amsterdam Kill, The	HK	1977	Robert Clouse	93	sc		GB	33
Angel At My Table, An	NZ	1990	Jane Campion	160		AE	GB	70
Anastasia	USA	1956	Anatole Litvak	105	sc/std		FB	18
Anatomy of a Murder	USA	1959	Otto Preminger	140			FB	15
Anatomy of an Opera: Jonathan Miller	GB	1978	Alan Benson	68			AC	19
Anchors Aweigh	USA	1945	George Sidney	140			FB	24
...And Justice For All	USA	1979	Norman Jewison	119			FB	33
And Now for Something Completely Different	GB	1971	Ian MacNaughton	88			FB	22
And Now the Screaming Starts!	GB	1973	Roy Ward Baker	91		GB	GB	22
And Soon the Darkness	GB	1970	Robert Fuest	100			FB	18
And the Ship Sails On	FR/IT	1983	Federico Fellini	128	eng		FB	70
And Then There Were None	USA	1945	René Clair	97			GB	16
Anderson Tapes, The	USA	1971	Sidney Lumet	98	std		FB	18
Andrei Rublev	USSR	1966	Andrei Tarkovsky	183	sc/est	AE	GB	70
Androcles and the Lion	USA	1952	Chester Erskine	98			GB	15
Andromeda Strain, The	USA	1970	Robert Wise	131	sc/std		FB	18
Andy Hardy Comes Home	USA	1958	Howard W. Koch	77			FB	15
Andy Hardy's Blonde Trouble	USA	1944	George B. Seitz	107			FB	15
Andy Hardy's Double Life	USA	1942	George B. Seitz	92			FB	15
Angel	EIRE	1982	Neil Jordan	92			BFI	35
Angel Dust	FR	1987	Edouard Niemens	95	est		GB	50
Angel Face	USA	1953	Otto Preminger	90		GB	GB	15
Angel Heart	USA	1987	Alan Parker	113			FB	60
Angel Wore Red, The	IT/USA	1960	Nunnally Johnson	99			FB	0
Angel's Holiday	CZ	1955	Martin Fric	63	est		ETV	10
Angela Davis: Portrait of a Revolutionary	USA	1971	Yolande Duluart	62			GB	15
Angels With Dirty Faces	USA	1938	Michael Curtiz	94			FB	22
Anger Magick Lantern Cycle	USA	1947-1970	Kenneth Anger	158	col/bw		BFI	60
Angry Hills, The	GB	1959	Robert Aldrich	105	std		FB	15
Angry Silence, The	GB	1960	Guy Green	95			FB	15
Animal Crackers	USA	1930	Victor Heerman	93			FB	15
Animal Farm	GB	1954	John Halas/Joy Batchelor	73		BFI	BFI	35
Animals Film, The	GB/USA	1981	Victor Schonfeld/ Myriam Alaux	136			CONC/GB	40
Ankur	INDIA	1974	Shyam Benegal	131	est		GB	30
Ann Vickers	USA	1933	John Cromwell	72			GB	15
Anna Christie	USA	1930	Clarence Brown	90			FB	22
Anna Karenina	USA	1935	Clarence Brown	93			FB	22

a	COUNTRY OF PRODUCTION	YEAR	DIRECTOR	RUNNING TIME	VERSION	35mm	16mm	16mm RENTAL FEE
Annabel Takes a Tour	USA	1938	Lew Landers	67			GB	15
Annapolis Salute	USA	1937	Christy Cabanne	65			GB	15
Anne Devlin	EIRE	1984	Pat Murphy	121		GB	GB	52
Anne of the Thousand Days	GB	1969	Charles Jarrott	146	std		FB	33
Anne of Windy Poplars	USA	1940	Jack Hively	86			GB	15
Anne Trister	CAN	1986	Lea Pool	105			GB	60
Annie	USA	1982	John Huston	128	sc/std		FB	60
Annie Hall	USA	1977	Woody Allen	93		UIP	FB	38
Annie Oakley	USA	1935	George Stevens	90			GB	15
Annie's Coming Out	AUSTR	1984	Gil Brealey	92			GB	50
Anno Uno (see Italy: Year One)								
Anoop and The Elephant	GB	1972	David Eady	55			GB	17
Another Country	GB	1984	Marek Kanievska	90			GB	50
Another Face	USA	1935	Christy Cabanne	70			GB	15
Another Man, Another Woman	FR	1977	Claude Lelouch	132			FB	18
Another Part of the Forest	USA	1948	Michael Gordon	108			FB	15
Another Shore	GB	1948	Charles Crichton	77			FB	15
Anou Banou or The Daughters of Utopia	FR W.GER	1983	Edna Politi	85	est		CIRC	15
Antagonists, The	USA	1980	Boris Sagal	121			FB	33
Any Number Can Play	USA	1949	Mervyn LeRoy	102			FB	18
Any Which Way You Can	USA	1980	Buddy Van Horn	115			FB	43
Anything for Laughs	USA	1961/61	Compilation	57			FB	15
Anything Goes	USA	1956	Robert Lewis	106			FB	15
Apache War Smoke	USA	1952	Harold F. Kress	67			FB	15
Aparajito	INDIA	1956	Satyajit Ray	113	est	CONT	GB	25
Apartment, The	USA	1960	Billy Wilder	125	sc/std		FB	22
Ape and Superape	HOLL/ USA	1972	Bert Haanstra	103			FB	18
Apple Dumpling Gang, The	USA	1975	Norman Tokar	100			FB	33
Apple, The	USA/ W.GER	1980	Menahem Golan	84	sc		FB	38
Appointment in Honduras	USA	1953	Jacques Tourneur	80			GB	27
Appointment With Death	USA	1988	Michael Winner	108			FB	45
Appointment, The	USA	1969	Sidney Lumet	136			FB	26
April Fools, The	USA	1969	Stuart Rosenberg	95	sc/std		GB	18
April in Paris	USA	1952	David Butler	101			FB	18
Arabella	IT	1967	Mauro Bolognini	88			FB	18
Arabian Adventure	GB	1979	Kevin Connor	98			FB	30
Arabian Nights	IT/FR	1974	Pier Paolo Pasolini	128	dub		FB	33
Arachnophobia	USA	1990	Frank Marshall	109			FB	65
Arch of Triumph	USA	1948	Lewis Milestone	120			GB	16
Are These Our Children?	USA	1931	Wesley Ruggles	83			GB	15
Are You Being Served?	GB	1977	Bob Kellett	95			FB	22
Aren't We Wonderful (see Wir Wunderkinder)								
Arena of Fear	AUST	1958	Arthur Maria Rabenalt	95	bw/dub		GB	15
Argent, L'	SWITZ/ FR	1983	Robert Bresson	85	est	AE	GB	50
Argie	ARG/FR	1984	Jorge Blanco	75			ICA	50
Aria	GB	1987	Nicolas Roeg/Charles Sturridge/ Jean-Luc Godard/Julien Temple/ Bruce Beresford/Robert Altman/ Franc Roddam/Ken Russell/ Bill Bryden	89			GB	35
Aria for an Athlete	POL	1979	Filip Bajon	108	est		FOP	0
Ariane	GB/GER	1931	Paul Czinner	70	est		GB	35
Ariel	FIN	1988	Aki Kaurismäki	72	st		GB	70
Arizona Raiders	USA	1965	William Witney	80	sc/std		FB	18
Arizona Ranger, The	USA	1948	John Rawlins	63			GB	15
Arme Mann Luther, Der	W.GER	1964	Franz Peter Wirth	114	est		GFL	0
Armed and Dangerous	USA	1986	Mark L. Lester	88			FB	50
Armoured Car Robbery	USA	1950	Richard Fleischer	68			GB	15

	COUNTRY OF PRODUCTION	YEAR	DIRECTOR	RUNNING TIME	VERSION	35mm	16mm	16mm RENTAL FEE
Army of Lovers	W.GER/ USA	1972/79	Rosa von Praunheim	107			MP	57.5
Arnold	USA	1973	Georg Fenady	95			FB	18
Around the World	USA	1943	Allan Dwan	81			GB	15
Around the World Under the Sea	USA	1966	Andrew Marton	111	std		FB	18
Arrangement, The	USA	1969	Elia Kazan	126	std		FB	18
Arsenal	USSR	1929	Alexander Dovzhenko	92	est/sd		GB	30
Arsenic and Old Lace	USA	1944	Frank Capra	118			FB	22
Art In Revolution	GB	1972	Lutz Becker	50	col/bw		AC	20
Art of Love, The	USA	1965	Norman Jewison	99			FB	18
Art of Worldly Wisdom, The	CAN	1979	Elder Bruce	55			LFMC	46.75
Arthur	USA	1981	Steve Gordon	97			FB	48
Arthur 2: On the Rocks	USA	1988	Bud Yorkin	113			FB	55
Arthur Penn: 1922 Themes and Variants	USA	1970	Robert Hughes	86			BFI	18
Artistes at the Top of the Big Top:Disorientated	W.GER	1968	Alexander Kluge	95	est		GFL	0
Arzt von Stalingrad, Der	W.GER	1958	Geza von Radvanyi	109	bw/est		GFL	0
As You Like It	GB/USA	1978	Basil Coleman	150			BBC	35
Ascendancy	GB	1982	Edward Bennett	85			BFI	40
Ascenseur pour l'Echafaud, L'	FR	1957	Louis Malle	90	est		GB	35
Ashanti	SWITZ	1979	Richard Fleischer	117	sc/std		FB	36
Ashes and Diamonds	POL	1958	Andrzej Wajda	104	est	CONT	GB	25
Ask Any Girl	USA	1959	Charles Walters	98	sc/std		FB	18
Aspern	PORT	1981	Eduardo de Gregorio	97	est		GB	30
Asphalt Jungle, The	USA	1950	John Huston	105			FB	16
Assam Garden, The	GB	1985	Mary McMurray	92			GB	55
Assault	GB	1970	Sidney Hayers	90			FB	18
Assault on a Queen	USA	1966	Jack Donohue	106	std		FB	18
Assault, The	HOLL	1986	Fons Rademakers	148	est		FB	70
Assignment K	GB	1967	Val Guest	97	sc/std		FB	18
Assignment to Kill	USA	1968	Sheldon Reynolds	93	std		FB	18
Asterix and Cleopatra	FR/BEL	1968	René Goscinny/Alberto Uderzo	73	dub	BFI	GB	35
Asterix the Gaul	FR	1967	René Goscinny/Alberto Uderzo	65	dub	BFI	GB	35
Asya's Happiness	USSR	1966	Andrei Milkhalkov-Konchalovsky	98	est		GB	60
Asylum	GB	1972	Roy Ward Baker	88			FB	18
At Close Range	USA	1985	James Foley	114	sc		FB	45
At Long Last Love	USA	1975	Peter Bogdanovich	114			FB	20
At Sword's Point	USA	1952	Lewis Allen	81	col/ bw		GB	20
At the Fountainhead (of German Strength)	GB	1980	Nick Burton/ Anthea Kennedy	96			BFI	35
Atalante, L'	FR	1934	Jean Vigo	85	est	AE	GB	45
Atlantic City USA	CAN/FR	1980	Louis Malle	105			GB	48
Atlantide, L'	FR	1921	Jacques Feyder	121	st/est		BFI	20
Atlantis the Lost Continent	USA	1961	George Pal	89			FB	18
Atomic Café	USA	1982	Kevin Rafferty/Jayne Loader/Pierce Rafferty	89			CONC	45
Atomic Submarine, The	USA	1959	Spencer G. Bennet	75			GB	15
Atragon	JAP	1964	Inoshiro Honda	79	sc/std/		FB	20
Att Älska (see To Love)								
Attack on the Iron Coast	GB	1967	Paul Wendkos	90			FB	18
Attica	USA	1973	Cinda Firestone	80			MP	35
Au Revoir les Enfants	FR/ W.GER	1987	Louis Malle	104	est	GA	GB	65
Audrey Rose	USA	1977	Robert Wise	113	std		FB	27
Augustine of Hippo	IT	1972	Roberto Rossellini	120	est		BFI	25
Aussie Assault	AUSTR	1983	Harvey Spencer	82			GB	35
Author! Author!	USA	1982	Arthur Hiller	110			FB	35
Autobus	FR	1991	Eric Rochant	85		AE	GB	80
Autre Homme une Autre Chance, Un (see Another Man, Another Woman)								
Autumn Afternoon, An	JAP	1962	Yasujiro Ozu	113	est		GB	35
Autumn Sonata	NOR/W.GER	1978	Ingmar Bergman	92	est		GB	38
Avalanche	GB	1975	Frederic Goode	55			GB	25
Avalon	USA	1990	Barry Levinson	126		C	FB	60

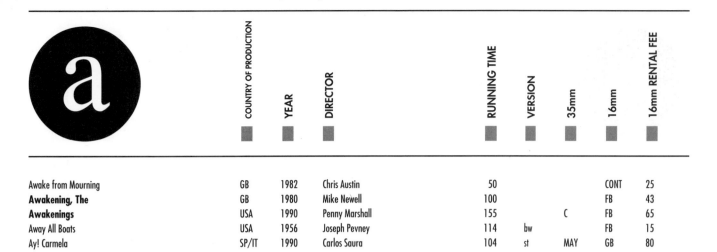

	COUNTRY OF PRODUCTION	YEAR	DIRECTOR	RUNNING TIME	VERSION	35mm	16mm	16mm RENTAL FEE
Awake from Mourning	GB	1982	Chris Austin	50			CONT	25
Awakening, The	GB	1980	Mike Newell	100			FB	43
Awakenings	USA	1990	Penny Marshall	155		C	FB	65
Away All Boats	USA	1956	Joseph Pevney	114	bw		FB	15
Ay! Carmela	SP/IT	1990	Carlos Saura	104	st	MAY	GB	80

Ay! Carmela

	COUNTRY OF PRODUCTION	YEAR	DIRECTOR	RUNNING TIME	VERSION	35mm	16mm	16mm RENTAL FEE
Babe	USA	1975	Buzz Kulik	99			FB	30
Babes in Toyland	USA	1961	Jack Donohue	105			FB	33
Babette's Feast	DEN	1987	Gabriel Axel	103	est		GB	60
Baby Blue Marine	USA	1976	John Hancock	90	std		FB	18
Baby Boom	USA	1987	Charles Shyer	111			FB	50
Baby It's You	USA	1982	John Sayles	104			GB	50
Baby Love	GB	1967	Alastair Reid	96			FB	18
Baby - Secret of the Lost Legend	USA	1984	B.W.L. Norton	93			FB	38
Babylon	GB	1980	Franco Rosso	95			GB	50
Bach & Broccoli	CA	1986	André Melançon	95			GB	40
Bachelor Apartment	USA	1931	Lowell Sherman	77			FB	15
Bachelor Bait	USA	1934	George Stevens	74			GB	20
Bachelor Girl Apartment	USA	1966	Robert Ellis Miller	85	bw		FB	15
Bachelor in Paradise	USA	1961	Jack Arnold	109	sc/std		FB	18
Bachelor Knight	USA	1947	Irving Reis	95			GB	15
Bachelor Mother	USA	1939	Garson Kanin	82			GB	15
Bachelor of Hearts	GB	1958	Wolf Rilla	94	bw		FB	15
Bachelor Party	USA	1984	Neal Israel	107			FB	45
Back Alley Princess	HK	1972	Lo Wei	96	std/dub		GB	22
Back and Forth (——)	CAN	1968/9	Michael Snow	52			BFI/LFC	25
Back From Eternity	USA	1956	John Farrow	97			GB	18
Backlash	USA	1956	John Sturges	83	bw		FB	15
Back Roads	USA	1981	Martin Ritt	95			FB	33
Back Street	USA	1941	Robert Stevenson	89			FB	15
Back Street	USA	1961	David Miller	107			FB	18
Back to Bataan	USA	1945	Edward Dmytryk	91			GB	18
Back to the Future	USA	1985	Robert Zemeckis	116		UIP	FB	55
Back to the Future: Part II	USA	1989	Robert Zemeckis	98		UIP	FB	70
Back to the Future: Part III	USA	1989	Robert Zemeckis	98		UIP	FB	65
Backdraft	USA	1991	Ron Howard	136		UIP	FB	75
Bad Boys	USA	1983	Rick Rosenthal	109			FB	38
Bad Company	USA	1931	Tay Garnett	62			GB	15
Bad Hats	GB	1982	Pascal Ortega	105			GB	45
Bad Lands	USA	1939	Lew Landers	71			GB	15
Bad Man's Territory	USA	1946	Tim Whelan	97			GB	15
Bad Medicine	USA	1985	Harvey Miller	97			FB	40
Bad News Bears	USA	1976	Michael Ritchie	103			FB	27
Bad News Bears in Breaking Training, The	USA	1977	Michael Pressman	100			FB	22
Bad Seed,The	USA	1956	Mervyn LeRoy	128			FB	15
Bad Timing	GB	1980	Nicolas Roeg	122	sc		FB	43
Badge 373	USA	1973	Howard W. Koch	104			FB	18
Badlanders,The	USA	1958	Delmer Daves	83	std		FB	18
Badlands	USA	1973	Terrence Malick	93			FB	18
Baffled!	GB	1972	Philip Leacock	90			GB	18
Bagdad Cafe	USA	1987	Percy Adlon	92			BFI	60
Baited Trap, The	USA	1958	Norman Panama	84	bw		FB	15
Balance, La	FR	1982	Bob Swaim	102	est		FB	60
Ballad of Narayama	JAP	1980	Shohei Imamura	130	est		FB	70
Ballad of a Soldier	USSR	1959	Grigori Chukhrai	87	est		GB	25
Ballad of Cable Hogue, The	USA	1970	Sam Peckinpah	119			FB	18
Ballad of Gregorio Cortez	MEX/USA	1982	Robert M. Young	130			GB	40
Ballad of Josie, The	USA	1967	Andrew V. McLaglen	102			FB	18
Ballad of the Sad Café, The	US	1990	Simon Callow	101		MAY	GB	70
Ballerina	USA/DEN	1965	Norman Campbell	95			FB	27
Ballet Black	GB	1986	Stephen Dwoskin	83			CONC	19
Baltimore Bullet	USA	1980	Robert Ellis Miller	103			FB	38
Bamba, La	USA	1986	Luis Valdez	108			FB	5
Bamboo Blonde	USA	1946	Anthony Mann	67			GB	15

b

	COUNTRY OF PRODUCTION	YEAR	DIRECTOR	RUNNING TIME	VERSION	35mm	16mm	16mm RENTAL FEE
Banana Ridge	GB	1941	Walter C. Mycroft	88			FB	15
Band Waggon	GB	1939	Marcel Varnel	85			FB	22
Bandit General	MEX/USA	1949	Emilio Fernandez	78			GB	15
Bandit of Sherwood Forest, The	USA	1946	Henry Levin/George Sherwin	87			FB	22
Bandit Trail, The	USA	1941	Edward Killy	60			GB	15
Bandits in Rome	IT	1968	Alberto De Martino	104	std/dub		FB	18
Bandolero	USA	1968	Andrew V. McLaglen	106	sc/std		FB	18
Bank Dick, The	USA	1941	Edward Cline	73			FB	15
Bank Shot, The	USA	1974	Gower Champion	84	sc/std		FB	18
Bankbreaker, The (see Kaleidoscope)								
Banner, The	W.GER	1977	Ottokar Runze	122	est		GFL	0
Banners of the Dawn	BOL	1978	Ukamau Group	90	est		WFA	45
Barabbas	IT	1961	Richard Fleischer	139	std		FB	18
Barbarella	FR/IT	1967	Roger Vadim	98	sc/std		FB	18
Barbarosa	USA	1982	Fred Schepisi	90	sc/std	BD	GB	38
Barefoot Executive, The	USA	1970	Robert Butler	96			FB	27
Bargee, The	GB	1964	Duncan Wood	106	std		FB	22
Barnacle Bill	GB	1957	Charles Frend	87			FB	15
Baron Munchhausen	CZ	1962	Karel Zeman	88	est		GB	26
Barquero	USA	1970	Gordon Douglas	109			FB	18
Barracuda	USA	1977	Harry Kerwin	96			FB	22
Barretts of Wimpole Street, The	USA	1956	Sidney A. Franklin	105	sc		FB	18
Barry Lyndon	GB	1975	Stanley Kubrick	187			FB	38
Barton Fink	USA	1991	Joel Coen	117		R	FB	75
Basic Instinct	USA	1992	Paul Verhoeven	128		GU	GU	100
Basic Training	USA	1971	Frederick Wiseman	89			GB	50
Bathing Beauty	USA	1944	George Sidney	101	bw		FB	15
Batman	USA	1989	Tim Burton	126	std	W	FB	65
Batman Returns	USA	1992	Tim Burton	127		W	FB	75
*batteries not included	USA	1987	Mathew Robbins	107			FB	50
Battle at Apache Pass, The	USA	1952	George Sherman	85			FB	18
Battle Beneath the Earth	GB	1967	Montgomery Tully	83			FB	18
Battle Beyond the Stars	USA	1980	Jimmy T. Murakami	102			FB	38
Battle for Anzio	IT	1968	Edward Dmytryk	117	std		FB	18
Battle for the Planet of the Apes	USA	1973	J. Lee Thompson	86	sc/std		FB	20
Battle Hymn	USA	1957	Douglas Sirk	108	sc/std		FB	18
Battle of Britain	GB	1969	Guy Hamilton	131	sc/std		FB	27
Battle of Algiers	IT/ALG	1965	Gillo Pontecorvo	125	est	BFI	BFI	55
Battle of Billy's Pond, The	GB	1976	Harley Cokliss	56			GB	17
Battle of Midway	USA	1976	Jack Smight	133	sc/std		FB	38
Battle of Russia, The	USA	1944	Anatole Litvak/Frank Capra	83			CFL	15
Battle of the Coronel and Falkland Islands, The	GB	1927	Walter Summers	116	st		BFI	15
Battle of the River Plate, The	GB	1956	Michael Powell/Emeric Pressburger	119	bw/std		FB	15
Battle of the Sexes, The	GB	1960	Charles Crichton	84			FB	15
Battle of the Ten Million, The	BEL/FR	1970	Chris Marker	58	est		MP	34.5
Battle of the Villa Fiorita, The	GB	1964	Delmer Daves	105	std		FB	18
Battle Rage (see Missing in Action)								
Battlefield	USA		Judd Taylor	60			FB	8
Battleship Potemkin	USSR	1925	Sergei Eisenstein	70	est/sd		GB	25
					est/st		BFI	20
Battlestar Galactica	USA	1978	Richard A. Colla	117			FB	43
Battling Bellhop (see Kid Galahad)								
Bawdy Adventures of Tom Jones, The	GB	1975	Cliff Owen	93			FB	22
Bawdy Tales	IT/FR	1973	Sergio Citti	82	dub		FB	27
Baxter!	GB/USA	1972	Lionel Jeffries	106			FB	18
Bayan Ko: My Own Country	PHIL/FR	1984	Lino Brocka	108	est		BFI	40
Be Upright and Walk Without Fear	W.GER	1971	Jutta Bruckner	60	dub		GFL	0
Beach of the War Gods	HK	1972	Wang Yu	82	std/dub		GB	22

	COUNTRY OF PRODUCTION	YEAR	DIRECTOR	RUNNING TIME	VERSION	35mm	16mm	16mm RENTAL FEE
Beach Party, The	USA	1963	William Asher	96	sc		FB	18
Beaches	USA	1988	Garry Marshall	123			FB	55
Bear Island	CAN/GB	1979	Don Sharp	118	sc/std		FB	43
Bear's Wedding, The	USSR	1926	Vladimir Gardin/Konstantin Eggert	90	st/est		BFI	30
Bear, The	FR	1988	Jean-Jacques Annaud	98		C	FB	60
Bears and I, The	USA	1974	Bernard McEveety	89			FB	27
Beast in the Cellar, The	GB	1970	James Kelly	87		GB	GB	25
Beast With a Million Eyes	USA	1955	David Kramarsky	80			FB	15
Beast With Five Fingers, The	USA	1946	Robert Florey	82			FB	22
Beast, The	FR	1975	Walerian Borowczyk	96	102/est		GB	40
Beast, The	F'OL	1977	J. Domaradzki	95	est		FOP	0
Beastmaster, The	USA	1982	Don Coscarelli	115			FB	38
"Beat" Girl	GB	1959	Edmond T. Greville	91		GB	GB	25
Beat the Band	USA	1947	John H. Auer	67			GB	15
Beat The Devil	GB	1953	John Huston	92			BFI	25
Beau Geste	USA	1939	William A. Wellman	114			FB	22
Beau Ideal	USA	1930	Herbert Brenon	81			GB	18
Beautiful Blonde From Bashful Bend, The	USA	1949	Preston Sturges	77			FB	18
Beautiful but Dangerous	USA	1954	Lloyd Bacon	92			GB	15
Beautiful Dreamers	CA	1990	John K. Harrison	108		BD	GB	70
Beautiful People	S.AFR	1974	Jamie Uys	93	sc/std		FB	22
Beauty For the Asking	USA	1939	Glenn Tryon	68			GB	15
Beauty Jungle, The	GB	1964	Val Guest	114	std		FB	18
Beaux Souvenirs, Les	CAN	1981	Francis Mankiewicz	113	fr dia		CHC	0
Because I am King	GB	1980	Stewart Mackinnon	76			MP	35
Because You're Mine	USA	1952	Alexander Hall	103			FB	24
Bed of Roses	USA	1933	Gregory La Cava	67			GB	15
Bedford Incident, The	GB	1965	James B. Harris	102			FB	15
Bedknobs and Broomsticks	USA	1971	Robert Stevenson	118			FB	38
Bedlam	USA	1946	Mark Robson	80			GB	15
Bedtime Story	USA	1963	Ralph Levy	99	col/bw		FB FB	18
Beekeeper, The	GR FR	1986	Theo Angelopoulos	121	est		GB	60
Beethoven	USA	1991	Brian Levant	87		UIP	FB	70
Beethoven	E.GER	1978		90			ETV	15
Beetle on an Extra Tour, A (see Kaefer Auf Extratour, Ein)								
Beetlejuice	USA	1988	Tim Burton	92			FB	65
Before Dawn	USA	1933	Irving Pichel	62			GB	15
Before Hindsight	GB	1977	Jonathan Lewis	81			BFI	30
Before Stonewall	USA	1983	Greta Schiller	87			MP	57.5
Before the Monsoon	GB	1979	Michael Grigsby	135			BFI	30
Before the Nickelodeon	USA	1982	Charles Musser	60			BFI	25
Before the Revolution	IT	1964	Bernardo Bertolucci	112	est		GB	25
Begging the Ring	GB	1978	Colin Gregg	55				0
Behave Yourself	USA	1951	George Beck	81			GB	15
Behind Convent Walls	IT	1977	Walerian Borowczyk	96	est		GB	40
Behind the Headlines	US	1937	Richard Rosson	58			GB	15
Behind the Rent Strike	GB	1974	Nick Broomfield	52			CONT	15
Behind the Lines	GB	1971	Margaret Dickinson	55			CONT	10
Behind the Mask	GB	1958	Brian Desmond Hurst	99			GB	25
Behind the Rising Sun	USA	1943	Edward Dmytryk	87			GB	15
Behind the Wall	POL	1971	Krzysztof Zanussi	60	est		FOP	0
Behold a Pale Horse	USA	1964	Fred Zinnemann	121			FB	15
Being There	USA	1979	Hal Ashby	130			GB	43
Believe In Me	USA	1971	Stuart Hagmann	86			FB	33
Believers, The	USA	1987	John Schlesinger	113			FB	55
Bell, Book and Candle	USA	1958	Richard Quine	102	col		FB	15
Bell-bottom George	GB	1944	Marcel Varnel	99			FB	15
Belle de Jour	FT/IT	1967	Luis Buñuel	100	st	ELEC	GB	70

	COUNTRY OF PRODUCTION	YEAR	DIRECTOR	RUNNING TIME	VERSION	35mm	16mm	16mm RENTAL FEE
Belle et la Bête, La	FR	1946	Jean Cocteau	89	est	BFI	GB	35
Belle Noiseus (Divertimenti, La)	FR	1991	Jacques Rivette	126		AE	GB	85
Bells Are Ringing, The	USA	1960	Vincente Minnelli	125	sc/std		FB	24
Belly of an Architect, The	GB/IT	1987	Peter Greenaway	118			GB	40
Beloved Rogue, The	USA	1927	Alan Crosland	99	sd		BFI	20
Belstone Fox, The	GB	1973	James Hill	103			FB	22
Ben	USA	1972	Phil Karlson	94		GB	GB	22
Ben-Hur	USA	1959	William Wyler	213	std		FB	43
Beneath the Planet of the Apes	USA	1969	Ted Post	94	sc/std		FB	20
Bengazi	USA	1955	John Brahm	79	std		GB	15
Benny Goodman Story, The	USA	1955	Valentine Davies	117	col		FB	18
					bw		FB	15
Beowulf	GB	1976	Don Fairservice	60			BFI	22.5
Bequest to the Nation	GB	1973	James Cellan Jones	117			FB	18
Berlin Express	USA	1948	Jacques Tourneur	87			GB	15
Berlin Symphony of a City	GER	1927	Walter J. Ruttmann	69	st		BFI	20
Berlinger	W.GER	1975	Bernhard Sinkel/Alf Brustellin	114	est		GFL	0
Best Age, The	CZ	1968	Jaroslav Papousek	80	est		ETV	15
Best Boy	USA	1979	Ira Wohl	111			CONC	38.4
Best Defence	USA	1984	Willard Huyck	94			FB	45
Best Friends	USA	1982	Norman Jewison	109			FB	40
Best House in London, The	GB	1968	Philip Saville	96			FB	18
Best Intentions, The	SWE	1992	Bille August	181		AE	GB	85
Best Little Whorehouse in Texas, The	USA	1982	Colin Higgins	114	sc/std		FB	43
Best Man, The	USA	1964	Franklin J. Schaffner	104			FB	15
Best of Benny Hill, The	GB	1974	John Robins	88			FB	18
Best of Enemies, The	IT	1961	Guy Hamilton	104	sc/std		FB	18
Best of Everything, The	USA	1959	Jean Negulesco	120	std		FB	18
Best of the Badmen	USA	1951	William D. Russell	84	bw/col		GB	15
Best of Times	USA	1985	Roger Spottiswoode	103			FB	35
Best of Walt Disney's True-Life Adventures, The	USA	1975	James Algar	89			FB	27
Best Seller	USA	1987	John Flynn	95			FB	55
Best Shot	USA	1986	David Anspaugh	115			FB	40
Best Things in Life Are Free, The	USA	1956	Michael Curtiz	104	sc/std		FB	18
Best Way To Walk, The (see Meilleure Facon de Marcher, La)								
Betrayal	GB	1983	David Jones	95			GB	43
Betrayal from the East	USA	1945	William Berke	82			GB	15
Betrayed	USA	1954	Gottfried Reinhardt	108			FB	18
Betrayed	GB/USA	1988	Costa-Gavras	126			FB	60
Betsy's Wedding	USA	1990	Alan Alda	98		W	FB	55
Betsy, The	USA	1978	Daniel Petrie	125			FB	38
Better a Widow	IT/FR	1968	Duccio Tessari	105	dub		FB	18
Better Active Today than Radio-active Tomorrow	W.GER	1977	Nina Gladitz	65	eng		GB	25
Betty Blue	FR	1986	Jean-Jacques Beineix	121	est		BFI	60
Between Heaven and Hell	USA	1956	Richard Fleischer	94	std		FB	18
Between the Lines	USA	1977	Joan Micklin Silver	101			CONC	44
Between Time and Eternity	W.GER	1956	Arthur Maria Rabenalt	98	dub		GB	15
Beverly Hills Cop	USA	1984	Martin Brest	105			FB	60
Beverly Hills Cop II	USA	1987	Tony Scott	103			FB	65
Beyond a Reasonable Doubt	USA	1956	Fritz Lang	80			BFI	20
Beyond the Curtain	GB	1960	Compton Bennett	88			GB	15
Beyond The Forest	GB	1991	Esther Ronay	52			AC	20
Beyond The Maypole	GB	1991	Mike Alexander	52			AC	20
Beyond the Plains Where Man Was Born	GB/FR	1976	Michael Raeburn	95			GB	25
Beyond the Poseidon Adventure	USA	1979	Irwin Allen	113	sc		FB	30
Beyond the River	USA	1956	Henry Hathaway	89	sc		FB	18
Beyond the Time Barrier	USA	1959	Edgar Ulmer	73			FB	15
Beyond the Valley of the Dolls	USA	1970	Russ Meyer	106	sc		FB	19

	COUNTRY OF PRODUCTION	YEAR	DIRECTOR	RUNNING TIME	VERSION	35mm	16mm	16mm RENTAL FEE
Beyond This Place	GB	1959	Jack Cardiff	89		GB	GB	25
Beyond Victory	USA	1931	John S. Robertson	73			GB	15
Bhumika (see Role,The)								
Bible . . . In the Beginning, The	IT/USA	1966	John Huston	159	sc/std		FB	30
Biches, Les	FR/IT	1968	Claude Chabrol	99	est		GB	30
Big	USA	1988	Penny Marshall	112			FB	60
Big Brawl, The	USA	1980	Robert Clouse	95	sc		FB	43
Big Bus, The	USA	1976	James Frawley	89	sc/std		FB	38
Big Business	USA	1988	Jim Abrahams	98			FB	55
Big Catch, The	GB	1968	Laurence Henson	55			GB	17
Big Chill, The	USA	1983	Lawrence Kasdan	105			FB	40
Big City	USA	1948	Norman Taurog	103			FB	15
Big Day, The	GB	1960	Peter Graham Scott	62			GB	15
Big Deal at Dodge City	USA	1966	Fielder Cook	92	bw		FB	15
Big Easy, The	USA	1986	Jim McBride	101			GB	50
Big Family, The	USSR	1954	Josef Heifitz	106	est		ETV	15
Big Fish, The	CZ		Bretislav Pojar	54	est		GB	12
Big Fix, The	USA	1978	Jeremy Paul Kagan	109			FB	38
Big Flame, The	GB	1969	Ken Loach	85			BFI	25
Big Gamble, The	USA	1931	Fred Niblo	63			GB	15
Big Game, The	USA	1936	George Nicholls Jr	75			GB	15
Big George is Dead	GB	1986	Henry Martin	60			KO	
Big Hangover, The	US	1949	Norman Krasna	82			FB	18
Big Heart, The (Miracle on 34th Street)	USA	1947	George Seaton	97			FB	15
Big Jake	USA	1971	George Sherman	110	sc		GB	18
Big Job, The	GB	1965	Gerald Thomas	88			FB	15
Big K	GB	1975	Antonia Caccia and Others	52			CONT	20
Big Land, The	USA	1957	Gordon Douglas	92			GB	18
Big Leaguer	USA	1953	Robert Aldrich	72			FB	15
Big Man	UK	1990	David Leland	116		MAY	GB	
Big Money, The	GB	1956	John Paddy Carstairs	85			FB	15
Big Noise, The	USA	1944	Mal St. Clair	75			FB	15
Big Parade of Comedy	USA	1964	Compilation	90			FB	15
Big Picture	USA	1988	Christopher Guest	101			GB	60
Big Red	USA	1961	Norman Tokar	89			FB	27
Big Red One, The	USA	1980	Samuel Fuller	113			GB	43
Big Shot, The	USA	1937	Edward Killy	82			GB	27
Big Shot, The	USA	1942	Lewis Seiler	82			GB	20
Big Sky, The	USA	1952	Howard Hawks	122		GB	GB	25
Big Sleep, The	USA	1946	Howard Hawks	114		UIP	FB	22
Big Sleep, The	GB	1978	Michael Winner	89			GB	33
Big Steal, The	USA	1949	Don Siegel	74			GB	15
Big Store	USA	1941	Charles F. Reisner	83			FB	15
Big Street, The	USA	1942	Irving Reis	87			GB	15
Big Town, The	USA	1987	Ben Bolt	109			FB	45
Big Trouble in Little China	USA	1986	John Carpenter	100	sc		FB	45
Big Wednesday	USA	1978	John Milius	119	sc		FB	33
Big Wheel, The	USA	1949	Edward Ludwig	92			GB	15
Big Wheels and Sailor	GB	1979	Doug Aitken	55			GB	17
Bigfoot and the Hendersons	USA	1987	William Dear	111			FB	45
Bigger Splash, A	GB	1974	Jack Hazan	105			GB	35
Biggest Bundle of Them All, The	USA	1967	Ken Annakin	98	std		FB	18
Bikini Beach	USA	1964	William Asher	99	sc		FB	18
Billion Dollar Brain	GB	1967	Ken Russell	108	sc/std		FB	18
Billion Dollar Threat	USA	1979	Barry Shear	97			FB	27
Billy Bathgate	USA	1991	Robert Benton	107		W	FB	70
Billy Liar	GB	1963	John Schlesinger	98			FB	15
Billy Two Hats	GB	1973	Ted Kotcheff	99			FB	18

	COUNTRY OF PRODUCTION	YEAR	DIRECTOR	RUNNING TIME	VERSION	35mm	16mm	16mm RENTAL FEE
Biloxi Blues	USA	1988	Mike Nichols	106			FB	55
Bingo Long Travelling All-Stars and Motor Kings, The	USA	1976	John Badham	111			FB	22
Bird	USA *	1988	Clint Eastwood	161			FB	65
Bird on a Wire	USA	1990	John Badham	111		UIP	FB	65
Birds and the Bees, The	USA	1956	Norman Taurog	94	bw		FB	15
Birds and the Bees, The	USA	1948	Fred M. Wilcox	115	bw		FB	15
Birds, The	USA	1963	Alfred Hitchcock	119		UIP	FB	27
Birdy	USA	1984	Alan Parker	120			FB	50
Birmingham Is What I Think With	GB	1991	Tom Pickard	50			AC	20
Birth of a Nation	W.GER	1973	Klaus Wyborny	70	mag		LFC	30
Birth of a Nation, The	USA	1915	D.W. Griffith	125	sd/col	BFI	BFI	30
Birth of The Beatles	GB	1979	Richard Marquand	108			GB	43
Bit of Fat, A	W.GER	1976	Michael Verhoeven	91	est		GFL	0
Bitch, The	GB	1979	Gerry O'Hara	94			GB	40
Bite the Bullet	USA	1975	Richard Brooks	130	sc/std		FB	22
Bitter Cane	HAITI	1983	Jacques Arcelin	75			MP	46
Bitter Tea of General Yen, The	USA	1932	Frank Capra	89			FB	15
Bitter Tears of Petra von Kant, The	W.GER	1972	R.W. Fassbinder	114	est	BFI	BFI	50
Black and Silver	GB	1981	William Raban/Marilyn Raban	75			RFI	30
Black Beauty	GB	1971	James Hill	106		GB	GB	25
Black Belt Jones	USA	1973	Robert Clouse	83			FB	18
Black Bird, The	USA	1975	David Giler	98			FB	18
Black Cat, The	USA	1934	Edgar Ulmer	66			FB	15
Black Dynasty	CZ	1962	Stepan Skalsky	94	est		ETV	10
Black Emanuelle	IT	1976	Adalberto Albertini	95	dub		FB	33
Black Eye	USA	1973	Jack Arnold	98			FB	18
Black Fox, The	USA	1962	Louis Clyde Stouman	90			GB	33
Black Girl	SEN	1965	Ousmane Sembene	60	est		MP	34.5
Black Gunn	USA	1972	Robert Hartford-Davis	95			FB	18
Black Hand, The	USA	1949	Richard Thorpe	92			FB	15
Black Hole, The	USA	1979	Gary Nelson	97			FB	38
Black Holiday	IT	1973	Marco Leto	112	est		MP	30
Black Island	GB	1978	Ben Bolt	57			GB	17
Black Joy	GB	1977	Anthony Simmons	97			GB	70
Black Legend, The	GB	1948	Alan Cooke/John Schlesinger	60			BFI	12
Black Man' Land								
Part I: Mau Mau	GB	1973		50			MP	27.6
Part 2: Kenyatta	GB	1973		52				
Black Narcissus	GB	1947	Michael Powell/Emeric Pressburger	100		BFI	BFI	45
Black Orchid, The	USA	1958	Martin Ritt	96	std		FB	15
Black Orpheus	FR IT/BRAZ	1958	Marcel Camus	106	dub		BFI	30
Black Rain	USA	1989	Ridley Scott	125		UIP	FB	68
Black Rain	JAP	1989	Shoei Imamura	123	est	AE	GB	70
Black Robe	CAN/AUSTR	1991	Bruce Beresford	100		ENT	FB	70
Black Sabbath	IT/FR	1963	Mario Bava	95	dub		FB	20
Black Shield of Falworth, The	USA	1954	Rudolph Maté	98	bw		FB	15
Black Stallion, The	USA	1979	Carroll Ballard	117			FB	38
Black Sunday	USA	1976	John Frankenheimer	142	std		FB	43
Black Swan, The	USA	1942	Henry King	82			FB	15
Black Wax	GB/USA	1982	Robert Mugge	79			GB	50
Black Widow	USA	1954	Nunnally Johnson	95	sc/std		FB	18
Black Widow	USA	1987	Bob Rafelson	95			FB	55
Black Windmill, The	USA	1974	Don Siegel	106	sc/std		FB	22
Blackbeard the Pirate	USA	1952	Raoul Walsh	98			GB	15
Blackbeard's Ghost	USA	1967	Robert Stevenson	106			FB	38
Blackbird Descending	GB	1977	Malcolm Le Grice	120			LFC	55
Blackboard Jungle	USA	1955	Richard Brooks	94			FB	15
Blackhill Campaign	GB	1963	Jack Parsons	52			BFI	9

	COUNTRY OF PRODUCTION	YEAR	DIRECTOR	RUNNING TIME	VERSION	35mm	16mm	16mm RENTAL FEE
Blacks Britannica	GB/USA	1978	David Koff/Musindo Mwinyipembe	57			MP	40
							ETV	52
Black Stuff, The	GB	1980	Jim Goddard	107			BFI	25
Blade Runner	USA	1982	Ridley Scott	117	sc		FB	40
Blaise Pascal	IT/FR	1972	Roberto Rossellini	135	est		BFI	25
Blame it on Rio	USA	1983	Stanley Donen	99			FB	45
Blame it on the Bellboy	GB	1991	Mark Herman	79		W	FB	65
Blanche	FR	1971	Walerian Borowczyk	90	est	CONT	GB	30
Blaze	USA	1989	Ron Shelton	117		W	FB	60
Blazing Saddles	USA	1974	Mel Brooks	93	sc/std		FB	33
Bleak Moments	GB	1971	Mike Leigh	111			RESP	35
Bless This House	GB	1972	Gerald Thomas	89			FB	22
Blind Adventure	USA	1933	Ernest Schoedsack	63			GB	15
Blind Alibi	USA	1938	Lew Landers	61			GB	15
Blind Date	GB	1959	Joseph Losey	95			GB	15
Blind Date	USA	1987	Blake Edwards	95			FB	55
Blind Fury	USA	1989	Phillip Noyce	86		C	FB	60
Blind Man's Buff	GB	1977	Gerry O'Hara	58			GB	17
Blind Man's Buff	W.GER	1972	Theodor Gradler	60	dub		GFL	0
Blind Spot	GER	1979	Claudia Alemann	111	est		CIRC	45
Blind Terror	GB	1971	Richard Fleischer	89			FB	18
Blindfold	USA	1965	Philip Dunne	102	bw/std		FB	15
Blindman	USA/IT	1971	Ferdinando Baldi	96			FB	18
Blinker's Spy Spotter	GB	1971	Harold Orton	58			GB	17
Bliss of Mrs. Blossom	GB	1968	Joseph McGrath	93			FB	18
Blithe Spirit	GB	1944	David Lean	96			FB	27
Blitz on Britain	GB	1960	Harry Booth	71			FB	15
Blob, The	USA	1958	Irvin S. Yeaworth Jr.	79			BFI	20
Block, The	GB	1972	Paul Watson (Prod)	75			CONC	15.8
Blockheads	USA	1938	John G. Blystone	60			GB	15
Blonde Cheat	USA	1938	Joseph Santley	62			GB	15
Blonde in Love, A	CZ	1965	Milos Forman	80	est		GB	25
Blonde Venus	USA	1932	Josef von Sternberg	89			BFI	25
Blood and Sand	USA	1941	Rouben Mamoulian	125			FB	18
Blood Feud	IT	1978	Lina Wertmuller	109	est		GB	33
Blood Money	HK/IT/	1974	Anthony M. Dawson	100	std		FB	18
Blood Oath	AUSTR	1990	Stephen Wallace	108		R	FB	60
Blood of a Poet. The (See Sang d'un Poete, Le)								
Blood of the Condor	BOL	1969	Jorge Sanjines	est			WFA	40
Blood of the Dragon (see Return of the Streetfighter, The)								
Blood on His Lips	USA	1959	Robert Clarke	60			GB	15
Blood on the Moon	USA	1948	Robert Wise	87			GB	15
Blood on the Sun	USA	1945	Frank Lloyd	94			GB	18
Blood Relatives	CAN/FR	1977	Claude Chabrol	94			FB	33
Blood Simple	USA	1984	Joel Coen	98			GB	50
Bloodbrothers	USA	1978	Robert Mulligan	116			FB	27
Bloodsport	USA	1987	Newt Arnold	92			FB	45
Blot, The	USA	1921	Lois Weber	90	st		CIRC	35
Blow Out	USA	1981	Brian De Palma	107	sc		FB	48
Blow Your Own Trumpet	GB	1958	Cecil Musk	56			GB	15
Blowup	GB/IT	1966	Michelangelo Antonioni	111			FB	28
Blowing Wild	USA	1953	Hugo Fregonese	90			GB	18
Blue Collar	USA	1978	Paul Schrader	114			FB	38
Blue Dahlia	USA	1945	George Marshall	99			FB	15
Blue Fantasies	W.GER	1978	Walter Boos	78	dub		FB	38
Blue Jeans	USA	1959	Philip Dunne	89	sc/std		FB	15
Blue Knight, The	USA	1973	Robert Butler	96			GB	20
Blue Lagoon, The	USA	1980	Randal Kleiser	104			FB	43

b

	COUNTRY OF PRODUCTION	YEAR	DIRECTOR	RUNNING TIME	VERSION	35mm	16mm	16mm RENTAL FEE
Blue Light, The	GER	1932	Leni Riefenstahl	70	est		BFI	25
Blue Max, The	GB	1966	John Guillermin	155	sc		FB	25
Blue Mountains	USSR	1983	Eldar Shengelaya	97	est	NP	MP	57.5
Blue Steel	US	1990	Kathryn Bigelow	102		FI	GB	70
Blue Sunshine	USA	1977	Jeff Lieberman	94			FB	22
Blue Thunder	USA	1983	John Badham	110	sc/std		FB	50
Blue Veil, The	USA	1951	Curtis Bernhardt	112			GB	15
Blue Velvet	USA	1986	David Lynch	120	std		BFI	60
Blue Water, White Death	USA	1971	Peter Gimbel/James Lipscomb	97	sc/std		GB	22
Blues Brothers, The	USA	1980	John Landis	133			FB	48
Blume in Love	USA	1973	Paul Mazursky	116			FB	18
BMX Bandits	AUSTR	1983	Brian Trenchard-Smith	91			FB	35
Boat, The	W.Ger	1981	Wolfgang Petersen	128	dub		FB	40
Boatniks, The	USA	1970	Norman Tokar	100			FB	27
Bob & Carol & Ted & Alice	USA	1969	Paul Mazursky	105			FB	18
Bob Roberts	USA	1992	Tim Robbins	103		R	FB	75
Bobo, The	GB	1967	Robert Parrish	103			FB	18
Body and Soul	USA	1947	Robert Rossen	106			GB	18
Body and Soul	USA	1981	George Bowers	105			FB	38
Body Double	USA	1985	Brian de Palma	115			FB	45
Body Heat	USA	1981	Lawrence Kasdan	116			FB	48
Body Rock	USA	1984	Marcelo Epstein	94			FB	35
Body Snatcher, The	USA	1945	Robert Wise	73			GB	15
Body, The	GB	1970	Roy Battersby	111			FB	24
Bodyguard	USA	1948	Richard Fleischer	62			GB	15
Bodystealers, The	GB/USA	1969	Gerry Levy	91		GB	GB	20
Boeing Boeing	USA	1965	John Rich	102			FB	18
Boesman and Lena	S.AFR	1973	Ross Devenish	102			GB	30
Bof!	FR	1971	Claude Farraldo	94	est		MP	51.75
Bofors Gun, The	GB	1968	Jack Gold	105	bw		FB	15
Bohemian Girl	USA	1936	James Horne/Charles Rogers	71			GB	20
Bohrer, Der	W.GER	1968	Erich Neureuther	65	dub		GFL	0
Bolero	USA	1984	John Derek	104			FB	45
Bomb, The	GB	1980	Jonathan Dimbleby	70			CONC	14.4
Bombardier, The	USA	1943	Richard Wallace	99			GB	15
Bon Voyage!	USA	1962	James Neilson	132			FB	27
Bond Street	GB	1948	Gordon Parry	107			GB	20
Bonfire of the Vanities	USA	1990	Brian de Palma	125		W	FB	60
Bonjour Tristesse	GB	1957	Otto Preminger	93	std		FB	18
Bonne Année, La	FR/IT	1973	Claude Lelouch	112	est		GB	27
Bonne Soupe, La	FR/IT	1963	Robert Thomas	97	std/est		FB	15
Bonnie and Clyde	USA	1967	Arthur Penn	111		W	FB	27
Bonnie Scotland	USA	1935	James W. Horne	80			FB	15
Bonus, The	USSR	1975	Sergei Michaelyan	85	est		ETV	15
Bonzo Goes to College	USA	1952	Frederick De Cordova	80			FB	15
Bookseller Who Gave Up Bathing, The	SWE	1968	Jarl Kulle	99	est		GB	30
Boom!	GB	1968	Joseph Losey	110	std		FB	18
Boom Town	USA	1940	Jack Conway	119			FB	15
Border Cafe	USA	1937	Lew Landers	68			GB	15
Border G-Man	USA	1938	David Howard	61			GB	15
Border Incident	USA	1949	Anthony Mann	93			FB	15
Border, The	USA	1981	Tony Richardson	109			FB	43
Borderline	USA	1980	Jerrold Friedman	97			GB	38
Borderline	GB	1930	Kenneth MacPherson	60	st		BFI	30
Born Free	GB	1965	James Hill	95	sc/std		FB	18
Born in 1921	CZ	1957	Vaclav Gajer	90	est		ETV	10
Born in Flames	USA	1982	Lizzie Borden	89			CNO	52
Born to be Bad	USA	1950	Nicholas Ray	80			GB	15

	COUNTRY OF PRODUCTION	YEAR	DIRECTOR	RUNNING TIME	VERSION	35mm	16mm	16mm RENTAL FEE
Born to Kill (see Lady of Deceit)								
Born to Love	USA	1931	Paul L. Stein	99			GB	15
Born to Sing	USA/AUSTR	1962	Steve Previn	92			FB	27
Borrowed Hero	US	1942	Lewis D. Collins	65			GB	25
Borsalino	FR/IT	1970	Jacques Deray	126	dub		FB	18
Boston Strangler, The	USA	1968	Richard Fleischer	114	sc/std		FB	19
Bostonians, The	USA	1984	James Ivory	120		MAY	GB	50
Bottoms Up!	GB	1959	Mario Zampi	87			FB	15
Boucher, Le	FR/IT	1969	Claude Chabrol	92	est	BFI	GB	35
Boudu Sauvé des Eaux	FR	1932	Jean Renoir	87	est		GB	25
Boulevard du Rhum (see Winner Takes All)								
Boulevard Nights	USA	1979	Michael Pressman	101			FB	30
Bound for Glory	USA	1976	Hal Ashby	148			FB	27
Bounty Hunters, The	IT	1970	Frank Kramer	106	sc/dub		FB	18
Bounty, The	GB	1984	Roger Donaldson	133	sc/std		FB	45
Boxcar Bertha	USA	1972	Martin Scorsese	87			FB	18
Boxer	POL	1966	Julian Dziedzina	80	est		APO	35
Boxer and Death, The	CZ	1963	Peter Solan	100	est		ETV	10
Boy Friend, The	GB	1971	Ken Russell	125	sc/std/109		FB	28
Boy Slaves	USA	1939	P.J. Wolfson	72			GB	15
Boy Soldier	GB	1986	Karl Francis	100	est		MP	57.5
Boy Who Stole an Elephant, The	USA	1970	Michael Caffey	78			FB	27
Boy Who Turned Yellow, The	GB	1972	Michael Powell	55			GB	17
Boy With Green Hair, The	US	1948	Joseph Losey	82	bw		GB	20
					col		GB	25
Boy With Two Heads, The (7 episodes)	GB	1974	Jonathan Ingrams	15-19 each			GB	6
Boy, Did I Get a Wrong Number!	USA	1966	George Marshall	99			FB	18
Boyars Plot, The (see Ivan the Terrible Part 2)								
Boys From Brazil	USA	1978	Franklin J. Schaffner	123			GB	40
Boys in Blue, The	GB	1983	Val Guest	90			FB	38
Boys in Company C, The	GB	1977	Sidney J. Furie	128	sc/std		GB	38
Boys in the Band, The	USA	1970	William Friedkin	119			GB	18
Boys Will Be Boys	GB	1935	William Beaudine	76			FB	15
Boys' Night Out	USA	1962	Michael Gordon	112	sc/std		FB	18
Boys' Ranch	USA	1946	Roy Rowland	96			FB	15
Boys' Town	USA	1938	Norman Taurog	93			FB	15
Boys, The	GB	1962	Sidney J. Furie	123	sc		FB	20
Boyz 'N the Hood	USA	1991	John Singleton	111		C	FB	75
Braddock: Missing in Action III	USA	1988	Aaron Norris	103			FB	45
Brainstorm	USA	1983	Douglas Trumbull	106			FB	38
Brannigan	GB	1975	Douglas Hickox	101	sc/std		FB	22
Brass Target	USA	1978	John Hough	111			FB	33
Bravados, The	USA	1958	Henry King	97	std		FB	18
Brazen Bell, The	USA	1962	James Sheldon	74	bw		FB	15
Brazil	GB	1985	Terry Gilliam	142			FB	50
Break of Hearts	USA	1935	Philip Moeller	80			GB	15
Break Out	GB	1984	Frank Godwin	62			FB	17
Breakdance	USA	1984	Joel Silberg	87			FB	40
Breakdance II	USA	1985	Sam Firstenberg	90			FB	40
Breaker Morant	AUSTR	1979	Bruce Beresford	107	std		GB	40
Breakfast for Two	USA	1937	Alfred Santell	65			GB	15
Breakheart Pass	USA	1975	Tom Gries	95			FB	33
Breaking Away	USA	1979	Peter Yates	101			FB	33
Breaking Glass	GB	1980	Brian Gibson	104	std	GB	GB	48
Breaking in Children	GB	1981	BBC 'Horizon'	60			CONC	23.8
Breaking of Bumbo, The	GB	1970	Andrew Sinclair	94			GB	25
Breaking Point	CAN	1976	Bob Clark	92			FB	18
Breakout	USA	1975	Tom Gries	96	sc/std		FB	27

b	COUNTRY OF PRODUCTION	YEAR	DIRECTOR	RUNNING TIME	VERSION	35mm	16mm	16mm RENTAL FEE
Breakout	GB	1959	Peter Graham Scott	62			GB	20
Breath of Scandal	USA/IT/AUST	1960	Michael Curtiz	98	col		FB	18
					bw		FB	15
Breathless	USA	1983	Jim McBride	100			FB	43
Bred and Born	GB	1983	Joanna Davis/Mary Pat Leece	75			CIRC	35
Breezy	USA	1973	Clint Eastwood	107			FB	27
Bremer Freiheit	W.GER	1973	R.W. Fassbinder	87	est		GFL	0
Brewster McCloud	USA	1970	Robert Altman	105	std		FB	22
Brewster's Millions	USA	1985	Walter Hill	97			FB	45
Bridal Path, The	GB	1959	Frank Launder	95			FB	18
Bride by Mistake	USA	1944	Richard Wallace	80			GB	15
Bride for Sale	USA	1949	William D. Russell	65			GB	15
Bride Goes Wild, The	USA	1948	Norman Taurog	98			FB	15
Bride Walks Out, The	USA	1936	Leigh Jason	81			GB	15
Bride, The	GB	1985	Franc Roddam	119			FB	45
Brides of Dracula, The	GB	1960	Terence Fisher	85	bw		FB	15
Brides of Fu Manchu, The	GB	1966	Don Sharp	95			FB	15
Bridge on the River Kwai, The	GB	1957	David Lean	161	sc/std		FB	27
Bridge to the Sun	USA/FR	1961	Etienne Perier	112	bw		FB	15
Bridge Too Far, A	GB	1977	Richard Attenborough	175	sc/std		FB	48
Bridge, The	W.GER	1959	Bernhard Wicki	105	dub		GFL	0
Bridges at Toko-Ri, The	USA	1954	Mark Robson	104	bw		FB	15
Brief Encounter	GB	1945	David Lean	86	R		FB	22
Brief Encounter	GB	1974	Alan Bridges	103			GB	22
Brigadista, El	CB	1977	Octavio Cortázar	113	est	MP	MP	
Brigadoon	USA	1954	Vincente Minnelli	102	sc/std		FB	27
Bright Lights, Big City	USA	1988	James Bridges	107			FB	55
Brightness (see Yeelen)								
Brighton Rock	GB	1947	John Boulting	90			FB	15
Brighton Strangler, The	USA	1945	Max Nosseck	67			GB	15
Brimstone and Treacle	GB	1982	Richard Loncraine	87			GB	43
Bring Me the Head of Alfredo Garcia	USA/MEX	1974	Sam Peckinpah	112			FB	33
Bringing Up Baby	USA	1938	Howard Hawks	102		GB	BFI	25
Brink's Job, The	USA	1978	William Friedkin	102			FB	33
Bristle Face	USA	1970	Bob Sweeney	91			FB	27
Britannia Hospital	GB	1982	Lindsay Anderson	116			FB	45
British Sounds	GB	1969	Jean-Luc Godard	52			MP	40.25
Brno Trail, The	CZ	1967	Radim Curcek	55			GB	12
Broadcast News	USA	1987	James Brooks	131			FB	55
Broadway Danny Rose	USA	1984	Woody Allen	85			FB	40
Broken Blossoms	USA	1919	D.W. Griffith	102	st		BFI	20
Broken Lance	USA	1954	Edward Dmytryk	96	std		FB	18
Broken Rainbow	USA	1984	Victoria Mudd	70			CONC	25
Bronco Billy	USA	1980	Clint Eastwood	116			FB	40
Bronco Bullfrog	GB	1971	Barney Platts-Mills	86			BFI	25
Brood, The	CAN	1979	David Cronenberg	92			GB	35
Brother Can You Spare a Dime?	GB	1975	Philippe Mora	109			GB	26
Brother from Another Planet	USA	1984	John Sayles	108			GB	55
Brother of the Wind	CAN/USA	1972	Dick Robinson	88			GB	35
Brother Orchid	USA	1940	Lloyd Bacon	87			FB	22
Brotherhood, The	USA	1968	Martin Ritt	96			FB	18
Brothers and Sisters	GB	1980	Richard Woolley	101			BFI	35
Brothers in Law	GB	1956	Roy Boulting	94			FB	15
Brothers Karamazov, The	USA	1958	Richard Brooks	145			FB	22
Brothers O'Toole, The	USA	1972	Richard Erdman	92			GB	27
Brothers, The	GB	1947	David MacDonald	91			BFI	30
Browning Version, The	GB	1951	Anthony Asquith	89			GB	30
Brubaker	USA	1980	Stuart Rosenberg	130			FB	40

	COUNTRY OF PRODUCTION	YEAR	DIRECTOR	RUNNING TIME	VERSION	35mm	16mm	16mm RENTAL FEE
Brutalization of Franz Blum, The	W.GER	1974	Reinhard Hauff	104	est		GFL	0
Brute, The	GB	1976	Gerry O'Hara	90			FB	33
Buck and the Preacher	USA	1972	Sidney Poitier	102			FB	18
Buck Rogers in the 25th Century	USA	1979	Daniel Haller	89			FB	38
Bucket of Blood, A	USA	1959	Roger Corman	66			FB	15
Buddies	USA	1985	Arthur J. Bressan Jr.	79			GB	45
Buddy Buddy	USA	1981	Billy Wilder	96			FB	43
Buddy Holly Story, The	USA	1978	Steve Rash	114			FB	38
Buffalo Bill in Tomahawk Territory	USA	1952	Bernard B. Ray	63			GB	15
Bug	USA	1975	Jeannot Szwarc	101			FB	22
Bugles in the Afternoon	USA	1952	Roy Rowland	85			GB	15
Bugsy	USA	1991	Barry Levinson	135		C	FB	75
Bugsy Malone	GB	1976	Alan Parker	93			FB	33
Build My Gallows High (see Out of the Past)								
Bulldog Breed, The	GB	1960	Robert Asher	97			FB	15
Bulldog Drummond Escapes	USA	1937	James Hogan	67			GB	27
Bullet for a Badman	USA	1964	R.G. Springsteen	80			FB	15
Bullet for the General, A	IT	1968	Damiano Damiani	76	std/dub		FB	18
Bullets or Ballots	USA	1936	William Keighley	81			FB	22
Bullfighters, The	USA	1945	Mal St. Clair	61			FB	15
Bullitt	USA	1968	Peter Yates	114			FB	18
Bunco Squad	USA	1950	Herbert I. Leeds	67			GB	15
Bundle of Joy	USA	1956	Norman Taurog	98	col		GB	18
Bungala Boys	AUSTR/GB	1961	Jim Jeffrey	61			GB	17
Bunny	GB	1972	Frank Cvitanovich	60	col		CONC	19.8
Bunny Lake Is Missing	GB	1965	Otto Preminger	107	sc/std		FB	15
Buona Sera, Mrs. Campbell	USA	1968	Melvin Frank	112			FB	18
'Burbs, The	USA	1989	Joe Dante	102			FB	55
Burden of Dreams	USA	1982	Les Blank	94	est		GB	40
Burglar	USA	1987	Hugh Wilson	102			FB	65
Burglars, The	FR/IT	1971	Henri Verneuil	113	sc/dub		FB	18
Burma Victory	GB	1945	Roy Boulting	62			CFL	15
Burning an Illusion	GB	1981	Menelik Shabazz	105			BFI	45
Burnt Offerings	USA	1976	Dan Curtis	115			FB	18
Bush Baby	GB	1968	John Trent	100			FB	18
Bush Christmas	GB	1947	Ralph Smart	81			FB	10
Buster	GB	1988	David Green	102			GB	60
Buster Keaton Story ,The	USA	1956	Sidney Sheldon	93			FB	15
Buster Keaton: A Hard Act to Follow	GB	1987	Kevin Brownlow/David Gill	159			BFI	20
Busting	USA	1973	Peter Hyams	93			FB	18
But Not For Me	USA	1959	Walter Lang	105			FB	15
Butch and Sundance: The Early Days	USA	1979	Richard Lester	111			FB	40
Butch Cassidy and the Sundance Kid	USA	1969	George Roy Hill	110	sc/std		FB	40
Butcher, The (see Boucher, Le)								
Buttercup Chain, The	GB	1970	Robert Ellis Miller	95	sc		FB	18
Butterfield 8	USA	1960	Daniel Mann	108	sc/std		FB	22
Butterflies Are Free	USA	1972	Milton Katselas	109			FB	18
By the Light of the Silvery Moon	USA	1953	David Butler	101	bw		FB	15
By Your Leave	USA	1934	Lloyd Corrigan	83			GB	15
Bye Bye Birdie	USA	1963	George Sidney	109	sc/std		FB	18
Bye Bye Red Riding Hood	CAN/HU	1989	Marta Meszaros	94		GB	GB	40
Byzantine Merchant's Treasure	CZ	1966	Ivor Novak	94	est		ETV	10

C

	COUNTRY OF PRODUCTION	YEAR	DIRECTOR	RUNNING TIME	VERSION	35mm	16mm	16mm RENTAL FEE
C'est La Vie	FR	1990	Diane Kurys	96	st	CONT	GB	80
C.C. and Company	USA	1970	Seymour Robbie	93			GB	22
Cabaret	USA	1972	Bob Fosse	123		BFI	GB	33
Cactus	AUSTR	1986	Paul Cox	96		BD	GB	60
Cactus Flower	USA	1969	Gene Saks	104			FB	18
Caddy, The	USA	1953	Norman Taurog	94			FB	15
Caddyshack	USA	1980	Harold Ramis	98			FB	30
Caesar and Cleopatra	GB	1945	Gabriel Pascal	128		R	FB	33
Cage Aux Folles II, La	FR/IT	1980	Edouard Molinaro	99	est		FB	43
Cage Aux Folles, La	FR'IT	1978	Edouard Molinaro	91	est		FB	43
Cahill	USA	1973	Andrew V McLaglen	102	std		FB	18
Caine Mutiny, The	USA	1954	Edward Dmytryk	124			FB	22
Cairo	USA	1963	Wolf Rilla	91			FB	12
Cairo Road	GB	1950	David MacDonald	95			GB	20
Cal	GB	1984	Pat O'Connor	103			FB	40
Calamity Jane	USA	1953	David Butler	101	col/bw		FB	18
Calamity the Cow	GB	1967	David Eastman	55			GB	12
Calcutta	FR	1968	Louis Malle	92			GB	25
California Dolls	USA	1981	Robert Aldrich	113			FB	38
California Holiday	USA	1966	Norman Taurog	93	std		FB	22
California Split	USA	1974	Robert Altman	109	std		FB	18
California Suite	USA	1978	Herbert Ross	103			FB	43
Call Harry Crown	USA	1974	John Frankenheimer	98	sc/std		FB	18
Call It Murder	US	1934	Chester Erskine	71			GB	20
Call of the Wild, The	GB/W.GER/ SP/IT/FR	1972	Ken Annakin	95			FB	18
Call Out the Marines	USA	1941	Frank Ryan/William Hamilton	67			GB	15
Callan	GB	1974	Don Sharp	106			FB	18
Cameraman, The	USA	1928	Edward Sedgwick	88	st		FB	27
Camerons, The	GB	1974	Frederick Wilson	56			GB	17
Camille	USA	1936	George Cukor	109			FB	22
Camouflage	POL	1977	Krzysztof Zanussi	106	st		GB	40
Campbell's Kingdom	GB	1957	Ralph Thomas	100	bw		FB	15
Can Be Done Amigo	IT/FR/SP	1971	Maurizio Lucidi				GB	30
Can She Bake a Cherry Pie?	USA	1983	Henry Jaglom	90			GB	43
Can't Buy Me Love	USA	1987	Steve Rash	93			FB	40
Can't Stop the Music	USA	1980	Nancy Walker	123	sc		FB	41
Can-Can	USA	1960	Walter Lang	131	std		FB	18
Canal Zone	USA	1977	Frederick Wiseman	174			GB	55
Canaris	W. GER	1954	Alfred Weidenmann	110	dub		GFL	0
Candidate, The	USA	1972	Michael Ritchie	110			FB	18
Candleshoe	USA/GB	1977	Norman Tokar	101			FB	38
Cannon for Cordoba	USA	1970	Paul Wendkos	103	sc		FB	18
Canterbury Tale, A	GB	1944	Michael Powell/Emeric Pressburger	124			BFI	30
Cape Fear	USA	1991	Martin Scorsese	127		UIP	FB	75
Cape Fear	USA	1961	J. Lee Thompson	99			FB	15
Capone	USA	1975	Steve Carver	101			FB	22
Capricious Summer	CZ	1968	Jiri Menzel	75	est		GB	30
Capricorn One	USA	1977	Peter Hyams	124	sc/std		GB	43
Captain Blood	USA	1936	Michael Curtiz	118	98		FB	22
Captain Clegg	GB	1962	Peter Graham Scott	82	col		FB	18
					bw		FB	15
Captain Johnno	AUSTR	1988	Mario Andreacchio	96	est/def		BFI	25
Captain Kronos - Vampire Hunter	GB	1972	Brian Clemens	91			FB	18
Captain Nemo and the Underwater City	GB	1969	James Hill	106	sc/std		FB	19
Captain Sinbad	USA/W.GER	1963	Byron Haskin	81	std		FB	18
Captain Stirrick	GB	1982	Colin Finbow	90		BD	GB	40
Captain's Table, The	GB	1958	Jack Lee	89			FB	18

	COUNTRY OF PRODUCTION	YEAR	DIRECTOR	RUNNING TIME	VERSION	35mm	16mm	16mm RENTAL FEE
Captains Courageous	USA	1937	Victor Fleming	116			FB	15
Captive du désert, La	FR	1990	Raymond Depardon	101	st	AE	GB	80
Car Trouble	GB	1985	David Green	93			FB	50
Car Wash	USA	1976	Michael Schultz	97			FB	38
Car, The	USA	1977	Elliot Silverstein	97	sc/std		FB	33
Carabiniers, Les	FR/IT	1963	Jean-Luc Godard	85	est		GB	45
Caravaggio	GB	1986	Derek Jarman	93		BFI	BFI	50
Caravan of Courage	USA	1984	John Korty	97			FB	40
Caravan to Vaccares	GB/FR	1974	Geoffrey Reeve	98	std		GB	33
Carbine Williams	USA	1952	Richard Thorpe	90			FB	15
Cardillac	W.GER	1969	Edgar Reitz	110	est		GFL	0
Cardinal, The	USA	1963	Otto Preminger	175	sc/std		FB	16
Care Bears Movie II : A New Generation	USA	1986	Dale Schott	76			FB	40
Carefree	USA	1938	Mark Sandrich	85			GB	15
Caretaker, The	GB	1963	Clive Donner	105			GB	25
Carey Treatment, The	USA	1972	Blake Edwards	101	sc/std		FB	22
Carmen	SP	1983	Carlos Saura	131	est		GB	50
Carmen	FR/IT	1984	Francesco Rosi	152	cst		GB	70
Carmen Jones	USA	1954	Otto Preminger	104	std		FB	18
Carnival	GER	1943	Veit Harlan	92	est		BFI	25
Carnival Boat	USA	1932	Albert S. Rogell	62			GB	15
Carnival Night, The	USSR	1956	Eldar Ryanazov	77			ETV	10
Carnival of Thieves	USA	1966	Russell Rouse	93	bw		FB	15
Carrie	USA	1976	Brian De Palma	97			FB	43
Carry Greenham Home	GB	1983	Beeban Kidron/Amanda Richardson	66			CONC/GB	25
Carry on Abroad	GB	1972	Gerald Thomas	89			FB	18
Carry on Admiral	GB	1957	Val Guest	82	bw/std/sc	GB	GB	15
Carry on Again Doctor	GB	1969	Gerald Thomas	89			FB	18
Carry on at Your Convenience	GB	1971	Gerald Thomas	90			FB	18
Carry on Behind	GB	1975	Gerald Thomas	90			FB	22
Carry on Cabby	GB	1963	Gerald Thomas	91			FB	15
Carry on Camping	GB	1969	Gerald Thomas	88			FB	18
Carry on Cleo	GB	1964	Gerald Thomas	92			FB	18
Carry on Constable	GB	1960	Gerald Thomas	86			FB	15
Carry on Cowboy	GB	1965	Gerald Thomas/Peter Bolton	92			FB	18
Carry on Cruising	GB	1962	Gerald Thomas	89			FB	18
Carry on Dick	GB	1974	Gerald Thomas	90			FB	22
Carry on Doctor	GB	1968	Gerald Thomas	95			FB	18
Carry on Emmannuelle	GB	1978	Gerald Thomas	98			GB	27
Carry on England	GB	1976	Gerald Thomas	95			FB	22
Carry on Girls	GB	1973	Gerald Thomas	88			FB	18
Carry on Henry	GB	1971	Gerald Thomas	90			FB	18
Carry on Jack	GB	1964	Gerald Thomas	92			FB	18
Carry on Loving	GB	1970	Gerald Thomas	90			FB	18
Carry on Matron	GB	1972	Gerald Thomas	89			FB	18
Carry on Nurse	GB	1959	Gerald Thomas	80			FB	15
Carry on Regardless	GB	1961	Gerald Thomas	90			FB	15
Carry on Screaming	GB	1966	Gerald Thomas	97	bw		FB	15
Carry on Sergeant	GB	1958	Gerald Thomas	85	bw		FB	15
Carry on Spying	GB	1964	Gerald Thomas	87	bw		FB	15
Carry on Teacher	GB	1959	Gerald Thomas	86			FB	15
Carry on up the Jungle	GB	1970	Gerald Thomas	90			FB	18
Carry on up the Khyber	GB	1968	Gerald Thomas	87			FB	18
Carve Her Name with Pride	GB	1958	Lewis Gilbert	119			FB	15
Casablanca	USA	1942	Michael Curtiz	103		UIP	FB	22
Casanova's Big Night	USA	1953	Norman McLeod	86	bw		FB	15
Case of the Witch that Wasn't	CAN		Jean Beaudry	92		GB	GB	40
Casey's Shadow	USA	1977	Martin Ritt	96			FB	27

	COUNTRY OF PRODUCTION	YEAR	DIRECTOR	RUNNING TIME	VERSION	35mm	16mm	16mm RENTAL FEE
Cass Timberlane	USA	1947	George Sidney	117			FB	15
Cassandra Crossing, The	GB/IT/W.GER	1976	George Pan Cosmatos	128			FB	30
Castaway	GB	1986	Nicolas Roeg	120			FB	45
Castaway Cowboy, The	USA	1974	Vincent McEveety	93			FB	27
Castle, The	W.GER	1968	Rudolf Noelte	91	est		GFL	0
Cat and Mouse	GB	1974	Daniel Petrie	90			FB	18
Cat and the Canary, The	GB	1978	Radley Metzger	106			GB	30
Cat Ballou	USA	1965	Elliot Silverstein	95			FB	18
Cat From Outer Space, The	USA	1978	Norman Tokar	98	103		FB	38
Cat Gang, The	GB	1958	Darrel Catling	50			GB	12
Cat O'Nine Tails	FR/IT/W.GER	1971	Dario Argento	104	dub		FB	22
Cat on a Hot Tin Roof	USA	1958	Richard Brooks	108			FB	22
Cat People	USA	1943	Jacques Tourneur	72		GB	BFI	20
Cat People	USA	1982	Paul Schrader	118			FB	43
Cat's Eye	USA	1984	Lewis Teague	94			FB	40
Catamount Killing, The	E.GER	1974	Krzysztof Zanussi	96			FB	18
Catch - 22	USA	1970	Mike Nichols	122	std		FB	22
Catholic Boys	USA	1985	Michael Dinner	103			FB	45
Cathy Come Home	GB	1966	Ken Loach	70			CONC	14.8
Catlow	GB	1971	Sam Wanamaker	101	std		FB	18
Caught	USA	1948	Max Ophuls	88			GB	15
Caught in the Net	GB	1960	John Haggarty	64			GB	12
Caught on a Train	GB	1980	Peter Duffell	80			BFI	25
Cavalier of the Gold Star	USSR	1951	Yuli Raizman	110	est		ETV	15
Caveman	USA	1981	Carl Gottlieb	97			FB	38
Caza, La	SP	1965	Carlos Saura	84	est		GB	25
Cecilia, La	FR/IT	1976	Jean-Louis Comolli	105	est		MP	46
Ceddo	SEN	1977	Ousmane Sembene	117	est		BFI	35
Celebration at Big Sur	USA	1971	Baird Bryant/Johanna Demetrakas	82			FB	18
Celia	AUSTR	1988	Ann Turner	103		CONT	GB	75
Céline et Julie Vont en Bateau	FR	1974	Jacques Rivette	180	est	CONT	GB	45
Central Bazaar	GB	1976	Steven Dwoskin	154			MP	51.75
Centre Forward	USSR		S. Derevyansky/I. Zemgano	70	est		ETV	12
Ceremony, The	USA/SP	1963	Laurence Harvey	107			FB	15
Chain Reaction, The	AUSTR	1980	Ian Barry	92			FB	43
Chain, The	GB	1984	Jack Gold	96			FB	40
Chair, The	USA	1962	Richard Leacock/D.A. Pennebaker	90			CONC	15.4
Chalk Garden	GB	1964	Ronald Neame	106			FB	18
Challenge for Robin Hood, A	GB	1967	C.M.Pennington Richards	96			FB	18
Challenge to be Free	US	1972	Tay Garnett	90			GB	45
Challenge to Lassie	USA	1949	Richard Thorpe	76	bw		FB	12
Challenge, The	USA	1975	Herbert Kline	104			GB	38
Chamber of Horrors	USA	1966	Hy Averback	81	bw		FB	15
Chameleon	USA	1978	Owen Shapiro	86			LFC	35
Champ, The	USA	1979	Franco Zeffirelli	121			FB	38
Champagne for Caesar	USA	1950	Richard Whorf	98			GB	15
Champagne Murders (see Scandale, Le)								
Champions	GB	1983	John Irvin	114			FB	55
Chan is Missing	USA	1981	Wayne Wang	75			BFI	45
Chance at Heaven	USA	1933	William A. Seiter	70			GB	15
Chance, History, Art...	GB	1980	James Scott	50			AC	20
Chandler	USA	1971	Paul Magwood	88	sc		FB	38
Change of Seasons	USA	1980	Richard Lang	101			FB	43
Changeling, The	CAN	1979	Peter Medak	107	std		GB	43
Chant of Jimmy Blacksmith, The	AUSTR	1978	Fred Schepisi	122	sc		GB	30
Chapel, The	CONGO	1979	Jean-Michel Tchissoukou	84	est		BFI	35
Chapter Two	USA	1979	Robert Moore	126			FB	38
Charge at Feather River, The	USA	1953	Gordon Douglas	94	bw		FB	20

	COUNTRY OF PRODUCTION	YEAR	DIRECTOR	RUNNING TIME	VERSION	35mm	16mm	16mm RENTAL FEE
Charge is Murder, The	USA	1963	Boris Sagal	104	sc/std		FB	12
Charge of the Light Brigade,The	USA	1936	Michael Curtiz	115			FB	22
Chariot of the Gods	W.GER	1969	Harald Reinl	98			FB	22
Chariots of Fire	GB	1981	Hugh Hudson	123			FB	40
Charles et Lucie	FR	1979	Nelly Kaplan	98	est		BFI	35
Charley and the Angel	USA	1973	Vincent McEveety	93			FB	27
Charley One-eye	GB	1972	Don Chaffey	94			GB	24
Charley Varrick	USA	1973	Don Siegel	111	std		FB	27
Charlie Bubbles	GB	1967	Albert Finney	89			FB	18
Charlie Chan and the Curse of the Dragon Queen	USA	1980	Clive Donner	97			FB	33
Charlotte's Web	USA	1972	Charles Nichols/Iwao Takamoto	96			GB	30
Charly	USA	1968	Ralph Nelson	103	sc/std	GB	GB	22
Charro!	USA	1969	Charles Marquis Warren	96			FB	27
Chase a Crooked Shadow	GB	1957	Michael Anderson	86			FB	15
Chase, The	USA	1966	Arthur Penn	122	sc		FB	18
Chasing Yesterday	USA	1935	George Nicholls Jr.	70			GB	15
Chastity Belt, The	IT	1967	Pasquale Festa Campanile	110			FB	18
Chat dans le sac, Le	CAN	1972	Gilles Groulx	74	fr dia		CHC	0
Chateau de ma mére, La (see My Mothers Castle)								
Chato's Land	GB	1971	Michael Winner	100			FB	18
Chatterbox	USA	1936	George Nicholls Jr.	68			GB	15
Che!	USA	1969	Richard Fleischer	96	sc/std		FB	18
Cheap Detective, The	USA	1978	Robert Moore	93	sc/std		FB	33
Check and Double Check	USA	1930	Melville Brown	76			GB	15
Checkpoint	GB	1956	Ralph Thomas	84	bw		FB	15
Cheer Boys Cheer	GB	1939	Walter Forde	87			FB	15
Chelsea Girls	USA	1966	Andy Warhol	110			GB	40
Cherry 2000	USA	1988	Steve De Jarnatt	90			FB	35
Cherry, Harry and Raquel	USA	1969	Russ Meyer	71			GB	40
Cheviot, the Stag and the Black Black Oil, The	GB	1974	John MacKenzie	90			BFI	25
Chicago Maternity Centre Story, The	USA	1977	Kartemquin Films	60			WFA	22.5
Chicken Ranch	USA	1982	Nick Broomfield	77			GB	35
Chiens, Les	FR	1978	Alain Jessua	100	est		GB	35
Chiffy Kids, The	GB	1976	(6 episodes)	17-20 each			GB	6
Child is Waiting, A	USA	1962	John Cassavetes	104			FB	15
Child of Divorce	USA	1946	Richard Fleischer	62			GB	15
Child's Play	USA	1988	Tom Holland	87			FB	55
Child's Play II	USA	1990	John Lafia	87		UIP	FB	55
Childhood of Maxim Gorky, The	USSR	1938	Mark Donskoi	110	est		GB	25
Children Are Watching Us, The	IT	1943	Vittorio De Sica	82	est		BFI	25
Children of a Lesser God	USA	1986	Randa Haines	119			FB	50
Children of Hiroshima	JAP	1953	Kaneto Shindo	85	s/t		GB	35
Children of the Damned	GB	1963	Anton M. Leader	90			FB	12
Chimes at Midnight	SP/SWITZ	1966	Orson Welles	115			FB	28
China	GB	1965	Felix Greene	70			GB	20
China Caravan	USA	1942	George B. Seitz	67			FB	10
China Clipper	USA	1936	Ray Enright	89			FB	22
China Passage	USA	1937	Edward Killy	64			GB	15
China Sky	USA	1945	Ray Enright	87			GB	15
China Syndrome,The	USA	1978	James Bridges	122			FB	53
Chinamans and MarriageSwindler	CZ	1964	Jiri Krejcik	110	est		ETV	10
Chinatown	USA	1974	Roman Polanski	131	sc/std	BFI	FB	38
Chinoise, La	FR	1967	Jean-Luc Godard	96	est	GB	GB	45
Chisum	USA	1970	Andrew V. McLaglen	110	sc/std		FB	27
Chitty Chitty Bang Bang	GB	1968	Ken Hughes	144	sc/std		FB	27
Chocolat	FR	1988	Claire Denis	105	est	ELEC	GB	70
Choirboys, The	USA	1977	Robert Aldrich	122			GB	38
Choose Me	USA	1984	Alan Rudolph	106		BD	GB	40

	COUNTRY OF PRODUCTION	YEAR	DIRECTOR	RUNNING TIME	VERSION	35mm	16mm	16mm RENTAL FEE
Chorus Line, A	USA	1985	Richard Attenborough	118	sc/std		FB	60
Chorus of Disapproval, A	GB	1989	Michael Winner	100		MAY	GB	75
Chosen Survivors	USA	1974	Sutton Roley	96			FB	18
Chosen, The	USA	1981	Jeremy Paul Kagan	106			GB	50
Christ Stopped at Eboli	IT/FR	1979	Francesco Rosi	152	est	AE	GB	55
Christian Licorice Store, The	USA	1971	James Frawley	90			GB	40
Christine	USA	1983	John Carpenter	110			FB	40
Christmas Carol, A	AUSTR	1982	Eddy Graham	72			FB	15
Christmas Carol, The	USA	1938	Edwin L. Marin	69			FB	10
Christmas Story, A	USA	1983	Bob Clark	93			FB	40
Christmas Tree, The	GB	1966	James Clark	57			GB	10
Christopher Columbus	GB	1948	David MacDonald	100			FB	18
Christopher Columbus - The Discovery	USA	1992	John Glen	121		R	FB	65
Christopher Strong	USA	1933	Dorothy Arzner	77			GB	16
Chronicle of a Death Foretold	IT/FR	1987	Francesco Rosi	110	est		GB	70
Chronicle of Anna Magdalena Bach, The	W.GER IT	1968	Jean-Marie Straub	93	est		GB	45
Chu-Chin-Chow	GB	1934	Walter Forde	102			FB	15
Chuck Berry - Hail! Hail! Rock'n'Roll	USA	1987	Taylor Hackford	121			FB	45
Chuka	USA	1967	Gordon Douglas	105			FB	18
Chump at Oxford, A	USA	1939	Alfred Goulding	62			BFI	15
							GB	5
Cimarron	USA	1960	Anthony Mann	135	sc/std		FB	22
Cincinatti Kid, The	USA	1965	Norman Jewison	102			FB	18
Cinderella Liberty	USA	1973	Mark Rydell	117	sc		FB	18
Cinema Paradiso	IT/FR	1988	Giuseppe Tornatore	123	s/t	MAY	GB	70
Circle of Gold	GB	1988	Uday Bhattacharya	52			BFI	35
Circus of Fear	GB	1966	John Moxey	83	bw		FB	15
Circus of Horrors	GB	1960	Sidney Hayers	91	bw		FB	15
Citizen Kane	USA	1941	Orson Welles	119			GB	35
Citizens Band	USA	1977	Jonathan Demme	98			GB	40
City Heat	USA	1984	Richard Benjamin	97			FB	50
City of Joy	GB/FR	1991	Roland Joffe	135		W	FB	TBA
City of Lost Souls	W.GER	1983	Rosa Von Praunheim	89	est		MP	51.75
City of Sadness	TAI	1989	Hou Hsiao-Hsien	160		AE	GB	70
City of Women	IT/FR	1980	Federico Fellini	139	est		GB	55
City on Fire	CAN/USA	1979	Alvin Rakoff	103			FB	33
City Slickers	US	1991	Ron Underwood	114		FI	GB	80
City Under the Sea	GB/USA	1965	Jacques Tourneur	84	bw/std		FB	15
Clambake	USA	1967	Arthur Nadel	99	sc		FB	22
Clandestine Nation, The	BOL	1989	Ukamau Group	100	est		WFA	50
Clarence, the Cross-Eyed Lion	USA	1965	Andrew Marton	98			FB	20
Clash by Night	USA	1951	Fritz Lang	105			GB	15
Clash of Steel	FR/IT	1962	Bernard Borderie	80	std/sc/dub		FB	15
Clash of the Titans	GB	1981	Desmond Davis	118			FB	53
Class	USA	1983	Lewis John Carlino	98			FB	38
Class of '44	USA	1973	Paul Bogart	102	sc		FB	18
Class Struggle (see Film from The Clyde)								
Claude Monet	GB	1976	John Read	50			AC	20
Claudine	USA	1974	John Berry	92			FB	18
Clavigo	W.GER	1970	Marcel Ophuls	130			GB	0
Cleopatra	USA	1934	Cecil B. DeMille	100			FB	22
Cleopatra	USA	1963	Joseph L. Mankiewicz	192	sc		FB	22
Cleopatra Jones	USA	1973	Jack Starrett	89			FB	18
Cleopatra Jones and the Casino of Gold	USA/HK	1975	Chuck Bail	96			FB	18
Climb Up The Wall	GB	1960	Michael Winner	72			GB	15
Cloak and Dagger	USA	1946	Fritz Lang	104			GB	15
Cloak, The	USSR	1926	Grigori Kozintsev/Leonid Trauberg	88	st/est		BFI	30
Clockwise	GB	1985	Christopher Morahan	96			FB	60

	COUNTRY OF PRODUCTION	YEAR	DIRECTOR	RUNNING TIME	VERSION	35mm	16mm	16mm RENTAL FEE
Close Encounters of the Third Kind (Special Edition)	USA	1977	Steven Spielberg	133	std	C	FB	50
Close My Eyes	GB	1991	Stephen Poliakoff	108		AE	GB	80
Close to the Wind	SWE	1969	Stellan Olsson	117	est		CONC	38.4
Close Up	GB	1983	Peter Gidal	70			LFC	45
Clouded Yellow	GB	1950	Ralph Thomas	95			GB	15
Club de Femmes	FR	1936	Jacques Deval	91	est		BFI	40
Clue	USA	1985	Jonathan Lynn	87			FB	45
Coal Miner's Daughter	USA	1980	Michael Apted	125			FB	43
Coast to Coast	USA	1980	Joseph Sargent	95			FB	38
Coastal Command	GB	1942	J.B. Holmes	73			CFL	19
Cobra	USA	1986	George Pan Cosmatos	87			FB	60
Cobweb, The	USA	1955	Vincente Minnelli	124	bw/std		FB	22
Cock of the Dawn	CZ		Vladimir Cech	95	est		ETV	10
Cockeyed Cavaliers	USA	1934	Mark Sandrich	71			GB	15
Cockleshell Heroes, The	GB	1955	José Ferrer	96	bw/std		FB	18
Cocktail	USA	1988	Roger Donaldson	104			FB	55
Cocoon	USA	1985	Ron Howard	117			FB	50
Code of Silence	USA	1985	Andy Davies	100			FB	45
Codename: The Soldier	USA	1982	James Glickenhaus	88			FB	43
Codex	GB	1979	Stuart Pound	60			LHA	30
Cold Eye	USA	1980	Babette Mangolte	90			CIRC	35
Cold River	US	1981	Fred G. Sullivan	94			GB	45
Cold Summer of 53, The	USSR	1987	Alexander Proshkin	101	est		GB	60
Cold Sweat	FR IT	1970	Terence Young	94			FB	18
Cold Turkey	USA	1970	Norman Lear	101			FB	18
Colditz Story, The	GB	1954	Guy Hamilton	97			FB	15
Collectionneuse, La	FR	1966	Eric Rohmer	80	est		GB	30
College	USA	1927	James W. Horne	65	sd		BFI	25
Colonel Redl	HUNG/ W.GER/AUST	1984	Istvan Szabo	149	est		FB	70
Color of Money, The	USA	1986	Martin Scorsese	119			FB	45
Color Purple, The	USA	1985	Steven Spielberg	154			FB	75
Colossus of Rhodes, The	IT/SP	1961	Sergio Leone	127	std/dub		FB	18
Colour of Pomegranates, The	USSR	1969	Sergo Paradjanov	73	est		BFI	35
Coma	USA	1977	Michael Crichton	113			FB	33
Comancheros, The	USA	1961	Michael Curtiz	106	std		FB	22
Come Back Africa	USA	1959	Lionel Rogosin	90			GB	40
Come Fly With Me	GB	1962	Henry Levin	109	sc/std		FB	14
Come Play With Me II	SWITZ	1980	Michael Thomas	80	92		FB	35
Come See the Paradise	USA	1990	Alan Parker	113		F	FB	60
Come September	USA	1961	Robert Mulligan	113	std		FB	18
Comedians, The	USA/BER	1967	Peter Glenville	147	std		FB	22
Comes A Horseman	USA	1978	Alan J. Pakula	118	sc/std		FB	27
Comfort and Joy	GB	1984	Bill Forsyth	106			FB	40
Comfort of Strangers, The	GB/IT	1990	Paul Schrader	105		R	FB	65
Comin' Thro' The Rye	GB	1923	Cecil Hepworth	88	st		BFI	20
Coming Home	USA	1978	Hal Ashby	128			FB	33
Coming to America	USA	1988	John Landis	116			FB	65
Command Decision	USA	1948	Sam Wood	111			FB	12
Command, The	USA	1954	David Butler	94	bw/std		FB	20
Commando	USA	1985	Mark L. Lester	90			FB	45
Commare Secca, La	IT	1962	Bernardo Bertolucci	91	est		BFI	30
Commissar, The	USSR	1967	Alexander Askoldov	108	sc/est		GB	60
Commitments, The	EIRE	1991	Alan Parker	118		F	FB	75
Committed	USA	1983	Sheila McLaughlin/Lynne Tillman	79			GB	52
Committee, The	GB	1968	Peter Sykes	56			GB	15
Common Law, The	USA	1931	Paul L. Stein	78			GB	15
Common Threads: Stories from the Quilt	USA	1990	Robert Epstein/Jeffrey Friedman	75		ICA	GB	50

	COUNTRY OF PRODUCTION	YEAR	DIRECTOR	RUNNING TIME	VERSION	35mm	16mm	16mm RENTAL FEE
Communist, The	USSR	1957	Yuli Raizman	115			ETV	10
Company Limited	INDIA	1971	Satyajit Ray	112	est		GB	25
Company of Cowards!	USA	1963	George Marshall	86	sc/std		FB	14
Company of Killers	USA	1970	Jerry Thorpe	86			FB	18
Company of Strangers, The	CAN	1990	Cynthia Scott	101		ELEC	GB	85
Company of Wolves	GB	1984	Neil Jordan	95			GB	70
Competition, The	USA	1980	Joel Oliansky	125			FB	43
Compromising Positions	USA	1985	Frank Perry	98			FB	45
Computer Wore Tennis Shoes,The	USA	1969	Robert Butler	90			FB	27
Comrade X	USA	1940	King Vidor	90			FB	22
Conan the Barbarian	USA	1981	John Milius	126	sc		FB	40
Conan the Destroyer	USA	1984	Richard Fleischer	101			FB	35
Condemned of Altona, The	IT/FR	1962	Vittorio De Sica	113			FB	15
Condemned Women	USA	1938	Lew Landers	77			GB	15
Condorman	USA	1981	Charles Jarrott	90			FB	38
Conduct Unbecoming	GB	1975	Michael Anderson	107			FB	27
Cone of Silence	GB	1960	Charles Frend	92			FB	15
Confessions from a Holiday Camp	GB	1977	Norman Cohen	88			FB	22
Confessions of a Driving Instructor	GB	1976	Norman Cohen	90			FB	22
Confessions of a Pop Performer	GB	1975	Norman Cohen	91			FB	22
Confessions of a Window Cleaner	GB	1974	Val Guest	90			FB	22
Confessions of the David Galaxy Affair	GB	1979	Willy Roe	96			GB	40
Confessions of Winifred Wagner, The	W.GER	1975	Hans-Jürgen Syberberg	104	est		GB	25
Conflict	USA	1945	Curtis Bernhardt	85			FB	22
Confrontation: Assassination in Davos	SWITZ	1975	Rolf Lyssy	115	est		GB	25
Congress Dances	GB/GER	1931	Erik Charrell	85	est		BFI	25
Connecticut Yankee in King Arthur's Court, A	USA	1949	Tay Garnett	107	col		FB	18
					bw		FB	15
Connection, The	USA	1961	Shirley Clarke	110			GB	25
Conquerors, The (see Pioneer Builders)								
Conquest of the Earth	USA	1980	Sidney Hayers/Sigmund Neufeld Jr./Barry Crane	99			FB	38
Conquest of the Planet of the Apes	USA	1972	J. Lee Thompson	85	sc		FB	20
Conquest of the South Pole	GB	1989	Gillies Mackinnon	95			GB	60
Conrack	USA	1974	Martin Ritt	106	sc		FB	18
Consolation Marriage	USA	1931	Paul Sloane	82			GB	15
Conspiracy	USA	1930	Christy Cabanne	72			GB	15
Conspiracy of Hearts	GB	1960	Ralph Thomas	111			FB	15
Conspirator, The	GB	1949	Victor Saville	87	bw		FB	14
Constant Husband, The	GB	1954	Sidney Gilliat	88			FB	18
Continent Aflame Part 1 Part 2	USSR	1973	Roman Karmen	72	eng		ETV	7
Continental Divide	USA	1981	Michael Apted	103			FB	38
Conversation, The	USA	1974	Francis Ford Coppola	113	GB		GB	55
Convict 99	GB	1939	Marcel Varnel	88			FB	15
Convoy	USA	1978	Sam Peckinpah	111	sc/std		FB	33
Coogan's Bluff	USA	1968	Don Siegel	94			FB	18
Cook The Thief His Wife & Her Lover	GB	1989	Peter Greenaway	124			GB	85
Cookie	USA	1989	Susan Seidelman	133	W		FB	55
Cool Breeze	USA	1972	Barry Pollack	102			FB	16
Cool World, The	USA	1963	Shirley Clarke	106		BFI	BFI	35
Cop au Vin	FR	1984	Claude Chabrol	108			GB	60
Cop, Le	FR	1984	Claude Zidi	107	est		FB	60
Cops and Robbers	USA	1972	Aram Avakian	89			FB	18
'Copter Kids, The	GB	1976	Ronald Spencer	57			GB	17
Coquet Meander	GB	1981	Upper Cocquetdale Film Group	100			NA	50
Cordelia	CAN	1979	Jean Beaudin	115	fr dia		CHC	0
Cornelius Cardew	GB	1986	Philippe Regniez	52			AC	20
Cornered	USA	1945	Edward Dmytryk	102			GB	15
Corridors of Blood	GB	1958	Robert Day	86			GB	15

Title	COUNTRY OF PRODUCTION	YEAR	DIRECTOR	RUNNING TIME	VERSION	35mm	16mm	16mm RENTAL FEE
Cossacks Beyond the Danube	USSR	1952	V. Lapoknysh	92	est		ETV	15
Cottage on Dartmoor	GB	1929	Anthony Asquith	103	st		BFI	20
Cotton Comes to Harlem	USA	1970	Ossie Davis	97			FB	18
Count of Monte Cristo, The	GB	1974	David Greene	104			GB	27
Count the Hours	USA	1953	Don Siegel	74			GB	15
Count Three and Pray	USA	1955	George Sherman	102	std		FB	18
Count Your Blessings	USA	1959	Jean Negulesco	102	std		FB	14
Counterfeit Traitor, The	USA	1961	George Seaton	138			FB	18
Counterpoint	USA	1967	Ralph Nelson	99	std		FB	18
Countess Dracula	GB	1970	Peter Sasdy	94			FB	18
Countess from Hong Kong, A	GB	1966	Charles Chaplin	120			FB	18
Country	GB	1981	Richard Eyre	80			BFI	25
Country Dance	GB	1969	J. Lee Thompson	112			FB	16
Country Doctor	USSR	1952	Sergei Gerasimov	100	est		ETV	10
Country Doctor	CZ	1961	Karel Kachyna	90	est		ETV	10
Country Girl, The	USA	1954	George Seaton	105	bw		FB	15
Country Girls, The	GB	1983	Desmond Davis	108			GB	40
Coup de Grâce, Le	W.GER/FR	1976	Volker Schlöndorff	95	est		GB	30
Coupe De Ville	USA	1990	Joe Roth	98		W	FB	70
Courage To Live	SWE	1977/80	Ingela Romare	84	est		GB	25
Court-martial of Billy Mitchell	US	1955	Otto Preminger	95	st/sc		GB	18
Courtesans of Bombay	GB	1982	Ismail Merchant	75			GB	35
Courtship of Eddie's Father	USA	1962	Vincente Minnelli	118	sc/std		FB	16
Cousins	USA	1989	Joel Schumacher	113		UIP	FB	55
Cover Girl	USA	1944	Charles Vidor	107			FB	18
Cow, The	IRAN	1968	Daryioush Mehrjui	100	est		GB	25
Coward, The	CZ	1962	Jiri Weiss	96	est		ETV	10
Cowboy	USA	1958	Delmer Daves	90	col		FB	18
Cowboys, The	USA	1971	Mark Rydell	121	std		FB	18
Crack-Up	USA	1946	Irving Reis	93			GB	15
Crack in the World	USA	1964	Andrew Marton	96	col		FB	18
					bw		FB	15
Cracked Nuts	USA	1931	Edward Cline	74			GB	15
Cracksman, The	GB	1963	Peter Graham Scott	112	std		FB	18
Cranes are Flying, The	USSR	1957	Mikhail Kalatozov	92	est/dub		GB	25
Crash	USA	1976	Alan Gibson	78	sc		FB	18
Crashing Hollywood	USA	1938	Lew Landers	61			GB	15
Crazy Family	JAP	1984	Sogo Ishii	106	est		MP	0
Creative Process: Norman McLaren, The	GB/CAN	1990	Donald McWilliams	116			BFI	50
Creature from the Black Lagoon	USA	1954	Jack Arnold	79	3D	GB	FB	15
							FB	43
Creatures	GB	1974	John Du Cane	80	st		LFC	30
Creatures the World Forgot	GB	1970	Don Chaffey	95			FB	18
Cree Hunters of Mistassini	CAN	1974	Boyce Richardson/Tony Ianzelo	60			CONC	20.2
Creggan	GB	1982	Michael Whyte/Mary Holland	60			BFI	20
Cremator, The	CZ	1968	Juraj Herz	102	est		GB	25
Crescendo	GB	1969	Alan Gibson	95			FB	18
Cria Cuervos	SP	1975	Carlos Saura	110	est		FB	40
Cries and Whispers	SWE	1972	Ingmar Bergman	91	est	BFI	GB	40
Crime and Punishment	USA	1935	Josef von Sternberg	90			FB	15
Crime de M. Lange, Le	FR	1935	Jean Renoir	80	est	BFI	GB	35
Crime in a Girls' School	CZ	1965	Ivo Novak/Jiri Menzel/Ladislav Rychman	110	est		ETV	12.5
Crime Ring	USA	1938	Leslie Goodwins	70			GB	15
Crimebusters	IT	1976	E.B. Clucher	97	dub		FB	22
Crimebusters, The	USA	1961	Boris Sagal	74			FB	10
Crimes of Passion	USA	1985	Ken Russell	106			FB	50
Crimes of the Future	CAN	1970	David Cronenberg	65			MP	
Crimewave	USA	1985	Sam Raimi	86			FB	45

	COUNTRY OF PRODUCTION	YEAR	DIRECTOR	RUNNING TIME	VERSION	35mm	16mm	16mm RENTAL FEE
Criminal Court	USA	1946	Robert Wise	60			GB	15
Criminal, The	GB	1960	Joseph Losey	97			FB	15
Crimson Pirate, The	GB	1952	Robert Siodmak	105			FB	18
Crisis	USA	1950	Richard Brooks	95			FB	12
Critic's Choice	USA	1962	Don Weis	100	std		FB	18
Critters	USA	1986	Stephen Herek	85			GB	60
Crocodile Dundee	USA	1986	Peter Faiman	96	est		FB	45
					deaf		BFI	25
Crocodile Dundee II	USA	1988	John Cornell	111			FB	65
Cromwell	GB	1970	Ken Hughes	139	sc/std		FB	27
Crooks and Coronets	GB	1969	Jim O'Connolly	106	bw		FB	15
Crooks Anonymous	GB	1962	Ken Annakin	87			FB	15
Crooks in Cloisters	GB	1963	Jeremy Summers	98	bw/std		FB	15
Cross	GB	1974	John Du Cane	60	st		LFC	25
Cross and Passion	GB	1981	Kim Longinotto/Claire Pollak	58			CFW	25
Cross of Iron	GB/W.GER	1977	Sam Peckinpah	133			FB	30
Cross-Country Romance	USA	1940	Frank Woodruff	66			GB	15
Crossfire	USA	1947	Edward Dmytryk	86			BFI	20
Crossing Delancey	USA	1988	Joan Micklin Silver	97			FB	60
Crossplot	GB	1969	Alvin Rakoff	97			FB	18
Crossways	JAP	1928	Teinosuke Kinugsa	86	st		BFI	20
Crucified Island	USSR		Shota Managazde	80	est		ETV	10
Cruel Garden	GB	1982	Colin Nears	77			CONC	19
Cry Danger	USA	1951	Robert Parrish	75			GB	15
Cry for Happy	USA	1960	George Marshall	101	sc		FB	18
Cry Freedom	GB	1987	Richard Attenborough	159			FB	60
Cry in the Dark, A	AUSTR	1988	Fred Schepisi	122			FB	60
Cry in the Night, The	USA	1956	Frank Tuttle	75			GB	27
Cry of the City	USA	1948	Robert Siodmak	96			FB	15
Cry Terror	USA	1958	Andrew Stone	94			FB	15
Cry Wolf	GB	1958	John Davis	58			GB	17
Cry, the Beloved Country	GB	1951	Zoltan Korda	103			GB	25
Crystal Gazing	GB	1982	Laura Mulvey/Peter Wollen	90			BFI	35
Cuba	USA	1979	Richard Lester	116			FB	33
Cuba Va	GB	1971	Felix Greene	78			GB	20
Cucumber Hero, The	CZ	1964	Cestmir Mlikovsky	110			ETV	10
Cujo	USA	1983	Lewis Teague	91			GB	43
Cul-de-Sac	GB	1966	Roman Polanski	111		GB	GB	30
Culloden	GB	1964	Peter Watkins	71	bw		BFI	20
Culpepper Cattle Co, The	USA	1972	Dick Richards	92			FB	18
Cup Fever	GB	1965	David Bracknell	63			GB	12
Cup Glory	GB	1971	Tony Maylam	82			GB	20
Curly Sue	USA	1991	John Hughes	102		W	FB	70
Curse of Simba	GB/USA	1964	Lindsay Shonteff	90			GB	15
Curse of the Cat People, The	USA	1944	Robert Wise/Gunther V. Fritsch	70			GB	15
Curse of the Crimson Altar	GB	1968	Vernon Sewell	89	std	GB	GB	20
Curse of the Fly	GB	1965	Don Sharp	86	sc		FB	15
Curse of the Pink Panther	GB	1983	Blake Edwards	110			FB	38
Curse of the Werewolf	GB	1961	Terence Fisher	88	col		FB	18
Curtain Call	USA	1940	Frank Woodruff	63			GB	15
Custard Boys, The	GB	1979	Colin Finbow	80			GB	40
Custer of the West	USA/SP	1966	Robert Siodmak	146	sc/std		GB	18
Cutter's Way	USA	1980	Ivan Passer	109			FB	38
Cutting Edge, The	CAN	1991	Paul M. Glaser	101		UIP	FB	65
Cycle, The	IRAN	1974	Daryioush Mehrjui	95	est		GB	35
Cyclone on Horseback	USA	1942	Edward Killy	60			GB	15
Cyrano de Bergerac	FR	1990	Jean-Paul Rappeneau	135	st	AE	GB	80

Films on Offer

27

	COUNTRY OF PRODUCTION	YEAR	DIRECTOR	RUNNING TIME	VERSION	35mm	16mm	16mm RENTAL FEE
D.A.R.Y.L.	GB	1985	Simon Wincer	100			FB	45
D.O.A	USA	1988	Rocky Morton/Annabel Jankel	97			FB	55
D.O.A.	USA	1950	Rudolph Maté	83			RESP	25
Dad's Army	GB	1970	Norman Cohen	95			FB	18
Daddie Nostalgie (see These Foolish Things)								
Daemon	GB	1986	Colin Finbow	71		BD	GB	40
Daisies	CZ	1966	Vera Chytilova	75	est		GB	30
Daisy Miller	USA	1974	Peter Bogdanovich	92			FB	18
Dam Busters, The	GB	1954	Michael Anderson	130			FB	15
Dames	USA	1934	Ray Enright	90			FB	15
Damien Omen II	USA	1978	Don Taylor	106	sc/std		FB	43
Damn Yankees	USA	1958	George Abbott/Stanley Donen	110			FB	18
Damnation Alley	USA	1977	Jack Smight	95	sc		FB	27
Damned, The	IT/ W.GER	1969	Luchino Visconti	155			FB	22
Damsel in Distress, A	USA	1937	George Stevens	100			GB	16
Dance Girl Dance	USA	1940	Dorothy Arzner	89			GB	20
Dance Little Lady	GB	1954	Val Guest	87		GB	GB	15
Dance of the Vampires	GB	1967	Roman Polanski	107	sc/std		FB	18
Dancers	USA	1987	Herbert Ross	99			FB	40
Dances of Our Nationalities	CHI			65			GB	15
Dances With Wolves	USA	1991	Kevin Costner	173		GU	GU	100
Dancing Masters, The	USA	1944	Mal St. Clair	64			FB	15
Dandy in Aspic	GB	1968	Anthony Mann	107	sc/std		FB	18
Danger on Dartmoor	GB	1980	David Eady	57			GB	17
Danger on the Danube	HUNG	1961	György Révész	54			GB	12
Danger Patrol	USA	1937	Lew Landers	60			GB	15
Danger Point	GB	1971	John Davis	56			GB	17
Danger Route	GB	1967	Seth Holt	92			FB	18
Danger Within	GB	1958	Don Chaffey	101			GB	20
Danger: Diabolik	IT/FR	1967	Mario Bava	88	bw/dub		FB	15
Dangerous Cargo	GB	1954	John Harlow	61			GB	20
Dangerous Corner	USA	1934	Phil Rosen	67			GB	15
Dangerous Days of Kiowa Jones, The	USA	1966	Alex March	99			FB	18
Dangerous Hours	USA	1920	Fred Niblo	84	st		BFI	15
Dangerous Liaisons	USA	1988	Stephen Frears	120			FB	65
Dangerous Mission	USA	1954	Louis King	75			GB	15
Dangerous Moonlight	GB	1941	Brian Desmond Hurst	98			GB	15
Dangerous Profession, A	USA	1949	Ted Tetzlaff	85			GB	15
Dangerous When Wet	USA	1953	Charles Walters	95			FB	16
Daniel Boone - Frontier Trail Rider	USA	1966	George Sherman	91			FB	18
Danton	FR	1983	Andrzej Wajda	136	s/t	AE	GB	55
Dark at the Top of the Stairs, The	USA	1960	Delbert Mann	124			FB	18
Dark Circle	USA	1982	Judy Irving/Chris Beaver/ Ruther Landy	81			CONC	45
							MP	51.75
Dark Crystal, The	GB	1982	Jim Henson/Frank Oz	92			FB	43
Dark Enemy	GB	1984	Colin Finbow	85		BD	GB	40
Dark Eyes	IT	1987	Nikita Mikhalkov	118	est	GA	GB	65
Dark Intruder	USA	1965	Harvey Hart	59			FB	15
Dark Passage	USA	1947	Delmer Daves	106			FB	22
Dark Victory	USA	1976	Robert Butler	100			FB	27
Darling	GB	1965	John Schlesinger	127	bw/std		FB	15
Darling Lili	USA	1969	Blake Edwards	136	sc/std		FB	22
Darwin Adventure	GB	1971	Jack Couffer	91			FB	18
Date with Judy, A	USA	1948	Richard Thorpe	113	bw		FB	12
Daughter of The Nile	TAI	1987	Hou-Hsiao Hsien	84	st	AE	GB	60
Daughter-in-Law	USSR	1972	Hodjakuli Narliyev	82	est		ETV	12
Daughters of China	CHI	1950	Ling Tzufong/Ti Chang	90	est		ETV	10
Daughters of Satan	USA	1972	Hollingsworth Morse	86			FB	18

	COUNTRY OF PRODUCTION	YEAR	DIRECTOR	RUNNING TIME	VERSION	35mm	16mm	16mm RENTAL FEE
David and Bathsheba	USA	1951	Henry King	116			FB	22
David Copperfield	USA	1934	George Cukor	130			FB	16
David Copperfield	GB	1970	Delbert Mann	118			FB	18
David Lean: A Self Portrait	GB	1971	Thomas Craven	60			GB	18
Davy	GB	1957	Michael Relph	82	std		FB	15
Davy Crockett and the River Pirates	USA	1956	Norman Foster	81			FB	27
Davy Crockett King of the Wild Frontier	USA	1955	Norman Foster	93			FB	27
Davy Jones Locker	GB		Frederic Goode	59			GB	17
Dawn Killer	GB	1959	Don Taylor	68			GB	12
Dawn Patrol	USA	1938	Edmund Goulding	107			FB	22
Dawning, The	GB	1988	Robert Knights	97			GB	50
Day After Trinity	USA	1980	Jon Else	88			GB	50
							CONC	28
Day and the Hour, The	FR /IT	1962	René Clément	115	std/dub		FB	15
Day at the Races, A	USA	1937	Sam Wood	109			FB	14
Day for Night (see Nuit Américaine, La)								
Day Mars Invaded Earth, The	USA	1962	Maury Dexter	70	std		FB	15
Day of the Animals	USA	1976	William Girdler	97	sc/std		FB	22
Day of the Dolphin, The	USA	1973	Mike Nichols	104	std		GR	27
Day of the Evil Gun	USA	1968	Jerry Thorpe	93	std		FB	18
Day of the Jackal	GB/FR	1973	Fred Zinnemann	142			FB	38
Day of the Wolves	USA	1971	Ferde Grofe Jr.	95			GB	22
Day Shall Dawn	PAK	1958	Aajeay Kardar	91	est		GB	25
Day the Bookies Wept, The	USA	1939	Leslie Goodwins	64			GB	15
Day the Earth Stood Still, The	USA	1951	Robert Wise	92			FB	15
Day They Gave Babies Away, The (see All Mine to Give)								
Day They Robbed the Bank ofEngland, The	GB	1959	John Guillermin	85			FB	14
Day with the Wind, A	W.GER	1978	Haro Senft	94	est		GFL	0
Daylight Robbery	GB	1964	Michael Truman	57			GB	12
Days and Nights in the Forest	INDIA	1970	Satyajit Ray	115	est		GB	25
Days of Glory	USA	1944	Jacques Tourneur	86			GB	15
Days of Heaven	USA	1978	Terrence Malick	94			FB	38
Days of Hope								
1916 Joining Up				95				
1921 Lockout				100				
1924 Labour Government				80				
1926 General Strike	GB		Ken Loach	135			BFI	25
Days of Thrills and Laughter	USA	1961	Robert Youngson	80			GB	15
Days of Thunder	USA	1990	Tony Scott	107		UIP	FB	65
Dead Again	USA	1991	Kenneth Branagh	101		UIP	FB	70
Dead Bang	USA	1989	John Frankenheimer	102		W	FB	60
Dead Calm	AUSTR	1989	Phillip Noyce	96		W	FB	60
Dead Cert	GB	1974	Tony Richardson	100			FB	18
Dead Heat on a Merry-go-Round	USA	1966	Bernard Girard	107			FB	18
Dead Men Don't Wear Plaid	USA	1982	Carl Reiner	89			FB	43
Dead of Night	GB	1945	Alberto Cavalcanti/ Charles Crichton/					
			Basil Dearden/Robert Hamer	104			FB	15
Dead Poets Society	USA	1989	Peter Weir	128		W	FB	60
Dead Pool, The	USA	1988	Buddy Van Horn	90			FB	65
Dead Reckoning	USA	1947	John Cromwell	101			FB	15
Dead Ringers	CAN	1988	David Cronenberg	115			FB	60
Dead, The	USA/GB	1987	John Huston	83			GB	60
Deadfall	GB	1968	Bryan Forbes	120			FB	18
Deadline at Dawn	USA	1946	Harold Clurman	82			GB	15
Deadly Affair, The	GB	1966	Sidney Lumet	107			FB	18
Deadly Females, The	GB	1976	Donovan Winter	105			GB	30
Deadly Friend	USA	1986	Wes Craven	90			FB	45
Deadly Game	USA	1986	Marshall Brickman	112			FB	45

	COUNTRY OF PRODUCTION	YEAR	DIRECTOR	RUNNING TIME	VERSION	35mm	16mm	16mm RENTAL FEE
Deadly Mantis, The	USA	1957	Nathan Juran	79			FB	15
Deadly Pursuit (Shoot to Kill)	USA	1988	Roger Spottiswoode	110			FB	55
Deadly Roulette	USA	1966	William Hale	90	bw		FB	15
Deadly Trackers	USA	1973	Barry Shear	105			FB	18
Deadly Trap	FR/IT	1971	René Clément	97			FB	18
Dealers	GB	1989	Colin Bucksey	91		R	FB	55
Dear Brigitte	USA	1965	Henry Koster	100	std		FB	18
Dear Inspector	FR	1977	Philippe de Broca	105	dub		FB	33
Dear John	SWE	1964	Lars Magnus Lindgren	105	est		GB	30
Dear Wife	USA	1949	Richard Haydn	88			FB	15
Death and the Singing Telegram	USA	1983	Mark Rance	114			LFC	59
Death at Broadcasting House	GB	1934	Reginald Denham	60			BFI	15
Death Before Dying	W.GER	1976	Rainer Wolffhardt	87	est		GFL	0
Death Comes in the Rain	CZ	1966	Andrej Lettrich	94	est		ETV	10
Death Hunt	USA	1981	Peter Hunt	97			FB	33
Death in a French Garden	FR	1985	Michel Deville	100	s/t	AE	GB	55
Death in Venice	IT	1971	Luchino Visconti	130			FB	22
Death of a Princess	GB/USA/NZ/							
	AUSTR/HOLL	1980	Anthony Thomas	115			BFI	25
Death of a Salesman	USA	1985	Volker Schlöndorff	136		AE	GB	60
Death of a Scoundrel	USA	1956	Charles Martin	119			GB	15
Death of Maria Malibran	W.GER	1972	Werner Schroeter	108	est		GFL	0
Death of Mario Ricci, The	W.GER/ FR	1983	Claude Goretta	101	est		FB	50
Death on the Nile	GB	1978	John Guillermin	140			FB	43
Death Race 2000	USA	1975	Paul Bartel	79			GB	30
Death Rides a Horse	IT	1967	Giulio Petroni	113	sc/dub		FB	18
Death Vengeance	USA	1982	Lewis Teague	96			FB	40
Death Watch	FR W.GER	1979	Bertrand Tavernier	128	sc/est		GB	40
Death Weekend	CAN	1976	William Fruet	84			GB	33
Death Wish	USA	1974	Michael Winner	94			FB	38
Death Wish 4: The Crackdown	USA	1987	J. Lee Thompson	98			FB	45
Death Wish II	USA	1981	Michael Winner	93			FB	45
Death Wish III	USA	1985	Michael Winner	90			FB	45
Deathtrap	USA	1982	Sidney Lumet	116			FB	40
Decameron, The	IT/FR/ W.GER	1970	Pier Paolo Pasolini	111	est		FB	22
Deceived	USA	1991	Damian Harris	108		W	FB	65
Deceivers, The	GB	1988	Nicholas Meyer	103			GB	55
December Bride	GB	1990	Thaddeus O'Sullivan	88			BFI	75
Decks Ran Red	USA	1958	Andrew Stone	84			FB	15
Decline and Fall of a Birdwatcher	GB	1968	John Krish	113			FB	18
Decline of the American Empire, The	CAN	1986	Denys Arcand	101	est		GB	60
Decline of Western Civilization, The	USA	1980	Penelope Spheeris	100			ICA	50
Deep End	W.GER/ USA	1970	Jerzy Skolimowski	88			GB	35
Deep Six, The	USA	1957	Rudolph Maté	110			GB	22
Deep Star Six	USA	1989	Sean S. Cunningham	99		GU	GU	80
Deep Waters	GB	1978	David Eady	55			GB	17
Deep, The	USA/GB	1977	Peter Yates	123	sc/std		FB	35
Deer Hunter, The	USA	1978	Michael Cimino	182	sc/std		FB	45
Defence of the Realm	GB	1985	David Drury	96			FB	40
Defending Your Life	USA	1991	Albert Brooks	111		W	FB	60
Degree of Murder, A	W.GER	1966	Volker Schlöndorff	87	dub		FB	18
Déjà Vu	GB	1984	Tony Richmond	90			FB	40
Delegation, Die	W.GER	1970	Rainer Erler	98	cst		GFL	0
Délicatessen	FR	1990	Jean-Pierre Jennet/Marc Caro	99	st	ELEC	GB	90
Delightful Rogue, The	USA	1929	Lynn Shores	73			GB	15
Deliverance	USA	1972	John Boorman	107	sc		FB	27
Delta Force	USA	1986	Menahem Golan	128			FB	45
Demetrius and the Gladiators	USA	1954	Delmer Daves	100	std		FB	18

d

	COUNTRY OF PRODUCTION	YEAR	DIRECTOR	RUNNING TIME	VERSION	35mm	16mm	16mm RENTAL FEE
Demi-Paradise, The	GB	1943	Anthony Asquith	111			BFI	30
Demon Seed	USA	1977	Donald Cammell	95	std		FB	33
Demons of the Mind	GB	1971	Peter Sykes	89			FB	18
Demons of the Swamp	USA	1958	Bernard Kowalski	61			FB	15
Dentellière, La	FR/ SWITZ	1976	Claude Goretta	106	est		GB	40
Dentist in the Chair	GB	1960	Don Chaffey	88	GB		GB	15
Dentist on the Job	GB	1961	C.M. Pennington Richards	88			FB	15
Depart, Le	BEL	1968	Jerzy Skolimowski	89	est		GB	25
Dersu Uzala	USSR/ JAP	1975	Akira Kurosawa	141	est	ELEC	GB	43
Desert Bloom	USA	1985	Eugene Corr	106			GB	70
Desert Fox The Story of Rommel, The	USA	1951	Henry Hathaway	89			FB	15
Desert Fury	USA	1947	Lewis Allen	96	bw		FB	15
Desert Hearts	USA	1985	Donna Deitch	91			BFI	55
Desert Mice	GB	1959	Michael Relph	83			GB	15
Desert Victory	GB	1943	Roy Boulting	60			CFL	13
Deserter, The	USSR	1933	Vsevolod Pudovkin	106	cst		BFI	30
Deserter, The	IT/YUGO	1970	Burt Kennedy	99	sc/std		FB	18
Design for Living	USA	1933	Ernst Lubitsch	95			FB	22
Designing Woman	USA	1957	Vincente Minnelli	118	std		FB	18
Desire in the Dust	USA	1960	William F. Claxton	102	sc/std		FB	15
Desire Me	USA	1947	George Cukor	91			FB	12
Despair	FR/ W.GER	1978	R.W. Fassbinder	119			FB	40
Desperados, The	USA	1968	Henry Levin	90			FB	18
Desperate	USA	1947	Anthony Mann	72			GB	15
Desperate Characters	USA	1971	Frank D. Gilroy	91			GB	22
Desperate Hours	USA	1955	William Wyler	113		F	FB	15
Desperately Seeking Susan	USA	1985	Susan Seidelman	103			FB	50
Destination Berlin	POL	1968	Jerzy Passendorfer	87	est		FOP	0
Destination Moon	USA	1950	Irving Pichel	94	bw		GB	15
Destinations	GB	1981	Russell Murray	70			YAA	0
Destiny	GER	1921	Fritz Lang	78	est/sd		BFI	20
Destiny	GB	1978	Mike Newell	105			BFI	20
Destry Rides Again	USA	1940	George Marshall	81			FB	15
Detective Story	USA	1951	William Wyler	104			FB	15
Detective, The	USA	1968	Gordon Douglas	114	sc/std		FB	18
Devices and Desires	GB	1975	Giles Foster	55			CONT	25
Devil and Daniel Webster, The	USA	1941	William Dieterle	106			GB	15
Devil and Max Devlin, The	USA	1981	Steven Stern	96			FB	38
Devil and The Nun, The	POL	1960	Jerzy Kawalerowicz	92	est		GB	25
Devil Bat's Daughter	USA	1946	Frank Wisbar	67			GB	15
Devil Bat, The	USA	1941	Jean Yarbrough	70			GB	15
Devil Doll	GB/USA	1963	Lindsay Shonteff	82			GB	15
Devil is a Woman, The	USA	1935	Josef von Sternberg	79			BFI	25
Devil Rides Out, The	GB	1967	Terence Fisher	95	bw		FB	15
Devil Thumbs a Ride, The	USA	1947	Felix Feist	63			GB	15
Devil's 8, The	USA	1968	Burt Topper	98	bw		FB	15
Devil's Brigade, The	USA	1968	Andrew V. McLaglen	130	sc		FB	18
Devil's Children, The	USA	1962	James Sheldon	75	bw		FB	15
Devil's Cleavage, The	USA	1975	George Kuchar	110			RESP	40
Devil's Doorway	USA	1950	Anthony Mann	83			FB	12
Devil's Eye, The	SWE	1960	Ingmar Bergman	90	est		GB	35
Devil's Pass, The	POL	1949	Tadeusz Kanski/Aldo Vergano	90	est		FOP	0
Devil's Wanton, The	SWE	1949	Ingmar Bergman	80	est		GB	25
Devil-Doll, The	USA	1936	Tod Browning	78			FB	22
Devils, The	GB	1971	Ken Russell	111	std		FB	33
Devotion	USA	1931	Robert Milton	80			GB	15
Diabolik (see Danger: Diabolik)								
Dial M for Murder	USA	1954	Alfred Hitchcock	105	bw		FB	25

d

	COUNTRY OF PRODUCTION	YEAR	DIRECTOR	RUNNING TIME	VERSION	35mm	16mm	16mm RENTAL FEE
Diamond Head	USA	1962	Guy Green	107	std		FB	18
Diamonds	USA	1975	Menahem Golan	110			FB	19
Diamonds are Forever	GB	1971	Guy Hamilton	119	sc/std		FB	38
Diamonds of the Night	CZ	1964	Jan Nemec	64	est		GB	20
Diary for My Children	HUNG	1982	Marta Meszaros	106	est		GB	55
Diary for My Loves	HUNG	1987	Marta Meszaros	130	est	AE	GB	60
Diary of a Chambermaid	FR	1965	Luis Buñuel	97	s/t	ELEC	GB	50
Diary of a Country Priest (see Journal d'un Cure de Campagne)								
Diary of a Mad Housewife	USA	1970	Frank Perry	95			FB	18
Diary of a Sane Man	GB	1989	Gad Hollander	88			BFI	60
Diary of a Shinjuku Thief	JAP	1969	Nagisa Oshima	94	est		GB	30
Diary of Anne Frank, The	USA	1959	George Stevens	150	std		FB	18
Dick Deadeye	GB	1975	Bill Melendez	77			GB	25
Dick Tracy	USA	1990	Warren Beatty	105		W	FB	65
Did You Hear the One About the Travelling Saleslady?	USA	1967	Don Weis	74	96/std		FB	18
Die Hard	USA	1988	John McTiernan	132		F	FB	60
Die Hard 2	USA	1989	Renny Harlin	123	sc	F	FB	75
Die to Live - Survivors of Die to Live - Survivors Hiroshima	GB	1975	BBC 'Horizon'	60			CONC	17
Digby the Biggest Dog in the World	GB	1973	Joseph McGrath	88			FB	22
Dillinger	USA	1973	John Milius	103			FB	18
Dim Sum A Little Bit of Heart	USA	1985	Wayne Wang	87	est		BFI	50
Dimension 5	USA	1966	Franklin Adreon	86	bw		FB	15
Dimenticare Venezia (see To Forget Venice)								
Dimples	USA	1936	William A. Seiter	78			FB	15
Diner	USA	1982	Barry Levinson	110			FB	43
Ding Dong Williams	USA	1946	William Berke	62			GB	15
Dingleton	GB	1971	Shirley Fisher	60			CONC	15.4
Dionne Quintuplets, The	CAN	1979	Donald Brittain	87			CONC	24.2
Diplomaniacs	USA	1933	William A. Seiter	63			GB	15
Dirt Cheap	AUSTR	1980	Marg Clancy/David Hay/Ned Lander	88			GB	25
Dirty Dancing	USA	1987	Emile Ardolino	100			GB	60
Dirty Dingus Magee	USA	1970	Burt Kennedy	91	sc/std		FB	24
Dirty Dozen, The	USA/GB	1967	Robert Aldrich	150			FB	38
Dirty Harry	USA	1971	Don Siegel	101	sc/std		FB	33
Dirty Mary, Crazy Larry	USA	1974	John Hough	93			FB	30
Dirty Money (see Flic, Un)								
Dirty O'Neil The Love Life of a Cop	USA	1974	Howard Freen/Lewis Teague	79			GB	30
Discovery on Fuzzy Hill	CZ		Karel Stekly	70	est		ETV	10
Discreet Charm of the Bourgeoisie	FR	1972	Luis Buñuel	101	s/t		GB	50
Dishonoured	USA	1931	Josef von Sternberg	91			BFI	25
Disorder and Early Suffering	W.GER	1977	Franz Seitz	90	est		GFL	0
Disorderly Orderly, The	USA	1964	Jerry Lewis	89	col		FB	18
					bw		FB	15
Distant Drums	USA	1951	Raoul Walsh	101	bw/ col		GB	18
							GB	20
Distant Thunder	INDIA	1973	Satyajit Ray	99	est		GB	38
Distant Trumpet, A	USA	1964	Raoul Walsh	117	std		FB	18
Distant Voices, Still Lives	GB	1988	Terence Davies	84		BFI	BFI	65
Diva	FR	1981	Jean-Jacques Beineix	110	est	ELEC	GB	76
Divine Comedy Purgatory, A (see Purgatorio)								
Divine Madness	USA	1980	Michael Ritchie	93	sc		FB	43
Divorce American Style	USA	1967	Bud Yorkin	108			FB	15
Dixiana	USA	1930	Luther Reed	99			GB	15
Do Not Disturb	USA	1965	Ralph Levy	102	sc		FB	18
Doberman Gang, The	USA	1972	Byron Chudgow	95			GB	38
Doberman Patrol	USA	1973	Frank de Felitta	87			FB	15
Doc	USA	1971	Frank Perry	91			FB	18
Doc Hollywood	USA	1991	Michael Caton-Jones	104		W	FB	70

Films on Offer

d

	COUNTRY OF PRODUCTION	YEAR	DIRECTOR	RUNNING TIME	VERSION	35mm	16mm	16mm RENTAL FEE
Doc Savage...The Man of Bronze	USA	1975	Michael Anderson	100			FB	18
Dock Brief, The	GB	1962	James Hill	88			FB	14
Doctor at Large	GB	1957	Ralph Thomas	104	bw		FB	18
Doctor Dolittle	GB	1966	Richard Fleischer	152	sc/std		FB	27
Doctor Faustus	GB/IT	1967	Richard Burton/Neville Coghill	92			FB	18
Doctor from Stalingrad (see Arzt Von Stalingrad. Der)								
Doctor in Clover	GB	1966	Ralph Thomas	101	col/ bw		FB	18
Doctor in Distress	GB	1963	Ralph Thomas	102			FB	18
Doctor in Love	GB	1960	Ralph Thomas	92	col		FB	18
Doctor in Trouble	GB	1970	Ralph Thomas	90			FB	18
Doctor Syn Alias the Scarecrow	USA	1964	James Neilson	98			FB	27
Doctor X	USA	1932	Michael Curtiz	76	bw		FB	22
Doctor You've Got to be Kidding	USA	1967	Peter Tewksbury	94	std		FB	16
Doctor Zhivago	USA	1965	David Lean	193	sc/std		FB	43
Doctor's Dilemma, The	GB	1958	Anthony Asquith	99			FB	15
Doctors' Wives	USA	1970	George Schaefer	102			FB	18
Dog Day Afternoon	USA	1975	Sidney Lumet	130			FB	27
Dog of Flanders, A	USA	1935	Edward Sloman	72			GB	15
Dog Soldiers	USA	1978	Karel Reisz	125			FB	27
Dog Star Man	USA	1961	Stan Brakhage	79			LFC	35
Dogs of War, The	GB	1980	John Irvin	119			FB	43
Dolce Vita, La	IT	1959	Federico Fellini	174	sc/est	BFI	BFI	60
Doll's Eye	GB	1982	Jan Worth	75			BFI	35
Domino Killings, The	USA	1976	Stanley Kramer	100			GB	33
Don Giovanni	FR/IT/ W.GER	1979	Joseph Losey	176		AE	GB	55
Don is Dead, The	USA	1973	Richard Fleischer	117			FB	18
Don Quixote	USSR	1957	Grigori Kozintsev	107	est		GB	25
Don't Bother to Knock	GB	1961	Cyril Frankel	89	bw/sc/ std		FB	15
Don't Go Near the Water	USA	1957	Charles Walters	107	std		FB	16
Don't Just Lie There Say Something	GB	1973	Bob Kellett	91			FB	18
Don't Just Stand There	USA	1967	Ron Winston	99	std		FB	18
Don't Look Back	USA	1967	D.A. Pennebaker	95			GB	60
Don't Lose Your Head	GB	1966	Gerald Thomas	90	bw		FB	15
Don't Make Waves	USA	1967	Alexander Mackendrick	85	sc		FB	16
Don't Tell the Wife	USA	1937	Christy Cabanne	63			GB	15
Don't Turn 'Em Loose	USA	1936	Ben Stoloff	67			GB	15
Dona Flor and Her Two Husbands	BRAZ	1977	Bruno Barreto	110	est		GB	20
Donna	IT/HOLL	1979	Yvonne Scholter	64	est		GB	35
Doomed to Die	USA	1940	William Nigh	65			GB	20
Doomsday Flight , The	USA	1966	William A. Graham	97	bw		FB	15
Doomwatch	GB	1972	Peter Sasdy	92		GB	GB	20
Doppelganger	GB	1969	Robert Parrish	101			FB	18
Double Danger	USA	1938	Lew Landers	62			GB	15
Double Dynamite	USA	1951	Irving Cummings	80			GB	15
Double Headed Eagle	GB	1973	Lutz Becker	90	est		GB	27
Double Indemnity	USA	1944	Billy Wilder	107		UIP	FB	22
Double Life of Veronique, The	FR	1991	Krzysztof Kieslowski	98			GB	100
Double Man, The	GB	1967	Franklin J. Schaffner	105			FB	18
Double Trouble	USA	1966	Norman Taurog	92	std		FB	22
Double Vision	GB	1986	Amber Films	60			AMB	TBC
Dove, The	USA	1974	Charles Jarrott	105	sc/std		FB	18
Doves, The	CAN	1972	Jean-Claude Lord	116	dub		FB	24
Down and Out in Beverly Hills	USA	1986	Paul Mazursky	103			FB	45
Down By Law	USA	1986	Jim Jarmusch	107			GB	60
Down the Corner	GB	1977	Joe Comerford	77	est		BFI	25
Down Three Dark Streets	USA	1954	Arnold Laven	84			GB	15
Down to Their Last Yacht	USA	1934	Paul Sloane	64			GB	15

d

	COUNTRY OF PRODUCTION	YEAR	DIRECTOR	RUNNING TIME	VERSION	35mm	16mm	16mm RENTAL FEE
Downhill Racer	USA	1969	Michael Ritchie	101			FB	22
Dr Ehrlich's Magic Bullet	USA	1939	William Dieterle	103			FB	22
Dr G and the Bikini Machine	USA	1965	Norman Taurog	90	std		FB	18
Dr Heckyl and Mr Hype	USA	1980	Charles B. Griffith	96			FB	38
Dr Jekyll & Mr Hyde	USA	1920	John S. Robertson	63	sd		BFI	15
Dr Jekyll & Sister Hyde	GB	1971	Roy Ward Baker	97			FB	18
Dr No	GB	1962	Terence Young	110			FB	33
Dr Phibes Rises Again	GB	1972	Robert Fuest	94			FB	18
Dr Strangelove	GB	1963	Stanley Kubrick	94			FB	15
Dr. Livingstone	GB			64	st		GB	20
Dr. Mabuse The Gambler								
Part One				102	est sd		BFI	
Part Two	GER	1921-22	Fritz Lang	92	sd			25
Dracula	USA	1930	Tod Browning	76			FB	22
Dracula	USA	1979	John Badham	112	std		FB	38
Dracula A.D. 1972	GB	1972	Alan Gibson	97			FB	18
Dragnet	USA	1987	Tom Mankiewicz	106			FB	45
Dragonslayer	GB	1981	Matthew Robbins	109	sc		FB	38
Draughtsman's Contract, The	GB	1982	Peter Greenaway	104			BFI	50
Dream Chasers	USA	1985	Arthur Dubs/David E. Jackson	95			FB	45
Dream Life	CAN	1972	Mireille Dansereau	72	est		FB	30
Dreamchild	GB	1985	Gavin Millar	94			FB	45
Dreams that Money Can Buy	USA	1947	Hans Richter	90			GB	25
Dreigroschenoper Die	GER	1931	G.W. Pabst	100	est		GB	25
Dresser, The	GB	1983	Peter Yates	118			FB	45
Dressmaker, The	GB	1987	Jim O Brien	92			FB	60
Drifters	GB	1929	John Grierson	50	st		CFL	21.74
Drive-in	USA	1976	Rod Amateau	96			FB	15
Driver, The	USA	1978	Walter Hill	90			FB	33
Driving Miss Daisy	USA	1989	Bruce Beresford	99		W	FB	65
Dr Jekyll & Mr Hyde	USA	1941	Victor Fleming	122			FB	14
Droids	FR/GB	1978	Jean-Pascal Auberge	75			LFC	30
Drôle de Drame	FR	1937	Marcel Carné	95	est		GB	25
Drop Dead Darling	GB	1966	Ken Hughes	100	std		FB	18
Drop Dead Fred	USA	1991	Ate de Jong	99		R	FB	65
Drowning by Numbers	GB	1988	Peter Greenaway	119			GB	75
Drowning Pool, The	USA	1975	Stuart Rosenberg	108	sc/std		FB	18
Drugstore Cowboy	US	1989	Gus Van Sant Jr.	101		FFC	GB	80
Drum Beat	USA	1954	Delmer Daves	109	std		GB	22
Drums Across the River	USA	1954	Nathan Juran	77	bw		FB	15
Drums Along the Mohawk	USA	1939	John Ford	104			FB	19
Drums of Africa	USA	1963	James B. Clark	90			FB	14
Drums of Destiny	S.AFR	1962	George Michael	80			GB	22
Drums of the Desert	USA	1940	George Waggner	65			GB	15
Dry White Season, A	USA	1989	Euzhan Palcy	107		UIP	FB	65
Drylanders	CAN	1962	Donald Haldane	69	bw		CHC	0
Du Land der Liebe	W GER	1978	Rolf von Sydow	60	est		GFL	0
Duchess and the Dirtwater Fox, The	USA	1976	Melvin Frank	104	sc/std		FB	25
Duchess of Idaho	USA	1950	Robert Z. Leonard	98	bw		FB	12
Duck Tales: The Movie	USA	1990	Bob Hathcock	65		D	FB	65
Dude Cowboy	USA	1941	David Howard	60			GB	15
Duel	USA	1971	Steven Spielberg	90			FB	27
Duel in the Jungle	GB	1954	George Marshall	101			FB	18
Duel in the Sun	USA	1946	King Vidor	135		GB	GB	22
Duellists, The	GB	1977	Ridley Scott	101			FB	33
Duet for One	USA	1986	Andrei Konchalovsky	107			FB	45
Duffy	GB	1968	Robert Parrish	101			FB	18
Duke Wore Jeans The	GB	1958	Gerald Thomas	90	bw		FB	15

	COUNTRY OF PRODUCTION	YEAR	DIRECTOR	RUNNING TIME	VERSION	35mm	16mm	16mm RENTAL FEE
Dulcima	GB	1971	Frank Nesbitt	98			FB	18
Dumbo	USA	1941	Ben Sharpsteen	64			FB	35
Dune	USA	1984	David Lynch	136			FB	50
Dunkirk	GB	1958	Leslie Norman	135			FB	18
Dunwich Horror, The	USA	1969	Daniel Haller	86			FB	18
Dust	BEL/FR	1985	Marion Hansel	88	BD		GB	60
Dying Young	USA	1991	Joel Schumacher	111	F		FB	65
Dyn Amo	GB	1972	Steve Dwoskin	120			MP	51.75
Dynamite Man from Glory Jail	USA	1971	Andrew V. McLaglen	98			FB	18

Chinatown

Dead of Night

e	COUNTRY OF PRODUCTION	YEAR	DIRECTOR	RUNNING TIME	VERSION	35mm	16mm	16mm RENTAL FEE
E'Lollipop	S.AFR	1975	Ashley Lazarus	93			FB	18
Each Dawn I Die	USA	1939	William Keighley	89			FB	22
Eadweard Muybridge – Zoopraxographer	USA	1975	Thom Andersen	60			GB	20
Eagle Has Landed, The	GB	1976	John Sturges	132	sc/std		GB	48
Eagle Rock	GB	1964	Henry Geddes	62			GB	17
Eagle's Wing, The	GB	1978	Anthony Harvey	104	111/sc/sd		FB	33
Eagle, The	USA	1925	Clarence Brown	86	st		BFI	20
Early Bird, The	GB	1965	Robert Asher	98	bw		FB	15
Early Spring	JAP	1956	Yasujiro Ozu	144	est		GB	45
Earth	USSR	1930	Alexander Dovzhenko	90	st	CONT	GB	25
Earth Girls Are Easy	USA	1988	Julien Temple	100			FB	55
Earth II	USA	1970	Tom Gries	75			FB	16
Earth is a Sinful Song	FIN	1973	Rauni Mollberg	102	est		GB	30
Earth Sings, The	CZ	1933	Karel Plicka	65	est		BFI	15
Earthquake	USA	1974	Mark Robson	123			FB	43
East is Red, The	CHI	1965/77	Collective	119	est		GB	25
East Wind (see Vent D'Est)								
Easter Parade	USA	1948	Charles Walters	103			FB	28
Easy Living	USA	1949	Jacques Tourneur	78			GB	15
Easy Money	USA	1982	Joe Signorelli	96			FB	38
Eat a Bowl of Tea	USA	1989	Wayne Wang	104		AE	GB	70
Eating Raoul	USA	1982	Paul Bartel	87			GB	48
Echo of the Badlands	GB	1976	David Eady/Tim King	56			GB	17
Echoes of a Summer	USA/ CAN	1975	Don Taylor	98			FB	18
Eddy Duchin Story, The	USA	1955	George Sidney	123	col/sc/ std		FB	18
Edison the Man	USA	1940	Clarence Brown	107			FB	15
Edna,the Inebriate Woman	GB	1971	Ted Kotcheff	90			CONC	13.20
Educating Rita	GB	1983	Lewis Gilbert	110			FB	48
Edward II	GB	1991	Derek Jarman	90		MAY	GB	80
Edward Scissorhands	USA	1991	Tim Burton	105		F	FB	70
Edward, My Son	GB	1949	George Cukor	112			FB	15
Effect of Gamma Rays on Man in the Moon Marigolds, The	USA	1972	Paul Newman	101			FB	18
Effi Briest	W GER	1974	R.W. Fassbinder	140	est	BFI	BFI	45
Egg and I, The	USA	1947	Chester Erskine	108			FB	15
Egghead's Robot	GB	1970	Milo Lewis	56			GB	17
Eiger Sanction, The	USA	1975	Clint Eastwood	118	sc/std		FB	33
Eight Minutes to Midnight	USA	1980	Mary Benjamin	55			GB	40
							CONC	20
84 Charing Cross Road	USA	1986	David Jones	99			FB	55
El	MEX	1952	Luis Buñuel	91	est		BFI	25
El Salvador: Another Vietnam	USA	1981	Glen Silber/ Tete Vasconellos	50			MP	40.25
El Salvador: The Decision to Win	EL SAL	1981	Cero a la Izquierda Collective	75	est		MP	40.25
El Salvador: The People Will Win	EL SAL	1980	Diego de la Texera	80	eng/est		MP	40.25
El Salvador: The Road to Victory	EL SAL	1984	El Salvador Film Institute	58	est		MP	34.5
Electra Glide in Blue	USA	1973	James William Guercio	113	sc		FB	27
Electric Blue: The Movie	GB	1980	Adam Cole	90			GB	40
Electric Dreams	GB/USA	1984	Steve Barron	111			GB	45
Electric Eskimo, The	GB	1979	Frank Godwin	60			GB	17
Electric Horseman, The	USA	1979	Sydney Pollack	120	std		FB	43
Element of Crime, The	DEN	1984	Lars von Trier	104			GB	50
Elephant Called Slowly, An	GB	1969	James Hill	91			FB	18
Elephant Man, The	USA	1980	David Lynch	127	sc		FB	43
Elephant Walk	USA	1954	William Dieterle	103	bw		FB	15
Elephants Never Forget	USA	1939	Gordon Douglas	74			BFI/ GB	15
Eleven Harrowhouse	GB	1974	Aram Avakian	95	sc/std		FB	18
Elizabeth of Ladymead	GB	1948	Herbert Wilcox	97			GB	25
Elizabeth The Queen	USA	1939	Michael Curtiz	106			FB	16
Ella Cinders	USA	1926	Alfred E. Green	65	st		BFI	15

	COUNTRY OF PRODUCTION	YEAR	DIRECTOR	RUNNING TIME	VERSION	35mm	16mm	16mm RENTAL FEE
Elstree Calling	GB	1930	Adrian Brunel	85			BFI	20
Elvira Madigan	SWE	1967	Bo Widerberg	95	est		APO	35
Elvis on Tour	USA	1972	Pierre Adidge/Robert Abel	93	sc/std		FB	27
Elvis That's the Way It Is	USA	1970	Denis Sanders	108	std/sc		FB	27
Elvis! Elvis!	SWE	1977	Kay Pollak	101	est		GB	30
Elvis: The Movie	USA	1979	John Carpenter	122			GB	43
Emanations	GB	1979	John Du Cane	60			LFC	25
Emanuelle Queen Bitch	GR	1979	Plias Milonakos	77			GB	40
Embassy	GB	1972	Gordon Hessler	90			GB	18
Emerald Forest, The	GB	1985	John Boorman	114			FB	50
Emergency Call	USA	1933	Edward Cahn	60			GB	15
Emigrants, The	SWE	1970	Jan Troell	151	dub		FB	27
Emil and the Detectives	USA	1964	Peter Tewksbury	98			FB	27
Emily (Third Party Speculation)	GB	1979	Malcolm LeGrice	60			LFC	30
Emmanuelle and the Last Cannibals	USA	1977	Joe D'Amato	82			FB	38
Emmanuelle in Soho	GB	1981	David Hughes	66			GB	40
Emperor of the North	USA	1973	Robert Aldrich	119			FB	18
Emperor's Naked Army Marches On, The	JAP	1987	Hara Kazuo	123	st	ICA	GB	50
Emperor, Citizens and Comrades	W GER	1971		92	est		GFL	0
Empire of the Sun	USA	1987	Steven Spielberg	152			FB	65
Empty Suitcases	USA	1980	Bette Gordon	55			BFI	22
En Compagnie de Max Linder (see Laugh with Max Linder)								
Enchanted April, The	USA	1935	Harry Beaumont	66			GB	15
Enchanted Cottage, The	USA	1945	John Cromwell	96			GB	15
Enchanted Island	USA	1958	Allan Dwan	94			GB	22
Encore	GB	1951	Pat Jackson	89		R	FB	15
End of a Business Trip, The	W. GER		Hans Dieter Schwarze	85	dub		GFL	0
End of an Agent	CZ	1967	Vaclav Vorlicek	88	est		ETV	12.50
End of St. Petersburg, The	USSR	1927	Vsevolod Pudovkin	105	st/est st/est		BFI	25
							GB	25
End of the Road	CZ	1960	Miroslav Akan	85	est		ETV	10
End of the Road	USA	1969	Aram Avakian	110			GB	30
End, The	USA	1978	Burt Reynolds	100			FB	27
Endurance	GB	1933	Frank Hurley	63			BFI	15
Enemy	GB	1974	Anthony Bagley	65			BFI	18
Enemy Below, The	USA	1957	Dick Powell	97	std		FB	18
Enemy Mine	USA	1985	Wolfgang Petersen	108			FB	45
Enfance Nue, L'	FR	1968	Maurice Pialat	90	est		AE	60
Enfant Sauvage, L' (see Wild Child)								
Enfants du Paradis, Les	FR	1943	Marcel Carné	188	est	AE	GB	40
Enfants Terribles, Les	FR	1949	Jean-Pierre Melville	106	st	CONT	GB	35
Enforcer, The	USA	1976	James Fargo	96	sc/std		FB	33
Enigma	GB/FR	1982	Jeannot Szwarc	101			FB	40
Enigma of Kaspar Hauser, The	W GER	1974	Werner Herzog	110	est		GB	35
Enigma Secret	POL	1979	R. Wionczek	159	est		FOP	0
Ensign Pulver	USA	1963	Joshua Logan	85	bw/std		FB	15
Enter Laughing	USA	1967	Carl Reiner	97			FB	18
Enter the Dragon	USA/HK	1973	Robert Clouse	98	std		FB	27
Enter the Ninja	USA	1981	Menahem Golan	94			FB	41
Enthusiasm	USSR	1931	Dziga Vertov	67	est		BFI	30
Entity, The	USA	1982	Sidney J. Furie	125	sc		FB	50
Entre tu et Vous	CAN	1969	Gilles Groulx	65	bw/fr dia		CHC	0
Epitaph to Barbara Rodziwill	POL	1982	Janusz Majewski	93	est		FOP	0
Equus	GB	1977	Sidney Lumet	137			FB	27
Erik the Viking	GB	1989	Terry Jones	107			FB	55
Erika's Passions	W GER	1976	Ulla Stöckl	68	est		GFL	0
Ernest Saves Christmas	USA	1988	John Cherry	91			FB	55
Ernie Game, The	CAN	1967	Don Owen	88			CHC	0

	COUNTRY OF PRODUCTION	YEAR	DIRECTOR	RUNNING TIME	VERSION	35mm	16mm	16mm RENTAL FEE
Eroica	POL	1957	Andrzej Munk	83	est		GB	25
Erotic Inferno	GB	1975	Trevor Wrenn	80			FB	33
Erotissimo	FR/IT	1968	Gerard Pires	85	est		GB	30
Escapade in Japan	USA	1957	Arthur Lubin	89	dub		GB	22
Escape from Alcatraz	USA	1979	Don Siegel	112			FB	48
Escape from East Berlin (see Tunnel 28)								
Escape from the Dark	USA	1976	Charles Jarrott	104			FB	33
Escape from the Planet of the Apes	USA	1971	Don Taylor	97	sc		FB	20
Escape From the Sea	GB	1968	Peter Seabourne	53			GB	17
Escape to Athena	GB	1979	George Pan Cosmatos	117	sc/std		GB	43
Escape to Witch Mountain	USA	1974	John Hough	97			FB	38
Escape, The	JAP		Tsuneo Kobayashi	90	dub		GB	15
Essene	USA	1972	Frederick Wiseman	86			GB	45
Eugene Atget	GB	1982	Peter Wyeth	50			AC	20
Eureka	GB/USA	1982	Nicolas Roeg	129			BFI	45
Europe After The Rain	GB	1978	Mick Gold	88			AC	20
Europeans, The	GB	1979	James Ivory	92			GB	45
Even Dwarfs Started Small	W.GER	1970	Werner Herzog	98	bw/est		MP	51.75
Evening with the Royal Ballet, An	GB	1963	Anthony Asquith/ Anthony Havelock-Allan	90			GB	22
Everybody's Fine	IT	1991	Guiseppe Tornatore	126		R	FB	75
Every Day's a Holiday	USA	1938	Edward Sutherland	79			FB	15
Every Girl Should be Married	USA	1948	Don Hartman	88			GB	15
Every Home Should Have One	GB	1970	Jim Clark	94			FB	22
Every Little Crook and Nanny	USA	1972	Cy Howard	92			FB	16
Every Picture tells a Story	GB	1984	James Scott	83			BFI	40
Every Which Way But Loose	USA	1978	James Fargo	114			FB	43
Everybody's Doing It	USA	1938	Christy Cabanne	67			GB	15
Everything for Sale	POL	1968	Andrzej Wajda	99	est		GB	30
Everything I Have is Yours	USA	1952	Robert Z. Leonard	92	bw		FB	15
Everything You Always Wanted To Know About Sex But Were Afraid to Ask	USA	1972	Woody Allen	87			FB	33
Everything's Rosie	USA	1931	Clyde Bruckman	76			GB	20
Evil Dead II	USA	1987	Sam Raimi	84			GB	70
Evil Dead, The	USA	1982	Sam Raimi	84			GB	48
Evil Eye, The	IT	1962	Mario Bava	92	bw/dub		FB	18
Evil that Men Do	USA	1984	J. Lee Thompson	88			GB	43
Evil Under the Sun	GB	1981	Guy Hamilton	113	117		FB	48
Ewiger Walzer	W.GER	1954	Paul Verhoeven	86	est		GFL	0
Ex-Mrs Bradford, The	USA	1936	Stephen Roberts	87			GB	15
Excalibur	USA	1981	John Boorman	140			FB	43
Exceptional Class, An	CZ	1966	Jiri Blazek	90	est		ETV	10
Exchange and Divide	GB	1980	Margaret Dickinson	50			BFI	18
Executioner's Song, The	USA	1982	Lawrence Schiller	135			GB	43
Executioner, The	GB	1970	Sam Wanamaker	111	std		FB	15
Executive Suite	USA	1954	Robert Wise	104			FB	15
Exile, The	USA	1947	Max Ophuls	91			BFI	25
Exit Smiling	USA	1926	Sam Taylor	71	bw/st		FB	22
Exorcist II: The Heretic	USA	1977	John Boorman	102			FB	33
Exorcist, The	USA	1973	William Friedkin	122			FB	33
Expelled from Paradise	WGER	1977	Niklaus Schilling	119	est		GFL	0
Experiment Perilous	USA	1945	Jacques Tourneur	92			GB	15
Experts, The	W.GER	1973	Norbert Kückelmann	100	est		GFL	0
Exploits at West Poley	GB	1986	Diarmuid Lawrence	63			FB	20
Explorers	USA	1985	Joe Dante	109		BD	GB	50
Exposed	USA/FR	1983	James Toback	99			FB	38
Extraordinary Adventures of Mister West in the Land of the Bolsheviks, The	USSR	1924	Lev Kuleshov	76	st/est		BFI	30
Extraordinary Seaman, The	USA	1968	John Frankenheimer	80	std		FB	18

	COUNTRY OF PRODUCTION	YEAR	DIRECTOR	RUNNING TIME	VERSION	35mm	16mm	16mm RENTAL FEE
Extreme Prejudice	USA	1987	Walter Hill	104			GU	80
Eye of the Cat	USA	1969	David Lowell Rich	99			FB	18
Eye of the Devil	GB	1966	J. Lee Thompson	90			FB	15
Eye of the Needle	GB	1981	Richard Marquand	112			FB	43
Eyes Do Not Want To Close At All Times	W GER/IT	1969	Jean-Marie Straub/ Danièle Huillet	83	est		GB	33
Eyes of Laura Mars	USA	1978	Irvin Kershner	103			FB	30
Eyes Without a Face (see Yeux Sans Visage, Les)								
Eyewitness	GB	1970	John Hough	92			FB	18

Edward Scissorhands

The Elephant Man

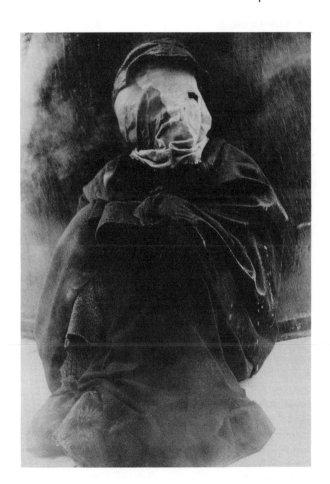

	COUNTRY OF PRODUCTION	YEAR	DIRECTOR	RUNNING TIME	VERSION	35mm	16mm	16mm RENTAL FEE
F.B.I. Story, The	USA	1959	Mervyn LeRoy	128			FB	18
F.I.S.T.	USA	1978	Norman Jewison	130			FB	33
F/X – Murder By Illusion	USA	1985	Robert Mandel	108		R	FB	45
Fabulous Baker Boys, The	USA	1990	Steve Kloves	114	his	R	BFI	25
						R	FB	65
Fabulous Dorseys, The	USA	1947	Alfred E. Green				GB	20
Face of Famine, The	GB	1975	BBC TV	75			CONC	19.8
Face of Fu Manchu, The	GB	1965	Don Sharp	94	bw/std		FB	15
Face, The	SWE	1958	Ingmar Bergman	102	est		GB	35
Faces in the Dark	GB	1960	David Eady	87			GB	15
Fahrenheit 451	GB	1966	François Truffaut	112			FB	22
Fail Safe	USA	1964	Sidney Lumet	111			FB	15
Fairly Decent Fellows				90	est		ETV	10
Falcon and the Snowman, The	USA	1985	John Schlesinger	131			FB	45
Falcon in Hollywood, The	USA	1944	Gordon Douglas	67			GB	15
Falcon in San Francisco, The	USA	1946	Joseph H. Lewis	67			GB	15
Falcon Out West, The	USA	1944	William Clemens	66			GB	15
Falcon Strikes Back, The	USA	1943	Edward Dmytryk	72			GB	15
Falcon Takes Over, The	USA	1942	Irving Reis	66			GB	22
Falcon's Adventure, The	USA	1946	William Berke	62			GB	15
Falcon's Alibi, The	USA	1946	Ray McCarey	66			GB	15
Falcon's Brother, The	USA	1942	Stanley Logan	65			GB	15
Fall of the Romanov Dynasty, The	USSR	1926	Esther Schub	66	sd		GB	20
Fall Guy, The	USA	1930	Leslie Pearce	70			GB	15
Fall of the House of Usher, The	FR	1928	Jean Epstein	38	st		BFI	12.5
Fallen Sparrow, The	USA	1943	Richard Wallace	94			GB	15
Falling in Love	USA	1984	Ulu Grosbard	106			FB	40
Falls, The	GB	1980	Peter Greenaway	194			BFI	40
False Witness	USA	1970	Richard A. Colla	88	sc/std		FB	15
Fame	USA	1980	Alan Parker	134			FB	48
Family Business	USA	1982	Tom Cohen	87			BFI	30
Family Fragments	GB	1983	Alan Fountain/Jeff Baggot	78			MP	40.25
Family Life	POL	1972	Krzysztof Zanussi	92	st		GB	40
Family Plot	USA	1976	Alfred Hitchcock	121			FB	33
Family Viewing	CAN	1987	Atom Egoyan	87			MP	69
Family Way, The	GB	1966	Roy Boulting	115			FB	18
Fan, The	USA	1981	Edward Bianchi	95			FB	38
Fanny and Alexander	SWE	1982	Ingmar Bergman	188	est	AE	GB	60
Fantasia	USA	1942	Ben Sharpsteen/Walt Disney	135		D	FB	100
Fantasist, The	EIRE	1986	Robin Hardy	98		BD	GB	60
Fantastic Voyage	USA	1966	Richard Fleischer	100	sc/std		FB	18
Far and Away	EIR	1992	Ron Howard	140		UIP	FB	70
Far Country, The	USA	1954	Anthony Mann	97	bw		FB	15
Far from Poland	USA	1984	Jill Godmilow	106			BFI	35
Far From the Madding Crowd	GB	1967	John Schlesinger	168	std		FB	30
Far From Vietnam (see Loin du Vietnam)								
Far North	USA	1988	Sam Shepard	89			FB	55
Farceur, Le	FR	1960	Philippe de Broca	85	est		GB	20
Farewell	USSR	1981	Elem Klimov	128	est		GB	60
Farewell My Lovely	USA	1945	Edward Dmytryk	95			GB	15
Farewell My Lovely	USA	1975	Dick Richards	95			FB	27
Farewell to Arms	USA	1958	Charles Vidor	149	std		GB	22
Farewell to Arms, A	USA	1932	Frank Borzage	78			FB	22
Fargo Kid	USA	1943	Edward Killy	73			GB	15
Farmer in the Dell, The	USA	1936	Ben Holmes	67			GB	15
Faro Document 1979	SWE	1980	Ingmar Bergman	103	est		GB	35
Fast and Furious	USA	1954	Ed Sampson/John Ireland	73			FB	15
Fast Charlie – The Moonbeam Rider	USA	1978	Steve Carver	99			FB	38

	COUNTRY OF PRODUCTION	YEAR	DIRECTOR	RUNNING TIME	VERSION	35mm	16mm	16mm RENTAL FEE
Fast Lady, The	GB	1962	Ken Annakin	95	col/ bw		FB FB	18
Fast Times at Ridgemont High	USA	1982	Amy Heckerling	90			FB	38
Faster, Pussycat! Kill! Kill!	USA	1965	Russ Meyer	83			GB	40
Fastest Guitar Alive, The	USA	1966	Michael Moore	87			FB	18
Fastest Gun Alive, The	USA	1956	Russell Rouse	89			FB	15
Fat City	USA	1972	John Huston	96			FB	18
Fata Morgana	W GER	1971	Werner Herzog	78	eng		MP	
Fatal Attraction	USA	1987	Adrian Lyne	120			FB	60
Father and Son	HK	1981	Allen Fong	96	est		BFI	40
Father Came Too	GB	1963	Peter Graham Scott	93			FB	18
Father Dear Father	GB	1972	William G. Stewart	99			FB	22
Father of the Bride	USA	1950	Vincente Minnelli	92			FB	15
Father of the Bride	USA	1991	Charles Shyer	105		W	FB	70
Father's Doing Fine	GB	1952	Henry Cass	83			FB	18
Father's Little Dividend	USA	1951	Vincente Minnelli	81			FB	15
Fathom	GB	1967	Leslie H. Martinson	99	sc/std		FB	18
Faust	GB	1980	Steve Rumbelow	75		BD	EMA	30
Favour, The Watch and the Very Big Fish, The	FR/GB	1991	Ben Lewin	89		R	FB	TBA
Favourites of the Moon	FR	1984	Otar Yosseliani	101	est		GR	55
Fear	IT/ W.GER	1954	Roberto Rossellini	75	est		BFI	25
Fear	CZ	1964	Petr Schulhoff	102	est		ETV	10
Fear Eats the Soul	W. GER	1973	R.W. Fassbinder	92	est		BFI	45
Fear in the Night	GB	1972	Jimmy Sangster	86			FB	18
Fear is the Key	GB	1972	Michael Tuchner	105	sc/std		FB	18
Fedora	W.GER	1978	Billy Wilder	113			GB	43
Feet First	USA	1930	Clyde Bruckman	78			GB	27
Fellini Satyricon	IT/FR	1969	Federico Fellini	129	std/dub		FB	27
Fellini's 8 1/2	IT	1963	Federico Fellini	137	est	BFI	BFI	55
Fellini's Casanova	IT	1976	Federico Fellini	154	std		FB	43
Fellini's Roma	IT/FR	1972	Federico Fellini	128	est		FB	27
Fellini: A Director's Notebook	USA	1969	Federico Fellini	53			BFI	15
Fellow Traveller	GB/ USA	1989	Philip Saville	97		BFI	BFI	65
Femme d'à Coté, La	FR	1981	François Truffaut	106	est		FB	45
Femme Marièe, Une	FR	1964	Jean-Luc Godard	95	est		BFI	25
Femmes Savantes, Les	FR	1965	Jean Meyer	100	bw/est		GB	35
Fern, The Red Deer	GB	1976	Jan Darnley-Smith	58			GB	17
Ferngully: The Last Rainforest	USA	1991	Bill Kroyer	76		F	FB	65
Ferris Bueller's Day Off	USA	1986	John Hughes	103			FB	45
Ferry to Hong Kong	GB	1959	Lewis Gilbert	113	bw/std		FB	15
Festival of Folk Heroes	USA			89			FB	27
Festival of Fools	GB	1973	Ian McMillan/ Peggy Seeger	60			GB	15
Feu Follet, Le	FR IT	1963	Louis Malle	121	est		GB	25
Fidanzati, I	IT	1962	Ermanno Olmi	76	est	BFI	GB	30
Fiddler on the Roof	USA	1971	Norman Jewison	181	sc		FB	38
Fiddlers Three	GB	1944	Henry Watt	85			FB	15
Fidelio	AUST	1956	Walter Felsenstein	88	est		GB	20
Field Diary	IS/FR	1982	Amos Gitai	83	est		BFI	35
Field of Dreams	USA	1990	Phil Arlen Robinson	106		GU	GU	80
Field, The	GB	1990	Jim Sheridan	110		ENT	GB	80
Fiend Without a Face	GB	1957	Arthur Crabtree	80			GB	15
Fiendish Plot of Dr Fu Manchu, The	USA	1980	Piers Haggard	108			FB	41
Fifteen Girls and a Coach	CHI	1957		93	est		ETV	10
Fifth Avenue Girl	USA	1939	Gregory La Cava	83			GB	15
52 Pick-up	USA	1986	John Frankenheimer	108			FB	45
Fight For Your Lady	USA	1937	Ben Stoloff	67			GB	15
Fighting 69th, The	USA	1940	William Keighley	88			FB	22
Fighting Father Dunne	USA	1947	Ted Tetzlaff	90			GB	15
Fighting Gringo	USA	1939	David Howard	60			GB	15

Films on Offer

f

	COUNTRY OF PRODUCTION	YEAR	DIRECTOR	RUNNING TIME	VERSION	35mm	16mm	16mm RENTAL FEE
Fighting Mad	USA	1976	Jonathan Demme	86			FB	18
Fighting Prince of Donegal, The	GB	1966	Michael O'Herlihy	104			FB	27
File of the Golden Goose, The	GB	1969	Sam Wanamaker	106			FB	18
Fillmore	USA	1972	Richard Heffron	106			FB	18
Film About A Woman Who . . .	USA	1974	Yvonne Rainer	105			BFI	35
Film and Reality	GB	1942	Alberto Cavalcanti	105			BFI	18
Film from the Clyde	GB	1977	Cinema Action	83			CA	20
Film Portrait	USA	1972	Jerome Hill	81			GB	40
Final Analysis	USA	1991	Phil Joanou	125		W	FB	70
Final Conflict, The	USA	1981	Graham Baker	108			FB	48
Final Hour, The	USA	1962	Robert Douglas	74	bw		FB	15
Final Programme	GB	1973	Robert Fuest	89			GB	25
Finders Keepers	GB	1966	Sidney Hayers	90	std		FB	18
Findhorn	GB	1977		62			CONC	27.40
Fine and Dandy	USA	1950	Roy Del Ruth	105			FB	15
Fine Madness, A	USA	1966	Irvin Kershner	104			FB	18
Fine Mess, A	USA	1986	Blake Edwards	90			FB	45
Finest Hours, The	GB	1964	Peter Baylis	116	col/bw	GB	GB	27
Finishing School	USA	1934	Wanda Tuchock/ George Nicholls Jr	73			GB	15
Finnegan's Chin – Temporal Economy	GB	1981	Malcolm Le Grice	85			BFI	30
Finnegan's Wake	USA	1965	Mary Ellen Bute	88			GB	25
Finye: The Wind	MALI	1982	Souleymane Cisse	105	est	BFI	BFI	45
Fire and Ice	USA	1982	Ralph Bakshi	81			FB	40
Fire at Midnight	W GER	1978	Gustaf Ehmck	100	est		GFL	0
Fire Down Below	GB	1957	Robert Parrish	116	std		FB	18
Fire Festival	JAP	1984	Mitsuo Yanagimachi	118	est		GB	50
Fire Sale	USA	1977	Alan Arkin	88	std		FB	18
Fire Walker	USA	1986	J. Lee Thompson	104			FB	45
Fire!	USA	1976	Earl Bellamy	97			FB	18
Fireball 500	USA	1966	William Asher	81			FB	18
Firechasers	GB	1970	Sidney Hayers	101			GB	18
Firecreek	USA	1967	Vincent McEveety	104	std		FB	18
Firefighters, The	GB	1974	Jonathan !ngrams	56			GB	17
Firefox	USA	1982	Clint Eastwood	135	sc/std		FB	45
Firepower	GB	1979	Michael Winner	104			GB	38
Fires Were Started (see I Was a Fireman)								
Firestarter	USA	1984	Mark L. Lester	114			FB	35
First Courier, The	USSR/BULG	1967	Vladimir Yanchev	90	est		ETV	10
First Great Train Robbery, The	GB	1978	Michael Crichton	110			FB	38
First Love	USA	1977	Joan Darling	92			FB	27
First Man into Space	GB	1958	Robert Day	80			GB	15
First Men in the Moon	GB	1964	Nathan Juran	102	sc/std		FB	18
First Monday in October	USA	1981	Ronald Neame	98			FB	43
First Name Carmen	FR/ SWITZ	1983	Jean-Luc Godard	84	est		GB	50
First Rescue Party	CZ	1959	Otakar Vavra	95	est		ETV	10
First Start, The	POL	1949	Leonard Buczkowski	100	est		FOP	0
First Teacher, The	USSR	1965	Andrei Mikhalkov Konchalovsky	96	est		GB	25
First Travelling Saleslady, The	USA	1956	Arthur Lubin	92			GB	22
First Yank into Tokyo	USA	1945	Gordon Douglas	72			GB	15
Fish Called Wanda, A	GB	1988	Charles Crichton	108			FB	65
Fisher King, The	USA	1991	Terry Gilliam	137		C	FB	70
Fitzcarraldo	W.GER	1982	Werner Herzog	158	est	NE	GB	55
Fitzwilly Strikes Back	USA	1967	Delbert Mann	102	sc/std		FB	18
Five Came Back	USA	1939	John Farrow	75			GB	15
Five Card Stud	USA	1968	Henry Hathaway	102			FB	18
Five Days One Summer	USA	1982	Fred Zinnemann	108			FB	35
Five Easy Pieces	USA	1970	Bob Rafelson	98			FB	22
Five Golden Dragons	GB	1967	Jeremy Summers	105	std		FB	18

Films on Offer

	COUNTRY OF PRODUCTION	YEAR	DIRECTOR	RUNNING TIME	VERSION	35mm	16mm	16mm RENTAL FEE
Five Man Army, The	IT	1969	Don Taylor	105	sc/dub		FB	18
Five Miles to Midnight	FR/IT	1962	Anatole Litvak	107			FB	15
Five Minutes to Midnight	GB			85			CONC	33
Five Pennies, The	USA	1959	Melville Shavelson	117	std		FB	18
Five Star Final	USA	1932	Mervyn LeRoy	87			FB	22
Five Thousand Fingers of Dr. T	USA	1953	Roy Rowland	88			FB	18
Fixer Dugan	USA	1939	Lew Landers	68			GB	15
Fixer, The	USA	1968	John Frankenheimer	132			FB	22
Flame and the Arrow. The	USA	1950	Jacques Tourneur	87			FB	18
Flame in the Streets	GB	1961	Roy Ward Baker	93	bw/std		FB	15
Flame of New Orleans, The	USA	1941	René Clair	79			FB	22
Flaming Star	USA	1960	Don Siegel	92	sc/std		FB	18
Flamingo Kid, The	USA	1984	Garry Marshall	100			GB	50
Flareup	USA	1969	James Neilson	90			FB	22
Flash and the Firecat	USA	1975	Fred Sebastion	83			GB	25
Flash Gordon	GB	1980	Mike Hodges	114	sc		FB	45
Flash the Sheep Dog	GB	1967	Laurence Henson	58			GB	17
Flashdance	USA	1983	Adrian Lyne	95			FB	48
Flashpoint	USA	1984	William Tannen	93			FB	35
Flatliners	USA	1990	Joel Schumacher	111		C	FB	65
Flavour of Green Tea Over Rice, The	JAP	1952	Yasujiro Ozu	115	est		GB	45
Flaw, The	GB	1955	Terence Fisher	62			GB	15
Flea in her Ear, A	USA/FR	1968	Jacques Charon	94	std		FB	18
Flesh and Blood	USA/HOLL	1985	Paul Verhoeven	127	sc		FB	40
Fletch	USA	1985	Michael Ritchie	96			FB	40
Fletch Lives	USA	1989	Michael Ritchie	95			FB	55
Flic, Un	FR/IT	1972	Jean-Pierre Melville	98	dub		FB	18
Flight for Freedom	USA	1943	Lothar Mendes	101			GB	15
Flight from Ashiya	USA/ JAP	1963	Michael Anderson	102	sc		FB	18
Flight from Glory	USA	1937	Lew Landers	67			GB	5
Flight of the Doves	GB	1971	Ralph Nelson	101			FB	18
Flight of the Lost Balloon	USA	1961	Nathan Juran	87	sc		FB	18
Flight of the Phoenix, The	USA	1965	Robert Aldrich	147			FB	22
Flight of the White Stallions, The	USA	1962	Arthur Hiller	112			FB	27
Flight to Berlin	GB	1983	Christopher Petit	90			BFI	40
Flipper and the Pirates	USA	1964	Leon Benson	98			FB	16
Flirting	AUSTR	1991	John Duigan	100		W	FB	65
Flood	USA	1976	Earl Bellamy	97			FB	18
Flood, The	GB	1963	Lionel Hoare	59			GB	12
Flowers Were Mourning, The	W GER	1971	Dietrich Haugk	60	est		GFL	0
Fluffy	USA	1964	Earl Bellamy	92	bw		FB	15
Fly, The	USA	1986	David Cronenberg	100			FB	55
Fly 2, The	USA	1989	Chris Walas	105		F	FB	55
Fly a Flag for Poplar	GB	1975	Collective	77			CONC	15.40
Flying Deuces	USA	1939	Edward Sutherland	69			GB	20
Flying Devils	USA	1933	Russell Birdwell	62			GB	15
Flying Down to Rio	USA	1933	Thornton Freeland	90			GB	16
Flying Irishman, The	USA	1938	Leigh Jason	72			GB	15
Flying Leathernecks	USA	1951	Nicholas Ray	100	col		GB	22
					bw		GB	17
Flying Sorcerer, The	GB	1975	Harry Booth	52			GB	17
FM	USA	1978	John Alonzo	105			FB	27
Foes	USA	1977	John Coates	90			GB	33
Fog, The	USA	1979	John Carpenter	89	sc		FB	43
Follow Me	GB	1971	Carol Reed	93	sc		FB	18
Follow a Star	GB	1959	Robert Asher	93			FB	15
Follow Me Boys	USA	1976	Norman Tokar	120	131		FB	27
Follow Me Quietly	USA	1949	Richard Fleischer	60			GB	15

	COUNTRY OF PRODUCTION	YEAR	DIRECTOR	RUNNING TIME	VERSION	35mm	16mm	16mm RENTAL FEE
Follow that Camel	GB	1967	Gerald Thomas	95	bw		FB	15
Follow that Dream	USA	1962	Gordon Douglas	109	sc		FB	18
Follow the Boys	USA	1963	Richard Thorpe	95	sc/std		FB	15
Follow the Fleet	USA	1936	Mark Sandrich	112			GB	18
Fool, The	GB	1990	Christine Edzard	140		MAY	GB	80
Foolish Wives	USA	1921	Erich von Stroheim	111	st	BFI	BFI	25
Fools of Fortune	GB	1990	Pat O'Connor	109		MAY	GB	75
Footlight Fever	USA	1941	Irving Reis	69			GB	15
Footlight Parade	USA	1933	Lloyd Bacon	101			FB	22
Footlight Varieties	USA	1951	Hal Yates	91			GB	15
Footloose	USA	1984	Herbert Ross	105			FB	35
For a Few Dollars More	IT/SP/ W.GER	1965	Sergio Leone	128	sc/std/ dub		FB	27
For Love of Ivy	USA	1968	Daniel Mann	102			GB	18
For Love or Money	USA	1963	Michael Gordon	108	col		FB	18
					bw		FB	15
For Me and My Gal	USA	1942	Busby Berkeley	109			FB	22
For Memory	GB	1984	Marc Karlin	120			BFI	35
For Pete's Sake	USA	1974	Peter Yates	90			FB	18
For the First Time	W.GER/USA	1958	Rudolph Maté	97	sc/std/ dub		FB	18
For Whom the Bell Tolls	USA	1943	Sam Wood	136			FB	22
For Your Eyes Only	GB	1981	John Glen	127			FB	53
Forbidden Planet	USA	1956	Fred M. Wilcox	97	sc/std		FB	22
Forbidden Volcano	FR	1965	Haroun Tazieff	53		CONT	GB	25
Forbin Project, The	USA	1969	Joseph Sargent	88	sc		FB	18
Force 10 From Navarone	GB	1978	Guy Hamilton	118	sc/std		FB	33
Force of Destiny	IT	1949	Carmine Gallone	95			GB	20
Force of Evil	USA	1949	Abraham Polonsky	76			GB	22
Fords on Water	GB	1983	Barry Bliss	83			BFI	35
Foreign Body	GB	1986	Ronald Neame	111			FB	50
Foreign Correspondent	USA	1940	Alfred Hitchcock	119			BFI	25
Foreigners	SWE	1972	Johan Bergenstrahle	113	est		GB	30
Forever Darling	USA	1954	Alexander Hall	92			FB	10
Forever Female	USA	1953	Irving Rapper	92			FB	15
Formula, The	USA	1980	John G Avildsen	117			FB	38
Forsyte Saga, The	USA	1949	Compton Bennett	113	bw		FB	15
Fort Apache	USA	1948	John Ford	127			GB	18
Fortini/Cani	IT/FR/ W.GER/USA	1976	Jean-Marie Straub/ Danièle Huillet	83	est	AE	GB	40
Fortunat	FR/IT/USA	1960	Alex Joffe	120	est		GB	25
Fortune Lane	GB	1947	John Baxter	60			FB	10
Fortune, The	USA	1974	Mike Nichols	90	sc/std		FB	22
4D Special Agents	GB	1981	Harold Orton	60			GB	17
48 Hrs.	USA	1982	Walter Hill	96			FB	40
Forty Four, The	CZ	1957	Palo Bielik	133	est		ETV	10
Forty Naughty Girls	USA	1937	Edward Cline	63			GB	15
Forty Ninth 49th Parallel	GB	1941	Michael Powell	123		R	FB	15
42nd Street	USA	1933	Lloyd Bacon	89			FB	22
Forward Together	CAN	1977		90			ETV	15
Foul Play	USA	1978	Colin Higgins	116			FB	48
Fountainhead, The	USA	1949	King Vidor	113			BFI	25
Four Questions About Art	GB	1979	Edward Bennett	50			AC	16
Four Adventures of Reinette and Mirabelle, The	FR	1986	Eric Rohmer	99	est	AE	GB	60
Four Feathers, The	USA	1929	Ernest Schoedsack	84	st		FB	18
Four Feathers, The	GB	1978	Don Sharp	104			GB	33
Four Flies on Grey Velvet	IT/FR	1971	Dario Argento	94	sc/dub		FB	18
Four for Texas	USA	1963	Robert Aldrich	115			FB	18
Four Horsemen of the Apocalypse, The	USA	1961	Vincente Minnelli	153	sc/std		FB	22

	COUNTRY OF PRODUCTION	YEAR	DIRECTOR	RUNNING TIME	VERSION	35mm	16mm	16mm RENTAL FEE
Four Jacks and a Jill	USA	1941	Jack Hively	68			GB	15
Four Seasons, The	USA	1981	Alan Alda	108			FB	43
Four Sons	USA	1928	John Ford	97	sd		BFI	25
Fourteen Americans	USA	1980	Michael Blackwood	88			AC	15
Fourth Man, The	HOLL	1983	Paul Verhoeven	95	es		GB	45
Fourth Protocol, The	GB	1987	John MacKenzie	119	sc		FB	50
Fox and His Friends	W.GER	1975	R.W. Fassbinder	123	est		BFI	45
Foxes	USA	1979	Adrian Lyne	105			FB	33
Fra Diavolo	USA	1933	Hal Roach	90			FB	15
Fragment of Fear	GB	1970	Richard C. Sarafian	95			FB	18
Framed	USA	1974	Phil Karlson	101			FB	33
Frances	USA	1982	Graeme Clifford	139			FB	40
Francis Joins the W.A.C.S.	USA	1954	Arthur Lubin	85			FB	15
Francis of Assisi	USA	1961	Michael Curtiz	105	bw/std		FB	15
Francis, God's Jester	IT	1950	Roberto Rossellini	85	est		BFI	25
Frankenstein Conquers the World	JAP/ USA	1965	Inoshiro Honda	87	sc/dub		FB	18
Frankenstein Meets the Wolfman	USA	1946	Roy William Neill	73			FB	15
Frankenstein Must Be Destroyed	GB	1969	Terence Fisher	97			FB	18
Frankenstein Unbound	USA	1991	Roger Corman	85		BD	FB	65
Frankenstein's Daughter	USA	1958	Richard E. Cunha	85			GB	22
Frankenstein: The True Story	GB	1973	Jack Smight	123			FB	22
Frankie & Johnny	USA	1991	Garry Marshall	117		UIP	FB	70
Frankie and Johnny	USA	1965	Frederick De Cordova	88			FB	18
Frantic	USA	1988	Roman Polanski	120			FB	65
Fraternally Yours	USA	1933	William A. Seiter	65			BFI GB	15
Frauen Siedlung	W.GER	1976	Wolfgang Storch	80	est		GFL	0
Freaks	USA	1932	Tod Browning	64			FB	18
Freaky Friday	USA	1976	Gary Nelson	98			FB	33
Freddy's Dead: The Final Nightmare	USA	1992	Rachel Talaley	89	Not 3d	GU	GU	100
Free the Army (see FTA)								
Free Voice of Labour: The Jewish Anarchists	USA	1980	Steven Fischler/Joel Sucher	60			GB	20
Freebie and the Bean	USA	1974	Richard Rush	112	std		FB	18
Freedom is Paradise	USSR	1990	Sergei Bodrov	75	st	AE	GB	70
Freejack	USA	1991	Geoff Murphy	100		W	FB	65
Freighters of Destiny	USA	1931	Fred Allen	60			GB	15
French Connection II	USA	1975	John Frankenheimer	95			FB	30
French Connection, The	USA	1971	William Friedkin	104			FB	30
French Dressing	GB	1963	Ken Russell	86	std		FB	15
French Lieutenant's Woman, The	GB	1981	Karel Reisz	121			FB	48
French Line	USA	1953	Lloyd Bacon	99	col		GB	22
					bw		GB	15
French Mistress, A	GB	1960	Roy Boulting	98			FB	15
Frenchman's Creek	USA	1944	Mitchell Leisen	112	bw		FB	15
Frenzy	SWE	1944	Alf Sjöberg	98	est		BFI	20
Frenzy	GB	1972	Alfred Hitchcock	116			FB	28
Freshman, The	USA	1990	Andrew Bergman	102		C	FB	65
Friday the 13th	USA	1980	Sean S. Cunningham	95			FB	43
Friday the 13th Pt. 2	USA	1981	Steve Miner	87			FB	43
Friday the 13th, A New Beginning	USA	1985	Danny Steinmann	92			FB	40
Friday the 13th: The Final Chapter	USA	1982	Steve Miner	95			FB	43
Fried Green Tomatoes at the Whistle Stop Cafe	USA	1992	Jon Avnet	130		R	FB	75
Friedrich Schiller	W.GER	1940	Herbert Maisch	107	est		BFI	25
Friend or Foe	GB	1982	John Krish	70			FB	17
Friends and Enemies	AUSTR	1986	Tom Zubrycki	89			WFA	30
Friends and Husbands — A Labour of Love	W.GER	1982	Margarethe von Trotta	105	est		GB	50
Friends and Lovers	USA	1931	Victor Schertzinger	96			GB	15
Friends of Eddie Coyle, The	USA	1973	Peter Yates	102			FB	22
Friendship's Death	GB	1987	Peter Wollen	80		BFI	BFI	50

	COUNTRY OF PRODUCTION	YEAR	DIRECTOR	RUNNING TIME	VERSION	35mm	16mm	16mm RENTAL FEE
Fright	GB	1971	Peter Collinson	87			FB	18
Fright Night	USA	1985	Tom Holland	106			FB	45
Fright Night II	USA	1988	Tommy Lee Wallace	110			FB	55
Frightened City	GB	1961	John Lamont	97			FB	15
Frisco Kid, The	USA	1979	Robert Aldrich	118			FB	38
Frog Prince, The	GB	1984	Brian Gilbert	90			FB	45
Frogs	USA	1972	George McCowan	90			FB	18
From a Far Country	IT/GB/POL	1981	Krzysztof Zanussi	119	140		GB	38
From Beyond the Grave	GB	1973	Kevin Connor	98			FB	18
From Hell to Borneo	USA	1964	George Montgomery	87			GB	27
From Hell to Victory	FR/IT/SP	1979	Umberto Lenzi	102	sc		FB	33
From Mao to Mozart – Isaac Stern in China	USA	1980	Murray Lerner	83			GB	40
From My Life	CZ	1955	Vaclav Krska	114	est		ETV	15
From Noon Till Three	USA	1975	Frank D. Gilroy	99			FB	27
From Russia With Love	GB	1963	Terence Young	115			FB	33
From the Earth to the Moon	USA	1958	Byron Haskin	100			GB	24
From the Terrace	USA	1960	Mark Robson	144	sc/std		FB	18
Front Page, The	USA	1974	Billy Wilder	105	sc/std		FB	33
Front, The	USA	1976	Martin Ritt	95			FB	22
FTA	USA	1972	Francine Parker	96			GB	30
Fugitive, The	USA	1947	John Ford	102			GB	15
Fugitives for a Night	USA	1938	Leslie Goodwins	63			GB	15
Full Confession	USA	1939	John Farrow	66			GB	15
Full Metal Jacket	GB	1987	Stanley Kubrick	116			FB	55
Full Moon in Paris	FR	1984	Eric Rohmer	102	est		GB	55
Fun and Fancy Free	USA	1947	Bill Roberts	83			FB	27
Fun Down There	USA	1988	Roger Stigliano	85			MP	50
Fun With Dick and Jane	USA	1976	Ted Kotcheff	99			FB	22
Funhouse	USA	1981	Tobe Hooper	96			FB	38
Funny Face	USA	1956	Stanley Donen	104			FB	18
Funny Girl	USA	1968	William Wyler	146	sc/std		FB	27
Funny Lady	USA	1975	Herbert Ross	138	sc/std		FB	27
Funny Thing Happened on the Way to the Forum, A	USA	1966	Richard Lester	98			FB	18
Further Adventures of the Wilderness Family, The	USA	1977	Frank Zuniga	90			GB	30
Fury	USA	1936	Fritz Lang	94			FB	22
Fury on Wheels	USA	1971	Joe Manduke	87			FB	30
Fury, The	USA	1978	Brian De Palma	118			FB	33
Future is Woman, The	IT/FR/ W GER	1984	Marco Ferreri	100	est		FB	60
Fuzis, Oz (see Guns. The)								
Fuzz	USA	1972	Richard A. Colla	92			FB	27

The Fabulous Baker Boys

g

	COUNTRY OF PRODUCTION	YEAR	DIRECTOR	RUNNING TIME	VERSION	35mm	16mm	16mm RENTAL FEE
'G' Men	USA	1935	William Keighley	84			FB	22
Gable and Lombard	USA	1976	Sidney J. Furie	116			FB	27
Gale is Dead	GB	1970	Jenny Barraclough	50	col		CONC	15.40
					bw		CONC	16
Gallipoli	AUSTR	1981	Peter Weir	111	sc/std		FB	48
Gambit	GB	1966	Ronald Neame	108			FB	18
Gambler, The	USA	1974	Karel Reisz	109			FB	27
Gambling House	USA	1951	Ted Tetzlaff	80			GB	15
Game for Vultures	GB	1979	James Fargo	106			FB	33
Game Without Rules	CZ	1969	Jindrich Polak	85	est		ETV	15
Games	USA	1967	Curtis Harrington	96	bw/std		FB	15
Games, The	GB	1969	Michael Winner	96	sc/std		FB	18
Gandhi	GB/INDIA	1982	Richard Attenborough	188	sc/std	C	FB	75
Gang That Couldn't Shoot Straight, The	USA	1971	James Goldstone	96			FB	16
Gang's All Here, The	GB	1938	Thornton Freeland	78			BFI	20
Gang, Le	FR/IT	1976	Jacques Deray	103	dub		FB	22
Gangbusters	USA	1955	Bill Karn	72			GB	15
Gangs Incorporated	USA	1941	Phil Rosen	72			GB	15
Gangster Wars	USA	1981	Richard C. Sarafian	122			FB	33
Gangway for Tomorrow	USA	1944	John H. Auer	76			GB	15
Garden, The	GB	1990	Derek Jarman	92		AE	GB	70
Garlic is as Good as Ten Mothers	USA	1980	Les Blank	54			GB/CONT	20
Gas House Kids	USA	1946	Sam Newfield	64			GB	15
Gas! Or It Became Necessary To Destroy the World In Order To Save It	USA	1970	Roger Corman	79			GB	38
Gathering of Eagles, A	USA	1962	Delbert Mann	115			FB	27
Gatling Gun, The	USA	1971	Robert Gordon	93	std		GB	24
Gator	USA	1976	Burt Reynolds	115	sc/std		FB	27
Gauguin the Savage	USA	1980	Fielder Cook	120			GB	41
Gauntlet, The	USA	1977	Clint Eastwood	109	sc/std		FB	33
Gawain and the Green Knight	GB	1983	Stephen Weeks	101			FB	33
Gay Diplomat, The	USA	1931	Richard Boleslawski	67			GB	15
Gay Divorcee, The	USA	1934	Mark Sandrich	107			GB	16
Gay Purr-ee	USA	1962	Abe Levitow	85			FB	22
Gazebo, The	USA	1959	George Marshall	102	sc/std		FB	14
Gelignite Gang, The	GB	1955	Francis Searle	76		GB	GB	15
General Died at Dawn, The	USA	1936	Lewis Milestone	98			FB	15
General Line, The	USSR	1929	Sergei Eisenstein/ Grigori Alexandrov	97	st		BFI	20
Generation	POL	1954	Andrzej Wajda	91	est	CONT	GB	25
Generation of Conquerors, A	USSR	1956	Vera Stroyeva	100			ETV	10
Genesis	FR/IND/ BEL/ SWITZ	1986	Mrinal Sen	105	est		GB	60
Genevieve	GB	1953	Henry Cornelius	86	bw		FB	15
Genghis Khan	USA/ W.GER/ YUGO	1965	Henry Levin	126	col/sc/ std		FB	18
Genius at Work	USA	1946	Leslie Goodwins	79			GB	15
Gentle Sex, The	GB	1943	Leslie Howard	92			BFI	30
Gentleman Jim	USA	1942	Raoul Walsh	104			FB	22
George and Mildred	GB	1980	Peter Frazer-Jones	93			GB	38
George Kuchar: The Comedy of the Underground	USA	1982	David Hallinger/ Gustavo Cortez	60			BFI	25
George White's Scandals	USA	1945	Felix Feist	95			GB	15
Georgia O'Keefe	USA	1978	Perry Miller Adato	60			AC	16
Georgia's Friends	USA	1981	Arthur Penn	115			FB	40
Georgy Girl	GB	1966	Silvio Narizzano	99			FB	15
German Sisters, The	W.GER	1981	Margarethe von Trotta	106	est		GB	50
German Story, The	E.GER	1954	Andrew Thorndike/ Annelie Thorndike	84	est		ETV	11
Germany – Year Zero	FR/ W.GER	1947	Roberto Rossellini	72	est		BFI	25
Geronimo	USA	1940	Paul Sloane	90			FB	18

	COUNTRY OF PRODUCTION	YEAR	DIRECTOR	RUNNING TIME	VERSION	35mm	16mm	16mm RENTAL FEE
Geronimo	USA/ MEX	1961	Arnold Laven	102	sc		FB	18
Gertrude Stein: When This You See, Remember Me	USA	1970	Perry Miller Adato	89			GB	25
Get Carter	GB	1971	Mike Hodges	112			FB	26
Get Out of Here	EQU	1977	Grupo Ukamau	95	est/bw		WFA	45
Getaway, The	USA	1972	Sam Peckinpah	123	std		FB	33
Getting of Wisdom, The	AUSTR	1977	Bruce Beresford	103			GB	35
Getting Straight	USA	1970	Richard Rush	125			FB	18
Ghare-Baire (see Home and the World)								
Ghost	USA	1990	Jerry Zucker	121		UIP	FB	70
Ghost Dance	GB	1983	Ken McMullen	100			MP	40.25
Ghost of a Chance, A	GB	1967	Jan Darnley-Smith	52			GB	17
Ghost of Dragstrip Hollow, The	USA	1959	William Hole, Jr.	65			FB	15
Ghost of St Michael's, The	GB	1941	Marcel Varnel	83			FB	15
Ghost Ship	GB	1952	Vernon Sewell	75			FB	15
Ghost Ship	USA	1943	Mark Robson	69			GB	15
Ghost Story	USA	1981	John Irvin	111			FB	38
Ghost Train, The	GB	1940	Walter Forde	89			FB	15
Ghostbusters	USA	1984	Ivan Reitman	105	sc/std	C	FB	60
Ghostbusters II	USA	1989	Ivan Reitman	108			FB	60
Giant of Marathon, The	IT/FR	1959	Jacques Tourneur	87	sc/std/ dub		GB	16
Gideon's Day	GB	1958	John Ford	91			FB	15
Gidget Goes Hawaiian	USA	1961	Paul Wendkos	101			FB	18
Gidget Goes to Rome	USA	1962	Paul Wendkos	104			FB	18
Gift for Heidi	USA	1958	George N. Templeton	72			GB	18
Gigi	USA	1958	Vincente Minnelli	115	sc/std		FB	27
Gilda	USA	1946	Charles Vidor	109			FB	15
Gildersleeve on Broadway	USA	1943	Gordon Douglas	65			GB	15
Gildersleeve's Bad Day	USA	1943	Gordon Douglas	62			GB	15
Gildersleeve's Ghost	USA	1944	Gordon Douglas	64			GB	15
Ginger and Fred	IT/FR/ W.GER	1986	Federico Fellini	127	est		GB	60
Girl and the General, The	IT/FR	1967	Pasquale Festa Campanile	89			FB	16
Girl Crazy	USA	1943	Norman Taurog	99			FB	22
Girl from Lorraine, A	FR/ SWITZ	1980	Claude Goretta	112	est		FB	45
Girl from Mexico, The	USA	1939	Leslie Goodwins	72			GB	15
Girl from Petrovka, The	USA	1974	Robert Ellis Miller	104	sc/std		FB	27
Girl Happy	USA	1965	Boris Sagal	96	std		FB	22
Girl in a Taxi	GB	1937	André Berthomieu	76			FB	15
Girl in Every Port, A	USA	1928	Howard Hawks	64	sd		BFI	25
Girl in Every Port, A	USA	1951	Chester Erskine	89			GB	15
Girl in the Picture	GB	1985	Cary Parker	91			FB	40
Girl Most Likely, The	USA	1956	Mitchell Leisen	98	bw col		GB	15
Girl Next Door, The	USA	1953	Richard Sale	92	bw		FB	15
Girl of the Grassland	CHI	1955	Hsu T'ao	85	est		ETV	10
Girl of the Port	USA	1930	Bert Glennon	69			GB	15
Girl of the Rio	USA	1932	Herbert Brenon	69			GB	15
Girl on a Motorcycle	GB	1968	Jack Cardiff	91			GB	30
Girl Rosemarie	W.GER	1958	Rolf Thiele	100	st		GB	30
Girl Rush	USA	1944	Gordon Douglas	65			GB	15
Girl Stroke Boy	GB	1971	Bob Kellett	88			GB	18
Girl with the Red Hair	HOLL	1982	Ben Verbong	116		BD	GB	50
Girl's War, The	W.GER	1977	Bernhard Sinkel/ Alf Brustellin	145	est		GFL	0
Girl, A Guy and a Gob, A	USA	1941	Richard Wallace	70			GB	15
Girlfriends	USA	1978	Claudia Weill	87			FB	20
Girls on Ice	CHI	1959	Wu Chao-Ti	105	est		ETV	10
Giro City	GB	1982	Karl Francis	104			GB	45
Give My Regards To Broad Street	GB	1984	Peter Webb	108			FB	40
Give Us This Day	GB	1982	Phil Mulloy	65			AC	19

g

	COUNTRY OF PRODUCTION	YEAR	DIRECTOR	RUNNING TIME	VERSION	35mm	16mm	16mm RENTAL FEE
Glass Bottom Boat, The	USA	1966	Frank Tashlin	110	std		FB	18
Glass Cell, The	W.GER	1977	Hans W. Geissendorfer	96	est		GFL	0
Glass Mountain, The	GB	1950	Henry Cass	86			GB	22
Glass Slipper, The	USA	1954	Charles Walters	94	col		FB	16
					bw		FB	12
Glastonbury Fayre	GB	1973	Peter Neal	100			GB	22
Gleaming the Cube	USA	1989	Graeme Clifford	105		GU	FB	55
Glengarry Glen Ross	USA	1992	James Foley	100		R	FB	
Glenn Miller Story, The	USA	1953	Anthony Mann	116	bw		FB	15
Glitterball, The	GB	1977	Harley Cokliss	56			GB	17
Global Affair, A	USA	1963	Jack Arnold	85			FB	15
Gloire de mon Père, La (See My Father's Glory)								
Gloria	USA	1980	John Cassavetes	121			FB	43
Glory Brigade, The	USA	1953	Robert Webb	82			FB	15
Glory Guys, The	USA	1965	Arnold Laven	111	sc		FB	18
Gnome-mobile, The	USA	1966	Robert Stevenson	84			FB	33
Go for a Take	GB	1972	Harry Booth	90			FB	18
Go Johnny Go	USA	1958	Paul Landres	75			GB	30
Go Kart Go	GB	1963	Jan Darnley-Smith	55			GB	12
Go Tell the Spartans	USA	1977	Ted Post	114			FB	30
Go to Blazes	GB	1961	Michael Truman	83	std		FB	18
Go West	USA	1940	Edward Buzzell	80			FB	15
Go West Young Man	USA	1936	Henry Hathaway	89			FB	15
Go-Between, The	GB	1970	Joseph Losey	116			FB	18
Goal Goal Another Goal	USSR	1968	V. Sadvosky	90	est		ETV	10
Goalkeeper's Fear of the Penalty, The	W.GER/ AUST	1971	Wim Wenders	101	est	BFI	BFI	46
Goat Horn, The	BULG	1972	Metodi Andonov	97	est		ETV	15
Godfather Part III, The	USA	1990	Francis Ford Coppola	160		UIP	FB	65
Godfather Part II, The	USA	1974	Francis Ford Coppola	200		UIP	FB	43
Godfather, The	USA	1971	Francis Ford Coppola	175		UIP	FB	43
Godsend, The	GB	1980	Gabrielle Beaumont	88			FB	38
Godspell	USA	1973	David Greene	110			FB	27
Godzilla vs. the Thing	JAP	1964	Inoshiro Honda	87	std/dub		FB	18
Goin' South	USA	1978	Jack Nicholson	111			FB	38
Goin' to Town	USA	1935	Alexander Hall	70			FB	15
Going My Way	USA	1944	Leo McCarey	124			FB	22
Gold Diggers of 1933	USA	1933	Mervyn LeRoy	96			FB	22
Gold Diggers of 1935	USA	1935	Mervyn LeRoy	95			FB	22
Gold for the Caesars	IT/FR	1962	André de Toth/Sabatino Ciuffini	66	dub		FB	18
Gold Racket, The	USA	1937	Louis J. Gasnier	66			GB	25
Golden Age of Comedy	USA	1957	Robert Youngson	78			GB	15
Golden Boy	USA	1939	Rouben Mamoulian	91			FB	15
Golden Braid	AUSTR	1989	Paul Cox	91		AE	GB	80
Golden Child, The	USA	1986	Michael Ritchie	94			FB	50
Golden Horde	USA	1951	George Sherman	76			FB	15
Golden Needles	USA	1974	Robert Clouse	92	sc/std		FB	18
Golden Rendezvous	USA	1977	Ashley Lazarus	102			FB	33
Golden Salamander, The	GB	1949	Ronald Neame	87		R	FB	15
Golden Seal, The	USA	1983	Frank Zuniga	94			GB	35
Golden Voyage of Sinbad, The	GB	1973	Gordon Hessler	105			FB	18
Goldengirl	USA	1979	Joseph Sargent	105			GB	33
Goldfinger	GB	1964	Guy Hamilton	109			FB	33
Goldie Gets Along	USA	1933	Malcolm St. Clair	68			GB	15
Gone to Earth	GB	1950	Michael Powell/ Emeric Pressburger	110			BFI	45
Gone With The Wind	USA	1939	Victor Fleming	222			FB	54
Good Earth, The	USA	1936	Sidney A. Franklin	138			FB	22
Good Father, The	GB	1986	Mike Newell	90			BFI	50

	COUNTRY OF PRODUCTION	YEAR	DIRECTOR	RUNNING TIME	VERSION	35mm	16mm	16mm RENTAL FEE
Good Guys and the Bad Guys, The	USA	1969	Burt Kennedy	90	sc/std		FB	18
Good Marriage, A	FR	1981	Eric Rohmer	93	97		FB	60
Good Morning (see Ohayo)								
Good Morning Babylon	IT/FR/ USA	1986	Paolo Taviani/ Vittorio Taviani	117			GB	60
Good Morning Vietnam	USA	1987	Barry Levinson	120			FB	60
Good Mother, The	USA	1988	Leonard Nimoy	103			FB	55
Good Neighbour Sam	USA	1964	David Swift	111	col		FB	18
Good, the Bad and the Ugly,The	IT	1966	Sergio Leone	148	sc/std/ dub		FB	27
Good-Time Girl	GB	1947	David MacDonald	92			BFI	30
Goodbye Again	USA/FR	1961	Anatole Litvak	120			FB	15
Goodbye Charlie	USA	1964	Vincente Minnelli	116	sc/std		FB	18
Goodbye Columbus	USA	1969	Larry Peerce	102			FB	18
Goodbye Emmanuelle	FR	1977	Francois Leterrier	98	sc/dub		FB	41
Goodbye Friends	BULG	1972	Borislav Sharaliev	100	est		ETV	10
Goodbye Girl, The	USA	1977	Herbert Ross	110			FB	33
Goodbye in the Mirror	USA	1964	Storm De Hirsch	80			LFC	18.75
Goodbye Mr. Chips	GB	1939	Sam Wood	113			FB	16
Goodbye Mr. Chips	GB	1969	Herbert Ross	147	sc/std		FB	22
Goodbye Porkpie	NZ	1980	Geoff Murphy	105			GB	38
Goodfellas	USA	1990	Martin Scorsese	145		W	FB	65
Goonies, The	USA	1985	Richard Donner	114	sc		FB	50
Goose Steps Out, The	GB	1942	Basil Dearden/Will Hay	79			FB	15
Gordon's War	USA	1973	Ossie Davis	90			FB	18
Gorillas in the Mist	USA	1988	Michael Apted	129			FB	60
Gorky Park	USA	1983	Michael Apted	128			FB	38
Gospel According to St. Matthew, The	IT/FR	1964	Pier Paolo Pasolini	142	est/dub	BFI	GB	35
Gothic	GB	1986	Ken Russell	87			GB	60
Goto Island of Love	FR	1968	Walerian Borowczyk	93	est		GB	30
Government Girl	USA	1943	Dudley Nichols	93			GB	15
Grabenplatz 17	W.GER	1958	Erich Engels	95	bw/est		GFL	0
Grace Quigley	USA	1984	Anthony Harvey	87			FB	40
Grand Blond Avec Une Chaussure Noire, Le	FR	1972	Yves Robert	89	dub		FB	18
Grand Canyon	USA	1991	Lawrence Kasdan	135		F	FB	70
Grand Chemin, Le	FR	1987	Jean-Loup Hubert	100	est		FB	60
Grand Hotel	USA	1932	Edmund Goulding	110			FB	22
Grand Jury	USA	1936	Albert S. Rogell	61			GB	15
Grand Meaulnes, Le	FR	1967	J.G. Albicocco	104	est		GB	40
Grand National Night	GB	1953	Bob McNaught	81			GB	15
Grand Old Girl, The	USA	1935	John S. Robertson	71			GB	20
Grand Opera	USA	1980	James Benning	90			LFC	35
Grand Prix	USA	1966	John Frankenheimer	175	std		FB	33
Grande Illusion, La	FR	1937	Jean Renoir	111	est		GB	30
Grape Dealer's Daughter, The	USA	1969	Walter Gutman	72			LFC	49
Grass	USA	1925	Merian C. Cooper/ Ernest Schoedsack	55	st st		CONC BFI	7.60
Gravy Train, The	USA	1974	Jack Starrett	95			FB	18
Gray Lady Down	USA	1977	David Greene	111	sc/std		FB	33
Grease	USA	1978	Randal Kleiser	110	sc/std		FB	53
Grease 2	USA	1982	Patricia Birch	114			FB	43
Greased Lightning	USA	1977	Michael Schultz	96			FB	22
Great Chase,The	USA	1962	Hardy Cort	80			GB	18
Great Consoler, The	USSR	1933	Lev Kuleshov	95	est		BFI	30
Great American Chase, The	USA	1979	Chuck Jones	97			FB	30
Great Bank Robbery, The	USA	1969	Hy Averback	95	std		FB	18
Great Charity Concert (see Grosse Wunschkonzert, Das)								
Great Dan Patch, The	USA	1949	Joeseph M. Newman	94			GB	15
Great Day	GB	1946	Lance Comfort	94			GB	15
Great Day in the Morning	USA	1955	Jacques Tourneur	91	std		GB	18
Great Erkel, The	HUN	1953	Marton Keleti	80	est		GB	20

	COUNTRY OF PRODUCTION	YEAR	DIRECTOR	RUNNING TIME	VERSION	35mm	16mm	16mm RENTAL FEE
Great Events and Ordinary People	FR	1978	Raul Ruiz	63	est		BFI	20
Great Expectations	GB	1946	David Lean	118		R	FB	15
Great Expectations	GB	1975	Joseph Hardy	124			GB	23
Great Gatsby, The	USA	1974	Jack Clayton	140			FB	33
Great Gildersleeve, The	USA	1942	Gordon Douglas	62			GB	15
Great Guns	USA	1941	Monty Banks	78			FB	15
Great Holiday Massacre, The	USA	1961	Ed Murrow	54			BFI	9
Great Imposter, The	USA	1960	Robert Mulligan	112			FB	15
Great Jasper	USA	1933	J. Walter Ruben	76			GB	15
Great King, The	GER	1942	Veit Harlan	93	est		BFI	25
Great Locomotive Chase, The	USA	1956	Francis D. Lyon	88	std		FB	27
Great Man Votes, The	USA	1939	Garson Kanin	72			GB	15
Great Man, The	USA	1956	José Ferrer	92			FB	15
Great Muppet Caper, The	GB	1981	Jim Henson	97			GB	35
Great Northfield Minnesota Raid, The	USA	1971	Philip Kaufman	90			FB	18
Great Pony Raid, The	GB	1958	Frederic Goode	58			GB	17
Great Riviera Bank Raid, The			Francis Megahy	96			GB	33
Great Rock 'N' Roll Swindle, The	GB	1979	Julien Temple	100			GB	48
Great Rupert, The	USA	1950	Irving Pichel	88			GB	15
Great Sacrifice, The	GER	1944	Veit Harlan	92	est		BFI	25
Great Santini, The	USA	1979	Lewis John Carlino	115			FB	41
Great Sharp, The	POL	1982	Sylvester Checinski	100	est		FOP	0
Great Sioux Massacre, The	USA	1965	Sidney Salkow	92	sc/std		FB	18
Great St. Trinian's Train Robbery, The	GB	1966	Frank Launder/Sidney Gilliat	94			FB	22
Great Waldo Pepper, The	USA	1975	George Roy Hill	109	sc/std		FB	27
Great Waltz, The	USA	1972	Andrew Stone	134	sc/std		FB	38
Great White Hope, The	USA	1970	Martin Ritt	103	sc		FB	18
Great Ziegfeld, The	USA	1936	Robert Z. Leonard	176			FB	30
Greatest, The	USA/GB	1977	Tom Gries	101			FB	30
Greed	USA	1923	Erich von Stroheim	104	st	UIP	FB	22
Greek Tycoon, The	USA	1978	J. Lee Thompson	107	std		FB	38
Green Berets, The	USA	1968	John Wayne/Ray Kellogg	138	std		FB	18
Green Card	AUSTR/ FR/US	1991	Peter Weir	107		W	FB	75
Green Helmet, The	GB	1961	Michael Forlong	88			FB	12
Green Ice	GB	1981	Ernest Day	116			GB	40
Green Man, The	GB	1956	Robert Day	80			FB	15
Green Mansions	USA	1959	Mel Ferrer	104	std		FB	14
Green Ray, The	FR	1986	Eric Rohmer	98	est	AE	GB	60
Green Slime, The	USA/ JAP	1968	Kinji Fukasaku	90			FB	27
Greengage Summer, The	GB	1961	Lewis Gilbert	99			FB	18
Greetings	USA	1968	Brian De Palma	88			GB	33
Gremlins	USA	1984	Joe Dante	106			FB	55
Grey Fox, The	CAN	1983	Phillip Borsos	92			GB	60
Grey Morning	W.GER	1971	Theodor Gradler	60	est		GFL	0
Greyfriars Bobby	GB	1961	Don Chaffey	91			FB	27
Greystoke – Legend of Tarzan Lord of the Apes	GB	1984	Hugh Hudson	130	sc/std		FB	55
Gridiron Flash	USA	1934	Glenn Tryon	64			GB	15
Grierson	CAN	1973	Roger Blais	60			CONC	18.4
Grifters, The	US	1990	Stephen Frears	110		MAY	GB	80
Grim Reaper, The (see Commare Secca, La)								
Grip of Fear	USA	1962	Blake Edwards	122			FB	15
Grip of the Strangler	GB	1958	Robert Day	80			GB	15
Grissom Gang, The	USA	1971	Robert Aldrich	128		GB	GB	22
Grizedale	GB	1989	Maggie Ellis	52			AC	20
Grizzly	USA	1976	William Girdler	89	sc/std		FB	22
Groove Tube, The	USA	1974	Ken Shapiro	73			GB	28
Grosse Wunschkonzert, Das	W.GER	1960	Arthur Maria Rabenalt	102	bw/est		GFL	0

	COUNTRY OF PRODUCTION	YEAR	DIRECTOR	RUNNING TIME	VERSION	35mm	16mm	16mm RENTAL FEE
Groundstar Conspiracy, The	USA	1972	Lamont Johnson	96	sc/std		FB	18
Group, The	GB	1973	Doc on Alcoholism	70			CONC	17.4
Grove Music	GB	1981	Henry Martin	50			AC	20
Grown Ups	GB	1980	Mike Leigh	95			BFI	25
Guadalcanal Diary	USA	1943	Lewis Seiler	93			FB	15
Guardian of the Wilderness	USA	1976	David O'Malley	110			GB	43
Guess Who's Coming to Dinner	USA	1967	Stanley Kramer	108			FB	18
Guide for the Married Man, A	USA	1967	Gene Kelly	91	sc/std		FB	18
Guilty By Suspicion	USA	1991	Irwin Winkler	105		W	FB	65
Gulliver's Travels	USA	1939	Dave Fleischer	85			APO	35
Gumball Rally, The	USA	1976	Chuck Bail	106	sc/std		FB	18
Gumshoe	GB	1971	Stephen Frears	95			FB	18
Gun Code	USA	1940	Peter Stewart	60			GB	15
Gun for a Coward	USA	1956	Abner Biberman	88	bw/std		FB	15
Gun Law	USA	1938	David Howard	60			GB	15
Gun Moll	USA	1949	Fletcher Markle	72			GB	25
Gun Point	USA	1956	Alfred Werker	85	std		FB	15
Gun Smugglers	USA	1948	Frank McDonald	61			GB	15
Gunfight at the O.K. Corral	USA	1957	John Sturges	122	std		FB	27
Gunfight in Abilene	USA	1966	William Hale	86	sc/std		FB	18
Gunfighter, The	USA	1951	Henry King	85			FB	15
Gunga Din	USA	1938	George Stevens	114			GB	22
Gunman's Walk	USA	1958	Phil Karlson	95	std		FB	18
Gunn	USA	1967	Blake Edwards	94			FB	18
Guns at Batasi	GB	1964	John Guillermin	103	sc/std		FB	15
Guns Don't Argue	USA	1955	Bill Karn/Richard C. Karn	68			GB	15
Guns for San Sebastian	FRI/T/ MEX	1967	Henri Verneuil	111	std		FB	18
Guns in the Afternoon	USA	1961	Sam Peckinpah	93	sc/std		FB	24
Guns in the Heather	GB	1968	Robert Butler	89			FB	27
Guns of Darkness	GB	1962	Anthony Asquith	102	bw		FB	15
Guns of Navarone, The	GB	1961	J. Lee Thompson	157	sc/std		FB	30
Guns of the Black Witch	IT/FR	1961	Domenico Paolella	83	sc/std		FB	18
Guns of the Magnificent Seven	USA	1968	Paul Wendkos	105	sc/std		FB	27
Guns of the Timberland	USA	1959	Robert D. Webb	91			GB	18
Guns of Wyoming	USA	1963	Tay Garnett	88			FB	16
Guns, The	BRAZ	1964	Ruy Guerra	110	est		MP	46
Gunslinger	USA	1956	Roger Corman	71	col		FB	18
Gypsy Colt	USA	1953	Andrew Marton	71			FB	15
Gypsy Moths, The	USA	1969	John Frankenheimer	106			FB	18

The Grifters

	COUNTRY OF PRODUCTION	YEAR	DIRECTOR	RUNNING TIME	VERSION	35mm	16mm	16mm RENTAL FEE
H.M.S. Defiant	GB	1962	Lewis Gilbert	100	std/sc		FB	18
Habañera, La	GB	1937	Douglas Sirk	95	est		BFI	25
Hail Mary	FR	1984	Jean-Luc Godard	110	est		MP	57.5
Hair	USA	1979	Milos Forman	118			FB	38
Hairdresser's Husband, The	FR	1990	Patrice Leconte	80	sc/st	MAY	GB	80
Hairspray	USA	1988	John Waters	92			GB	80
Half a Sixpence	GB/USA	1967	George Sidney	147	sc/std		FB	18
Half Life	AUSTR	1985	Dennis O'Rourke	84			MP	51.5
Half Shot at Sunrise	USA	1930	Paul Sloane	78			GB	15
Half-Naked Truth, The	USA	1932	Gregory La Cava	67			GB	15
Halfway House	GB	1943	Basil Dearden	95			FB	15
Hallelujah the Hills	USA	1963	Adolfas Mekas	82		GB	GB	40
Hallelujah Trail, The	USA	1965	John Sturges	146	sc		FB	22
Halloween II	USA	1981	Rick Rosenthal	92			FB	43
Halloween III: Season of the Witch	USA	1982	Tommy Lee Wallace	97	sc/std		FB	40
Halls of Montezuma	USA	1950	Lewis Milestone	122	bw		FB	15
Hamburger Hill	USA	1987	John Irvin	110			GB	75
Hamlet	GB/USA	1980	Rodney Bennett	210			BBC	35
Hamlet	GB	1976	Celestino Coronado	67		R	GB	25
Hamlet	GB	1948	Laurence Olivier	158			FB	22
Hamlet	USSR	1964	Grigori Kozintsev	149	std/est		GB	35
Hamlet	GB	1969	Tony Richardson	117			FB	33
Hamlet	GB	1990	Franco Zeffirelli	134		GU	GU	100
Hammer	USA	1972	Bruce Clark	89			FB	18
Hammerhead	GB	1968	David Miller	98			FB	18
Hammersmith is Out	USA	1972	Peter Ustinov	114			GB	27
Hammett	USA	1982	Wim Wenders	98		BFI	BFI	50
Hamsin Eastern Wind	IS	1982	Daniel Wachsmann	87	est		GB	45
Hand that Rocks the Cradle	USA	1991	Curtis Hanson	110		W	FB	70
Handful of Dust, A	GB	1987	Charles Sturridge	118			GB	70
Handful of Love, A	SWE	1974	Vilgot Sjöman	130	est		GB	35
Handle with Care	USA	1958	David Friedkin	82			FB	10
Handmaid's Tale, The	USA/ GER	1990	Volker Schlöndorff	108			GB	80
Hands Across the Table	USA	1935	Mitchell Leisen	81			FB	22
Hands of the Ripper	GB	1971	Peter Sasdy	85			FB	18
Hands Over the City	IT	1963	Francesco Rosi	105	est		GB	25
Handsworth Songs	GB	1986	John Akomfrah	60			BAFC	70
Hang 'Em High	USA	1967	Ted Post	114			FB	27
Hangmen Also Die	USA	1943	Fritz Lang	134			BFI	20
Hanky Panky	USA	1982	Sidney Poitier	107			FB	40
Hannah And Her Sisters	USA	1986	Woody Allen	107			FB	60
Hannibal Brooks	GB	1968	Michael Winner	102			FB	18
Hannie Caulder	GB	1971	Burt Kennedy	85	sc/std		GB	20
Hanover Street	GB	1979	Peter Hyams	109	sc		FB	36
Hans Brinker or the Silver Skates	W.GER	1962	Norman Foster	90	dub		FB	27
Happiest Days of Your Life, The	GB	1950	Frank Launder	81			GB	25
Happiest Millionaire, The	USA	1967	Norman Tokar	159			FB	27
Happiness	USSR	1934	Alexander Medvedkin	74			MP	
Happiness in 20 Years	FR	1971	Albert Knobler	90			GB	22
Happy Ending, The	USA	1969	Richard Brooks	112	sc		FB	18
Happy Ever After	GB	1954	Mario Zampi	87	bw		FB	15
Happy Go Lovely	GB	1950	H. Bruce Humberstone	97			FB	18
Hard Contract	USA	1969	S. Lee Pogostin	106	sc		FB	18
Hard Country	USA	1981	David Greene	101			GB	33
Hard Times	GB/ PORT	1988	João Botelho	96	est		GB	60
Hard Way, The	USA	1991	John Badham	111		UIP	FB	65
Hardcore Life, The	USA	1978	Paul Schrader	107			FB	33
Harem Holiday	USA	1965	Gene Nelson	84			FB	22

h

	COUNTRY OF PRODUCTION	YEAR	DIRECTOR	RUNNING TIME	VERSION	35mm	16mm	16mm RENTAL FEE
Harlem Globetrotters	USA	1951	Phil Brown	77			FB	15
Harlem Jazz Festival	USA	1955	Joseph Kohn	50			CONT	15
Harlow	USA	1965	Gordon Douglas	125	sc		FB	18
Harold and Maude	USA	1971	Hal Ashby	92			FB	22
Harrad Experiment, The	GB/USA	1973	Ted Post	92			GB	20
Harry and Tonto	USA	1974	Paul Mazursky	115			FB	18
Harry and Walter Go to New York	USA	1976	Mark Rydell	111	sc/std		FB	22
Harry in your Pocket	USA	1973	Bruce Geller	103	std		FB	18
Harry Munter	SWE	1969	Kjell Grede	101	est		GB	30
Harvest	USSR	1953	Vsevolod Pudovkin	110	est		ETV	15
Harvey Middleman, Fireman	USA	1965	Ernest Pintoff	76			FB	18
Hasek's Stories	CZ	1952	Miroslav Hubacek	90			ETV	10
Hasty Heart, The	GB	1949	Vincent Sherman	106			FB	15
Hat, Coat and Glove	USA	1934	Worthington Miner	64			GB	15
Hate for Hate	IT	1967	Domenico Paolella	91	dub/std		FB	15
Hatful of Rain, A	USA	1957	Fred Zinnemann	109	sc/std		FB	15
Hatter's Castle	GB	1941	Lance Comfort	101			FB	15
Haunt of Man, The	GB	1982	Mischa Scorer	60			CONC	23.8
Haunted and the Hunted, The	EIRE/ USA	1963	Francis Ford Coppola	73			GB	15
Haunted Honeymoon	USA	1986	Gene Wilder	84			FB	45
Haunted House of Horror, The	GB	1969	Michael Armstrong	91			GB	20
Haunted Palace, The	USA	1963	Roger Corman	86	sc		FB	18
Haunters of the Deep	GB	1984	Andrew Bogle	61			FB	17
Haunting, The	GB	1963	Robert Wise	112			FB	15
Havana	USA	1990	Sydney Pollack	144		U	FB	60
Having A Wonderful Crime	USA	1945	Edward Sutherland	70			GB	15
Having a Wonderful Time	USA	1938	Alfred Santell	70			GB	15
Hawk the Slayer	GB	1980	Terry Marcel	94			GB	38
Häxan (see Witchcraft Throughout the Ages)								
He Died With His Eyes Open	FR	1985	Jacques Deray	106	est		FB	60
He Knew Women	USA	1930	Hugh Herbert/Lynn Shores	70			GB	15
He Knows You're Alone	USA	1980	Armand Mastroianni	94			FB	38
He Who Gets Slapped	USA	1924	Victor Sjöström	77	st		FB	22
Head, The	W.GER	1959	Victor Trivas	95	dub		GB	15
Headless Ghost, The	GB	1959	Peter Graham Scott	61			FB	15
Headline	GB	1943	John Harlow	71				
Headline Hunters	GB	1968	Jonathan Ingrams	60			GB	17
Headline Shooter	USA	1933	Otto Brower	61			GB	15
Headlines for Murder	W.GER	1970	Heinz Schirck	63	est		GFL	0
Heads They Win, Tails You Lose	GB	1975	BBC tv	60			CONC	18.4
Hear My Song	GB	1990	Peter Chelsom	105		MAY	GB	85
Heart Beat	USA	1979	John Byrum	108			FB	41
Heart of a Child	GB	1958	Clive Donner	77			FB	15
Heart of Glass	W.GER	1976	Werner Herzog	93	est		GB	35
Heart of Russia, The	USSR	1971	Vera Stroyeva	105	est		ETV	10
Heart of Texas Ryan	USA	1917	E.A. Martin	61	st		BFI	15
Heartbeat	USA	1946	Sam Wood	103			GB	15
Heartbreak Ridge	USA	1986	Clint Eastwood	130			FB	55
Heartburn	USA	1986	Mike Nichols	109			FB	50
Heartland	USA	1979	Richard Pearce	95			GB	45
Hearts of Darkness: A Filmmakers Apocalypse	USA	1991	Fax Bahr/ George Hickenlooper	96		BD	GB	90
Hearts of the World	USA	1918	D.W. Griffith	105	st		BFI	25
Heat	USA	1986	Dick Richards	101			FB	40
Heat and Dust	GB	1982	James Ivory	130			GB	50
Heaven and Earth Magic Feature, The	USA	1968	Harry Smith	70			AC	10
Heaven Can Wait	USA	1978	Warren Beatty/Buck Henry	101			FB	38
Heaven Knows, Mr. Allison	USA	1957	John Huston	106	std		FB	15
Heaven With a Gun	USA	1968	Lee H. Katzin	98	sc/std		FB	18

h

	COUNTRY OF PRODUCTION	YEAR	DIRECTOR	RUNNING TIME	VERSION	35mm	16mm	16mm RENTAL FEE
Heavenly Days	USA	1944	Howard Estabrook	71			GB	15
Heavenly Kid, The	USA	1985	Gary Medoway	89			FB	40
Heavenly Pursuits	GB	1986	Charles Gormley	91			GB	60
Heavens Above	GB	1963	John Boulting	118			FB	15
Heavens Gate	USA	1980	Michael Cimino	148	sc		FB	43
Heavy Metal	USA	1981	Gerald Potterton	90			FB	48
Heidelberger Romance	W.GER	1952	Paul Verhoeven	97	est		GFL	0
Heidi	USA	1937	Allan Dwan	82			FB	15
Heidi's Song	USA/FR	1982	Robert Taylor	94			FB	38
Heist, The	USA	1971	Richard Brooks	120			FB	18
Helen of Troy	USA	1955	Robert Wise	114	bw		FB	15
Hell Bent for Leather	USA	1959	George Sherman	82	bw/std		FB	15
Hell Boats	GB	1969	Paul Wendkos	96			FB	18
Hell Divers	USA	1932	George Hill	107			FB	22
Hell Drivers	GB	1957	Cy Endfield	108	std		FB	15
Hell in the Pacific	USA	1968	John Boorman	102	std	GB	GB	18
Hell is a City	GB	1959	Val Guest	96	sc/std		FB	15
Hell is for Heroes	USA	1962	Don Siegel	89			FB	15
Hell on Frisco Bay	USA	1955	Frank Tuttle	93	std		GB	22
Hell with Heroes, The	USA	1968	Joseph Sargent	102	std		FB	18
Hell's Angels	USA	1930	Howard Hughes	125			BFI	30
Hell's Angels '69	USA	1969	Lee Madden	98			FB	18
Hell's Belles	USA	1969	Maury Dexter	95			FB	18
Hell's Highway	USA	1932	Rowland Brown	60			GB	15
Hellbenders, The	IT/SP	1966	Sergio Corbucci	92	dub		FB	18
Heller in Pink Tights	USA	1960	George Cukor	101	bw		FB	15
Hellfighters	USA	1968	Andrew V. McLaglen	110	sc/std		FB	18
Hello — Goodbye	USA	1970	Jean Negulesco	101			FB	18
Hello Again	USA	1987	Frank Perry	96			FB	50
Hello Down There	USA	1968	Jack Arnold	88			FB	18
Hello, Dolly!	USA	1969	Gene Kelly	145	sc/std		FB	27
Hellstrom Chronicle, The	USA	1971	Walon Green	90			FB	20
Hemingway's Adventures of a Young Man	USA	1962	Martin Ritt	142	sc/std		FB	18
Henry IV (Part I & Part 2)	GB/USA	1979	David Giles	155			BBC	35
Henry V	GB	1989	Kenneth Branagh	135		MAY	GB	95
Henry V	GB	1944	Laurence Olivier	137		R	FB	27
Henry V	GB/USA	1979	David Giles	170			BBC	35
Henry VIII	GB/USA	1979	Kevin Billington	160			BBC	35
Henry VIII and his Six Wives	GB	1972	Waris Hussein	106			FB	18
Henry: Portrait of A Serial Killer	USA	1986	John McNaughton	82		ELEC	GB	80
Her Alibi	USA	1989	Bruce Beresford	95			FB	55
Her Crime Was Love (see Ihr Verbrechen War Liebe)								
Her Favourite Husband	GB	1950	Mario Soldati	80			GB	15
Her First Affair	GB	1932	Allan Dwan	72			GB	15
Her Majesty, Love	USA	1931	William Dieterle	75			FB	22
Herbie Goes Bananas	USA	1980	Vincent McEveety	92			FB	38
Herbie Goes to Monte Carlo	USA	1977	Vincent McEveety	105			FB	38
Herbie Rides Again	USA	1973	Robert Stevenson	88			FB	38
Hercules Against Kung Fu	IT	1973	Anthony M. Dawson	104	sc/dub/88		FB	22
Hercules and the Captive Women	IT/FR	1961	Vittorio Cottafavi	95	std/dub		GB	18
Herd, The	TURK	1979	Zeki Ökten	122	est		BFI	35
Here Come the Girls	USA	1953	Claude Binyon	87	bw		FB	15
Here Comes the Groom	USA	1951	Frank Capra	114			FB	15
Here We Go Again	USA	1942	Allan Dwan	77			GB	15
Here We Go Round the Mulberry Bush	GB	1967	Clive Donner	94			FB	18
Heretic, The (see Exorcist II: The Heretic)								
Hero	GB	1982	Barney Platts-Mills	92	est		BFI	30
Hero at Large	USA	1980	Martin Davidson	99			FB	38

h

	COUNTRY OF PRODUCTION	YEAR	DIRECTOR	RUNNING TIME	VERSION	35mm	16mm	16mm RENTAL FEE
Heroes	USA	1977	Jeremy Paul Kagan	107			FB	33
Heroes of Shipka	BULG/USSR	1955	Sergei Vasiliev	112	est		ETV	10
Heroes of Telemark, The	GB	1965	Anthony Mann	131	std		FB	22
Heroin Gang, The	USA	1967	Brian G. Hutton	89	sc/std		FB	16
Herostratus	GB	1967	Don Levy	142			BFI	35
Herr Arnes Pengar	SWE	1919	Mauritz Stiller	100	est/st		GB	20
Hester Street	USA	1974	Joan Micklin Silver	86			GB	25
Hi Gaucho	USA	1935	Tommy Atkins	59			GB	20
Hi, Mom	USA	1969	Brian De Palma	87			GB	23
Hickey & Boggs	USA	1972	Robert Culp	111			FB	18
Hidden Agenda	GB	1990	Ken Loach	108			GB	80
Hidden Eye, The	USA	1945	Richard Whorf	69			FB	10
Hidden Heritage	GB	1990	Andrew Piddington	52			AC	20
Hide and Seek	GB	1972	David Eady	61			GB	17
Hide in Plain Sight	USA	1980	James Caan	92	std		FB	38
Hideaway	USA	1937	Richard Rosson	60			GB	15
Hier Kein Ausgang Nur Ubergang	W.GER	1977	Rainer Wolffhardt	88	est		GFL	0
High Anxiety	USA	1977	Mel Brooks	94			FB	36
High Barbaree	USA	1947	Jack Conway	91			FB	10
High Bright Sun, The	GB	1965	Ralph Thomas	114			FB	18
High Command, The	GB	1937	Thorold Dickinson	74			FB	15
High Cost of Loving, The	USA	1958	José Ferrer	87			FB	12
High Fire	GB	1983	John Tchalenko	52			AC	20
High Flyers	USA	1937	Edward Cline	70			GB	15
High Heels	SP	1987	Pedro Almódovar	114		R	FB	70
High Hopes	GB	1988	Mike Leigh	112			GB	80
High Plains Drifter	USA	1972	Clint Eastwood	102	std		FB	27
High Rise Donkey	GB	1980	Michael Forlong	57			GB	20
High School	USA	1968	Frederick Wiseman	75			GB	45
High Sierra	USA	1941	Raoul Walsh	100			FB	22
High Society	USA	1956	Charles Walters	107			FB	27
High Spirits	USA	1988	Neil Jordan	96			GB	75
High Stakes	USA	1931	Lowell Sherman	69			GB	15
High Time	USA	1960	Blake Edwards	104	sc/std		FB	18
High Wall	CZ	1963	Karel Kachyna	79	est		ETV	10
High Wind in Jamaica, A	GB	1965	Alexander Mackendrick	103	sc/std		FB	18
Higher and Higher	USA	1944	Tim Whelan	91			GB	16
Highlander	GB	1986	Russell Mulcahy	116			FB	45
Highways by Night	USA	1942	Peter Godfrey	63			GB	15
Hijack	GB	1975	Michael Forlong	59			GB	17
Hilda Was a Goodlooker	GB	1983	Anna Thew	60			LFC	
Hill 24 Doesn't Answer	IS	1954	Thorold Dickinson	106			GB	25
Hill in Korea, A	GB	1956	Julian Amyes	81			FB	15
Hill's Angels	USA	1978	Bruce Bilson	99			FB	38
Hill, The	GB	1965	Sidney Lumet	123			FB	27
Hindenburg, The	USA	1975	Robert Wise	106	sc/std		FB	33
Hindle Wakes	GB	1952	Arthur Crabtree	90			GB	15
Hintertreppe, Die	GER	1921	Leopold Jessner	60	est/st		GB	0
Hips, Hips, Hooray!	USA	1934	Mark Sandrich	69			GB	15
Hired Gun	USA	1958	Ray Nazarro	64			FB	10
Hired Hand, The	USA	1971	Peter Fonda	102			FB	18
Hireling, The	GB	1973	Alan Bridges	108			FB	18
His and Hers	GB	1960	Brian Desmond Hurst	94			GB	15
His Family Tree	USA	1935	Charles Vidor	68			GB	15
His Greatest Gamble	USA	1934	John S. Robertson	70			GB	15
His Kind of Woman	USA	1951	John Farrow	120			GB	15
His Other Woman	USA	1957	Walter Lang	103	std		FB	18
His Picture in the Papers	USA	1916	John Emerson	69			BFI	15

	COUNTRY OF PRODUCTION	YEAR	DIRECTOR	RUNNING TIME	VERSION	35mm	16mm	16mm RENTAL FEE
History Book, The	DEN	1974	Jannik Hastrup/Li Vilstrup		15-20 each		MP	23
History Lessons	IT/ W.GER	1972	Jean-Marie Straub/ Danièle Huillet	85	est		GB	40
History of Mr Polly, The	GB	1948	Anthony Pélissier	94			FB	15
Hit	USA	1973	Sidney J. Furie	134	sc		FB	27
Hit the Deck	USA	1955	Roy Rowland	112	sc		FB	18
Hit, The	GB	1984	Stephen Frears	98			GB	50
Hitch	USA	1974	Irving Jacoby	90			CONC	35
Hitch in Time, A	GB	1978	Jan Darnley-Smith	60			GB	17
Hitcher, The	USA	1986	Robert Harmon	97	sc/std		FB	50
Hitler's Children	USA	1943	Edward Dmytryk	84			GB	15
Hitler's Madman	USA	1943	Douglas Sirk	84			FB	18
Hitler: The Last Ten Days	GB/IT	1973	Ennio De Concini	104			FB	33
Hitlerjunge Quex	GER	1931	Hans Steinhoff	101	est		BFI	20
Hitting a New High	USA	1937	Raoul Walsh	85			GB	15
Hoffman	GB	1969	Alvin Rakoff	113			FB	18
Holcroft Covenant, The	GB	1985	John Frankenheimer	112			FB	40
Hold 'Em Jail	USA	1932	Norman Taurog	75			GB	15
Hold Back the Dawn	USA	1941	Mitchell Leisen	116			FB	15
Holiday Affair	USA	1949	Don Hartman	87			GB	15
Holiday on the Buses	GB	1973	Bryan Izzard	87			FB	18
Holidays with Minka	CZ	1960	Josef Pinkava	85	est		ETV	10
Hollywood Blue	USA	1981	Alan Roberts	85			FB	38
Hollywood Canteen	USA	1944	Delmer Daves	125			FB	22
Hollywood Cowboy	USA	1975	Howard Zieff	103			FB	27
Hollywood Hotel	USA	1938	Busby Berkeley	110			FB	22
Hollywood: The Selznick Years	USA	1970	Marshall Flaum	60			FB	22
Holocaust 2000	GB/IT	1977	Alberto De Martino	102			FB	38
Hombre	USA	1966	Martin Ritt	110	sc/std		FB	18
Home Alone	USA	1990	Chris Columbus	95		F	FB	65
Home and the World	IND	1985	Satyajit Ray	140	st		GB	55
Home at Seven	GB	1952	Ralph Richardson	85			GB	20
Hondo and the Apaches	USA	1966	Lee H. Katzin	86			FB	15
Honey Pot, The	USA/IT	1966	Joseph L. Mankiewicz	150	131		FB	18
Honeymoon	USA	1947	William Keighley	77			GB	15
Honeymoon Hotel	USA	1964	Henry Levin	87	sc/std		FB	15
Honeymoon Killers, The	USA	1969	Leonard Kastle	106			BFI	30
Honeymoon Machine, The	USA	1961	Richard Thorpe	87	sc/std		FB	16
Honeysuckle Rose	USA	1980	Jerry Schatzberg	119			FB	40
Honkers, The	USA	1971	Steve Ihnat	102			FB	18
Honky Tonk Freeway	USA	1981	John Schlesinger	107			FB	38
Honorary Consul, The	GB	1983	John Mackenzie	103			GB	50
Hook	USA	1991	Steven Spielberg	140		C	FB	75
Hook, Line and Sinker	USA	1930	Edward Cline	72			GB	15
Hook, The	USA	1962	George Seaton	98	sc/std		FB	12
Hooper	USA	1978	Hal Needham	99			FB	30
Hooray for Love	USA	1935	Walter Lang	73			GB	15
Hootenanny Hoot	USA	1963	Gene Nelson	91			FB	12
Hooties Blues (see Kansas City)								
Hope and Glory	GB	1987	John Boorman	112			FB	55
Hopscotch	USA	1980	Ronald Neame	107	sc/std		FB	43
Horizons West	USA	1952	Budd Boetticher	81			FB	18
Horizontal Lieutenant, The	USA	1962	Richard Thorpe	90			FB	16
Hornets' Nest	GB	1955	Charles Saunders	64			FB	18
Horror Hospital	GB	1973	Anthony Balch	91			GB	27
Horror of Frankenstein, The	GB	1970	Jimmy Sangster	95			FB	18
Horse Called Jester, A	GB	1979	Ken Fairbairn	55			GB	17
Horse Feathers	USA	1932	Norman Z. McLeod	67			FB	15
Horse in the Gray Flannel								

	COUNTRY OF PRODUCTION	YEAR	DIRECTOR	RUNNING TIME	VERSION	35mm	16mm	16mm RENTAL FEE
Horse Without A Head, The	GB	1963	Don Chaffey	89			FB	27
Horse's Mouth, The	GB	1958	Ronald Neame	95			GB	24
Horsemen, The	USA	1970	John Frankenheimer	109	sc		FB	18
Hospital	USA	1970	Frederick Wiseman	84			GB	50
Hospital, The	USA	1971	Arthur Hiller	102			FB	22
Hostage Tower, The	USA	1980	Claudio Guzman	97			FB	41
Hostages, The	GB	1975	David Eady	59			GB	17
Hostess	E.GER	1976	Rolf Romer	90			ETV	10
Hot Acts of Love	FR	1974	Jean-Marie Pallardy	73	dub		FB	20
Hot Bubblegum	IS/W.GER	1981	Boaz Davidson	94	dub		FB	33
Hot Enough for June	GB	1963	Ralph Thomas	98			FB	18
Hot Lead and Cold Feet	USA	1978	Robert Butler	90			FB	33
Hot Millions	GB	1968	Eric Till	106			FB	18
Hot One, The	USA	1978	Matthew Robbins	104			FB	30
Hot Pepper	USA	1973	Les Blank	54			GB	20
Hot Shots!	USA	1991	Jim Abrahams	84		F	FB	70
Hot Spell	USA	1958	Daniel Mann	84			FB	15
Hot Spot, The	**USA**	**1990**	**Dennis Hopper**	**130**		**R**	**FB**	**60**
Hot Stuff	USA	1979	Dom DeLuise	91			FB	27
Hot Summer Night	USA	1956	David Friedkin	81			FB	15
Hot Tip	USA	1935	Ray McCarey/James Gleason	69			GB	15
Hotel	USA	1967	Richard Quine	110			FB	18
Hotel Paradiso	GB	1966	Peter Glenville	99			FB	18
Hotel Reserve	USA	1944	Lance Comfort/Max Greene	89			GB	15
Hound Dog Man	USA	1959	Don Siegel	87	sc/std		FB	18
Hounds of Spring, The	SWE	1976	Erland Josephson	68	est		GB	25
Hour of the Furnaces								
Part 1	ARG	1968	Fernando E. Solanas	95	est		MP	46
Part 2 & 3				165				51
Parts 1,2,& 3				260				75
Hour of the Gun	USA	1967	John Sturges	101	sc		FB	18
Hour of the Star	BRAZ	1985	Suzana Amaral	96			GB	50
Hour of the Wolf	SWE	1967	Ingmar Bergman	90	est		FB	22
House	IS	1981	Amos Gitai	50	est		BFI	25
House Across the Lake	GB	1954	Ken Hughes	68			FB	15
House at the Crossroads	CZ	1959	Vladimir Bahna	85	est		ETV	10
House Calls	USA	1978	Howard Zieff	98			FB	43
House in Nightmare Park, The	GB	1973	Peter Sykes	95			FB	18
House in the Square	GB	1951	Roy Ward Baker	91	bw		FB	15
House of Cards	USA	1968	John Guillermin	103	sc/std		FB	18
House of Dark Shadows	USA	1970	Dan Curtis	97			FB	15
House of Games	USA	1987	David Mamet	101			FB	40
House of Mortal Sin	GB	1975	Peter Walker	104			FB	18
House of Mystery	GB	1961	Vernon Sewell	56			FB	15
House of Numbers	USA	1957	Russell Rouse	92	sc/std		FB	12
House of Rothschild, The	USA	1934	Alfred Werker	87			WEB	20
House of Secrets, The	USA	1937	Roland D. Reed	68			GB	15
House of the Long Shadows	GB	1983	Peter Walker	102			FB	38
House of the Seven Gables, The	USA	1940	Joe May	89			FB	15
House of the Seven Hawks, The	GB	1959	Richard Thorpe	92			FB	12
House of Wax	USA	1953	André de Toth	87	bw/std		FB	15
House on 92nd Street, The	USA	1945	Henry Hathaway	88			FB	15
House on Carroll Street, The	USA	1988	Peter Yates	101			FB	60
House on Trubnaya Square	USSR	1928	Boris Barnet	77	st/est	BFI	BFI	30
House that Dripped Blood, The	GB	1970	Peter Duffell	102			GB	22
House That Screamed, The	SP	1969	Narciso Serrador	76	sc/dub		FB	18
Houseboat	USA	1958	Melville Shavelson	110	bw/std		FB	15
Householder, The	INDIA	1963	James Ivory	101			GB	25

h	COUNTRY OF PRODUCTION	YEAR	DIRECTOR	RUNNING TIME	VERSION	35mm	16mm	16mm RENTAL FEE
Houses are Full of Smoke, The	USA	1987	Allan Francovich	176			BFI	50
Housesitter	USA	1992	Frank Oz	102		UIP	FB	70
Hoverbug	GB	1971	Jan Darnley-Smith	57			GB	17
How Do I Love Thee?	USA	1970	Michael Gordon	98	(109)		GB	18
How Does It Feel	GB	1976	Mick Csaky	60			AC	16
How Green Was My Valley	USA	1941	John Ford	118			FB	16
How the West Was Won	USA	1961	Henry Hathaway/John Ford/George Marshall	155	std		FB	38
How to Be Very, Very Popular	USA	1955	Nunnally Johnson	90	std		FB	18
How to Beat the High Cost of Living	USA	1980	Robert Scheerer	97			GB	38
How to Destroy the Reputation of the Greatest Secret Agent	FR/IT	1973	Philippe de Broca	92	std/dub		FB	18
How to Get Ahead in Advertising	GB	1989	Bruce Robinson	93			GB	85
How to Murder Your Wife	USA	1964	Richard Quine	118			FB	18
How to Save a Marriage . . . and Ruin Your Life	USA	1967	Fielder Cook	102	sc/std		FB	18
How to Steal a Diamond in 4 Uneasy Lessons	USA	1972	Peter Yates	101	sc/std		FB	25
How to Steal a Million	USA	1966	William Wyler	123	sc/std		FB	18
How to Steal the World	USA	1968	Sutton Roley	89			FB	16
How's Business?	GB	1990	Colin Finbow	71			GB	40
Howard – A New Breed of Hero	USA	1986	Willard Huyck	110			FB	45
Howard's End	GB	1991	James Ivory	142		MAY	GB	80
Huckleberry Finn	USA	1974	J. Lee Thompson	114	sc/std		FB	22
Hucksters, The	USA	1947	Jack Conway	115			FB	14
Hudson Hawk	USA	1990	Michael Lehmann	95		C	FB	55
Hue and Cry	GB	1946	Charles Crichton	81			FB	15
Hugo and Josefin	SWE	1967	Kjell Grede	82	est		GB	30
Hugo the Hippo	USA	1975	Bill Feigenbaum	78			GB	30
Hugs and Kisses	SWE	1966	Jonas Cornell	93	est		GB	30
Hullabaloo Over Georgie and Bonnie's Pictures	GB	1978	James Ivory	82			GB	35
Human Desire	USA	1954	Fritz Lang	91			FB	15
Human Factor, The	GB/USA	1979	Otto Preminger	115	std		FB	38
Humanoid, The	IT	1979	George B. Lewis	99	eng		FB	27
Hunch, The	GB	1967	Sarah Erulkar	55			GB	17
Hunchback of Notre Dame, The	USA	1923	Wallace Worsley	93	st		BFI	20
Hunchback of Notre Dame, The	USA	1939	William Dieterle	112			GB	15
100 Rifles	USA	1968	Tom Gries	109			FB	20
Hunger, The	USA	1983	Tony Scott	96			FB	38
Hunt, The (see Caza, La)								
Hunted in Holland	GB	1961	Derek Williams	61			GB	17
Hunted, The	USA	1987	Joe Camp	89			FB	40
Hunter, The	USA	1980	Buzz Kulik	98			FB	43
Hunting Instinct, The	USA	1962	Wolfgang Reitherman	70			FB	27
Hurricane	USA	1979	Jan Troell	119	sc		GB	38
Hurry Charlie Hurry	USA	1941	Charles E. Roberts	65			GB	15
Hurry Tomorrow	USA	1976	Richard Cohen/Kevin Rafferty	80			GB	20
Hush . . Hush Sweet Charlotte	USA	1964	Robert Aldrich	132	std		FB	15
Hush A Bye Baby	EIRE	1989	Margo Harkin	72			BFI	
Hustle	USA	1975	Robert Aldrich	118			FB	27
Hustler, The	USA	1961	Robert Rossen	135	std		FB	17
Hyena's Sun	HOLL/ TUN	1977	Ridha Behi	100	est		CONC	33
Hypothesis of the Stolen Painting	FR	1978	Raul Ruiz	66	est		BFI	30

	COUNTRY OF PRODUCTION	YEAR	DIRECTOR	RUNNING TIME	VERSION	35mm	16mm	16mm RENTAL FEE
I A Woman	DEN/SWE	1965	Mac Ahlberg	90	st		GB	35
I Accuse	GB	1957	José Ferrer	84	std		FB	10
I am a Dancer	FR/GB	1972	Pierre Jourdain	93			FB	18
I am a Fugitive from a Chain Gang	USA	1932	Mervyn LeRoy	90			FB	22
I am Curious – Blue	SWE	1968	Vilgot Sjöman	103	est/107		GB	30
I am Curious – Yellow	SWE	1967	Vilgot Sjöman	110	est/121		GB	30
I Be Done Was Is	USA	1983	Debra J. Robinson	58			CN	41
I Bought A Vampire Motorcyle	GB	1989	Dirk Campbell	105		MAY	GB	60
I Confess	USA	1953	Alfred Hitchcock	95			FB	25
I Could Go On Singing	GB	1963	Ronald Neame	100	sc		FB	18
I Crossed the Colour Line	USA	1966	Ted V. Mikels	88			GB	25
I Deal in Danger	USA	1966	Walter Grauman	89			FB	18
I Dream Too Much	USA	1935	John Cromwell	95			GB	15
I Escaped From Devil's Island	USA	1973	William Witney	87			FB	18
I Killed Geronimo	USA	1950	John Hoffman	69			GB	5
I Killed That Man	USA	1942	Phil Rosen	75			GB	5
I Know Where I'm Going!	GB	1945	Michael Powell/Emeric Pressburger	91		R	FB	30
I Live in Fear	JAP	1955	Akira Kurosawa	100	est		BFI	55
I Love My Wife	GB	1971	Mel Stuart	95			FB	18
I Love You – I Kill You	W.GER	1970	Uwe Brandner	94	est		GFL	0
I Married a Communist (see Woman on Pier 13)								
I Married a Woman	USA	1956	Hal Kanter	85	sc		GB	15
I Only Want You To Love Me	W.GER	1976	R.W. Fassbinder	114	est		GFL	0
I Remember Mama	USA	1948	George Stevens	115		GB	GB	15
I Saw What You Did	GB	1965	William Castle	82			FB	15
I See Ice	GB	1938	Anthony Kimmins	82			FB	15
I Shall Return	GB	1950	Fritz Lang	104	bw		FB	15
I Start Counting	GB	1969	David Greene	105			FB	18
I Thank a Fool	GB	1962	Robert Stevens	100	sc/std		FB	16
I the Jury	USA	1981	Richard Heffron	109			FB	43
I Walk the Line	USA	1970	John Frankenheimer	97	sc		FB	18
I Wanna Hold Your Hand	USA	1978	Robert Zemeckis	99			FB	33
I Want What I Want	GB	1971	John Dexter	91	GB		GB	22
I Was a Fireman	GB	1943	Humphrey Jennings	74		BFI	BFI	20
				65			CFL	17.50
I Was Born But	JAP	1932	Yasujiro Ozu	88	sd/est		BFI	25
I Was Happy Here	GB	1965	Desmond Davis	91			FB	15
I Was Monty's Double	GB	1958	John Guillermin	100			FB	15
I'd Rather be Rich	USA	1964	Jack Smight	96	bw		FB	15
I'll Cry Tomorrow	USA	1955	Daniel Mann	119			FB	12
I'll Never Forget What's 'is name	GB	1967	Michael Winner	97			FB	18
I'm All Right Jack	GB	1959	John Boulting	105			FB	15
I'm From the City	USA	1938	Ben Holmes	66			GB	15
I'm No Angel	USA	1933	Wesley Ruggles	89			FB	15
I'm Still Alive	USA	1940	Irving Reis	72			GB	15
I've Heard the Mermaids Singing	CAN	1987	Patricia Rozema	83			GB	75
I, Monster	GB	1970	Stephen Weeks	75			GB	25
Ice Age	NOR/W.GER	1975	Peter Zadek	108	est		GFL	0
Ice Castles	USA	1978	Donald Wrye	109			FB	30
Ice Cold in Alex	GB	1958	J. Lee Thompson	130			FB	15
Ice Pirates	USA	1984	Stewart Raffill	92			FB	35
Ice Station Zebra	USA	1968	John Sturges	145	sc/std		FB	33
Identification of a Woman	IT/FR	1982	Michelangelo Antonioni	130	est		GB	50
Idiot, The	JAP	1951	Akira Kurosawa	165			GB	25
Idolmaker, The	USA	1980	Taylor Hackford	117			FB	38
If a Man Answers	USA	1962	Henry Levin	102	bw		FB	15

	COUNTRY OF PRODUCTION	YEAR	DIRECTOR	RUNNING TIME	VERSION	35mm	16mm	16mm RENTAL FEE
If I Had a Million	USA	1932	Ernst Lubitsch/Norman Taurog/ Stephen Roberts/Norman Z.McLeod/ James Cruze/William A. Seiter/ H. Bruce Humberstone	76			FB	15
If I Were Free	USA	1933	Elliott Nugent	66			GB	15
If It's Tuesday, This Must Be Belgium	USA	1969	Mel Stuart	98			FB	18
If You Feel Like Singing	USA	1950	Charles Walters	103			FB	14
If You Knew Susie	USA	1948	Gordon Douglas	90			GB	15
IF....	GB	1968	Lindsay Anderson	111		UIP	FB	27
Ihr Verbrechen War Liebe	W.GER	1958	Geza Radvanyi	98	est		GFL	0
Ikiru	JAP	1952	Akira Kurosawa	130	est		GB	30
Ill Met by Moonlight	GB	1956	Michael Powell/Emeric Pressburger	104	std		FB	15
Illuminated Texts	USA	1985	Bruce Elder	180			LFC	60
Illumination	POL	1972	Krzysztof Zanussi	92			GB	30
Illusive Crime	GB	1976	Richard Woolley	33			LFC	16.5
Image Con Text: One	GB	1984	Mike Leggett	50			LFMC	42.5
Image Con Text: Two	GB	1984	Mike Leggett	50			LFMC	42.5
Images	EIRE	1972	Robert Altman	101	std		GB	18
Imagine: John Lennon	USA	1988	Andrew Solt	106			FB	50
Imitation Game, The	GB	1980	Richard Eyre	95			BFI	25
Imitation General	USA	1958	George Marshall	88			FB	12
Imitation of Life	USA	1934	John M. Stahl	109			BFI	25
Imitation of Life	USA	1959	Douglas Sirk	124			BFI	30
Immoral Tales	FR	1974	Walerian Borowczyk	103	est		GB	40
Immortal Garrison, The	USSR	1956	Z. Agranenko	96	est		ETV	10
Immortal Story, The	FR	1968	Orson Welles	60			GB	25
Impact	USA	1949	Arthur Lubin	111			GB	24
Impasse	USA	1968	Richard Benedict	99			FB	18
Impossible Years, The	USA	1968	Michael Gordon	98	sc/std		FB	16
Impostors	USA	1979	Mark Rappaport	110			BFI	35
Improper Channels	CAN	1979	Eric Till	93			FB	33
Improper Conduct	FR	1983	Nestor Almendros/Orlando Leal	114	est		ICA	50
Impudent Girl, An	FR	1985	Claude Miller	97	est		GB	60
In Cold Blood	USA	1967	Richard Brooks	134	sc		FB	15
In Defence of the People	IR USA	1981	Rafigh Pooya	100	est		MP	57.5
In Fading Light	GB	1989	Amber Films				GB	
In for Treatment	HOLL	1979	Erik Van Zuylen/Marja Kok	92	est		CONC	38.4
In Harm's Way	USA	1965	Otto Preminger	154	bw/std		FB	15
In Like Flint	USA	1967	Gordon Douglas	115	sc/std		FB	18
In Love and War	USA	1958	Philip Dunne	115	sc/std		FB	18
In Name Only	USA	1939	John Cromwell	94			GB	15
In Person	USA	1935	William A. Seiter	87			GB	15
In Praise of Older Women	CAN	1977	George Kaczender	116			FB	38
In Search of the Castaways	GB	1961	Robert Stevenson	100			FB	35
In the Cool of the Day	USA	1962	Robert Stevens	88	std		FB	16
In the Doghouse	GB	1961	Darcy Conyers	92			FB	15
In the Forest	GB	1978	Phil Mulloy	80			BFI	30
In the King of Prussia	USA	1982	Emile de Antonio	90			CONC	30
In the Name of the Father	IT	1971	Marco Bellocchio	107	est		MP	51.75
In the Nick	GB	1959	Ken Hughes	105	std		FB	15
In the Quiet of the Night	POL	1978	Tadeusz Chmielewski	120	est		FOP	0
In the Realm of the Senses	FR/JAP	1976	Nagisa Oshima	104	est	BFI	BFI	75
In The Shadow of the Sun	GB	1972/80	Derek Jarman	54			BFI	20
In the White City	PORT/ SWITZ	1983	Alain Tanner	108	est		GB	50
In-laws, The	USA	1979	Arthur Hiller	102			FB	43
Incident At Midnight	GB	1962	Norman Harrison	56			GB	20
Incident at Phantom Hill	USA	1965	Earl Bellamy	87	bw		FB	15

	COUNTRY OF PRODUCTION	YEAR	DIRECTOR	RUNNING TIME	VERSION	35mm	16mm	16mm RENTAL FEE
Incredible Journey, The	USA	1963	Fletcher Markle	80			FB	38
Incredible Shrinking Woman, The	USA	1981	Joel Schumacher	89			FB	38
Incubus, The	CAN	1981	John Hough	78			GB	38
Indian Tomb, The	FR/IT/ W.GER	1958	Fritz Lang	97	est		BFI	25
Indiana Jones and the Last Crusade	USA	1989	Steven Spielberg	127			FB	65
Indiana Jones and the Temple of Doom	USA	1984	Steven Spielberg	117			FB	60
Inferno	USA	1953	Roy Ward Baker	83	bw		FB	15
Inferno	IT	1980	Dario Argento	106	eng		FB	33
Informer, The	USA	1935	John Ford	88			BFI	20
Inglorious Bastards, The	IT	1978	Enzo G. Castellari	82	dub		FB	33
Inherit the Wind	USA	1960	Stanley Kramer	128			FB	22
Inn of the Sixth Happiness, The	GB	1958	Mark Robson	159	sc/std		FB	19
Inner Circle	USA/ SWE/IT	1991	Andrei Konchalovsky	134		C	FB	70
Innerspace	USA	1987	Joe Dante	119			FB	50
Innocent Sinners	GB	1958	Philip Leacock	95	bw		FB	15
Innocent Sorcerers	POL	1960	Andrzej Wajda	86	est		GB	25
Innocents, The	GB	1961	Jack Clayton	99	sc		FB	15
Inquisitor, The	FR	1981	Claude Miller	88	est		FB	55
Inseparable Friends	USSR	1952	V. Zhuralev	80	est		ETV	10
Inserts	GB	1976	John Byrum	1 17			FB	27
Inside Job	USA	1973	Robert Michael Lewis	86			FB	22
Inside North Vietnam	USA	1967	Felix Greene	81			GB	20
Inside Out	GB/ W.GER	1975	Peter Duffell	97			FB	22
Insignificance	GB	1985	Nicolas Roeg	109			GB	60
Inspecteur Lavardin	FR	1986	Claude Chabrol	100	est		GB	60
Inspector Clouseau	GB	1968	Bud Yorkin	96	sc		FB	27
Institution, The	GB	1978	Ian Breakwell/Kevin Coyne	50			LFMC	42.5
Intelligence Men, The	GB	1965	Robert Asher	104	bw		FB	15
Intent to Kill	GB	1958	Jack Cardiff	89	sc/std		FB	15
Interiors	USA	1978	Woody Allen	91			FB	27
Interlude	USA	1958	Douglas Sirk	89	std		FB	22
Interlude	GB	1968	Kevin Billington	113			FB	18
Intermezzo	USA	1939	Gregory Ratoff	71			GB	22
International Velvet	GB	1978	Bryan Forbes	127			FB	33
Intimate Lighting	CZ	1965	Ivan Passer	72	est		GB	25
Into the Night	USA	1984	John Landis	115			FB	40
Intolerance	USA	1916	D.W Griffith	160	st		BFI	30
Intruder in the Dust	USA	1949	Clarence Brown	86			FB	10
Intruder, The	GB	1953	Guy Hamilton	84			GB	20
Invaders from Mars	USA	1953	William Cameron Menzies	75			GB	30
Invaders from Mars	USA	1986	Tobe Hooper	100			FB	40
Invaders, The	GB	1977	Nick May	87			NFS	14.55
Invasion	GB	1966	Alan Bridges	82			FB	15
Invasion of the Body Snatchers, The	USA	1978	Philip Kaufman	115			FB	38
Invasion Quartet	GB	1961	Jay Lewis	87			FB	12
Invasion USA	USA	1985	Joseph Zito	107			FB	40
Investigation of a Citizen Above Suspicion	IT	1970	Elio Petri	115	dub		FB	18
Investigation of Murder, An	USA	1973	Stuart Rosenberg	112			FB	18
Invisible Adversaries	AUST	1977	Valie Export	109	mag/est		CIRC	35
Invisible Boy, The	USA	1957	Herman Hoffman	82			FB	12
Invitation to the Dance	GB	1954	Gene Kelly	62			FB	14
Invitation, L'	FR/SWITZ	1973	Claude Goretta	100	est		GB	25
Invocation – Maya Deren	GB	1987	Jo Ann Kaplan	53			AC	20
Ipcress File, The	GB	1965	Sidney J. Furie	108	col/sc		FB	18
					bw/std		FB	15
Iphigenia	GR	1976	Michael Cacoyannis	129	est		FB	22

	COUNTRY OF PRODUCTION	YEAR	DIRECTOR	RUNNING TIME	VERSION	35mm	16mm	16mm RENTAL FEE
Irene	USA	1940	Herbert Wilcox	104			GB	15
Irishman, The	AUSTR	1978	Donald Crombie	108			GB	35
Irma la Douce	USA	1963	Billy Wilder	141	sc		FB	18
Iron Duke, The	GB	1935	Victor Saville	89			FB	22
Iron Eagle	USA	1985	Sidney J. Furie	119			FB	45
Iron Eagle II	USA	1989	Sidney J. Furie	98		GU	GU	80
Iron Horse, The	USA	1924	John Ford	119	t/sd		BFI	25
Iron Maiden, The	GB	1962	Gerald Thomas	98	bw		FB	15
Iron Major, The	USA	1943	Ray Enright	130			GB	22
Ironweed	USA	1987	Hector Babenco	135			FB	50
Is My Face Red?	USA	1932	William A. Seiter	66			GB	15
Is Paris Burning?	FR	1965	René Clément	165	bw/sc		FB	15
Isadora	GB	1968	Karel Reisz	138			FB	18
Ishtar	USA	1987	Elaine May	107			FB	50
Island at the Top of the World, The	USA	1973	Robert Stevenson	94			FB	35
Island in the Sun	GB	1957	Robert Rossen	119	sc/std		FB	20
Island of Lost Women	USA	1959	Frank Tuttle	72			GB	27
Island, The	GB	1980	Michael Ritchie	114	std		FB	35
Islands in the Stream	USA	1976	Franklin J. Schaffner	105	std		FB	27
Isle of the Dead	USA	1945	Mark Robson	72			GB	15
It Came from Beneath the Sea	USA	1955	Robert Gordon	77			FB	15
It Happened at the World's Fair	USA	1962	Norman Taurog	106	sc/std		FB	22
It Happened Here	GB	1963	Kevin Brownlow/Andrew Mollo	95			FB	15
It Happened One Night	USA	1934	Frank Capra	105			FB	15
It Happened to Jane	USA	1959	Richard Quine	97	col		FB	18
It Lives Again	USA	1978	Larry Cohen	90			FB	18
It Only Hurts When I Laugh	USA	1981	Glenn Jordan	120			FB	38
It Started in Naples	USA	1960	Melville Shavelson	100	std		FB	18
It Started with a Kiss	USA	1959	George Marshall	104	sc/std		FB	15
It's a Big Country	USA	1951	Richard Thorpe/John Sturges/ Charles Vidor/Don Weis/ Clarence Brown/William Wellman/ Don Hartman	89			FB	18
It's a Gift	USA	1934	Norman Z. McLeod	71			FB	15
It's a Great Feeling	USA	1949	David Butler	85	bw		FB	15
It's a Wonderful World	GB	1956	Val Guest	89	sc std	GB	GB	25
It's Alive	USA	1973	Larry Cohen	91			FB	18
It's All Happening	GB	1963	Don Sharp	101			GB	25
It's Always Fair Weather	USA	1955	Gene Kelly/Stanley Donen	101	sc/std		FB	22
It's Great to be Young	GB	1956	Cyril Frankel	95			FB	15
It's That Man Again	GB	1942	Walter Forde	84			FB	22
Italian Graffiti	IT	1973	Alfio Caltabiano	85	dub		GB	22
Italian Job, The	GB	1969	Peter Collinson	100	std		FB	27
Italian Straw Hat, An	FR	1927	René Clair	99	st		BFI	25
Italy: Year One	IT	1974	Roberto Rossellini	123	est		BFI	25
Ivan the Terrible Part 2	USSR	1943/6	Sergei Eisenstein	88	est	CONT	GB	25
Ivan the Terrible Part 1	USSR	1944	Sergei Eisenstein	99	est	CONT	GB	25
Ivan's Childhood	USSR	1962	Andrei Tarkovsky	97	est	AE	GB	0
Ivanhoe	GB	1952	Richard Thorpe	107			FB	22
Ivy	USA	1947	Sam Wood	99			FB	15

j

	COUNTRY OF PRODUCTION	YEAR	DIRECTOR	RUNNING TIME	VERSION	35mm	16mm	16mm RENTAL FEE
J.A. Martin Photographer	CAN	1976	Jean Beaudin	101			GB	35
Ja Ja Mein General (see Which Way to the Front)								
Jabberwocky	GB	1977	Terry Gilliam	101			FB	22
Jack and the Beanstalk	USA	1952	Jean Yarbrough	78	bw		GB	15
Jack of Diamonds	USA/W.GER	1967	Don Taylor	108	std/108		FB	18
Jack the Skinner	W.GER	1958	Helmut Käutner	120	est		GFL	0
Jackal of Nahueltoro, The	CHILE	1969	Miguel Littin	88	est		MP	40
Jackson County Jail	USA	1976	Michael Miller	84			FB	27
Jacob Epstein	GB	1987	Catherine Collis	52			AC	20
Jacob's Ladder	USA	1991	Adrian Lyne	113			GU	0
Jagged Edge	USA	1985	Richard Marquand	109			FB	60
Jaguar Lives	USA	1979	Ernest Pintoff	90			FB	33
Jalna	USA	1935	John Cromwell	75			GB	15
James Baldwin: The Price of the Ticket	USA	1989	Karen Thorsen	87		BFI	BFI	60
James Brothers, The	USA	1956	Nicholas Ray	92	std		FB	18
James Dean the First American Teenager	GB	1975	Ray Connolly	80			GB	22
Jane and the Lost City	GB	1987	Terry Marcel	92		BD	GB	60
Jane Austen in Manhattan	GB/USA	1980	James Ivory	108			GB	30
Jane Eyre	USA	1943	Robert Stevenson	97			FB	15
Jane Eyre	USA	1971	Delbert Mann	109			GB	33
Jane is Jane Forever	W.GER	1977	Walter Bockmeyer/Rolf Buhrmann	85	est		GFL	0
Janitor, The	USA	1981	Peter Yates	108			FB	38
January Man, The	USA	1989	Pat O'Connor	97		UIP	FB	55
Japan Live Performance	GB	1989	Philip Day	52			AC	20
Jason and the Argonauts	GB	1963	Don Chaffey	103		C	FB	18
Jaws	USA	1975	Steven Spielberg	125	sc/std		FB	53
Jaws 2	USA	1978	Jeannot Szwarc	116	sc/std		FB	53
Jaws 3	USA	1983	Joe Alves	98			FB	48
Jaws – The Revenge	USA	1987	Joseph Sargent	90	sc		FB	45
Jazz Heaven	USA	1929	Melville Brown	71			GB	15
Jazz on a Summer's Day	USA	1959	Bert Stern	90			GB	25
Jazz Singer, The	USA	1927	Alan Crosland	90			FB	22
Jazz Singer, The	USA	1980	Richard Fleischer	106			FB	40
Je Tu Il Elle	BELG/ FR	1974	Chantal Akerman	85	est		MP	57.5
Jeanne Dielman, 23 Quai Du Commerce, 1080 Bruxelles	BELG/ FR	1975	Chantal Akerman	201	est		MP	80.5
Jennifer on my Mind	USA	1971	Noel Black	84			FB	18
Jeremiah Johnson	USA	1972	Sydney Pollack	108	sc/std		FB	18
Jeremy	USA	1973	Arthur Barron	90			FB	18
Jericho Mile, The	USA	1979	Michael Mann	97			GB	38
Jerk, The	USA	1979	Carl Reiner	94			FB	33
Jerusalem File, The	USA/IS	1971	John Flynn	96			FB	18
Jesus Christ Superstar	USA	1973	Norman Jewison	107	sc/std		FB	38
Jesus of Montreal	CAN/FR	1989	Denys Arcand	120	est	AE	GB	70
Jet Pilot	USA	1951	Josef von Sternberg	112			BFI	30
Jetsons: The Movie	USA	1990	William Hanna/Joseph Barbera	81		UIP	FB	40
Jewel of the Nile, The	USA	1985	Lewis Teague	106			FB	55
Jezebel	USA	1938	William Wyler	106			FB	22
JFK	USA	1991	Oliver Stone	120		W	FB	75
Jigsaw	GB	1980	Robina Rose	67			CIRC	30
Jim Stirling's Architecture	GB	1973	Ron Parks	50			AC	20
Jitterbugs	USA	1943	Mal St. Clair	75			FB	15
Joan of Arc	USA	1948	Victor Fleming	100			GB	18
Joan of Paris	USA	1942	Robert Stevenson	90			GB	15
Joanna	GB	1968	Michael Sarne	113	std		FB	18
Joaquin Murieta	USA	1970	Earl Bellamy	83			FB	18
Joe	USA	1970	John G. Avildsen	106			FB	26
Joe Kidd	USA	1972	John Sturges	87	sc/std		FB	22
Joe Palooka in Humphrey Takes a Chance	USA	1950	Jean Yarbrough	62			GB	20

j

Title	Country of Production	Year	Director	Running Time	Version	35mm	16mm	16mm Rental Fee
Joe Versus the Volcano	USA	1990	John Patrick Shanley	102		W	FB	60
Joey	GB	1974	Brian Gibson	70			CONC	18.6
Joey Boy	GB	1965	Frank Launder	91			FB	15
John and Mary	USA	1969	Peter Yates	92	sc		FB	18
John Cooper-Clarke Ten Years in an Open-Necked Shirt	GB	1982	Nick Day/David Kelly	52			AC	16
John Everett Millais	GB	1979	Anita Sterner	60			AC	16
John Goldfarb, Please Come Home!	USA	1964	J. Lee Thompson	96	sc		FB	18
John Heartfield Fotomonteur	W.GER	1976	Helmut Herbst	63	eng		BFI	25
Johnny Angel	USA	1945	Edwin L. Marin	79			GB	15
Johnny Belinda	USA	1948	Jean Negulesco	124			FB	22
Johnny Come Lately	USA	1943	William K. Howard	97			GB	18
Johnny Dangerously	USA	1984	Amy Heckerling	90			FB	40
Johnny Handsome	USA	1990	Walter Hill	94		GU	GU	80
Johnny Shiloh	USA	1963	James Neilson	90			FB	27
Johnstown Monster, The	GB	1971	Olaf Pooley	54			GB	17
Joker is Wild, The	USA	1957	Charles Vidor	126			FB	15
Jokers, The	GB	1967	Michael Winner	94			FB	18
Joli Mai, Le	FR	1962	Chris Marker	118	est		GB	20
Jolson Sings Again	USA	1949	Henry Levin	95			FB	18
Jolson Story, The	USA	1946	Alfred E. Green	130			FB	18
Jonah, Who Will Be 25 in theYear 2000	FR	1976	Alain Tanner	115	est		GB	35
Jory	USA/ MEX	1972	Jorge Fons	97			GB	25
Joseph Andrews	GB	1976	Tony Richardson	104			FB	22
Jour de Fête	FR	1949	Jacques Tati	81	est	BFI	BFI	30
Jour se Léve, Le	FR	1939	Marcel Carné	93	est	BFI	GB	30
Journal D'un Curé De Campagne, Le	FR	1951	Robert Bresson	110	est		GB	30
Journey into Autumn	SWE	1954	Ingmar Bergman	86	est		GB	35
Journey into Fear	USA	1942	Norman Foster	71			GB	16
Journey Through Fire	USSR	1969	Samson Samsonov	74	est		ETV	10
Journey to the Centre of the Earth	USA	1959	Henry Levin	130	std		FB	18
Journey, The	USA	1959	Anatole Litvak	125			FB	18
Joy in the Morning	USA	1964	Alex Segal	78			FB	15
Joy of Living	USA	1938	Tay Garnett	90			GB	15
Ju Dou	JAP/CHI	1990	Zhang Yimou/Yang Fengliang	95	st	BD	GB	80
Juarez	USA	1939	William Dieterle	128	121		FB	22
Jubilee	GB	1978	Derek Jarman	104		BFI	BFI	40
Judex	FR/IT	1963	Georges Franju	95	est	CONT	GB	25
Judge Steps Out, The	USA	1949	Boris Ingster	91			GB	15
Judith	USA/IS	1965	Daniel Mann	109	std		FB	18
Judith of Bethulia	USA	1913	D.W. Griffith	62	st		BFI	15.5
Juggernaut	GB	1974	Richard Lester	110			FB	27
Jules et Jim	FR	1961	François Truffaut	105	est/sc	GALA	GB	70
Jules Verne's Rocket to the Moon	GB	1967	Don Sharp	101	sc/std		FB	18
Julia	USA	1977	Fred Zinnemann	117			FB	29
Julia Misbehaves	USA	1948	Jack Conway	99			FB	15
Julie	USA	1956	Andrew Stone	97			FB	15
Julius Caesar	GB/USA	1979	Herbert Wise	170			BBC	35
Jumbo	USA	1962	Charles Walters	124	sc/std		FB	18
Jumpin' Jack Flash	USA	1986	Penny Marshall	100			FB	40
Jumping Jacks	USA	1952	Norman Taurog	96			FB	15
Jungle Book	USA	1942	Zoltan Korda	115			APO	25
Jungle Cat	USA	1960	James Algar	70			FB	27
Jungle Fever	USA	1991	Spike Lee	110		UIP	FB	75
Jungle Man	USA	1942	Harry Fraser	62			GB	15
Junior Bonner	USA	1972	Sam Peckinpah	103	sc/std		GB	18
Junket 89	GB	1970	Peter Plummer	56			GB	17
Junoon	INDIA	1978	Shyam Benegal	141	est		GB	45
Just a Gigolo	W.GER	1978	David Hemmings	105			GB	30

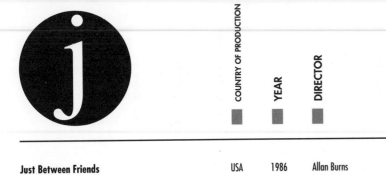

	COUNTRY OF PRODUCTION	YEAR	DIRECTOR	RUNNING TIME	VERSION	35mm	16mm	16mm RENTAL FEE
Just Between Friends	USA	1986	Allan Burns	111	120		FB	40
Just Like a Woman	GB	1966	Robert Fuest	90			GB	18
Just Like a Woman	GB	1992	Christopher Monger	106	R		FB	65
Just My Luck	GB	1957	John Paddy Carstairs	86			FB	15
Just This Once	USA	1951	Don Weis	91			FB	15
Just What Is It?	GB	1984	Geoff Dunlop	52			AC	20
Justine	USA	1969	George Cukor	96	sc/std		FB	18
Justine	GB	1976	Stewart Mackinnon/Clive Myers/Nigel Perkins	90			MP	27.5
Juvenile Court	USA	1973	Frederick Wiseman	135			GB	55
Juvenile Liaison	GB	1975	Nick Broomfield/ Joan Churchill	101			GB	30

Jubilee

k

	COUNTRY OF PRODUCTION	YEAR	DIRECTOR	RUNNING TIME	VERSION	35mm	16mm	16mm RENTAL FEE
K-9	USA	1989	Rod Daniel	102		W	FB	55
Kaadu	INDIA	1974	Garish Karnad	123	est		GB	25
Kadoyng	GB	1972	Ian Shand	58			GB	17
Kafer Auf Extratour, Ein	W.GER	1973	Rudolf Zehetgruber	106	est		GFL	0
Kagemusha	JAP	1980	Akira Kurosawa	159	std/est		FB	48
Kaleidoscope	GB	1966	Jack Smight	103			FB	18
Kameradschaft	GER	1931	G.W. Pabst	83	est		GB	25
Kamikaze Hearts	USA	1988	Juliet Bashore	80			MP	
Kanal	POL	1956	Andrzej Wajda	96	est	CONT	GB	25
Kansas City Bomber	USA	1972	Jerrold Freedman	99			FB	22
Karate Kid, The	USA	1984	John G. Avildsen	127			FB	40
Karate Kid. Part II, The	USA	1986	John G. Avildsen	113			FB	50
Karate Kid III, The	USA	1989	John G. Avildsen	111		C	FB	55
Karate Killers, The	USA	1967	Barry Shear	92			FB	18
Kashima Paradise	FR	1973	Yann le Masson/ Bernie Deswarte	110			MP	35
Kazablan	IS	1973	Menahem Golan	95	std		FB	28
Keep 'em Rolling	USA	1934	George Archainbaud	69			GB	15
Keep Fit	GB	1937	Anthony Kimmins	85			FB	15
Keep, The	USA	1984	Michael Mann	95			FB	35
Keeping Time	GB	1983	Murray Martin	60			NA	25
Kelek	W.GER	1968	Werner Nekes	60			LFC	34
Kelly's Heroes	USA/ YUGO	1970	Brian G. Hutton	143	sc/std		FB	38
Kemira Diary of a Strike	AUSTR	1984	Tom Zubrycki	62			MP	25
Kentucky Kernels	USA	1934	George Stevens	75			GB	15
Kept Husbands	USA	1931	Lloyd Bacon	76			GB	15
Kerosene Seller's Wife, The	USSR	1988	Alexander Kaidanovsky	100	est		AE	70
Kes	GB	1969	Ken Loach	113			FB	27
Kettledrummer, The	W.GER	1968	Volker Schlöndorff	96	est		GFL	0
Kettles in the Ozarks, The	USA	1955	Charles Lamont	81			FB	15
Key Largo	USA	1948	John Huston	100			FB	22
Key to the City	USA	1949	George Sidney	98			FB	15
Key, The	GB	1958	Carol Reed	126	sc/std		FB	18
Key, The	CZ	1971	Vladimir Cech	88	est		ETV	10
Khartoum	USA/GB	1966	Basil Dearden	128	sc/std		FB	27
Kid Blue	USA	1973	James Frawley	100	sc/std		FB	18
Kid From Canada, The	GB	1957	Kay Mander	57			GB	12
Kid Galahad	USA	1937	Michael Curtiz	102			FB	22
Kid Galahad	USA	1962	Phil Karlson	96			FB	22
Kidnapped	USA	1938	Alfred Werker	89			FB	15
Kidnapped	GB	1959	Robert Stevenson	95			FB	27
Kidnapped	GB	1971	Delbert Mann	107	std		FB	27
Kidnappers, The	GB	1953	Philip Leacock	95			FB	15
Kill Me Tomorrow	GB	1956	Terence Fisher	81		GB	GB	15
Kill or Cure	GB	1962	George Pollock	88			FB	15
Killer Elite, The	USA	1975	Sam Peckinpah	122	sc/std		FB	27
Killer Fish	BRAZ/FR	1978	Anthony M. Dawson	100			GB	27
Killer McCoy	USA	1948	Roy Rowland	103			FB	15
Killer of Sheep	USA	1977	Charles Burnett	84			BFI	30
Killer on a Horse	USA	1966	Burt Kennedy	105	103		FB	22
Killer! (see Que la Bete Meure)								
Killer's Kiss	USA	1955	Stanley Kubrick	67			BFI	25
Killers, The	USA	1946	Robert Siodmak	103			BFI	25
Killers, The	USA	1964	Don Siegel	94	bw		FB	15
Killing Fields, The	GB	1984	Roland Joffe	142			FB	75
Killing Floor	USA	1985	Bill Duke	118			BFI	55
Killing Game, The	FR	1967	Alain Jessua	94	dub		FB	18
Killing of a Chinese Bookie, The	USA	1976	John Cassavetes	133			BFI	45
Killing of Sister George, The	USA	1968	Robert Aldrich	138		GB	GB	22

	COUNTRY OF PRODUCTION	YEAR	DIRECTOR	RUNNING TIME	VERSION	35mm	16mm	16mm RENTAL FEE
Killing, The	USA	1956	Stanley Kubrick	84			BFI	25
Kim	USA	1950	Victor Saville	112	bw		FB	15
Kimberley Jim	S.AFR	1965	Emil Nofal	82	std		GB	25
Kind Hearts and Coronets	GB	1949	Robert Hamer	105		MAY	FB	15
Kind of Loving, A	GB	1962	John Schlesinger	112			FB	15
Kindergarten Cop	USA	1990	Ivan Reitman	111		UIP	FB	65
King Blank	USA	1982	Michael Oblowitz	73			BFI	30
King Carnival	GB	1972	Horace Ové	50			CONT	25
King David	USA	1985	Bruce Beresford	114			FB	45
King Kong	USA	1933	Ernest Schoedsack/ Merian C. Cooper	99		GB	GB	27
King Lear	USSR	1970	Grigori Kozintsev	137	sc/est		GB	30
King Lear	GB/DEN	1970	Peter Brook	137			FB	33
King of Kings	USA	1961	Nicholas Ray	160	sc		FB	38
King of Marvin Gardens	USA	1972	Bob Rafelson	104			FB	22
King of the Grizzlies	USA	1969	Ron Kelly	93			FB	27
King of the Gypsies	USA	1978	Frank Pierson	113			FB	33
King Ralph	USA	1991	David S. Ward	96		UIP	FB	55
King Rat	USA	1965	Bryan Forbes	134			FB	15
King Solomon's Mines	USA	1950	Compton Bennett/ Andrew Marton		bw		FB	27
King Solomon's Mines	USA	1985	J. Lee Thompson	100			FB	45
King's Story, A	GB	1965	Jack Le Vien	102		GB	GB	27
King's Thief, The	USA	1955	Robert Z. Leonard	79	sc/std		FB	18
Kingdom for a House	HOLL	1980	Tilt Film/Meat Ball	70	mag		MP	25
Kings of the Road	W.GER	1975	Wim Wenders	180	est	BFI	BFI	45
Kings Row	USA	1941	Sam Wood	127			FB	15
Kismet	USA	1955	Vincente Minnelli	113	std		FB	27
Kiss Me Deadly	USA	1955	Robert Aldrich	104		UIP	FB	15
Kiss Me Kate	USA	1953	George Sidney	109			FB	27
Kiss Me Stupid	USA	1964	Billy Wilder	124	sc		FB	15
Kiss of Death	USA	1947	Henry Hathaway	99			FB	20
Kiss of the Spider Woman	BRAZ	1985	Hector Babenco	121			GB	60
Kiss the Blood Off My Hands	USA	1948	Norman Foster	80			FB	15
Kiss Tomorrow Goodbye	USA	1950	Gordon Douglas	102			GB	18
Kiss, The	USA	1929	Jacques Feyder	64	st		FB	18
Kiss, The	USA	1988	Pen Densham	98			FB	55
Kissin' Cousins	USA	1963	Gene Nelson	93	sc/std		FB	22
Kitchen	USA	1966	Andy Warhol	60			LFC	30
Kitchen, The	GB	1961	James Hill	74			GB	25
Kitten with a Whip	USA	1964	Douglas Heyes	83			FB	15
Kittens Not Carried	CZ	1967	Josef Pinkava	82	est		ETV	10
Kitty Foyle	USA	1941	Sam Wood	108			GB	15
Kitty Return to Auschwitz	GB	1980	Peter Morley	90			CONC	24
Klondike Annie	USA	1936	Raoul Walsh	83			FB	22
Klute	USA	1971	Alan J. Pakula	114	sc/std		FB	18
Knack, The	GB	1965	Richard Lester	84			FB	15
Knife in the Back, The	W.GER	1975	Ottokar Runze	100	est		GFL	0
Knife in the Head	W.GER	1978	Reinhard Hauff	113	est		GB	40
Knife in the Water	POL	1962	Roman Polanski	94	est	BFI	GB	25
Knights of the Black Eagle	GER/IT	1937	Luis Trenker	99	est		BFI	25
Knights of the Round Table, The	GB	1953	Richard Thorpe	115			FB	22
Knowledge, The	GB	1979	Bob Brooks	89			GB	45
Komischer Heiliger, Ein	W.GER	1978	Klaus Lemke	83	est		GFL	0
Konfrontation(see Confrontation: Assassination in Davos)								
Konga	GB	1960	John Lemont	90	bw		FB	15
Kotch	USA	1971	Jack Lemmon	114			GB	18
Krakatit	CZ	1948	Otakar Vavra	104	est		ETV	15
Krakatoa – East of Java	USA	1968	Bernard Kowalski	143	std	GB	GB	22
Kramer vs. Kramer	USA	1979	Robert Benton	104			FB	45

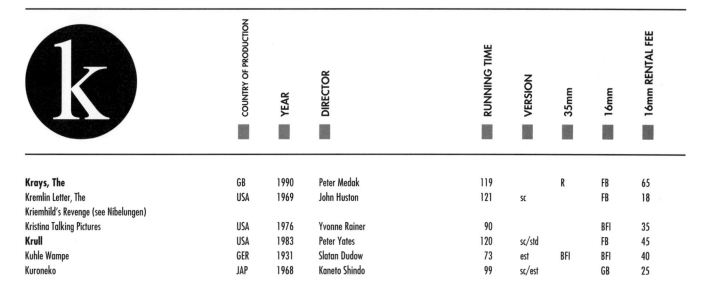

	COUNTRY OF PRODUCTION	YEAR	DIRECTOR	RUNNING TIME	VERSION	35mm	16mm	16mm RENTAL FEE
Krays, The	GB	1990	Peter Medak	119		R	FB	65
Kremlin Letter, The	USA	1969	John Huston	121	sc		FB	18
Kriemhild's Revenge (see Nibelungen)								
Kristina Talking Pictures	USA	1976	Yvonne Rainer	90			BFI	35
Krull	USA	1983	Peter Yates	120	sc/std		FB	45
Kuhle Wampe	GER	1931	Slatan Dudow	73	est	BFI	BFI	40
Kuroneko	JAP	1968	Kaneto Shindo	99	sc/est		GB	25

Kes

	COUNTRY OF PRODUCTION	YEAR	DIRECTOR	RUNNING TIME	VERSION	35mm	16mm	16mm RENTAL FEE
L-Shaped Room, The	GB	1962	Bryan Forbes	126			FB	15
LA Story	USA	1991	Mick Jackson	94		GU	GU	80
Labour of Love, A (see Friends and Husbands a Labour of Love)								
Labyrinth	GB	1986	Jim Henson	101			FB	45
Lacemaker, The (see Dentellière, La)								
Lacey Rituals, The	GB	1973	Bruce Lacey and Family	63			AC	19
Ladder of Swords	GB	1988	Norman Hull	98		MAY	GB	70
Ladies of the Jury	USA	1932	Lowell Sherman	64			GB	15
Ladies Who Do	GB	1963	C.M. Pennington Richards	85			FB	15
Ladies' Day	USA	1943	Leslie Goodwins	62			GB	15
Lady Caroline Lamb	GB/IT	1972	Robert Bolt	123	sc/std		FB	24
Lady Chatterley's Lover	GB/FR	1981	Just Jaeckin	103			FB	48
Lady Confesses, The	USA	1945	Sam Newfield	70			GB	25
Lady Consents, The	USA	1936	Stephen Roberts	76			GB	15
Lady in Cement	USA	1968	Gordon Douglas	94	sc/std		FB	18
Lady in the Car with Glasses and a Gun, The	FR	1970	Anatole Litvak	101	dub/sc		FB	18
Lady in the Lake	USA	1946	Robert Montgomery	103			FB	15
Lady is a Square, The	GB	1958	Herbert Wilcox	98			FB	15
Lady Jane	GB	1985	Trevor Nunn	142			FB	40
Lady L	FR IT	1965	Peter Ustinov	124	std		FB	18
Lady Luck	USA	1946	Edwin L. Marin	97			GB	15
Lady of Deceit	USA	1947	Robert Wise	93			GB	15
Lady Refuses, The	USA	1931	George Archainbaud	72			GB	15
Lady Takes a Chance, A	USA	1943	William Seiter	86			GB	15
Lady Vanishes, The	GB	1938	Alfred Hitchcock	97		R	FB	25
Lady Vanishes, The	GB	1979	Anthony Page	99	sc/std		FB	33
Lady With A Lamp, The	GB	1951	Herbert Wilcox	106			FB	15
Lady With a Past	USA	1932	Edward H. Griffith	80			GB	15
Lady Without a Passport, A	USA	1950	Joseph H. Lewis	74			FB	15
Ladyhawke	USA	1985	Richard Donner	120			FB	45
Lake of Peculiarity	POL	1972	Jan Batory	90	est		FOP	0
Lamb	GB	1985	Colin Gregg	110			FB	60
Land of Promise	POL	1974	Andrzej Wajda	180	est		FOP	0
Land of the Open Range	USA	1942	Edward Killy	60			GB	15
Land Raiders	USA	1969	Nathan Juran	101			FB	18
Land That Time Forgot, The	GB	1974	Kevin Connor	90			FB	33
Land Unknown	USA	1957	Virgil Vogel	77	sc/std/bw		FB	15
Landscape After Battle	POL	1970	Andrzej Wajda	105	est		GB	30
Landscape in the Mist	GR	1988	Theo Angelopoulos	126	est		GB	60
Larceny, Inc.	USA	1942	Lloyd Bacon	95			FB	22
Las Vegas Story, The	USA	1952	Robert Stevenson	88			GB	15
Lassiter	USA	1983	Roger Young	100			FB	30
Last American Hero, The	USA	1973	Lamont Johnson	95	sc/std		FB	18
Last American Virgin	USA	1982	Boaz Davidson	93			FB	33
Last Boy Scout, The	USA	1991	Tony Scott	105	W		FB	70
Last Chance	IT	1973	Maurizio Lucidi	102	est		GB	30
Last Days of Pompeii, The	USA	1935	Ernest Schoedsack	108			GB	18
Last Days of Pompeii, The	IT	1913	Mario Caserini	92	st		BFI	14
Last Detail, The	USA	1973	Hal Ashby	103			FB	18
Last Dragon, The	USA	1985	Michael Schultz	108			FB	45
Last Embrace	USA	1979	Jonathan Demme	101			FB	33
Last Emperor, The	CHI/IT	1987	Bernardo Bertolucci	160	sc		FB	75
Last Escape, The	USA	1969	Walter Grauman	90			FB	18
Last Exit to Brooklyn	GER	1990	Uli Edel	103		GU	GU	80
Last Flight of Noah's Ark, The	USA	1980	Charles Jarrott	98			FB	38
Last Flight, The	USA	1931	William Dieterle	77			FB	15
Last Grenade	GB	1969	Gordon Flemyng	94			GB	25
Last Hard Men, The	USA	1976	Andrew V. McLaglen	97	sc		FB	22

	COUNTRY OF PRODUCTION	YEAR	DIRECTOR	RUNNING TIME	VERSION	35mm	16mm	16mm RENTAL FEE
Last Holiday	GB	1950	Henry Cass	88			FB	15
Last Hours, The	GB	1959	Cyril Butcher	83			BFI	15.5
Last Hunt, The	USA	1955	Richard Brooks	98	std		FB	18
Last Hurrah, The	USA	1958	John Ford	122			FB	15
Last Laugh, The	GER	1925	F.W. Murnau	73	st/sd	BFI	BFI	25
Last Married Couple in America, The	USA	1979	Gilbert Cates	102			FB	38
Last Movie, The	USA	1971	Dennis Hopper	108			MP	57.5
Last Night At The Alamo	USA	1984	Eagle Pennell	80			RESP	25
Last of Sheila, The	USA	1973	Herbert Ross	119			FB	18
Last Of The Blue Devils (see Kansas City)								
Last of the Cuiva	GB	1971		67			CONC	26.4
Last of the Fast Guns	USA	1958	George Sherman	82	col/std		FB	18
					bw/std		FB	15
Last Outlaw, The	USA	1936	Christy Cabanne	80			GB	15
Last Picture Show, The	USA	1971	Peter Bogdanovich	118			FB	15
Last Remake of Beau Geste, The	USA	1977	Marty Feldman	85			FB	38
Last Resort, The	USA	1978	Daniel Keller	60			CONC	24
Last Run, The	USA	1971	Richard Fleischer	95	sc/std		FB	18
Last Safari, The	GB	1967	Henry Hathaway	99			FB	18
Last Snows of Spring, The	IT	1973	Raimondo Del Balzo	90			GB	38
Last Straw, The	CAN	1987	Giles Walker	95			MP	69
Last Supper, The	CB	1976	Tomás Gutiérrez Alea	113	est		GB	30
Last Tango in Paris	IT/FR	1972	Bernardo Bertolucci	129		UIP	FB	43
Last Temptation of Christ, The	USA	1988	Martin Scorsese	163		UIP	BFI	60
Last Unicorn, The	USA	1982	Arthur Rankin/Jules Bass	92			GB	40
Last Valley, The	GB	1970	James Clavell	129	std	GB	GB	27
Last Voyage, The	USA	1959	Andrew Stone	91			FB	18
Last Wagon, The	USA	1956	Delmer Daves	98	sc/std		FB	18
Last Waltz, The	USA	1978	Martin Scorsese	116			FB	38
Last Waltz, The	W.GER	1953	Arthur Maria Rabenalt	93	est		GFL	0
Last Warrior, The	USA	1970	Carol Reed	106	std		FB	15
Last Wave, The	AUSTR	1977	Peter Weir	106			FB	26
Late Mathias Pascal, The	FR	1925	Marcel L'Herbier	176	st/est		BFI	20
Late Show, The	USA	1977	Robert Benton	93			FB	22
Late Spring	JAP	1949	Yasujiro Ozu	108	est		GB	45
Laugh and Get Rich	USA	1931	Gregory La Cava	72			GB	15
Laugh with Max Linder	FR	1963	Maud Max Linder	88			GB	33
Laughter in Paradise	GB	1951	Mario Zampi	93			GB	25
Laughterhouse	GB	1984	Richard Eyre	93			GB	50
Laura	USA	1944	Otto Preminger	88		F	FB	15
Laurel and Hardy's Laughing 20s	USA	1965	Robert Youngson	90			FB	15
Lavender Hill Mob, The	GB	1951	Charles Crichton	81			FB	15
Law West of Tombstone, The	USA	1938	Glenn Tryon	75			GB	15
Law And Disorder	GB	1958	Charles Crichton	76			FB	15
Law and Jake Wade, The	USA	1958	John Sturges	86	sc/std		FB	18
Law and Order	USA	1969	Frederick Wiseman	81			GB	55
Law and Order: A Detective's Tale	GB	1978	Les Blair	80			BFI	25
Law of the Underworld	USA	1938	Lew Landers	61			GB	15
Lawbreakers, The	USA	1960	Joseph M. Newman	79			FB	15
Lawman	USA	1970	Michael Winner	98			FB	18
Lawrence of Arabia	GB	1962	David Lean	206	sc/std	C	FB	38
Lawyer, The	USA	1968	Sidney J. Furie	120			FB	18
Le Mans	USA	1971	Lee H. Katzin	108	std		GB	22
League of Gentlemen, The	GB	1960	Basil Dearden	116			FB	15
Lectrice, La	FR	1988	Michel Deville	99	est	CU	GB	75
Left Handed Gun, The	USA	1958	Arthur Penn	102			FB	15
Left, Right and Centre	GB	1959	Sidney Gilliat	92			FB	15
Legal Eagles	USA	1986	Ivan Reitman	116			FB	60

	COUNTRY OF PRODUCTION	YEAR	DIRECTOR	RUNNING TIME	VERSION	35mm	16mm	16mm RENTAL FEE
Legend of Frenchie King, The	FR/IT/ SP/GB	1971	Christian-Jaque	96	dub		GB	18
Legend of Hell House, The	GB	1973	John Hough	94			FB	18
Legend of Lylah Clare, The	USA	1969	Robert Aldrich	130			FB	26
Legend of the 7 Golden Vampires, The	GB/HK	1974	Roy Ward Baker	89	sc/std		FB	18
Legend of the Holy Drinker, The	IT	1988	Ermanno Olmi	125		AE	GB	60
Legend of the Lone Ranger, The	USA	1981	William Fraker	97	sc/std		GB	43
Legend of Young Dick Turpin, The	GB	1965	James Neilson	84			FB	27
Legendary Champions, The	USA	1968	Harry F. Chapin	102			GB	15
Leila And The Wolves	GB	1984	Heiny Srour	93			GB	52
Lemon Popsicle	IS	1977	Boaz Davidson	92	dub		FB	38
Lenin in 1918	USSR	1943	Mikhail Romm	133	est		ETV	20
Lenin in October	USSR	1937	Mikhail Romm	97	est/103		ETV	20
Leningrad Cowboys Go America	FIN/SWE	1989	Aki Kaurismäki	82		AE	GB	70
Leningrad Fights	USSR	1942	Paul Capon	60			CFL	15
Lenny	USA	1974	Bob Fosse	111			FB	33
Lenny Bruce Performance Film, The	USA	1966	John Magnuson	65			GB	43
Leone Have Sept Cabezas, Der (see Lion Has Seven Heads, The)								
Leopard Man, The	USA	1943	Jacques Tourneur	66			GB	15
Lepke	USA	1974	Menahem Golan	110	sc/std		FB	18
Les Girls	USA	1957	George Cukor	114	sc/std		FB	22
Lesson in Love, A	SWE	1963	Ingmar Bergman	97	est		GB	35
Let George Do It	GB	1940	Marcel Varnel	83			FB	15
Let The Balloons Go	AUSTR	1976	Oliver Howes	78			GB	30
Let the Good Times Roll	USA	1973	Sid Levin/Robert Abel	99	sc		FB	22
Let's Be Famous	GB	1939	Walter Forde	82			FB	15
Let's Dance	USA	1950	Norman Z. McLeod	112	bw		FB	15
Let's Do It Again	USA	1976	Sidney Poitier	113			FB	18
Let's Hope It's A Girl	IT/FR	1986	Mario Monicelli	114	est		GB	60
Let's Kill Uncle	USA	1966	William Castle	89	bw		FB	15
Let's Make Music	USA	1940	Leslie Goodwins	87			GB	15
Let's Scare Jessica To Death	USA	1971	John Hancock	89			FB	18
Let's Spend the Night Together	USA	1981	Hal Ashby	91			FB	38
Let's Try Again	USA	1934	Worthington Miner	67			GB	15
Lethal Weapon	USA	1987	Richard Donner	109			FB	60
Lethal Weapon II	USA	1989	Richard Donner	113			FB	65
Lethal Weapon III	USA	1992	Richard Donner	117		W	FB	75
Letter From an Unknown Wornan	USA	1947	Max Ophuls	87			GB	40
Letter From My Village	SEN	1973	Safi Faye	98	est		BFI	35
Letter From the Wife	INDIA	1974	Purnendu Pattrea	98	est		GB	35
Letter of Introduction	USA	1938	John M. Stahl	103			BFI	25
Letter to Brezhnev	GB	1985	Chris Bernard	95			GB	60
Letter to Jane, A	FR	1972	Jean-Luc Godard/ Jean-Pierre Gorin	55			MP	27.6
Letter with the Feathers	CHI	1953	Shih Hui	90	est		GB	15
Letters From a Dead Man	USSR	1986	Konstantin Lopushansky	89	est		GB	60
Lianna	USA	1982	John Sayles	112			GB	45
Libel	GB	1959	Anthony Asquith	100			FB	15
Licence To Kill	USA	1989	John Glen	133		UIP	FB	60
Licking Hitler	GB	1978	David Hare	64			BFI	25
Lie Detector, The	USA	1947	Lew Landers	65			GB	15
Lies My Father Told Me	CAN	1975	Jan Kadar	102			FB	22
Life & Times of Lord Louis Mountbatten (12 parts)				50			GB	20
Life and Death of Colonel Blimp, The	GB	1943	Michael Powell/ Emeric Pressburger	163		BFI	BFI	50
Life and Nothing But	FR	1989	Bertrand Tavernier	134	sc/est	AE	GB	70
Life and Times of Judge Roy Bean, The	USA	1972	John Huston	123			FB	30
Life and Times of Rosie the Riveter, The	USA	1980	Connie Field	65			MP	40.25
Life Apart, A	GB	1973	Michael Grigsby	70			CONC	19.8
Life at the Top	GB	1965	Ted Kotcheff	117			FB	15

	COUNTRY OF PRODUCTION	YEAR	DIRECTOR	RUNNING TIME	VERSION	35mm	16mm	16mm RENTAL FEE
Life for Christine	GB	1980	John Goldschmidt	90			CONC	25
Life for Ruth	GB	1962	Basil Dearden	91			FB	15
Life in the Arctic	RUS	1953	Alexander Zguridi	70	eng/nar		GB	20
Life is Sweet	GB	1990	Mike Leigh	103		MAY	GB	80
Life of O-Haru, The	JAP	1952	Kenji Mizoguchi	134	est		BFI	50
Life of the Party, The	USA	1937	William A. Seiter	77			GB	15
Life Story of Baal, The	GB	1978	Edward Bennett	57			BFI	25
Life Upside Down (see Vie A l'Envers, La)								
Lifeboat	USA	1943	Alfred Hitchcock	96			FB	25
Lifeforce	USA	1985	Tobe Hooper	101			FB	50
Lifeguard	USA	1976	Daniel Petrie	96			FB	22
Lift to the Scaffold	FR	1957	Louis Malle	90	s/t		GB	35
Lift, The	HOLL	1983	Dick Maas	99	dub		FB	35
Light In The Piazza, The	GB	1961	Guy Green	101	sc/std		FB	18
Light Up the Sky	GB	1960	Lewis Gilbert	90			FB	15
Lighthorseman, The	AUSTR	1987	Simon Wincer	131			GB	55
Lightning Strikes Twice	USA	1935	Ben Holmes	66			GB	15
Lights of Variety	IT	1950	Alberto Lattuada/ Federico Fellini	93	est		BFI	20
Like Father Like Son	USA	1987	Rod Daniel	98			FB	50
Likely Lads, The	GB	1976	Michael Tuchner	90			FB	18
Likely Story, A	USA	1947	H.C. Potter	90			GB	15
Lili Marlene	GB	1950	Arthur Crabtree	90			GB	15
Lilies of the Field	USA	1963	Ralph Nelson	94			FB	15
Lilith	USA	1964	Robert Rossen	114			FB	15
Limousine Daimler-Benz, The	POL	1981	Filip Bajon	94	est		FOP	0
Lina Brooke	GB	1979	Anthony Harrild	75			BFI	30
Line Up, The	USA	1958	Don Siegel	86			FB	15
Link	GB	1985	Richard Franklin	116			FB	45
Lion Has Seven Heads, The	IT/FR	1970	Glauber Rocha	97	est		MP	30
Lion in Winter, The	GB	1968	Anthony Harvey	134	sc/ sd		GB	33
Lion's Den	PERU/SP	1988	Francisco J. Lombardi	116	st		GB	60
Lion, The	GB	1962	Jack Cardiff	96	sc/std		FB	18
Lionheart	GB	1968	Michael Forlong	57			GB	17
Lions Love	USA	1969	Agnes Varda	115			GB	30
Lipstick	USA	1976	Lamont Johnson	90			FB	38
Liquidator, The	GB	1965	Jack Cardiff	104	sc/std		FB	18
Lisa — Indispensable	W.GER	1973	Rolf Biesch	94	est		GFL	0
Lisztomania	GB	1975	Ken Russell	104			FB	27
Little Ark	USA	1971	James B. Clark	101	sc		GB	18
Little Ballerina, The	GB	1947	Lewis Gilbert	60			FB	10
Little Big Shot	GB	1952	Jack Raymond	91			FB	15
Little Boy Lost	USA	1953	George Seaton	95			FB	15
Little Caesar	USA	1930	Mervyn LeRoy	80		U	FB	22
Little Darlings	USA	1980	Ronald F. Maxwell	95	sc		FB	38
Little Drummer Girl, The	USA	1984	George Roy Hill	130			FB	50
Little Girl Who Lives Down the Lane, The	CAN/FR/ USA	1976	Nicolas Gessner	91			FB	22
Little Hut, The	USA	1957	Mark Robson	90			FB	18
Little Ida	SWE/ NOR	1981	Laila Mikkelsen	79	est		BFI	40
Little Lord Fauntleroy	GB	1980	Jack Gold	103			GB	40
Little Man, What Now?	USA	1934	Frank Borzage	90			BFI	25
Little Mermaid, The	USA	1989	Ron Clements/ John Musker	82		D	FB	75
Little Minister, The	USA	1934	Richard Wallace	110			GB	15
Little Miss Broadway	USA	1939	Irving Cummings	71			FB	15
Little Miss Marker	USA	1934	Alexander Hall	79			FB	22
Little Miss Marker	USA	1980	Walter Bernstein	103			FB	38
Little Mister Jim	USA	1946	Fred Zinnemann	92			FB	15
Little Orvie	USA	1940	Ray McCarey	66			GB	15

Films on Offer

	COUNTRY OF PRODUCTION	YEAR	DIRECTOR	RUNNING TIME	VERSION	35mm	16mm	16mm RENTAL FEE
Little People, The	W.GER	1956	Hubert Schonger	75	dub		GFL	0
Little Romance, A	USA	1979	George Roy Hill	110	sc/std		FB	36
Little Savage, The	USA	1959	Byron Haskin	78	std		FB	15
Little Shop of Horrors,The	USA	1986	Frank Oz	94			FB	65
Little Women	USA	1949	Mervyn LeRoy	122			FB	15
Littlest Outlaw, The	USA	1955	Robert Gavaldon	72			FB	27
Live a Life	GB	1982	Maxim Ford	80			CONC	15
							MP	23
Live a Little, Love a Little	USA	1968	Norman Taurog	90	sc/std		FB	22
Live a Little, Steal a Lot	USA	1974	Marvin Chomsky	90			GB	22
Lives of a Bengal Lancer, The	USA	1934	Henry Hathaway	111			FB	22
Lives of Performers	USA	1972	Yvonne Rainer	90			BFI	35
Living (see Ikiru)								
Living Apart Together	GB	1983	Charles Gormley	98			GB	45
Living Corpse, The	USSR/ GER	1928	Feodor Ozep	142	st/est		BFI	20
Living Daylights, The	GB	1987	John Glen	131			FB	65
Living Dead, The	GER	1932	Richard Oswald	85	est		GB	20
Living Desert, The	USA	1953	James Algar	75			FB	31
Living Free	GB	1972	Jack Couffer	92			FB	18
Living on the Edge	GB	1987	Michael Grigsby	89			BFI	35
Local Color	USA	1977	Mark Rappaport	115			BFI	30
Local Hero	GB	1983	Bill Forsyth	111			FB	55
Lock Up	USA	1990	John Flynn	109		GU	GU	80
Locket, The	USA	1946	John Brahm	86			GB	15
Lodger, The	GB	1926	Alfred Hitchcock	89	t/st	BFI	BFI	20
Logan's Run	USA	1976	Michael Anderson	118	sc/std		FB	33
Logical Propositions	GB	1973	Mike Dunford	60			LFC	34
Loin de Vietnam	FR	1967	Alain Resnais/Jean-Luc Godard/ Agnes Varda/Claude Lelouch/ William Klein/Joris Ivens	115	est		GB	30
Lola	W.GER	1981	R.W. Fassbinder	115	est	ELEC	GB	50
Lolita	GB	1961	Stanley Kubrick	153		R	FB	22
London Connection, The	GB	1979	Robert Clouse	84			FB	33
Lone Rider in Cheyenne	USA	1940	Sam Newfield	60			GB	15
Lone Rider Rides On	USA	1941	Sam Newfield	60			GB	15
Lone Rider's Texas Justice	USA	1942	Sam Newfield	60			GB	15
Lone Star	USA	1951	Vincent Sherman	94			FB	15
Lone Wolf McQuade	USA	1983	Steve Carver	107			FB	38
Loneliness of the Long Distance Runner, The	GB	1962	Tony Richardson	104			FB	15
Lonely Man	USA	1957	Henry Levin	88			FB	15
Lonely Passion of Judith Hearne, The	GB	1987	Jack Clayton	116			GB	80
Lonely Wives	USA	1931	Russell Mack	90			GB	15
Long Arm, The	GB	1956	Charles Frend	96			GB	20
Long Day Closes, The	GB	1992	Terrence Davies	85		MAY	GB	80
Long Duel, The	GB	1966	Ken Annakin	115	std		FB	22
Long Good Friday, The	GB	1979	John MacKenzie	114			GB	35
Long Goodbye, The	USA	1973	Robert Altman	111	sc		FB	18
Long Gray Line, The	USA	1955	John Ford	137	std		FB	15
Long Holidays of 1936, The	SP	1976	Jaime Camino	107	est		GB	35
Long Hot Summer, The	USA	1958	Martin Ritt	117	std		FB	18
Long Live the Lady!	IT	1987	Ermanno Olmi	115	est		GB	60
Long Lost Father	USA	1934	Ernest Schoedsack	63			GB	15
Long Ride Home, The	USA	1967	Phil Karlson	88	sc		FB	18
Long Ride, The	USA/HUNG	1983	Pal Gabor	93			FB	30
Long Riders, The	USA	1980	Walter Hill	100			FB	38
Long Shot	GB	1978	Maurice Hatton	85			BFI	30
Long Time Companion	USA	1990	Norman Rene	99		MAY	GB	70
Long Voyage Home, The	USA	1940	John Ford	104			BFI	25

	COUNTRY OF PRODUCTION	YEAR	DIRECTOR	RUNNING TIME	VERSION	35mm	16mm	16mm RENTAL FEE
Long, and the Short and the Tall, The	GB	1960	Leslie Norman	105			FB	15
Longest Day, The	USA	1962	Ken Annakin/Andrew Marton/ Bernhard Wicki	176	sc/std		FB	30
Look Up and Laugh	GB	1935	Basil Dean	77			FB	15
Look Who's Talking	USA	1989	Amy Heckerling	96		C	FB	60
Look Who's Talking Too	USA	1990	Amy Heckerling	86		C	FB	60
Looking for Daddy	CZ	1967	Franjisek Daniel	88	est		ETV	10
Looking for Love	USA	1964	Don Weis	83	sc/std		FB	18
Looking for Mr. Goodbar	USA	1977	Richard Brooks	136			FB	38
Looking Glass War, The	GB	1969	Frank Pierson	107	sc		FB	18
Looking On The Bright Side	GB	1932	Basil Dean/Graham Cutts	78			BFI	30
Loom, The	USA		Stan Brakhage	50			LFMC	42.5
Loophole	GB	1980	John Quested	105			GB	38
Loot	GB	1971	Silvio Narizzano	101			FB	18
Lord Jim	GB	1964	Richard Brooks	153	sc/std		FB	22
Lord of the Flies	GB	1962	Peter Brook	91			FB	27
Lord of the Flies	USA	1990	Harry Hook	90			GB	80
Lord of the Rings	USA	1978	Ralph Bakshi	134			FB	43
Lord von Barmbeck, Der	W.GER	1973	Ottokar Runze	107	dub		GFL	0
Lords of Discipline, The	USA/GB	1983	Franc Roddam	103			FB	38
Lorna Doone	USA	1951	Phil Karlson	82			FB	18
Lorna Doone	GB	1934	Basil Dean	90			GB	20
Losers, The	USA	1970	Jack Starrett	95			GB	30
Lost and Found	GB	1979	Melvin Frank	105			FB	38
Lost Boys, The	USA	1987	Joel Schumacher	97			FB	45
Lost Command, The	USA	1966	Mark Robson	130	sc/std		FB	18
Lost Continent, The	GB	1968	Michael Carreras	98			FB	15
Lost Honour of Katherina Blum, The	W.GER	1975	Volker Schlöndorff	105	est		GB	35
Lost Horizon	USA	1937	Frank Capra	120			FB	15
Lost Horizon	USA	1972	Charles Jarrott	143	sc/std		FB	27
Lost in a Harem	USA	1944	Charles F. Reisner	89			FB	15
Lost In America	USA	1985	Albert Brooks	91			FB	45
Lost Life	W.GER	1975	Ottokar Runze	94	est		GFL	0
Lost Man, The	USA	1969	Robert Alan Aurthur	110	sc		FB	18
Lost Moment The	USA	1947	Martin Gabel	89			GB	22
Lost One, The	W.GER	1951	Peter Lorre	90	est		BFI	25
Lost Patrol, The	USA	1934	John Ford	75			GB	15
Lost Squadron, The	USA	1932	George Archainbaud	79			GB	15
Lost Weekend, The	USA	1945	Billy Wilder	99			FB	22
Lotna	POL	1959	Andrzej Wajda	89	est		GB	30
Lotte in Italia	FR IT	1970	Dziga Vertov Group	60	est		MP/ETV	35
Louisiana Purchase	USA	1942	Irving Cummings	98			FB	18
Louisiana Story	USA	1948	Robert Flaherty	77			GB	15
Louisiana Territory	USA	1953	Harry Smith	65			GB	18
Loulou	FR	1980	Maurice Pialat	105	est	AE	GB	50
Love and Bullets	USA	1978	Stuart Rosenberg	101	sc/std		GB	33
Love and Death	USA	1975	Woody Allen	85			FB	27
Love and Pain and the Whole Damn Thing	USA	1972	Alan J. Pakula	110			FB	18
Love Ban, The	GB	1973	Ralph Thomas	96			FB	18
Love Bewitched, A	SP	1986	Carlos Saura	98	est		GB	75
Love Bug, The	USA	1969	Robert Stevenson	108			FB	38
Love Cage. The	FR	1964	René Clément	97	std		FB	15
Love Comes Along	USA	1930	Rupert Julian	78			GB	15
Love Crazy	USA	1941	Jack Conway	99			FB	15
Love God, The	USA	1969	Nat Hiken	110	std		FB	18
Love Goddesses, The	USA	1965	Graeme Ferguson/Saul Turell (Prods)	87			GB	22
Love in Germany, A	FR/ W.GER	1983	Andrzej Wajda	115	est		GB	55
Love in Las Vegas	USA	1963	George Sidney	83	sc/std		FB	22

	COUNTRY OF PRODUCTION	YEAR	DIRECTOR	RUNNING TIME	VERSION	35mm	16mm	16mm RENTAL FEE
Love Is a Many-Splendored Thing	USA	1955	Henry King	102	std		FB	18
Love Lottery, The	GB	1953	Charles Crichton	89			FB	18
Love Me Or Leave Me	USA	1955	Charles Vidor	122	std		FB	33
Love Me Tender	USA	1956	Robert D. Webb	89	sc/std		FB	17
Love On a Bet	USA	1936	Leigh Jason	77			GB	15
Love On the Dole	GB	1941	John Baxter	98			BFI	25
Love Story	USA	1970	Arthur Hiller	100			FB	33
Love Streams	USA	1984	John Cassavetes	141			FB	60
Love Thy Neighbour	GB	1973	John Robins	95			FB	18
Love With the Proper Stranger	USA	1963	Robert Mulligan	100			FB	15
Love, Life and Laughter	GB	1934	Maurice Elvey	83			FB	15
Loved One, The	USA	1965	Tony Richardson	120			FB	22
Lovejoy's Nuclear War	USA	1975	Dan Keller/ Chuck Light	60			CONC	15.40
Lovely To Look At	USA	1952	Mervyn LeRoy	102	bw		FB	15
Lovely Way To Go, A	USA	1968	David Lowell Rich	103	std		FB	18
Lover Come Back	USA	1961	Delbert Mann	107	col/bw		FB FB	18
Lovers and Other Strangers	USA	1969	Cy Howard	106			GB	18
Lovers!	GB	1972	Herbert Wise	89			FB	18
Lovers, The (see Amants, Les)								
Lovesick	USA	1983	Marshall Brickman	95			FB	40
Lovin' the Ladies	USA	1930	Melville Brown	65			GB	15
Loving Memory	GB	1969	Tony Scott	57			BFI	15.5
Lt. Robinson Crusoe	USA	1966	Byron Paul	114			FB	27
Lucia	CB	1969	Humberto Solas	160	bw/est	MP	MP	–
Lucky Boy	USA	1928	Norman Taurog	77	sd		BFI	20
Lucky Devils	USA	1933	Ralph Ince	60			GB	15
Lucky Jim	GB	1957	John Boulting	95			FB	15
Lucky Lady	USA	1975	Stanley Donen	117			FB	30
Lucky Luke-Daisy Town	FR/BEL	1971	René Goscinny	76			GB	35
Lucky Partners	USA	1940	Lewis Milestone	99			GB	15
Ludwig: Requiem for a Virgin King	W.GER	1972	Hans-Jürgen Syberberg	139	est		GB	40
Lullaby of Broadway	USA	1951	David Butler	92			FB	18
Luna, La	IT	1979	Bernardo Bertolucci	142			FB	38
Lust for a Vampire	GB	1970	Jimmy Sangster	95			FB	18
Lust For Life	USA	1956	Vincente Minnelli	122	std		FB	27
Lusty Men, The	USA	1952	Nicholas Ray	112			GB	15
Luxury Liner	USA	1948	Richard Whorf	98	bw		FB	15

Leningrad Cowboys Go America

	COUNTRY OF PRODUCTION	YEAR	DIRECTOR	RUNNING TIME	VERSION	35mm	16mm	16mm RENTAL FEE
m								
M	GER	1931	Fritz Lang	106	est	BFI	BFI	30
M'Liss	USA	1936	George Nicholls Jr.	66			GB	15
M. Hulot's Holiday	FR	1953	Jacques Tati	86	est	BFI	BFI	30
Mac And Me	USA	1989	Stewart Raffill	99		GU	GU	80
Macao	USA	1952	Josef von Sternberg	81			GB	15
MacArthur the Rebel General	USA	1977	Joseph Sargent	130			FB	33
Macbeth	USA	1948	Orson Welles	109			GB	27
Macbeth	GB	1971	Roman Polanski	140	sc/std		FB	33
Machine Gun McCain	IT	1968	Giuliano Montaldo	96	sc		FB	18
Machine That Kills, The	IT	1948	Roberto Rossellini	83	est		BFI	25
Macho Callahan	USA	1970	Bernard Kowalski	100	std		GB	18
Mackenna's Gold	USA	1968	J. Lee Thompson	125	sc/std		FB	22
Mackintosh Man, The	GB	1973	John Huston	99			FB	18
Mad About Men	GB	1954	Ralph Thomas	85			FB	18
Mad Adventures of Rabbi Jacob, The	FR/IT	1973	Gérard Oury	94	est		FB	27
Mad Love (see Hands of Orlac , 1935)								
Mad Max	AUSTR	1979	George Miller	91	sc		FB	43
Mad Max 2	AUSTR	1981	George Miller	95	sc		FB	48
Mad Max Beyond Thunderdome	AUSTR	1985	George Miller/George Ogilvie	107	sc/std		FB	45
Mad Miss Manton	USA	1938	Leigh Jason	80			GB	15
Mad Monkey	SP	1990	Fernando Truenda	108	eng	MAY	GB	60
Mad Wednesday	USA	1946	Preston Sturges	77			BFI	25
Madame Bovary	USA	1949	Vincente Minnelli	114			FB	15
Madame Claude	FR	1976	Just Jaeckin	110	dub		FB	41
Madame Curie	USA	1943	Mervyn LeRoy	124	bw		FB	15
Madame Dubarry	GER	1919	Ernst Lubitsch	86	st/gst		GFL	0
Madame Sin	GB	1972	David Greene	90			GB	18
Made in Paris	USA	1966	Boris Sagal	103	std		FB	18
Madeleine – Tel 136211	W.GER	1958	Kurt Meisel	86	est		GB	25
Mademoiselle	GB/FR	1966	Tony Richardson	103	est/sc/ dub		FB	15
Mademoiselle Fifi (see Silent Bell, The)								
Madhouse	GB	1974	Jim Clark	92			FB	18
Madhouse	USA	1990	Tom Ropelewski	90		C	FB	60
Madigan	USA	1968	Don Siegel	101	std		FB	18
Madonna of the Seven Moons	GB	1944	Arthur Crabtree	110			BFI	30
Madres The Mothers of Plaza de Mayo, Las	USA	1985	Susana Munoz/Lourdes Portillo	65	est		GB	35
Madwoman of the Chaillot, The	GB	1969	Bryan Forbes	137	std		FB	18
Maeve	GB	1981	Pat Murphy/John Davies	109			BFI	40
Maggie, The	GB	1953	Alexander Mackendrick	92			FB	16
Magic	USA	1978	Richard Attenborough	107			FB	35
Magic Boy	JAP	1960	Akira Daikubara	75	sc/dub		FB	18
Magic Flute, The	SWE	1974	Ingmar Bergman	135			BFI	45
Magic Lotus Lantern, The	CHI	1959	Yeh Ming	81	eng		GB	25
Magic of Lassie, The	USA	1978	Don Chaffey	79			GB	35
Magic Town	USA	1947	William Wellman	103			GB	15
Magician of Lublin, The	W.GER/ IS	1978	Menahem Golan	113			FB	38
Magnificent 7 Deadly Sins, The	GB	1971	Graham Stark	107		GB	GB	25
Magnificent Ambersons, The	USA	1942	Orson Welles	88			GB	22
Magnificent Obsession	USA	1935	John M. Stahl	102			BFI	25
Magnificent Obsession	USA	1954	Douglas Sirk	108	bw		FB	15
Magnificent Rebel, The	USA/ W.GER	1960	Georg Tressler	94			FB	27
Magnificent Seven Ride, The	USA	1972	George McCowan	100			FB	27
Magnificent Two, The	GB	1967	Cliff Owen	100			FB	18
Magnum Force	USA	1973	Ted Post	122	sc/std		FB	33
Mahler	GB	1974	Ken Russell	115			GB	27
Maid's Night Out	USA	1938	Ben Holmes	64			GB	15
Main Attraction, The	GB	1962	Daniel Petrie	90			FB	18
Main Event, The	USA	1979	Howard Zieff	109			FB	37

	COUNTRY OF PRODUCTION	YEAR	DIRECTOR	RUNNING TIME	VERSION	35mm	16mm	16mm RENTAL FEE
Majdhar	GB	1985	Ahmed A Jamal	76			JB	–
Major and the Minor, The	USA	1942	Billy Wilder	100			FB	22
Major Barbara	GB	1941	Gabriel Pascal	90			GB	15
Major Dundee	USA	1964	Sam Peckinpah	119	sc/std		FB	22
Major League	USA	1989	David S. Ward	107			FB	55
Make Mine A Million	GB	1959	Lance Comfort	82			FB	15
Make Mine Laughs	USA	1949	Richard Fleischer	63			GB	20
Make Way for a Lady	USA	1936	David Burton	65			GB	20
Mala Noche	USA	1985	Gus Van Sant	78			RESP	40
Mala The Magnificent	USA	1934	W.S. Van Dyke	108	bw		FB	15
Malachi's Cove	GB	1974	Henry Herbert	89			GB	20
Malcolm	AUSTR	1986	Nadia Tass	86			BFI	45
Mambo Kings, The	USA	1992	Arne Glimcher	130		W	FB	70
Man Alive	USA	1945	Ray Enright	70			GB	20
Man and Child	FR	1956	Raoul Andre	89			GB	20
Man Called Horse	USA	1970	Elliot Silverstein	114			GB	25
Man Eater of Kumaon	USA	1948	Byron Haskin	80			GB	15
Man Escaped, A	FR	1956	Robert Bresson	102	est	AE	AE	45
Man For All Seasons, A	GB	1966	Fred Zinnemann	120			FB	33
Man Friday	GB	1975	Jack Gold	109			GB	22
Man From Alamo, The	USA	1953	Budd Boetticher	79	col		FB	18
					bw			15
Man From Hong Kong, The	AUSTR/HK	1975	Brian Smith	103	sc/std		GB	27
Man From Laramie	USA	1955	Anthony Mann	101	sc/std		FB	18
Man From Nowhere, The	GB	1976	James Hill	58			GB	17
Man From Snowy River	AUSTR	1982	George Miller	93			FB	35
Man From the First Century, The	CZ	1961	Oldrich Lipsky	95	est		ETV	10
Man Hunt	USA	1933	Irving Cummings	68			GB	15
Man in Grey, The	GB	1943	Leslie Arliss	116			BFI	30
Man in the Iron Mask, The	GB/USA	1976	Mike Newell	105			GB	25
Man in the Sky	GB	1956	Charles Crichton	87			FB	15
Man In the White Suit	GB	1951	Alexander MacKendrick	85			FB	15
Man in the Wilderness	USA	1971	Richard C. Sarafian	107			FB	18
Man Is Not Alone, A	CZ	1971	Josef Mach	90			ETV	10
Man Like Eva, A	GER	1983	Radu Gabrea	89	st		GB	60
Man of Aran	GB	1933	Robert Flaherty	76		R	FB	55
Man of Flowers	AUSTR	1983	Paul Cox	90			GB	45
Man of Iron	POL	1981	Andrzej Wajda	150	est		GB	55
Man of La Mancha	IT	1972	Arthur Hiller	132			FB	27
Man of the East	IT/FR	1972	E.B. Clucher	124	sc/dub		FB	18
Man of Two Worlds	USA	1934	J. Walter Ruben	97			GB	15
Man on a Swing	USA	1974	Frank Perry	108	std		FB	27
Man on Fire	USA	1957	Ranald McDougall	95			FB	15
Man on the Eiffel Tower, The	FR	1948	Burgess Meredith	98			GB	20
Man on the Flying Trapeze	USA	1935	Clyde Bruckman	66			FB	15
Man Proof	USA	1937	Richard Thorpe	75			FB	15
Man Who Fell To Earth, The	GB	1976	Nicolas Roeg	140			FB	38
Man Who Finally Died, The	GB	1962	Quentin Lawrence	100			FB	15
Man Who Found Himself, The	USA	1936	Lew Landers	67			GB	15
Man Who Had His Hair Cut Short, The	BELG	1966	André Delvaux	94	est		GB	25
Man Who Had Power Over Women, The	GB	1970	John Krish	89			FB	18
Man Who Haunted Himself, The	GB	1970	Basil Dearden	94			FB	18
Man Who Knew Too Much, The	USA	1955	Alfred Hitchcock	120			FB	35
Man Who Loved Cat Dancing, The	USA	1973	Richard C. Sarafian	114			FB	24
Man Who Loved Women, The	USA	1983	Blake Edwards	105			FB	38
Man Who Saw Tomorrow, The	USA	1981	Robert Guenette	88			FB	27
Man Who Walked Alone	USA	1945	Christy Cabanne	60			GB	25
Man Who Would Be King, The	USA	1975	John Huston	128	sc/std		FB	27

m

Title	COUNTRY OF PRODUCTION	YEAR	DIRECTOR	RUNNING TIME	VERSION	35mm	16mm	16mm RENTAL FEE
Man with a Cloak	USA	1951	Fletcher Markle	80			FB	15
Man with a Gun	USSR	1938	Sergei Yutkevitch	85	est		ETV	10
Man With One Red Shoe, The	USA	1984	Stan Dragoti	93			FB	40
Man With the Deadly Lens	USA	1982	Richard Brooks	118	sc		FB	45
Man with the Golden Gun, The	GB	1974	Guy Hamilton	125			FB	43
Man With the Movie Camera	USSR	1928	Dziga Vertov	67	st/sd		BFI	25
Man with Two Lives, The	USA	1942	Phil Rosen	67			GB	15
Man without a Body, The	GB	1957	W. Lee Wilder/Charles Saunders	80			GB	15
Man without a Star	USA	1955	King Vidor	89			FB	18
Man You Loved to Hate, The	USA	1979	Patrick Montgomery	90			BFI	25
Man, Woman and Child	USA	1982	Dick Richards	100			FB	40
Mandrake, The	IT/FR	1965	Alberto Lattuada	99	est		GB	30
Mandy	GB	1952	Alexander MacKendrick	93			FB	15
Maneater of Kumaon	USA	1948	Byron Haskin	80			GB	20
Manganinnie	AUSTR	1980	John Honey	90			GB	30
Manhattan	USA	1979	Woody Allen	96	sc/std		FB	43
Manhunter	USA	1986	Michael Mann	102	sc		GB	75
Mani Sulla Citta (see Hands Over the City)								
Manila	PHIL	1975	Lina Brocka	124	est	BFI	BFI	60
Manitou	USA	1978	William Girdler	105			GB	25
Mannequin	USA	1987	Michael Gottlieb	90			FB	50
Mano Destra	SWITZ	1985	Uebelmann Cleo	53			LFMC	45.05
Manoeuvre	USA	1979	Frederick Wiseman	115			GB	35
Manon des Sources	FR/IT/ SWITZ	1986	Claude Berri	114	est	GALA	FB	100
Manon of the Spring (see Manon des Sources)								
Manpower	USA	1941	Raoul Walsh	103			FB	22
Many Rivers to Cross	USA	1954	Roy Rowland	94	col/sc/ std		FB	18
Mapantsula	S.AFR	1988	Oliver Schmitz	104			GB	70
Maracaibo	USA	1958	Cornel Wilde	88	bw/std		FB	15
Maragoli	GB/USA	1977	Sandra Nichols	60			CONC	22
Marathon Man	USA	1976	John Schlesinger	126			FB	48
March or Die	GB	1977	Dick Richards	107			FB	33
Marco Polo	IT/FR	1961	Hugo Fregonese	91	sc/dub		FB	18
Mare's Tail	GB	1969	David Larcher	150			LFC	24
Maria Horzeck	W.GER	1976	Horst Flick	92	est		GFL	0
Maria's Lovers	USA	1984	Andrei Konchalovsky	107			FB	40
Marie	USA	1985	Roger Donaldson	112			FB	45
Marie Antoinette	USA	1938	W.S. Van Dyke	139			FB	15
Marie Walewska	USA	1937	Clarence Brown	112			FB	22
Marigolds in August	S.AFR	1980	Ross Devenish	87			GB	40
Marilyn	USA	1963	Compilation	83			FB	15
Marine Raiders	GB	1944	Harold Schuster	91			GB	15
Marines Fly High	USA	1940	George Nicholls Jr	68			GB	15
Marjorie Morningstar	USA	1958	Irving Rapper	123	bw		GB	18
Mark of the Vampire	USA	1935	Tod Browning	61			FB	18
Mark of Zorro, The	USA	1920	Fred Niblo	90	st		BFI	18
Marlowe	USA	1969	Paul Bogart	95			FB	22
Maroc 7	GB	1967	Gerry O'Hara	91	std		FB	18
Marooned	USA	1969	John Sturges	128	sc/std		FB	22
Marriage of Figaro, The	W.GER	1949	Georg Wildhagen	87	est		GB	25
Marriage of Maria Braun, The	W.GER	1978	R.W. Fassbinder	120	est/dub		GB	50
Marriage on the Rocks	USA	1965	Jack Donohue	101	sc/std		FB	18
Married and in Love	USA	1940	John Farrow	59			GB	20
Married Couple, A	CAN	1969	Allan King	97			GB	30
Marseillaise, La	FR	1937	Jean Renoir	130	est		GB	25
Marseille Contract, The	GB/FR	1974	Robert Parrish	90			FB	18
Marshal of Mesa City, The	USA	1939	David Howard	62			GB	15

	COUNTRY OF PRODUCTION	YEAR	DIRECTOR	RUNNING TIME	VERSION	35mm	16mm	16mm RENTAL FEE
Martha Graham Dance Company,The	USA	1976	Merrill Brockway	90			AC	19
Martin Luther	USA/W.GER	1953	Irving Pichel	106			CTVC	9
Martyrs of Love	CZ	1967	Jan Nemec	70	est		GB	25
Marusya's First Year at School	USSR	1951	Ilya Frez	72	est		ETV	10
Marvellous Mum	CZ	1965	Vladislav Pavlovic	85	est		ETV	10
Mary of Scotland	USA	1936	John Ford	123			GB	15
Mary Poppins	USA	1964	Robert Stevenson	95			FB	38
Mary, Queen of Scots	GB	1971	Charles Jarrott	128	sc/std		FB	27
MASH	USA	1969	Robert Altman	115	sc/std	F	FB	31
Mask	USA	1985	Peter Bogdanovich	120			FB	40
Mask of Dimitrios, The	USA	1944	Jean Negulesco	95			FB	22
Mask of Fu Manchu, The	USA	1932	Charles Brabin	67			FB	22
Masked Raiders	USA	1949	Lesley Selander	60			GB	15
Masque of the Red Death, The	GB	1964	Roger Corman	84	sc		FB	18
Masquerade	USA	1988	Bob Swaim	92			FB	50
Masquerade	GB	1964	Basil Dearden	102			FB	18
Masques	FR	1987	Claude Chabrol	100	est		FB	70
Mass Appeal	USA	1984	Glenn Jordan	99			FB	35
Massacre of Kaffr Kassem, The	LEB/SYRIA	1973	Borhan Alaouie	100	est		WFA	45
Master of Lassie	USA	1948	Fred M. Wilcox	97	bw/col		FB	18
Master of the Islands	USA	1970	Tom Gries	132	sc		FB	18
Master of the World	USA	1961	William Witney	98			FB	15
Master Race, The	USA	1945	Herbert J. Biberman	96	bw		GB	15
Master, The	POL	1966	Jerzy Antczak	60	est		FOP	0
Masters of the Universe	USA	1987	Gary Goddard	106			FB	50
Mat (see Mother)								
Mata Hari	USA	1985	Curtis Harrington	108			FB	40
Matchmaker, The	USA	1957	Joseph Anthony	101	std		FB	15
Mating Game, The	USA	1958	George Marshall	96	sc/std		FB	18
Matter of Who, A	GB	1961	Don Chaffey	90			FB	10
Maurice	GB	1987	James Ivory	140		MAY	GB	75
Mauro the Gypsy	GB	1972	Lawrence Henson	58			GB	17
Mauvais Sang (see Night is Young, The)								
Maxie	USA	1985	Paul Aaron	98			FB	45
Maximka	USSR	1952	Vladimir Braun	90	est		ETV	10
Mayday at 40,000 Feet	USA	1976	Robert Butler	94			FB	18
Mayerling	FR/GB	1968	Terence Young	141	sc/std		FB	18
Mayor of 44th Street	USA	1942	Alfred E. Green	88			GB	20
McHale's Navy	USA	1964	Edward J. Montagne	93			FB	15
McKenzie Break, The	GB	1970	Lamont Johnson	106			FB	18
McMasters Tougher than theWest Itself	USA	1969	Alf Kjellin	83			GB	18
McQ	USA	1974	John Sturges	111	sc/std		FB	18
McVicar	GB	1980	Tom Clegg	112			GB	43
Me Natalie	USA	1969	Fred Coe	111			GB	18
Mean Machine, The	USA	1974	Robert Aldrich	122			FB	38
Mean Season, The	USA	1985	Phillip Borsos	104			FB	40
Meanest Gal in Town, The	USA	1934	Russell Mack	67			GB	15
Measure For Measure	GB/USA	1979	Desmond Davis	145			BBC	35
Meat	USA	1976	Frederick Wiseman	113			GB	50
Meatballs	CAN	1979	Ivan Reitman	94			FB	38
Mechanic, The	USA	1972	Michael Winner	100	std		FB	27
Medicine Man	USA	1992	John McTiernan	105	sc	GU	GU	100
Medusa Touch, The	GB/FR	1978	Jack Gold	109			GB	43
Meet Me After the Show	USA	1951	Robert Sale	87			FB	18
Meet Me in St. Louis	USA	1944	Vincente Minnelli	113			FB	30
Meet Mr. Lucifer	GB	1953	Anthony Pélissier	83			FB	15
Meet the Missus	USA	1937	Joseph Santley	60			GB	15
Meeting Venus	GB/US	1991	István Szabó	119		W	FB	70

	COUNTRY OF PRODUCTION	YEAR	DIRECTOR	RUNNING TIME	VERSION	35mm	16mm	16mm RENTAL FEE
Meetings with Remarkable Men	USA	1978	Peter Brook	107			GB	40
Mein Kampf	SWE	1959	Erwin Leiser	118	est		GB	30
Melancholia	GB/W.GER	1989	Andi Engel	88		AE	BFI	65
Melody (See S.W.A.L.K.)								
Melody Time	USA	1948	Walt Disney	75			FB	27
Melvin and Howard	USA	1980	Jonathan Demme	95			FB	33
Member of the Government	USSR	1940	Alex Zarkhi/Josef Heifitz	94	est		ETV	10
Memoirs of an Invisible Man	USA	1992	John Carpenter	95		W	FB	65
Memorandum	CAN	1966	Donald Brittain/John Spotton	60			CONC	11.20
Memorias del Subdesarrollo (see Memories of Undervelopment)								
Memories of Underdevelopment	CB	1968	Tomás Gutiérrez Alea	97	bw/est	MP	MP	
Memphis Belle	GB	1990	Michael Caton-Jones	102		W	FB	65
Men	W.GER	1985	Doris Dörrie	99	est		GB	60
Men Against the Sky	USA	1940	Leslie Goodwins	75			GB	15
Men Against the Sun	KEN	1953	Brendan J. Stafford	72			GB	15
Men of America	USA	1932	Ralph Ince	75			GB	15
Men of Boy's Town	USA	1941	Norman Taurog	106			FB	18
Men of Chance	USA	1932	George Archainbaud	63			GB	20
Menace	FR	1971	Sergio Gobbi	90	dub		FB	18
Menace on the Mountain	USA	1972	Vincent McEveety	90			FB	27
Menilmontant	FR	1924	Dimitri Kirsanoff	50	st/sd		BFI	15
Mensch Mutter	W.GER	1977	Peter Wehage	80	est		GFL	0
Menschen am Sonntag	GER	1929	Robert Siodmak/Edgar Ulmer	89	est		GB	25
Mercenaries, The	GB	1967	Jack Cardiff	100	std		FB	24
Merchant of Four Seasons, The	W.GER	1972	R.W. Fassbinder	90	est	BFI	BFI	45
Merci La Vie	FR	1992	Bertrand Blier	117	st	AE	GB	80
Mermaids	USA	1990	Richard Benjamin	110		R	FB	60
Merrill's Marauders	USA	1962	Samuel Fuller	91	bw/std		FB	15
Merrily We Go to Hell	USA	1932	Dorothy Arzner	83			BFI	25
Merry Andrew	USA	1958	Michael Kidd	103	sc/std		FB	18
Merry Christmas, Mr. Lawrence	GB	1982	Nagisa Oshima	123			GB	48
Merry Widow, The	USA	1952	Curtis Bernhardt	105			FB	16
Merry Wives of Windsor, The	GB	1964	Georg Tressler	97			GB	22
Messer im Kopf (see Knife in the Head)								
Messidor	FR/SWITZ	1978	Alain Tanner	120	est		FB	40
Meteor	USA	1979	Ronald Neame	107	sc		FB	43
Metropolis	GER	1926	Fritz Lang	119	sd/st	BFI	BFI	25
Metropolitan	USA	1989	Whit Stillman	98			BFI	85
Mexican Spitfire at Sea	USA	1941	Leslie Goodwins	73			GB	15
Mexican Spitfire out West	USA	1940	Leslie Goodwins	76			GB	15
Mexican Spitfire Sees a Ghost	USA	1942	Leslie Goodwins	70			GB	15
Mexican Spitfire's Baby	USA	1941	Leslie Goodwins	70			GB	15
Mexican Spitfire's Elephant	USA	1942	Leslie Goodwins	64			GB	15
Miami Blues	USA	1990	George Armitage	97		R	FB	60
Mickey Mouse Anniversary Show	USA	1968	Ward Kimball/Robert Stevenson	89			FB	27
Mickey One	USA	1965	Arthur Penn	93			FB	15
Micki And Maude	USA	1985	Blake Edwards	117			FB	40
Middle Man, The	INDIA	1975	Satyajit Ray	134	est		GB	25
Midnight	USA	1938	Mitchell Leisen	94			FB	15
Midnight Blue	USA	1980	Gerard Damiano	62	71		FB	35
Midnight Cowboy	USA	1969	John Schlesinger	113			FB	27
Midnight Express	GB	1978	Alan Parker	121			FB	43
Midnight Madness	USA	1980	Michael Hankin/David Wechter	110			FB	38
Midnight Man, The	USA	1974	Roland Kibbee/Burt Lancaster	116			FB	27
Midnight Mystery	USA	1930	George B. Seitz	69			GB	20
Midnight Run	USA	1988	Martin Brest	127			FB	60
Midshipman Easy	GB	1934	Carol Reed	74			FB	15
Midshipman Jack	USA	1933	Christy Cabanne	65			GB	20

	COUNTRY OF PRODUCTION	YEAR	DIRECTOR	RUNNING TIME	VERSION	35mm	16mm	16mm RENTAL FEE
Midsummer Night's Dream, A	CZ	1958	Jiri Trnka	76	sc		GB	25
Midsummer Night's Dream, A	GB/SP	1984	Celestino Coronado	78			GB	45
Midsummer Night's Dream, A	USA	1935	Max Reinhardt/William Dieterle	120			FB	22
Midsummer Night's Sex Comedy, A	USA	1982	Woody Allen	87			FB	40
Mighty Joe Young	USA	1949	Ernest Schoedsack	93			GB	16
Mikado, The	GB	1938	Victor Schertzinger	90		R	FB	22
Mikado, The	GB	1966	Stuart Burge	130			GB	22
Milagro Beanfield War, The	USA	1987	Robert Redford	118			FB	60
Mildred Pierce	USA	1945	Michael Curtiz	111			BFI	25
Milestones	USA	1975	Robert Kramer/John Douglas	210			GB	50
Military Policemen	USA	1952	George Marshall	89			FB	15
Millennium	USA	1989	Michael Anderson	105		R	FB	55
Miller's Crossing	USA	1990	Joel Coen	115		F	FB	90
Millhouse: A White Comedy	USA	1971	Emile De Antonio	93			GB	55
Millie	USA	1931	John Francis Dillon	85			GB	15
Million Dollar Duck	USA	1971	Vincent McEveety	92			FB	27
Million Pound Note	GB	1953	Ronald Neame	91	bw		FB	15
Millionaire Playboy	USA	1937	David Howard	64			GB	15
Millions Like Us	GB	1943	Frank Launder/Sidney Gilliat	103			BFI	25
Milou en Mai	FR/IT	1989	Louis Malle	107	est	GA	GB	75
Minamata	JAP	1971	Noriaki Tsuchimoto	122	est		GB	25
Mine Own Executioner	GB	1947	Anthony Kimmins	108			GB	25
Miniver Story, The	GB	1950	H.C. Potter	104			FB	15
Miracle of Fatima	USA	1952	John Brahm	105	bw		FB	15
Miracle, The	GB	1990	Neil Jordan	97		MAY	GB	80
Miracles	USA	1985	Jim Kouf	87			FB	45
Mirage	USA	1965	Edward Dmytryk	109	bw		FB	15
Mirror	USSR	1974	Andrei Tarkovsky	106	est	AE	GB	50
Mirror Crack'd, The	GB	1980	Guy Hamilton	106			FB	48
Misadventures of Merlin Jones, The	USA	1964	Robert Stevenson	91			FB	33
Misbehaving Husbands	USA	1940	William Beaudine	65			GB	15
Mischief	GB	1969	Ian Shand	57			GB	17
Mischief	USA	1984	Mel Damski	97			FB	45
Misery	USA	1990	Rob Reiner	107		FI	GB	80
Mishima: A Life In Four Chapters	JAP/USA	1985	Paul Schrader	120			FB	75
Miss Julie	SWE	1950	Alf Sjöberg	87	est		GB	30
Missing	USA	1981	Costa-Gavras	122			FB	43
Missing In Action	USA	1984	Joseph Zito	96			FB	35
Missing Note, The	GB		Michael Brandt	56			GB	12.9
Mission Galactica: The Cylon Attack	USA	1979	Vince Edwards/Christian Nyby II	107			FB	38
Mission Impossible v. The Mob	USA	1969	Paul Stanley	86			FB	18
Mission, The	USA/W.GER	1983	Parvis Sayyad	101	est		GB	45
Mission, The	GB	1986	Roland Joffe	125	std		FB	75
Missionary, The	GB	1981	Richard Loncraine	86			GB	35
Mississippi Gambler	USA	1952	Rudolph Maté	98	col		FB	18
Mississippi Masala	USA	1991	Mira Nair	113			GB	80
Mississippi Mermaid (see Sirene du Mississippi)								
Missouri Breaks, The	USA	1976	Arthur Penn	126			FB	33
Missouri Traveller, The	USA	1958	Jerry Hopper	104			GB	15
Mister Lucky	USA	1943	H.C. Potter	100			GB	15
Mister Moses	USA	1965	Ronald Neame	116	sc		FB	18
Mister Roberts	USA	1955	John Ford/Mervyn LeRoy	120	bw/std		FB	15
Mister Ten Per Cent	GB	1967	Peter Graham Scott	84	bw/std		FB	15
Mixed Company	USA	1974	Melville Shavelson	109			FB	18
Mo' Better Blues	USA	1991	Spike Lee	137		UIP	FB	60
Moana	USA	1926	Robert Flaherty	84	st		BFI	20
Model	USA	1980	Frederick Wiseman	125			GB	55
Moderato Cantabile	FR IT	1960	Peter Brook	90	std/est		GB	35

m

	COUNTRY OF PRODUCTION	YEAR	DIRECTOR	RUNNING TIME	VERSION	35mm	16mm	16mm RENTAL FEE
Modesty Blaise	GB	1966	Joseph Losey	119			FB	18
Mogambo	USA	1953	John Ford	116			FB	18
Moi, Pierre Rivière	FR	1976	René Allio	125	est		MP	51.75
Mole People. The	USA	1956	Virgil Vogel	78			FB	15
Mommie Dearest	USA	1981	Frank Perry	129			FB	43
Mon Oncle	FR	1956	Jacques Tati	116	est	BFI	BFI	35
Mon Oncle Antoine	CAN	1971	Claude Jutra	110	est		CHC	0
Mon Oncle d'Amérique	FR	1980	Alain Resnais	126	est		FB	50
Mona Lisa	GB	1986	Neil Jordan	104			GB	90
Money from Home	USA	1953	George Marshall	100	bw		FB	15
Money Movers	AUSTR	1979	Bruce Beresford	97			GB	35
Money Pit, The	USA	1985	Richard Benjamin	91			FB	40
Money Trap, The	USA	1965	Burt Kennedy	79	std		FB	12
Monihara	IND	1961	Satyajit Ray	52	est		CONT	20
Monkey Business	USA	1931	Norman Z. McLeod	77			FB	15
Monkey Grip	AUSTR	1981	Ken Cameron	105			FB	40
Monkey Shines	USA	1988	Georges Romero	100		R	FB	6
Monkey's Uncle, The	USA	1964	Robert Stevenson	90			FB	27
Monsieur Hire	FR	1989	Patrice Leconte	79	sc/ st	MAY	GB	80
Monsieur Vincent	FR	1947	Maurice Cloche	118	dub/est		GB	25
Monsignor	USA	1982	Frank Perry	121			FB	38
Monster	USA	1980	Barbara Peeters	81			FB	33
Monster, The	USA	1925	Roland West	72	st		FB	22
Monster Club, The	GB	1980	Roy Ward Baker	90			GB	33
Monster of Highgate Ponds	GB	1960	Alberto Cavalcanti	59			GB	12
Monster of Piedras Blancas	USA	1958	Irvin Berwick	71			GB	5
Montana Belle	USA	1952	Allan Dwan	82	bw		GB	15
Monte Carlo	USA	1930	Ernst Lubitsch	95			FB	22
Monte Walsh	USA	1970	William Fraker	99	sc/std		GB	18
Montenegro	SWE/GB	1981	Dusan Makavejev	95			GB	40
Monterey Pop	USA	1968	D.A. Pennebaker	72		BD	GB	38
Month in the Country, A	GB	1987	Pat O'Connor	96			FB	50
Montreal Main	CAN	1974	Frank Vitale	88			FB	22
Monty Python and the Holy Grail	GB	1974	Terry Gilliam/Terry Jones	92			FB	38
Monty Python's Life of Brian	GB	1979	Terry Jones	90			GB	50
Monty Python's The Meaning of Life	GB	1983	Terry Jones	106			FB	48
Moon in the Gutter, The	FR/IT	1983	Jean Jacques Beineix	130	sc/est		GB	45
Moon Over the Alley	GB	1975	Joseph Despins	101			BFI	30
Moon Pilot	USA	1961	James Neilson	98			FB	27
Moon Zero Two	GB	1969	Roy Ward Baker	100			FB	18
Moonraker	GB/FR	1979	Lewis Gilbert	126	sc/std		FB	53
Moonraker, The	GB	1958	David Macdonald	82			FB	18
Moonrunners	USA	1974	Cy Waldron	101			FB	18
Moonshine War, The	USA	1970	Richard Quine	100	std		FB	18
Moonspinners, The	GB	1964	James Neilson	119			FB	27
Moonstruck	USA	1987	Norman Jewison	102			FB	50
Moonwalker	USA	1988	Jerry Kramer/Colin Chilvers	93			FB	60
More American Graffitti	USA	1979	B.W.L. Norton	109			FB	38
More Dead than Alive	USA	1968	Robert Sparr	99			FB	18
Morgan – A Suitable Case For Treatment	GB	1966	Karel Reisz	97			FB	15
Morgan the Pirate	IT/FR	1960	André de Toth	95	dub/std		FB	16
Moritz Lieber Moritz	W.GER	1978	Hark Bohm	96	est		APO	30
Morning Departure	GB	1952	Roy Ward Baker	101			FB	15
Morning Glory	USA	1933	Lowell Sherman	72			GB	15
Morocco	USA	1930	Josef von Sternberg	92			BFI	25
Morons From Outer Space	GB	1985	Mike Hodges	91			FB	35
Mortal Thoughts	USA	1991	Alan Rudolph	102		C	FB	70
Moscow On The Hudson	USA	1984	Paul Mazursky	117			FB	35

m

	COUNTRY OF PRODUCTION	YEAR	DIRECTOR	RUNNING TIME	VERSION	35mm	16mm	16mm RENTAL FEE
Moses	IT/GB	1975	Gianfranco De Bosio	141			GB	27
Most Dangerous Man in the World, The	GB	1969	J. Lee Thompson	99	sc/std		FB	18
Motel Hell	USA	1980	Kevin Connor	102	106		FB	33
Mother	USSR	1926	Vsevolod Pudovkin	85	sd		GB	25
				93	st		BFI	25
Mother	USSR	1955	Mark Donskoi	100	est		ETV	10
Mother Carey's Chickens	USA	1938	Rowland V. Lee	84			GB	15
Mother Joan of the Angels (see Devil and the Nun, The)								
Mother's Loyalty, A	USSR	1967	Mark Donskoi	82			ETV	10
Mother, Jugs and Speed	USA	1976	Peter Yates	98	sc		FB	18
Moulin Rouge	GB	1928	E.A. Dupont	85	sd		BFI	20
Mountain	USA	1956	Edward Dmytryk	105	bw		FB	15
Mountain Family Robinson	USA	1979	John Cotter	102			GB	45
Mountain Men, The	USA	1979	Richard Lang	101	sc		FB	41
Mountains of the Moon	USA	1990	Bob Rafelson	135		GU	GU	80
Mourir a Madrid, A (see To Die in Madrid)								
Mouse on the Moon, The	GB	1963	Richard Lester	85			FB	18
Mouse that Roared, The	GB	1959	Jack Arnold	83			FB	18
Moussorgsky	USSR	1950	Grigori Roshal	99	est		GB	25
Movie Movie	USA	1978	Stanley Donen	105			GB	33
Moving Target, The	USA	1966	Jack Smight	121	bw/std		FB	15
Moving Violations	USA	1985	Neal Israel	86			FB	40
Mr Blot's Academy	POL	1983	Krzysztof Gradowski	140	est		FOP	0
Mr. Forbush And The Penguins	GB	1971	Al Viola	101			FB	18
Mr. & Mrs. Bridge	USA	1990	James Ivory	125		MAY	GB	80
Mr. and Mrs. Smith	USA	1941	Alfred Hitchcock	88			GB	18
Mr. Billion	USA	1977	Jonathan Kaplan	92			FB	20
Mr. Blandings Builds his Dream House	USA	1948	H.C. Potter	92			GB	15
Mr. Deeds Goes to Town	USA	1936	Frank Capra	117			FB	15
Mr. Doodle Kicks Off	USA	1938	Leslie Goodwins	76			GB	15
Mr. Griggs Returns	USA	1946	S. Sylvan Simon	82			FB	10
Mr. Horatio Nibbles	GB	1971	Robert Hird	60			GB	17
Mr. Jericho	GB	1969	Sidney Hayers	85			GB	20
Mr. Kingstreet's War	USA	1973	Percival Rubens	105			GB	18
Mr. Majestyk	USA	1974	Richard Fleischer	103			FB	18
Mr. Mum	USA	1984	Stan Dragoti	91			FB	45
Mr. Music	USA	1950	Richard Haydn	113			FB	15
Mr. North	USA	1988	Danny Huston	92			FB	60
Mr. Ricco	USA	1975	Paul Bogart	98	sc/std		FB	31
Mr. Robinson Crusoe	USA	1932	Edward Sutherland	72			GB	20
Mr. Selkie	GB	1978	Anthony Squire	52			GB	17
Mr. Skeeter	GB	1985	Colin Finbow	78		BD	GB	40
Mr. Smith Goes to Washington	USA	1939	Frank Capra	115			FB	15
Mr. Superinvisible	IT/SP/ W.GER	1970	Anthony M. Dawson	90	std/dub		GB	18
Mr. Symbol Man	AUST/ CAN	1975	Bruce Moir/Bob Kingsbury	60			CONC	19.80
Mrs. Pollifax — Spy	USA	1970	Leslie H. Martinson	100			FB	18
Mrs. Soffel	USA	1984	Gillian Armstrong	111			FB	40
Muddy River	JAP	1981	Koshei Oguri	105	est		GB	35
Müde Tod, Der (see Destiny) (1921)								
Mummy's Boys	USA	1936	Fred Guiol	68			GB	15
Munna	INDIA	1954	Ahmad Abbas	85	est		GB	25
Muppet Movie, The	USA	1979	Jim Henson	97			GB	35
Muppets Take Manhattan, The	USA	1984	Frank Oz	94			FB	40
Murder	GB	1930	Alfred Hitchcock	108			FB	25
Murder Ahoy	GB	1964	George Pollock	74			FB	15
Murder at Midnight	US	1931	Frank R. Strayer	64			GB	20
Murder at the Gallop	GB	1956	George Pollock	81			FB	12

m	COUNTRY OF PRODUCTION	YEAR	DIRECTOR	RUNNING TIME	VERSION	35mm	16mm	16mm RENTAL FEE
Murder by Death	USA	1973	Robert Moore	95	std		FB	27
Murder By Television	USA	1935	Clifford Sanforth	55			GB	20
Murder in the Cathedral	GB	1951	George Hoellering	113			BFI	35
Murder Incorporated	USA	1951	Bretaigne Windust	88			GB	20
Murder Most Foul	GB	1964	George Pollock	91			FB	12
Murder on a Bridle Path	USA	1936	Edward Killy/William Hamilton	66			GB	15
Murder on a Honeymoon	USA	1935	Lloyd Corrigan	73			GB	15
Murder on the Blackboard	USA	1934	George Archainbaud	71			GB	15
Murder on the Orient Express	GB	1974	Sidney Lumet	127			FB	40
Murder She Said	GB	1961	George Pollock	86			FB	12
Murderers	USA	1966	Henry Levin	105			FB	15
Murders in the Rue Morgue	USA	1971	Gordon Hessler	87			FB	18
Murphy's Law	USA	1985	J. Lee Thompson	100			FB	40
Murphy's Romance	USA	1985	Martin Ritt	118			FB	40
Murphy's War	GB	1971	Peter Yates	106	std		GB	22
Muscle Beach Party	USA	1964	William Asher	95	std		FB	18
Music Box	USA	1990	Costa-Gavras	126		GU	GU	80
Music for Madame	USA	1937	John Blystone	81			GB	15
Music for Millions	USA	1945	Henry Koster	117			FB	10
Music from the Flames: Shostakovich	GB	1974	Ian Engelman	64			AC	16
Music Hall	GB	1934	John Baxter	75			BFI	15
Music in Manhattan	USA	1943	John H. Auer	80			GB	15
Music Lovers, The	GB	1970	Ken Russell	124	sc		FB	27
Music Machine, The	GB	1979	Ian Sharp	90			FB	30
Muss 'Em Up	USA	1936	Charles Vidor	68			GB	20
Mustang Country	USA	1976	John Champion	80			FB	22
Mutations, The	GB	1973	Jack Cardiff	92			FB	18
Mutiny on the Bounty	USA	1935	Frank Lloyd	133			FB	22
Mutiny on the Bounty	USA	1962	Lewis Milestone	178	std		FB	33
Mutiny on the Buses	GB	1972	Harry Booth	88			FB	18
Mutter Krausens Fahrt ins Gluck	GER	1929	Piel Jutzi	109	st/ger		GB	0
My Ain Folk	GB	1973	Bill Douglas	55			BFI	25
My Apprenticeship	USSR	1939	Mark Donskoi	98	est		ETV	20
My Beautiful Laundrette	GB	1984	Stephen Frears	94			BFI	45
My Bloody Valentine	CAN	1980	George Mihalka	91			FB	43
My Blue Heaven	USA	1990	Herbert Ross	96		W	FB	60
My Bodyguard	USA	1980	Tony Bill	96			FB	33
My Boy	USA	1921	Victor Heerman/Albert Austin	65	st		BFI	15
My Cousin Vinny	USA	1992	Jonathon Lynn	119		F	FB	65
My Daughter	USSR		V. Zhilia	95	est		ETV	10
My Dear Secretary	USA	1948	Charles Martin	83			GB	15
My Father's Glory	FR	1990	Yves Robert	111	st	MAY	GB	80
My Favourite Spy	USA	1942	Tay Garnett	86			GB	15
My Favourite Wife	USA	1940	Garson Kanin	88			GB	15
My Favourite Year	USA	1982	Richard Benjamin	92			FB	38
My First Wife	AUSTR	1984	Paul Cox	97			GB	55
My Forbidden Past	USA	1951	Robert Stevenson	75			GB	15
My Geisha	USA/ JAP	1961	Jack Cardiff	120	sc		FB	18
My Girl	USA	1991	Howard Zieff	102		C	FB	70
My Girl Tisa	USA	1948	Elliott Nugent	95			GB	18
My Girlfriend's Boyfriend	FR	1987	Eric Rohmer	102	est	AE	GB	60
My Grandmother	USSR	1929	Kote Mikarberidze	66	sd/est		BFI	30
My Lady of Whims	USA	1926	Dallas M. Fitzgerald	66	st		BFI	15
My Learned Friend	GB	1943	Basil Dearden/ Will Hay	74			FB	15
My Left Foot	GB	1989	Jim Sheridan	98		MAY	GB	70
My Life As A Dog	SWE	1985	Lasse Hallström	100	est	AE	GB	60
My Life With Caroline	USA	1941	Lewis Milestone	81			GB	15
My Lover, My Son	GB	1969	John Newland	95			FB	22

	COUNTRY OF PRODUCTION	YEAR	DIRECTOR	RUNNING TIME	VERSION	35mm	16mm	16mm RENTAL FEE
My Man Godfrey	USA	1936	Gregory La Cava	90			FB	22
My Mother's Castle	FR	1990	Yves Robert	98	st	MAY	GB	80
My Own Private Idaho	USA	1991	Gus Van Sant	104		ELEC	GB	90
My Pal Wolf	USA	1944	Alfred Werker	76			GB	15
My Side of the Mountain	CAN	1969	James B. Clark	101	sc/std		FB	15
My Sister, My Love	SWE	1966	Vilgot Sjöman	96	est		GB	30
My Stepmother is an Alien	USA	1988	Richard Benjamin	107			FB	55
My Survival As An Aboriginal	AUSTR	1979	Essie Coffey	50			GB	30
My Universities	USSR	1940	Mark Donskoi	98			GB	35
My Way Home	GB	1977	Bill Douglas	72			BFI	35
Myra Breckinridge	USA	1970	Michael Sarne	91	sc		FB	18
Mysterians, The	JAP	1958	Inoshiro Honda	85	std		GB	22
Mysteries of July	GB	1991	Reece Auguiste	52			BAFC	75
Mysterious Desperado, The	USA	1949	Lesley Selander	61			GB	15
Mysterious Invader, The	USA	1957	Ronnie Ashcroft	60			FB	15
Mysterious Island	GB	1961	Cy Endfield	100			FB	18
Mysterious Wreck, The	E.GER	1953	Herbert Ballman	59			GB	12
Mystery in Mexico	USA	1948	Robert Wise	66			GB	20

My Life As A Dog

n

	COUNTRY OF PRODUCTION	YEAR	DIRECTOR	RUNNING TIME	VERSION	35mm	16mm	16mm RENTAL FEE
Nabonga	USA	1944	Sam Newfield	75			GB	15
Nada	FR/IT	1974	Claude Chabrol	134	est		GB	30
Nadine	USA	1987	Robert Benton	85			FB	45
Naked and the Dead, The	USA	1958	Raoul Walsh	131	bw/sc/		GB	15
Naked Civil Servant, The	GB	1981	Jack Gold	82			GB	50
Naked Earth	GB	1957	Vincent Sherman	96	std		FB	15
Naked Face, The	USA	1984	Bryan Forbes	103			FB	45
Naked Gun 2 1/2: The Smell of Fear, The	USA	1991	David Zucker	81		UIP	FB	70
Naked Gun, The	USA	1988	David Zucker	85			FB	55
Naked Jungle, The	USA	1953	Byron Haskin	94			FB	15
Naked Kiss, The	USA	1964	Samuel Fuller	90			BFI	55
Naked Spaces	W.AFR/USA	1985	Trinh T. Minh-Ha	135			CIRC	50
Naked Spur, The	USA	1952	Anthony Mann	91	bw		FB	14
Naked Street, The	USA	1955	Maxwell Shane	85			GB	20
Naked Truth, The	GB	1957	Mario Zampi	92			FB	15
Namu, the Killer Whale	USA	1966	Laslo Benedek	76			FB	18
Nana	IT	1982	Dan Wolman	100			FB	38
Nanny, The	GB	1965	Seth Holt	93			FB	15
Nanook of the North	USA	1922	Robert Flaherty	64			GB	15
Napoleon and Samantha	USA	1972	Bernard McEveety	91			FB	27
Narrow Margin, The	USA	1950	Richard Fleischer	70			GB	20
Narrow Margin	USA	1991	Peter Hyams	87	ws	GU	GU	80
Nashville	USA	1975	Robert Altman	161	sc		FB	38
Nashville Sound. The	USA	1970	Robert Elfstrom/ David Hoffman	85		GB	GB	22
National Health, The	GB	1973	Jack Gold	98			FB	18
National Lampoon's Animal House, The	USA	1978	John Landis	109			FB	38
National Lampoon's Class Reunion	USA	1982	Michael Miller	85			FB	38
National Lampoon's European Vacation	USA	1985	Amy Heckerling	99			FB	45
National Lampoon's Vacation	USA	1983	Harold Ramis	98			FB	45
National Velvet	USA	1945	Clarence Brown	123			FB	22
Natural, The	USA	1984	Barry Levinson	122			FB	50
Nature of the Beast, The	GB	1988	Franco Rosso	96	GB		GB	45
Naughty Nineties	USA	1945	Jean Yarbrough	75			FB	15
Navajo	USA	1951	Norman Foster	70			BFI	20
Navajo Run	USA	1963	Johnny Seven	79			FB	15
Navigator	AUSTR	1988	Vincent Ward	91			GB	70
Navy Comes Through, The	USA	1942	Edward Sutherland	81			GB	15
Navy Seals	USA	1990	Lewis Teague	113		R	FB	55
Ned Kelly	GB	1970	Tony Richardson	103			FB	18
Neither the Sea nor the Sand	GB	1972	Fred Burnley	94			GB	20
Neptune Factor, The	CAN	1973	Daniel Petrie	98	sc		FB	18
Nest of Gentlefolk, A	USSR	1969	Andrei Mikhalkov-Konchalovsky	106	est		GB	30
Nest, The (see Nido, El)								
Network	USA	1976	Sidney Lumet	121			FB	38
Nevada Smith	USA	1966	Henry Hathaway	120	std		FB	18
Never a Dull Moment	USA	1967	Jerry Paris	100			FB	27
Never a Dull Moment	USA	1950	George Marshall	89			GB	15
Never Cry Wolf	USA	1983	Carroll Ballard	105			FB	38
Never Give an Inch	USA	1971	Paul Newman	110	sc/std		FB	18
Never Let Go	GB	1960	John Guillermin	91			FB	15
Never Mind the Quality Feel the Width	GB	1972	Ronnie Baxter	88			FB	18
Never Put It in Writing	GB	1963	Andrew Stone	90			FB	15
Never So Few	USA	1959	John Sturges	124	sc/std		FB	18
Never Steal Anything Small	USA	1958	Charles Lederer	94	std		FB	18
Never too Late	USA	1965	Bud Yorkin	104	std		FB	18
Neverending Story II: The Next Chapter, The	GER	1989	George Miller	89		W	FB	60
Neverending Story, The	W.GER	1984	Wolfgang Petersen	94			FB	45
New Land, The	SWE	1973	Jan Troell	161	dub		FB	27

	COUNTRY OF PRODUCTION	YEAR	DIRECTOR	RUNNING TIME	VERSION	35mm	16mm	16mm RENTAL FEE
New Leaf, A	USA	1970	Elaine May	102			FB	18
New Adventures of Highwayman Hotzenplotz	W.GER	1971	Gustav Ehmck	103	est		GFL	0
New Face in Hell	USA	1967	John Guillermin	106	std		FB	18
New Faces of 1937	USA	1937	Leigh Jason	102			GB	15
New Heroes Will Arise	CZ	1951	Jiri Weiss	100	est		ETV	10
New Jack City	USA	1991	Mario Van Peebles	100		W	FB	70
New Kind of Love, A	USA	1962	Melville Shavelson	109	col		FB	18
					bw		FB	15
New Year Sacrifice	CHI	1957	Sang Hu	85	est		GB	25
New York New York	USA	1977	Martin Scorsese	137			FB	38
New York Stories	USA	1989	Martin Scorsese/ Francis Ford Coppola/ Woody Allen	125		W	FB	60
Newman's Law	USA	1974	Richard Heffron	99			FB	18
News Boys/Newsies	USA	1992	Kenny Ortega	122		D	FB	65
News from Home	BELG/ FR/W.GER	1976	Chantal Akerman	90			MP	51.75
Next of Kin	USA	1989	John Irvin	109		W	FB	55
Next Stop, Greenwich Village	USA	1976	Paul Mazursky	111			FB	23
Nibelungen, Die Part Two: Kriemhild's Revenge	GER	1923/4	Fritz Lang	60	sd		BFI	25
Nicholas and Alexandra	USA	1971	Franklin J. Schaffner	169	sc		FB	33
Nicholas Nickleby	GB	1947	Alberto Cavalcanti	108			FB	15
Nickel Queen	AUSTR	1971	John McCallum	90			FB	18
Nickelodeon	USA/GB	1976	Peter Bogdanovich	122			FB	25
Nico – Above the Law	USA	1988	Andrew Davis	99			FB	55
Nido, El	SP	1980	Jaime de Armiñan	97	est		GB	50
Night after Night	USA	1932	Archie Mayo	75			FB	22
Night at the Opera, A	USA	1935	Sam Wood	94		UIP	FB	14
Night Crossing	USA	1982	Delbert Mann	107			FB	38
Night Cry	USA	1926	Herman C. Raymaker	69	st		BFI	15
Night Duty	W.GER	1975	Krzyztof Zanussi/ Edward Zebrowski	64	est		GFL	0
Night Ferry	GB	1976	David Eady	60			GB	17
Night Full of Rain. A	IT/USA	1977	Lina Wertmuller	104			FB	33
Night in Casablanca, A	USA	1946	Archie Mayo	90			GB	20
Night is my Future	SWE	1947	Ingmar Bergman	90	est		GB	25
Night is Young, The	FR	1986	Leos Carax	110	est	AE	GB	60
Night Moves	USA	1975	Arthur Penn	99			FB	18
Night Must Fall	GB	1964	Karel Reisz	101			FB	15
Night of Adventure, A	USA	1944	Gordon Douglas	65			GB	20
Night of Counting the Years, The	UAR	1970	Shadi Abdelsalam	100	est		GB	30
Night of San Lorenzo, The	IT	1981	Paolo Taviani/Vittorio Taviani	107	est		GB	50
Night of the Blood Beast	USA	1958	Bernard Kowalski	63			FB	15
Night of the Eagle	GB	1961	Sidney Hayers	87			FB	15
Night of the Following Day, The	USA	1968	Hubert Cornfield	93			FB	18
Night of the Generals, The	GB/FR	1966	Anatole Litvak	147	sc/std		FB	18
Night of the Hunter, The	USA	1955	Charles Laughton	92			BFI	25
Night of the Iguana, The	USA	1964	John Huston	118			FB	16
Night of the Lepus	USA	1972	William Claxton	88			FB	16
Night of the Living Dead, The	USA	1969	George A. Romero	96			FB	40
Night on the Town	USA	1987	Chris Columbus	102			FB	45
Night Shift	USA	1982	Ron Howard	106			FB	40
Night Song	USA	1947	John Cromwell	102			GB	15
Night Sun	IT/FR/ GER	1990	Paolo Taviani/Vittorio Taviani	113	st	AE	GB	80
Night the Lights Went out in Georgia, The	USA	1981	Ronald F. Maxwell	101			GB	33
Night to Remember, A	GB	1958	Roy Ward Baker	123			FB	15
Night Waitress	USA	1936	Lew Landers	65			GB	20
Night Walker, The	USA	1964	William Castle	86	std		FB	15
Night Was Our Friend	GB	1951	Michael Anderson	65			GB	20
Night We Dropped a Clanger, The	GB	1959	Darcy Conyers	88			GB	15

	COUNTRY OF PRODUCTION	YEAR	DIRECTOR	RUNNING TIME	VERSION	35mm	16mm	16mm RENTAL FEE
Night We Got The Bird, The	GB	1960	Darcy Conyers	82			FB	15
Nightcaller	FR/IT	1975	Henri Verneuil	93	dub		FB	18
Nightcomers, The	GB	1971	Michael Winner	96			GB	28
Nighthawks	USA	1981	Bruce Malmuth	99			FB	43
Nightmare	GB	1963	Freddie Francis	82	sc/std		FB	15
Nightmare Alley	USA	1947	Edmund Goulding	111			FB	15
Nightmare on Elm Street 3: Dream Warriors, A	USA	1987	Chuck Russell	89			GB	70
Nightmare on Elm Street 4: The Dream Master, A	USA	1987	Renny Harlin	93			GB	75
Nightmares	USA	1982	Joseph Sargent	99			FB	38
Nightshade	W.GER	1971	Niklaus Schilling	96	est		GFL	0
Nightshift	GB	1981	Robina Rose	75			CIRC	35
Nightwing	NETH	1979	Arthur Hiller	105			FB	30
Nikita	FR/IT	1990	Luc Besson	117	sc st	MAY	GB	80
Nikki, Wild Dog of the North	CAN/USA	1960	Don Haldane/Jack Couffer	70			FB	35
Nine Lives of Elfego Baga	USA	1959	Norman Foster	80			FB	27
Nine to Five	USA	1980	Colin Higgins	110			FB	38
1984	GB	1984	Michael Radford	110			GB	60
1900 Part One	IT/FR/	1976	Bernardo Bertolucci	129			FB	30
Part Two	W.GER			119			FB	30
1941	USA	1979	Steven Spielberg	118	std		FB	38
Nineteen Nineteen	GB	1984	Hugh Brody	99			BFI	40
Ninety Degrees South	GB	1933	Herbert Ponting	73			BFI	15
99 River Street	USA	1953	Phil Karlson	70			GB	25
92 in the Shade	USA/GB	1975	Thomas McGuane	95			GB	22
90 Days	CAN	1985	Giles Walker	99			MP	69
Ninja III: The Domination	USA	1984	Sam Firstenberg	92			FB	35
Ninotchka	USA	1939	Ernst Lubitsch	110			FB	22
Nitwits, The	USA	1935	George Stevens	82			GB	15
No Blade of Grass	GB	1970	Cornel Wilde	96	sc/std/74		FB	18
No Deposit, No Return	USA	1976	Norman Tokar	111			FB	27
No End	POL	1984	Krzysztof Kieslowski	108	est		GB	60
No Limit	GB	1935	Monty Banks	81			FB	15
No Love for Johnnie	GB	1960	Roy Ward Baker	110	sc		FB	15
No Man's Land	USA	1987	Peter Werner	105			FB	55
No Marriage Ties	USA	1933	J. Walter Ruben	73			GB	15
No Mercy	USA	1986	Richard Pearce	108			FB	50
No Minor Vices	USA	1948	Lewis Milestone	96			GB	27
No Nukes	USA	1980	Julian Schlossberg/ Danny Goldberg/ Anthony Potenza	103			GB	48
No Other Woman	USA	1933	J. Walter Ruben	58			GB	15
No Return Ticket	CZ	1973	Dusan Klein/Miroslav Sobota	78	est		ETV	10
No Sex Please We're British	GB	1973	Cliff Owen	92			FB	18
No Trees In The Street	GB	1958	J. Lee Thompson	96			FB	15
No Way Out	USA	1987	Roger Donaldson	114			FB	55
No Way Out Only Across (see Hier Kein Ausgang Nur Übergang)								
No Way to Treat a Lady	USA	1967	Jack Smight	108			FB	18
No, My Darling Daughter	GB	1961	Ralph Thomas	96			FB	15
Nobody Runs Forever	GB/USA	1968	Ralph Thomas	101			FB	22
Nobody's Kid	USA	1921	Howard Hickman	65	st		BFI	15
Nobody's Perfect	USA	1967	Alan Rafkin	102			FB	18
Nocturne	USA	1947	Edwin L. Marin	90			GB	15
None But the Brave	USA/ JAP	1965	Frank Sinatra	105	std		FB	18
None But the Lonely Heart	USA	1945	Clifford Odets	113			GB	15
Norma Rae	USA	1979	Martin Ritt	115	sc/std		FB	33
Norman . . . Is That You?	USA	1976	George Schlatter	92			FB	38
Norte, El	USA	1983	Gregory Nava	140	est		BFI	45
North by Northwest	USA	1959	Alfred Hitchcock	136			FB	28
North Dallas Forty	USA	1979	Ted Kotcheff	119			FB	38

	COUNTRY OF PRODUCTION	YEAR	DIRECTOR	RUNNING TIME	VERSION	35mm	16mm	16mm RENTAL FEE
North Sea Hijack	GB	1979	Andrew V. McLaglen	100			FB	43
North to Alaska	USA	1960	Henry Hathaway	122	std		FB	18
Nosey Dobson	GB	1976	Michael Alexander	59			GB	17
Nosferatu	GER	1922	F.W. Murnau	63	sd	BFI	BFI	25
Nosferatu the Vampire	FR/W.GER	1979	Werner Herzog	96	96/dub	F	FB	38
Nostalgia	IT/USSR	1983	Andrei Tarkovsky	125	est	AE	GB	55
Not a Love Story	CAN	1981	Bonnie Sher Klein	69			GB	40
Not As a Stranger	USA	1955	Stanley Kramer	136			FB	15
Not Now, Comrade	GB	1976	Harold Snoad/Ray Cooney	90			FB	18
Not Now, Darling	GB	1972	Ray Cooney/David Croft	97			GB	20
Not Quite Jerusalem	GB	1984	Lewis Gilbert	114			FB	40
Not Reconciled	W.GER	1965	Jean-Marie Straub	53	est		GB	35
Not Wanted on Voyage	GB	1956	Maclean Rogers	82		GB	GB	15
Not With My Wife You Don't	USA	1966	Norman Panama	119			FB	18
Noted Eel and Pie Houses	GB	1975	David Furnham	50			CONT	20
Nothing But the Best	GB	1964	Clive Donner	116			FB	18
Nothing But the Night	GB	1972	Peter Sasdy	90			FB	18
Nothing But Trouble	USA	1991	Dan Ackroyd	93	W		FB	65
Nothing But Trouble	USA	1944	Sam Taylor	69			FB	12
Nothing in Common	USA	1986	Garry Marshall	119			FB	50
Nothing Sacred	USA	1937	William A. Wellman	85			BFI	20
Nouveaux Messieurs, Les	FR	1928	Jacques Feyder	135	st		BFI	20
November Plan, The	USA	1976	Don Medford	103			FB	27
Novembermoon	FR/W.GER	1984	Alexandra von Grote	106	GB		CN	52
Now About These Women	SWE	1964	Ingmar Bergman	80	est		GB	35
Now that the Buffalo's Gone	GB	1969	Ross Devenish	60			CONC	14.6
Now Voyager	USA	1942	Irving Rapper	117			FB	22
Now You See Him Now You Don't	USA	1972	Robert Butler	88			FB	27
Nowhere to Go	GB	1958	Seth Holt	87			FB	15
Nude Bomb, The	USA	1980	Clive Donner	94			FB	33
Nuit Américaine, La	FR/IT	1973	François Truffaut	116	dub		FB	22
Numero Deux	FR	1975	Jean-Luc Godard	89	est		MP	51.75
Nuns on the Run	GB	1990	Jonathan Lynn	92	st/dub		GB	80
Nuremberg Trials, The	W.GER	1958	Felix von Podmanitsky (prod)	80			GB	15
Nutcracker	GB	1982	Anwar Kawadri	101			FB	38
Nuts	USA	1987	Martin Ritt	116			FB	55
Nutty Professor, The	USA	1962	Jerry Lewis	112	bw	U	FB	15

Nosferatu the Vampire

O

	COUNTRY OF PRODUCTION	YEAR	DIRECTOR	RUNNING TIME	VERSION	35mm	16mm	16mm RENTAL FEE
O Lucky Man!	GB	1973	Lindsay Anderson	166			FB	22
O'Rourke of the Royal Mounted	USA	1954	Raoul Walsh	87	bw		FB	15
O.K...La Liberté	CAN	1973	Marcel Carrière	112	fr dia		CHC	0
O.S.S.	USA	1946	Irving Pichel	107			FB	15
Oberwald Mystery, The	IT/W.GER	1980	Michelangelo Antonioni	127	est	AE	GB	50
Objective Burma!	USA	1945	Raoul Walsh	142	111		FB	22
Obliging Young Lady	USA	1941	Richard Wallace	80			GB	15
Oblomov	USSR	1979	Nikita Mikhalkov	140	est		GB	45
Oblong Box, The	GB	1969	Gordon Hessler	91			FB	18
Obsession	USA	1976	Brian De Palma	98	sc/std		FB	22
Obsession	GB	1948	Edward Dmytryk	98			GB	30
Ocean's Eleven	USA	1960	Lewis Milestone	127	sc/std		FB	18
October	USSR	1928	Sergei Eisenstein/Grigori Alexandrov	140	st/sd	CONT	BFI/GB	25
October Days	USSR	1958	Sergei Vasiliev	110	est		ETV	10
Octopussy	GB	1983	John Glen	130			FB	53
Odd Angry Shot, The	AUSTR	1979	Tom Jeffrey	92			GB	35
Odd Man Out	GB	1947	Carol Reed	117		R	FB	15
Odds and Evens	IT	1978	Sergio Corbucci	116	dub		FB	22
Ode to Billy Joe	USA	1976	Max Baer	106			FB	18
Odessa File, The	GB/W.GER	1974	Ronald Neame	129	sc/std		FB	27
Odette	GB	1950	Herbert Wilcox	117			FB	15
Oedipus Rex	IT	1967	Pier Paolo Pasolini	104	est		GB	30
Oedipus the King	GB	1967	Philip Saville	97			FB	18
Of Human Bondage	GB	1963	Ken Hughes	99			FB	15
Of Mice and Men	USA	1940	Lewis Milestone	107			GB	25
Offbeat	GB	1960	Cliff Owen	94			GB	20
Offence, The	GB	1972	Sidney Lumet	112			FB	18
Officer and a Gentleman, An	USA	1981	Taylor Hackford	124			FB	43
Officers	USSR	1971	Vladimir Rogovoi	93	est		ETV	10
Official Version, The	ARG	1985	Luis Puenzo	114	est		GB	60
Oh God!	USA	1977	Carl Reiner	104			FB	33
Oh Heavenly Dog	USA	1980	Joe Camp	102			FB	35
Oh Mother! (see Mensch Mutter)								
Oh! What a Lovely War	GB	1969	Richard Attenborough	144	sc/std		FB	27
Oh, Mr. Porter!	GB	1937	Marcel Varnel	85			FB	15
Ohayo	JAP	1959	Yasujiro Ozu	94	est		GB	45
Oklahoma Crude	USA	1973	Stanley Kramer	111	std		FB	18
Oklahoma Kid	USA	1939	Lloyd Bacon	81			FB	22
Oklahoma!	USA	1955	Fred Zinnemann	143	std		GB	48
Old Fashioned Way, The	USA	1934	William Beaudine	70			FB	15
Old Gringo	USA	1989	Luis Puenzo	120		C	FB	55
Old Man Rhythm	USA	1935	Edward Ludwig	82			GB	15
Old Mother Riley Headmistress	GB	1950	John Harlow	76			GB	15
Old Mother Riley Meets the Vampire	GB	1952	John Gilling	75			GB	15
Old Mother Riley's Jungle Treasure	GB	1951	Maclean Rogers	75		GB	GB	15
Old Mother Riley's New Venture	GB	1949	John Harlow	80			GB	15
Old New World, The	E.GER	1977	Andrew Thorndike	105			ETV	12
Old Yeller	USA	1947	Robert Stevenson	83			FB	30
Oliver Twist	GB	1948	David Lean	116			FB	15
Oliver!	GB	1968	Carol Reed	145	sc/std		FB	27
Oliver's Story	USA	1978	John Korty	91			FB	33
Olivia	FR	1951	Jacqueline Audry	96	est/bw		CIRC	35
Olympia Olympia	W.GER	1972	Olympic Games History	97	eng		GFL	0
Olympics '40	POL	1980	Andrzej Kotkowski	100			FOP	0
Omaha Trail, The	USA	1942	Edward Buzzell	62			FB	15
Omar Khayam	USA	1956	William Dieterle	99	col/std		FB	18
					bw/std		FB	15
Omega Man, The	USA	1971	Boris Sagal	98	sc/std		FB	18

	COUNTRY OF PRODUCTION	YEAR	DIRECTOR	RUNNING TIME	VERSION	35mm	16mm	16mm RENTAL FEE
Omen II (see Damien Omen II)								
Omen, The	USA	1976	Richard Donner	111	sc		FB	40
On a Clear Day You Can See Forever	USA	1970	Vincente Minnelli	130	sc/std		FB	22
On a Paving Stone Mounted	GB	1978	Thaddeus O'Sullivan	96			BFI	30
On Again – Off Again	USA	1937	Edward Cline	68			GB	15
On an Island With You	USA	1948	Richard Thorpe	107	bw		FB	15
On Any Sunday	USA	1971	Bruce Brown	86			GB	22
On Borrowed Time	W.GER	1971	Manfred Bieler	86	est		GFL	0
On Dangerous Ground	USA	1951	Nicholas Ray	81			BFI	25
On Giant's Shoulders	GB	1979	Anthony Simmons	92			CONC	30
On Golden Pond	USA	1981	Mark Rydell	109			FB	48
On Her Majesty's Secret Service	GB	1969	Peter Hunt	133	sc/std		FB	33
On l'Appelle France	FR	1967	Serge Leroy	75			FI	2.5
On ne Badine pas Avec l'Amour	FR	1961	Jean Desailly	87	fr dia		GB	25
On Sacred Ground	AUSTR	1982	Film Australia	65			MP	35
On the Air: Workers' Playtime	GB	1983	Frank Abbott	55			BFI	25
On the Beat	GB	1962	Robert Asher	106			FB	15
On the Black Hill	GB	1987	Andrew Grieve	116		BFI	BFI	60
					est /deaf			25
On the Bowery	USA	1955	Lionel Rogosin	65			GB	40
On the Buses	GB	1971	Harry Booth	88			FB	18
On The Run	GB	1969	Pat Jackson	57			GB	17
On the Way to Berlin	USSR	1970		76	est		ETV	6
On Trial: Criminal Justice	USA	1970	Paul Galan	90			CONC	26.40
Once a Thief	USA/FR	1965	Ralph Nelson	106	sc/std		FB	15
Once More with Feeling!	USA	1959	Stanley Donen	92			FB	18
Once Upon a Family	USA	1980	Richard Michaels	120			FB	33
Once Upon a Honeymoon	USA	1942	Leo McCarey	115			GB	15
Once Upon a Horse	USA	1958	Hal Kanter	85	sc/std		FB	15
Once Upon a Time in America	USA	1983	Sergio Leone	140			FB	55
One and Only, The	USA	1977	Carl Reiner	98			FB	38
One Born Every Minute	USA	1967	Irvin Kershner	104	sc/std		FB	18
One Crowded Night	USA	1940	Irving Reis	68			GB	15
One Day in the Life of Ivan Denisovich	GB/NOR	1971	Casper Wrede	100			GB	27
One Deadly Summer	FR	1983	Jean Becker	130	est		FB	70
One from the Heart	USA	1982	Francis Ford Coppola	101			BFI	50
One Good Turn	GB	1954	John Paddy Carstairs	90			FB	15
One Hour to Doomsday	USA	1970	Irwin Allen	93			FB	18
One Hour to Zero	GB	1976	Jeremy Summers	55			GB	17
One is a Lonely Number	USA	1972	Mel Stuart	97			FB	27
One Little Indian	USA	1973	Bernard McEveety	90			FB	27
One Magic Christmas	CAN	1985	Phillip Borsos	85			FB	40
One Man	CAN	1977	Robin Spry	87			CHC	0
One Man's China Part One	GB	1972	Felix Greene	75			GB	30
Part Two				100			GB	30
One Man's War	FR/W.GER	1981	Edgardo Cozarinsky	106	est		GB	50
One Man's Way	USA	1963	Denis Sanders	106			CTVC	12
One Million Years B.C.	GB	1966	Don Chaffey	100			FB	18
One Minute to Zero	USA	1951	Tay Garnett	105			GB	15
One More Chance	USA		Sam Firstenberg	86			FB	38
One More Train to Rob	USA	1971	Andrew V. McLaglen	108			FB	18
One Night of Love	USA	1934	Victor Schertzinger	75			FB	10
One of Our Dinosaurs Is Missing	USA	1975	Robert Stevenson	94			FB	33
One Of Our Spies Is Missing	USA	1966	E. Darrell Hallenbeck	91			FB	18
One on One	USA	1977	Lamont Johnson	97			FB	22
One or the Other	W.GER	1974	Wolfgang Petersen	109	est		GFL	0
One Plus One (see Sympathy for the Devil)								
One Potato, Two Potato	USA	1964	Larry Peerce	79			FB	15

O	COUNTRY OF PRODUCTION	YEAR	DIRECTOR	RUNNING TIME	VERSION	35mm	16mm	16mm RENTAL FEE
One Spy Too Many	USA	1965	Joseph Sargent	101			FB	18
One That Got Away, The	GB	1957	Roy Ward Baker	115			FB	15
One Way or Another	CB	1977	Sara Gómez	79	bw/ eng nar		MP	57.50
One Way Pendulum	GB	1964	Peter Yates	84			FB	15
One-Armed Boxer	HK	1972	Wang Yu	79	dub		GB	18
One-Piece Bathing Suit, The	USA	1952	Mervyn LeRoy	89	bw		FB	22
Onion Field, The	USA	1979	Harold Becker	126			GB	38
Only Angels Have Wings	USA	1939	Howard Hawks	121		C	FB	15
Only Game in Town, The	USA	1968	George Stevens	113			FB	18
Only the Valiant	USA	1950	Gordon Douglas	105			GB	18
Only When I Larf	GB	1968	Basil Dearden	103			FB	18
Only Yesterday	USA	1933	John M. Stahl	105			BFI	25
Ooh! You Are Awful	GB	1972	Cliff Owen	97			FB	22
Open Season	SP/ SWITZ	1974	Peter Collinson	104	std		FB	18
Operation Amsterdam	GB	1959	Michael McCarthy	100			FB	15
Operation Cupid	GB	1959	Charles Saunders	67			GB	15
Operation Daybreak	USA	1975	Lewis Gilbert	105			FB	22
Operation Heartbeat	USA	1973	Boris Sagal	79			FB	33
Operation Kid Brother	IT	1967	Alberto De Martino	105	sc/dub		FB	18
Operation Third Form	GB	1966	David Eady	58			GB	12
Operation Undercover	USA	1974	Milton Katselas	112			FB	18
Opfergang (see Great Sacrifice, The)								
Opium War, The	CHI	1959	Cheng Chun-Li/ Chen Fan	108	est		GB	15
Opposite Sex, The	USA	1956	David Miller	116	sc		FB	18
Optimists of Nine Elms, The	GB	1973	Anthony Simmons	110			GB	22
Orchestra Rehearsal	IT/FR/ W.GER	1978	Federico Fellini	70	est		GB	30
Orders	CAN	1975	Michel Brault	108	est		GB	30
Orders from Above	GB	1975	Robert Vas	89			CONC	16.40
Ordinary People	USA	1980	Robert Redford	125			FB	43
Oregon Trail	USA	1959	Gene Fowler Jr	86	sc/std		FB	18
Organisation, The	USA	1971	Don Medford	107			FB	18
Orphans of the Storm	USA	1922	D.W. Griffith	125	sd	BFI	BFI	25
Orphée	FR	1950	Jean Cocteau	95	est	BFI	GB	35
Oscar	USA	1991	John Landis	106		W	FB	65
Oscar, The	USA	1965	Russell Rouse	121			FB	18
Oskar Fischinger Programme	GER/USA	1928-47		52	bw/col		BFI	15
Ossessione	IT	1942	Luchino Visconti	140	est	BFI	BFI	40
Osterman Weekend, The	USA	1983	Sam Peckinpah	105			FB	45
Othello	GER	1922	Dimitri Buchowetzki	80	st/est		BFI	15
Othello	MOR	1950	Orson Welles	90			BFI	25
Othello	GB	1965	Stuart Burge	170	std		GB	30
Other People's Money	USA	1991	Norman Jewison	101		W	FB	70
Other Side of Midnight, The	USA	1977	Charles Jarrott	166	std		FB	38
Other Side of the Underneath, The	GB	1972	Jane Arden	135			GB	30
Othon (see Eyes Do Not Want to Close at All Times)								
Otley	GB	1968	Dick Clement	98			FB	18
Our Betters	USA	1933	George Cukor	72			GB	15
Our Business is Fun	GB	1975	Michael Whyte	60			AC	16
Our Girl Friday	GB	1953	Noel Langley	75		GB	GB	15
Our Man Flint	USA	1965	Daniel Mann	108	sc		FB	18
Our Man in Havana	GB	1959	Carol Reed	107	sc/std		FB	15
Our Man in Marrakesh	GB	1966	Don Sharp	94			FB	18
Our Miss Fred	GB	1972	Bob Kellett	96			FB	18
Our Mother's House	GB	1967	Jack Clayton	105			FB	18
Our Story	FR	1974	Bertrand Blier	111	est	BFI	BFI	55
Out of Africa	USA	1985	Sydney Pollack	161			FB	60
Out of an Old Man's Head	SWE	1968	Tage Danielsson	85			GB	30

	COUNTRY OF PRODUCTION	YEAR	DIRECTOR	RUNNING TIME	VERSION	35mm	16mm	16mm RENTAL FEE
Out Of Darkness	GB	1985	John Krish	68			FB	20
Out of Order	GB	1987	Jonnie Turpie	98			BFI	50
Out of Reach of the Devil	CZ	1958	Zdenek Podskalsky	86	est		ETV	10
Out of Season	GB	1975	Alan Bridges	90			FB	18
Out of the Clouds	GB	1954	Basil Dearden/ Michael Relph	88			GB	20
Out of the Past	USA	1947	Jacques Tourneur	96			BFI	25
Out-of-Towners, The	USA	1969	Arthur Hiller	97			FB	18
Outcasts of Poker Flat, The	USA	1936	Christy Cabanne	68			GB	15
Outfit, The	USA	1973	John Flynn	103			FB	28
Outland	GB	1981	Peter Hyams	109	sc		FB	48
Outlaw Blues	USA	1977	Richard Heffron	100			FB	33
Outlaw Josey Wales, The	USA	1976	Clint Eastwood	134	sc/std		FB	38
Outlaw, The	USA	1946	Howard Hughes	120			GB	18
Outrage, The	USA	1964	Martin Ritt	96	std		FB	16
Outrageous Fortune	USA	1987	Arthur Hiller	99			FB	50
Outside In	GB/W.GER	1981	Steve Dwoskin	100			MP	45
Outside Man, The	FR/IT	1972	Jacques Deray	104	std		FB	18
Outside-In	GB	1973	Jonathan Lewis	50			AC	20
Outsider, The	USA	1961	Delbert Mann	93	108		FB	15
Outsiders, The	IND	1977	Mrinal Sen	115	est		GB	30
Outsiders, The	USA	1983	Francis Ford Coppola	91	sc		FB	40
Outskirts	USSR	1933	Boris Barnet	96	est		BFI	30
Over the Brooklyn Bridge	USA	1983	Menahem Golan	106			FB	38
Over the Top	USA	1986	Menahem Golan	93			FB	45
Overboard	USA	1987	Garry Marshall	112			FB	55
Overlanders, The	GB	1946	Harry Watt	89			FB	15
Overlord	GB	1975	Stuart Cooper	83			FB	17
Owl and the Pussycat, The	USA	1970	Herbert Ross	97	sc		FB	22

Our Man in Havana

p

	COUNTRY OF PRODUCTION	YEAR	DIRECTOR	RUNNING TIME	VERSION	35mm	16mm	16mm RENTAL FEE
P4W: Prison for Women	CAN	1981	Janis Cole/Holly Dale	81			GB	25
Pablo Picasso: The Legacy of a Genius	USA	1982	Michael Blackwood	90			AC	19
Pace that Thrills, The	USA	1952	Leon Barsha	64			GB	20
Pacific Heights	USA	1990	John Schlesinger	110		F	FB	70
Pack up your Troubles	USA	1932	George Marshall/Ray McCarey	67			GB	15
Pack, The	USA	1977	Robert Clouse	98			FB	18
Pad (And How To Use It), The	USA	1966	Brian G. Hutton	86			FB	15
Padre Padrone	IT	1980	Paolo Taviani/ Vittorio Taviani	114	st	AE	GB	55
Paganini Strikes Again	GB	1973	Gerry O'Hara	59			GB	17
Page of Madness, A	JAP	1926	Teinosuke Kinugasa	60	sd		MP	30
							BFI	20
Paint Your Wagon	USA	1969	Joshua Logan	127	std/sc		FB	33
Painted Boats	GB	1945	Charles Crichton	65			FB	15
Painted Desert, The	USA	1938	David Howard	83			GB	15
Painted Hills	USA	1951	Harold F. Kress	67	bw/87		FB	15
Painters Painting	USA	1972	Emile de Antonio	116			GB	55
Pair of Briefs, A	GB	1961	Ralph Thomas	90			FB	15
Paisa	IT	1946	Roberto Rossellini	117	est		BFI	25
Pajama Game	USA	1957	George Abbott/Stanley Donen	101			FB	18
Pal Joey	USA	1957	George Sidney	107	std/col		FB	18
Palaces of a Queen	GB	1966	Michael Ingrams	80			FB	18
Pale Rider	USA	1985	Clint Eastwood	115			FB	50
Paleface	USA	1948	Norman Z. Macleod	91	bw		FB	15
Palm Beach Story, The	USA	1942	Preston Sturges	84		C	FB	15
Pan Americana	USA	1945	John H. Auer	84			GB	15
Panama Flo	USA	1932	Ralph Murphy	73			GB	15
Panama Lady	USA	1939	Jack Hively	65			GB	15
Pandora's Box	GER	1928	G.W. Pabst	110	st/sd	CONT	GB	25
Panic in Needle Park	USA	1971	Jerry Schatzberg	109			FB	18
Panic in Year Zero!	USA	1962	Ray Milland	92	sc		FB	15
Paolozzi Story, The	W.GER	1980	Al Lauder	120			GB	40
Paper Chase, The	USA	1973	James Bridges	112	sc/std		FB	18
Paper Moon	USA	1973	Peter Bogdanovich	103			FB	27
Paracelsus	GER	1943	G.W. Pabst	104	est		BFI	25
Parachute Battalion	USA	1941	Leslie Goodwins	75			GB	15
Parade	FR	1974	Jacques Tati	85	est		BFI	35
Paradine Case, The	USA	1947	Alfred Hitchcock	110		GB	GB	25
Paradis des Riches, Le	FR	1978	Paul Barge	90	est		GB	30
Paradise	USA	1991	Mary A. Donoghue	111		T	FB	65
Paradise Alley	USA	1978	Sylvester Stallone	109			FB	33
Paradise Now	USA	1970	Sheldon Rochlin	90			GB	
Parallax View, The	USA	1974	Alan J. Pakula	102	std		FB	18
Paranoiac	GB	1962	Freddie Francis	80	std		FB	15
Pardners	USA	1956	Norman Taurog	88	bw/std		FB	15
Parent Trap, The	USA	1961	David Swift	129			FB	27
Paris 1900	FR	1947	Nicole Vedres	93			GB	20
Paris by Night	GB	1989	David Hare	103		FFC	GB	75
Paris Vu Par...	FR	1964	Jean Douchet/Jean Rouch/Jean-Daniel Pollet/ Eric Rohmer/Jean-Luc Godard/Claude Chabrol	98	est		APO	35
Paris When it Sizzles	USA	1964	Richard Quine	111	bw/std		FB	18
Paris, Texas	FR/ W.GER	1984	Wim Wenders	114			GB	70
Park Row	USA	1952	Samuel Fuller	83			BFI	25
Parting Glances	USA	1985	Bill Sherwood	90			GB	60
Partners	USA	1982	James Burrows	92			FB	43
Party and the Guests, The	CZ	1966	Jan Nemec	70	est		GB	25
Party, The	USA	1968	Blake Edwards	99	sc		FB	18
Party Girl	USA	1958	Nicholas Ray	98	sc/std		FB	18
Party Party	GB	1983	Terry Winsor	98			FB	40

	COUNTRY OF PRODUCTION	YEAR	DIRECTOR	RUNNING TIME	VERSION	35mm	16mm	16mm RENTAL FEE
Party's Over, The	GB	1963	Guy Hamilton	95			GB	25
Pas de Deux	GB/INDIA	1981	Prakash Jha	50			CONT	20
Pascali's Island	GB	1988	James Dearden	104			GB	80
Passage Through: A Ritual	USA	1990	Stan Brakhage	50			LFMC	42.50
Passage to India, A	GB	1984	David Lean	163			FB	75
Passage to Marseille	USA	1944	Michael Curtiz	109			FB	22
Passage, The	GB	1978	J. Lee Thompson	98	sc/std		GB	43
Passenger	POL	1963	Andrzej Munk/Witold Lesiewicz	62	sc/est	GB	GB	20
Passion	FR/SWITZ	1982	Jean-Luc Godard	88	est	AE	GB	50
Passion of Joan of Arc, The	FR	1928	Carl Dreyer	82	est	CONT	GB	50
Passion of Remembrance, The	GB	1986	Maureen Blackwood/Isaac Julien	82			SAN	55
Passion, A	SWE	1969	Ingmar Bergman	100	est		FB	22
Passionates, The	W.GER	1982	Thomas Koerfer	111	est		GFL	0
Passport to Destiny	USA	1944	Ray McCarey	64			GB	15
Password is Courage, The	GB	1962	Andrew Stone	116			FB	15
Pat and Mike	USA	1952	George Cukor	95			FB	22
Pat Garrett & Billy the Kid	USA	1973	Sam Peckinpah	106	sc/std		FB	27
Patch of Blue, A	USA	1965	Guy Green	105			FB	15
Paternity	USA	1981	David Steinberg	93			FB	43
Pather Panchali	INDIA	1955	Satyajit Ray	115	est	CONT	GB	30
Pathfinder	FIN	1988	Nils Gaup	86	eng/nar	GU	GU	80
Paths of Glory	USA	1957	Stanley Kubrick	87	UA		BFI	25
Patrick	AUSTR	1978	Richard Franklin	110			GB	33
Patriot Game, The	FR	1978	Arthur MacCaig	93			MP	35
Patriot Games	USA	1992	Phillip Noyce	116		UIP	FB	75
Patriot, The	W.GER	1979	Alexander Kluge	121	est		MP	50
Patton: Lust for Glory	USA	1969	Franklin J. Schaffner	170	sc		FB	30
Patu	NZ	1983	Merata Mita	110			GB	30
Paul Jacobs and the Nuclear Gang	USA	1979	Jack Willis/Saul Landau	60			CONC	13
Paule Paulander	W.GER	1975	Reinhard Hauff	94	est		GFL	0
Pauline at the Beach	FR	1982	Eric Rohmer	95	est		FB	60
Pavel Korchagin	USSR		Alexander Alov/ Vladimir Naumov	95			ETV	10
Payroll	GB	1961	Sidney Hayers	105			FB	15
Peach O' Reno	USA	1932	William A. Seiter	70			GB	15
Pearl in the Crown	POL	1972	Kazimierz Kutz	110	est		FOP	0
Peasants Part One: Boryna								
Part Two: Jagna	POL			90	dub		FOP	0
Pee-Wee's Big Adventure	USA	1985	Tim Burton	91			GB	50
Peeper	USA	1975	Peter Hyams	87	std		FB	18
Peeping Tom	GB	1960	Michael Powell	101			BFI	50
Peggy Sue Got Married	USA	1986	Francis Ford Coppola	103			FB	50
Peking Medallion, The	W.GER/FR	1966	James Hill	90	sc/std		FB	18
Pelle the Conqueror	DEN/SWE	1987	Bille August	150	est	CZ	GB	60
Penal Colony, The	CHILE	1971	Raúl Ruiz	68	est		BFI	30
Pendulum	USA	1968	George Schaefer	102			FB	18
Penelope	USA	1966	Arthur Hiller	98	sc		FB	18
Penguin Pool Murder, The	USA	1932	George Archainbaud	70			GB	15
Pennies from Heaven	USA	1981	Herbert Ross	107			FB	38
People Next Door, The	USA	1968	David Greene	79			CONC	15.20
People of Ireland	GB	1973	Cinema Action	105			CA	20
People on Sunday (see Menschen am Sonntag)								
People on Wheels	CZ	1966	Martin Fric	87	est		ETV	10
People Organised, The	USA/MOZ	1976	Robert Van Lierop	67	eng		MP	22
People Under the Stairs, The	USA	1992	Phillip Noyce	116		UIP	FB	70
Peppermint Frappé	SP	1967	Carlos Saura	93	est		BFI	25
Peppermint Freedom	W.GER	1983	Marianne Rosenbaum	100	est		MP	50
Percy	GB	1971	Ralph Thomas	103			FB	18
Percy's Progress	GB	1974	Ralph Thomas	101			FB	18

Title	COUNTRY OF PRODUCTION	YEAR	DIRECTOR	RUNNING TIME	VERSION	35mm	16mm	16mm RENTAL FEE
Peregrine Hunters, The	GB	1978	Cecil Petty	56			GB	17
Perfect	USA	1985	James Bridges	120			FB	45
Perfect Couple, A	USA	1979	Robert Altman	112			FB	27
Perfect Friday	GB	1970	Peter Hall	95			GB	18
Perfect Strangers	GB	1945	Alexander Korda	102			FB	15
Perils of Pauline	USA	1947	George Marshall	94	bw		FB	15
Period of Adjustment	USA	1962	George Roy Hill	110			FB	15
Permission to Kill	USA/ AUST	1975	Cyril Frankel	96	sc/std		FB	18
Perri	USA	1957	N. Paul Kenworthy/Ralph Wright	74			FB	22
Personal History of the Australian Surf, A	AUSTR	1981	Michael Blakemore	52		CONT	GB	20
Pete 'n' Tillie	USA	1972	Martin Ritt	101	sc/std		FB	18
Pete's Dragon	USA	1977	Don Chaffey	127			FB	38
Peter and Pavla	CZ	1963	Milos Forman	85	est		GB	25
Peter Ibbetson	USA	1935	Henry Hathaway	85			BFI	25
Peter the Great Part I	USSR	1937	Vladimir Petrov	98	est		GB	20
Peter's Friends	GB	1992	Kenneth Branagh	102		ENT	FB	TBA
Petersen	AUSTR	1974	Tim Burstall	107			FB	22
Petit Soldat, Le	FR	1960	Jean-Luc Godard	88	est		GB	45
Petrified Forest, The	USA	1936	Archie Mayo	92			FB	22
Petticoat Larceny	USA	1943	Ben Holmes	61			GB	15
Petticoat Pirates	GB	1961	David Macdonald/ Jeremy Summers	87	std		FB	18
Peyton Place	USA	1957	Mark Robson	155	std		FB	18
Phantasm	USA	1978	Don Coscarelli	96			GB	38
Phantom Carriage, The	SWE	1920	Victor Sjöström	83	st/est		GB	20
Phantom from 10,000 Leagues, The	USA	1955	Dan Milner	81			FB	15
Phantom Lady	USA	1944	Robert Siodmak	87			BFI	25
Phantom of 42nd Street	USA	1945	Albert Herman	60			GB	25
Phantom of Crestwood, The	USA	1932	J. Walter Ruben	77			GB	15
Phantom of the Opera	USA	1943	Arthur Lubin	92			FB	18
Phantom of the Opera, The	USA	1923	Rupert Julian	75	sd		BFI	25
Phantom of the Paradise	USA	1974	Brian De Palma	91			FB	25
Phantom Planet, The	USA	1961	William Marshall	82			FB	15
Phantom Tollbooth, The	USA	1969	Chuck Jones/Abe Levitow	90			FB	18
Phar Lap Heart of a Nation	AUSTR	1982	Simon Wincer	107			FB	45
Phase IV	GB	1973	Saul Bass	84			FB	18
Philosopher's Stone, The	INDIA	1958	Satyajit Ray	90	est		GB	25
Physical Evidence	USA	1989	Michael Crichton	99		R	FB	55
Piccadilly Third Stop	GB	1960	Wolf Rilla	90			GB	15
Pickwick Papers, The	GB	1952	Noel Langley	109		GB	GB	18
Picnic at Hanging Rock	AUSTR	1975	Peter Weir	115			GB	35
Pictorial Documentary	W.GER		German Silent Cinema	125			GFL	0
Picture of Dorian Gray, The	USA	1945	Albert Lewin	111			FB	22
Picture Show Man, The	AUSTR	1977	John Power	99			GB	35
Pictures of the Lost World	W.GER	1974	Wyborny Klaus	50			LFMC	42.5
Picturing Derry	GB	1985	Dave Fox	52			AC	20
Piece of the Action, A	USA	1977	Sidney Poitier	135			FB	22
Pied Piper	CZECH/ W.GER	1985	Jiri Barta	57		BFI	BFI	30
Pierrot le Fou	FR	1965	Jean-Luc Godard	110	est	ELEC	GB	60
Pigs	EIRE	1984	Cathal Black	79			RITZY	45
Pillars of Society	GER	1935	Douglas Sirk	81	est		BFI	25
Pillow to Post	USA	1945	Vincent Sherman	92			FB	15
Pineapple	FR	1983	Amos Gitai	73			BFI	30
Ping Pong	GB	1986	Po Chih Leong	100			GB	50
Pink Floyd The Wall	GB	1982	Alan Parker	95			FB	38
Pink Jungle, The	USA	1968	Delbert Mann	93	std		FB	18
Pink Panther	USA	1963	Blake Edwards	89	sc/std		FB	27
Pink Panther Strikes Again, The	GB	1976	Blake Edwards	103	sc/std		FB	43

	COUNTRY OF PRODUCTION	YEAR	DIRECTOR	RUNNING TIME	VERSION	35mm	16mm	16mm RENTAL FEE
Pink String and Sealing Wax	GB	1949	Robert Hamer	90			FB	15
Pioneer Builders	USA	1932	William A. Wellman	80			GB	15
Piotr Pervyi (see Peter the Great Part I)								
Piranha	USA	1978	Joe Dante	94			FB	33
Piranha II Flying Killers	HOLL	1981	James Cameron	95	dub		FB	28
Pirate and the Slave Girl, The	IT	1959	Piero Pierotti	87			GB	18
Pirate Movie, The	AUSTR	1982	Ken Annakin	105			FB	30
Pirate, The	USA	1948	Vincente Minnelli	102			FB	32
Pirates	FR	1986	Roman Polanski	124			FB	45
Pirates of Penzance	GB	1982	Wilford Leach	112			FB	38
Pirosmani	USSR	1971	Georgy Shengelaya	85	est		GB	40
Pistol Harvest	USA	1951	Lesley Selander	60			GB	15
Pistol, The	SWE	1973	Jiri Tirl	84	est		GB	20
Pistolero of Red River, The	USA	1967	Richard Thorpe	96	sc/std		FB	18
Pixote	BRAZ	1981	Hector Babenco	120	est		GB	48
Place for Lovers, A	IT/FR	1968	Vittorio De Sica	88			FB	18
Places in the Heart	USA	1984	Robert Benton	111			FB	45
Plague Dogs, The	USA	1982	Martin Rosen	103			FB	38
Plague of the Zombies, The	GB	1966	John Gilling	91	bw		FB	15
Plague on your Children, A	GB	1968	Arthur Malone (prod)	70			CONC	7
Plainsman, The	USA	1936	Cecil B. DeMille	91			FB	22
Plainsman, The	USA	1966	David Lowell Rich	81	bw		FB	15
Plan Nine from Outer Space	USA	1958	Edward D. Wood	79			GB	24
Planes, Trains and Automobiles	USA	1987	John Hughes	93			FB	50
Planet of the Apes	USA	1967	Franklin J. Schaffner	112	sc/std		FB	20
Platinum Blonde	USA	1931	Frank Capra	90			FB	15
Platoon	USA	1986	Oliver Stone	120			FB	65
Play Dirty	GB	1968	André deToth	117	sc/std		FB	33
Play for Life	CZ	1956	Jiri Weiss	100	est		ETV	15
Play Girl	USA	1941	Frank Woodruff	77			GB	15
Play It Again Sam	USA	1972	Herbert Ross	86			FB	27
Play it Cool	GB	1962	Michael Winner	91			FB	15
Play Misty for Me	USA	1971	Clint Eastwood	96	96		FB	33
Playbirds	GB	1978	Willy Roe	94			GB	22
Players	USA	1979	Anthony Harvey	120			FB	10
Playgirls and the Vampire	IT	1960	Pierre Regnoli	75	dub		GB	15
Playmates	USA	1941	David Butler	96			GB	15
Playtime	FR	1967	Jacques Tati	152	123/std		BFI	35
Plaza Suite	USA	1970	Arthur Hiller	114			FB	18
Please Believe Me	USA	1950	Norman Taurog	87			FB	18
Please Don't Eat The Daisies	USA	1960	Charles Walters	111	sc/std		FB	18
Please Sir	GB	1971	Mark Stuart	101			FB	22
Pleasure at Her Majesty's	GB	1976	Roger Graef	105			CONC	38.40
Pleasure of His Company, The	USA	1961	George Seaton	114	col/std		FB	18
					bw/std			15
Pleasure Seekers, The	USA	1964	Jean Negulesco	107	std		FB	18
Plenty	USA	1985	Fred Schepisi	124	sc		FB	50
Plot Against Harry, The	US	1970	Michael Roemer	81			GB	60
Plot Thickens, The	USA	1936	Ben Holmes	69			GB	15
Plough and the Stars, The	USA	1936	John Ford	78			GB	18
Ploughman's Lunch, The	GB	1983	Richard Eyre	104			GB	48
Plumber, The	AUSTR	1979	Peter Weir	72			GB	35
Plymouth Adventure	USA	1952	Clarence Brown	104			FB	18
Pocketful of Miracles	USA	1961	Frank Capra	137	sc		FB	18
Point Break	USA	1991	Kathryn Bigelow	120		F	FB	70
Point Blank	USA	1967	John Boorman	92	sc/std		FB	28
Point Counterpoint	GB	1979	Ann Turner	70			AC	19
Poison Pen	GB	1939	Paul L. Stein	78			FB	18

	COUNTRY OF PRODUCTION	YEAR	DIRECTOR	RUNNING TIME	VERSION	35mm	16mm	16mm RENTAL FEE
Police	FR	1985	Maurice Pialat	113	est	AE	GB	55
Police Academy	USA	1984	Hugh Wilson	96		W	FB	55
Police Academy 2: Their First Assignment	USA	1985	Jerry Paris	87		W	FB	55
Police Academy 3: Back in Training	USA	1986	Jerry Paris	84		W	FB	55
Police Academy 4: Citizens on Patrol	USA	1988	Jim Drake	90		W	FB	55
Police Academy 5: Assignment Miami Beach	USA	1987	Alan Myerson	87		W	FB	55
Police Academy 6: City Under Siege	USA	1989	Peter Bonerz	84		W	FB	55
Police Story	USA	1973	William Graham	96			FB	18
Policeman, The	IS	1971	Ephraim Kishon	88	est		GB	30
Polikushka	USSR	1919	Alexander Sanin	67	st		BFI	15
Pollyanna	USA	1960	David Swift	134			FB	27
Poltergeist	USA	1982	Tobe Hooper	114			FB	43
Poltergeist III	USA	1988	Gary A. Sherman	98			FB	55
Poltergeist II: The Other Side	USA	1986	Brian Gibson	91			FB	50
Pony Express	USA	1925	James Cruze	78	st		BFI	15
Poor Cow	GB	1967	Kenneth Loach	101			FB	18
Poor Man Luther (see Arme Mann Luther, Der)								
Pop Always Pays	USA	1940	Leslie Goodwins	67			GB	15
Pop Pirates	GB	1984	Jack Grossman	58			FB	17
Pope of Greenwich Village, The	USA	1984	Stuart Rosenberg	120			FB	35
Popeye	USA	1980	Robert Altman	97			FB	38
Popi	USA	1969	Arthur Hiller	98	113		FB	18
Porky's	CAN	1981	Bob Clark	98			FB	48
Porky's II: The Next Day	CAN	1983	Bob Clark	98			FB	40
Porky's Revenge	USA	1985	James Komack	91			FB	48
Porridge	GB	1979	Dick Clement	93			GB	38
Port of Call	SWE	1948	Ingmar Bergman	100	est		GB	35
Port of Escape	GB	1954	Tony Young	76	GB		GB	22
Port of New York	USA	1949	Laslo Benedek	82			GB	15
Portnoy's Complaint	USA	1972	Ernest Lehman	99	std		FB	22
Portrait in Black	USA	1960	Michael Gordon	113			FB	18
Portrait of Alison	GB	1955	Guy Green	88			FB	15
Portrait of Clare	GB	1950	Lance Comfort	98			GB	20
Portrait of the Artist as a Young Man	GB	1977	Joseph Strick	92			GB	35
Poseidon Adventure, The	USA	1972	Ronald Neame	117	sc/std		FB	33
Posse	USA	1975	Kirk Douglas	93			FB	27
Posse from Hell	USA	1961	Herbert Coleman	89	std		FB	18
Possessed	USA	1947	Curtis Bernhardt	108			FB	15
Possession of Joel Delaney, The	USA	1971	Waris Hussein	108			GB	18
Postcards From the Edge	USA	1991	Mike Nichols	202		C	FB	65
Postman's Knock	GB	1961	Robert Lynn	87			FB	15
Posto, Il	IT	1961	Ermannno Olmi	90	est		GB	25
Poto and Cabengo	USA	1979	Jean-Pierre Gorin	75			MP	40
Powder Town	USA	1942	Rowland V. Lee	79			GB	15
Powdersmoke Range	USA	1935	Wallace Fox	71			GB	16
Power and the Prize. The	USA	1956	Henry Koster	97	std		FB	15
Power of One	USA	1992	John G. Avildsen	125		W	FB	70
Power Play	CAN/GB	1978	Martyn Burke	102			FB	27
Power, The	USA	1967	Byron Haskin	108	std		FB	18
Prague: Zero Hour	E.GER	1965	Milos Macovec	75	est		ETV	10
Praise Marx and Pass the Ammunition	GB	1968	Maurice Hatton	90			GB	30
Pram, The	SWE	1962	Bo Widerberg	84	est		APO	35
Pravda	FR	1969	Jean-Luc Godard/Jean-Pierre Gorin	58			MP	25.40
Prayer for the Dying, A	GB	1987	Mike Hodges	108	GU		GU	80
Precinct 45 Los Angeles Police	USA	1972	Richard Fleischer	100	std		FB	18
Predator	USA	1987	John McTiernan	107			FB	50
Preservation Order	W.GER	1975	Eberhard Fechner	91	dub		GFL	0
Presidio, The	USA	1988	Peter Hyams	98			FB	55

	COUNTRY OF PRODUCTION	YEAR	DIRECTOR	RUNNING TIME	VERSION	35mm	16mm	16mm RENTAL FEE
Press for Time	GB	1966	Robert Asher	102	bw		FB	15
Pressure	GB	1974	Horace Ové	120			BFI	35
Prestige	USA	1932	Tay Garnett	71			GB	15
Presumed Innocent	USA	1990	Alan J. Pakula	127		W	FB	65
Pretty Baby	USA	1977	Louis Malle	110			FB	43
Pretty in Pink	USA	1986	Howard Deutch	97			FB	40
Pretty Maids all in a Row	USA	1971	Roger Vadim	91			FB	18
Pretty Poison	USA	1968	Noel Black	89			FB	18
Pretty Polly	GB	1967	Guy Green	102	std		FB	18
Price of a Union, The	FR	1977		70			CONC	27
Prick Up Your Ears	GB	1987	Stephen Frears	110		MF	GB	60
Pride and Prejudice	USA	1940	Robert Z. Leonard	H9			FB	15
Pride and the Passion, The	USA	1957	Stanley Kramer	132	bw/std		FB	15
Priest's Wife, The	IT/FR	1970	Dino Risi	103	dub		FB	18
Primary	USA	1960	D. A. Pennebaker	52			BFI	15
Primate	USA	1974	Frederick Wiseman	105			GB	45
Prime Cut	USA	1972	Michael Ritchie	86	sc/std		GB	18
Prime of Miss Jean Brodie, The	GB	1968	Ronald Neame	116			FB	22
Primel Kloines Maedchan Za Verleihen	W.GER	1979	Monika Teuber	86	est		GFL	0
Primrose Path	USA	1925	Harry O. Hoyt	70	St		BFI	15
Primrose Path	USA	1940	Gregory La Cava	93			GB	15
Prince and the Pauper, The	USA	1937	William Keighley	118			FB	22
Prince and the Pauper, The	GB	1962	Don Chaffey	93			FB	27
Prince of the City	USA	1981	Sidney Lumet	167			FB	45
Prince of Tides	USA	1991	Barbra Streisand	131		C	FB	70
Princes, Les	FR	1983	Tony Gatlif	105	est		GB	45
Princess Bride	USA	1987	Rob Reiner	98			GB	60
Principal Enemy, The	PERU	1974	Grupo Ukamau	100	bw/est		WFA	45
Principal, The	USA	1987	Christopher Cain	109			FB	45
Prise du Pouvoir par Louis XIV, La	FR	1966	Roberto Rossellini	100	est		GB	40
Prisoner of Second Avenue, The	USA	1975	Melvin Frank	98	std		FB	18
Prisoner of Shark Island, The	USA	1936	John Ford	94			FB	15
Prisoner of Zenda, The	USA	1952	Richard Thorpe	100			FB	26
Prisoner of Zenda, The	USA	1979	Richard Quine	109			FB	38
Prisoner, The	GB	1955	Peter Glenville	94			FB	15
Private Benjamin	USA	1980	Howard Zieff	110			FB	43
Private Enterprise, A	GB	1974	Peter Smith	78			BFI	30
Private Function, A	GB	1984	Malcolm Mowbray	94			GB/BFI	45
Private Information	GB	1952	Fergus McDonell	65			GB	25
Private Life	USSR	1982	Yuli Raizman	102	est		GB	50
Private Life of Sherlock Holmes, The	GB	1970	Billy Wilder	125	Sc		FB	18
Private Lives of Elizabeth and Essex, The (see Elizabeth the Queen)								
Private Popsicle	IS/ W.GER	1982	Boaz Davidson	100			FB	33
Private Potter	GB	1962	Casper Wrede	100			FB	18
Private Wore Skirts, The	USA	1952	Norman Z. McLeod	84			GB	30
Private's Affair, A	USA	1959	Raoul Walsh	92	sc/std		FB	20
Private's Progress	GB	1956	John Boulting	102			GB	25
Privates On Parade	GB	1982	Michael Blakemore	112			GB	42
Privilege	GB	1967	Peter Watkins	100			FB	18
Privileged	GB	1982	Michael Hoffman	94	96		GB	38
Prize, The	USA	1963	Mark Robson	135	sc/std		FB	24
Problem Child	USA	1990	Dennis Dugan	80		UIP	FB	60
Professional Gun, A	IT/SP	1968	Sergio Corbucci	104	sc/dub		FB	18
Professional Sweetheart	USA	1933	William A. Seiter	68			GB	15
Professor Popper's Problems (6 episodes)	GB	1974	Gerry O'Hara	14 -16 each			GB	6
Progress of Peoples, The	GB	1975	Kieron Moore	79	75		GB	15
Project X	USA	1967	William Castle	97	bw		FB	15
Projected Man, The	GB	1966	Ian Curteis	90	sc/std		GB	20

	COUNTRY OF PRODUCTION	YEAR	DIRECTOR	RUNNING TIME	VERSION	35mm	16mm	16mm RENTAL FEE
Promise Her Anything	GB	1965	Arthur Hiller	95	col bw		FB	18
Promise, The	USA	1978	Gilbert Cates	97	sc/std		FB	38
Promised Lands	FR	1974	Susan Sontag	87			GB	25
Proof	AUSTR	1991	Jocelyn Moorhouse	90		AE	GB	80
Prophecy	USA	1979	John Frankenheimer	102	sc		FB	43
Prospero's Books	NETH	1991	Peter Greenaway	120		MAY	GB	80
Prostitute	GB	1980	Tony Garnett	96			GB	50
Protocol	USA	1984	Herbert Ross	95			FB	50
Proud and the Damned, The	USA	1973	Ferde Grofe Jr	90			GB	27
Proud Ones, The	USA	1956	Robert D. Webb	94	std		FB	18
Proud Valley, The	GB	1939	Pen Tennyson	77			BFI	25
Prudence and the Pill	GB	1968	Fielder Cook	88			FB	22
Psycho II	USA	1982	Richard Franklin	113		UIP	FB	43
Psycho III	USA	1986	Anthony Perkins	93		UIP	FB	43
Puberty Blues	AUSTR	1981	Bruce Beresford	81			FB	35
Public Defender, The	USA	1931	J. Walter Ruben	71			GB	22
Public Enemy	USA	1931	William A. Wellman	84		UIP	FB	22
Pull My Daisy	USA	1958	Robert Frank	27			GB	10
Pulp	GB	1972	Mike Hodges	95			FB	18
Pumpkin Eater, The	GB	1964	Jack Clayton	110		C	FB	15
Punch and Judy Man, The	GB	1962	Jeremy Summers	96			FB	15
Punchline	USA	1988	David Seltzer	122			FB	60
Punishment Park	USA	1971	Peter Watkins	89			MP	40
Punk in London	W.GER	1977	Wolfgang Buld	92	mag		CONC	38.4
Pure Hell of St. Trinian's, The	GB	1960	Frank Launder	94			FB	15
Purgatorio	SWE	1974	Michael Meschke	86			GB	30
Purple Haze	USA	1982	David Burton Morris	97	104		FB	60
Purple Heart, The	USA	1944	Lewis Milestone	100			FB	15
Purple Rain	USA	1984	Albert Magnoli	111		W	FB	40
Purple Rose of Cairo, The	USA	1985	Woody Allen	82			FB	45
Pursued	USA	1947	Raoul Walsh	101			GB	18
Pussycat, Pussycat, I Love You	USA	1970	Rod Amateau	100			FB	18
Putney Swope	USA	1969	Robert Downey	84			GB	15
Pygmalion	GB	1938	Anthony Asquith/Leslie Howard	90			GB	18
Pyjama Party	USA	1963	Don Weis	85		UIP	FB	18

Paleface

q

	COUNTRY OF PRODUCTION	YEAR	DIRECTOR	RUNNING TIME	VERSION	35mm	16mm	16mm RENTAL FEE
Q – The Winged Serpent	USA	1982	Larry Cohen	94			GB	35
Q&A	USA	1990	Sidney Lumet	132			GB	80
Quack, The	POL	1982	Jerzy Hoffman	135	est		FOP	0
Quadrophenia	GB	1979	Franc Roddam	120		GB	GB	43
Quality Street	USA	1937	George Stevens	83			GB	16
Quartet	GB/FR	1981	James Ivory	101			FB	38
Quatermass and the Pit	GB	1967	Roy Ward Baker	87			FB	15
Que la Bête Meure	FR/IT	1969	Claude Chabrol	110	85/dub		GB	30
Queen Christina	USA	1934	Rouben Mamoulian	100		U	FB	22
Queen is Crowned, A	GB	1953	Castleton Knight	80			FB	22
Queen Kelly	USA	1928	Erich von Stroheim	96		CONT	GB	45
Queen of Hearts	GB	1989	Jon Amiel	12			GB	70
Queen of Hearts	GB	1936	Monty Banks	78			FB	15
Queen of the Blues	GB	1979	Willy Roe	62			GB	40
Queen, The	USA	1968	Frank Simon	68			GB	20
Querelle	FR/ W.GER	1982	R.W. Fassbinder	106	sc		GB	48
Quest for Fire	CAN/FR	1981	Jean-Jacques Annaud	100	sc/std		FB	40
Quest for Love	GB	1971	Ralph Thomas	91			FB	18
Quick Before It Melts	USA	1964	Delbert Mann	98	std		FB	18
Quick Billie	USA	1968/70	Bruce Baillie	60			LFC	25
Quick Change	USA	1990	Howard Franklin/ Bill Murray	89		W	FB	60
Quick Money	USA	1937	Edward Killy	59			GB	15
Quicksand	USA	1951	Irving Pichel	79			GB	15
Quicksilver	USA	1986	Tom Donnelly	106			FB	35
Quiet American, The	USA	1957	Joseph L. Mankiewicz	121			FB	18
Quiet One, The	USA	1949	Sidney Meyers	67			CONC	15.4
Quiet Please: Stand By to Shoot 'The Magic Flute'	SWE	1975	Katrinka Faragó/Hans Reutersvärd	64			GB	15
Quiet Weekend	GB	1946	Harold French	92			GB	20
Quiller Memorandum, The	GB/USA	1966	Michael Anderson	103	sc		FB	18
Quintet	USA	1979	Robert Altman	118			FB	27

Quadrophenia

r

	COUNTRY OF PRODUCTION	YEAR	DIRECTOR	RUNNING TIME	VERSION	35mm	16mm	16mm RENTAL FEE
Ra: The Path of the Sun God	GB	1990	Lesley Keen	72			BFI	50
Rabbits in the Tall Grass	CZ	1962	Vaclav Gajer	90	est		ETV	10
Rabid	CAN	1976	David Cronenberg	91			GB	35
Race For Your Life, Charlie Brown	USA	1977	Bill Melendez	76			FB	33
Race Street	USA	1948	Edwin L. Marin	80			GB	15
Race with the Devil	USA	1975	Jack Starrett	88			FB	22
Rachel and the Beelzebub Bombardiers	GB	1977	Peter Ormrod	51			GB	25
Rachel and the Stranger	USA	1947	Norman Foster	93			GB	15
Rachel, Rachel	USA	1968	Paul Newman	101			FB	18
Racing With The Moon	USA	1984	Richard Benjamin	108		UIP	FB	35
Racket Busters	USA	1938	Lloyd Bacon	71			FB	22
Racket, The	USA	1951	John Cromwell	89			GB	15
Radio City Revels	USA	1938	Ben Stoloff	90			GB	15
Radio Days	USA	1987	Woody Allen	88			FB	60
Radio On	GB/W.GER	1979	Christopher Petit	102			BFI	35
Radio Parade of 1935	GB	1934	Arthur Woods	94			BFI	15
Radio Stars on Parade	USA	1945	Leslie Goodwins	69			GB	15
Rafferty and the Gold Dust Twins	USA	1975	Dick Richards	91	sc/std		FB	22
Raga	USA	1971	Howard Worth	96			GB	25
Rage in Harlem, A	GB	1991	Bill Duke	108		MAY	GB	80
Rage to Live, A	USA	1964	Walter Grauman	101	sc		FB	15
Raggedy Rawney	GB	1988	Bob Hoskins	103			GB	80
Raging Bull	USA	1980	Martin Scorsese	129			FB	48
Raging Moon, The	GB	1970	Bryan Forbes	111			FB	18
Ragtime	USA	1981	Milos Forman	155	sc		FB	40
Raid on Rommel	USA	1971	Henry Hathaway	98	sc		FB	18
Raid, The	USA	1954	Hugo Fregonese	81	bw		FB	15
Raiders	USA	1952	Lesley Selander	80			FB	15
Raiders of the Lost Ark	USA	1981	Steven Spielberg	115	sc/std		FB	48
Rails into Laramie	USA	1954	Jesse Hibbs	81	bw		FB	15
Railway Children, The	GB	1970	Lionel Jeffries	95		MAY	FB	27
Rain Man	USA	1988	Barry Levinson	134			FB	65
Rainbow, The	USSR	1944	Mark Donskoi	85	est		ETV	15
Rainmaker, The	USA	1956	Joseph Anthony	121			FB	15
Rainmakers, The	USA	1935	Fred Guiol	75			GB	15
Raintree County	USA	1957	Edward Dmytryk	166	sc/std		FB	18
Raise the Red Lantern	HK	1991	Zhang Yimou	125	st	ELEC	GB	80
Raise the Titanic	U5A	1980	Jerry Jameson	114	sc/std		GB	43
Raisin in the Sun	USA	1961	Daniel Petrie	127			FB	15
Raising A Riot	GB	1955	Wendy Toye	81			FB	15
Raising Arizona	USA	1987	Joel Coen	94			FB	50
Raising the Roof	GB	1971	Michael Forlong	54			GB	17
Raising the Wind	GB	1961	Gerald Thomas	91			FB	18
Raison Avant la Passion, La	CAN	1969	Joyce Wieland	80			LFC	18.75
Rambo III	USA	1988	Peter MacDonald	101	sc		FB	60
Rampage	USA	1962	Phil Karlson	93			FB	18
Ramparts of Clay	FR/ALG	1970	Jean-Louis Bertuccelli	87	est		GB	30
Rancho Deluxe	USA	1974	Frank Perry	94			FB	18
Rancho Notorious	USA	1952	Fritz Lang	90			GB	24
Random Harvest	USA	1942	Mervyn LeRoy	126			FB	15
Rangi's Catch (8 episodes)	GB	1972	Michael Forlong	14-18 each			GB	6
Ransom	GB	1974	Casper Wrede	97			FB	33
Ransom for a Dead Man	USA	1971	Richard Irving	95			FB	18
Ransom, A	USA	1956	Alex Segal	102			FB	14
Rappin'	USA	1985	Joel Silberg	92			FB	40
Rapunzel, Let Down Your Hair	GB	1978	Esther Ronay/Sue Shapiro/ Francine Winham	78			BFI	30
Rare Breed, The	USA	1965	Andrew V. McLaglen	97	std		FB	18
Rascal	USA	1969	Norman Tokar	85			FB	27

r

	COUNTRY OF PRODUCTION	YEAR	DIRECTOR	RUNNING TIME	VERSION	35mm	16mm	16mm RENTAL FEE
Rashomon	JAP	1951	Akira Kurosawa	83	est	BFI	GB	35
Rat Race, The	USA	1960	Robert Mulligan	105	bw		FB	15
Rat-Trap	INDIA	1981	Adoor Gopalakrishnan	121	est		BFI	40
Rate It X	USA	1985	Paula de Koenigsberg/ Lucy Winer	93		BD	GB	50
Rattle of a Simple Man	GB	1964	Muriel Box	95			FB	15
Raven's Dance	FIN/SWE	1980	Markku Lehmuskallio	80			GB	35
Raven's End	SWE	1964	Bo Widerberg	100	est		APO	35
Raw Deal	AUSTR	1977	Russell Hagg	94			GB	35
Rawhide Years	USA	1955	Rudolph Maté	85			FB	18
Razor's Edge, The	USA	1946	Edmund Goulding	146			FB	15
Reach for the Sky	GB	1956	Lewis Gilbert	136			FB	15
Reaching for the Moon	USA	1931	Edmund Goulding	73			GB	25
Real Genius	USA	1985	Martha Coolidge	106			FB	40
Rear Window	USA	1954	Alfred Hitchcock	112			FB	35
Reason to Live, A Reason to Die, A	IT/FR/ SP/W.GER	1972	Tonino Valerii	91	std/dub		GB	18
Rebel, The	GB	1960	Robert Day	105			FB	18
Rebound	USA	1931	Edward H. Griffith	73			GB	15
Recipe for a Crime	CZ	1967	Martin Fric	100	est		ETV	10
Reckoning, The	GB	1969	Jack Gold	111			FB	18
Record of a Tenement Gentleman, The	JAP	1947	Yasujiro Ozu	72	est		GB	45
Red Badge of Courage, The	USA	1951	John Huston	69			FB	16
Red Baron, The	USA	1971	Roger Corman	97			FB	18
Red Beret, The	GB	1953	Terence Young	88			FB	18
Red Danube	USA	1949	George Sidney	119			FB	15
Red Dawn	USA	1984	John Milius	114			FB	40
Red Detachment of Women	CHI	1970	Hsieh Tsin	120	est		GB	25
Red Dust	USA	1932	Victor Fleming	79			FB	27
Red Ensign	GB	1934	Michael Powell	69			BFI	20
Red Heat	USA	1988	Walter Hill	104			FB	55
Red Line 7000	USA	1965	Howard Hawks	110			FB	22
Red Morning	USA	1934	Wallace Fox	63			GB	15
Red Mountain	USA	1951	William Dieterle	84	bw		FB	15
Red Psalm	HUNG	1971	Miklos Jancso	88	est		AE	45
Red River	USA	1946	Howard Hawks	125		UIP	FB	15
Red Shoes, The	GB	1948	Michael Powell/Emeric Pressburger	134		R	FB	55
Red Sonja	USA	1985	Richard Fleischer	89			FB	35
Red Sorghum	CHI	1987	Zhang Yimou	92	est		GB	80
Red Square Part 1	USSR	1970	Vasily Ordynski	65	est		ETV	10
Part 2				60				10
Red Sun	FR	1971	Terence Young	107			FB	18
Red Tent, The	IT/USSR	1969	Mikhail Kalatozov	121			FB	18
Red Wedding (see Noces Rouges, Les)								
Reds	USA	1981	Warren Beatty	196			FB	48
Redupers (see All Round Reduced Personality, The)								
Reflections in a Golden Eye	USA	1967	John Huston	109	sc/bw		FB	15
Refusal	AUSTR	1972	Axel Corti	95			GB	25
Reg'lar Fellers	USA	1941	Arthur Dreifuss	72			GB	15
Regarding Henry	USA	1991	Mike Nichols	107		UIP	FB	70
Reggae	GB	1970	Horace Ové	59	mag		GB	25
Region Centrale, La	CAN	1971	Michael Snow	180			LFC	70
Règle du Jeu, La	FR	1939	Jean Renoir	110	est	CONT	GB	35
Rehearsal Goes On, The	CZ	1960	Jaroslav Balik	90	est		ETV	10
Reign of Terror	USA	1949	Anthony Mann	90			GB	15
Reivers, The	USA	1969	Mark Rydell	112	sc/std		GB	18
Reluctant Astronaut, The	USA	1967	Edward Montagne	102			FB	18
Reluctant Debutante, The	USA	1958	Vincente Minnelli	96	sc/std		FB	18
Reluctant Saint, The	IT/ USA	1962	Edward Dmytryk	105			FB	15

	COUNTRY OF PRODUCTION	YEAR	DIRECTOR	RUNNING TIME	VERSION	35mm	16mm	16mm RENTAL FEE
Remember Me This Way	GB	1974	Ron Inkpen/Bob Foster	60			GB	18
Remember my Name	USA	1978	Alan Rudolph	94	std		FB	33
Remo Unarmed and Dangerous	USA	1985	Guy Hamilton	116	121		FB	40
Rendez-vous d'Anna, Les	BELG/ FR/ W.GER	1978	Chantal Akerman	122	est		MP	57.5
Renegade Ranger, The	USA	1939	David Howard	60			GB	15
Renegades	US	1989	Jack Sholder	105			GB	70
Reno	USA	1939	John Farrow	73			GB	15
Rentadick	GB	1972	Jim Clark	94			FB	18
Repeater	GB	1980	Chris Monger	78			BFI	27.5
Repent at Leisure	USA	1941	Frank Woodruff	66			GB	15
Repulsion	GB	1965	Roman Polanski	106		GB	GB	30
Requiem for a Gunfighter	USA	1965	Spencer G. Bennet	91	sc/std		GB	20
Requiem for a Village	GB	1975	David Gladwell	68			BFI	25
							CONC	27.40
Rescue Squad, The	GB	1963	Colin Bell	54			GB	12
Rescuers Down Under, The	USA	1991	Hendel Butoy/ Mike Gabriel	77		D	FB	50
Resistance	GB	1974	Ken McMullen	90			BFI	35
Resistance to Hitler	W.GER			60			GFL	0
Respectable Life, A	SWE	1979	Stefan Jarl	102	est		GB	35
Restless Eye: Eugene Delacroix (1798-1863), The	GB	1981	Colin Nears	60			AC	16
Restless Natives	GB	1985	Michael Hoffman	89			FB	40
Resurrected	GB	1989	Paul Greenglass	92			GB	60
Resurrected Fields	CAN		Henry Jesionka	55			LFMC	46.75
Resurrection	USA	1980	Daniel Petrie	103			FB	38
Resurrection of Zachary Wheeler	USA	1971	Bob Wynn	100			GB	38
Retour d'un Repere	FR		Rose Lowder	55			LFMC	46.75
Retreat Hell	USA	1952	Joseph H. Lewis	95			GB	18
Return from the Ashes	GB	1965	J. Lee Thompson	104	sc		FB	15
Return from the Gallows	CZ			90	est		ETV	10
Return from Witch Mountain	USA	1978	John Hough	94			FB	38
Return of a Man Called Horse, The	USA	1976	Irvin Kershner	125	sc		FB	27
Return of Count Yorga, The	USA	1971	Robert Kelljan	97			FB	18
Return of Doctor X, The	USA	1939	Vincent Sherman	66			FB	22
Return of Martin Guerre, The	FR	1982	Daniel Vigne	110	est		GB	45
Return of Peter Grimm, The	USA	1935	George Nicholls Jr.	82			GB	15
Return of Sabata	IT/FR/ W.GER	1971	Frank Kramer	89	sc		FB	18
Return of the Badmen	USA	1948	Ray Enright	93			GB	15
Return of the Dragon	HK	1972	Shen Chiang	87	dub/sc		FB	22
Return of the Gunfighter	USA	1966	James Neilson	98			FB	18
Return of the Pink Panther	GB	1974	Blake Edwards	113	sc/std		FB	43
Return of the Secaucus Seven	USA	1979	John Sayles	110			BFI	35
Return of the Soldier, The	GB	1982	Alan Bridges	101			FB	45
Return to Oz	USA	1985	Walter Murch	109			FB	45
Return to Peyton Place	USA	1961	José Ferrer	121	sc/std		FB	18
Return to Yesterday	GB	1939	Robert Stevenson	68			GB	20
Reuben, Reuben	USA	1982	Robert Ellis Miller	100			GB	45
Revenge	GB	1971	Sidney Hayers	89			FB	18
Revenge in El Paso	IT	1968	Giuseppe Colizzi	103	sc/dub		FB	18
Revenge of the Creature	USA	1955	Jack Arnold	82	3D		FB	43
Revenge of the Nerds	USA	1984	Jeff Kanew	90			FB	45
Revenge of the Ninja	USA	1983	Sam Firstenberg	84			FB	35
Revenge of the Pink Panther	GB	1978	Blake Edwards	100	sc/dub		FB	43
Revengers, The	USA/ MEX	1972	Daniel Mann	108	sc		GB	18
Reversal of Fortune	USA	1990	Barbet Schroeder	105		R	FB	65
Revolution	GB	1985	Hugh Hudson	125	sc/std		FB	50
Reward, The	USA	1965	Serge Bourguignon	91	sc		FB	18

	COUNTRY OF PRODUCTION	YEAR	DIRECTOR	RUNNING TIME	VERSION	35mm	16mm	16mm RENTAL FEE
Rex Whistler	GB	1980	Derek Bailey (Prod)	60			AC	16
Rhapsody	USA	1954	Charles Vidor	116			FB	22
Rhapsody in Blue	USA	1945	Irving Rapper	141			FB	18
Rhinestone	USA	1984	Bob Clark	111			FB	45
Rhino	USA	1963	Ivan Tors	91			FB	18
Ricco (see Dirty Mob)								
Rich and Famous	USA	1981	George Cukor	117			FB	43
Rich and Strange	GB	1932	Alfred Hitchcock	92			FB	25
Rich Full Life	USA	1947	Robert Z. Leonard	98			FB	15
Rich Kids	USA	1979	Robert M. Young	96			FB	22
Richard II	GB/USA	1978	David Giles	150			BBC	35
Richard III	GB	1955	Laurence Olivier	158			FB	22
Richard Pryor Live in Concert	USA	1979	Jeff Margolis	79			FB	43
Richest Girl in the World, The	USA	1934	William A. Seiter	76			GB	15
Riddle of the Sands, The	GB	1978	Tony Maylam	102	sc/std		FB	38
Riddles of the Sphinx	GB	1977	Laura Mulvey/Peter Wollen	90			BFI	35
Ride a Wild Pony	USA	1975	Don Chaffey	91			FB	33
Ride to Hangman's Tree, The	USA	1966	Alan Rafkin	88	bw		FB	15
Ride, Vaquero!	USA	1953	John Farrow	98			FB	18
Riders from Tucson	USA	1952	Lesley Selander	60			GB	15
Riders of the New Forest	GB	1949	Philip Leacock	60			FB	10
Riding Shotgun	USA	1954	André de Toth	75			FB	18
Riff Raff	USA	1947	Ted Tetzlaff	82			GB	15
Riff-Raff	GB	1990	Ken Loach	95	117	MAY	GB	65
Rififi	FR	1954	Jules Dassin	115	dub/117/est		GB	35
Rififi in Tokyo	FR/IT	1961	Jacques Deray	90	dub		FB	15
Right Cross	USA	1950	John Sturges	90			FB	15
Right Out of History: The Making of Judy Chicago's Dinner Party	USA	1980	Johanna Demetrakas	75			AC	19
Right Stuff, The	USA	1983	Philip Kaufman	192			FB	50
Right to Romance, The	USA	1933	Alfred Santell	70			GB	15
Ring of Bright Water	GB	1969	Jack Couffer	107	GB		GB	30
Ring of Fire	USA	1961	Andrew Stone	90			FB	18
Ring, The	GB	1927	Alfred Hitchcock	115	st		FB	25
Ringo and his Golden Pistol	IT	1966	Sergio Corbucci	98	dub		FB	18
Rio Bravo	USA	1959	Howard Hawks	140		W	FB	18
Rio Conchos	USA	1964	Gordon Douglas	105	sc/std		FB	18
Rio Grande	USA	1950	John Ford	105			GB	22
Rio Lobo	USA	1970	Howard Hawks	113			GB	18
Riot in Cell Block 11	USA	1954	Don Siegel	80			APO	35
Rise and Fall of Legs Diamond, The	USA	1959	Budd Boetticher	101			FB	15
Rise To Power (see Prise du Pouvoir par Louis XIV, La)								
Rising Damp	GB	1980	Joe McGrath	98			GB	38
Rising of the Moon, The	EIRE	1957	John Ford	80			FB	15
Risky Business	USA	1983	Paul Brickman	99			FB	45
Rite, The	SWE	1969	Ingmar Bergman	75	est		GB	30
Rites of Spring	CAN	1980	Michael Checnik	60			CONC	19.8
Ritz, The	GB	1976	Richard Lester	91			FB	22
River's Edge	USA	1986	Tim Hunter	100			GB	70
River's Edge, The	USA	1956	Allan Dwan	87	sc		FB	18
River, The	USA	1984	Mark Rydell	124			FB	40
Riverboat Rhythm	USA	1946	Leslie Goodwins	65			GB	15
Road Agent	USA	1952	Lesley Selander	60			GB	15
Road Movie	GB	1984	Richard Philpott	59			GB	35
Road to Hong Kong, The	GB	1961	Norman Panama	91			FB	15
Road to Life	USSR	1931	Nikolai Ekk	95	est		ETV	20
Road to Morocco	USA	1942	David Butler	85			FB	15
Road to Utopia	USA	1945	Hal Walker	89			FB	15
Roadblock	USA	1951	Harold Daniels	73			GB	150

	COUNTRY OF PRODUCTION	YEAR	DIRECTOR	RUNNING TIME	VERSION	35mm	16mm	16mm RENTAL FEE
Roadhouse Murder, The	USA	1932	J Walter Ruben	73			GB	15
Roadie	USA	1980	Alan Rudolph	90			FB	33
Roar of the Dragon	USA	1932	Wesley Ruggles	77			GB	15
Roaring Twenties, The	USA	1939	Raoul Walsh	107			FB	22
Rob Roy the Highland Rogue	GB	1953	Harold French	82			FB	27
Robbers of the Range	USA	1941	Edward Killy	61			GB	15
Robbery	GB	1967	Peter Yates	114			GB	18
Robbery Under Arms	GB	1957	Jack Lee	93	bw		FB	15
Robe, The	USA	1953	Henry Koster	134	std		FB	22
Robin and Marian	USA	1976	Richard Lester	107			FB	27
Robin and the 7 Hoods	USA	1964	Gordon Douglas	123		W	FB	18
Robin Hood	USA	1973	Wolfgang Reitherman	83		D	FB	50
Robin Hood	USA	1991	John Irvin	104		F	FB	65
Robin Hood Junior	GB	1975	Matt McCarthy/John Black	61			GB	17
Robin Hood: Prince of Thieves	USA	1991	Kevin Reynolds	143		W	FB	70
Robinson Crusoe	USSR	1972	Stanislas Govorukin	92	dub		GB	12
Robocop	USA	1987	Paul Verhoeven	103			FB	55
Rocco and his Brothers	IT/FR	1960	Luchino Visconti	176	est/dub	BFI	GB	45
Rock-A-Doodle	USA	1991	Don Bluth	74		R	FB	65
Rocketeer, The	USA	1991	Joe Johnston	108		D	FB	70
Rockets Galore	GB	1958	Michael Relph	91			FB	18
Rockets in the Dunes	GB	1960	William Hammond	57			GB	12
Rocking the Foundations	AUSTR	1974-84	Pat Fiske	92			WFA	30
Rocky	USA	1976	John G. Avildsen	119		UIP	FB	43
Rocky II	USA	1979	Sylvester Stallone	117		UIP	FB	43
Rocky III	USA	1982	Sylvester Stallone	99		UIP	FB	43
Rocky IV	USA	1985	Sylvester Stallone	91		UIP	FB	60
Rocky V	USA	1990	John G Avildsen	104		UIP	FB	60
Rocky Horror Picture Show, The	GB	1975	Jim Sharman	100		F	FB	33
Rocky Mountain	USA	1951	William Keighley	82			FB	15
Rogues of Sherwood Forest	USA	1950	Gordon Douglas	80	col		FB	18
Role, The	INDIA	1977	Shyam Benegal	140	est		GB	45
Rollerball	USA	1975	Norman Jewison	125	std		FB	38
Rollercoaster	USA	1977	James Goldstone	118	sc/std		FB	43
Rolling Down the Great Divide	USA	1942	Sam Newfield	60			GB	15
Rollover	USA	1981	Alan J. Pakula	116		W	FB	35
Romance in a Minor Key	GER	1943	Helmut Käutner	98	est		BFI	25
Romance in Manhattan	USA	1935	Stephen Roberts	77			GB	15
Romance of Heidelberg, The (see Heidelberger Romanze)								
Romancing the Stone	USA	1984	Robert Zemeckis	105	sc		FB	55
Romantic Comedy	USA	1983	Arthur Hiller	101			FB	40
Romantic Englishwoman, The	GB/FR	1975	Joseph Losey	116			FB	33
Rome, Open City	IT	1945	Roberto Rossellini	102	est		BFI	25
Romeo and Juliet	GB	1966	Paul Czinner	126			FB	18
Romeo and Juliet	GB/IT	1968	Franco Zeffirelli	152	139		FB	33
Romeo and Juliet	GB/USA	1978	Alvin Rakoff	170			BBC	35
Rommel The Desert Fox (see Desert Fox The Story of Rommel, The)								
Romuald et Juliette	FR	1989	Coline Serreau	112	st		GB	60
Ronde, La	FR	1950	Max Ophuls	92	est	BFI	BFI	35
Rookie Cop, The	USA	1939	David Howard	60			GB	15
Rookie, The	USA	1990	Clint Eastwood	115		W	FB	60
Rookies in Burma	USA	1943	Leslie Goodwins	62			GB	15
Room at the Top	GB	1959	Jack Clayton	117			GB	25
Room Film	GB	1973	Peter Gidal	55	st		LFMC	46.75
Room in the House	GB	1955	Maurice Elvey	74			GB	20
Room Service	USA	1938	William A. Seiter	78			GB	15
Room With A View, A	GB	1985	James Ivory	117			GB	50
Rooster Cogburn	USA	1975	Stuart Millar	108	sc/std		FB	33

Title	Country of Production	Year	Director	Running Time	Version	35mm	16mm	16mm Rental Fee
Rope	USA	1948	Alfred Hitchcock	81			FB	35
Rosa Luxemburg	GER	1986	Margarethe Von Trotta	124	st	AE	GB	60
Rosalie Goes Shopping	W.GER	1989	Percy Adlon	94		ML	BFI	70
Rose, The	USA	1979	Mark Rydell	134			FB	35
Rosebud	USA	1974	Otto Preminger	126	sc/std		FB	22
Roseland	USA	1977	James Ivory	103		BD	GB	33
Rosemary's Killer	USA	1981	Josef Zito	87			FB	38
Rosencrantz & Guildenstern are Dead	USA	1990	Tom Stoppard	118			GB	80
Rosenkavalier, Der	GB	1961	Paul Czinner	192			FB	33
Roses in December	USA	1982	Ana Carrigan/Bernard Stone	56			GB	25
Rosie	USA	1967	David Lowell Rich	98	bw/std		FB	15
Rosie Dixon Night Nurse	GB	1978	Justin Cartwright	88			FB	38
Rotten To The Core	GB	1965	John Boulting	90			FB	15
Rough and the Smooth, The	GB	1959	Robert Siodmak	100		GB	GB	25
Rough Company	USA	1954	Rudolph Maté	95	std/col		FB	18
Rough Cut	USA	1980	Don Siegel	112			FB	38
Rough Cut and Ready Dubbed	GB	1982	Hasan Shah/Don Shaw	58			BFI	25
Rough Night in Jericho	USA	1967	Arnold Laven	102	std		FB	18
Roughshod	USA	1949	Mark Robson	88			GB	15
Round Midnight	USA/FR	1986	Bertrand Tavernier	133	sc	W	FB	55
Round-Up, The	HUNG	1965	Miklos Jancso	94	sc/est	CONT	GB	25
Rounders, The	USA	1964	Burt Kennedy	84	std		FB	18
Roxanne	USA	1987	Fred Schepisi	107			FB	55
Royal Bed, The	USA	1931	Lowell Sherman	75			GB	15
Royal Family	GB	1969	Richard Cawston (Prod)	90			BBC	13
Royal Flash	GB	1975	Richard Lester	102			FB	30
Royal Wedding	USA	1951	Stanley Donen	93			FB	33
Ruby	USA	1977	Curtis Harrington	85			GB	22
Ruby	USA	1992	John Mackenzie	111		R	FB	70
Ruby Gentry	USA	1952	King Vidor	82			GB	25
Ruddigore	GB	1967	Joy Batchelor	60		GB	GB	22
Rude Boy	GB	1980	Jack Hazan/David Mingay	133			GB	35
Rue Cases-Negres	FR/ MART	1983	Euzhan Palcy	106	est	AE	GB	55
Ruggles of Red Gap	USA	1934	Leo McCarey	90			FB	22
Rumblefish	USA	1983	Francis Ford Coppola	94		UIP	FB	40
Rumpelstiltskin	W.GER	1955	Herbert Fredersdorf	82			GB	8
Run for Your Money	GB	1949	Charles Frend	84			FB	15
Run of the Arrow	USA	1956	Samuel Fuller	85	std/col		GB	22
Run on Gold, A	USA	1969	Alf Kjellin	104			GB	22
Run Wild Run Free	GB	1969	Richard C. Sarafian	98			FB	18
Runaway	USA	1984	Michael Crichton	97	sc	C	FB	40
Runaway Bride	USA	1930	Donald Crisp	69			GB	15
Runaway Daughters	USA	1956	Edward L. Cahn	91			GB	15
Runaway Railway	GB	1965	Jan Darnley-Smith	55			GB	12
Runaway Train	USA	1985	Andrei Konchalovsky	111			FB	45
Runaway Train, The	USA	1973	David Lowell Rich	87			FB	27
Running Brave	CAN	1983	D.S. Everett	102			GB	35
Running Man, The	GB	1963	Carol Reed	103	sc/std	C	FB	18
Running on Empty	USA	1988	Sidney Lumet	117			FB	60
Rupture, La	BEL/FR/IT	1970	Claude Chabrol	125	est		GB	25
Rush to Judgment	USA	1967	Emile de Antonio	110			GB	50
Russia House, The	USA	1990	Fred Schepisi	124		UIP	FB	60
Russian Miracle Part One	E.GER	1961-63	Andrew Thorndike/Annelise Thorndike	105			ETV	10
Part Two				100				
Russian Roulette	USA	1975	Lou Lombardo	93			GB	22
Russians are Coming, the Russians are Coming, The	USA	1965	Norman Jewison	125	sc/std	UIP	FB	18
Ruth Halbfass	W.GER	1971	Volker Schlöndorff	92	est		GFL	0
Ruthless People	USA	1986	Jim Abrahams/David Zucker/ Jerry Zucker	94		T	FB	60

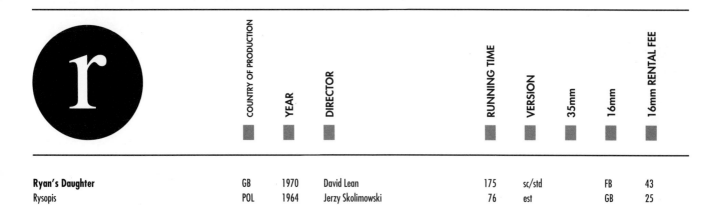

	COUNTRY OF PRODUCTION	YEAR	DIRECTOR	RUNNING TIME	VERSION	35mm	16mm	16mm RENTAL FEE
Ryan's Daughter	GB	1970	David Lean	175	sc/std		FB	43
Rysopis	POL	1964	Jerzy Skolimowski	76	est		GB	25

Rosalie Goes Shopping

	COUNTRY OF PRODUCTION	YEAR	DIRECTOR	RUNNING TIME	VERSION	35mm	16mm	16mm RENTAL FEE
S.O.B.	USA	1981	Blake Edwards	120	sc		GB	43
S.O.S. Pacific	GB	1959	Guy Green	92			GB	15
S.O.S. Titanic	GB	1979	William Hale	102			FB	28
S.W.A.L.K.	GB	1971	Waris Hussein	107			FB	18
Sabata	IT	1969	Frank Kramer	106	sc/dub		FB	18
Saboteur Code Name Morituri	USA	1965	Bernhard Wicki	122	std/bw		FB	15
Sabotage	GB	1936	Alfred Hitchcock	76		R	FB	25
Sabrina Fair	USA	1954	Billy Wilder	114			FB	15
Sacred Ground	USA	1977	Rodney H. Jacobs	100			GB	45
Sacred Hearts	GB	1984	Barbara Rennie	93			GB	45
Sacrifice Area	HOLL	1980	Erica Damon	63			CONC	23.80
Sacrifice, The	SWE/FR	1986	Andrei Tarkovsky	149	est	AE	GB	60
Sacrificed Youth	CHI	1985	Zhang Nuanxin	96	est		GB	60
Sad Horse, The	USA	1959	James B. Clark	78	std		FB	18
Saddle Buster, The	USA	1932	Fred Allen	60			GB	15
Saddle the Wind	USA	1958	Robert Parrish	84	sc/std		FB	18
Saddled with Five Girls	CZ	1967	Ewald Schorm	88	est		ETV	15
Safecracker, The	GB	1957	Ray Milland	96			FB	15
Sahara	USA	1983	Andrew V. McLaglen	106			FB	30
Saigon	USA	1988	Christopher Crowe	102			FB	55
Sailor Beware	GB	1956	Gordon Parry	81			FB	20
Sailor from the Comet, The	USSR	1958	Isider Annensky	90	est		ETV	10
Sailors Three	GB	1940	Walter Forde	85			FB	15
Saint in London, The	GB	1939	John Paddy Carstairs	77			GB	15
Saint in New York, The	USA	1938	Ben Holmes	72			GB	15
Saint in Palm Springs, The	USA	1941	Jack Hively	68			GB	15
Saint Strikes Back, The	USA	1939	John Farrow	66			GB	15
Saint's Double Trouble, The	USA	1940	Jack Hively	68			GB	15
Saint's Vacation, The	GB	1940	Leslie Fenton	78			GB	15
Salaam Bombay!	GB/FR/ IND	1988	Mira Nair	113			BFI	70
Salamander, The	GB/IT USA	1980	Peter Zinner	102			GB	43
Salamandre, La	SWITZ	1971	Alain Tanner	129	est		GB	25
Sally in Our Alley	GB	1931	Maurice Elvey	76			FB	15
Sally of the Sawdust	USA	1925	D.W. Griffith	100	sd		BFI	20
Salon Kitty	IT/ W.GER	1976	Tinto Brass	127	dub		FB	38
Salsa	USA	1988	Boaz Davidson	96			FB	40
Salt & Pepper	GB	1968	Richard Donner	101			FB	18
Salvador	USA	1986	Oliver Stone	122			GB	70
Salzburg Connection, The	USA	1972	Lee H. Katzin	93	std		FB	18
Sam Whiskey	USA	1969	Arnold Laven	97			FB	18
Same Time, Next Year	USA	1978	Robert Mulligan	120			FB	38
Sammy and Rosie Get Laid	5B	1987	Stephen Frears	101			GB	70
Sammy's Super T- Shirt	GB	1978	Jeremy Summers	58			GB	20
Samson and Delilah	USA	1949	Cecil B. DeMille	128			FB	18
Samson and the 7 Miracles	IT/FR	1961	Riccardo Freda	76	sc/dub		FB	18
Samson and the Slave Queen	IT	1963	Umberto Lenzi	92	sc/dub		FB	18
San Francisco	USA	1936	W.S. Van Dyke	115			FB	16
San Francisco Story, The	USA	1952	Robert Parrish	80			GB	15
San Quentin	USA	1946	Gordon Douglas	60			GB	15
San Quentin	USA	1937	Lloyd Bacon	70			FB	22
Sand Pebbles, The	USA	1966	Robert Wise	180	sc		FB	22
Sandpiper, The	USA	1965	Vincente Minnelli	117	sc/std		FB	18
Sands of Iwo Jima	USA	1949	Allan Dwan	110			GB	27
Sands of the Desert	GB	1960	John Paddy Carstairs	92			FB	18
Sands of the Kalahari	GB	1965	Cy Endfield	119	sc/std		FB	18
Sandwich Man, The	GB	1966	Robert Hartford-Davis	112		R	FB	18
Sang d'un Poète, Le	FR	1932	Jean Cocteau	53	est		GB	25
Sanjuro	JAP	1962	Akira Kurosawa	96	cst/sc		GB	25

	COUNTRY OF PRODUCTION	YEAR	DIRECTOR	RUNNING TIME	VERSION	35mm	16mm	16mm RENTAL FEE
Sans Soleil	FR	1983	Chris Marker	100	eng		MP	51.75
Sansho Dayu	JAP	1954	Kenji Mizoguchi	123	bw/est	BFI	BFI	55
Santa Claus – The Movie	GB	1985	Jeannot Szwarc	108		R	FB	50
Santa Fe Trail	USA	1940	Michael Curtiz	109			FB	22
Santee	USA	1972	Gary Nelson	90			FB	18
Sapphire	GB	1959	Basil Dearden	92	bw	R	FB	15
Saps at Sea	USA	1940	Gordon Douglas	57		BFI	GB	10
Saraband for Dead Lovers	GB	1948	Basil Dearden	91	bw		FB	15
Saragossa Manuscript, The	POL	1964	Wojciech Jerzy Has	124	est/sc		GB	30
Satan Bug, The	USA	1964	John Sturges	113	sc		FB	18
Satanic Rites of Dracula, The	GB	1973	Alan Gibson	87			FB	18
Saturday Night Fever	USA	1977	John Badham	119	cert x		FB	53
					cert a		FB	53
Saturday's Heroes	USA	1937	Edward Killy	60			GB	15
Saturn 3	GB	1980	Stanley Donen	86			GB	38
Savage Eye, The	USA	1959	Ben Maddow/Sidney Meyers/Joseph Strick	68			GB	25
Savage Guns, The	SP/USA	1962	Michael Carreras	83	sc/std		FB	18
Savage Islands	NZ	1983	Ferdinand Fairfax	99			FB	43
Savage Messiah	GB	1972	Ken Russell	103	99		FB	26
Savage Sam	USA	1962	Norman Tokar	104			FB	27
Savages	USA	1972	James Ivory	105		BD	GB	33
Save the Tiger	USA	1972	John G. Avildsen	101			FB	18
Say Anything	USA	1988	Cameron Crowe	100			FB	55
Say Hello to Yesterday	GB	1970	Alvin Rakoff	92	GB		GB	22
Say It With Flowers	GB	1934	John Baxter	73			BFI	20
Scalawag	US/IT	1973	Kirk Douglas	93			FB	22
Scalphunters, The	USA	1968	Sydney Pollack	103	sc/std		FB	18
Scamp, The	GB	1957	Wolf Rilla	90			GB	15
Scandal	GB	1989	Michael Caton-Jones	114		MAY	GB	80
Scandal at Scourie	USA	1953	Jean Negulesco	90			FB	15
Scandale, Le	FR	1967	Claude Chabrol	98	sc/dub		FB	18
Scanners	CAN	1980	David Cronenberg	103			GB	43
Scapegoat, The	GB	1958	Robert Hamer	92			FB	15
Scarecrow	USA	1973	Jerry Schatzberg	103	std		FB	18
Scared Stiff	USA	1963	George Marshall	107			FB	15
Scarface	USA	1932	Howard Hawks	93			BFI	30
Scarface	USA	1983	Brian De Palma	170		UIP	FB	53
Scarlet Blade, The	GB	1963	John Gilling	82	std		FB	18
Scarlet Buccaneer, The	USA	1976	James Goldstone	102	sc/std		FB	27
Scarlet Coat, The	USA	1955	John Sturges	88			FB	27
Scarlet Hour, The	USA	1955	Michael Curtiz	93	bw/std		FB	15
Scarlet Letter, The	USA	1926	Victor Sjöström	91	st	UIP	FB	22
Scarlet Spear	GB	1953	George Breakston/Ray Stahl	78	bw		GB	15
Scarlet Street	USA	1945	Fritz Lang	101			BFI	25
Scavengers, The	PHIL/ USA	1959	John Cromwell	179			GB	15
Scenes From A Mall	USA	1990	Paul Mazursky	88		T	FB	70
Scenes from a Marriage	SWE	1973	Ingmar Bergman	168	st		GB	40
Scenes of Battle	POL	1965	Jerzy Passendorfer	100	est		FOP	0
Scenic Route, The	USA	1978	Mark Rappaport	76			BFI	30
Schatten (see Warning Shadows)								
Schizo	GB	1976	Peter Walker	109			FB	18
Schlussakkord	GER	1936	Douglas Sirk	100	est		BFI	25
School for Scoundrels	GB	1960	Robert Hamer	95			FB	15
School for Vandals	GB	1986	Colin Finbow	80			GB	20
School Photo Memories – of German Citizens Part I	W.GER	1970	Eberhard Fechner	84	dub		GFL	0
Part 2				96	dub			
Schoolmaster Hofer	W.GER	1975	Peter Lilienthal	111	est		GFL	0
Scorpio	USA	1972	Michael Winner	114			FB	18

	COUNTRY OF PRODUCTION	YEAR	DIRECTOR	RUNNING TIME	VERSION	35mm	16mm	16mm RENTAL FEE
Scorpio Letters, The	USA	1966	Richard Thorpe	80	97		FB	18
Scotch Myths	GB	1982	Murray Grigor	90			BFI	25
Scott of the Antarctic	GB	1949	Charles Frend	101			FB	18
Scoundrel in White	FR/IT	1972	Claude Chabrol	101			FB	27
Scramble	GB	1970	David Eady	61			GB	17
Scream and Scream Again	GB	1969	Gordon Hessler	95			FB	18
Scream from Silence, A	CAN	1979	Anne-Clair Poirier	96			CHC	51.75
Screaming Skull, The	USA	1958	Alex Nicol	68			FB	15
Scrooge	GB	1951	Brian Desmond Hurst	86	bw		GB	20
Scrooge	GB	1970	Ronald Neame	118	sc/std	GB	GB	29
Scrooged	USA	1988	Richard Donner	101			FB	60
Scum	GB	1979	Alan Clarke	96		GB	GB	50
Sea Chase	USA	1955	John Farrow	117			FB	15
Sea Devils	USA	1936	Ben Stoloff	90			GB	15
Sea Devils, The	GB	1952	Raoul Walsh	85	bw		GB	15
Sea Hawk, The	USA	1940	Michael Curtiz	128	bw/123		FB	22
Sea of Sand	GB	1958	Guy Green	97			FB	15
Sea Wolf	USA	1941	Michael Curtiz	81			FB	22
Sea Wolves, The	GB/SWITZ/ USA	1980	Andrew V. McLaglen	120			FB	48
Seacoal	GB	1985	Amber Films	83			AMB	60
Seagull, The	USSR	1971	Yuli Karasik	98	sc/est		GB	30
Seal Island	GB	1977	Ronald Spencer	57			GB	17
Sealed Cargo	USA	1951	Alfred Werker	90			GB	15
Seance on a Wet Afternoon	GB	1964	Bryan Forbes	116			FB	15
Search for Sandra Laing, The	GB	1979	Anthony Thomas	60			CONC	21.60
Searchers, The	USA	1956	John Ford	117	col	W	FB	22
Sebastian	GB	1967	David Greene	99			FB	18
Sebastiane	GB	1976	Derek Jarman/ Paul Humfress	86	est	GB	BFI	40
Second Awakening of Christa Klages, The	W.GER	1977	Margarethe von Trotta	93	est	BD	GB	2
Second Chance	USA	1953	Rudolph Maté	80			GB	15
Second Chorus	USA	1941	H.C. Potter	82			GB	15
Second Wife	USA	1936	Edward Killy	74			GB	20
Second Woman, The	USA	1950	James V. Kern	91			GB	15
Seconds	USA	1966	John Frankenheimer	105	std		FB	18
Secret Admirer	USA	1985	David Greenwalt	98			FB	40
Secret Agent	GB	1936	Alfred Hitchcock	85		R	FB	25
Secret Agents	W.GER	1971	Eberhard Fechner	94	est		GFL	0
Secret Beyond the Door...	USA	1948	Fritz Lang	79			GB	22
Secret Ceremony	GB	1968	Joseph Losey	109			FB	18
Secret Garden, The	USA	1949	Fred M. Wilcox	92			FB	16
Secret Honour	USA	1984	Robert Altman	90			GB	60
Secret Interlude	USA	1955	Philip Dunne	97	sc		FB	18
Secret Invasion, The	USA	1964	Roger Corman	98	sc		FB	18
Secret Life of an American Wife, The	USA	1968	George Axelrod	92			FB	18
Secret Love Games	FR	1975	Edgar P. Sullivan	71	dub		FB	20
Secret Man, The	GB	1958	Ronald Kinnoch	68			GB	15
Secret of Blood Island, The	GB	1964	Quentin Lawrence	84	bw		FB	15
Secret of Eternal Night	USSR	1956	D. Vasiliev	75			ETV	6
Secret of My Success, The	USA	1987	Herbert Ross	111		UIP	FB	50
Secret of My Success, The	GB	1965	Andrew Stone	103	sc/std		FB	18
Secret of Nimh, The	USA	1982	Don Bluth	83			FB	38
Secret of Santa Vittoria, The	USA	1969	Stanley Kramer	140	sc/std		FB	18
Secret Partner	GB	1961	Basil Dearden	91	bw		FB	15
Secret People	GB	1951	Thorold Dickinson	96			GB	20
Secret Service	USA	1931	J. Walter Ruben	68			GB	15
Secret War of Harry Frigg, The	USA	1967	Jack Smight	110	std		FB	18
Secret Ways, The	USA	1961	Phil Karlson	111			FB	15

S

	COUNTRY OF PRODUCTION	YEAR	DIRECTOR	RUNNING TIME	VERSION	35mm	16mm	16mm RENTAL FEE
Secret, The	FR	1974	Robert Enrico	102	est		GB	30
Secrets of Life	USA	1956	James Algar	69			FB	22
Secrets of Sex	GB	1969	Anthony Balch	92			GB	40
Secrets of the French Police	USA	1932	Edward Sutherland	58			GB	15
Seduction of Joe Tynan, The	USA	1979	Jerry Schatzberg	107			FB	33
Seduction of Julia, The	AUST/FR	1962	Alfred Weidenmann	97	dub		GB	15
See No Evil, Hear No Evil	USA	1989	Arthur Hiller	107		C	FB	55
Seedling, The (see Ankur)								
Seems Like Old Times	USA	1980	Jay Sandrich	102			FB	41
Sell Out, The	GB/IT	1975	Peter Collinson	102			FB	18
Semaine de Vacances, Une	FR	1980	Bertrand Tavernier	100	est		GB	50
Semi-Tough	USA	1977	Michael Ritchie	107		UIP	FB	27
Sense of Loss, A	GB	1972	Marcel Ophuls	132			GB	25
Senso	IT	1954	Luchino Visconti	100	est	BFI	BFI	30
Sentenced to Success	HOLL	1978	Union of Atomic Energy Workers	70			CONC	22
Sentinel, The	USA	1976	Michael Winner	92			FB	38
Separate Beds	USA	1963	Arthur Hiller	105	sc/std		FB	18
September Affair	USA	1950	William Dieterle	105			FB	15
September Wheat	W.GER	1980	Peter Krieg	96	eng		WFA	35
Serail	FR	1975	Eduardo De Gregorio	90	sc/est		GB	35
Serengeti Shall Not Die	W.GER	1959	Michael Grzimek	87			GFL	0
Serfs	CHI	1964	Li Jun	95	est		GB	15
Sergeant Deadhead	USA	1965	Norman Taurog	89	sc/std		FB	18
Sergeant Rutledge	USA	1960	John Ford	111		W	FB	20
Sergeant York	USA	1941	Howard Hawks	134			FB	22
Sergei Eisenstein	USSR	1958	V. Katanyan	52		CONT	GB	15
Serpent and the Rainbow, The	USA	1988	Wes Craven	98			FB	55
Serpico	USA	1973	Sidney Lumet	130			FB	33
Servant, The	GB	1963	Joseph Losey	116		MAY	FB	15
Servante et Maitresse	FR	1977	Bruno Gantillon	90	est		GB	25
Serving Two Masters	USA	1987	Edward Tim Lewis	bw			BFI	25
Set-Up, The	USA	1948	Robert Wise	72			GB	15
Sett for Sunday	GB		Upper Coquetdale Film Group	70			NA	30
7 Women	USA	1965	John Ford	93	sc/std	UIP	FB	22
Seven Brides for Seven Brothers	USA	1953	Stanley Donen	102	sc/std	UIP	FB	27
Seven Days a Week	CZ	1968	Pavel Kohout	102	est		ETV	10
Seven Days Ashore	USA	1944	John H. Auer	74			GB	15
Seven Days Leave	USA	1942	Tim Whelan	87			GB	15
Seven Deadly Sins	FR/IT	1952	Eduardo De Filippo/Jean Dréville/ Yves Allégret/Roberto Rossellini/Carlo Rim/ Claude Autant-Lara/Georges Lacombe	140			GB	25
Seven Faces of Dr. Lao	USA	1964	George Pal	99			FB	20
Seven Hills of Rome	USA/IT	1958	Roy Rowland	103	sc/std		FB	18
Seven Keys to Baldpate	USA	1947	Lew Landers	68			GB	15
Seven Keys to Baldpate	USA	1930	Reginald Barker	75			GB	15
Seven Keys to Baldpate	USA	1935	William Hamilton/Edward Killy	80			GB	15
Seven Miles from Alcatraz	USA	1942	Edward Dmytryk	62			GB	15
Seven Nights in Japan	GB/FR	1976	Lewis Gilbert	104			FB	18
Seven Plus Seven	GB	1970	Seven Interviews	55			BFI	14
Seven Samurai	JAP	1954	Akira Kurosawa	200	est/155	BFI	GB	40
Seven Seas to Calais	USA/IT	1962	Rudolph Maté	101	sc/std		FB	18
Seven Sinners	USA	1940	Tay Garnett	87			FB	22
Seven Songs about Armenia	USSR			66			ETV	5
Seven Ways from Sundown	USA	1960	Harry Keller	86	col		FB	18
					bw		FB	15
Seven Year Itch, The	USA	1955	Billy Wilder	105	std	F	FB	18
Seven-per-cent Solution, The	USA	1976	Herbert Ross	114			FB	27
Seven-Ups, The	USA	1973	Philip D'Antoni	103			FB	18

S

	COUNTRY OF PRODUCTION	YEAR	DIRECTOR	RUNNING TIME	VERSION	35mm	16mm	16mm RENTAL FEE
Seventeen	DEN	1965	Annelise Meineche	88	est		FB	25
1776	USA	1972	Peter Hunt	132	sc/std		FB	18
7th Heaven	USA	1927	Frank Borzage	119	sd/t		BFI	25
7th Voyage of Sinbad, The	USA	1958	Nathan Juran	79		C	FB	18
Seventh Dawn, The	USA/GB	1964	Lewis Gilbert	123			FB	18
Seventh Seal, The	SWE	1957	Ingmar Bergman	95	est		GB	35
Seventh Sign, The	USA	1988	Carl Schultz	97			FB	60
Seventh Veil, The	GB	1945	Compton Bennett	94			BFI	25
Seventh Victim, The	USA	1943	Mark Robson	71			GB	15
Seventy Deadly Pills	GB	1963	Pat Jackson	55			GB	12
Severed Head, A	GB	1970	Dick Clement	98			FB	18
Sex and the Single Girl	USA	1964	Richard Quine	110			FB	18
Sex With the Stars	GB	1980	Anwar Kawadri	92			GB	40
sex, lies and videotape	USA	1989	Steven Soderbergh	100		FFC	GB	90
Sgt. Pepper's Lonely Hearts Club Band	USA/ W.GER	1978	Michael Schultz	111	sc/std	UIP	FB	33
Shadow of a Doubt	HOLL	1975	Rolf Orthel	53			CONT	20
Shadow of Terror	USA	1945	Lew Landers	60			GB	25
Shadow of the Cat, The	GB	1961	John Gilling	79			FB	15
Shadow of the Hawk	CAN	1976	George McCowan	92			FB	18
Shaft	USA	1971	Gordon Parks	100			FB	22
Shaft in Africa	USA	1973	John Guillermin	109	sc/std		FB	22
Shaft's Big Score	USA	1972	Gordon Parks	105	sc/std		FB	22
Shag	USA	1987	Zelda Barron	100			FB	5
Shaggy D.A., The	USA	1976	Robert Stevenson	92		D	FB	33
Shaggy Dog, The	USA	1959	Charles Barton	104			FB	22
Shake Hands With Murder	USA	1944	Albert Herman	60			GB	20
Shakedown, The	GB	1959	John Lamont	94			GB	15
Shakespeare Wallah	INDIA	1965	James Ivory	125			GB	25
Shakiest Gun in the West	USA	1967	Alan Rafkin	88	std		FB	18
Shalako	GB	1968	Edward Dmytryk	113	std		FB	18
Shall We Dance?	USA	1937	Mark Sandrich	116			GB	16
Shame	SWE	1967	Ingmar Bergman	103	est		FB	22
Shampoo	USA	1975	Hal Ashby	110		C	FB	27
Shane	USA	1952	George Stevens	116		UIP	FB	27
Shanghai Express	USA	1932	Josef von Sternberg	81			BFI	25
Shanghai Surprise	GB	1986	Jim Goddard	97			FB	45
Shark Reef	USA	1957	Roger Corman	62	col		FB	18
Shark's Treasure	USA	1974	Cornel Wilde	95			FB	18
Sharkey's Machine	USA	1981	Burt Reynolds	121			FB	40
Shattered	FR/IT	1976	Serge Leroy	103	est		FB	22
Shattered	USA	1991	Wolfgang Petersen	98			GB	80
She	GB	1965	Robert Day	105	std/sc		FB	18
She Demons	USA	1957	Richard E. Cunha	80			GB	15
She Must Be Seeing Things	USA	1987	Sheila McLaughlin	94			MP	69
She Wore a Yellow Ribbon	USA	1949	John Ford	100			GB	24
She'll Have To Go	GB	1962	Robert Asher	90			GB	20
She's Got Everything	USA	1938	Joseph Santley	72			GB	15
She's Gotta Have It	USA	1986	Spike Lee	85			GB	60
She's My Weakness	USA	1930	Melville Brown	74			GB	15
Sheba Baby	USA	1975	William Girdler	80			GB	22
Sheepman, The	USA	1958	George Marshall	86	sc/std		FB	18
Sheltering Sky, The	GB	1990	Bernardo Bertolucci	138		MAY	GB	80
Sheriff of Fractured Jaw, The	GB	1958	Raoul Walsh	103	sc/std		FB	14
Sherlock Holmes and the Secret Weapon	USA	1943	Roy William Neill	67			GB	15
Sherman's March	USA	1986	Ross McElwee	155			GB	60
Shine So Hard	GB	1981	John Smith/Bill Butt	32/15			GB	25
Shining, The	GB	1980	Stanley Kubrick	119	144		FB	50
Ship of Fools	USA	1965	Stanley Kramer	143			FB	15

	COUNTRY OF PRODUCTION	YEAR	DIRECTOR	RUNNING TIME	VERSION	35mm	16mm	16mm RENTAL FEE
Ship that Died of Shame, The	GB	1955	Basil Dearden/Michael Relph	91			FB	15
Ships With Wings	GB	1941	Sergei Nolbandov	103			GB	20
Shipwreck	USA	1978	Stewart Raffill	102			FB	30
Shiralee	GB	1957	Leslie Norman	99			FB	15
Shirin's Wedding	W.GER	1976	Helke Sanders-Brahms	116	est		MP	46
Shirley Valentine	USA	1989	Lewis Gilbert	108			FB	65
Shock	IT	1977	Mario Bava	87	dub		GB	33
Shock Corridor	USA	1963	Samuel Fuller	101			BFI	55
Shock Treatment	GB	1981	Jim Sharman	95			FB	40
Shoes of the Fisherman, The	USA	1968	Michael Anderson	155	sc/std		FB	30
Shoot Out	USA	1971	Henry Hathaway	94			FB	18
Shoot the Moon	USA	1981	Alan Parker	124			FB	38
Shoot the Pianist (see Tirez Sur le Pianiste)								
Shooting Party, The	GB	1984	Alan Bridges	101	MAY		GB	50
Shooting Stars	GB	1927	Anthony Asquith/ A. V. Bramble	96	st		BFI	20
Shootist, The	USA	1976	Don Siegel	100		UIP	FB	38
Shop Around the Corner, The	USA	1939	Ernst Lubitsch	99			FB	18
Shop On the High Street	CZ	1964	Jan Kadar/Elmar Klos	128	est		GB	30
Short Circuit	USA	1986	John Badham	98			FB	50
Short Time	USA	1987	Gregg Champion	97		R	FB	55
Short Weights	W.GER	1971	Bernhard Wicki	131	est		GFL	0
Shot in the Dark, A	GB	1964	Blake Edwards	100	sc		FB	27
Shout at the Devil	GB	1976	Peter Hunt	147	sc/std		GB	40
Shout, The	GB	1978	Jerzy Skolimowski	86			FB	33
Show Business	USA	1944	Edwin L. Marin	95			GB	15
Show Goes On, The	GB	1937	Basil Dean	94			BFI	30
Show of Shows	USA	1929	John G. Adolfi	124			FB	15
Showdown	USA	1963	R.G. Springsteen	79			FB	15
Showdown	USA	1972	George Seaton	99	sc/std		FB	18
Shrike, The	USA	1955	José Ferrer	88			FB	15
Siberian Lady Macbeth	YUGO	1961	Andrzej Wajda	92	sc/est		BFI	25
Sicilian Clan, The	FR	1968	Henri Verneuil	117	sc		FB	18
Sid and Nancy	GB	1986	Alex Cox	114			GB	60
Sid Caesar's Hour	USA	1959	A Sid Caesar Show	54			BFI	9
Side by Side	GB	1975	Bruce Beresford	85			GB	24
Sidecar Racers	USA	1974	Earl Bellamy	100			FB	18
Sidewalks of New York	USA	1931	Jules White/Zion Myers	74			FB	27
Sidney Sheldon's Bloodline	USA/ W.GER	1979	Terence Young	117			FB	38
Siege at Red River	USA	1954	Rudolph Maté	85			FB	18
Siege of Pinchgut, The	GB	1959	Harry Watt	104			FB	15
Sierra Baron	USA	1958	James B. Clark	79	sc/std		FB	18
Siesta	USA	1987	Mary Lambert	100			FB	60
Sign Is A Fine Investment, A	GB	1983	Judith Williamson	50			AC	20
Sign of the Cross, The	USA	1932	Cecil B. DeMille	107	120		FB	22
Sign of the Pagan	USA	1954	Douglas Sirk	92	std		FB	27
Sign of Zorro, The	USA	1958	Norman Foster/Lewis Foster	90			FB	22
Signora di Tutti, La	IT	1934	Max Ophuls	89	est	BFI	BFI	30
Signora Senza Camelie, La	IT	1953	Michelangelo Antonioni	101	est		BFI	25
Signpost to Murder	USA	1964	George Englund	69			FB	15
Signs of Life	W.GER	1968	Werner Herzog	89	bw/est		MP	51.75
Silence of the Lambs	USA	1991	Jonathan Demme	119			R	0
Silence, The	SWE	1963	Ingmar Bergman	94	est		GB	35
Silent Bell, The	USA	1944	Robert Wise	70			GB	15
Silent Flute, The	USA	1978	Richard Moore	95			FB	27
Silent Minority	GB	1981	Nigel Evans	60			CONC	19.2
Silent Movie	USA	1976	Mel Brooks	87			FB	33
Silent Running	USA	1971	Douglas Trumbull	89			FB	18
Silent Voice	USA	1987	Mike Newell	115			FB	40

	COUNTRY OF PRODUCTION	YEAR	DIRECTOR	RUNNING TIME	VERSION	35mm	16mm	16mm RENTAL FEE
Silk Stockings	USA	1957	Rouben Mamoulian	117	sc/std		FB	22
Silly Billies	USA	1936	Fred Guiol	64			GB	15
Silver Bears	GB	1977	Ivan Passer	113	sc/std		FB	24
Silver Bullet	USA	1985	Daniel Attias	94	sc		FB	40
Silver Dream Racer	GB	1979	David Wickes	111	sc		FB	38
Silver Horde	USA	1930	George Archainbaud	76			GB	15
Silver Streak	USA	1976	Arthur Hiller	113			FB	30
Silver Streak, The	USA	1934	Tommy Atkins	72			GB	15
Silverado	USA	1985	Lawrence Kasdan	132	sc/std		FB	55
Simba	GB	1955	Brian Desmond Hurst	98			FB	18
Simon	USA	1980	Marshall Brickman	97			FB	41
Sin of Harold Diddlebock. The (see Mad Wednesday)								
Sin Ship, The	USA	1931	Louis Wolheim	65			GB	15
Sin Takes a Holiday	USA	1930	Paul L. Stein	81			GB	15
Sinai Field Mission	USA	1978	Frederick Wiseman	127			GB	35
Sinbad and the Eye of the Tiger	GB	1977	Sam Wanamaker	113			FB	22
Sinbad the Sailor	USA	1947	Richard Wallace	115	col		GB	22
					bw		GB	18
Since You Went Away	USA	1944	John Cromwell	136			GB	22
Sinful Davey	GB	1968	John Huston	95	sc		FB	18
Sing	USA	1989	Richard Baskin	98		C	FB	55
Sing and Like It	USA	1934	William A. Seiter	72			GB	15
Sing As We Go	GB	1934	Basil Dean	77			BFI	30
Sing Your Way Home	USA	1945	Anthony Mann	72			GB	15
Sing Your Worries Away	USA	1942	Edward Sutherland	71			GB	15
Singer Not the Song, The	GB	1960	Roy Ward Baker	132	bw/std		FB	15
Singing Nun, The	USA	1965	Henry Koster	96	std		FB	18
Sink the Bismarck!	GB	1960	Lewis Gilbert	98	sc		FB	15
Sirène du Mississippi, La	FR/IT	1969	François Truffaut	109	std/dub		FB	18
Sister Kenny	USA	1946	Dudley Nichols	118			GB	15
Sisters or the Balance of Happiness	W. GER	1980	Margarethe von Trotta	95	est	BD	GB	60
Sitting Ducks	USA	1978	Henry Jaglom	88			MP	45
Sitting in Limbo	CAN	1986	John N. Smith	95			MP	50
Sitting Target	GB	1972	Douglas Hickox	93			FB	24
Six Days in Soweto	GB	1976	Anthony Thomas	60			CONC	21.60
6.5 Special	GB	1958	Alfred Shaughnessy	85			FB	13
Six Gun Law	USA	1962	Christian Nyby	78			FB	27
Six Inches Tall	USA	1957	Bert I. Gordon	78			FB	15
633 Squadron	GB	1964	Walter Grauman	94	std		FB	22
Six Weeks	USA	1982	Tony Bill	107			FB	38
Sixth of the Earth, A	USSR	1926	Dziga Vertov	60	est/st		GB	35
Sixty Four Day Hero	GB	1985	Franco Rosso	92			BFI	40
Skanderberg	ALB/ USSR	1953	Sergei Yutkevitch	78	est/110		ETV	10
Skateboard	USA	1977	George Gage	95			FB	27
Skates	USA	1962	Norman Foster	90	dub		FB	27
Ski Party	USA	1965	Alan Rafkin	80	sc/std		FB	18
Ski Raiders, The	USA	1972	George Englund	90	sc		FB	18
Skin Deep	USA	1989	Blake Edwards	101		F	FB	55
Skin Game	USA	1971	Paul Bogart	102	sc/std		FB	18
Skip Tracer	CAN	1977	Zale Dalen	92			GB	35
Skipper Surprised His Wife	USA	1950	Elliott Nugent	85			FB	15
Sky Bike, The	GB	1967	Charles Frend	62			GB	17
Sky Devils	USA	1931	Edward Sutherland	89			BFI	25
Sky Giant	USA	1938	Lew Landers	81			GB	15
Sky on Location, The	USA	1983	Babette Mangolte	90			CIRC	35
Sky Pirates	GB	1976	C. M. Pennington Richards	60			GB	17
Sky West and Crooked	GB	1965	John Mills	102	bw		FB	15
Sky's the Limit, The	USA	1942	Edward H. Griffith	91			GB	15

	COUNTRY OF PRODUCTION	YEAR	DIRECTOR	RUNNING TIME	VERSION	35mm	16mm	16mm RENTAL FEE
Skyjacked	USA	1972	John Guillermin	101	sc/std		FB	26
Skyriders	USA	1976	Douglas Hickox	91	sc/std		FB	22
SL-I	USA	1983	Dianne Orr/C. Larry Roberts	60			MP	28.75
Slams, The	USA	1973	Jonathan Kaplan	97			FB	38
Slander	USA	1956	Roy Rowland	76			FB	15
Slap Shot	USA	1977	George Roy Hill	124			FB	43
Slaughter on Tenth Avenue	USA	1957	Arnold Laven	103			FB	15
Slaughterhouse – Five	USA	1972	George Roy Hill	103			FB	18
Slaves of New York	USA	1989	James Ivory	125		C	FB	55
Sleep My Love	USA	1947	Douglas Sirk	95			GB	15
Sleeper	USA	1973	Woody Allen	88		UIP	FB	27
Sleeping Tiger, The	GB	1954	Joseph Losey	89			FB	15
Sleeping With The Enemy	USA	1991	Joseph Ruben	94			F	0
Sleuth	GB	1972	Joseph L. Mankiewicz	138			FB	27
Slim Carter	USA	1957	Richard H. Bartlett	81			FB	15
Slipper and the Rose, The	GB	1976	Bryan Forbes	143	sc/std	GB	GB	45
Slither	USA	1973	Howard Zieff	96			FB	18
Slow Dancing in the Big City	USA	1978	John G. Avildsen	110			FB	22
Slumber Party '57	USA	1976	William A. Levey	87			FB	27
Small Back Room, The	GB	1949	Michael Powell/ Emeric Pressburger	107			BFI	25
Small Circle of Friends, A	USA	1980	Rob Cohen	113			FB	33
Small Girl to Let (see Primel – Kleines Mädchen Zu Verleihen)								
Small Summer Blues	CZ	1968	Jiri Hanibal	74			ETV	10
Smallest Show on Earth, The	GB	1957	Basil Dearden				GB	80
Smart Money	USA	1931	Alfred E. Green	83			FB	22
Smashing the Rackets	USA	1938	Lew Landers	60			GB	15
Smashing Time	GB	1967	Desmond Davis	96			FB	18
Smile	USA	1974	Michael Ritchie	113			FB	22
Smile Orange	JAM	1974	Trevor D. Rhone	88			GB	50
Smiles of a Summer Night	SWE	1955	Ingmar Bergman	105	est		GB	35
Smokey and the Bandit	USA	1977	Hal Needham	97			FB	43
Smokey and the Bandit Ride Again	USA	1980	Hal Needham	101			FB	43
Smokey Joe's Revenge	GB	1974	Ronald Spencer	57			GB	17
Smooth Talk	USA	1985	Joyce Chopra	91			GB	60
Smouldering Fires	USA	1924	Clarence Brown	94	st		BFI	15
Smugglers of Death	CZ	1961		90	est		ETV	10
Snoopy Come Home	USA	1972	Bill Melendez	80			GB	25
Snow Queen, The	USSR	1966	Gennadi Kazanski	80	dub		GB	20
Snowball Express	USA	1972	Norman Tokar	93	col/std		FB	33
So Dear to My Heart	USA	1948	Harold Schuster	82			FB	27
So Fine	USA	1981	Andrew Bergman	91			FB	33
So Ist Das Leben (see Such Is Life)								
So Little Time	GB	1952	Compton Bennett	90			GB	20
So That You Can Live	GB	1982	Cinema Action	81			CA/BFI	35
So Well Remembered	GB	1947	Edward Dmytryk	114			GB	15
Soap Box Derby, The	GB	1957	Darcy Conyers	64			GB	12
Soapdish	USA	1991	Michael Hoffman	96		UIP	FB	70
Soft Beds, Hard Battles	GB	1973	Roy Boulting	98			FB	27
Soir, Un Train, Un	BELG/ FR	1968	André Delvaux	89	dub/est		FB	18
Solaris	USSR	1972	Andrei Tarkovsky	165	est		GB	38
Soldier and the Lady, The	USA	1937	George Nicholls Jr	84			GB	15
Soldier Blue	USA	1970	Ralph Nelson	114	sc/std		FB	30
Soldier Girls	GB	1981	Nick Broomfield/ Joan Churchill	90			GB	30
Soldier's Story, A	USA	1984	Norman Jewison	101		C	FB	45
Soldier's Tale, The	GB	1963	Michael Birkett	55			GB	18
Soldiers of the Revolution	USSR	1972	Kamil Yarmatov	90	est		ETV	10
Some Came Running	USA	1958	Vincente Minnelli	136	sc/std		FB	18
Some Girls Do	GB	1969	Ralph Thomas	93			FB	18

	COUNTRY OF PRODUCTION	YEAR	DIRECTOR	RUNNING TIME	VERSION	35mm	16mm	16mm RENTAL FEE
Some Like It Hot	USA	1959	Billy Wilder	121		UIP	FB	27
Some People	GB	1962	Clive Donner	93			GB	25
Some Will, Some Won't	GB	1959	Duncan Wood	90			FB	18
Somebody Up There Likes Me	USA	1956	Robert Wise	110			FB	15
Someone from the Welfare	GB	1973	Jenny Barraclough	69			CONC	14.20
Someone to Watch Over Me	USA	1987	Ridley Scott	107			FB	55
Something Always Happens	GB	1934	Michael Powell	69			BFI	20
Something Big	USA	1971	Andrew V. McLaglen	108			GB	18
Something Short of Paradise	USA	1979	Fred Barron	91			GB	27
Something Wicked This Way Comes	USA	1982	Jack Clayton	95			FB	38
Something Wild	USA	1986	Jonathan Demme	114			FB	50
Somewhere in Hackney	GB	1980	Ron Orders (Community Arts)	50			AC	20
Somewhere in Time	USA	1980	Jeannot Szwarc	104			FB	38
Son of Ali Baba	USA	1952	Kurt Neumann	75	bw		FB	15
Son of Frankenstein	USA	1938	Rowland V. Lee	95			FB	15
Son of Kong	USA	1933	Ernest Schoedsack	72			GB	16
Son of Sinbad	USA	1955	Ted Tetzlaff	86	std		GB	22
Son of Spartacus	IT	1962	Sergio Corbucci	100	sc/std		FB	18
Son of the Sheik, The	USA	1926	George Fitzmaurice	90	st/sd		BFI	25
Song of Bernadette, The	USA	1944	Henry King	156			FB	15
Song of Youth	CHI	1959	Cui Wei/Chen Huaiai	170	st		GB	40
Song of Love	USA	1947	Clarence Brown	118			FB	15
Song of Norway	USA	1970	Andrew Stone	141	sc/std		GB	33
Song of the Shirt, The	GB	1979	Susan Clayton/ Jonathan Curling	135			MP	50.60
Song of the South	USA	1946	Harve Foster/ Wilfred Jackson	95			FB	33
Song Remains the Same, The	GB	1976	Peter Clifton/Joe Massot	137			FB	33
Song to Remember, A	USA	1944	Charles Vidor	110			FB	18
Song Without End	USA	1960	Charles Vidor	130	sc/std		FB	18
Sons and Daughters	CHI	1951	Sze Tung-San	90			ETV	10
Sons of Katie Elder, The	USA	1965	Henry Hathaway	122	sc/std		FB	18
Sons of the Desert (see Fraternally Yours)								
Sophie's Choice	USA	1982	Alan J. Pakula	151			FB	38
Sorrowful Jones	USA	1948	Sidney Lanfield	88			FB	15
Sound and the Fury, The	USA	1959	Martin Ritt	115	std		FB	18
Sound of Music, The	USA	1965	Robert Wise	174	sc/std		FB	63
Sources of Creation	USSR	1975		60			ETV	7
South of St. Louis	USA	1949	Ray Enright	88	bw		GB	18
					col		GB	20
South of the Border	AUSTR	1988	David Bradbury	63			WFA	30
South Pacific	USA	1958	Joshua Logan	139			GB	53
South, The (see Sur, El)								
Southern Comfort	USA	1981	Walter Hill	105			FB	43
Southern Star, The	GB	1968	Sidney Hayers	105	sc/std		FB	18
Southwest to Sonora	USA	1966	Sidney J. Furie	98	bw/std		FB	15
Soviet Art	GB	1983	Binia Tymieniecka	60			AC	16
Soviet Concert	USSR	1967		90			ETV	5
Soylent Green	USA	1973	Richard Fleischer	97	sc/std		FB	26
Spaceballs	USA	1987	Mel Brooks	98			FB	50
Spaceman and King Arthur, The	USA	1979	Russ Mayberry	93			FB	38
Spanish Fly	GB	1975	Bob Kellett	86			FB	18
Spanish Gardener, The	GB	1956	Philip Leacock	97	bw		FB	15
Spanish Main, The	USA	1945	Frank Borzage	105	col/bw		GB	15
Spare a Copper	GB	1940	John Paddy Carstairs	79			FB	15
Spare the Rod	GB	1961	Leslie Norman	93			FB	15
Sparrows Can't Sing	GB	1962	Joan Littlewood	94			FB	15
Spartacus the Gladiator	IT	1953	Riccardo Freda	95	dub		GB	15
Speaking Directly	USA	1974	Jon Jost	106			BFI	35
Special Delivery	USA	1976	Paul Wendkos	98			FB	18

	COUNTRY OF PRODUCTION	YEAR	DIRECTOR	RUNNING TIME	VERSION	35mm	16mm	16mm RENTAL FEE
Special Investigator	USA	1936	Louis King	61			GB	15
Speedway	USA	1968	Norman Taurog	94	sc/std		FB	22
Spellbound	USA	1945	Alfred Hitchcock	111		GB	GB	25
Spencer's Mountain	USA	1963	Delmer Daves	106			FB	18
Sphinx	USA	1980	Franklin J. Schaffner	118	sc		FB	41
Spider's Stratagem	IT	1970	Bernardo Bertolucci	97	st		GB	40
Spiderman	USA	1977	E.W. Swackhamer	93			FB	25
Spiderman – the Dragon's Challenge	USA	1979	Don McDougall	96			FB	25
Spiders, The	GER	1919	Fritz Lang	137	sd/cst		BFI	25
Spies Like Us	USA	1985	John Landis	102			FB	50
Spikes Gang, The	USA	1974	Richard Fleischer	96			FB	18
Spinster, The	USA	1961	Charles Walters	99	sc/std		FB	18
Spiral Road, The	USA	1962	Robert Mulligan	136	std/col		FB	18
					bw		FB	15
Spiral Staircase, The	USA	1946	Robert Siodmak	83			GB	15
Spiral Staircase, The	GB	1975	Peter Collinson	89			FB	18
Spiral, The	FR	1976	Armand Mattelart/Jacqueline Meppiel/	145	eng		MP	51.75
			Valerie Mayoux/Chris Marker/					
			Jean-Michel Folon/Pierre Flament					
Spiral, The	POL	1978	Krzysztof Zanussi	90	est		FOP	0
Spirit is Willing, The	USA	1966	William Castle	92			FB	18
Spirit of the Beehive	SP	1973	Victor Erice	98	est		GB	40
Spirit of the People, The	USA	1940	John Cromwell	110			GB	15
Spitfire	USA	1934	John Cromwell	88			GB	16
Splash	USA	1984	Ron Howard	110		T	FB	38
Split Second	USA	1953	Dick Powell	89			GB	15
Spongers, The	GB	1978	Roland Joffe	103			CONC	24
Sport Parade, The	USA	1932	Dudley Murphy	65			GB	15
Spot	CAN	1974	Jeffrey Bloom	88			GB	18
Spring and Port Wine	GB	1969	Peter Hammond	101			FB	18
Spy in the Green Hat, The	USA	1966	Joseph Sargent	92			FB	18
Spy in Your Eye	IT	1965	Vittorio Sala	105	dub		FB	18
Spy Who Loved Me, The	GB	1977	Lewis Gilbert	125	sc		FB	53
Spy With My Face, The	USA	1964	John Newland	86			FB	18
Spy, The	GER	1928	Fritz Lang	114	st/est		BFI	25
SPYS	GB	1974	Irvin Kershner	104			FB	18
Square of Violence	USA/ YUGO	1961	Leonardo Bercovici	93			FB	15
Square Peg, The	GB	1958	John Paddy Carstairs	89			FB	15
Square Ring	GB	1953	Michael Relph/Basil Dearden	83			GB	20
Squeeze a Flower	AUSTR	1969	Marc Daniels	90			FB	18
Squeeze, The	GB	1977	Michael Apted	106			FB	27
St. Elizabeth's Square	CZ	1965	Vladimir Bahna	88	est		ETV	10
St. Elmo's Fire	USA	1985	Joel Schumacher	106	sc/std		FB	45
St. Ives	USA	1976	J. Lee Thompson	94			FB	18
St. Valentine's Day Massacre	USA	1967	Roger Corman	99	sc/std		FB	18
Stage Struck	USA	1959	Sidney Lumet	95			GB	18
Stagecoach	USA	1939	John Ford	95		BFI	BFI	25
Stagecoach	USA	1966	Gordon Douglas	114	sc/std		FB	18
Stagecoach Kid	USA	1949	Lew Landers	60			GB	15
Stage Door	USA	1937	Gregory La Cava	92			GB	15
Stages – Peter Brook and CICT in Australia	AUS	1980	Macau Lightfilms	50			AC	20
			Produced by Brian Adams					
Stakeout	USA	1987	John Badham	117			FB	50
Stalker	USSR	1979	Andrei Tarkovsky	161	est		GB	50
Stand and Deliver	USA	1988	Ramon Menendez	104			FB	50
Stand By Me	USA	1986	Rob Reiner	89		W	FB	50
Stand Up and Fight	USA	1939	W.S. Van Dyke	97		W	FB	15
Stand Up Virgin Soldiers	GB	1977	Norman Cohen	91			FB	22

	COUNTRY OF PRODUCTION	YEAR	DIRECTOR	RUNNING TIME	VERSION	35mm	16mm	16mm RENTAL FEE
Stand-In	USA	1937	Tay Garnett	90			BFI	20
Stanley and Livingstone	USA	1940	Henry King	101			FB	15
Star	USA	1968	Robert Wise	120	sc/std		FB	22
Star 80	USA	1983	Bob Fosse	103			FB	50
Star Is Born, A	USA	1976	Frank R. Pierson	140		W	FB	33
Star of India	GB	1953	Arthur Lubin	90			GB	15
Star of Midnight	USA	1935	Stephen Roberts	90			GB	15
Star Spangled Rhythm	USA	1942	George Marshall	85			FB	15
StarTrek II – The Wrath of Khan	USA	1982	Nicholas Meyer	113	sc/std		FB	48
Star Trek III – The Search for Spock	USA	1984	Leonard Nimoy	105		UIP	FB	45
Star Trek the Motion Picture	USA	1979	Robert Wise	132	std	UIP	FB	48
Star Trek V: The Final Frontier	USA	1989	William Shatner	107		UIP	FB	55
Star Trek VI: The Undiscovered Country	USA	1991	Nicholas Meyer	117		UIP	FB	70
Star Wars	USA	1977	George Lucas	121	sc/std	F	FB	60
Stardust	GB	1974	Michael Apted	113			FB	19
Stardust Memories	USA	1980	Woody Allen	89		UIP	FB	43
Starflight One	USA	1983	Jerry Jameson	114			FB	43
Starman	USA	1984	John Carpenter	115			FB	50
Stars and Bars	USA	1988	Pat O'Connor	94			FB	50
Stars Look Down, The	GB	1939	Carol Reed	99			BFI	20
Start the Revolution Without Me	USA	1969	Bud Yorkin	90			FB	18
Starting Over	USA	1979	Alan J. Pakula	106			FB	38
State Fair	USA	1962	José Ferrer	118	sc/std		FB	18
State of Grace	USA	1990	Phil Joanou	134		R	FB	60
State of Siege	FR/IT/ W.GE R	1973	Costa-Gavras	120	est		MP	51.75
Static	USA	1985	Mark Romanek	88		BD	GB	60
Station West	USA	1948	Sidney Lanfield	96			GB	15
Stay Away Joe	USA	1968	Peter Tewksbury	97	std		FB	22
Stay Hungry	USA	1976	Bob Rafelson	102			FB	18
Staying Alive	USA	1983	Sylvester Stallone	96			FB	48
Steam-Roller – The Violin, The	USSR	1961	Andrei Tarkovsky	50	est		GB	20
Steamboat Round the Bend	USA	1935	John Ford	81			FB	15
Steel	USA	1979	Steven Carver	101			FB	27
Steelyard Blues	USA	1972	Alan Myerson	93			FB	18
Step by Step	USA	1946	Phil Rosen	62			GB	15
Step Lively	USA	1944	Tim Whelan	90			GB	16
Stepford Wives, The	USA	1975	Bryan Forbes	115			GB	40
Steppenwolf	USA	1974	Fred Haines	106			GB	35
Stepping Out	USA	1991	Lewis Gilbert	108		F	FB	70
Steptoe and Son	GB	1972	Cliff Owen	97			FB	18
Steptoe and Son Ride Again	GB	1973	Peter Sykes	98			FB	18
Stereo	CAN	1969	David Cronenberg	65			MP	34.50
Stiletto	USA	1969	Bernard Kowalski	99			GB	18
Still Image	GB	1976	Mike Dunford	60	mag		BFI	15
Still of the Night	USA	1982	Robert Benton	90			FB	38
Sting II, The	USA	1982	Jeremy Paul Kagan	101			FB	38
Sting, The	USA	1973	George Roy Hill	129			FB	48
Stir Crazy	USA	1980	Sidney Poitier	111			FB	41
Stitch in Time, A	GB	1963	Robert Asher	94	bw		FB	15
Stone	AUSTR	1974	Sandy Harbutt	100			GB	38
Stone Killer, The	USA	1973	Michael Winner	96			FB	18
Stooge, The	USA	1951	Norman Taurog	98			FB	15
Stooges Go West, The	USA	1951	Edward Bernds	62			GB	15
Stop Or My Mom Will Shoot	USA	1991	Roger Spottiswoode	87		UIP	FB	65
Stopover Tokyo	USA	1957	Richard L. Breen	100	sc/std		FB	18
Stories from a Flying Trunk	GB	1979	Christine Edzard	87			FB	33
Storm Over Asia	USSR	1928	Vsevolod Pudovkin	87	sd/est		GB	20

	COUNTRY OF PRODUCTION	YEAR	DIRECTOR	RUNNING TIME	VERSION	35mm	16mm	16mm RENTAL FEE
Storm Warning	USA	1951	Stuart Heisler	90			FB	15
Stormy Monday	GB	1987	Mike Figgis	93			GB	75
Story of Gilbert and Sullivan	GB	1953	Sidney Gilliat	109	col		GB	25
Story of Louis Pasteur	USA	1935	William Dieterle	85			FB	22
Story of Night, The	SWITZ	1979	Clemens Klopfenstein	63	mag		LFC	30
Story of Robin Hood and His Merrie Men, The	GB	1952	Ken Annakin	84			FB	27
Story of Sea Biscuit	USA	1949	David Butler	93	bw		FB	15
Story of Three Loves, The	USA	1952	Gottfried Reinhardt/Vincente Minnelli	122	bw		FB	15
Story of Vernon and Irene Castle	USA	1939	H.C. Potter	99			GB	16
Story on Page One, The	USA	1959	Clifford Odets	123	sc/std		FB	15
Strada, La	IT	1954	Federico Fellini	104	est		GB	35
Straight On Till Morning	GB	1972	Peter Collinson	96			FB	18
Straight Time	USA	1977	Ulu Grosbard	114			FB	27
Strange Affair, The	GB	1968	David Greene	105	std		FB	18
Strange Bedfellows	USA	1965	Melvin Frank	99			FB	18
Strange Justice	USA	1932	Victor Schertzinger	72			GB	15
Strange Lady in Town	USA	1955	Melvyn LeRoy	112			FB	18
Strange Place to Meet, A	FR	1988	François Dupeyron	100	est		GB	60
Strange Vengeance of Rosalie, The	USA	1971	Jack Starrett	106			FB	18
Stranger in my Arms, A	USA	1958	Helmut Käutner	88	std		FB	15
Stranger in Town	USA	1953	Roy Rowland	67			FB	15
Stranger on the Third Floor	USA	1940	Boris Ingster	62			GB	15
Stranger Than Fiction	GB	1985	Ian Potts	88			BFI	35
Stranger, The	IJSA	1946	Orson Welles	94			BFI	25
Strangers All	USA	1935	Charles Vidor	69			GB	20
Strangers When We Meet	USA	1960	Richard Quine	117	col/sc		FB	18
Strangler of the Swamp	US	1945	Frank Wisbar	60			GB	25
Strapless	GB	1988	David Hare	100			GB	70
Strategia del Ragno (see Spider's Stratagem)								
Strategy of Acceleration, The	USSR	1986	Vladlen Troshkin	75	eng		ETV	12
Strategy of Terror	USA	i964	Jack Smight	90			FB	18
Stratton Story, The	USA	1949	Sam Wood	100			FB	15
Straw Dogs	GB	1971	Sam Peckinpah	118		GB	GB	38
Strawberry Blonde	USA	1941	Raoul Walsh	99			FB	22
Strawberry Statement, The	USA	1970	Stuart Hagmann	109			FB	18
Street Angel	USA	1928	Frank Borzage	101	sd		BFI	25
Street Angel	CHI	1937	Yuan Muzhi	93	est		BFI	25
Street Fleet	USA	1983	Joel Schumacher	99			FB	35
Street Girl	USA	1929	Wesley Ruggles	91			GB	15
Street Smart	USA	1987	Jerry Schatzberg	97			FB	40
Street Walker	FR	1976	Walerian Borowczyk	91	st		GB	40
Streetfighter, The	USA	1975	Walter Hill	93	sc/std		FB	22
Streets of Fire	USA	1984	Walter Hill	94			FB	40
Streets of Laredo	USA	1949	Leslie Fenton	92	bw		FB	15
Streetwise	USA	1984	Martin Bell	92			BFI/CONC	45
Strictly Ballroom	AUSTR	1992	Baz Luhrmann	94		R	FB	70
Strictly Confidential	GB	1959	Charles Saunders	64			GB	15
Strictly Dynamite	USA	1934	Elliott Nugent	71			GB	20
Strike	USSR	1924	Sergei Eisenstein	82	sd	CONT	GB	25
				94	st		GB	25
Strike and Occupation of a Print Shop	IT	1969	Cinegionali Liberi Collective	60			WFA	24
Strikebound	AUSTR	1984	Richard Lowenstein	100			MP	57.50
Strip Jack Naked	GB	1991	Ron Peck	91			BFI	75
Stripes	USA	1981	Ivan Reitman	106			FB	43
Strohfeuer	W.GER	1972	Volker Schlöndorff	105	est		GFL	0
Stromboli	IT	1950	Roberto Rossellini	81	eng (107)		BFI	25
Strongest Man in the World, The	USA	1975	Vincent McEveety	92			FB	33
Stroszek	W GER	1976	Werner Herzog	107	est		GB	40

	COUNTRY OF PRODUCTION	YEAR	DIRECTOR	RUNNING TIME	VERSION	35mm	16mm	16mm RENTAL FEE
Struggle for China	GB	1969	Tony Essex (Prod)	73			BFI	14
Stud, The	GB	1978	Quentin Masters	90			GB	40
Student von Prag, Der	GER	1913	Stellan Rye/Paul Wegener	60	gst/st		GFL	0
Study in Terror, A	GB	1965	James Hill	95			GB	20
Stunt Man, The	USA	1979	Richard Rush	131			FB	36
Stunts	USA	1977	Mark L. Lester	84			GB	38
Stutzen der Gesellschaft, Die (see Pillars of Society)								
Stylus	GB	1980	Stuart Pound	60	mag		LHA	30
Subterfuge	GB	1968	Peter Graham Scott	86			FB	18
Subterraneans, The	USA	1960	Ranald McDougall	89	std		FB	15
Subway	FR	1985	Luc Besson	102	est/sc		GB	55
Success At Any Price	USA	1934	J. Walter Ruben	77			GB	15
Such Good Friends	USA	1971	Otto Preminger	102			FB	18
Such Is Life	GER	1929	Karl Junghans	66	est/sd		BFI	15
Such Men Are Dangerous	USA	1955	Henry Hathaway	92	st-l		FB	18
Sudden Fortune of the Poor People of Kombach, The	W GER	1971	Volker Schlöndorff	80	est		GFL	0
Sudden Impact	USA	1983	Clint Eastwood	117		W	FB	55
Suddenly Last Summer	GB	1959	Joseph L. Mankiewicz	114			FB	15
Sued for Libel	USA	1940	Leslie Goodwins	69			GB	15
Suez	USA	1938	Allan Dwan	100			FB	15
Sugarbaby	W.GER	1985	Percy Adlon	86	est		GB	45
Sugarland Express	USA	1974	Steven Spielberg	110	sc/std	UIP	FB	18
Suicide Fleet	USA	1931	Albert S. Rogell	88			GB	15
Suit, The	USA	1968	Norman Tokar	113			FB	27
Summer Place	USA	1959	Delmer Daves	120	bw		FB	15
Summer Guests	W.GER	1976	Peter Stein	120	est		GFL.	0
Summer Holiday	GB	1962	Peter Yates	92	std/sc		FB	18
Summer Interlude	SWE	1950	Ingmar Bergman	97	est		GB	35
Summer Madness (see Summertime)								
Summer Magic	USA	1962	James Neilson	104			FB	27
Summer of '42	USA	1971	Robert Mulligan	104			FB	18
Summer of Fear	IJSA	1978	Wes Craven	93			GB	38
Summer of the Colt	CAN	1989	André Melançon	100			GB	0
Summer Paradise	SWE	1977	Gunnel Lindblom	113	est		GB	35
Summer Soldiers	JAP	1971	Hiroshi Teshigahara	103	est		APO	35
Summer Story, A	GB	1987	Piers Haggard	97			FB	55
Summer With Monika	SWE	1952	Ingmar Bergman	97	est		GB	35
Summertime	GB/USA	i955	David Lean	100			GB	18
Summer Wishes Winter Dreams	USA	1973	Gilbert Cates	88			FB	18
Sun Comes Up, The	USA	1949	Richard Thorpe	93			FB	15
Sunday Bloody Sunday	GB	1971	John Schlesinger	110		UIP	FB	22
Sunday in New York	IJSA	1963	Peter Tewksbury	105			FB	18
Sunday In The Country	FR	1984	Bertrand Tavernier	94	est		GB	55
Sundowners, The	AUSTR/GB	1960	Fred Zinemann	132			FB	18
Sunless (see Sans Soleil)								
Sunrise	USA	1927	F.W. Murnau	95	sd		BFI	25
Sunset	USA	1988	Blake Edwards	107	std/sc		FB	55
Sunshine	USA	1973	Joseph Sargent	103			FB	18
Sunshine Boys, The	USA	1975	Herbert Ross	112			FB	33
Sunstruck	GB	1972	James Gilbert	75			FB	18
Super Sleuth	USA	1937	Ben Stoloff	70			GB	15
Superbeast	USA	1972	George Schenck	92			FB	18
Supercops, The	USA	1973	Gordon Parks	94			FB	20
Superdad	USA	1974	Vincent McEveety	95			FB	27
Superfly	USA	1972	Gordon Parks Jr	97			FB	18
Superman The Movie	GB	1978	Richard Donner	143	sc/std	W	FB	50
Superman II	GB	1980	Richard Lester	127	sc/std	W	FB	50
Superman III	GB	1983	Richard Lester	125		W	FB	60

	COUNTRY OF PRODUCTION	YEAR	DIRECTOR	RUNNING TIME	VERSION	35mm	16mm	16mm RENTAL FEE
Superman IV: The Quest for Peace	USA	1987	Sidney J. Furie	89	sc		FB	60
Supersnooper	USA	1980	Sergio Corbucci	92			FB	33
Support Your Local Gunfighter	USA	1971	Burt Kennedy	92			FB	18
Support Your Local Sheriff	USA	1968	Burt Kennedy	93			FB	18
Suppose They Gave a War and Nobody Came	USA	1969	Hy Averback	113		GB	GB	18
Sur, El	SP	1983	Victor Erice	94	est	BFI	GB	40
Sure Thing, The	USA	1985	Rob Reiner	94			FB	40
Surrender	USA	1987	Jerry Belson	95			FB	50
Sürü (see The Herd)								
Survival 67	USA	1970	Jules Dassin	70			GB	20
Survival Run	HOLL	1977	Paul Verhoeven	120			FB	27
Susan Slept Here	USA	1954	Frank Tashlin	98			GB	15
Suspect	USA	1987	Peter Yates	121			FB	55
Suspect, The	USA	1944	Robert Siodmak	85			FB	22
Suspended Vocation	FR	1977	Raul Ruiz	97	est		BFI	35
Suspicion	USA	1941	Alfred Hitchcock	100			GB	35
Sven Klang's Combo	SWE	1976	Stellan Olsson	109	est		CONC	35
Svengali	USA	1931	Archie Mayo	81			FB	15
Svengali	GB	1954	Noel Langley	83	bw	GB	GB	15
Svetlana			Mike Hoolboom	55			LFMC	46.75
Swallows and Amazons	GB	1974	Claude Whatham	92			FB	25
Swamp of the Lost Monsters	MEX	1964	Rafael Baledon	75			GB	20
Swann in Love	FR/ W.GER	1984	Volker Schlöndorff	110	est	AE	GB	55
Swap, The	USA	1975	John Shade	90			FB	33
Swarm in May	GB	1983	Colin Finbow	90		BD	GB	40
Swarm, The	USA	1978	Irwin Allen	116	sc		FB	33
Swastika	GB	1973	Philippe Mora	100			GB	30
Sweeney	GB	1976	David Wickes	97			FB	27
Sweeney 2	GB	1978	Tom Clegg	108			FB	27
Sweepings	USA	1933	John Cromwell	80			GB	15
Sweepstakes	USA	1931	Albert S. Rogell	77			GB	15
Sweet Bird of Youth	USA	1961	Richard Brooks	120	sc/std		FB	18
Sweet Charity	USA	1968	Bob Fosse	132	sc/std		FB	18
Sweet Dreams	USA	1985	Karel Reisz	115			FB	40
Sweet Games of Last Summer	CZ	1969	Juraj Herz	67	est		GB	30
Sweet Jesus, Preacher Man	USA	1973	Henning Schellerup	103			FB	38
Sweet Liberty	USA	1985	Alan Alda	107		UIP	FB	40
Sweet November	USA	1968	Robert Ellis Miller	94	113		FB	18
Sweet Revenge	USA	1976	Jerry Schatzberg	90	sc/std		FB	28
Sweetie	AUSTR	1989	Jane Campion	100		ELEC	GB	80
Swept Away	IT	1975	Lina Wertmuller	120	est		GB	33
Swimmer, The	USA	1968	Frank Perry	94			FB	18
Swimming to Cambodia	USA	1987	Jonathan Demme	85			BFI	55
Swing Time	USA	1936	George Stevens	85			GB	22
Swing, The	W.GER	1983	Percy Adlon	133	est		GB	55
Swinging Summer, A	USA	1965	Robert Sparr	80	std		GB	22
Swiss Conspiracy, The	USA/W.GER	1975	Jack Arnold	80			FB	18
Swiss Family Robinson	USA	1960	Ken Annakin	126	sc/std		FB	38
Swiss Miss	USA	1938	John Blystone	65			GB	15
Swissmakers, The	SWITZ	1978	Rolf Lyssy	107	est		GB	40
Switch	USA	1991	Blake Edwards	103			FB	65
Switching Channels	USA	1988	Ted Kotcheff	105			FB	55
Sword and the Sorcerer, The	USA	1982	Albert Pyun	99		R	FB	38
Sword in the Stone, The	USA	1983	Wolfgang Reitherman	80		D	FB	35
Sword of Ali Baba, The	USA	1964	Virgil Vogel	81	bw		FB	15
Sword of Sherwood Forest	GB	1960	Terence Fisher	80	sc/std		FB	18
Sword of the Valiant: The Legend of Gawain and the Green Giant	GB	1973	Stephen Weeks	93	sc		FB	18

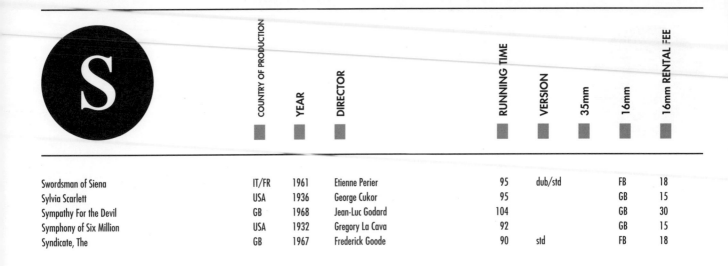

	COUNTRY OF PRODUCTION	YEAR	DIRECTOR	RUNNING TIME	VERSION	35mm	16mm	16mm RENTAL FEE
Swordsman of Siena	IT/FR	1961	Etienne Perier	95	dub/std		FB	18
Sylvia Scarlett	USA	1936	George Cukor	95			GB	15
Sympathy For the Devil	GB	1968	Jean-Luc Godard	104			GB	30
Symphony of Six Million	USA	1932	Gregory La Cava	92			GB	15
Syndicate, The	GB	1967	Frederick Goode	90	std		FB	18

Salaam Bombay!

	COUNTRY OF PRODUCTION	YEAR	DIRECTOR	RUNNING TIME	VERSION	35mm	16mm	16mm RENTAL FEE
T-Wo-Men	W.GER	1972	Werner Nekes	90			LFC	45
T. Dan Smith	GB	1987	Amber Films	85			BFI	35
Table for Five	USA	1983	Robert Lieberman	121			FB	43
Tadelloser & Wolff	W.GER	1975	Eberhard Fechner	195	est		GFL	0
Tadpole and the Whale	CAN	1988	Jean-Claude Lord	90			GB	40
Taggart	USA	1965	R.G. Springsteen	85	bw		FB	15
Take a Girl Like You	GB	1970	Jonathan Miller	98			FB	15
Take a Hard Ride	USA/IT	1975	Anthony M. Dawson	103			FB	18
Take Me as I Am	FR/IT	1959	Maurice Labro	92	dub		GB	25
Take Me High	GB	1973	David Askey	90			FB	18
Take the High Ground!	USA	1954	Richard Brooks	100			FB	15
Take the Money and Run	USA	1969	Woody Allen	85			GB	27
Taking of Pelham 123, The	USA	1974	Joseph Sargent	104	sc/std		FB	33
Taking Off	USA	1971	Milos Forman	92			FB	18
Taking Tiger Mountain by Strategy	CHI	1970	Collective	129	est		GB	25
Talacre School Film	GB	1976	George King	90			BFI	25
Tale of Springtine, A	FR	1989	Eric Rohmer	112	st	AE	GB	70
Tale of Two Cities, A	USA	1935	Jack Conway	128			FB	22
Tale of Two Cities, A	GB	1958	Ralph Thomas	117			FB	15
Tales From the Crypt	GB	1972	Freddie Francis	92		GB	GB	22
Tales of Beatrix Potter	GB	1971	Reginald Mills	91		SQ	FB	27
Tales of Hasek	CZ	1952	Miroslav Hubacek	90	est		ETV	10
Tales of Terror	USA	1962	Roger Corman	88	sc		FB	18
Talk of the Town, The	USA	1942	George Stevens	117			FB	15
Talk Radio	USA	1988	Oliver Stone	108			FB	65
Tall Guy, The	GB	1989	Mel Smith	90			GB	70
Tall in the Saddle	USA	1944	Edwin L. Marin	87			GB	15
Tall Men, The	USA	1955	Raoul Walsh	122	std		FB	18
Tall Target, The	USA	1951	Anthony Mann	78			FB	15
Tamahine	GB	1962	Philip Leacock	96	std		FB	18
Tamarind Seed, The	GB	1974	Blake Edwards	125	std		GB	27
Taming of the Shrew	W.GER	1977	Cranko Ballet	85	sc/std		GFL	0
Taming of the Shrew, The	USA/IT	1966	Franco Zeffirelli	122	sc/std	C	FB	33
Tammy and the Millionaire	USA	1967	Sidney Miller	88			FB	18
Tammy Tell Me True	USA	1961	Harry Keller	97	col		FB	18
					bw		FB	15
Tampopo	JAP	1986	Juzo Itami	114	est		GB	75
Tangled Web	GB	1989	Raj Patel	101			SP	0
Tank	USA	1984	Marvin J. Chomsky	113			FB	35
Tanned Legs	USA	1929	Marshall Neilan	71			GB	15
Tansy	GB	1922	Cecil Hepworth	74	st		BFI	15
Tap	USA	1988	Nick Castle	111			FB	55
Taps	USA	1981	Harold Becker	126			FB	43
Taras Bulba	USA	1962	J. Lee Thompson	123	sc		FB	18
Target	USA	1952	Stuart Gilmore	60			GB	15
Target for Tonight	GB	1941	Harry Watt	50			CFL	21.53
Targets	USA	1967	Peter Bogdanovich	80	91		FB	22
Tarka the Otter	GB	1978	David Cobham	91			FB	30
Tarnished Angel	USA	1938	Leslie Goodwins	68			GB	15
Tarnished Angels, The	USA	1957	Douglas Sirk	93	std		FB	15
Tartars, The	IT	1960	Richard Thorpe	83	sc/std		FB	18
Tartuffe, Le	FR	1963	Jean Meyer	98	est		GB	35
Tarzan the Ape Man	USA	1981	John Derek	92			FB	43
Tarzan the Ape Man	USA	1959	Joseph M. Newman	80	bw		FB	15
Tarzan the Ape Man	USA	1932	W.S. Van Dyke	100	bw		FB	22
Tarzan's Secret Treasure	USA	1941	Richard Thorpe	81			FB	22
Tashkent Earthquake	USSR	1968		70			ETV	6
Taste the Blood of Dracula	GB	1969	Peter Sasdy	95			FB	18

t

	COUNTRY OF PRODUCTION	YEAR	DIRECTOR	RUNNING TIME	VERSION	35mm	16mm	16mm RENTAL FEE
Tatie Danielle	FR	1990	Etienne Chatiliez	106	st		GB	80
Tattooed Stranger, The	USA	1950	Edward J. Montagne	64			GB	15
Tattooed Tears	USA	1978	Nick Broomfield/ Joan Churchill	88			GB	30
Taxi Driver	USA	1976	Martin Scorsese	113		BFI	FB	22
Taxi Zum Klo	W.GER	1980	Frank Ripploh	92	est	MP	MP	69
Taxing Woman, A	JAP	1987	Juzo Itami	127	est		GB	60
Tchaikovsky Music Festival	USSR	1963		80			ETV	5
Tea and Sympathy	USA	1956	Vincente Minnelli	122			FB	22
Teacher's Pet	USA	1957	George Seaton	120	bw/std		FB	15
Teachers	USA	1984	Arthur Hiller	106			FB	35
Teen Agent	USA	1991	William Dear	89		W	FB	65
Teenage Mutant Ninja Turtles	USA	1990	Steve Barron	92			GB	60
Teenage Mutant Ninja Turtles II: The Secret of the Ooze	USA	1991	Michael Pressman	84		F	FB	65
Telefon	USA	1977	Don Siegel	103			FB	38
Television and the World	GB	1962	Richard Cawston	83			BFI	15
Tell England	GB	1931	Anthony Asquith/ Geoffrey Barkas	86			BFI	20
Telling Tales	GB	1978	Richard Woolley	88			MP/LFC	40.25
Tempest	USA	1928	Sam Taylor	102	sd		BFI	18
Tempest, The	GB	1979	Derek Jarman	95		BFI	BFI	45
Tempest, The	GB/USA	1980	John Gorrie	125			BBC	35
Tempesta, La	FR/IT/ YUGO	1958	Alberto Lattuada	122	sc		FB	18
10	USA	1979	Blake Edwards	122	sc/std		FB	48
Ten Commandments, The	USA	1956	Cecil B. DeMille	222	std		FB	33
Ten Little Indians	GB	1965	George Pollock	91			FB	15
Ten Little Niggers (see And Then There Were None)								
Ten Thousand Bedrooms	USA	1957	Richard Thorpe	114	sc		FB	18
Ten Who Dared	USA	1960	William Beaudine	92			FB	27
Ten10 to Midnight	USA	1983	J. Lee Thompson	102			FB	43
Tenant, The	FR	1976	Roman Polanski	126			FB	33
Tender Comrade	USA	1945	Edward Dmytryk	102			GB	15
Tender Mercies	USA	1982	Bruce Beresford	91			FB	38
Tender Trap, The	USA	1955	Charles Walters	111	std		FB	18
Tender Warrior	USA	1970	Stewart Raffill	60			FB	18
Tennessee Johnson	USA	1943	William Dieterle	86			FB	18
Tennessee's Partner	USA	1955	Allan Dwan	95			GB	18
Tension	USA	1949	John Berry	91			FB	15
Tension at Table Rock	USA	1956	Charles Marquis Warren	93	bw/col		GB	15
Tentacles	IT	1976	Oliver Hellman	102	sc/std		FB	22
Tenue de Soirée	FR	1986	Bertrand Blier	85	est		GB	70
Tequila Sunrise	USA	1988	Robert Towne	116			FB	60
Terence Davies Trilogy Children Madonna and Child Death and Transfiguration	GB	1976-1983	Terence Davies	101			BFI	50
Term of Trial	GB	1962	Peter Glenville	130			FB	15
Terminator II	USA	1992	James Cameron	136		GU	GU	100
Terminator, The	USA	1984	James Cameron	107		R	FB	45
Terms of Endearment	USA	1983	James L. Brooks	132			FB	43
Terra em Transe	BRAZ	1966	Glauber Rocha	110	est		MP	40.25
Terror Eyes	USA	1980	Ken Hughes	88			FB	33
Terror in the Aisles	USA	1985	Andrew J. Kuehn	83			GB	50
Terror Train	CAN	1979	Roger Spottiswoode	97			FB	36
Terry Fox Story, The	CAN	1983	Ralph L. Thomas	97			GB	35
Terry on the Fence	GB	1985	Frank Godwin	70			FB	20
Testament	GB	1988	John Akomfrah	86			BAFC	80
Testament	USA	1983	Lynne Littman	90			FB	35
Testament d' Orphée, Le	FR	1959	Jean Cocteau	83	est		GB	30
Testament von Dr. Mabuse, Das	GER	1933	Fritz Lang	120	est		GB	25
Tex	USA	1982	Tim Hunter	103			FB	38

t	COUNTRY OF PRODUCTION	YEAR	DIRECTOR	RUNNING TIME	VERSION	35mm	16mm	16mm RENTAL FEE
Texas Across the River	USA	1966	Michael Gordon	101	std		FB	15
Texas John Slaughter	USA	1958	Harry Keller	74			FB	27
Text of Light	USA	1974	Stan Brakhage	70			LFC	39
Thank God It's Friday	USA	1978	Robert Klane	89			FB	33
Thank Your Lucky Stars	USA	1943	David Butler	127			FB	22
That Certain Feeling	USA	1956	Norman Panama/ Melvin Frank	103			FB	15
That Championship Season	USA	1982	Jason Miller	110			FB	38
That Christmas	CZ	1958	Karel Kachyna	95	est		ETV	10
That Darn Cat	USA	1965	Robert Stevenson	116			FB	33
That Funny Boy From Form B	USSR		Ilya Frez	85	est		ETV	10
That Funny Feeling	USA	1965	Richard Thorpe	93	bw		FB	15
That God Should Be on the Side of the People Is Not Enough	LEB	1978	Borhan Alaouie/Lofti Thabet	70	est		WFA	32
That Kind of Woman	USA	1958	Sidney Lumet	92			FB	15
That Man Bolt	USA	1973	Henry Levin/David Lowell Rich	103			FB	22
That Man in Istanbul	SP/IT/FR	1964	Anthony Isasi	117	sc/dub/ std		FB	18
That Obscure Object of Desire	FR/SP	1977	Luis Buñuel	100	st	ELEC	GB	50
That Riviera Touch	GB	1966	Cliff Owen	98	bw		FB	15
That Sinking Feeling	GB	1979	Bill Forsyth	90			GB	38
That Summer!	GB	1979	Harley Cokliss	94			FB	27
That Woman Opposite	GB	1957	Compton Bennett	86			GB	15
That's Life	USA	1986	Blake Edwards	102			FB	45
That'll Be the Day	GB	1973	Claude Whatham	91			FB	25
That's Carry On	GB	1977	Gerald Thomas	95			FB	27
That's Dancing	USA	1985	Jack Haley Jr	104			FB	40
That's Entertainment Pt. II	USA	1976	Gene Kelly	126	133		FB	38
That's Entertainment!	USA	1974	Jack Haley Jr	135	std		FB	38
That's Right — You're Wrong	USA	1939	David Butler	89			GB	15
That's Your Funeral	GB	1972	John Robins	82			FB	18
Theatre Girls	GB	1978	Kim Longinotto/Claire Pollak	82			NFS	13.8
Theatre of Blood	GB	1973	Douglas Hickox	102			FB	18
Theatre of Death	GB	1966	Samuel Gallu	91	std		FB	20
Theatre of Mr. And Mrs. Kabal	FR	1967	Walerian Borowczyk	80	est		GB	25
Their Big Moment	USA	1934	James Cruze	64			GB	15
Thelma & Louise	USA	1991	Ridley Scott	130		UIP	FB	75
Them!	USA	1954	Gordon Douglas	94			FB	15
Themroc	FR	1972	Claude Faraldo	110			MP	51.75
Theorem	IT	1969	Pier Paolo Pasolini	98	eng		BFi	50
There Goes My Girl	USA	1937	Ben Holmes	73			GB	15
There Goes the Groom	USA	1937	Joseph Santley	65			GB	15
There Was a Crooked Man...	USA	1970	Joseph L. Mankiewicz	125	std		FB	18
There's A Girl In My Soup	GB	1970	Roy Boulting	96			FB	18
Thérèse	FR	1986	Alain Cavalier	91	est		FB	70
These Dangerous Years	GB	1957	Herbert Wilcox	92			GB	20
These Foolish Things	FR	1990	Bertrand Tavernier	107	sc/st		GB	90
These Thousand Hills	USA	1958	Richard Fleischer	95	sc/std		FB	18
They All Kissed the Bride	USA	1941	Alexander Hall	87			FB	15
They Call Me Trinity	IT	1970	E.B. Clucher	93	dub/std		GB	22
They Call Us Misfits	SWE	1967	Jan Lindquist/Stefan Jarl	101	est		GB	30
They Died With their Boots On	USA	1942	Raoul Walsh	142			FB	22
They Drive by Night	USA	1940	Raoul Walsh	95			FB	22
They Found a Cave	AUSTR	1962	Andrew Steane	63			GB	17
They Knew What They Wanted	USA	1940	Garson Kanin	96			GB	15
They Live	USA	1989	John Carpenter	95	sc	GU	GU	80
They Live by Night	USA	1948	Nicholas Ray	96			BFI	25
They Love Sex	SWE	1974	Calvin Floyd	78	dub		FB	33
They Made Her A Spy	USA	1939	Jack Hively	70			GB	15
They Met in Argentina	USA	1941	Leslie Goodwins	77			GB	15
They Might Be Giants	USA	1971	Anthony Harvey	86			FB	18

	COUNTRY OF PRODUCTION	YEAR	DIRECTOR	RUNNING TIME	VERSION	35mm	16mm	16mm RENTAL FEE
They Only Kill Their Masters	USA	1972	James Goldstone	98			FB	18
They Shoot Horses Don't They?	USA	1969	Sydney Pollack	120	sc	GB	GB	22
					std		GB	22
They Wanted to Marry	USA	1937	Lew Landers	68			GB	15
They Were Not Divided	GB	1950	Terence Young	100			FB	15
They Were Sisters	GB	1944	Arthur Crabtree	115			BFI	30
They Who Dare	GB	1953	Lewis Milestone	107			GB	25
They Won't Believe Me	USA	1947	Irving Pichel	98			GB	15
They're a Weird Mob	AUSTR/ GB	1966	Michael Powell	112			FB	18
Thief of Bagdad, The	USA	1924	Raoul Walsh	139	sd		BFI	25
Thief of Bagdad, The	GB./FR	1978	Clive Donner	102			FB	27
Thief of Hearts	USA	1984	Douglas Day Stewart	101			FB	45
Thief Who Came to Dinner, The	USA	1973	Bud Yorkin	106			FB	18
Thief, The	USA	1952	Russell Rouse	85			GB	18
Thieves Like Us	USA	1973	Robert Altman	123			FB	22
Thin Blue Line, The	USA	1988	Errol Morris	106			BFI	60
Thing From Another World, The	USA	1951	Christian Nyby	87		GB	GB	18
Thing, The	USA	1982	John Carpenter	109			FB	38
Things Change	USA	1988	David Mamet	100			FB	50
Third Man on the Mountain	GB	1959	Ken Annakin	105			FB	27
Third Man, The	GB	1949	Carol Reed	103		MF	FB	22
13 Rue Madeleine	USA	1941	Henry Hathaway	97			FB	15
Thirty Nine Steps, The	GB	1978	Don Sharp	102			FB	33
39 Steps, The	GB	1959	Ralph Thomas	93	col		FB	18
					bw		FB	15
36 Hours	USA	1964	George Seaton	115	sc/std		FB	15
'36 to '77	GB	1978	Marc Karlin/John Saunders/James Scott/ Humphrey Trevelyan	97			BFI	30
This Could Be the Night	USA	1957	Robert Wise	104	std		FB	15
This Gun for Hire	USA	1942	Frank Tuttle	81			FB	15
This Happy Breed	GB	1944	David Lean	110			BFI	30
This Is a Hijack	USA	1973	Barry Pollack	90			GB	27
This Is Elvis	USA	1981	Malcolm Leo/Andrew Solt	91			FB	43
This is Spinal Tap	USA	1983	Rob Reiner	83			GB	50
This Is the BBC	GB	1959	Richard Cawston	68			CFL	10
This Land is Mine	USA	1943	Jean Renoir	103	72		GB	15
This Man is Mine	USA	1934	John Cromwell	76			GB	15
This Marriage Business	USA	1938	Christy Cabanne	71			GB	20
This Week: 1844	GB	1978	Richard Broad	72			BFI	20
Thomas Graal's Best Film	SWE	1917	Mauritz Stiller	75	est/st		GB	30
Thomas l'Imposteur	FR	1964	Georges Franju	94	est		APO	35
Thoroughly Modern Millie	USA	1967	George Roy Hill	138			FB	18
Thoroughly Uncared-For Girl, A	W.GER	1977	Jutta Bruckner	80	est		GFL	0
Those Calloways	USA	1964	Norman Tokar	119	131		FB	27
Those Endearing Young Charms	USA	1945	Lewis Allen	89			GB	15
Those Magnificent Men in Their Flying Machines	GB	1965	Ken Annakin	132	sc/std		FB	26
Those Wonderful Movie Cranks	CZ	1978	Jiri Menzel	86	est		GB	40
Thousand Clarinets, A	CZ	1978	Jan Rohac/Vladimir Suitacek	132	est		ETV	10
Thousand Clowns, A	USA	1965	Fred Coe	115			FB	15
Thousand Eyes of Dr. Mabuse, The	FR./IT/ W.GER	1960	Fritz Lang	103	est		BFI	25
Thousand Plane Raid, The	USA	1968	Boris Sagal	92			FB	18
Three	GB	1969	James Salter	95			FB	18
Three Men and a Little Lady	USA	1991	Emile Ardolino	104		T	FB	65
3 Godfathers	USA	1949	John Ford	106	bw	UIP	FB	15
Three Amigos!	USA	1986	John Landis	104			FB	40
Three Bites of the Apple	USA	1966	Alvin Ganzer	88	std		FB	18
Three Brave Men	USA	1956	Philip Dunne	88	sc		FB	15

	COUNTRY OF PRODUCTION	YEAR	DIRECTOR	RUNNING TIME	VERSION	35mm	16mm	16mm RENTAL FEE
Three Brothers	IT/FR	1981	Francesco Rosi	113	est		GB	50
Three Caballeros, The	USA	1944	Norman Ferguson	72			FB	27
Three Cases of Murder	GB	1954	George More O'Ferrall/David Eady/Wendy Toye	99			GB	18
Three Comrades	USA	1938	Frank Borzage	98			FB	22
Three Daughters	INDIA	1961	Satyajit Ray	171	est		GB	25
Three Days in Szczecin	GB	1976	Leslie Woodhead	90			BFI	25
Three Days of the Condor	USA	1975	Sydney Pollack	118	sc/std		FB	33
Three Fugitives	USA	1989	Francis Veber	97			FB	60
Three Guns for Texas	USA	1968	David Lowell Rich	99			FB	18
Three Hats for Lisa	GB	1965	Sidney Hayers	99	sc/std		FB	18
Three Husbands	USA	1950	Irving Reis	80			GB	15
Three in the Cellar	USA	1970	Theodore J. Flicker	94			GB	40
Three Into Two Won't Go	GB	1968	Peter Hall	94			FB	18
Three Little Words	USA	1950	Richard Thorpe	102	bw		FB	15
Three Lives of Thomasina, The	GB	1963	Don Chaffey	97			FB	27
3 Men and a Baby	USA	1987	Leonard Nimoy	102			FB	50
3 Women	USA	1977	Robert Altman	123	sc		FB	30
Three Men in White	USA	1944	Willis Goldbeck	85			FB	15
Three Musketeers, The	USA	1936	Rowland V. Lee	100			GB	15
Three Musketeers, The	USA	1948	George Sidney	125			FB	24
Three On a Couch	USA	1966	Jerry Lewis	109			FB	15
Three Secrets	USA	1950	Robert Wise	98			GB	18
Three Sisters	GB	1970	Laurence Olivier	165			FB	22
Three Songs of Lenin	USSR	1934	Dziga Vertov	55			ETV	15
3.10 to Yuma	USA	1957	Delmer Daves	92		C	FB	15
Three Violent People	USA	1956	Rudolph Maté	100			FB	15
3 Worlds of Gulliver, The	GB/SP/USA	1959	Jack Sher	99			FB	18
Three Who Loved	USA	1931	George Archainbaud	78			GB	15
Threepenny Opera, The (see Dreigroschenoper, Die)								
Throne of Blood	JAP	1957	Akira Kurosawa	105	est	BFI	BFI	45
Through a Glass Darkly	SWE	1961	Ingmar Bergman	91	est		GB	35
Thunder and Lightning	USA	1977	Corey Allen	93			FB	27
Thunder in the Sun	USA	1958	Russell Rouse	79			FB	15
Thunder Mountain	USA	1947	Lew Landers	60			GB	15
Thunder of Drums, A	USA	1961	Joseph M. Newman	96	sc/std		FB	18
Thunder on the Hill	USA	1951	Douglas Sirk	85			FB	15
Thunder Rock	GB	1942	Roy Boulting	111			BFI	20
Thunderball	FB	1965	Terence Young	130	sc/std		FB	33
Thunderbolt	USA	1929	Josef von Sternberg	94			FB	15
Thunderbolt and Lightfoot	USA	1974	Michael Cimino	115	sc		FB	33
Tiara Tahiti	GB	1962	Ted Kotcheff	100			FB	18
Tibet	GB	1976	Felix Greene	60			GB	30
Tick...Tick...Tick	USA	1969	Ralph Nelson	97	sc/std		FB	18
Ticket to Tomahawk	USA	1949	Richard Sale	91			FB	15
Tickle Me	USA	1965	Norman Taurog	90	std		FB	18
Ticklish Affair, A	USA	1963	George Sidney	88	sc/std		FB	18
Tie Me Up! Tie Me Down!	SP	1989	Pedro Almodóvar	102	est		GB	80
Ties That Bind, The	USA	1984	Friedrich Su	55	bw		LFMC	46.75
Tiger Bay	GB	1959	J. Lee Thompson	105			FB	15
Tiger Fangs	USA	1944	Sam Newfield	61			GB	15
Tiger in the Smoke	GB	1956	Roy Ward Baker	94			FB	15
Tiger of Eschnapur, The	W.GER/IT/FR	1958	Fritz Lang	101	est		BFI	25
Tiger Shark	USA	1932	Howard Hawks	77			FB	22
Tightrope	USA	1984	Richard Tuggle	114			FB	45
Tightrope to Terror	GB	1982	Bob Kellett	52			FB	20
Tiko and the Shark	IT/FR	1962	Folco Quilici	88			FB	18
Tilaï	BF	1990	Idrissa Ouedraogo	81	est	AE	GB	70

Title	COUNTRY OF PRODUCTION	YEAR	DIRECTOR	RUNNING TIME	VERSION	35mm	16mm	16mm RENTAL FEE
Till Death Us Do Part	GB	1969	Norman Cohen	100			FB	18
Till the End of Time	USA	1946	Edward Dmytryk	105			GB	15
Time after Time	USA	1979	Nicholas Meyer	112	sc/std		FB	30
Time and Judgement	GB	1988	Menelik Shabazz	80			CEDDO	—
Time Bandit	CZ	1957	Jaroslav Balik	90	est		ETV	10
Time Bandits	GB	1981	Terry Gilliam	110			GB	40
Time Bomb	USA	1953	Ted Tetzlaff	72			FB	15
Time for Loving	GB	1971	Christopher Miles	104			GB	18
Time Gentlemen	CZ	1961		95	est		ETV	10
Time in the Sun	USA/USSR	1930/40	Sergei Eisenstein	60	eng nar		GB	20
Time of His Life	GB	1955	Leslie Hiscott	74		GB	GB	15
Time to Die, A	COL/CB	1985	Jorge Ali Triana	98	est		GB	60
Time to Love and a Time to Die, A	USA	1958	Douglas Sirk	131	std	UIP	FB	22
Times of Harvey Milk, The	USA	1984	Robert Epstein	87			GB	40
Times Square	USA	1980	Alan Moyle	111			FB	38
Timetable 2000	E.GER			60			ETV	45
Tin Men	USA	1987	Barry Levinson	112			FB	50
Tin Star, The	USA	1957	Anthony Mann	93		UIP	FB	15
Tip Off, The	USA	1931	Albert S. Rogell	78			GB	15
Tirez sur le Pianiste	FR	1960	François Truffaut	80	sc/std/ est		GB	25
'Tis Pity She's a Whore	IT	1971	Giuseppe Patroni Griffi	102			GB	30
Titanic	GER	1943	Herbert Selpin/Werner Klingler	87	est		BFI	25
Titanic	USA	1953	Jean Negulesco	98			FB	15
Titfield Thunderbolt, The	GB	1952	Charles Crichton	134	bw		FB	15
Title Shot	CAN	1979	Les Rose	88			GB	35
To Be or Not to Be	USA	1942	Ernst Lubitsch	105		BFI	BFI	30
To Be or Not To Be	USA	1983	Alan Johnson	108		F	FB	50
To Beat the Band	USA	1936	Ben Stoloff	70			GB	15
To Begin Again	SP	1981	Jose Luis Garci	92	cst	GB	GB	40
To Catch a Thief	USA	1955	Alfred Hitchcock	107	b v		FB	27
To Die in Madrid	FR	1962	Frédéric Rossif	87	eng nar		GB	25
					fr nar		GB	25
To Dorothy a Son	GB	1954	Muriel Box	84			GB	15
To Each His Own	USA	1946	Mitchell Leisen	124			FB	15
To Find a Man	USA	1972	Buzz Kulik	94			FB	18
To Forget Venice	IT/FR	1979	Franco Brusati	110			GB	35
To Have and Have Not	USA	1944	Howard Hawks	100		UIP	FB	22
To Hell and Back	USA	1955	Jesse Hibbs	106	col/std		FB F	18
					bw/sc		FB	18
To Kill a Clown	GB	1971	George Bloomfield	84			FB	18
To Kill a Mockingbird	USA	1962	Robert Mulligan	129			FB	27
To Live and Die in L.A.	USA	1985	William Friedkin	116			FB	35
To Live in Freedom	GB	1974	Simon Louvish et al	54		CONT	GB	15
To Love	SWE	1964	Jörn Donner	93	est		GB	30
To New Shores	GER	1937	Douglas Sirk	102	cst		BFI	25
To Our Loves	FR	1983	Maurice Pialat	102	est		GB	55
To Please a Lady	USA	1950	Clarence Brown	91			FB	15
To Sir With Love	GB	1966	James Clavell				FB	22
To the Devil a Daughter	GB/ W.GER	1976	Peter Sykes	93			FB	18
To Trap a Spy	USA	1965	Don Medford	92			FB	18
Toast	POL	1969	Jan Lomnicki	67	est		FOP	0
Toast of New Orleans	USA	1950	Norman Taurog	97			FB	24
Toast of New York, The	USA	1937	Rowland V. Lee	107			GB	12
Tobacco Road	USA	1941	John Ford	84			FB	15
Tobruk	USA	1966	Arthur Hiller	109	std		FB	18
Toby Tyler	USA	1959	Charles Barton	96			FB	27
Today Is Forever	USA	1976	Daryl Duke	96			GB	27
Today It's Me – Tomorrow You	IT	1968	Tonino Cervi	95	dub		TCM	15

	COUNTRY OF PRODUCTION	YEAR	DIRECTOR	RUNNING TIME	VERSION	35mm	16mm	16mm RENTAL FEE
Together	GB	1955	Lorenza Mazzetti	50			BFI	15.50
Tokyo Story	JAP	1953	Yasujiro Ozu	135	est	AE	GB	45
Tol'able David	USA	1921	Henry King	103	st		BFI	20
Tom Brown's Schooldays	GB	1951	Gordon Parry	96			GB	18
Tom Dick and Harry	USA	1941	Garson Kanin	86			GB	15
Tom Horn	USA	1980	William Wiard	97	sc		FB	43
Tom Phillips	GB	1977	David Rowan	50			AC	20
Tom Sawyer	USA	1973	Don Taylor	103	sc/std		FB	22
Tom Thumb	GB	1958	George Pal	92			FB	25
Tom Tit Tot	W GER	1955	Herbert B. Fredersdorf	79	est		GFL	0
Tom Tom the Pipers Son	USA	1968	Ken Jacobs	86			LFC	45
Tomb of Ligeia, The	GB	1964	Roger Corman	81	sc		FB	18
Tommy	GB	1975	Ken Russell	111			GB	0
Tommy Trickery and the Stamp Traveller	CAN		Michael Rubbo	101			GB	40
Tomorrow Never Comes	CAN/GB	1977	Peter Collinson	106			FB	38
Tongpan	THAI	1977	Yuthalla Mukdallsallit/Surachi Janthimathorn	65			CONC	16.60
Tongues Untied	USA	1990	Marlon T. Riggs	55			BFI	55
Tonight and Every Night	USA	1944	Victor Saville	92	col		FB	18
Tonight We Sing	USA	1953	Mitchell Leisen	110			FB	18
Tonio Kröger	W.GER/FR	1964	Rolf Thiele	90	est		GFL	0
Tonka	USA	1958	Lewis Foster	97			FB	27
Tons of Trouble	GB	1956	Leslie Hiscott	77			GB	15
Tony Rome	USA	1967	Gordon Douglas	110	sc/std		FB	18
Too Beautiful For You	FR	1989	Bertrand Blier	91	sc/est	AE	GB	70
Too Early, Too Late	FR/EGY	1982	Jean-Marie Straub	110	est		GB	50
Too Hot to Handle	USA	1991	Jerry Rees	117	79	T	FB	70
Too Late the Hero	USA	1969	Robert Aldrich	144	std		GB	27
Too Many Chefs	USA	1978	Ted Kotcheff	112			GB	33
Too Many Cooks	USA	1931	William A. Seiter	77			GB	15
Too Many Crooks	GB	1959	Mario Zampi	87		R	FB	15
Too Many Girls	USA	1940	George Abbott	85			GB	15
Too Many Thieves	USA	1966	Abner Biberman	96			GB	18
Too Many Wives	USA	!937	Ben Holmes	61			GB	15
Too Young to Love	GB	1959	Muriel Box	87			GB	25
Tootsie	USA	1982	Sydney Pollack	116	sc/std	C	FB	55
Top Gun	USA	1986	Tony Scott	110			FB	55
Top Hat	USA	1935	Mark Sandrich	108		GB	GB	15
Top Secret	GB	1953	Mario Zampi	94			FB	15
Top Secret	USA	1983	Jim Abrahams/David Zucker/ Jerry Zucker	90			FB	40
Topaz	USA	1969	Alfred Hitchcock	125			FB	28
Topkapi	USA	1964	Jules Dassin	120			FB	18
Topper	USA	1937	Norman Z. McLeod	85			GB	15
Tora! Tora! Tora!	JAP/USA	1970	Richard Fleischer	142	sc/std		FB	30
Tora-No-O	JAP	1951	Akira Kurosawa	60	est		GB	25
Torch Song Trilogy	USA	1989	Paul Bogart	119			GB	85
Torch, The (see Bandit General)								
Torches, The	CZ	1960	Vladimir Cech	90	cst		ETV	10
Tortilla Flat	USA	1942	Victor Fleming	106			FB	22
Tortured Dust	USA	1984	Stan Brakhage	90			LFC	60
Total Recall	USA	1990	Paul Verhoeven	109		GU	GU	80
Toto and the Poachers	GB	1956	Brian Salt	50			GB	17
Toto the Hero	BEL	1991	Jaco Van Dormael	91	est	ELEC	GB	90
Touch of Evil	USA	1957	Orson Welles	109		UIP	FB	22
Touch of Love, A	GB	1969	Waris Hussein	107			FB	15
Touch, The	SWE/USA	1970	Ingmar Bergman	113			GB	27
Touchez Pas au Grisbi	FR	1953	Jacques Becker	94	cst		GB	35
Tough Guys	USA	1986	Jeff Kanew	103			FB	60
Touki-Bouki	SEN	1973	Djibril Diop-Mambety	95	est		BFI	35

	COUNTRY OF PRODUCTION	YEAR	DIRECTOR	RUNNING TIME	VERSION	35mm	16mm	16mm RENTAL FEE
Tout Va Bien	FR/IT	1972	Jean-Luc Godard/ Jean-Pierre Gorin	95	est	MP	MP	51.75
Toute une Nuit	BEL/FR	1982	Chantal Akerman	90	cst		MP	57.50
Tower of Evil	GB/USA	1972	Jim O'Connolly	89			GB	20
Towering Inferno, The	USA	1974	John Guillermin	165	sc/std		FB	43
Town Bloody Hall	USA	1979	D.A. Pennebaker/ Chris Hegedus	85			BFI	35
Town Like Alice, A	GB	1956	Jack Lee	117			FB	15
Town Without Pity	W.GER/USA	1961	Gottfried Reinhardt	105	112		FB	15
Toy Soldiers	USA	1991	Daniel Petrie Jr.	112		C	FB	65
Track 29	GB	1987	Nicolas Roeg	90			GB	75
Trackdown	USA	1976	Richard Heffron	97			FB	18
Tracks	USA	1976	Henry Jaglom	90			MP	51.75
Trader Horn	USA	1931	W.S. Van Dyke	119			FB	15
Trader Horn	USA	1973	Reza S. Badiyi	106			FB	33
Trading Places	USA	1983	John Landis	116			FB	43
Trail of the Pink Panther	GB	1982	Blake Edwards	96			FB	43
Trail Street	USA	1947	Ray Enright	85			GB	15
Train Robbers, The	USA	1973	Burt Kennedy	92	sc/std		FB	18
Train, The	USA/FR/IT	1964	John Frankenheimer	140			FB	22
Trained to Kill	USA	1975	Daniel J. Vance	91			FB	33
Trans-Europe Express	FR	1966	Alain Robbe-Grillet	95	est		GB	30
Trap, The	CZ	1950	Martin Fric	100	est		ETV	10
Trap, The	GB/CAN	1966	Sidney Hayers	106	std		FB	18
Trapped	USA	1949	Richard Fleischer	83			GB	20
Traveller	GB	1981	Joe Comerford	81			BFI	35
Travelling Husbands	USA	1931	Paul Sloane	75			GB	20
Travelling North	AUSTR	1986	Carl Schultz	95			GB	75
Travels With My Aunt	USA	1972	George Cukor	109			FB	26
Traviata, La	IT	1966	Mario Lanfranchi	120			GB	22
Traviata, La	IT	1982	Franco Zeffirelli	105			GB	43
Tread Softly Stranger	GB	1958	Gordon Parry	92			GB	15
Treasure Island	USA	1934	Victor Fleming	103			FB	15
Treasure Island	USA	1950	Byron Haskin	96			FB	33
Treasure Island	GB/FR/ W.GER	1971	John Hough	95			FB	22
Treasure Island	USSR	1971	Eugen Fridman	76	dub		GB	18
Treasure Island			Nick Nicholson/Roger Muir	76			GB	18
Treasure of Kalifa	USA	1953	E.A. Dupont	87			GB	15
Treasure of Matecumbe	USA	1976	Vincent McEveety	117			FB	33
Treasure of Pancho Villa, The	USA	1955	George Sherman	95	bw/std		GB	15
Treasure of San Teresa, The	GB	1959	Alvin Rakoff	82			GB	15
Treasure of the Sierra Madre, The	USA	1947	John Huston	126			FB	22
Treasure, The	POL	1950	Leonard Buczkowski	77	est		FOP	0
Trenchcoat	USA	1983	Michael Tuchner	91		D	FB	38
Trent's Last Case	GB	1952	Herbert Wilcox	90			GB	20
Treve, La	FR	1968	Claude Guillemot	90	est		APO	35
Trial by Combat	GB	1976	Kevin Connor	90			FB	18
Trials of Alger Hiss, The	USA	1980	John Lowenthal	166			SCFL	35
Tribute	CAN/ USA	1980	Bob Clark	125			FB	38
Trinity Is Still My Name	IT	1971	E.B. Clucher	90	sc std/		GB	22
Trip to Bountiful, The	USA	1985	Peter Masterson	107			BFI	50
Trip to Kill	USA	1971	Tom Stern/Lane Slate	97			TCM	15
Trip, The	USA	1967	Roger Corman	85			GB	30
Triple Cross	USA	1966	Terence Young	126			TCM	25
Triple Echo, The	GB	1972	Michael Apted	94			GB	32
Trojan Women, The	USA	1971	Michael Cacoyannis	110			GB	27
Tron	USA	1982	Steven Lisberger	96		D	FB	38
Trop Belle Pour Toi (see Too Beautiful For You)								
Trouble Brewing	GB	1938	Anthony Kimmins	87			FB	20

	COUNTRY OF PRODUCTION	YEAR	DIRECTOR	RUNNING TIME	VERSION	35mm	16mm	16mm RENTAL FEE
Trouble in Mind	USA	1985	Alan Rudolph	112			GB	60
Trouble in Paradise	USA	1932	Ernst Lubitsch	95			FB	22
Trouble in Store	GB	1953	John Paddy Carstairs	85			FB	15
Trouble Man	USA	1972	Ivan Dixon	99			FB	18
Trouble with 2B (6 episodes)	GB	1972	Peter Smith	14-22 each			GB	6
Trouble With Girls	USA	1969	Peter Tewksbury	79	std		FB	22
Trouble with Harry, The	USA	1956	Alfred Hitchcock	99			FB	35
Troublemaker, The	USA	1964	Theodore J. Flicker	80			GB	15
Troublesome Double, The	GB	1971	Milo Lewis	57			GB	17
True Confessions	USA	1981	Ulu Grosbard	108			FB	43
True Glory, The	GB	1945	Garson Kanin/Carol Reed	87			CFL	23
True Heart Susie	USA	1919	D.W. Griffith	82	st		BFI	20
True Identity	USA	1991	Charles Lane	94		T	FB	65
True Stories	USA	1986	David Byrne	89		W	FB	65
Trust	USA	1990	Hal Hartley	106		MAY	GB	80
Truth Game, The	GB	1983	Central TV	90			CONC	30
Tsar's Bride, The	USSR	1956	Vladimir Gorriker	95	est		ETV	20
Tschetan Der Indianerjunge	W.GER	1972	Hark Bohm	96	dub		GFL	0
Tsiamelo: A Place of Goodness	GB	1983	Ellen Kuzwayo/Blanche Tsimatsima/Betty Wolpet	56			GB	20
Tucker: The Man and His Dreams	USA	1988	Francis Ford Coppola	111		UIP	FB	65
Tumbleweeds	USA	1925	King Baggot	84	sd		BFI	15
Tunes of Glory	GB	1960	Ronald Neame	107			GB	26
Tunisian Victory	GB	1943	Roy Boulting/Frank Capra	79			CFL	19
Tunnel 28	W.GER/ USA	1962	Robert Siodmak	89	dub		FB	15
Tunnel of Love	USA	1958	Gene Kelly	98	std		FB	15
Turk 182!	USA	1984	Bob Clark	98		F	FB	45
Turned Out Nice Again	GB	1941	Marcel Varnel	81			FB	15
Turning Point, The	USA	1977	Herbert Ross	115			FB	33
Tuttles of Tahiti	USA	1942	Charles Vidor	91			GB	33
Twelfth Hour	CZ	1959	Josef Medved/Andrej Lettrich	80	est		ETV	10
Twelfth Night	GB/USA	1980	John Gorrie	128			BBC	35
Twelfth Night	USSR	1955	Yan Fried	90	est		GB	25
Twelve Angry Men	USA	1957	Sidney Lumet	96		UIP	FB	30
Twelve Crowded Hours	USA	1938	Lew Landers	64			GB	15
Twelve O'Clock High	USA	1949	Henry King	130			FB	30
Twelve Views Of Kensal House	GB	1984	Peter Wyeth	55			AC	50
Twentieth Century	USA	1934	Howard Hawks	91			FB	15
20,000 Leagues Under The Sea	USA	1954	Richard Fleischer	126			FB	38
Twenty Mule Team	USA	1940	Richard Thorpe	83			FB	15
Twenty Thousand Years in Sing Sing	USA	1933	Michael Curtiz	78			FB	22
Twenty-Fifth Hour, The	FR IT/YUGO	1967	Henri Verneuil	118	std		FB	18
28 Up	GB	1984	Michael Apted	62/73			CONC	20
Twice Blessed	USA	1945	Harry Beaumont	76			FB	15
Twilight City	GB	1989	Reece Auguste	53			BAFC	70
Twilight Zone – The Movie	USA	1983	John Landis/Steven Spielberg/ Joe Dante/George Miller	101		W	FB	40
Twinky	GB	1969	Richard Donner	98	bw		FB	15
Twins	USA	1988	Ivan Reitman	107			FB	60
Twins of Evil	GB	1971	John Hough	87			FB	18
Twist of Sand	GB	1968	Don Chaffey	89			FB	18
Twisted Nerve	GB	1968	Roy Boulting	86	118		FB	27
2001: A Space Odyssey	GB	1968	Stanley Kubrick	141	sc/std	UIP	FB	43
Two Alone	USA	1934	Elliott Nugent	74			GB	20
Two Daughters	INDIA	1961	Satyajit Ray	110	est		GB	25
Two for the Road	GB	1966	Stanley Donen	111	sc/std		FB	18
Two for the Seesaw	USA	1962	Robert Wise	119	sc		FB	15
Two in Revolt	USA	1936	Glenn Tryon	64			GB	15
Two in the Dark	USA	1936	Ben Stoloff	73			GB	15

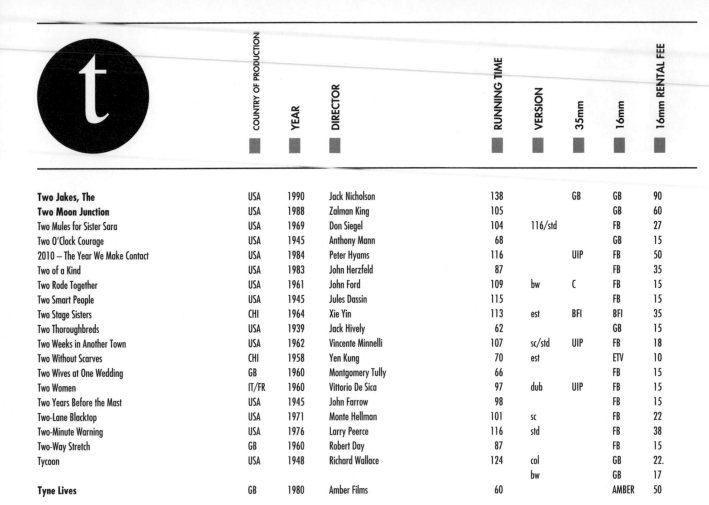

	COUNTRY OF PRODUCTION	YEAR	DIRECTOR	RUNNING TIME	VERSION	35mm	16mm	16mm RENTAL FEE
Two Jakes, The	USA	1990	Jack Nicholson	138		GB	GB	90
Two Moon Junction	USA	1988	Zalman King	105			GB	60
Two Mules for Sister Sara	USA	1969	Don Siegel	104	116/std		FB	27
Two O'Clock Courage	USA	1945	Anthony Mann	68			GB	15
2010 – The Year We Make Contact	USA	1984	Peter Hyams	116		UIP	FB	50
Two of a Kind	USA	1983	John Herzfeld	87			FB	35
Two Rode Together	USA	1961	John Ford	109	bw	C	FB	15
Two Smart People	USA	1945	Jules Dassin	115			FB	15
Two Stage Sisters	CHI	1964	Xie Yin	113	est	BFI	BFI	35
Two Thoroughbreds	USA	1939	Jack Hively	62			GB	15
Two Weeks in Another Town	USA	1962	Vincente Minnelli	107	sc/std	UIP	FB	18
Two Without Scarves	CHI	1958	Yen Kung	70	est		ETV	10
Two Wives at One Wedding	GB	1960	Montgomery Tully	66			FB	15
Two Women	IT/FR	1960	Vittorio De Sica	97	dub	UIP	FB	15
Two Years Before the Mast	USA	1945	John Farrow	98			FB	15
Two-Lane Blacktop	USA	1971	Monte Hellman	101	sc		FB	22
Two-Minute Warning	USA	1976	Larry Peerce	116	std		FB	38
Two-Way Stretch	GB	1960	Robert Day	87			FB	15
Tycoon	USA	1948	Richard Wallace	124	col		GB	22.
					bw		GB	17
Tyne Lives	GB	1980	Amber Films	60			AMBER	50

Tales of Beatrix Potter

	COUNTRY OF PRODUCTION	YEAR	DIRECTOR	RUNNING TIME	VERSION	35mm	16mm	16mm RENTAL FEE
U2: Rattle and Hum	USA	1988	Phil Joanou	105			FB	40
Ugetsu Monogatari	JAP	1953	Kenji Mizoguchi	89	est		GB	30
Ugly American, The	USA	1962	George Englund	120			FB	18
Ugly Dachshund, The	USA	1965	Norman Tokar	93			FB	33
Ultima Cena, La (see Last Supper, The)								
Ultimate Warrior, The	USA	1975	Robert Clouse	94			FB	18
Ulysses	GB	1967	Joseph Strick	132	sc/std		GB	30
Ulzana's Raid	USA	1972	Robert Aldrich	100		UIP	FB	18
Umberto D	IT	1952	Vittorio De Sica	82	est		BFI	30
Unbearable Lightness of Being, The	USA	1987	Philip Kaufman	172			FB	65
Unbelievable Truth	USA	1989	Hal Hartley	90		ELEC	GB	70
Unbroken Arrow, The	GB	1976	Matt McCarthy (6 episodes)	20-21 each			GB	6
Uncanny, The	CAN/GB	1977	Denis Heroux	85			FB	27
Uncle Buck	USA	1991	John Hughes	106		UIP	FB	60
Uncle Vanya	GB	1963	Stuart Burge	117			GB	30
Uncle Vanya	USSR	1971	Andrei Konchalovsky	102	est		GB	30
Uncommon Valour	USA	1983	Ted Kotcheff	105			FB	35
Unconquered	USA	1947	Cecil B. DeMille	146	col		FB	18
					bw		FB	15
Undefeated, The	USA	1969	Andrew V. McLaglen	118	sc/std		FB	18
Under Capricorn	GB	1949	Alfred Hitchcock	117			GB	28
Under Fire	USA	1983	Roger Spottiswoode	128		R	FB	43
Under Milk Wood	GB	1971	Andrew Sinclair	88		BFI	GB	33
Under Suspicion	USA	1991	Simon Moore	100		R	FB	70
Under Ten Flags	USA/IT	1960	Duilio Coletti/Silvio Narizzano	111			FB	15
Under the Tonto Rim	USA	1947	Lew Landers	61			GB	15
Under The Volcano	USA	1984	John Huston	112		F	FB	45
Under the Yum Yum Tree	USA	1963	David Swift	101			FB	18
Undercurrent	USA	1946	Vincente Minnelli	116			FB	15
Underdog, The	W.GER	1951	Wolfgang Staudte	90	est		GB	25
Underground	USA	1970	Arthur H. Nadel	95			FB	18
Underground USA	USA	1980	Eric Mitchell	85			GB	50
Underwater Warrior	USA	1958	Andrew Marton	92	sc/std		FB	15
Underwater!	USA	1954	John Sturges	90	col/std		GB	22
Unfaithfully Yours	USA	1983	Howard Zieff	96			FB	45
Unforgiven	USA	1992	Clint Eastwood	130		W	FB	75
Unheimliche Geschichten, Grausige Nachte	W.GER	1919	Richard Oswald	70	est		GFL	0
Unholy Three, The	USA	1930	Jack Conway	72			FB	22
Unholy Wife, The	USA	1956	John Farrow	94			GB	18
Union of Soviet Peoples	USSR			60			ETV	5
Union Pacific	USA	1939	Cecil B. DeMille	130			FB	15
Union Station	USA	1950	Rudolph Maté	81			FB	15
Unknown Chaplin (3 parts)	GB	1983	Kevin Brownlow/David Gill	3x52			BFI	20
Unknown Soldier, The	FIN	1955	Edvin Laine	132	est		GB	25
Unman, Wittering and Zigo	GB	1971	John Mackenzie	102		UIP	FB	18
Unmarried Woman, An	USA	1977	Paul Mazursky	124			FB	33
Unsinkable Molly Brown, The	USA	1964	Charles Walters	127	sc/std		FB	18
Unstable Elements: Atomic Stories 1939-1985	GB	1985	Andy Metcalf/Paul Morrison	90		CONC	GB	30
Unsuitable Job for A Woman, An	GB	1981	Christopher Petit	95			BFI	35
Untamed Frontier	USA	1952	Hugo Fregonese	76			FB	15
Untouchables, The	USA	1987	Brian De Palma	120			FB	65
Unvanquished, The (see Aparajito)								
Up	USA	1976	Russ Meyer	80			GB	40
Up in Smoke	USA	1978	Lou Adler	87			FB	38
Up in the Air	GB	1968	Jan Darnley-Smith	55			GB	17
Up in the World	GB	1956	John Paddy Carstairs	91			FB	15
Up Pompeii	GB	1971	Bob Kellett	90			FB	18
Up She Goes	USA	1946	Harry Beaumont	89			FB	15

	COUNTRY OF PRODUCTION	YEAR	DIRECTOR	RUNNING TIME	VERSION	35mm	16mm	16mm RENTAL FEE
Up The Chastity Belt	GB	1971	Bob Kellett	94			FB	18
Up the Front	GB	1972	Bob Kellett	95			FB	18
Up the Sandbox	USA	1972	Irvin Kershner	98			FB	27
Uproar in Heaven	CHI	1965	Wan Lai-Ming	120			WFA	34
Upside Down Feature	GB	1967/72	Peter Gidal	76			LFC	30
Upstairs and Downstairs	GB	1959	Ralph Thomas	101			FB	15
Uranium Conspiracy, The	IT	1978	Menahem Golan	101	dub		FB	33
Uranus	FR	1991	Claude Berri	100	est	AE	GB	80
Urban Cowboy	USA	1980	James Bridges	135	std		FB	38
Used Cars	USA	1980	Robert Zemeckis	101			FB	33

Valentino

V

	COUNTRY OF PRODUCTION	YEAR	DIRECTOR	RUNNING TIME	VERSION	35mm	16mm	16mm RENTAL FEE
V. I. Warshawski	USA	1991	Jeff Kanew	89		W	FB	70
V.I.P.s, The	GB	1963	Anthony Asquith	119	sc/std/91		FB	18
Va Banque	POL	1981	Juliusz Machulski	109			FOP	0
Vacation in Reno	USA	1946	Leslie Goodwins	60			GB	15
Vagabond Lover	USA	1929	Marshall Neilan	69			GB	15
Vagabonde	FR	1985	Agnès Varda	106	est		BFI	45
Valdez is Coming	USA	1970	Edwin Sherin	91			FB	18
Valdez the Halfbreed	IT/SP/FR	1973	John Sturges	97	dub		FB	22
Valentino	GB	1977	Ken Russell	126			FB	33
Valerie and Her Week of Wonders	CZ	1969	Jaromil Jires	77	est		GB	30
Valley of Bees, The	CZ	1968	Frantisek Vlacil	97	est		ETV	15
Valley of Decision	USA	1945	Tay Garnett	118			FB	15
Valley of Eagles	GB	1951	Terence Young	85			GB	15
Valley of Gwangi	USA	1968	Jim O'Connolly	95	bw		FB	15
Valley of Mystery	USA	1967	Joseph Leytes	94			FB	18
Valley of the Dolls	USA	1967	Mark Robson	123	std		FB	18
Valley of the Kings	USA	1954	Robert Pirosh	86			FB	18
Valley of the Sun	USA	1942	George Marshall	79			GB	15
Valmont	FR/UK	1989	Milos Forman	140	sc	AE	GB	80
Vampira	GB	1974	Clive Donner	88			FB	18
Vampire Bat, The	USA	1933	Frank R. Strayer	61			GB	18
Vampire Circus	GB	1972	Robert Young	87			FB	18
Vampire Lovers, The	GB	1970	Roy Ward Baker	91			FB	18
Vampyres	GB	1974	Joseph Larraz	84			FB	18
Van Gogh	FR	1991	Maurice Pialat	158		AE	GB	80
Vanishing Corporal, The	FR	1962	Jean Renoir	106	est		GB	25
Vanishing Point	GB	1971	Richard C. Sarafian	99			FB	22
Vanishing Prairie, The	USA	1954	James Algar	69			FB	27
Variety	USA	1983	Bette Gordon	100			BFI	40
Vassa	USSR	1983	Gleb Panfilov	140	est		GB	50
Vault of Horror, The	GB	1973	Roy Ward Baker	86			GB	22
Velvet Touch, The	USA	1948	John Gage	97			GB	15
Vendetta	SP	1964	George Sherman	107			FB	18
Vendetta	USA	1950	Mel Ferrer	84			BFI	25
Venetian Affair, The	USA	1966	Jerry Thorpe	92	std		FB	18
Vengeance of She, The	GB	1967	Cliff Owen	101			FB	18
Vengeance Valley	USA	1950	Richard Thorpe	82			FB	15
Vent d'Est	FR/IT/ W.GER	1970	Jean-Luc Godard	90		AE	GB	40
Venus Peter	GB	1989	Ian Sellar	94			GB	70
Verboten!	USA	1958	Samuel Fuller	88			GB	15
Verdict, The	USA	1982	Sidney Lumet	128		F	FB	50
Verdict, The	USA	1946	Don Siegel	86			FB	22
Verlorene, Der (see Lost One, The)								
Vernon, Florida	USA	1981	Errol Morris	60			BFI	40
Veronico Cruz	ARG/GB	1987	Miguel Pereira	96			GB	75
Veronika Voss	W.GER	1981	R.W. Fassbinder	105	est		GB	50
Vertigo	USA	1958	Alfred Hitchcock	99		UIP	FB	35
Vertigo	CZ	1963	Karel Kachyna	80	est		ETV	10
Very Important Person	GB	1961	Ken Annakin	98			FB	15
Very Special Favour, A	USA	1965	Michael Gordon	105	bw		FB	15
Via Luonge, Le (see Shine So Hard)								
Viaggio in Italia (see Voyage to Italy)								
Vibes	USA	1988	Ken Kwapis	99			FB	40
Vice Squad	USA	1981	Gary A. Sherman	93			GB	23
Vice Versa	USA	1988	Brian Gilbert	98			FB	50
Vice Versa	GB	1947	Peter Ustinov	102			FB	15
Victor Sjöström	SWE	1981	Gösta Werner	65	est		GB	15

V

	COUNTRY OF PRODUCTION	YEAR	DIRECTOR	RUNNING TIME	VERSION	35mm	16mm	16mm RENTAL FEE
Victor/Victoria	GB	1982	Blake Edwards	134			FB	38
Victors, The	GB	1963	Carl Foreman	159	sc/std		FB	15
Victory at Entebbe	USA	1976	Marvin Chomsky	119			FB	22
Videodrome	CAN	1982	David Cronenberg	89			GB	48
Vie A l'Envers, La	FR	1963	Alain Jessua	92	est		GB	35
Vie de Chateau, La	FR	1965	Jean-Paul Rappeneau	93	est		FB	15
Vieille Dame Indigne, La	FR	1964	René Allio	90	est		GB	25
View to a Kill, A	GB	1985	John Glen	131			FB	60
Vigil in the Night	USA	1940	George Stevens	97			GB	15
Vigilante Force	USA	1975	George Armitage	89			FB	22
Viking Queen, The	GB	1966	Don Chaffey	89			FB	18
Villa Rides	USA	1968	Buzz Kulik	124	std		FB	18
Villa!!	USA	1958	James B. Clark	72	sc/std		FB	18
Village of Daughters	GB	1961	George Pollock	86			FB	15
Village of the Damned	GB	1960	Wolf Rilla	77			FB	15
Village Tale	USA	1935	John Cromwell	79			GB	15
Village Teacher	USSR	1947	Mark Donskoi	106	est		ETV	15
Village, The	GB/SWE	1953	Leopold Lindtberg	83			FB	15
Villain	GB	1971	Michael Tuchner	98	sc/std		FB	18
Vincent	AUSTR	1987	Paul Cox	105			GB	0
Vincent and Theo	FR/UK	1990	Robert Altman	140	est	BD	GB	80
Viol, Le	SWE/FR	1967	Jacques Doniol-Valcroze	84	est		GB	20
Viola and Sebastian	W.GER	1972	Wilmar R. Guertler/Ottokar Runze	93	est		GFL	0
Violent Saturday	USA	1955	Richard Fleischer	90	sc/std		FB	18
Violent Streets	USA	1981	Michael Mann	122	123		FB	43
Violent Summer	FR	1961	Michel Boisrond	86	est		GB	15
Virgin	FR	1988	Catherine Breillat	88	est	ELEC	GB	60
Virgin and the Gypsy, The	GB	1970	Christopher Miles	95			GB	18
Virgin Soldiers, The	GB	1969	John Dexter	96			FB	18
Virgin Spring, The	SWE	1959	Ingmar Bergman	85	est		GB	35
Virginia City	USA	1940	Michael Curtiz	121			FB	22
Viridiana	SP/MEX	1961	Luis Buñuel	91	est	CONT	GB	35
Visions of Eight	USA	1973	Milos Forman/John Schlesinger/Kon Ichikawa/ Claude Lelouch/Yuri Ozerov/Mai Zetterling/ Arthur Penn/Michael Pfleghar	110	std		FB	18
Visit To Alberti	W.GER	1970	Wolfgang Staudte	60	est		GFL	0
Visiting Hours	CAN	1981	Jean-Claude Lord	104	105		FB	41
Vita Futurista	GB	1987	Lutz Becker	52			AC	20
Vitelloni, I	IT/FR	1953	Federico Fellini	104	bw/est		BFI	35
Viva Knievel!	USA	1977	Gordon Douglas	104	sc/std		FB	22
Viva La Muerte	FR/TUN	1970	Fernando Arrabal	90	est		APO	35
Viva Las Vegas!	USA	1956	Roy Rowland	112	sc/std		FB	18
Viva Maria!	FR/IT	1965	Louis Malle	120	dub/sc/ std		FB	18
Viva Portugal	FR/ W.GER	1975	Collective	99			CA	15
Vivacious Lady	USA	1941	George Stevens	90			GB	15
Vivre sa Vie	FR	1962	Jean-Luc Godard	82	est		GB	30
Vivre pour Vivre	FR/IT	1967	Claude Lelouch	130	est		FB	18
Vixen	USA	1968	Russ Meyer	71			GB	40
Von Ryan's Express	USA	1965	Mark Robson	116	sc/std		FB	18
Voyage Imaginaire, Le	FR	1925	René Clair	72	st/est		BFI	20
Voyage of the Damned	GB	1976	Stuart Rosenberg	137	155		FB	27
Voyage to Italy	IT/FR	1953	Roberto Rossellini	84	eng		BFI	30
Voyage to the End of the Universe	CZ	1962	Jindrich Polak	65	duh		FB	15
Vyborg Side, The	USSR	1939	Grigori Kozintsev/ Leonid Trauberg	110	est		ETV	15

W

	COUNTRY OF PRODUCTION	YEAR	DIRECTOR	RUNNING TIME	VERSION	35mm	16mm	16mm RENTAL FEE
W.C. Fields and Me	USA	1976	Arthur Hiller	112			FB	22
W.W. and the Dixie Dancekings	USA	1975	John G. Avildsen	91			FB	22
Wabash Avenue	USA	1950	Henry Koster	93			FB	18
Wages of Fear	USA	1977	William Friedkin	92	121		FB	33
Wagon Master	USA	1950	John Ford	89			GB	15
Wait Until Dark	USA	1967	Terence Young	108			FB	18
Waiting for Fidel	CAN	1976	Michael Rubro	60			CONC	15.2
Walk Don't Run	USA	1966	Charles Walters	114	sc/std		FB	18
Walk in the Spring Rain, A	USA	1969	Guy Green	98	sc/std		FB	18
Walk on the Wild Side, A	USA	1962	Edward Dmytryk	113			FB	15
Walk Softly Stranger	USA	1950	Robert Stevenson	84			GB	15
Walk the Proud Land	USA	1956	Jesse Hibbs	88	sc/std		FB	18
Walking Dead, The	USA	1936	Michael Curtiz	66			FB	15
Walking on Air	USA	1936	Joseph Santley	69			GB	15
Walking Stick, The	GB	1970	Eric Till	101	sc/std		FB	18
Walking Tall	W.GER	1976	Christian Ziewer	124	est		GFL	0
Walking Tall	USA	1973	Phil Karlson	100			FB	33
Wall Of Light	GB	1986	John Tchalenko	52			AC	20
Wall Street	USA	1987	Oliver Stone	126		F	FB	55
Walter	GB	1982	Stephen Frears	75			CONC	28
Waltz King, The	AUST/ USA	1963	Steve Previn	95			FB	27
Wanderer, The (see Grand Meaulnes, Le)								
Wanderers, The	USA/ HOLL	1979	Philip Kaufman	112			GB	38
Wanted: Jane Turner	USA	1936	Edward Killy	69			GB	15
War at Home, The	USA	1979	Glen Silber/Barry Alexander Brown	100			MP	46
War of the Gods	GB	1971	Granada TV	70			CONC	19.4
War of the Mummies	CH/ E.GER	1970-73	Walter Heynowski/Gerhard Scheumann	90			ETV	10
War of the Roses, The	USA	1989	Danny DeVito	116		F	FB	65
War Story, A	CAN	1981	Anne Wheeler	82			CHC	0
War Wagon, The	USA	1967	Burt Kennedy	101	sc/std		FB	18
War Games	USA	1983	John Badham	113		UIP	FB	53
Warlords of Atlantis	GB	1978	Kevin Connor	96			FB	27
Warm December, A	GB/USA	1972	Sidney Poitier	100			FB	25
Warm Nights, Hot Pleasures	GER	1980	Hubert Frank	90			GB	35
Warmth of Your Hands	USSR	1972	Nodar Managadze/Shota Managadze	90	est		ETV	10
Warning Shadows	GER	1923	Arthur Robison	95	st		BFI	18
Warning Shot	USA	1966	Buzz Kulik	100	col		FB	18
					bw		FB	15
Warning Sign	USA	1985	Hal Barwood	95			FB	40
Warrendale	CAN	1966	Allan King	100			GB	25
Warriors, The	USA	1979	Walter Hill	94			FB	38
Watch Out, We're Mad	IT/SP	1974	Marcello Fondato	102			FB	18
Watchers In The Woods	USA	1982	John Hough	83			FB	38
Watchmaker of Saint Paul, The	FR	1974	Bertrand Tavernier	105	est		GB	35
Water Babies, The	GB/POL	1978	Lionel Jeffries	92			GB	35
Waterloo	IT/USSR	1970	Sergei Bondarchuk	132	sc/std		FB	33
Waterloo Bridge	USA	1940	Mervyn LeRoy	102			FB	15
Watership Down	GB	1989	Martin Rosen	92		GU	GU	80
Watusi	USA	1958	Kurt Neumann	85			FB	18
Way Ahead, The	GB	1944	Carol Reed	91			FB	8
Way Back Home	USA	1932	William A. Seiter	82			GB	15
Way Back, The	CZ	1958	Vaclav Krska	95	est		ETV	10
Way of the Wicked	FR	1958	Luis Saslavsky	93	est		GB	15
Way Out West	USA	1937	James W. Horne	64			GB	15
Way We Were, The	USA	1973	Sydney Pollack	122	sc/std		FB	25
Way West, The	USA	1967	Andrew V. McLaglen	122	sc/std		FB	18
Wayne's World	USA	1992	Penelope Spheeris	95		UIP	FB	75
Wayward Bus, The	USA	1957	Victor Vicas	89	std		FB	15

	COUNTRY OF PRODUCTION	YEAR	DIRECTOR	RUNNING TIME	VERSION	35mm	16mm	16mm RENTAL FEE
We Are the Guinea Pigs	USA	1980	Joan Harvey	90			CONC	35
We are the Lambeth Boys	GB	1959	Karel Reisz	52			BFI	15
							CONC	88
We Joined the Navy	GB	1962	Wendy Toye	105	std		FB	18
We Make Dances	USA	1976	Michael Blackwood	88			AC	19
We of the Never Never	AUSTR	1982	Igor Auzins	134	sc		GB	48
We Think the World of You	GB	1988	Colin Gregg	94			GB	
We Who Are About To Die	USA	1936	Christy Cabanne	81			GB	15
We're Alive	USA	1974	UCLA Women's Film Workshop	50			GB	30
We're on the Jury	USA	1937	Ben Holmes	71			GB	15
We're Only Human	USA	1935	James Flood	80			GB	15
We're Rich Again	USA	1934	William A. Seiter	72			GB	15
We've a Lion at Home	CZ		Pavel Hobl	84	est		ETV	10
Weak and the Wicked, The	GB	1953	J. Lee Thompson	88			GB	20
Weapon, The	GB	1956	Val Guest	81			GB	25
Wedding in Galilee	BEL/FR	1987	Michel Khleifi	116	est		WFA	45
Wedding of Lili Marlene	GB	1953	Arthur Crabtree	92			GB	15
Wedding, A	USA	1978	Robert Altman	125	sc/std		FB	38
Wedding, The	POL	1972	Andrzej Wajda	110	est		FOP	0
Wednesday's Child	USA	1934	John S. Robertson	70			GB	15
Week-end	FR/IT	1967	Jean-Luc Godard	95	est		GB	45
Weekend at Bernies	USA	1989	Ted Kotcheff	99	sc/std		FB	55
Weekend for Three	USA	1941	Irving Reis	66			GB	15
Weekend of a Champion	GB	1971	Frank Simon	81			FB	18
Weekend with Lulu	GB	1960	John Paddy Carstairs	89			FB	15
Weird Science	USA	1985	John Hughes	94			FB	45
Welcome Home	USA	1989	Franklin J. Schaffner	92			FB	55
Welcome to Blood City	CAN/GB	1976	Peter Sasdy	96			FB	18
Welcome to Britain	GB	1976	Ben Lewin	70			BFI	35
Welcome to Cuba	CB/ USSR	1974		60			ETV	6
Welfare	USA	1975	Frederick Wiseman	167			GB	45
Well, The	USA	1951	Leo Popkin/Russell Rouse	85			GB	22
Went the Day Well?	GB	1942	Alberto Cavalcanti	92			BFI	20
West of Montana	USA	1963	Burt Kennedy	83	sc/std		FB	18
West of the Pecos	USA	1945	Edward Killy	88			GB	15
Western Approaches	GB	1944	Pat Jackson	82			CFL	23
Western Heritage	USA	1948	Wallace A. Grissell	61			GB	15
Westfront 1918	GER	1930	G.W. Pabst	103	est		GB	25
Westward Passage	USA	1932	Robert Milton	72			GB	15
Westward the Women	USA	1951	William Wellman	114			FB	15
Westworld	USA	1973	Michael Crichton	89			FB	27
Wetherby	GB	1984	David Hare	102			GB	60
Whales of August, The	USA	1987	Lindsay Anderson	91		MAY	GB	65
What a Blonde	USA	1944	Leslie Goodwins	71			GB	15
What a Way To Go	USA	1963	J. Lee Thompson	111	std		FB	22
What About Bob?	USA	1991	Frank Oz	99		T	FB	70
What Changed Charley Farthing?	GB	1974	Sidney Hayers	101			FB	22
What Did You Do In the War Daddy?	USA	1966	Blake Edwards	116	sc/std		FB	18
What Ever Happened to Aunt Alice?	USA	1969	Lee H. Katzin	101			GB	18
What Ever Happened to Baby Jane?	USA	1962	Robert Aldrich	133			FB	15
What Maisie Knew	USA	1975	Babette Mangolte	60			CIRC	35
What Next?	GB	1974	Peter Smith	56			GB	17
What Price Glory?	USA	1926	Raoul Walsh	122	t/sd		BFI	25
What Price Hollywood?	USA	1932	George Cukor	88			GB	15
What You Take for Granted	USA	1983	Michelle Citron	75			GB	41
What's Good for the Goose	GB	1969	Menahem Golan	104			GB	20
What's New Pussycat?	USA/FR	1965	Clive Donner	108			FB	18
What's So Bad about Feeling Good?	USA	1968	George Seaton	93			FB	18

	COUNTRY OF PRODUCTION	YEAR	DIRECTOR	RUNNING TIME	VERSION	35mm	16mm	16mm RENTAL FEE
W								
What's the Matter With Helen?	USA	1971	Curtis Harrington	100			FB	18
What's Up Doc?	USA	1972	Peter Bogdanovich	94			FB	27
What's Up Superdoc?	GB	1978	Derek Ford	93			FB	38
Wheelchair, The	SP	1959	Marco Ferreri	82	est		GB	25
When Comedy Was King	USA	1959	Robert Youngson	72			GB	15
When Dinosaurs Ruled the Earth	GB	1969	Val Guest	100			FB	18
When Father Was Away on Business	YUGO	1985	Emir Kusturica	136	est		FB	70
When Harry Met Sally...	USA	1989	Rob Reiner	95		MAY	GB	70
When the Legends Die	USA	1972	Stuart Millar	105			FB	18
When the North Wind Blows	USA	1974	Stewart Raffill	113			GB	43
When The Wind Blows	GB	1986	Jimmy T. Murakami	84			GB	75
When Time Ran Out...	USA	1980	James Goldstone	109	sc/std		FB	38
When Tomorrow Comes	USA	1939	John M. Stahl	92			FB	15
When Worlds Collide	USA	1951	Rudolph Maté	82			FB	18
Where Angels Fear to Tread	GB	1991	Charles Sturridge	113		R	FB	70
Where Angels Go ... Trouble Follows	USA	1967	James Neilson	93			FB	18
Where Danger Lives	USA	1950	John Farrow	81			GB	15
Where Does It Hurt?	USA	1971	Rod Amateau	85			GB	18
Where Eagles Dare	GB	1968	Brian G. Hutton	155	sc/std		FB	38
Where It's At	USA	1969	Garson Kanin	106			FB	18
Where No Vultures Fly	GB	1951	Harry Watt	109			FB	18
Where Sinners Meet	USA	1931	J. Walter Ruben	73			GB	15
Where the Boys Are	USA	1960	Henry Levin	99	sc/std		FB	18
Where The Boys Are	USA	1984	Hy Averback	94			GB	35
Where the Bullets Fly	USA	1966	John Gilling	90			GB	30
Where the North Begins	USA	1923	Chester M. Franklin	76	st		BFI	15
Where the River Bends	GB	1965	Val Guest	113	sc/std		FB	18
Where Were You When the Lights Went Out?	USA	1968	Hy Averback	91	std		FB	18
Where's Jack?	GB	1968	James Clavell	119			FB	18
Where's Johnny	GB	1974	David Eady	59			GB	17
Wherever She Goes	AUSTR	1950	Michael S. Gordon	81			FB	15
Which Way to the Front?	USA	1970	Jerry Lewis	96			FB	18
While the City Sleeps	USA	1956	Fritz Lang	99			BFI	20
Whip Hand, The	USA	1951	William Cameron Menzies	81			GB	15
Whisky Galore!	GB	1948	Alexander Mackendrick	83			FB	15
Whisperers, The	GB	1966	Bryan Forbes	106		UIP	FB	15
Whistle Blower, The	GB	1986	Simon Langton	104			FB	50
Whistle Down the Wind	GB	1961	Bryan Forbes	99			FB	15
White Buffalo, The	USA	1977	J. Lee Thompson	97			FB	18
White Cargo	USA	1942	Richard Thorpe	87			FB	15
White Cliffs of Dover, The	USA	1944	Clarence Brown	126			FB	15
White Coup, The	E.GER	1977	Walter Heynowski/Gerhard Scheumann	85	eng		ETV	12
White Dog	USA	1981	Samuel Fuller	90			BFI	40
White Fang	IT/SP/FR	1974	Lucio Fulci	101			FB	18
White Fang	USA	1991	Randal Kleiser	109		W	FB	65
White Gold	USA	1927	William K. Howard	60			GB	20
White Haired Girl	CHI	1972	Wang Pu/Shui Hua	102			ETV	20
							GB	25
White Heat	USA	1949	Raoul Walsh	110		UIP	FB	22
White Hell of Pitz Palu	GER	1929	Arnold Fanck/G.W. Pabst	76			BFI	20
White Lightning	USA	1973	Joseph Sargent	101			FB	18
White Line Fever	USA	1975	Jonathan Kaplan	89			FB	18
White Men Can't Jump	USA	1992	Ron Shelton	115		F	FB	70
White Mischief	GB	1987	Michael Radford	107			FB	60
White Nights	IT/FR	1957	Luchino Visconti	102	107/est		GB	25
White Nights	USA	1985	Taylor Hackford	134		C	FB	55
White Palace	USA	1991	Luis Mandoki	102		UIP	FB	60
White Rock	GB	1976	Tony Maylam	76	sc		FB	18

W	COUNTRY OF PRODUCTION	YEAR	DIRECTOR	RUNNING TIME	VERSION	35mm	16mm	16mm RENTAL FEE
White Room, The	BULG	1968	Metodi Andonov	90	est		ETV	10
White Sands	USA	1992	Roger Donaldson	101		W	FB	60
White Tower, The	USA	1950	Ted Tetzlaff	98	bw		GB	18
					col		GB	22
White Wall	SWE	1975	Stig Björkman	80	est		GB	30
White Wilderness	USA	1958	James Algar	72			FB	27
Whitney Brothers Programme	USA	1957-72		56	col		GB	30
Who Dares Wins	GB	1982	Ian Sharp	125			FB	48
Who Framed Roger Rabbit	USA	1988	Robert Zemeckis	104			FB	65
Who Needs a Heart?	GB	1991	John Akomfrah	90			BAFC	–
Who's Afraid of Virginia Woolf?	USA	1966	Mike Nichols	133			FB	22
Who's Got the Action?	USA	1962	Daniel Mann	93	bw/sc		FB	15
Who's Harry Crumb?	USA	1989	Paul Flaherty	95			FB	55
Who's Minding the Mint?	USA	1966	Howard Morris	97	col		FB	18
Who's Minding the Store?	USA	1963	Frank Tashlin	90	col		FB	18
					bw		FB	15
Who's That Girl	USA	1987	James Foley	92		W	FB	50
Whole Town's Talking, The	USA	1935	John Ford	86			FB	15
Whose Life is it Anyway?	USA	1981	John Badham	119			FB	38
Why Shoot the Teacher?	CAN	1976	Silvio Narizzano	99			GB	25
Wicked Lady, The	GB	1945	Leslie Arliss	103			BFI	30
Wicked Wicked	USA	1973	Richard Bare	95	sc		FB	35
Wicker Man, The	GB	1973	Robin Hardy	86		R	FB	22
Widow, The	IT/USA	1955	Lewis Milestone	95			GB	15
Wife, The	USSR	1955	Yuli Raizman	102	est		ETV	10
Wilby Conspiracy, The	GB	1974	Ralph Nelson	105			FB	22
Wild and the Willing, The	GB	1962	Ralph Thomas	114			FB	15
Wild and Wonderful	USA	1963	Michael Anderson	88			FB	18
Wild Angels, The	USA	1966	Roger Corman	83	std		GB	30
Wild At Heart	USA	1990	David Lynch	124	sc/est	MAY	GB	80
Wild Bunch, The	USA	1969	Sam Peckinpah	145	sc/std	BFI	FB	27
Wild Child	FR	1969	François Truffaut	84	dub		FB	22
Wild Country, The	USA	1970	Robert Totten	100	std		FB	27
Wild Duck, The	W.GER/ AUST	1976	Hans W. Geissendorfer	105	est		GFL	0
Wild Game (see Wildwechsel)								
Wild Geese II	GB	1985	Peter Hunt	124			FB	55
Wild Geese, The	GB	1977	Andrew V. McLaglen	134			FB	48
Wild Horse Mesa	USA	1947	George B. Seitz	60			GB	15
Wild Is the Wind	USA	1957	George Cukor	114	std		FB	15
Wild North, The	USA	1951	Andrew Marton	95			FB	27
Wild One, The	USA	1953	Laslo Benedek	79		C	FB	15
Wild River	USA	1960	Elia Kazan	110	sc!std		FB	18
Wild Rovers	USA	1971	Blake Edwards	132	std/107		FB	22
Wild Season	S.AFR	1967	Emil Nofal	92			FB	18
Wild Strawberries	SWE	1957	Ingmar Bergman	92	est	BFI	GB	35
Wild Style	USA	1982	Charlie Ahearn	82		BD	GB	50
Wildcat Bus	USA	1940	Frank Woodruff	64			GB	15
Wildcats	USA	1986	Michael Ritchie	106			FB	40
Wildwechsel	W.GER	1972	R.W. Fassbinder	102	est		GB	30
Will Any Gentleman?	GB	1953	Michael Anderson	85			FB	18
Will Penny	USA	1967	Tom Gries	108			FB	18
Willard	USA	1970	Daniel Mann	95			GB	22
Willie and Phil	USA	1980	Paul Mazursky	116			FB	30
Willow	USA	1988	Ron Howard	126			FB	55
Wilt	GB	1989	Michael Tuchner	92		R	FB	55
Winchester '73	USA	1950	Anthony Mann	91		UIP	FB	15
Wind and the Lion, The	USA	1975	John Milius	119	sc/std		FB	22

W

	COUNTRY OF PRODUCTION	YEAR	DIRECTOR	RUNNING TIME	VERSION	35mm	16mm	16mm RENTAL FEE
Wind, The	MALI	1982	Souleymane Cisse	100	est		BFI	40
Windbag the Sailor	GB	1936	William Beaudine	85			FB	15
Windflowers	USA	1967	Adolfas Mekas	64			LFC	25
Window to the Sky	USA	1975	Larry Peerce	104			FB	22
Window, The	USA	1948	Ted Tetzlaff	73			GB	15
Windwalker	USS	1980	Keith Merrill	106			GB	45
Windy Mountain	CZ	1956	Jiri Sequens	110	est		ETV	10
Wine of Youth	USA	1924	King Vidor	74	st		FB	22
Wings	USA	1927	William Wellman	136	sd		FB	22
Wings and the Woman	USA	1942	Herbert Wilcox	95			GB	15
Wings of Desire	FR/ W.GER	1987	Wim Wenders	128			GB	70
Wings of Eagles	USA	1956	John Ford	110			FB	18
Wings of Mystery	GB	1963	Gilbert Gunn	55			GB	12
Winning	USA	1969	James Goldstone	123	sc/std		FB	18
Winstanley	GB	1975	Kevin Brownlow/Andrew Mollo	96			BFI	35
Winter A-Go-Go	USA	1965	Richard Benedict	71			FB	15
Winter Soldier	USA	1972	Winterfilm Collective	99			GB	20
Winterspelt	GER	1978	Eberhard Fechner	111	est		GFL	0
Wir Wunderkinder	W.GER	1958	Kurt Hoffmann	96	est		GB	25
Wired	USA	1989	Larry Peerce	100		ENT	FB	60
Wise Blood	USA/W.GER	1979	John Huston	108		AE	GB	50
Wise Girl	USA	1937	Leigh Jason	72			GB	15
Wish You Were Here	GB	1987	David Leland	92			GB	75
Witchcraft Throught he Ages	SWE	1922	Benjamin Christensen	76	eng/com		GB	30
Witches of Eastwick, The	USA	1987	George Miller	118			FB	55
Witchfinder General	GB	1968	Michael Reeves	87			GB	25
With Six You Get Eggroll	USA	1968	Howard Morris	95	std		FB	18
Withnail and I	GB	1986	Bruce Robinson	107			GB	70
Without a Clue	GB	1988	Thom Eberhardt	107			FB	60
Without A Trace	USA	1983	Stanley R. Jaffe	116			FB	45
Without Orders	USA	1936	Lew Landers	69			GB	15
Without Prejudice	USSR	1947	Alexander Zagummy	95	est		GB	25
Without Reservations	USA	1946	Mervyn LeRoy	107			GB	15
Witness	USA	1985	Peter Weir	112			FB	55
Witness Chair, The	USA	1935	George Nicholls Jr	64			GB	15
Witness for the Prosecution	USA	1957	Billy Wilder	116			FB	15
Witness in the Dark	GB	1959	Wolf Rilla	63			GB	15
Witness, The	HUN	1968	Peter Basco	108	est		GB	55
Wives	NOR	1975	Anja Breien	84	est		GB	30
Wiz, The	USA	1978	Sidney Lumet	136			FB	43
Wizard of Speed and Time, The	USA	1988	Mike Jittlov	98			GB	50
Wizards	USA	1977	Ralph Bakshi	81			FB	22
Wobblies, The	USA	1979	Stewart Bird/Deborah Shaffer	89			MP	46
Wolfen	USA	1981	Michael Wadleigh	114			FB	38
Wolfman, The	USA	1941	George Waggner	79			FB	15
Woman Between, The	USA	1931	Victor Schertzinger	73			GB	15
Woman in Flames	W.GER	1983	Robert van Ackeren	100			FB	70
Woman in Green, The	USA	1945	Roy William Neill	68			GB	15
Woman in Question, The	GB	1950	Anthony Asquith	88			GB	27
Woman In Red	USA	1984	Gene Wilder	86			FB	45
Woman in the Window	USA	1944	Fritz Lang	99			BFI	25
Woman Next Door, The (see Femme d'a Cote, La)								
Woman of Straw	GB	1964	Basil Dearden	117			FB	18
Woman of Summer	USA	1963	Franklin J. Schaffner	94	std		FB	15
Woman of the Dunes	JAP	1964	Hiroshi Teshigahara	127	est		APO	35
Woman on Pier 13	USA	1949	Robert Stevenson	75			GB	15
Woman on the Beach	USA	1947	Jean Renoir	70			BFI	20
Woman Rebels, A	USA	1936	Mark Sandrich	88			GB	16

W

Title	Country of Production	Year	Director	Running Time	Version	35mm	16mm	16mm Rental Fee
Woman with No Name, The	GB	1950	Ladislas Vajda	80			GB	15
Woman Without a Face	USA	1965	Delbert Mann	95			FB	15
Woman's Angle, The	GB	1952	Leslie Arliss	86			GB	20
Woman's Estate, A (see Frauen Siedlung)								
Woman's Secret, A	USA	1948	Nicholas Ray	72			GB	15
Wombling Free	GB	1977	Lionel Jeffries	96			FB	33
Women Are Like That	FR	1960	Bernard Borderie	82	dub		GB	15
Women from South Lebanon	LEB	1986	Mai Masri/Jean Chamoun	71			CN	55
Women in Love	GB	1969	Ken Russell	130		UIP	FB	22
Women in Prison	GB	1971	Jenny Barraclough (Prod)	70			CONC	15.2
Women of Pleasure	W.GER	1965	Manfred Durneck	89			GB	25
Women, The	USA	1939	George Cukor	132			FB	15
Won Ton Ton, the Dog Who Saved Hollywood	USA	1975	Michael Winner	92			FB	27
Wonder Woman	USA	1973	Robert O'Neil	88			GB	25
Wonderful Life	GB	1964	Sidney J. Furie	113	std		FB	18
Woo Woo Kid, The	USA	1987	Phil Alden Robinson	98			FB	80
Woodstock	USA	1970	Michael Wadleigh	184	sc		FB	33
Word Is Out	USA	1977	Mariposa Film Group	135			MP	51.75
Work They Say is Mine, The	GB	1986	Rosie Gibson	50			CN	30
Working Girl	USA	1988	Mike Nichols	114			FB	65
Working Girls	USA	1986	Lizzie Borden	91			GB	60
Working Title: Journeys from Berlin/1971	GB/ W.GER	1980	Yvonne Rainer	125			BFI	30
World Apart, A	GB	1987	Chris Menges	113			GB	80
World Is Full of Married Men, The	GB	1979	Robert Young	107			GB	40
World of Abbott and Costello	USA	1968	Max Rosenberg/Milton Subotsky (Prods)	84			FB	15
World of Apu	INDIA	1958	Satyajit Ray	106	est	CONT	GB	25
World of Gilbert and George, The	GB	1981	Gilbert and George	69			AC	19
World of Hans Christian Andersen	USA	1971	Chuck McCann/Al Kilgore	72	std		GB	25
World of Strangers	DEN	1961	Henning Carlsen	92	est		GB	2World on
That Day April 22nd, The	USSR	1970		70	eng		ETV	6
World Without Pity, A	FR	1989	Eric Rochant	88	est	AE	GB	70
World Without Sun	FR/IT	1964	Jacques Cousteau	92			FB	18
World's Greatest Athlete, The	USA	1973	Robert Scheerer	92			FB	33
World's Greatest Lover, The	USA	1977	Gene Wilder	87			FB	22
World, the Flesh and the Devil, The	USA	1958	Ranald McDougall	95	std		FB	15
Worm's Eye View	GB	1951	Jack Raymond	78			FB	15
Woyzeck	W.GER	1978	Werner Herzog	80	est		GB	40
Wozzeck	W.GER	1947	Georg C. Klaren	66	est		GB	25
WR Mysteries of the Organism	W.GER/ YUGO	1971	Dusan Makavejev	86	est		GB	35
Wrath of God, The	USA	1972	Ralph Nelson	111	sc/std		FB	22
Wreck of Mary Deare, The	USA	1959	Michael Anderson	104	sc/std		FB	18
Wreck Raisers	GB	1972	Harold Orton	56			GB	17
Written on the Wind	USA	1956	Douglas Sirk	99		UIP	BFI	30
Wrong Box, The	GB	1966	Bryan Forbes	110			FB	18
Wrong Man, The	USA	1956	Alfred Hitchcock	104			FB	25
WUSA	USA	1970	Stuart Rosenberg	114	sc		FB	18
Wuthering Heights	GB	1970	Robert Fuest	104			FB	22

	COUNTRY OF PRODUCTION	YEAR	DIRECTOR	RUNNING TIME	VERSION	35mm	16mm	16mm RENTAL FEE
Xala	SEN	1974	Ousmane Sembene	123	est		GB	30
Xanadu	USA	1980	Robert Greenwald	96			FB	38
Xtro	GB	1982	Harry Bromley Davenport	86			GB	38

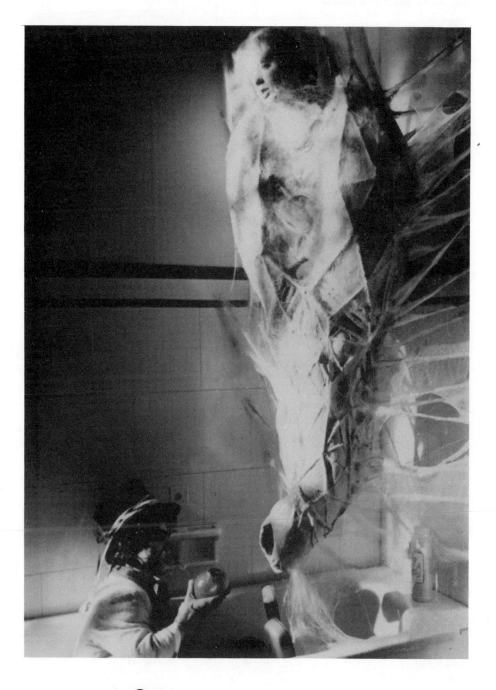

Xtro

	COUNTRY OF PRODUCTION	YEAR	DIRECTOR	RUNNING TIME	VERSION	35mm	16mm	16mm RENTAL FEE
Yaaba	B/F	1989	Idrissa Ouedraogo	90	est	Oasis	GB	70
Yangtse Incident	GB	1956	Michael Anderson	113			GB	20
Yank at Oxford, A	GB	1938	Jack Conway	97			FB	15
Yank in Ermine, A	GB	1955	Gordon Parry	85	bw		GB	15
Yanks	GB	1979	John Schlesinger	139			FB	43
Year My Voice Broke, The	AUSTR	1987	John Duigan	104			GB	75
Year of Living Dangerously, The	AUSTR/ PHIL	1982	Peter Weir	114			FB	38
Year of the Dragon	USA	1985	Michael Cimino	134			FB	55
Year of the Quiet Sun, A	POL/ W.GER	1984	Krzysztof Zanussi	91	108/est	BD	GB	60
Year of the Torturer	GB	1974	Leslie Woodhead	89			CONC	20.6
Year Zero the Silent Death of Cambodia	GB	1979	John Pilger	60			CONC	5.2
Yearling, The	USA	1946	Clarence Brown	135			FB	30
Years of Lightning, Day of Drums	USA	1964	Bruce Herschensohn	85			BFI	15
Yeelen	MALI	1987	Souleymane Cisse	105	st	AE	GB	60
Yellow Cab Man, The	USA	1949	Jack Donohue	84			FB	15
Yellow Canary	GB	1943	Herbert Wilcox	98			GB	18
Yellow Earth	CHI	1984	Chen Kaige	89	est		BFI	40
Yellow Rolls-Royce, The	GB	1964	Anthony Asquith	122	sc/std		FB	22
Yellowbeard	GB/MEX	1983	Mel Damski	96		UIP	FB	38
Yentl	GB	1983	Barbra Streisand	133			FB	43
Yesterday Girl	W.GER	1966	Alexander Kluge	90	est		GB	25
Yeux Sans Visage, Les	FR	1959	Georges Franju	90	est		GB	30
Yield to the Night	GB	1956	J. Lee Thompson	100			FB	15
Yojimbo	JAP	1961	Akira Kurosawa	112	sc/est		GB	25
You and Me	USA	1938	Fritz Lang	94			BFI	25
You Can't Buy Luck	USA	1937	Lew Landers	61			GB	20
You Can't Escape	GB	1956	Wilfred Eades	77			GB	20
You Can't Have Everything	USA	1970	Martin Zweiback	91			GB	18
You Can't Run Away From It	USA	1956	Dick Powell	108			FB	18
You Can't Take It With You	USA	1938	Frank Capra	126			FB	15
You Can't Win 'em All	GB	1970	Peter Collinson	99	sc/std		FB	18
You Know What Sailors Are	GB	1953	Ken Annakin	89			FB	18
You Light Up My Life	USA	1977	Joseph Brooks	91			FB	27
You Only Live Once	USA	1937	Fritz Lang	84			BFI	25
You Only Live Twice	GB	1967	Lewis Gilbert	116	sc/std		FB	33
You Were Never Lovelier	USA	1942	William A. Seiter	91			FB	15
You'll Find Out	USA	1940	David Butler	97			GB	15
You'll Like My Mother	USA	1972	Lamont Johnson	93			FB	18
You'll Never Get Rich	USA	1972	Sidney Lanfield	83			FB	15
You're Lying	SWE	1969	Vilgot Sjöman	107	est		GB	30
You're Never Too Young	USA	1955	Norman Taurog	103	bw		FB	15
Young Americans	USA	1967	Alex Grasshoff	79			FB	15
Young and the Brave, The	USA	1963	Francis D. Lyon	84			FB	15
Young Aphrodites	GR	1962	Nikos Koundouros	87	dub		GB	25
Young Bess	USA	1953	George Sidney	112			FB	18
Young Billy Young	USA	1969	Burt Kennedy	89			FB	18
Young Bride	USA	1932	William A. Seiter	76			GB	20
Young Cassidy	GB	1964	Jack Cardiff	110			FB	18
Young Doctors in Love	USA	1982	Garry Marshall	95			FB	48
Young Einstein	AUSTR	1989	Yahoo Serious	91		W	FB	60
Young Frankenstein	USA	1974	Mel Brooks	106			FB	33
Young Guard Part I	USSR	1948	Sergei Gerasimov	82	est		ETV	10
Part 2				72				
Young Guns	USA	1988	Christopher Cain	107			GB	60
Young Lions, The	USA	1958	Edward Dmytryk	167			FB	16
Young Magician	CAN	1986	Waldemar Dziki	101			GB	

40

y

	COUNTRY OF PRODUCTION	YEAR	DIRECTOR	RUNNING TIME	VERSION	35mm	16mm	16mm RENTAL FEE
Young Man of Music	USA	1950	Michael Curtiz	111			FB	15
Young Ones, The	GB	1961	Sidney J. Furie	108	std		FB	18
Young Racers, The	USA	1963	Roger Corman	84			FB	20
Young Sherlock Holmes and the Pyramid of Fear	USA	1985	Barry Levinson	109			FB	45
Young Stranger, The	USA	1957	John Frankenheimer	80			GB	15
Young Torless	W.GER/ FR	1966	Volker Schlöndorff	85	est		APO	30
Young Visiters, The	GB	1984	James Hill	93			GB	45
Young Warriors	USA	1983	Lawrence D. Foldes	102			FB	38
Young Warriors, The	USA	1966	John Peyser	93	std		FB	18
Young Winston	GB	1972	Richard Attenborough	156	163/sc/ std		FB	28
Youngblood	USA	1986	Peter Markle	110			FB	40
Youngblood Hawke	USA	1965	Delmer Daves	120			FB	15
Your Cheatin' Heart	USA	1964	Gene Nelson	96	std		FB	15
Your Money or Your Wife	GB	1959	Anthony Simmons	92			GB	15
Yours Mine and Ours	USA	1968	Melville Shavelson	110			FB	18
Youth of Maxim, The	USSR	1935	Grigori Kozintsev/ Leonid Trauberg	95	est		BFI	30

The Year My Voice Broke

	COUNTRY OF PRODUCTION	YEAR	DIRECTOR	RUNNING TIME	VERSION	35mm	16mm	16mm RENTAL FEE
Z	FR/ALG	1968	Costa-Gavras	125	dub		MP	51.75
Zabriskie Point	USA	1969	Michelangelo Antonioni	110	sc/std		FB	27
Zachariah	USA	1970	George Englund	93			GB	22
Zardoz	GB	1973	John Boorman	106	sc/std		FB	29
Zazie Dans le Metro	FR	1960	Louis Malle	88	est		GB	35
Zebra in the Kitchen	USA	1965	Ivan Tors	93			FB	20
Zee and Co.	GB	1971	Brian G. Hutton	108			FB	18
Zelig	USA	1983	Woody Allen	79		W	FB	45
Zemlya (see Earth)								
Zero Hour	W.GER	1976	Edgar Reitz	108	est		GFL	0
Ziegfeld Girl	USA	1941	Robert Z. Leonard	132			FB	15
Zimbabwe The Struggle for Health	GB	1983	Central TV	60			CONC	20.4
Zoltan ...Hound of Dracula	USA	1977	Albert Band	88			FB	18
Zombies on Broadway	USA	1945	Gordon Douglas	68			GB	15
Zoo Robbery, The	GB	1973	Matt McCarthy/John Black	64			GB	17
Zorns Lemma	USA	1970	Hollis Frampton	60			LFC	25
Zorro the Gay Blade	USA	1981	Peter Medak	94			FB	38
Zu Neuen Ufern (see To New Shores)								
Zulu	GB	1963	Cy Endfield	138	std		FB	33
Zulu Dawn	USA/ HOLL	1979	Douglas Hickox	117	sc		GB	35

Zelig

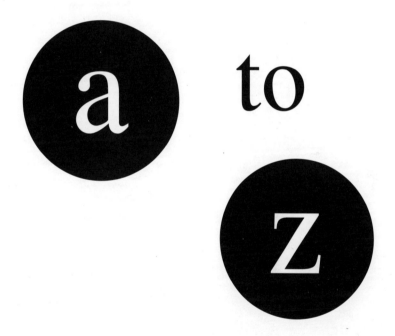

AARON, Paul
Maxie

ABBAS, Ahmad
Munna

ABBOTT, Frank
On the Air: Workers Playtime

ABBOTT, George
Damn Yankees (Co)
Pajama Game (Co)
Too Many Girls

ABDELSALAM, Shadi
Night of Counting the Years, The

ABEL, Robert
Elvis on Tour (Co)
Let the Good Times Roll (Co)

ABRAHAMS, Jim
Airplane! (Co)
Big Business
Hot Shots!
Ruthless People (Co)
Top Secret (Co)

ABRAHAMSON, Christen
American Dream, The

ACEVSKI, Jon
Freddie as F.R.O.7.

ACKROYD, Dan
Nothing But Trouble

ADATO, Perry Miller
Georgia O'Keefe
Gertrude Stein: When This
    You See, Remember Me

ADIDGE, Pierre
Elvis on Tour (Co)

ADLER, Lou
Up in Smoke

ADLON, Percy
Bagdad Café
Rosalie Goes Shopping
Sugarbaby
Swing, The

ADOLFI, John G.
Show of Shows

ADREON, Franklin
Dimension 5

AGRANENKO, Zakhar
Immortal Garrison, The

AHEARN, Charlie
Wild Style

AHLBERG, Mac
I A Woman

AITKEN, Doug
Big Wheels and Sailor

AKAN, Miroslav
End of the Road

AKERMAN, Chantal
Jeanne Dielman, 23 Quai
    Du Commerce, 1080, Bruxelles
Je Tu Il Elle

News from Home
Rendez-vous d'Anna, Les
Toute une Nuit

AKOMFRAH, John
Handsworth Songs
Testament
Who Needs a Heart?

ALAOUIE, Borhan
Massacre of Kaffr Kassem, The
That God Should Be on the Side of
    the People Is not Enough (Co)

ALAUX, Myriam
Animals Film, The (Co)

ALBERTINI, Adalberto
Black Emmanuelle

ALBICOCCO, J.G.
Grand Meaulnes, Le

ALDA, Alan
Betsy's Wedding
Four Seasons, The
Sweet Liberty

ALDRICH, Robert
Angry Hills, The
Big Leaguer
California Dolls
Choirboys, The
Dirty Dozen, The
Emperor of the North
Flight of the Phoenix, The
Four for Texas
Frisco Kid, The
Grissom Gang, The
Hush... Hush, Sweet Charlotte
Hustle
Killing of Sister George, The
Kiss Me Deadly
Legend of Lylah Claire, The
Mean Machine, The
Thieves Like Us
Too Late the Hero
Ulzana's Raid
Whatever Happened to Baby Jane?

ALEMANN, Claudia
Blind Spot

ALEXANDER, Michael
Beyond the Maypole
Nosey Dobson

ALEXANDROV, Grigori
General Line, The (Co)
October (Co)

ALGAR, James
Adventures of Ichabod and
    Mr. Toad, The (Co)
African Lion, The
Best of Walt Disney's True-
    Life Adventures, The
Jungle Cat
Living Desert, The
Secrets of Life
Vanishing Prairie, The
White Wilderness

ALLEN, Corey
Thunder and Lightning

ALLEN, Fred
Freighters of Destiny
Saddle Buster, The

ALLEN, Irwin
Beyond the Poseidon Adventure

One Hour to Doomsday
Swarm, The

ALLEN, Lewis
At Sword's Point
Desert Fury
Those Endearing Young Charms

ALLEN, Woody
Alice
Annie Hall
Broadway Danny Rose
Everything You Always Wanted to
    Know About Sex But Were Afraid
    to Ask
Hannah And Her Sisters
Interiors
Love and Death
Manhattan
Midsummer Night's Sex Comedy, A
New York Stories (Ep)
Purple Rose of Cairo, The
Radio Days
Sleeper
Stardust Memories
Take the Money and Run
Zelig

ALLIO, René
Moi, Pierre Rivière
Vieille Dame Indigne, La

ALMENDROS, Nestor
Improper Conduct (Co)

ALMODÓVAR, Pedro
High Heels
Tie Me Up! Tie Me Down!

ALONZO, John
FM

ALOV, Alexander
Pavel Korchagin (Co)

ALTMAN, Robert
Aria (Ep)
Brewster McCloud
California Split
Images
Long Goodbye, The
M.A.S.H.
Nashville
Perfect Couple, A
Popeye
Quintet
Secret Honour
Thieves Like Us
3 Women
Vincent and Theo
Wedding, A

ALVES, Joe
Jaws 3

AMARAL, Suzana
Hour of the Star

AMATEAU, Rod
Drive-in
Pussycat, Pussycat, I Love You
Where Does It Hurt?

AMBER
Double Vision
Dream On
In Fading Light
Seacoal
T. Dan Smith
Tyne Lives

AMIEL, Jon
Queen of Hearts

AMYES, Julian
Hill in Korea, A

ANDERSEN, Thom
Eadweard Muybridge -
    Zoopraxographer

ANDERSON, Lindsay
Britannia Hospital
IF...
O Lucky Man!
Whales of August, The

ANDERSON, Michael
All the Fine Young Cannibals
Chase a Crooked Shadow
Conduct Unbecoming
Dam Busters, The
Doc Savage... The Man of
    Bronze
Flight from Ashiya
Logan's Run
Millennium
Night Was Our Friend
Quiller Memorandum, The
Shoes of the Fisherman, The
Wild and Wonderful
Will Any Gentleman?
Wreck of the Mary Deare, The
Yangtse Incident

ANDONOV, Metodi
Goat Horn, The
White Room, The

ANDRE, Raoul
Man and Child

ANDREACCHIO, Mario
Captain Johnno

ANGELOPOULOS, Theo
Beekeeper, The
Landscape in the Mist

ANGER, Kenneth
Anger Magick Lantern Cycle

ANNAKIN, Ken
Biggest Bundle of Them All, The
Call of the Wild, The
Crooks Anonymous
Fast Lady, The
Long Duel, The
Longest Day, The (Co)
Pirate Movie, The
Story of Robin Hood and
    His Merrie Men, The
Swiss Family Robinson
Third Man on the Mountain
Those Magnificent Men in
    Their Flying Machines
Very Important Person
You Know What Sailors Are

ANNAUD, Jean - Jacques
Bear, The
Quest for Fire

ANNENSKY, Isider
Sailor from the Comet, The

ANSPAUGH, David
Best Shot

ANTCZAK, Jerzy
Master, The

ANTHONY, Joseph
Matchmaker, The
Rainmaker, The

ANTONIONI, Michelangelo
Amiche, Le
Amore in Citta (Ep)
Blow-Up
Identification of a Woman
Oberwald Mystery, The
Signora Senza Camelie, La
Zabriskie Point

APTED, Michael
Agatha
Coal Miner's Daughter
Continental Divide
Gorillas in the Mist
Gorky Park
Squeeze, The
Stardust
Triple Echo, The
28 Up

ARCAND, Denys
Decline of the American
 Empire, The
Jesus of Montreal

ARCELIN, Jacques
Bitter Cane

ARCHAINBAUD, George
After Tonight
Alias French Gertie
Keep 'em Rolling
Lady Refuses, The
Lost Squadron, The
Men of Chance
Murder on the Blackboard
Penguin Pool Murder, The
Silver Horde
Three Who Loved

ARDEN, Jane
Other Side of the Underneath, The

ARDOLINI, Emile
Dirty Dancing
Three Men and a Little Lady

ARGENTO, Dario
Cat O'Nine Tails
Four Flies on Grey Velvet
Inferno

ARKIN, Alan
Fire Sale

ARLISS, Leslie
Man in Grey, The
Wicked Lady, The
Woman's Angle, The

ARMITAGE, George
Miami Blues
Vigilante Force

ARMSTRONG, Gillian
Mrs. Soffel

ARMSTRONG, Michael
Haunted House of Horror, The

ARNOLD, Jack
Bachelor in Paradise
Black Eye
Creature from the Black
 Lagoon
Global Affair, A
Hello Down There
Mouse that Roared, The

Revenge of the Creature
Swiss Conspiracy, The

ARNOLD, Newt
Bloodsport

ARRABAL, Fernando
Viva La Muerte

AURTHUR, Robert Alan
Lost Man, The

ARZNER, Dorothy
Christopher Strong
Dance, Girl, Dance
Merrily We Go to Hell

ASHBY, Hal
Being There
Bound for Glory
Coming Home
Harold and Maude
Last Detail, The
Let's Spend the Night Together
Shampoo

ASHCROFT, Ronnie
Mysterious Invader, The

ASHER, Robert
Bulldog Breed, The
Early Bird, The
Follow a Star
Intelligence Men, The
On the Beat
Press for Time
She'll Have to Go
Stitch in Time, A

ASHER, William
Beach Party, The
Bikini Beach
Fireball 500
Muscle Beach Party

ASKEY, David
Take Me High

ASKOLDOV, Alexander
Commissar, The

ASQUITH, Anthony
Browning Version, The
Cottage on Dartmoor
Demi-Paradise, The
Doctor's Dilemma, The
Evening with the Royal
 Ballet, An (Co)
Guns of Darkness
Libel
Pygmalion (Co)
Shooting Stars (Co)
Tell England (Co)
V.I.P.s., The
Woman in Question, The
Yellow Rolls-Royce, The

ATKINS, Tommy
Hi Gaucho
Silver Streak, The

ATTENBOROUGH, Richard
Bridge Too Far, A
Chorus Line, A
Cry Freedom
Gandhi
Magic
Oh! What a Lovely War
Young Winston

ATTIAS, Daniel
Silver Bullet

AUBERGE, Jean-Pascal
Droids

AUDLEY, Michael
Mark of the Hawk

AUDRY, Jacqueline
Olivia

AUER, John H.
Beat the Band
Gangway for Tomorrow
Music in Manhattan
Pan Americana
Seven Days Ashore

AUGUST, Bille
Pelle the Conqueror
Best Intentions, The

AUGUSTE, Reece
Twilight City

AUSTIN, Albert
My Boy (Co)

AUTANT-LARA, Claude
Seven Deadly Sins (Ep)

AUZINS, Igor
We of the Never Never

AVAKIAN, Aram
Cops and Robbers
Eleven Harrowhouse
End of the Road

AVERBACK, Hy
Chamber of Horrors
Great Bank Robbery, The
Suppose They Gave a War
 and Nobody Came
Where The Boys Are
Where Were You When
 the Lights Went Out?

AVILDSEN, John G.
Formula, The
Joe
Karate Kid, The
Karate Kid: Part II, The
Karate Kid: Part III, The
Power of One
Rocky
Rocky V
Save the Tiger
Slow Dancing in the Big City
W.W. and the Dixie Dancekings

AVNET, Jon
Fried Green Tomatoes at the
 Whistle Stop Cafe

AXEL, Gabriel
Babette's Feast

AXLEROD, George
Secret Life of an American Wife, The

BABENCO, Hector
Ironweed
Kiss of the Spider Woman
Pixote

BACON, Lloyd
Action in the North Atlantic
Beautiful but Dangerous
Brother Orchid
Footlight Parade

Forty Second Street
French Line
Kept Husbands
Larceny, Inc.
Oklahoma Kid
Racket Busters
San Quentin

BADHAM, John
Bingo Long Travelling All-Stars and
 Motor Kings, The
Bird on a Wire
Blue Thunder
Dracula
Hard Way, The
Saturday Night Fever
Short Circuit
Stakeout
War Games
Whose Life is it Anyway?

BADIYI, Reza S.
Trader Horn

BAER, Max
Ode to Billy Joe

BAGGOTT, Jeff
Family Fragments (Co)

BAGGOT, King
Tumbleweeds

BAGLEY, Anthony
Enemy

BAHNA, Vladimir
House at the Crossroads
St. Elizabeth's Square

BAHR, Fax
Hearts of Darkness: A Filmmaker's
 Apocalypse (Co)

BAIL, Chuck
Cleopatra Jones and the Casino of
 Gold
Gumball Rally, The

BAILEY, Derek
Rex Whistler (Prod)

BAILLIE, Bruce
Quick Billie

BAJON, Filip
Aria for an Athlete
Limousine Daimler-Benz, The

BAKER, Graham
Final Conflict, The

BAKER, Roy Ward
And Now the Screaming Starts!
Asylum
Dr. Jekyll & Sister Hyde
Flame in the Streets
House in the Square
Inferno
Legend of the 7 Golden Vampires,
 The
Monster Club, The
Moon Zero Two
Morning Departure
Night to Remember, A
No Love for Johnnie
One That Got Away, The
Quatermass and the Pit
Singer Not the Song, The
Tiger in the Smoke
Vampire Lovers, The
Vault of Horror, The

BAKSHI, Ralph
Fire and Ice
Lord of the Rings
Wizards

BALCH, Anthony
Horror Hospital
Secrets of Sex

BALDI, Ferdinando
Blindman

BALEDON, Rafael
Swamp of the Lost Monster

BALIK, Jaroslav
Rehearsal Goes On, The
Time Bandit

BALLARD, Carroll
Black Stallion, The
Never Cry Wolf

BALLMAN, Herbert
Mysterious Wreck, The

BAND, Albert
Zoltan... Hound of Dracula

BANKS, Monty
Great Guns
No Limit
Queen of Hearts

BARBERA, Joseph
Jetsons: The Movie

BARE, RICHARD
Wicked Wicked

BARGES, Paul
Paradis des Riches, Le

BARKAS, Geoffrey
Tell England (Co)

BARKER, Reginald
Seven Keys to Baldpate

BARNET, Boris
House on Trubnaya Square
Outskirts

BARRACLOUGH, Jenny
Gale is Dead
Someone from the Welfare (Prod)
Women in Prison (Prod)

BARRETO, Bruno
Doña Flor and Her Two Husbands

BARRON, Arthur
Jeremy

BARRON, Fred
Something Short of Paradise

BARRON, Steve
Electric Dreams
Teenage Mutant Ninja Turtles

BARRON, Zelda
Shag

BARRY, Ian
Chain Reaction, The

BARSHA, Leon
Pace that Thrills, The

BARTA, Jiří
Pied Piper

BARTEL, Paul
Death Race 2000
Eating Raoul

BARTLETT, Richard H.
Slim Carter

BARTON, Charles
Shaggy Dog, The
Toby Tyler

BARWOOD, Hal
Warning Sign

BASCO, Peter
Witness, The

BASHORE, Juliet
Kamikaze Hearts

BASKIN, Richard
Sing

BASS, Jules
Last Unicorn, The (Co)

BASS, Saul
Phase IV

BATCHELOR, Joy
Animal Farm (Co)
Ruddigore

BATORY, Jan
Lake of Peculiarity

BATTERSBY, Roy
Body, The

BAVA, Mario
Black Sabbath
Danger: Diabolik
Evil Eye, The
Shock

BAXLEY, Craig R.
Stone Cold

BAXTER, John
Fortune Lane,
Love On the Dole
Music Hall
Say It With Flowers

BAXTER, Ronnie
Never Mind the Quality Feel the
  Width

BAYLIS, Peter
Finest Hours, The

BEARD, David
Scorchers

BEATTY, Warren
Dick Tracy
Heaven Can Wait
Reds

BEAUDIN, Jean
Cordelia
J.A. Martin, Photographe

BEAUDINE, William
Boys Will Be Boys
Misbehaving Husbands
Old Fashioned Way, The
Ten Who Dared
Windbag the Sailor

BEAUDRY, Jean
Case of the Witch that Wasn't

BEAUMONT, Gabrielle
Godsend, The

BEAUMONT, Harry
Alias A Gentleman
Enchanted April, The
Twice Be Blessed
Up She Goes

BEAVER, Chris
Dark Circle (Co)

BECK, George
Behave Yourself

BECKER, Harold
Onion Field, The
Taps

BECKER, Jacques
Touchez Pas au Grisbi

BECKER, Jean
One Deadly Summer

BECKER, Lutz
Double Headed Eagle, The
Vita Futurista

BEHI, Ridha
Hyena's Sun

BEINEIX, Jean-Jacques
Betty Blue
Diva
Moon in the Gutter, The

BELL, Colin
Rescue Squad, The

BELL, Martin
Streetwise

BELLAMY, Earl
Fire!
Flood
Fluffy
Incident at Phantom Hill
Joaquin Murieta
Sidecar Racers

BELLOCCHIO, Marco
In the Name of the Father

BELSON, Jerry
Surrender

BENEDEK, Laslo
Namu, the Killer Whale
Port of New York
Wild One, The

BENEDICT, Richard
Impasse
Winter A-Go-Go

BENEGAL, Shyam
Ankur
Junoon
Role, The

BENJAMIN, Mary
Eight Minutes to Midnight

BENJAMIN, Richard
City Heat
Mermaids
Money Pit, The
My Favourite Year
My Stepmother is an Alien
Racing With the Moon

BENNETT, Compton
Beyond the Curtain
Forsyte Saga
King Solomon's Mines (Co)
Seventh Veil, The
So Little Time
That Woman Opposite

BENNETT, Edward
Ascendancy
Life Story of Baal, The

BENNETT, Rodney
Hamlet

BENNET, Spencer G.
Atomic Submarine, The
Requiem for a Gunfighter

BENNING, James
Grand Opera

BENSON, Alan
Anatomy of an Opera:
  Jonathan Miller

BENSON, Leon
Flipper and the Pirates

BENTON, Robert
Billy Bathgate
Kramer vs. Kramer
Late Show, The
Nadine
Places in the Heart
Still of the Night

BERCOVICI, Leonardo
Square of Violence

BERESFORD, Bruce
Adventures of Barry
  Mackenzie, The
Aria (Ep)
Black Robe
Breaker Morant
Driving Miss Daisy
Getting of Wisdom, The
Her Alibi
King David
Money Movers
Puberty Blues
Side by Side
Tender Mercies

**BERGENSTRÅHLE,
Johan**
Foreigners

BERGMAN, Andrew
Freshman, The
So Fine

BERGMAN, Ingmar
Autumn Sonata
Cries and Whispers
Devil's Eye, The
Devil's Wanton, The
Face, The
Fanny and Alexander
Faro Document 1979
Hour of the Wolf
Journey into Autumn
Lesson in Love, A
Magic Flute, The
Night is my Future
Now About These Women
Passion, A
Port of Call
Quiet Please: Stand By
  to Shoot "The Magic Flute"
Rite, The

Scenes from a Marriage
Seventh Seal, The
Shame
Silence, The
Smiles of a Summer Night
Summer Interlude
Summer With Monika
Through a Glass Darkly
Touch, The
Virgin Spring, The
Wild Strawberries

BERKE, William
Betrayal from the East
Ding Dong Williams
Falcon's Adventure, The

BERKELEY, Busby
For Me and My Gal
Hollywood Hotel

BERNARD, Chris
Letter to Brezhnev

BERNDS, Edward
Stooges Go West, The

BERNHARDT, Curtis
Blue Veil, The
Conflict
Merry Widow, The
Possessed

BERNSTEIN, Walter
Little Miss Marker

BERRI, Claude
Manon des Sources
Uranus

BERRY, John
Claudine
Tension

BERTHOMIEU, Andre
Girl in a Taxi

BERTOLUCCI, Bernardo
Before the Revolution
Commare Secca, La
Last Emperor, The
Last Tango in Paris
Luna, La
1900
Sheltering Sky, The
Spider's Stratagem

BERTUCCELLI, Jean-Louis
Ramparts of Clay

BERWICK, Irvin
Monster of Piedras Blancas

BESSON, Luc
Nikita
Subway

BHATTACHARYA, Uday
Circle of Gold

BIANCHI, Edward
Fan, The
Off and Running

BIBERMAN, Abner
Gun for a Coward
Too Many Thieves

BIBERMAN, Herbert J.
Master Race, The

BIELER, Manfred
On Borrowed Time

BIESCH, Rolf
Lisa-Indispensable

BIGELOW, Kathryn
Blue Steel
Point Break

BILL, Tony
My Bodyguard
Six Weeks

BILLINGTON, Kevin
Henry VIII
Interlude

BILSON, Bruce
Hill's Angels

BINYON, Claude
Here Come the Girls

BIRCH, Patricia
Grease 2

BIRD, Stewart
Wobblies, The (Co)

BIRDWELL, Russell
Flying Devils

BIRKETT, Michael
Soldier's Tale, The

BIELIK, Palo
Forty Four, The

BJORKMAN, Stig
White Wall, The

BLACK, Cathal
Pigs

BLACK, John
Robin Hood Junior (Co)
Zoo Robbery, The (Co)

BLACK, Noel
Jennifer on my Mind
Pretty Poison

BLACKWOOD, Maureen
Passion of Remembrance, The (Co)

BLACKWOOD, Michael
Fourteen Americans
Pablo Picasso: The Legacy of a
    Genius
We Make Dances

BLAIR, Les
Law and Order: A Detective's Tale

BLAIS, Roger
Grierson

BLAKEMORE, Michael
Privates On Parade

BLANCO, Jorge
Argie

BLANK, Les
Always for Pleasure
Burden of Dreams
Garlic is as Good as Ten Mothers
Hot Pepper

BLAZEK, Jiri
Exceptional Class, An

BLIER, Bertrand
Merci La Vie
Our Story
Tenue de Soirée
Too Beautiful for You

BLISS, Barry
Fords on Water

BLOOM, Jeffrey
Spot

BLOOMFIELD, George
To Kill a Clown

BLUTH, Don
All Dogs Go to Heaven
Rock-A-Doodle
Secret of Nimh, The

BLYSTONE, John
Blockheads
Music for Madame
Swiss Miss

BOCKMEYER, Walter
Jane is Jane Forever (Co)

BODROV, Sergei
Freedom is Paradise

BOETTICHER, Budd
Horizons West
Man from Alamo, The
Rise and Fall of Legs Diamond, The

BOGART, Paul
Class of '44
Marlowe
Mr. Ricco
Skin Game
Torch Song Trilogy

BOGDANOVICH, Peter
At Long Last Love
Daisy Miller
Last Picture Show, The
Mask
Nickelodeon
Paper Moon
Targets
What's Up Doc?

BOGLE, Andrew
Haunters of the Deep

BOHM, Hark
Moritz Lieber Moritz
Tschetan - Der Indianerjunge

BOISROND, Michel
Violent Summer

BOLESLAWSKI, Richard
Gay Diplomat, The

BOLOGNINI, Mauro
Arabella

BOLT, Ben
Big Town, The
Black Island

BOLT, Robert
Lady Caroline Lamb

BONDARCHUK, Sergei
Waterloo

BONERZ, Peter
Police Academy 6: City Under Siege

BOORMAN, John
Deliverance
Emerald Forest, The
Excalibur
Exorcist II: The Heretic
Hell in the Pacific
Hope and Glory
Point Blank
Zardoz

BOOS, Walter
Blue Fantasies

BOOTH Harry
Blitz on Britain
Flying Sorcerer, The
Go for a Take
Mutiny on the Buses
On the Buses

BORDEN, Lizzie
Born in Flames
Working Girls

BORDERIE, Bernard
Clash of Steel
Women Are Like That

BOROWCZYK, Walerian
Beast, The
Behind Convent Walls
Blanche
Goto, Island of Love
Immoral Tales
Streetwalker, The
Theatre of Mr. and Mrs. Kabal

BORSOS, Phillip
Grey Fox, The
Mean Season, The
One Magic Christmas

BORZAGE, Frank
Farewell to Arms, A
Little Man, What Now?
7th Heaven
Spanish Main, The
Street Angel
Three Comrades

BOTELHO, Joao
Hard Times

BOULTING, John
Brighton Rock
Heavens Above
I'm All Right Jack
Lucky Jim
Private's Progress
Rotten to the Core

BOULTING, Roy
Brothers in Law
Burma Victory
Desert Victory
Family Way, The
French Mistress, A
Soft Beds, Hard Battles
There's A Girl in My Soup
Thunder Rock
Tunisian Victory (Co)
Twisted Nerve

BOWERS, George
Body and Soul

BOURGUIGNON, Serge
Reward, The

BOX, Muriel
Rattle of a Simple Man

To Dorothy a Son
Too Young to Love

BRABIN, Charles
Mask of Fu Manchu, The

BRACKNELL, David
Cup Fever

BRADBURY, David
South of the Border

BRAHM, John
Bengazi
Locket, The
Miracle of Fatima

BRAKHAGE, Stan
Dog Star Man
Text of Light
Tortured Dust

BRAMBLE, A.V.
Shooting Stars (Co)

BRANAGH, Kenneth
Dead Again
Henry V
Peter's Friends

BRANDNER, Uwe
I Love You - I Kill You

BRANDT, Michael
Missing Note, The

BRASS, Tinto
Salon Kitty

BRAULT, Michel
Orders

BRAUN, Valdimir
Maximka

BREAKSTON, George
Scarlet Spear

BREALEY, Gil
Annie's Coming Out

BREEN, Richard L.
Stopover Tokyo

BREILLAT, Catherine
Virgin

BREIEN, Anja
Wives

BRENON, Herbert
Beau Ideal
Girl of the Rio

BRESSAN Jr, Arthur J.
Buddies

BRESSON, Robert
Argent, L'
Journal D'un Curé De Campagne, Le

BREST, Martin
Beverly Hills Cop
Midnight Run

BRICKMAN, Marshall
Deadly Game
Lovesick
Simon

BRICKMAN, Paul
Risky Business

BRIDGES, Alan
Age of Innocence
Brief Encounter
Hireling, The
Invasion
Out of Season
Return of the Soldier, The
Shooting Party, The

BRIDGES, James
Bright Lights, Big City
China Syndrome, The
Paper Chase, The
Perfect
Urban Cowboy

BRITTAIN, Donald
Dionne Quintuplets, The
Memorandum (Co)

BROAD, Richard
This Week: 1844

BROCKA, Lino
Bayan Ko: My Own Country
Manila

BROCKWAY, Merrill
Martha Graham Dance
    Company, The

BRODY, Hugh
Nineteen Nineteen

BROOK, Peter
King Lear
Lord of the Flies
Meetings With Remarkable Men
Moderato Cantabile

BROOKS, Albert
Defending Your Life
Lost in America

BROOKS, Bob
Knowledge, The

BROOKS, James L.
Broadcast News
Terms of Endearment

BROOKS, Joseph
You Light Up My Life

BROOKS, Mel
Blazing Saddles
High Anxiety
Silent Movie
Spaceballs
Young Frankenstein

BROOKS, Richard
Bite the Bullet
Blackboard Jungle
Brothers Karamazov, The
Cat on a Hot Tin Roof
Crisis
Happy Ending, The
Heist, The
In Cold Blood
Last Hunt, The
Looking for Mr. Goodbar
Lord Jim
Man With the Deadly Lens
Sweet Bird of Youth
Take the High Ground!

BROOMFIELD, Nick
Behind the Rent Strike
Chicken Ranch
Juvenile Liaison (Co)
Soldier Girls (Co)

Tattooed Tears (Co)

BROWER, Otto
Headline Shooter

BROWN, Barry Alexander
War at Home, The (Co)

BROWN, Bruce
On Any Sunday

BROWN, Clarence
Anna Christie
Anna Karenina
Eagle, The
Edison the Man
Intruder in the Dust
It's a Big Country (Ep)
Marie Walewska
National Velvet
Plymouth Adventure
Smouldering Fires
Song of Love
To Please a Lady
White Cliffs of Dover, The
Yearling, The

BROWN, Melville
Check and Double Check
Jazz Heaven
Lovin' the Ladies
She's My Weakness

BROWN, Phil
Harlem Globetrotters

BROWN, Rowland
Hell's Highway

BROWN, William O.
Witchmaker, The

BROWNING, Tod
Devil-Doll, The
Dracula
Freaks
Mark of the Vampire

BROWNLOW, Kevin
Abel Gance - The Charm of
    Dynamite
Buster Keaton: A Hard Act to
    Follow (Co)
It Happened Here (Co)
Unknown Chaplin (Co)
Winstanley (Co)

BRUCKMAN, Clyde
Everything's Rosie
Feet First
Man on the Flying Trapeze

BRUCKNER, Jutta
Be Upright and Walk Without Fear
Thoroughly Uncared-For Girl, A

BRUNEL, Adrian
Elstree Calling

BRUSATI, Franco
To Forget Venice

BRUSTELLIN, Alf
Berlinger (Co)
Girl's War, The (Co)

BRYANT, Baird
Celebration at Big Sur (Co)

BRYDEN, Bill
Aria (Ep)

BUCHOWETZKI, Dimitri
Othello

BUCKSEY, Colin
Dealers

BUCZKOWSKI, Leonard
First Start, The
Treasure, The

BUHRMANN, Rolf
Jane is Jane Forever (Co)

BULD, Wolfgang
Punk in London

BUÑUEL, Luis
Age D'Or, L'
Belle de Jour
Diary of a Chambermaid
Discreet Charm of the
    Bourgeoisie, The
El
That Obscure Object of Desire

BURCH, Noël
Impersonation, The

BURGE, Stuart
Mikado, The
Othello
Uncle Vanya

BURKE, Martyn
Power Play

BURNETT, Charles
Killer of Sheep

BURNLEY, Fred
Neither the Sea nor the Sand

BURNS, Allan
Just Between Friends

BURROWS, James
Partners

BURSTALL, Tim
Alvin Purple
Petersen

BURTON, David
Make Way for a Lady

BURTON, Nick
At the Fountainhead (of German
    Strength) (Co)

BURTON, Richard
Doctor Faustus (Co)

BURTON, Tim
Batman
Batman Returns
Beetlejuice
Edward Scissorhands
Pee-Wee's Big Adventure

BUTCHER, Cyril
Last Hours, The

BUTE, Mary Ellen
Finnegan's Wake

BUTLER, David
April in Paris
By the Light of the Silvery Moon
Calamity Jane
Command, The
Guns in the Heather
It's a Great Feeling

Lullaby of Broadway
Playmates
Road to Morocco
Story of Sea Biscuit, The
Thank Your Lucky Stars
That's Right You're Wrong
You'll Find Out

BUTLER, Robert
Barefoot Executive, The
Blue Knight, The
Computer Wore Tennis Shoes, The
Dark Victory
Guns in the Heather
Hot Lead and Cold Feet
Mayday at 40,000 Feet
Now You See Him Now You Don't

BUTOY, Hendel
Rescuers Down Under, The (Co)

BUTT, Bill
Shine So Hard (Co)

BUZZELL, Edward
Marx Brothers Go West
Omaha Trail, The

BYRNE, David
True Stories

BYRUM, John
Heart Beat
Inserts

CAAN, James
Hide in Plain Sight

CABANNE, Christy
Annapolis Salute
Another Face
Conspiracy
Don't Tell the Wife
Everybody's Doing It
Man Who Walked Alone
Last Outlaw, The
Midshipman Jack
Outcasts of Poker Flat, The
This Marriage Business
We Who Are About To Die

CACOYANNIS, Michael
Iphigenia
Trojan Women, The

CAESER, Imruh
Mark of the Hand, The

CAFFEY, Michael
Boy Who Stole an Elephant, The

CAHN, Edward
Emergency Call
Runaway Daughters

CAIN, Christopher
Principal, The
Young Guns

CALLOW, Simon
Ballad of the Sad Cafe, The

CALTABIANO, Alfio
Italian Graffiti

CAMERON, James
Aliens
Piranha II - Flying Killers
Terminator, The

Terminator II

CAMERON, Ken
Monkey Grip

CAMINO, Jaime
Long Holidays of 1936, The

CAMMELL, Donald
Demon Seed

CAMP, Joe
Hunted, The

CAMPBELL, Dirk
I Bought a Vampire Motorcycle

CAMPBELL, Norman
Ballerina

CAMPION, Jane
Angel at My Table, An
Sweetie

CAMUS, Marcel
Black Orpheus

CAPON, Paul
Leningrad Fights

CAPRA, Frank
Arsenic and Old Lace
Battle of Russia, The (Co)
Bitter Tea of General Yen, The
Here Comes the Groom
It Happened One Night
Lost Horizon
Mr. Deeds Goes to Town
Mr. Smith Goes to Washington
Platinum Blonde
Pocketful of Miracles
Tunisian Victory (Co)
You Can't Take It With You

CARAX, Leos
Amants du Pont Neuf, Les
Night is Young, The

CARDIFF, Jack
Beyond This Place
Girl on a Motorcycle
Intent to Kill
Lion, The
Liquidator, The
Mercenaries, The
Mutations, The
My Geisha
Young Cassidy

CARLINO, Lewis John
Class
Great Santini, The

CARLO-RIM
Seven Deadly Sins (Ep)

CARLSEN, Henning
World of Strangers

CARNÉ, Marcel
Drôle de Drame
Enfants du Paradis, Les
Jour se lève, Le

CARO, Marc
Délicatessen (Co)

CARPENTER, John
Big Trouble in Little China Christine
Elvis: The Movie
Fog, The
Memoirs of an Invisible Man

Starman
They Live
Thing, The

CARRERAS, Michael
Lost Continent, The
Savage Guns, The

CARRIERE, Marcel
O.K... La Liberté

CARRIGAN, Ana
Roses in December

CARSON, L.M. Kit
American Dreamer (Co)

CARSTAIRS, John Paddy
Big Money, The
Just My Luck
One Good Turn
Saint in London, The
Sands of the Desert
Spare a Copper
Square Peg, The
Trouble in Store
Up in the World
Weekend with Lulu

CARTWRIGHT, Justin
Rosie Dixon Night Nurse

CARVER, Steve
Capone
Fast Charlie - The Moonbeam Rider
Lone Wolf McQuade
Steel

CASERINI, Mario
Last Days of Pompeii, The

CASS, Henry
Father's Doing Fine
Glass Mountain, The
Last Holiday

CASSAVETES, John
Child is Waiting, A
Gloria
Killing of a Chinese Bookie, The
Love Streams

CASTELLARI, Enzo G.
Inglorious Bastards, The

CASTLE, Nick
Tap

CASTLE, William
I Saw What You Did
Let's Kill Uncle
Night Walker, The
Project X
Spirit is Willing, The

CATES, Gilbert
Affair, The
Last Married Couple in
  America, The
Promise, The
Summer Wishes Winter Dreams

CATLING, Darrel
Cat Gang, The

CATON-JONES, Michael
Doc Hollywood
Memphis Belle
Scandal

CAVALCANTI, Alberto
Dead of Night (Ep)

Film and Reality
Monster of Highgate Ponds
Nicholas Nickleby
Went the Day Well?

CAVALIER, Alain
Thérèse

CAVANI, Liliana
Night Porter, The

CAWSTON, Richard
Television and the World
This is the BBC

CECH, Vladimir
Alibi is Not Everything, An
Cock of the Dawn
Key, The
Torches, The

CERVI, Tonino
Today It's Me - Tomorrow You

CHABROL, Claude
Biches, Les
Blood Relatives
Boucher, Le
Cop Au Vin
Inspecteur Lavardin
Killer!
Masques
Nada
Noces Rouges, Les
Paris Vu Par (Ep)
Que la Bête Meure
Rupture, La
Scandale, Le
Scoundrel in White

CHAFFEY, Don
Charley One-eye
Creatures the World Forgot
Danger Within
Dentist in the Chair
Greyfriars Bobby
Horse Without a Head, The
Jason and the Argonauts
Magic of Lassie, The
Matter of Who, A
One Million Years B.C.
Pete's Dragon
Prince and the Pauper, The
Ride a Wild Pony
Three Lives of Thomasina, The
Twist of Sand
Viking Queen, The

CHAMOUN, Jean
Women from South Lebanon (Co)

CHAMPION, Gower
Bank Shot

CHAMPION, Gregg
Short Time

CHAMPION, John
Mustang Country

CHAPIN, Harry F.
Legendary Champions, The

CHAPLIN, Charles
Countess from Hong Kong, A

CHARELL, Erik
Congress Dances

CHARON, Jacques
Flea in her Ear, A

CHATILIEZ, Etienne
Tatie Danielle

CHECINSKI, Sylvester
Great Sharp, The

CHECNIK, Michael
Rites of Spring

CHELSOM, Peter
Hear My Song

CHEN Fan
Opium War, The (Co)

CHENG Chun-Li
Opium War, The (Co)

CHEN Huai-ai
Song of Youth (Co)

CHEN Kaige
Yellow Earth

CHILVERS, Colin
Moonwalker (Co)

CHMIELEWSKI, Tadeusz
In the Quiet of the Night

CHOMSKY, Marvin
Tank
Victory at Entebbe

CHOPRA, Joyce
Smooth Talk

CHRISTENSEN, Benjamin
Witchcraft Through the Ages

CHRISTIAN-JAQUE
Legend of Frenchie King, The

CHUDNOW, Byron
Doberman Gang, The

CHUKHRAI, Grigori
Ballad of a Soldier

CHURCHILL, Joan
Juvenile Liaison (Co)
Soldier Girls (Co)
Tattooed Tears (Co)

CHYTILOVA, Vera
Daisies

CIMINO, Michael
Deer Hunter, The
Heaven's Gate
Thunderbolt and Lightfoot
Year of the Dragon

CISSE, Souleymane
Finye: The Wind
Yeelen

CITRON, Michelle
What You Take for Granted

CITTI, Sergio
Bawdy Tales

CIUFFINI, Sabatino
Gold for the Caesars (Co)

CLAIR, René
And Then There Were None
Flame of New Orleans, The
Italian Straw Hat, An
Voyage Imaginaire, Le

CLANCY, Marg
Dirt Cheap (Co)

CLARK, Bob
Breaking Point
Christmas Story, A
Porky's
Porky's II: The Next Day
Rhinestone
Tribute
Turk 182!

CLARK, Bruce
Hammer

CLARK, James
Christmas Tree, The

CLARK, James B.
Drums of Africa
Little Ark
My Side of the Mountain
Sad Horse, The
Sierra Baron
Villa!!

CLARK, Jim
Every Home Should Have One
Madhouse
Rentadick

CLARKE, Alan
Scum

CLARKE, Robert
Blood on His Lips

CLARKE, Shirley
Connection, The
Cool World, The

CLAVELL, James
Last Valley, The
To Sir With Love
Where's Jack?

CLAXTON, William F.
Desire in the Dust
Night of the Lepus

CLAYTON, Jack
Great Gatsby, The
Innocents, The
Lonely Passion of Judith Hearne, The
Our Mother's House
Pumpkin Eater, The
Room at the Top
Something Wicked This Way Comes

CLAYTON, Susan
Song of the Shirt, The (Co)

CLEGG, Tom
McVicar
Sweeney 2

CLEMENS, Brian
Captain Kronos - Vampire Hunter

CLEMENS, William
Falcon Out West, The

CLEMENT, DICK
Otley
Porridge
Severed Head, A

CLEMENT, Rene
Day and the Hour, The
Deadly Trap
Is Paris Burning?
Love Cage, The

CLEMENTS, Ron
Little Mermaid, The (Co)

CLIFFORD, Graeme
Frances
Gleaming the Tube

CLIFTON, Peter
Song Remains the Same, The (Co)

CLINE, Edward
Bank Dick, The
Cracked Nuts
Forty Naughty Girls
High Flyers
Hook, Line and Sinker
On Again - Off Again

CLOCHE, Maurice
Monsieur Vincent

CLOUSE, Robert
Amsterdam Kill, The
Big Brawl, The
Black Belt Jones
Enter the Dragon
Golden Needles
London Connection, The
Pack, The
Ultimate Warrior, The

CLOUZOT, Henri - Georges
Diaboliques, Les
Wages of Fear, The

CLUCHER, E.B.
Crimebusters
Man of the East
They Call Me Trinity
Trinity Is Still My Name

CLURMAN, Harold
Deadline at Dawn

COATES, John
Foes

COATES, Lewis
Adventures of Hercules II

COBHAM, David
Tarka the Otter

COCTEAU, Jean
Belle et la Bête, La
Orphée
Sang d'un Poète, Le
Testament d'Orphée, Le

COE, Fred
Me Natalie
Thousand Clowns, A

COEN, Joel
Barton Fink
Blood Simple
Miller's Crossing
Raising Arizona

COFFEY, Essie
My Survival as an Aboriginal

COGHILL, Neville
Doctor Faustus (Co)

COHEN, Larry
It Lives Again
It's Alive
Q - The Winged Serpent

COHEN, Norman
Adolf Hitler - My Part In His

Downfall
Confessions from a Holiday Camp
Confessions of a Driving Instructor
Confessions of a Pop Performer
Dad's Army
Stand Up Virgin Soldiers
Till Death Us Do Part

COHEN, Richard
Hurry Tomorrow (Co)

COHEN, Rob
Small Circle of Friends, A

COHEN, Tom
Family Business

COKLISS, Harley
Battle of Billy's Pond, The
Glitterball, The
That Summer!

COLE, Adam
Electric Blue: The Movie

COLE, Janis
P4W: Prison for Women (Co)

COLEMAN, Basil
As You Like It

COLEMAN, Herbert
Posse from Hell

COLETTI, Duilio
Under Ten Flags (Co)

COLIZZI, Giuseppe
Revenge in El Paso

COLLA, Richard A.
Battlestar Galactica
False Witness
Fuzz

COLLINS, Lewis D.
Borrowed Hero

COLLINSON, Peter
Fright
Italian Job, The
Open Season
Sell-Out, The
Spiral Staircase, The
Straight On Till Morning
Tomorrow Never Comes
You Can't Win 'Em All

COLLIS, Catherine
Jacob Epstein

COLUMBUS, Chris
Home Alone
Night On the Town
Only the Lonely

COMERFORD, Joe
Down the Corner
Traveller

COMFORT, Lance
Great Day
Hatter's Castle
Make Mine a Million
Portrait of Clare

COMOLLI, Jean-Louis
Cecilia, La

CONNOLLY, Ray
James Dean the First American
Teenager

CONNOR, Kevin
Arabian Adventure
From Beyond the Grave
Land That Time Forgot, The
Motel Hell
Trial by Combat
Warlords of Atlantis

CONWAY, Jack
Boom Town
High Barbaree
Hucksters, The
Julia Misbehaves
Love Crazy
Tale of Two Cities
Unholy Three, The
Yank at Oxford, A

CONYERS, Darcy
In the Doghouse
Night We Dropped a Clanger, The
Night We Got the Bird, The
Soap Box Derby, The

COOK, Fielder
Big Deal at Dodge City
Gauguin the Savage
How to Save a Marriage...
  and Ruin Your Life
Prudence and the Pill

COOKE, Alan
Black Legend (Co)

COOLIDGE, Martha
Real Genius

COONEY, Ray
Not Now, Comrade (Co)
Not Now, Darling (Co)

COOPER, Merian C.
Grass (Co)
King Kong (Co)

COOPER, Stuart
Overlord

COPPOLA, Francis Ford
Conversation, The
Godfather, The
Godfather Part II, The
Godfather III, The
Haunted and the Hunted, The
New York Stories (Ep)
One from the Heart
Outsiders, The
Peggy Sue Got Married
Rumble Fish
Tucker: The Man and His Dreams

CORBUCCI, Sergio
Hellbenders, The
Odds and Evens
Professional Gun, A
Ringo and his Golden Pistol
Son of Spartacus
Supersnooper

CORMAN, Roger
Bucket of Blood, A
Frankenstein Unbound
Gas! Or It Became Necessary
  To Destroy the World In Order To
  Save It
Gunslinger
Haunted Palace, The
Masque of the Red Death, The
Red Baron, The
St. Valentine's Day
Secret Invasion, The
Shark Reef

Tales of Terror
Tomb of Ligeia, The
Trip, The
Wild Angels, The
Young Racers, The

CORNELIUS, Henry
Genevieve

CORNELL, John
Almost an Angel
Crocodile Dundee II

CORNELL, Jonas
Hugs and Kisses

CORNFIELD, Hubert
Night of the Following Day, The

CORONADO, Celestino
Hamlet
Midsummer Night's Dream, A

CORR, Eugene
Desert Bloom

CORRIGAN, Lloyd
By Your Leave
Murder on a Honeymoon

CORT, Hardy
Great Chase, The

CORTAZAR, Octavio
Brigadista, El

CORTEZ, Gustavo
George Kuchar: The Comedy of
  the Underground (Co)

CORTI, Alex
Refusal

COSCARELLI, Don
Beastmaster
Phantasm

COSMATOS, George Pan
Cassandra Crossing, The
Cobra
Escape to Athena

COSTA-GAVRAS
Betrayed
Missing
Music Box
State of Siege
Z

COSTNER, Kevin
Dances With Wolves

COTTAFAVI, Vittorio
Hercules and the Captive Women

COTTER, John
Mountain Family Robinson

COUFFER, Jack
Darwin Adventure
Living Free
Nikki, Wild Dog of the North (Co)
Ring of Bright Water

COUSTEAU, Jacques
World Without Sun

COX, Alex
Sid & Nancy

COX, Paul
Cactus

Golden Braid
Man of Flowers
My First Wife
Vincent

COZARINSKY, Edgardo
One Man's War

CRABTREE, Arthur
Fiend Without a Face
Hindle Wakes
Lili Marlene
Madonna of the Seven Moons
They Were Sisters
Wedding of Lili Marlene, The

CRANE, Barry
Conquest of the Earth (Co)

CRAVEN, Thomas
David Lean: A Self Portrait

CRAVEN, Wes
Deadly Friend
People Under the Stairs, The
Serpent and the Rainbow, The
Summer of Fear, The

CRICHTON, Charles
Another Shore
Battle of the Sexes, The
Dead of Night (Ep)
Fish Called Wanda, A
Hue and Cry
Lavender Hill Mob, The
Law and Disorder
Love Lottery, The
Man in the Sky
Painted Boats
Titfield Thunderbolt, The

CRICHTON, Michael
Coma
First Great Train Robbery, The
Physical Evidence
Runaway
Westworld

CRISP, Donald
Runaway Bride

CROFT, David
Not Now, Darling (Co)

CROMBIE, Donald
Irishman, The

CROME, John
Naked Cell

CROMWELL, John
Ann Vickers
Dead Reckoning
Enchanted Cottage, The
I Dream Too Much
In Name Only
Jalna
Night Song
Racket, The
Scavengers, The
Since You Went Away
Spirit of the People, The
Spitfire
Sweepings
This Man is Mine
Village Tale

CRONENBERG, David
Brood, The
Crimes of the Future
Dead Ringers
Fly, The

Rabid
Scanners
Stereo
Videodrome

CROSLAND, Alan
Beloved Rogue, The
Jazz Singer, The

CROWE, Cameron
Say Anything

CROWE, Christopher
Saigon

CRUZE, James
If I Had a Million (Ep)
Pony Express
Their Big Moment

CSAKY, Mick
How Does it Feel

CUI Wei
Song of Youth (Co)

CUKOR, George
Actress, The
Adam's Rib
Camille
David Copperfield
Desire Me
Edward, My Son
Heller in Pink Tights
Justine
Les Girls
Our Betters
Pat and Mike
Rich and Famous
Sylvia Scarlett
Travels With My Aunt
What Price Hollywood?
Wild Is the Wind
Women, The

CULP, Robert
Hickey and Boggs

CUMMINGS, Irving
Double Dynamite
Little Miss Broadway
Louisiana Purchase

CUNHA, Richard E.
Frankenstein's Daughter
She Demons

CUNNINGHAM, Sean S.
Deep Star Six
Friday the 13th

CURCEK, Radim
Brno Trail, The

CURLING, Jonathan
Song of the Shirt, The (Co)

CURRAN, Peter
Penelope "Pulls It Off"

CURTEIS, Ian
Projected Man, The

CURTIS, Dan
Burnt Offerings
House of Dark Shadows

CURTIZ, Michael
Adventures of Huckleberry Finn, The
Adventures of Robin Hood, The (Co)
Angels With Dirty Faces
Best Things In Life Are Free, The

Breath of Scandal
Captain Blood
Casablanca
Charge of the Light Brigade, The
Comancheros, The
Doctor X
Elizabeth The Queen
Francis of Assisi
Kid Galahad
Mildred Pierce
Passage to Marseilles
Santa Fe Trail
Scarlet Hour, The
Sea Hawk, The
Sea Wolf, The
Twenty Thousand Years in Sing
   Sing
Virginia City
Walking Dead, The
Young Man of Music

CUTTS, Graham
Looking On the Bright Side (Co)

CVITANOVICH, Frank
Bunny

CZINNER, Paul
Ariane
Romeo and Juliet
Rosenkavalier, Der

DAIKUBARA, Akira
Magic Boy

DALE, Holly
P4W: Prison for Women (Co)

DALEN, Zale
Skip Tracer

D'AMATO, Joe
Emmanuelle and the Last Cannibals

DAMIANI, Damiano
Bullet for the General, A
Amityville Horror II: The Possession

DAMIANO, Gerard
Midnight Blue

DAMON, Erica
Sacrifice Area

DAMSKI, Mel
Mischief
Yellowbeard

DANIEL, Franjisek
Looking for Daddy

DANIEL, Rod
K-9
Like Father, Like Son

DANIELS, Harold
Roadblock

DANIELS, Marc
Squeeze a Flower

DANIELSSON, Tage
Out of an Old Man's Head

DANSEREAU, Mireille
Dream Life

DANTE, Joe
'Burbs, The

Explorers
Gremlins
Innerspace
Piranha
Twilight Zone - The Movie (Ep)

D'ANTONI, Philip
Seven-Ups, The

DARLING, Joan
First Love

DARNLEY-SMITH, Jan
Fern, The Red Deer
Ghost of a Chance, A
Go Kart Go
Hitch in Time, A
Hoverbug
Runaway Railway
Up in the Air

DASSIN, Jules
Rififi
Survival 67
Topkapi
Two Smart People

DAVENPORT, Harry Bromley
Xtro

DAVES, Delmer
Badlanders, The
Battle of the Villa Fiorita, The
Cowboy
Dark Passage
Demetrius and the Gladiators
Drum Beat
Hollywood Canteen
Last Wagon, The
Spencer's Mountain
Summer Place
Three Ten to Yuma
Youngblood Hawke

DAVIDSON, Boaz
Hot Bubblegum
Last American Virgin
Lemon Popsicle
Private Popsicle
Salsa

DAVIDSON, Martin
Almost Summer
Hero at Large

DAVIES, John
Maeve (Co)

DAVIES, Terence
Distant Voices, Still Lives
Long Day Closes, The
Terence Davies Trilogy

DAVIES, Valentine
Benny Goodman Story, The

DAVIS, Andrew
Code of Silence
Nico - Above the Law

DAVIS, Desmond
Clash of the Titans
Country Girls, The
I Was Happy Here
Measure for Measure
Smashing Time

DAVIS, Joanna
Bred and Born (Co)

DAVIS, John
Cry Wolf

Danger Point

DAVIS, Ossie
Cotton Comes to Harlem
Gordon's War

DAWSON, Anthony M.
Blood Money
Hercules Against Kung Fu
Killer Fish
Mr. Superinvisible
Take a Hard Ride

DAY, Ernest
Green Ice

DAY, Nick
John Cooper-Clarke - Ten Years
   in an Open-Necked Shirt (Co)

DAY, Philip
Japan Live Performance

DAY, Robert
Corridors of Blood
First Man into Space
Green Man, The
Grip of the Strangler
Rebel, The
She
Two-Way Stretch

DEAN, Basil
Looking On the Bright Side (Co)
Look Up and Laugh
Lorna Doone
Show Goes On, The
Sing As We Go

DE ANTONIO, Emile
In the King of Prussia
Millhouse: A White Comedy
Painters Painting
Rush to Judgement

DEAR, William
Bigfoot and the Hendersons
Teen Agent

DEARDEN, Basil
Dead of Night (Ep)
Goose Steps Out, The (Co)
Halfway House
Khartoum
League of Gentlemen, The
Life for Ruth
Man Who Haunted Himself, The
Masquerade
My Learned Friend
Only When I Larf
Out of the Clouds (Co)
Sapphire
Saraband for Dead Lovers
Secret Partner
Ship that Died of Shame, The (Co)
Smallest Show on Earth, The
Square Ring, The (Co)
Woman of Straw

DEARDEN, James
Kiss Before Dying, A
Pascali's Island

DE ARMINAN, Jaime
Nido, El

DE BOSIO, Gianfranco
Moses

DE BROCA, Philippe
Dear Inspector
Farceur, Le

How to Destroy the Reputation of
   the Greatest Secret Agent

DE CONCINI, Ennio
Hitler: The Last Ten Days

DE CORDOVA, Frederick
Bonzo Goes to College
Frankie and Johnny

DE FELITTA, Frank
Doberman Patrol

DE FILIPPO, Eduardo
Seven Deadly Sins (Ep)

DE GREGORIO, Eduardo
Aspern
Serail

DE HIRSCH, Storm
Goodbye in the Mirror

DEITCH, Donna
Desert Hearts

DE JARNATT, Steve
Cherry 2000

DE JONG, Ate
Drop Dead Fred
Highway to Hell

DE KOENIGSBERG, Paula
Rate it X (Co)

DE LA TEXERA, Diego
El Salvador - The People Will Win

DEL BALZO, Raimondo
Last Snows of Spring, The

DEL RUTH, Roy
Fine and Dandy

DELUISE, Dom
Hot Stuff

DELVAUX, Andre
Man Who Had His Hair Cut
   Short, The
Soir, Un Train, Un

DE MARTINO, Alberto
Bandits in Rome
Holocaust 2000
Operation Kid Brother

DEMETRAKAS, Johanna
Celebration at Big Sur (Co)
Right Out of History: The
   Making of Judy Chicago's Dinner
   Party

DEMILLE, Cecil B.
Cleopatra
Plainsman, The
Samson and Delilah
Sign of the Cross, The
Ten Commandments, The
Unconquered
Union Pacific

DEMME, Jonathan
Citizens Band
Fighting Mad
Last Embrace
Melvin and Howard
Silence of the Lambs
Something Wild
Swimming to Cambodia

DENHAM, Reginald
Death at Broadcasting House

DENIS, Claire
Chocolat

DENSHAM, Pen
Kiss, The

DE PALMA, Brian
Blow Out
Body Double
Bonfire of the Vanities
Carrie
Fury, The
Greetings
Hi, Mom
Obsession
Phantom of the Paradise
Scarface
Untouchables, The

DEPARDON, Raymond
Captive du Désert, La

DERAY, Jacques
Borsalino
Gang, Le
He Died With His Eyes Open
Outside Man, The
Rififi in Tokyo

DEREK, John
Bolero
Tarzan the Ape Man

DEREVYANSKY, S.
Centre Forward (Co)

DESAILLY, Jean
On ne Badine pas Avec l'Amour

DE SICA, Vittorio
After the Fox
Children Are Watching Us, The
Condemned of Altona, The
Place for Lovers, A
Two Women
Umberto D

DESPINS, Joseph
Moon over the Alley

DESWARTE, Bernie
Kashima Paradise (Co)

DE TOTH, Andre
Gold for the Caesars (Co)
House of Wax
Morgan the Pirate
Play Dirty
Riding Shotgun

DEUTCH, Howard
Pretty in Pink

DEVAL, Jacques
Club de Femmes

DEVENISH, Ross
Boesman and Lena
Marigolds in August
Now that the Buffalo's Gone

DEVILLE, Michel
Death in a French Garden
Lectrice, La

DEVITO, Danny
War of the Roses, The

DEXTER, John
I Want What I Want
Virgin Soldiers, The

DEXTER, Maury
Day Mars Invaded Earth, The
Hell's Belles

DICKINSON, Margaret
Against the Grain
Behind the Lines
Exchange and Divide

DICKINSON, Thorold
High Command
Hill 24 Doesn't Answer
Secret People

DIETERLE, William
Dr. Ehrlich's Magic Bullet
Elephant Walk
Her Majesty, Love
Hunchback of Notre Dame, The
Juarez
Last Flight, The
Midsumer Night's Dream, A (Co)
Omar Khayam
Red Mountain
September Affair
Story of Louis Pasteur, The
Tennessee Johnson

DILLON, John Francis
Millie

DIMBLEBY, Jonathan
Bomb, The

DINNER, Michael
Catholic Boys

DIOP-MAMBETY, Djibril
Touki-Bouki

DISNEY, Walt
Melody Time

DIXON, Ivan
Trouble Man

DMYTRYK, Edward
Alvarez Kelly
Back to Bataan
Battle for Anzio
Behind the Rising Sun
Broken Lance
Caine Mutiny, The
Cornered
Crossfire
Falcon Strikes Back, The
Farewell My Lovely
Hitler's Children
Mirage
Mountain
Obsession
Raintree Country
Reluctant Saint, The
Seven Miles from Alcatraz
Shalako
So Well Remembered
Tender Comrade
Till the End of Time
Walk on the Wild Side, A
Young Lions

DOMARADZKI, Jerzy
Beast, The

DONALDSON, Roger
Bounty, The
Cocktail
Marie

No Way Out
White Sands

DONEN, Stanley
Blame it on Rio
Damn Yankees (Co)
Funny Face
It's Always Fair Weather (Co)
Lucky Lady
Movie Movie
Once More with Feeling
Pajama Game (Co)
Royal Wedding
Saturn 3
Seven Brides for Seven Brothers
Two for the Road

DONIOL - VALCROZE, Jacques
Viol, Le

DONNELLY, Tom
Quicksilver

DONNER, Clive
Alfred the Great
Caretaker, The
Charlie Chan and the Curse
  of the Dragon Queen
Heart of a Child
Here We Go Round the
  Mulberry Bush
Nothing But the Best
Nude Bomb, The
Some People
Thief of Baghdad, The
Vampira
What's New Pussycat?

DONNER, Jörn
To Love

DONNER, Richard
Goonies, The
Ladyhawke
Lethal Weapon
Lethal Weapon 2
Lethal Weapon 3
Omen, The
Salt & Pepper
Scrooged
Superman The Movie
Twinky

DONOGHUE, Mary A.
Paradise

DONOHUE, Jack
Assault on a Queen
Babes in Toyland
Marriage on the Rocks
Yellow Cab Man, The

DONSKOI, Mark
Childhood of Maxim Gorky, The
Mother
Mother's Loyalty, A
My Apprenticeship
My Universities
Rainbow, The
Village Teacher

DORRIE, Doris
Men

DOUCHET, Jean
Paris Vu Par (Ep)

DOUGLAS, Bill
My Ain Folk
My Childhood
My Way Home

DOUGLAS, Gordon
Barquero
Big Land, The
Charge at Feather River, The
Chuka
Detective, The
Elephants Never Forget
Falcon in Hollywood, The
First Yank into Tokyo
Follow that Dream
Gildersleeve on Broadway
Gildersleeve's Bad Day
Gildersleeve's Ghost
Girl Rush
Great Gildersleeve, The
Harlow
If You Knew Susie
In Like Flint
Kiss Tomorrow Goodbye
Lady in Cement
Night of Adventure, A
Only the Valiant
Rio Conchos
Robin and the 7 Hoods
Rogues of Sherwood Forest
San Quentin
Saps at Sea
Stagecoach
Them!
Tony Rome
Viva Knievel!
Zombies on Broadway

DOUGLAS, John
Milestones (Co)

DOUGLAS, Kirk
Posse
Scalawag

DOUGLAS, Robert
Final Hour, The

DOVZHENKO, Alexander
Arsenal
Earth

DOWNEY, Robert
Putney Swope

DRAGOTI, Stan
Man With One Red Shoe, The
Mr. Mum
Necessary Roughness

DRAKE, Jim
Police Academy 4: Citizens on
  Patrol

DREIFUSS, Arthur
Reg'lar Fellers

DREVILLE, Jean
Seven Deadly Sins (Ep)

DREYER, Carl
Passion of Joan of Arc, The

DRURY, David
Defence of the Realm

DUBS, Arthur
Dream Chasers (Co)

DU CANE, John
Creatures
Cross
Emanations

DUDOW, Slatan
Kuhle Wampe

DUFFELL, Peter
Caught on a Train
House that Dripped Blood, The
Inside Out

DUGAN, Dennis
Problem Child

DUIGAN, John
Flirting
Year My Voice Broke, The

DUKE, Bill
Killing Floor
Rage in Harlem, A

DUKE, Daryl
Today Is Forever

DU LUART, Yolande
Angela Davis: Portrait of a
Revolutionary

DUNFORD, Mike
Logical Proposition
Still Image

DUNNE, Philip
Blindfold
Blue Jeans
In Love and War
Secret Interlude
Three Brave Men

DUNLOP, Jeff
Just What Is It

DUPEYRON, François
Strange Place to Meet, A

DUPONT, E.A.
Moulin Rouge
Treasure of Kalifa

DURNECK, Manfred
Women of Pleasure

DWAN, Allan
Around the World
Enchanted Island
Heidi
Here We Go Again
Her First Affair
Montana Belle
River's Edge, The
Sands of Iwo Jima
Suez
Tennessee's Partner

DWOSKIN, Stephen
Ballet Black, A
Central Bazaar
Dyn Amo
Outside In

DZIEDZINA, Julian
Boxer

DZIGA VERTOV GROUP
Lotte in Italia

DZIKI, Waldemar
Young Magician

EADES, Wilfrid
You Can't Escape

EADY, David
Anoop The Elephant

Danger on Dartmoor
Deep Waters
Echo of the Badlands (Co)
Faces in the Dark
Hide and Seek
Hostages, The
Night Ferry
Operation Third Form
Scramble
Three Cases of Murder (Ep)
Where's Johnny?

EASTMAN, David
Calamity the Cow

EASTWOOD, Clint
Bird
Breezy
Bronco Billy
Eiger Sanction, The
Firefox
Gauntlet, The
Heartbreak Ridge
High Plains Drifter
Outlaw Josey Wales, The
Pale Rider
Play Misty for Me
Rookie, The
Sudden Impact
Unforgiven

EBERHARDT, Thom
Without a Clue

EDEL, Uli
Last Exit to Brooklyn

EDWARDS, Blake
Blind Date
Carey Treatment, The
Curse of the Pink Panther
Darling Lili
Fine Mess, A
Grip of Fear
Gunn
High Time
Man Who Loved Women, The
Micki and Maude
Party, The
Pink Panther
Pink Panther Strikes Again, The
Return of the Pink Panther, The
Revenge of the Pink Panther
Shot in the Dark, A
Skin Deep
SOB
Sunset
Switch
Tamarind Seed, The
"10"
"That's Life"
Trail of the Pink Panther
Victor/Victoria
What Did You Do in the War,
  Daddy?
Wild Rovers

EDWARDS, Vince
Mission Galactica: The Cyclon
  Attack (Co)

EDZARD, Christine
Fool, The
Stories from a Flying Trunk

EGGERT, Konstantin
Bear's Wedding, The (Co)

EGOYAN, Atom
Family Viewing

EHMCK, Gustav
Fire at Midnight
New Adventures of Highwayman
  Hotzenplotz

EISENSTEIN, Sergei
Alexander Nevsky (Co)
Battleship Potemkin
General Line, The (Co)
Ivan the Terrible Part I
Ivan the Terrible Part 2
October (Co)
Strike
Time in the Sun

EKK, Nikolai
Road to Life

ELDER, Bruce
Illluminated Texts

ELFSTROM, Robert
Nashville Sound, The (Co)

ELLIS, Maggie
Grizedale

ELSE, Jon
Day After Trinity

ELVEY, Maurice
Love, Life and Laughter
Room in the House
Sally in Our Alley

EMERSON, John
His Picture in the Papers

ENDFIELD, Cy
Hell Drivers
Mysterious Island
Sands of the Kalahari
Zulu

ENGEL, Andy
Melancholia

ENGELMAN, Ian
Music from the Flames: Shostakovich

ENGELS, Erich
Grabenplatz 17

ENGLUND, George
Signpost to Murder
Ski Raiders, The
Ugly American, The
Zachariah

ENRICO, Robert
Secret, The

ENRIGHT, Ray
China Clipper
China Sky
Dames
Iron Major, The
Man Alive
Return of the Badmen
South of St. Louis
Trail Street

EPSTEIN, Jean
Fall of the House of Usher, The

EPSTEIN, Marcelo
Body Rock

EPSTEIN, Robert
Common Threads: Stories from the
  Quilt (Co)
Times of Harvey Milk, The

ERDMAN, Richard
Brothers O'Toole, The

ERICE, Victor
Spirit of the Beehive
Sur, El

ERLER, Rainer
Delegation, Die

ERSKINE, Chester
Androcles and the Lion
Call It Murder
Egg and I, The
Girl in Every Port, A

ERULKAR, Sarah
Hunch, The

ESSEX, Tony
Struggle for China (Prod)

ESTABROOK, Howard
Heavenly Days

EVANS, Nigel
Silent Minority

EVERETT, D.S.
Running Brave

EXPORT, Valie
Invisible Adversaries

EYRE, Richard
Country
Imitation Game, The
Laughterhouse
Ploughman's Lunch

FAIMAN, Peter
"Crocodile" Dundee

FAIRBAIRN, Ken
All at Sea
Horse Called Jester, A

FAIRFAX, Ferdinand
Savage Island

FAIRSERVICE, Don
Beowulf

FANCK, Arnold
White Hell of Pitz Palu (Co)

FARGO, James
Enforcer, The
Every Which Way But Loose
Game for Vultures

FARRALDO, Claude
BOF!
Themroc

FARROW, John
Alias Nick Beal
Back From Eternity
Five Came Back
Full Confession
His Kind of Woman
Married and in Love
Reno
Ride, Vaquero!
Saint Strikes Back, The
Sea Chase
Two Years Before the Mast
Unholy Wife, The
Where Danger Lives

FASSBINDER, R.W.
Bitter Tears of Petra von Kant, The
Bremer Freiheit
Despair
Effi Briest
Fear Eats the Soul
Fox and His Friends
I Only Want You to Love Me
Lola
Marriage of Maria Braun, The
Merchant of Four Sesons, The
Querelle
Veronika Voss
Wildwechsel

FAYE, Safi
Letter From My Village

FECHNER, Eberhard
Preservation Order
School Photo - Memories of
    German Citizens
Secret Agents
Tadelloser & Wolff
Winterspelt

FEIGENBAUM, Bill
Hugo the Hippo

FEIST, Felix
Devil Thumbs a Ride, The
George White's Scandals

FELDMAN, Marty
Last Remake of Beau Geste, The

FELLINI, Federico
Amarcord
Amore in Citte (Ep)
And the Ship Sails On
City of Women
Dolce Vita, La
Fellini - A Director's Notebook
Fellini Satyricon
Fellini's Casanova
Fellini's 8
Fellini's Roma
Ginger and Fred
Lights of Variety (Co)
Orchestra Rehearsal
Strada, La
Vitelloni, I

FELSENSTEIN, Walter
Fidelio

FENADY, Georg
Arnold

FENTON, Leslie
Saint's Vacation, The
Streets of Laredo

FERGUSON, Graeme
Love Goddesses, The (Co Prod)

FERGUSON, Norman
Three Caballeros, The

FERNANDEZ, Emilio
Bandit General

FERRER, José
Cockleshell Heroes
Great Man, The
High Cost of Loving, The
I Accuse
Return to Peyton Place
Shrike, The
State Fair

FERRER, Mel
Green Mansions
Vendetta

FERRERI, Marco
Future is Woman, The
Wheelchair, The

FESTA CAMPANILE, Pasquale
Chastity Belt, The
Girl and the General, The

FEYDER, Jacques
Atlantide, L'
Kiss, The
Nouveaux Messieurs, Les

FIELD, Connie
Life and Times of Rosie the
    Riveter, The

FIGGIS, Mike
Stormy Monday

FINBOW, Colin
Captain Stirrick
Custard Boys, The
Daemon
Dark Enemy
How's Business
Mr. Skeeter
School for Vandals
Swarm in May

FINCHER, David
Alien 3

FINKLEMAN, Ken
Airplane II - The Sequel

FINNEY, Albert
Charlie Bubbles

FIRESTONE, Cinda
Attica

FIRSTENBERG, Sam
American Ninja
American Ninja II: The Confrontation
Breakdance II
Ninja III: The Domination
One More Chance
Revenge of the Ninja

FISCHLER, Steven
Free Voice of Labour: The Jewish
    Anarchists (Co)

FISHER, Shirley
Dingleton

FISHER, Terence
Brides of Dracula, The
Curse of the Werewolf
Devil Rides Out, The
Flaw, The
Frankenstein Must Be Destroyed
Kill Me Tomorrow
Sword of Sherwood Forest

FISKE, Pat
Rocking the Foundations

FITZGERALD, Dallas M.
My Lady of Whims

FITZMAURICE, George
Son of the Sheik, The

FLAHERTY, Paul
Who's Harry Crumb?

FLAHERTY, Robert
Louisiana Story
Man of Aran
Nanook of the North
Moana

FLAMENT, Pierre
Spiral, The (Ep)

FLAUM, Marshall
Hollywood: The Selznick Years

FLEISCHER, Dave
Gulliver's Travels

FLEISCHER, Richard
Armoured Car Robbery
Ashanti
Barabbas
Between Heaven and Hell
Blind Terror
Bodyguard
Boston Strangler, The
Che!
Child of Divorce
Conan the Destroyer
Doctor Dolittle
Don is Dead, The
Fantastic Voyage
Follow Me Quietly
Jazz Singer, The
Last Run, The
Make Mine Laughs
Mr. Majestyk
Narrow Margin, The
Precinct 45 Los Angeles Police
Red Sonja
Soylent Green
Spikes Gang, The
These Thousand Hills
Tora! Tora! Tora!
Trapped
20,000 Leagues Under the Sea
Violent Saturday

FLEMING, Victor
Captains Courageous
Dr. Jekyll & Mr. Hyde
Gone With the Wind
Joan of Arc
Red Dust
Tortilla Flat
Treasure Island

FLEMYNG, Gordon
Last Grenade, The

FLICK, Horst
Maria Horzeck

FLICKER, Theodore J.
Three in the Cellar
Troublemaker, The

FLOOD, James
We're Only Human

FLOREY, Robert
Beast With Five Fingers, The

FLOYD, Calvin
They Love Sex

FLYNN, John
Best Seller
Jerusalem File, The
Lock Up
Outfit, The

FOLDES, Lawrence D.
Young Warriors

FOLEY, James
At Close Range
Glengarry Glen Ross
Who's that Girl

FOLON, Jean-Michel
Spiral, The (Ep)

FONDA, Peter
Hired Hand, The

FONDATO, Marcello
Watch Out, We're Mad

FONG, Allen
Father and Son

FONS, Jorge
Jory

FORBES, Bryan
Deadfall
International Velvet
King Rat
L-Shaped Room, The
Madwoman of Chaillot, The
Naked Face, The
Raging Moon, The
Seance on a Wet Afternoon
Slipper and the Rose, The
Stepford Wives, The
Whisperers, The
Whistle Down the Wind
Wrong Box, The

FORD, Derek
What's Up Superdoc?

FORD, John
Drums Along the Mohawk
Fort Apache
Four Sons
Fugitive, The
Gideon's Day
How Green Was My Valley
How The West Was Won (Co)
Informer, The
Iron Horse, The
Last Hurrah, The
Long Gray Line, The
Long Voyage Home, The
Lost Patrol, The
Mary of Scotland
Mister Roberts (Co)
Mogambo
Plough and the Stars, The
Prisoner of Shark Island, The
Rio Grande
Rising of the Moon, The
Searchers, The
Sergeant Rutledge
7 Women
She Wore a Yellow Ribbon
Stagecoach
Steamboat Round the Bend
3 Godfathers, The
Tobacco Road
Two Rode Together
Wagonmaster
Whole Town's Talking, The
Wings of the Eagles, The

FORD, Maxim
Live a Life

FORDE, Walter
Cheer Boys Cheer
Chu-Chin-Chow
Ghost Train, The
It's That Man Again
Let's Be Famous
Sailors Three

FOREMAN, Carl
Victors, The

FORLONG, Michael
Green Helmet, The
High Rise Donkey
Hijack
Lionheart
Raising the Roof
Rangi's Catch

FORMAN, Milos
Blonde in Love, A
Hair
Peter and Pavla
Ragtime
Taking Off
Valmont
Visions of Eight (Ep)

FORSYTH, Bill
Comfort and Joy
Local Hero
That Sinking Feeling

FOSSE, Bob
All That Jazz
Cabaret
Lenny
Star 80
Sweet Charity

FOSTER, Bob
Remember Me This Way (Co)

FOSTER, Giles
Devices and Desires

FOSTER, Harve
Song of the South (Co)

FOSTER, Lewis
Sign of Zorro, The (Co)
Tonka

FOSTER, Norman
Davy Crockett and the River Pirates
Davy Crockett King of the Wild Frontier
Hans Brinker or the Silver Skates
Journey into Fear
Kiss the Blood Off My Hands
Navajo
Nine Lives of Elfego Baga
Rachel and the Stranger
Sign of Zorro, The (Co)

FOUNTAIN, Alan
Family Fragments (Co)

FOWLER Jr, Gene
Oregon Trail

FOX, Wallace W.
Powdersmoke Range
Red Morning

FRAKER, William A.
Monte Walsh
Legend of the Lone Ranger, The

FRAMPTON, Hollis
Zorns Lemma

FRANCIS, Freddie
Nightmare
Paranoiac
Tales From the Crypt

FRANCIS, Karl
Above Us the Earth
Boy Soldier

Giro City

FRANCOVICH, Allan
Houses are Full of Smoke

FRANJU, Georges
Judex
Thomas l'Imposteur
Yeux Sans Visage, Les

FRANK, Hubert
Warm Nights, Hot Pleasures

FRANK, Melvin
Buona Sera, Mrs. Campbell
Duchess and the Dirtwater Fox, The
Lost and Found
Prisoner of Second Avenue, The
Strange Bedfellows
That Certain Feeling (Co)

FRANK, Robert
Pull My Daisy

FRANKEL, Cyril
Alive and Kicking
Don't Bother to Knock
It's Great to be Young
Permission to Kill

FRANKENHEIMER, John
All Fall Down
Black Sunday
Call Harry Crown
Dead Bang
Extraordinary Seaman, The
52 Pick-Up
Fixer, The
French Connection II
Grand Prix
Gypsy Moths, The
Holcroft Covenant, The
Horsemen, The
I Walk the Line
Prophecy
Seconds
Train, The
Young Stranger, The

FRANKLIN, Chester M.
Where the North Begins

FRANKLIN, Howard
Quick Change (Co)

FRANKLIN, Richard
Link
Patrick
Psycho II

FRANKLIN, Sidney A.
Good Earth, The

FRASER, Harry
Jungle Man

FRAWLEY, James
Big Bus, The
Christian Licorice Store, The
Kid Blue

FREARS, Stephen
Dangerous Liaisons
Grifters, The
Gumshoe
Hit, The
My Beautiful Laundrette
Prick Up Your Ears
Sammy and Rosie Get Laid
Walter

FREDA, Riccardo
Samson and the 7 Miracles
Spartacus the Gladiator

FREDERSDORF, Herbert
Rumpelstiltskin
Tom Tit Tot

FREEDMAN, Jerrold
Borderline
Kansas City Bomber

FREELAND, Thornton
Flying Down to Rio
Gang's All Here, The

FREEN, Howard
Dirty O'Neil - The Love Life of a Cop (Co)

FREGONESE, Hugo
Blowing Wild
Marco Polo
Raid, The
Untamed Frontier

FRENCH, Harold
Quiet Weekend
Rob Roy the Highland Rogue

FREND, Charles
Barnacle Bill
Cone of Silence
Long Run, The
Run for Your Money
Scott of the Antarctic
Sky Bike, The

FREZ, Ilya
Marusya's First Year at School
That Funny Boy From Form B

FRIC, Martin
Angel's Holiday
People on Wheels
Recipe for a Crime
Trap, The

FRIDMAN, Eugen
Treasure Island

FRIED, Yan
Twelth Night

FRIEDKIN, David
Handle with Care
Hot Summer Night

FRIEDKIN, William
Boys in the Band
Brinks Job, The
Exorcist, The
French Connection, The
To Live and Die in L.A.
Wages of Fear

FRIEDMAN, Gerald
Borderline

FRIEDMAN, Jeffrey
Common Threads: Stories from the Quilt (Co)

FRITSCH, Gunther V.
Curse of the Cat People, The (Co)

FRUET, William
Death Weekend

FUEST, Robert
Abominable Dr. Phibes, The
And Soon the Darkness

Dr. Phibes Rises Again
Final Programme, The
Just Like a Woman
Wuthering Heights

FUKASAKU, Kinji
Green Slime, The

FULCI, Lucio
White Fang

FULLER, Samuel
Big Red One, The
Merrill's Marauders
Naked Kiss, The
Park Row
Run of the Arrow
Shock Corridor
Verboten!
White Dog

FURIE, Sidney J.
Boys, The
Boys in Company C, The
Entity, The
Gable and Lombard
Hit
Ipcress File, The
Iron Eagle
Iron Eagle II
Lawyer, The
Southwest to Sonora
Superman IV: The Quest for Peace
Wonderful Life
Young Ones, The

GABEL, Martin
Lost Moment, The

GABOR, Pal
Long Ride, The

GABREA, Radu
Man Like Eva, A

GABRIEL, Mike
Rescuers Down Under, The (Co)

GAGE, George
Skateboard

GAGE, John
Velvet Touch, The

GAJER, Vaclav
Born in 1921
Rabbits in the Tall Grass

GALAN, Paul
On Trial: Criminal Justice

GALLONE, Carmine
Force of Destiny

GALLU, Samuel
Theatre of Death

GANTILLON, Bruno
Servante et Maitresse

GANZER, Alvin
Three Bites of the Apple

GARCI, José Luis
To Begin Again

GARDIN, Vladimir
Bear's Wedding, The (Co)

GARNETT, Tay
Arthur's Court, A
Bad Company
Challenge to Be Free
Connecticut Yankee in King Guns of
  Wyoming
Joy of Living
My Favourite Spy
One Minute to Zero
Prestige
Seven Sinners
Stand - In
Valley of Decision, The

GARNETT, Tony
Prostitute

GASNIER, Louis J.
Gold Racket, The

GATLIF, Tony
Princes, Les

GAUP, Nils
Pathfinder

GAVALDON, Robert
Littlest Outlaw, The

GEDDES, Henry
Eagle Rock

GEISSENDORFER, Hans W.
Glass Cell, The
Wild Duck, The

GELLER, Bruce
Harry in Your Pocket

GERASIMOV, Sergei
Country Doctor
Young Guard

GERONIMI, Clyde
Adventures of Ichabod and
  Mr. Toad, The (Co)
Alice in Wonderland (Co)

GESSNER, Nicolas
Little Girl Who Lives Down the
  Lane, The

GIBSON, Alan
Crash
Crescendo
Dracula A.D. 1972
Satanic Rites of Dracula, The

GIBSON, Brian
Breaking Glass
Joey
Poltergeist II: The Other Side

GIBSON, Rosie
Work They Say Is Mine, The

GIDAL, Peter
Close Up
Room Film
Upside Down Feature

GILBERT AND GEORGE
World of Gilbert and George, The

GILBERT Brian
Frog Prince, The
Vice Versa

GILBERT, James
Sunstruck

GILBERT, Lewis
Alfie
Carve Her Name with Pride
Educating Rita
Ferry to Hong Kong
Greengage Summer, The
H.M.S. Defiant
Johnny on the Run
Light Up the Sky
Little Ballerina, The
Moonraker
Not Quite Jerusalem
Operation Daybreak
Reach for the Sky
Seven Nights in Japan
Seventh Dawn, The
Shirley Valentine
Sink the Bismarck!
Spy Who Loved Me, The
Stepping Out
You Only Live Twice

GILER, David
Black Bird, The

GILES, David
Henry V
Henry IV (Part 1 & Part 2)
Richard II

GILL, David
Buster Keaton: A Hard Act to
  Follow (Co)
Unknown Chaplin (Co)

GILLIAM, Terry
Brazil
Fisher King, The
Jabberwocky
Monty Python and the Holy
  Grail(Co)
Time Bandits

GILLIAT, Sidney
Constant Husband, The
Great St. Trinian's Train
  Robbery, The (Co)
Left, Right and Centre
Millions Like Us (Co)
Story of Gilbert and Sullivan, The

GILLING, John
Old Mother Riley Meets the Vampire
Plague of the Zombies, The
Scarlet Blade, The
Shadow of the Cat, The
Where the Bullets Fly

GILMORE, Stuart
Target

GILROY, Frank D.
Desperate Characters
From Noon Till Three

GIMBEL, Peter
Blue Water, White Death (Co)

GIRARD, Bernard
Dead Heat on a Merry-go-Round

GIRDLER, William
Day of the Animals
Grizzly
Manitou
Sheba Baby

GITAI, Amos
Field Diary
House
Pineapple
Wadi

GLADITZ, Nina
Better Active Today than Radio
  Active Tomorrow

GLADWELL, David
Requiem for a Village

GLASSER, Paul M.
Cutting Edge

GLEASON, James
Hot Tip (Co)

GLEN, John
Christopher Columbus - Discovery
For Your Eyes Only
Licence to Kill
Living Daylights, The
Octopussy
View to a Kill, A

GLENNON, Bert
Girl of the Port

GLENVILLE, Peter
Comedians, The
Hotel Paradiso
Prisoner, The
Term of Trial

GLICKENHAUS, James
Codename: The Soldier

GLIMCHER, Arne
Mambo Kings, The

GOBBI, Sergio
Menace

GODARD, Jean-Luc
A Bout de Souffle
Alphaville (Co)
Aria (Ep)
British Sounds
Carabiniers, Les
Chinoise, La
Detective
Femme Mariée, Une
First Name Carmen
Hail Mary
Letter to Jane, A (Co)
Loin du Viêt-nam (Ep)
Numéro Deux
Paris Vu Par (Ep)
Passion
Petit Soldat, Le
Pierrot le Fou
Pravda (Co)
Sympathy for the Devil
Tout va Bien (Co)
Vent d'Est
Vivre sa Vie
Week-end

GODBOUT, Jacques
Alias Will James

GODDARD, Gary
Masters of the Universe

GODDARD, Jim
Blackstuff
Shanghai Surprise

GODFREY, Peter
Highways by Night

GODMILOW, Jill
Far From Poland

GODWIN, Frank
Break Out

Flectric Eskimo, The
Terry on the Fence

GOLAN, Menahem
Apple, The
Delta Force
Diamonds
Enter the Ninja
Kazablan
Lepke
Magician of Lublin, The
Over the Brooklyn Bridge
Over the Top
Uranium Conspiracy, The
What's Good for the Goose

GOLD, Jack
Aces High
Bofors Gun, The
Chain, The
Little Lord Fauntleroy
Man Friday
Medusa Touch, The
Naked Civil Servant, The
National Health, The
Reckoning, The

GOLD, Mick
Europe After the Rain

GOLDBECK, Willis
Three Men in White

GOLDBERG, Danny
No Nukes (Co)

GOLDSCHMIDT, John
Life for Christine

GOLDSTONE, James
Gang that Couldn't Shoot
  Straight, The
Rollercoaster
Scarlet Buccaneer, The
They Only Kill Their Masters
When Time Ran Out...
Winning

GOMEZ, Sara
One Way or Another

GOODE, Frederic
Avalanche
Davy Jones Locker
Great Pony Raid, The
Syndicate, The

GOODWINS, Leslie
Adventures of a Rookie
Almost a Gentleman
Crime Ring
Day the Bookies Wept, The
Fugitives for a Night
Genius at Work
Girl from Mexico, The
Ladies Day
Let's Make Music
Men Against the Sky
Mexican Spitfire at Sea
Mexican Spitfire Out West
Mexican Spitfire's Baby
Mexican Spitfire Sees a Ghost
Mexican Spitfire's Elephant
Mr. Doodle Kicks Off
Parachute Battalion
Pop Always Pays
Radio Stars on Parade
Riverboat Rhythm
Rookies in Burma
Sued for Libel
Tarnished Angel
They Met in Argentina

Vacation in Reno
What a Blonde

GOPALAKRISHNAN, Adoor
Rat-Trap

GORDON, Bert I.
Empire of the Ants
Six Inches Tall

GORDON, Bette
Empty Suitcases
Variety

GORDON, Michael
Act of Murder
Another Part of the Forest
Boys' Night Out
For Love or Money
How Do I Love Thee?
Impossible Years, The
Portrait in Black
Texas Across the River
Very Special Favour, A

GORDON, Michael S.
Wherever She Goes

GORDON, Robert
Gatling Gun, The
It Came from Beneath the Sea

GORDON, Steve
Arthur

GORETTA, Claude
Death of Mario Ricci, The
Dentelliäre, La
Girl from Lorraine, A
Invitation, L'

GORIN, Jean-Pierre
Letter to Jane, A (Co)
Poto and Cabengo
Pravda (Co)
Tout Va Bien (Co)

GORMLEY, Charles
Heavenly Pursuits
Living Apart Together

GORRIE, John
Tempest, The
Twelth Night

GORRIKER, Vladimir
Tsar's Bride, The

GOSCINNY, René
Asterix and Cleopatra (Co)
Asterix the Gaul (Co)
Lucky Luke - Daisy Town

GOTTLIEB, Carl
Caveman

GOTTLIEB, Michael
Mannequin

GOULDING, Alfred
Chump at Oxford, A

GOULDING, Edmund
Dawn Patrol
Grand Hotel
Nightmare Alley
Razor's Edge, The
Reaching for the Moon

GOVORUKIN, Stanislas
Robinson Crusoe

GRADLER, Theodor
Blind Man's Buff
Grey Morning

GRADOWSKI, Krzysztof
Mr. Blot's Academy

GRAEF, Roger
Pleasure at Her Majesty's

GRAHAM, Eddy
Christmas Carol, A

GRAHAM, William A.
Amazing Howard Hughes, The
Doomsday Flight, The
Police Story

GRANT, James Edward
Angel and the Badman

GRASSHOFF, Alex
Young Americans

GRAUMAN, Walter
I Deal in Danger
Last Escape, The
Rage to Live, A
633 Squadron

GREDE, Kjell
Harry Munter
Hugo and Josefin

GREEN, Alfred E.
Ella Cinders
Fabulous Dorseys, The
Jolson Story, The
Mayor of 44th Street
Smart Money

GREEN, David
Buster
Car Trouble

GREEN, Guy
Angry Silence, The
Diamond Head
Light In the Piazza, The
Magus, The
Patch of Blue, A
Portrait of Alison
Pretty Polly
Sea of Sand
S.O.S. Pacific
Walk in the Spring Rain, A

GREEN, Walon
Hellstrom Chronicle, The

GREENAWAY, Peter
Belly of an Architect, The
Cook, The Thief, His Wife
  & Her Lover, The
Draughtsman's Contract, The
Drowning by Numbers
Falls, The
Prospero's Books
Zed and Two Noughts, A

GREENE, David
Count of Monte Cristo, The
Godspell
Gray Lady Down
Hard Country
I Start Counting
Madame Sin
People Next Door, The
Sebastian
Strange Affair, The

GREENE, Felix
China
Cuba Va
Inside North Vietnam
One Man's China
Tibet

GREENGLASS, Paul
Resurrected

GREENWALD, Robert
Xanadu

GREENWALT, David
Secret Admirer

GREGG, Colin
Begging the Ring
Lamb
We Think the World of You

GREVILLE, Edmond T.
"Beat" Girl

GRIERSON, John
Drifters

GRIES, Tom
Breakheart Pass
Breakout
Earth II
Greatest, The
Master of the Islands
100 Rifles
Will Penny

GRIEVE, Andrew
On the Black Hill

GRIFFITH, Charles B.
Dr. Heckyl and Mr. Hype

GRIFFITH, D.W.
Abraham Lincoln
Birth of a Nation, The
Broken Blossoms
Hearts of the World
Intolerance
Judith of Bethulia
Orphans of the Storm
Sally of the Sawdust
True Heart Susie

GRIFFITHS, Edward H.
Lady With a Past
Rebound
Sky's the Limit, The

GRIGOR, Murray
Scotch Myths

GRIGSBY, Michael
Before the Monsoon
Life Apart, A
Living on the Edge

GRISSELL, Wallace A.
Western Heritage

GROFE Jr, Ferde
Day of the Wolves
Proud and the Damned, The

GROSBARD, Ulu
Falling in Love
Straight Time
True Confessions

GROSSMAN, Jack
Pop Pirates

GROTE, Alexandra von
Novembermoon

GROULX, Gilles
Chat dans le Sac, Le
Entre Tu et Vous

GRZIMEK, Michael
Serengeti Shall Not Die

GUENETTE, Robert
Man Who Saw Tomorrow, The

GUERCIO, James William
Electra Glide in Blue

GUERRA, Ruy
Guns, The

GUERTLER, Wilmar R.
Viola and Sebastian (Co)

GUEST, Christopher
Big Picture

GUEST, Val
Assignment K
Beauty Jungle, The
Boys in Blue, The
Carry on Admiral
Confessions of a Window
  Cleaner, The
Dance Little Lady
Hell is a City
It's a Wonderful World
Weapon, The
When Dinosaurs Ruled the Earth
Where the River Bends

GUILLERMIN, John
Blue Max, The
Day They Robbed the Bank of
  England, The
Death on the Nile
Guns at Batasi
House of Cards
I Was Monty's Double
Never Let Go
New Face in Hell
Shaft in Africa
Sheena
Skyjacked
Towering Inferno, The

GUIOL, Fred
Mummy's Boys
Rainmakers, The
Silly Billies

GUNN, Gilbert
Wings of Mystery

GUTIERREZ ALEA, Tomas
Last Supper, The
Memories of Underdevelopment

GUTMAN, Walter
Grape Dealer's Daughter, The

GUZMAN, Claudio
Hostage Tower, The

HAANSTRA, Bert
Ape and Superape

HACKFORD, Taylor
Against All Odds
Chuck Berry - Hail! Hail Rock
  'n' Roll

Idolmaker, The
Officer and a Gentleman, An
White Nights

HAGG, Russell
Raw Deal

HAGGARD, Piers
Fiendish Plot of Dr. Fu Manchu, The
Summer Story, A

HAGGARTY, John
Caught in the Net

HAGMANN, Stuart
Believe in Me
Strawberry Statement, The

HAINES, Fred
Steppenwolf

HAINES, Randa
Children of a Lesser God
Doctor

HALAS, John
Animal Farm (Co)

HALDANE, Donald
Drylanders
Nikki, Wild Dog of the North (Co)

HALE, William
Deadly Roulette
Gunfight in Abilene
S.O.S. Titanic

HALEY Jr, Jack
That's Dancing
That's Entertainment

HALL, Alexander
Because You're Mine
Forever Darling
Goin' to Town
Little Miss Marker
They All Kissed the Bride

HALL, Peter
Perfect Friday
Three Into Two Won't Go

HALLENBECK, E. Darrell
One of Our Spies Is Missing

HALLER, Daniel
Buck Rogers in the 25th Century
Dunwich Horror, The

HALLINGER, David
George Kuchar: The Comedy of the
Underground (Co)

HALLSTRÖM, Lasse
Abba - The Movie
My Life As a Dog

HAMER, Robert
Dead of Night (Ep)
Kind Hearts and Coronets
Pink String and Sealing Wax
Scapegoat, The
School for Scoundrels

HAMILTON, Guy
Battle of Britain
Best of Enemies, The
Colditz Story, The
Diamonds are Forever
Evil under the Sun
Force 10 from Navarone
Goldfinger

Intruder, The
Man with the Golden Gun, The
Mirror Crack'd The
Party's Over, The
Remo - Unarmed and Dangerous

HAMILTON, William
Call Out the Marines (Co)
Murder on a Bridal Path (Co)
Seven Keys to Baldpate (Co)

HAMMOND, Peter
Spring and Port Wine

HAMMOND, William
Rockets in the Dunes

HANBURY, Victor
Hotel Reserve

HANCOCK, John
Baby Blue Marine
Let's Scare Jessica To Death

HANIBAL, Jiri
Small Summer Blues

HANKIN, Michael
Midnight Madness (Co)

HANNA, William
Jetsons: The Movie (Co)

HANSEL, Marion
Dust

HANSON, Curtis
Hand that Rocks the Cradle, The

HARBUTT, Sandy
Stone

HARDY, Joseph
Great Expectations

HARDY, Robin
Fantasist, The
Wicker Man, The

HARE, David
Licking Hitler
Paris by Night
Strapless
Wetherby

HARLAN, Veit
Carnival
Great King, The
Great Sacrifice, The

HARKIN, Margo
Hush A Bye Baby

HARLIN, Renny
Die Hard II
Nightmare on Elm Street 4: The
Dream Master

HARLOW, John
Dangerous Cargo
Headline
Old Mother Riley's New Venture
Old Mother Riley Headmistress

HARMON, Robert
Hitcher, The

HARRILD, Anthony
Lina Brooke

HARRINGTON, Curtis
Games

Mata Hari
Ruby
What's the Matter With Helen?

HARRIS, Damian
Deceived

HARRIS, James B.
Bedford Incident, The

HARRISON, John K.
Beautiful Dreamers

HARRISON, Norman
Incident at Midnight

HART, Harvey
Dark Intruder

HARTFORD-DAVIS, Robert
Black Gunn
Sandwich Man, The

HARTLEY, Hal
Trust
Unbelievable Truth

HARTMAN, Don
Every Girl Should Be Married
Holiday Affair
It's a Big Country (Ep)

HARVEY, Anthony
Abdication, The
Eagle's Wing, The
Grace Quigley
Lion in Winter, The
Players
They Might Be Giants

HARVEY, Joan
America - from Hitler to M - X
We Are the Guinea Pigs

HARVEY, Laurence
Ceremony, The

HAS, WojciechJerzy
Saragossa Manuscript, The

HASKIN, Byron
Captain Sinbad
From the Earth to the Moon
Little Savage, The
Man-Eater of Kumaon
Naked Jungle, The
Power, The
Treasure Island

HASTRUP, Jannik
History Book, The (Co)

HATHAWAY, Henry
Beyond the River
Desert Fox The Story of
Rommel, The
Five Card Stud
Go West Young Man
House on 92nd Street, The
How the West Was Won (Co)
Kiss of Death
Last Safari, The
Lives of a Bengal Lancer, The
Nevada Smith
North to Alaska
Peter Ibbetson
Raid On Rommel
Shoot Out
Sons of Katie Elder, The
Such Men Are Dangerous
13 Rue Madeleine

HATHCOCK, Bob
Duck Tales: The Movie

HATTON, Maurice
Long Shot
Praise Marx and Pass the
Ammunition

HAUFF, Reinhard
Brutalization of Franz Blum, The
Knife in the Head
Paule Paulander

HAUGK, Dietrich
Flowers Were Mourning, The

HAVELOCK-ALLAN, Anthony
Evening with The Royal Ballet,
An (Co)

HAWKS, Howard
Air Force
Big Sky, The
Big Sleep, The
Bringing Up Baby
Girl in Every Port, A
Only Angels Have Wings
Red Line 7000
Red River
Rio Bravo
Rio Lobo
Scarface
Sergeant York
Tiger Shark
To Have and Have Not
Twentieth Century

HAY, David
Dirt Cheap (Co)

HAY, Will
Goose Steps Out, The (Co)

HAYDN, Richard
Dear Wife
Mr. Music

HAYERS, Sidney
All Coppers Are...
Assault
Circus of Horrors
Conquest of the Earth (Co)
Finders Keepers
Firechasers
Mr. Jericho
Night of the Eagle
Payroll
Revenge
Southern Star, The
Three Hats for Lisa
Trap, The
What Changed Charley Farthing?

HAZAN, Jack
Bigger Splash, A
Rude Boy (Co)

HECKERLING, Amy
Fast Times at Ridgemont High
Johnny Dangerously
Look Who's Talking
Look Who's Talking Too
National Lampoon's European
Vacation

HEERMAN, Victor
Animal Crackers
My Boy (Co)

HEFFRON, Richard
Fillmore
I the Jury

Newman's Law
Outlaw Blues
Trackdown

HEGEDUS, Chris
Town Bloody Hall (Co)

HEIFITZ, Josef
Big Family, The
Member of the Government (Co)

HEISLER, Stuart
Among the Living
Storm Warning

HELLMAN, Monte
Two-Lane Blacktop

HELLMAN, Oliver
Tentacles

HEMMINGS, David
Just a Gigolo

HENRY, Buck
Heaven Can Wait (Co)

HENSON, Jim
Dark Crystal, The (Co)
Great Muppet Caper, The
Labyrinth
Muppet Movie, The

HENSON, Laurence
Big Catch, The
Flash the Sheep Dog
Mauro the Gypsy

HEPWORTH, Cecil
Comin' Thro' the Rye
Tansy

HERBERT, Henry
Malachi's Cove

HERBERT, Hugh
He Knew Women

HERBST, Helmut
John Heartfield - Fotomonteur

HEREK, Stephen
Critters

HERMAN, Albert
Phantom of 42nd Street, The
Shake Hands With Murder

HERMAN, Mark
Blame It On the Bellboy

HEROUX, Denis
Uncanny, The

HERSCHENSOHN, Bruce
Years of Lightning, Day of Drums

HERZ, Juraj
Cremator, The
Sweet Games of Last Summer

HERZFELD, Jon
Two of a Kind

HERZOG, Werner
Aguirre, The Wrath of God
Enigma of Kaspar Hauser, The
Even Dwarfs Started Small
Fata Morgana
Fitzcarraldo
Heart of Glass
Nosferatu the Vampire

Signs of Life
Stroszek
Woyzeck

HESSLER, Gordon
Embassy
Golden Voyage of Sinbad, The
Murders in the Rue Morgue
Oblong Box, The
Scream and Scream Again

HEYES, Douglas
Kitten With a Whip

HEYNOWSKI, Walter
War of the Mummies (Co)
White Coup, The (Co)

HIBBS, Jesse
Rails into Laramie
To Hell and Back
Walk the Proud Land

HICKENLOOPER, George
Hearts of Darkness: A Filmmaker's
  Apocalypse (Co)

HICKMAN, Howard
Nobody's Kid

HICKOX, Douglas
Brannigan
Sitting Target
Skyriders
Theatre of Blood
Zulu Dawn

HIGGINS, Colin
Best Little Whorehouse in Texas, The
Foul Play
Nine to Five

HIKEN, Nat
Love God, The

HILL, George
Hell Divers

HILL, George Roy
Butch Cassidy and the Sundance Kid
Great Waldo Pepper, The
Little Drummer Girl, The
Little Romance, A
Period of Adjustment
Slap Shot
Slaughterhouse Five
Sting, The
Thoroughly Modern Millie

HILL, James
Belstone Fox, The
Black Beauty
Born Free
Captain Nemo and the Underwater
  City
Dock Brief, The
Elephant Called Slowly, An
Kitchen, The Man From Nowhere,
  The
Peking Medallion, The
Study in Terror, A
Young Visitors, The

HILL, Jerome
Film Portrait

HILL, Walter
Brewster's Millions
Driver, The
Extreme Prejudice
48 HRS.
Johnny Handsome

Long Riders, The
Red Heat
Southern Comfort
Streetfighter, The
Streets of Fire
Warriors, The

HILLER, Arthur
Author! Author!
Filofax
Flight of the White Stallions, The
Hospital, The
In-laws, The
Love Story
Man of La Mancha
Nightwing
Out-of-Towners, The
Outrageous Fortune
Penelope
Plaza Suite
Popi
Promise Her Anything
Romantic Comedy
See No Evil, Hear No Evil
Separate Beds
Silver Streak
Teachers
Tobruk
W.C. Fields and Me

HIRD, Robert
Mr. Horatio Nibbles

HISCOTT, Leslie
Time of His Life
Tons of Trouble

HITCHCOCK, Alfred
Birds, The
Dial M for Murder
Family Plot
Foreign Correspondent
Frenzy
I Confess
Lady Vanishes, The
Lifeboat
Lodger, The
Man Who Knew Too Much, The
Mr. and Mrs. Smith
Murder
North by Northwest
Paradine Case, The
Rear Window
Rich and Strange
Ring, The
Rope
Sabotage
Secret Agent
Spellbound
Suspicion
To Catch a Thief
Topaz
Trouble with Harry, The
Under Capricorn
Vertigo
Wrong Man, The

HIVELY, Jack
Ann of Windy Poplars
Four Jacks and a Jill
Panama Lady
Saint in Palm Springs, The
Saint's Double Trouble, The
They Made Her a Spy
Two Thoroughbreds

HOARE, Lionel
Flood, The

HOBL, Pavel
We've a Lion at Home

HODGES, Mike
Flash Gordon
Get Carter
Morons From Outer Space
Prayer for the Dying, A
Pulp

HOELLERING, George
Murder in the Cathedral

HOFFMAN, David
Nashville Sound, The (Co)

HOFFMAN, Herman
Invisible Boy

HOFFMAN, Jerzy
Quack, The

HOFFMAN, John
I Killed Geronimo

HOFFMAN, Michael
Privileged
Restless Natives
Soapdish

HOFFMANN, Kurt
Wir Wunderkinder

HOGAN, James
Bulldog Drummond Escapes

HOLE Jr, William
Ghost of Dragstrip Hollow, The

HOLLAND, Mary
Creggan (Co)

HOLLAND, Tom
Child's Play
Fright Night

HOLLANDER, Gad
Diary of a Sane Man

HOLMES, Ben
Farmer in the Dell, The
I'm From the City
Lightning Strikes Twice
Maid's Night Out
Petticoat Larceny
Plot Thickens, The
Saint in New York, The
There Goes My Girl
Too Many Wives
We're on the Jury

HOLMES, J.B.
Coastal Command

HOLT, Seth
Danger Route
Nanny, The
Nowhere to Go

HONDA, Inoshiro
Atragon
Frankenstein Conquers the World
Godzilla vs. the Thing
Mysterians, The

HONEY, John
Manganinnie

HOOK, Harry
Lord of the Flies

HOOPER, Tobe
Funhouse
Invaders from Mars
Lifeforce

Poltergeist

HOPKINS, Stephen
Predator 2

HOPPER, Dennis
Last Movie, The
Hot Spot, The

HOPPER, Jerry
Missouri Traveller

HORNBLOW, Arthur Jr
Desire Me

HORNE, James W.
Bohemian Girl (Co)
Bonnie Scotland
College
Way Out West

HOSKINS, Bob
Raggedy Rawney, The

HOUGH, John
Brass Target
Dirty Mary, Crazy Larry
Escape to Witch Mountain
Eyewitness
Incubus, The
Legend of Hell House, The
Return from Witch Mountain
Treasure Island
Twins of Evil
Watchers in the Woods

HOWARD, Cy
Every Little Crook and Nanny
Lovers and Other Strangers

HOWARD, David
Border G Man
Dude Cowboy
Fighting Gringo
Gun Law
Marshal of Mesa City, The
Millionaire Playboy
Painted Desert, The
Renegade Ranger, The
Rookie Cop, The

HOWARD, Leslie
Gentle Sex, The
Pygmalion (Co)

HOWARD, Ron
Backdraft
Cocoon
Far and Away
Night Shift
Splash
Willow

HOWARD, William K.
Johnny Come Lately
White Gold

HOWES, Oliver
Let The Balloons Go

HOYT, Harry D.
Primrose Path

HSIAO HSIEN, Hou
City of Sadness
Daughter of the Nile

HSIEH Tsin
Red Detachment of Women

HSU T'ao
Girl of the Grassland

HUBACEK, Miroslav
Hasek's Stories
Tales of Hasek

HUBERT, Jean-Loup
Grand Chemin, Le

HUDSON, Hugh
Chariots of Fire
Greystoke Legend of Tarzan Lord
of the Apes
Revolution

HUGHES, David
Emmanuelle in Soho

HUGHES, Howard
Hell's Angels
Outlaw, The

HUGHES, John
Curly Sue
Ferris Bueller's Day Off
Planes, Trains and Automobiles
Uncle Buck
Weird Science

HUGHES, Ken
Alfie Darling
Chitty Chitty Bang Bang
Cromwell
Drop Dead Darling
House Across the Lake
In the Nick
Of Human Bondage
Terror Eyes

HUGHES, Robert
Arthur Penn: 1922 Themes and
Variants

HUILLET, Daniele
Eyes Do Not Want to Close at
All Times (Co)
Fortini/Cani (Co)
History Lessons (Co)

HULL, Norman
Ladder of Swords

HUMBERSTONE, H Bruce
Happy Go Lovely
If I Had a Million (Ep)

HUMFRESS, Paul
Sebastiane (Co)

HUNT, Peter
Death Hunt
On Her Majesty's Secret Service
1776
Shout at the Devil
Wild Geese II

HUNTER, Tim
River's Edge
Tex

HURLEY, Frank
Endurance

HURST, Brian Desmond
Behind the Mask
Dangerous Moonlight
His and Hers
Scrooge
Simba

HUSSEIN, Waris
Henry VIII and His Six Wives
Possession of Joel Delaney, The
S.W.A.L.K.

Touch of Love, A

HUSTON, Danny
Mr. North

HUSTON, John
Across the Pacific
African Queen
Annie
Asphalt Jungle, The
Beat the Devil
Bible... In the Beginning, The
Dead, The
Fat City
Heaven Knows, Mr.Allison
Key Largo
Kremlin Letter, The
Life and Times of Judge Roy
Bean, The
Mackintosh Man, The
Man Who Would Be King, The
Night of the Iguana, The
Red Badge of Courage, The
Reflections in a Golden Eye
Sinful Davey
Treasure of the Sierra Madre, The
Under the Volcano
Wise Blood

HUTTON, Brian G.
Heroin Gang, The
Kelly's Heroes
Night Watch
Pad (And How To Use It), The
Where Eagles Dare
Zee and Co.

HUYCK, Willard
Best Defence
Howard - A New Breed of Hero

HYAMS, Peter
Busting
Capricorn One
Hanover Street
Narrow Margin, The
Outland
Peeper
Presidio, The
2010

IANZELO, Tony
Cree Hunters of Mistassini (Co)

ICHIKAWA, Kon
Actor's Revenge, An
Visions of Eight (Ep)

IHNAT, Steve
Honkers, The

IMAGE, Jean
Aladdin and His Magic Lamp

IMAMURA, Shohei
Ballad of Narayama
Black Rain

INCE, Ralph
Lucky Devil
Men of America

INGRAMS, Jonathan
Boy With Two Heads, The
Firefighters, The
Headline Hunters

INGRAMS, Michael
Palaces of a Queen

INGSTER, Boris
Judge Steps Out, The
Stranger on the Third Floor

INKPEN, Ron
Remember Me This Way (Co)

IRELAND, John
Fast and Furious (Co)

IRVIN, John
Champions
Dogs of War, The
Ghost Story
Hamburger Hill
Next of Kin
Robin Hood

IRVING, Judy
Dark Circle (Co)

IRVING, Richard
Ransom for a Dead Man

ISASI, Anthony
That Man in Istanbul

ISHII, Sogo
Crazy Family

ISRAEL, Neal
Bachelor Party
Moving Violations

ITAMI, Juzo
Tampopo
Taxing Woman, A

IVENS, Joris
Loin du Viêt-nam (Ep)

IVORY, James
Adventures of a Brown Man in
Search of Civilisation
Bostonians, The
Europeans, The
Heat and Dust
Householder, The
Hullabaloo Over Georgie and
Bonnie's Pictures
Jane Austen in Manhattan
Maurice
Mr. and Mrs. Bridge
Quartet
Room With A View, A
Roseland
Savages
Shakespeare Wallah
Slaves of New York

IZZARD, Bryan
Holiday on the Buses

JACKSON, David E.
Dream Chasers (Co)

JACKSON, Mick
LA Story

JACKSON, Pat
On the Run
Seventy Deadly Pills
Western Approaches

JACKSON, Wilfred
Song of the South (Co)
Alice in Wonderland (Co)

JACOBS, Ken
Tom Tom the Pipers Son

JACOBS, Rodney H.
Sacred Ground

JACOBY, Irving
Hitch

JAECKIN, Just
Lady Chatterley's Lover
Madame Claude

JAFFE Stanley R.
Without a Trace

JAGLOM, Henry
Can She Bake a Cherry Pie?
Sitting Ducks
Tracks

JAMAL, Ahmed A.
Majdhar

JAMESON, Jerry
Airport '77
Raise the Titanic
Starflight One

JANCSO, Miklos
Red Psalm
Round-Up, The

JANKEL, Annabel
D.O.A. (Co)

JANTHIMATHORN, Surachai
Tongpan (Co)

JARL, Stefan
Respectable Life, A
They Call Us Misfits (Co)

JARMAN, Derek
Aria (Ep)
Caravaggio
Edward II
Garden, The
In the Shadow of the Sun
Jubilee
Sebastiane (Co)
Tempest, The

JARMUSCH, Jim
Down by Law

JARROTT, Charles
Amateur, The
Anne of the Thousand
Days
Condorman
Dove, The
Escape from the Dark
Last Flight of Noah's Ark, The
Lost Horizon
Mary, Queen of Scots
Other Side of Midnight, The

JASON, Leigh
Bride Walks Out, The
Flying Irishman, The
Love On a Bet
Mad Miss Manton
New Faces of 1937
Wise Girl

JEFFREY, Jim
Bungala Boys

JEFFREY, Tom
Odd Angry Shot, The

JEFFRIES, Lionel
Amazing Mr. Blunden, The
Baxter!
Railway Children, The
Water Babies, The
Wombling Free

JENNINGS, Humphrey
I Was a Fireman

JESSNER, Leopold
Hintertreppe, Die

JESSUA, Alain
Chiens, Les
Killing Game, The
Vie A l'Envers, La

JEUNET, Jean-Pierre
Délicatessen (Co)

JEWISON, Norman
... And Justice for All
Agnes of God
Art of Love, The
Best Friends
Cincinatti Kid, The
Fiddler on the Roof
F.I.S.T.
Jesus Christ Superstar
Moonstruck
Other People's Money
Rollerball
Russians are Coming, The Russians
  are Coming, The
Soldier's Story, A

JHA, Prakash
Pas de Deux

JIRES, Jaromil
Valerie and Her Week of Wonders

JITTLOV, Mike
Wizard of Speed and Time, The

JOANOU, Phil
Final Analysis
State of Grace
U2: Rattle and Hum

JOFFÉ, Alex
Fortunat

JOFFÉ, Roland
City of Joy
Killing Fields, The
Mission, The
Spongers, The

JOHNSON, Alan
To Be or Not To Be

JOHNSON, Lamont
Groundstar Conspiracy, The
Last American Hero, The
Lipstick
McKenzie Break, The
One on One
You'll Like My Mother

JOHNSON, Nunnally
Angel Wore Red, The
Black Widow, The
How to Be Very, Very Popular

JOHNSTON, Joe
Rocketeer, The

JONES, Chuck
Great American Chase, The
Phantom Tollbooth, The (Co)

JONES, David
Betrayal
84 Charing Cross Road

JONES, James Cellan
Bequest to the Nation

JONES, Peter Frazer
George and Mildred

JONES, Terry
Erik the Viking
Monty Python and the Holy Grail
  (Co)
Monty Python's Life of Brian
Monty Python's The Meaning of Life

JORDAN, Glenn
It Only Hurts When I Laugh
Mass Appeal

JORDAN, Neil
Angel
Company of Wolves
High Spirits
Miracle, The
Mona Lisa

JOSEPHSON, Erland
Hounds of Spring, The

JOST, Jon
Speaking Directly

JOURDAIN, Pierre
I am a Dancer

JULIAN, Rupert
Love Comes Along
Phantom of the Opera, The

JULIEN, Isaac
Passion of Remembrance, The (Co)

JUNGHANS, Karl
Such Is Life

JURAN, Nathan
Deadly Mantis, The
Drums Across the River
First Men in the Moon
Flight of the Lost Balloon
Land Raiders
7th Voyage of Sinbad, The

JUTRA, Claude
Mon Oncle Antoine

JUTZI, Piel
Mutter Krausens Fahrt ins Gluck

KACHYNA, Karel
Country Doctor
High Wall
That Christmas
Vertigo

KACZENDER, George
In Praise of Older Women

KADAR, Jan
Lies My Father Told Me
Shop On the High Street, A (Co)

KAGAN, Jeremy Paul
Big Fix, The
Chosen, The
Heroes
Sting II, The

KAIDANOVSKY, Alexander
Kerosene Seller's Wife, The

KALATOZOV, Mikhail
Cranes are Flying, The
Red Tent, The

KANEW, Jeff
Revenge of the Nerds
Tough Guys
V.I. Warshawski

KANIEVSKA, Marek
Another Country

KANIN, Garson
Bachelor Mother
Great Man Votes, The
My Favourite Wife
They Knew What They Wanted
Tom, Dick and Harry
True Glory, The (Co)
Where It's At

KANSKI, Tadeusz
Devil's Pass, The (Co)

KANTER, Hal
I Married a Woman
Once Upon a Horse

KAPLAN, Jo Ann
Invocation - Maya Deren

KAPLAN, Jonathan
Accused, The
Mr. Billion
Slams, The
White Line Fever

KAPLAN, Nelly
Charles et Lucie

KARASIK, Yuli
Seagull, The

KARDAR, Aajeay
Day Shall Dawn

KAREL, Russ
Almonds and Raisins

KARLIN, Marc
For Memory
'36 to '77 (Co)

KARLSON, Phil
Ben
Framed
Gunman's Walk
Kid Galahad
Long Ride Home, The
Lorna Doone
99 River Street
Rampage
Secret Ways, The
Walking Tall

KARMEN, Roman
Continent Aflame

KARN, Bill
Gangbusters
Guns Don't Argue (Co)

KARN, Richard C.
Guns Don't Argue (Co)

KARNAD, Garish
Kaadu

KASDAN, Lawrence
Big Chill, The
Body Heat
Grand Canyon
Silverado

KASTLE, Leonard
Honeymoon Killer, The

KATSELAS, Milton
Butterflies Are Free
Operation Undercover

KATZIN, Lee H.
Heaven With a Gun
Hondo and the Apaches
Le Mans
Salzburg Connection, The
Whatever Happened to Aunt Alice?

KAUFMAN, Philip
Great Northfield Minnesota Raid,
  The
Invasion of the Bodysnatchers, The
Right Stuff, The
Unbearable Lightness of Being, The
Wanderers, The

KAURISMÄKI, Aki
Ariel
Leningrad Cowboys Go America

KAUTNER, Helmut
Jack the Skinner
Romance in a Minor Key
Stranger in My Arms, A

KAWADRI, Anwar
Nutcracker
Sex with the Stars

KAWALEROWICZ, Jerzy
Devil and the Nun, The

KAZAN, Elia
Arrangement, The
Splendour in the Grass
Wild River

KAZANSKY, Guenady
Snow Queen, The

KAZUO, Hara
Emperor's Naked Army Marches On

KEEN, Lesley
Ra: The Path of the Son God

KEIGHLEY, William
Adventures of Robin Hood, The (Co)
Bullets or Ballots
Each Dawn I Die
Fighting 69th, The
"G" Men
Honeymoon
Prince and the Pauper, The
Rocky Mountain

KELETI, Marton
Great Erkel, The

KELLER, Daniel
Last Resort, The
Lovejoy's Nuclear War (Co)

KELLER, Harry
Seven Ways from Sundown
Tammy Tell Me True
Texas John Slaughter

KELLETT, Bob
Alf Garnett Saga, The
Are You Being Served?
Don't Just Lie There, Say Something
Girl Stroke Boy
Our Miss Fred
Spanish Fly
Tightrope to Terror
Up Pompeii
Up the Chastity Belt
Up the Front

KELLJAN, Robert
Return of Count Yorga, The

KELLMAN, Barnet
Straight Talk

KELLOGG, Ray
Green Berets, The (Co)

KELLY, David
John Cooper-Clarke - Ten Years in
  an Open-Necked Shirt (Co)

KELLY, Gene
Guide for the Married
Man, A
Hello Dolly
Invitation to the Dance
It's Always Fair Weather (Co)
That's Entertainment Pt II
Tunnel of Love

KELLY, James
Beast in the Cellar, The

KELLY, Ron
King of the Grizzlies

KENNEDY, Anthea
At the Fountainhead (of German
  Strength) (Co)

KENNEDY, Burt
Deserter, The
Dirty Dingus Magee
Good Guys and Bad Guys, The
Hannie Caulder
Killer on a Horse
Money Trap, The
Rounders, The
Support Your Local Gunfighter
Support Your Local Sheriff
Train Robbers, The
War Wagon, The
West of Montana
Young Billy Young

KENWORTHY, N. Paul
Perri (Co)

KERN, James V.
Second Woman

KERSHNER, Irvin
Eyes of Laura Mars
Fine Madness, A
One Born Every Minute
Return of a Man Called Horse, The
S.P.Y.S.
Up the Sandbox

KERWIN, Harry
Barracuda

KHLEIFI, Michel
Wedding in Galilee

KIBBEE, Roland
Midnight Man, The (Co)

KIDD, Michael
Merry Andrew

KIDRON, Beeban
Carry Greenham Home (Co)

KIESLOWSKI, Krzysztof
Double Life of Veronique, The
No End

KILGORE, Al
World of Hans Christian Andersen
  (Co)

KILLY, Edward
Along the Rio Grande
Bandit Trail, The
Big Shot, The
China Passage
Cyclone on Horseback
Fargo Kid
Land of the Open Range
Murder on a Bridal Path (Co)
Quick Money
Robbers of the Range
Saturday's Heroes
Second Wife
Seven Keys to Baldate (Co)
Wanted! Jane Turner
West of the Pecos

KIMBALL, Ward
Mickey Mouse Anniversary
  Show (Co)

KIMMINS, Anthony
Amorous Prawn, The
I See Ice
Keep Fit
Mine Own Executioner
Trouble Brewing

KING, Allan
Married Couple, A
Warrendale

KING, George
Talacre School Film

KING, Henry
Black Swan, The
Bravados, The
David and Bathsheba
Gunfighter, The
Love Is a Many Splendoured Thing
Song of Bernadette, The
Stanley and Livingstone
Tol'able David
Twelve O'Clock High

KING, Louis
Dangerous Mission
Special Investigator

KING, Tim
Echo of the Badlands (Co)

KING, Zalman
Two Moon Junction

KINGSBURY, Bob
Mr. Symbol Man (Co)

KINNEY, Jack
Adventures of Ichabod and
  Mr.Toad, The (Co)

KINNOCH, Ronald
Secret Man, The

KINUGASA, Teinosuke
Crossways
Page of Madness, A

KIRSANOFF, Dimitri
Menilmontant

KISHON, Ephraim
Policeman, The

KJELLIN, Alf
McMasters Tougher than the West
  Itself
Run on Gold, A

KLANE, Robert
Thank God It's Friday

KLAREN, Georg C.
Wozzeck

KLAUS, Wyborny
Pictures of the Lost World

KLEIN, Bonnie Sher
Not a Love Story

KLEIN, Dusan
No Return Ticket (Co)

KLEIN, William
Loin du Viêt-nam (Ep)

KLEISER, Randal
Blue Lagoon
Grease
White Fang

KLIMOV, Elem
Farewell

KLINE, Herbert
Challenge, The

KLINGLER, Werner
Titanic (Co)

KLOPFENSTEIN, Clemens
Story of Night, The

KLOS, Elmar
Shop on the High Street, A (Co)

KLOVES, Steve
Fabulous Baker Boys, The

KLUGE, Alexander
Artistes at the Top of the Big Top:
  Disorientated
Patriot, The
Yesterday Girl

KNIGHT, Castleton
Queen is Crowned, A

KNIGHTS, Robert
Dawning, The

KNOBLER, Albert
Happiness in 20 Years

KOBAYASHI, Tsuneo
Escape, The

KOCH, Howard W.
Andy Hardy Comes Home
Badge 373

KOERFER, Thomas
Passionates, The

KOFF, David
Black Man's Land (Co)
Blacks Britannica (Co)

KOHN, Joseph
Harlem Jazz Festival

KOHOUT, Pavel
Seven Days a Week

KOK, Marja
In for Treatment (Co)

KOMACK, James
Porky's Revenge

KONCHALOVSKY, Andrei
see Andrei Mikhalkov-Konchalovsky

KORDA, Alexander
Perfect Strangers

KORDA, Zoltan
Cry, the Beloved Country
Jungle Book

KORTY, John
Alex and the Gypsy
Caravan of Courage
Oliver's Story

KOSTER, Henry
Dear Brigitte
Man Called Peter, A
Music for Millions
Power and the Prize, The
Robe, The
Singing Nun, The
Wabash Avenue

KOTCHEFF, Ted
Billy Two-hats
Edna, the Inebriate Woman
Fun With Dick and Jane
Life at the Top
North Dallas Forty
Switching Channels
Tiara Tahiti
Too Many Chefs
Uncommon Valour
Weekend at Bernies

KOTKOWSKI, Andrzej
Olympics, '40

KOUF, Jim
Miracles

KOUNDOUROS, Nikos
Young Aphrodites

KOWALSKI, Bernard
Demons of the Swamp
Krakatoa - East of Java
Macho Callahan
Night of the Blood Beast
Stiletto

KOZINTSEV, Grigori
Cloak, The (Co)
Don Quixote
Hamlet
King Lear
Vybourg Side, The (Co)
Youth of Maxim, The (Co)

KRAMARSKY, David
Beast With a Million Eyes

KRAMER, Frank
Bounty Hunters, The
Return of Sabata
Sabata

KRAMER, Jerry
Moonwalker (Co)

KRAMER, Robert
Milestones (Co)

KRAMER, Stanley
Domino Killings, The
Guess Who's Coming to Dinner
Inherit the Wind
Not As a Stranger
Oklahoma Crude
Pride and Passion, The
Secret of Santa Vittoria, The
Ship of Fools,

KRASNA, Norman
Big Hangover, The

KREJCIK, Jiri
Chintamans and Marriage Swindler

KRESS Harold F.
Apache Warsmoke
Painted Hills

KRIEG, Peter
September Wheat

KRISH, John
Decline and Fall... of a Birdwatcher
Friend or Foe
Man Who Had Power Over
Women, The
Out of Darkness

KRSKA, Vaclav
From My Life
Way Back, The

KUBRICK, Stanley
Barry Lyndon
Dr. Strangelove
Full Metal Jacket
Killer's Kiss
Killing, The
Lolita
Paths of Glory
Shining, The
2001: A Space Odyssey

KUCHAR, George
Devil's Cleavage, The

KUCKELMANN, Norbert
Experts, The

KUEHN, Andrew J.
Terror in the Aisles

KULESHOV, Lev
Extraordinary Adventures of Mister
West in the Land of the
Bolsheviks, The
Great Consoler, The

KULIK, Buzz
Babe
Hunter, The
To Find a Man
Villa Rides
Warning Shot

KULLE, Jarl
Bookseller Who Gave Up Bathing,
The

KUROSAWA, Akira
Akira Kurosawa's Dreams
Dersu Uzala
Idiot, The
Ikiru
I Live in Fear
Kagemusha
Rashomon

Sanjuro
Seven Samurai
Throne of Blood
Tora-No-O
Yojimbo

KURYS, Diane
C'est La Vie

KUSTURICA, Emir
When Father Was Away on
Business

KUTZ, Kazimierz
Pearl in the Crown

KWAPIS, Ken
Vibes

LABRO, Maurice
Take Me as I Am

LA CAVA, Gregory
Age of Consent
Bed of Roses
Fifth Avenue Girl
Half-Naked Truth, The
Laugh and Get Rich
My Man Godfrey
Primrose Path
Stagedoor
Symphony of Six Million

LACOMBE, Georges
Seven Deadly Sins (Ep)

LAFIA, John
Child's Play II

LAFORET, Georg
Kettledrummer, The (Ep)

LAINE, Edvin
Unknown Soldier, The

LAMBERT, Mary
Siesta

LAMONT, Charles
Abbott and Costello in the Foreign
Legion
Abbott and Costello Meet Captain
Kidd
Abbott and Costello Go to Mars
Abbott and Costello Meet the
Keystone Cops
Kettles in the Ozarks, The

LANCASTER, Burt
Midnight Man, The (Co)

LANDAU, Saul
Paul Jacobs and the Nuclear Gang
(Co)

LANDER, Ned
Dirt Cheap (Co)

LANDERS, Lew
Annabel Takes a Tour
Bad Lands
Blind Alibi
Border Cafe
Condemned Women
Crashing Hollywood
Danger Patrol
Double Danger
Fixer Dugan
Flight from Glory

Law of the Underworld
Lie Detector, The
Man Who Found Himself, The
Night Waitress
Seven Keys to Baldpate
Shadow of Terror
Sky Giant
Smashing the Rackets
Stagecoach Kid
They Wanted to Marry
Thunder Mountain
Twelve Crowded Hours
Under the Tonto Rim
Without Orders
You Can't Buy Luck

LANDIS, John
Blues Brothers, The
Coming to America
Into the Night
National Lampoon's Animal House,
The
Oscar
Spies Like Us
Three Amigos!
Trading Places
Twilight Zone - The Movie (Ep)

LANDRES, Paul
Go Johnny Go

LANDY, Ruther
Dark Circle (Co)

LANE, Charles
True Identity

LANFIELD, Sidney
Sorrowful Jones
Station West
You'll Never Get Rich

LANFRANCHI, Mario
Traviata, La

LANG, Fritz
Beyond a Reasonable Doubt
Clash by Night
Cloak and Dagger
Destiny
Dr. Mabuse the Gambler
Fury
Hangmen Also Die
Human Desire
Indian Tomb, The
I Shall Return
M
Metropolis
Nibelungen, Die
Rancho Notorious
Scarlet Street
Secret Beyond the Door
Spiders, The
Spy, The
Testament von Dr. Mabuse, Das
Thousand Eyes of Dr. Mabuse, The
Tiger of Eschnapur, The
While the City Sleeps
Woman in the Window, The
You and Me
You Only Live Once

LANG, Richard
Change of Seasons
Mountain Men, The

LANG, Walter
But Not For Me
Can-Can
His Other Woman
Hooray for Love

LANGLEY, Noel
Our Girl Friday
Pickwick Papers, The
Svengali

LANGTON, Simon
Whistle Blower, The

LANZMANN, Claude
Shoah

LAPOKNYSH, V.
Cossacks Beyond the Danube

LARCHER, David
Mare's Tail

LARRAZ, Joseph
Vampyres

LATTUADA, Alberto
Amore in Città (Ep)
Lights of Variety (Co)
Mandrake, The
Tempesta, La

LAUDER, Al
Paolozzi Story, The

LAUGHTON, Charles
Night of the Hunter, The

LAUNDER, Frank
Bridal Path, The
Great St. Trinian's Train Robbery,
  The (Co)
Happiest Days of Your Life, The
Joey Boy
Millions Like Us (Co)
Pure Hell of St Trinian's, The

LAVEN, Arnold
Down Three Dark Streets
Geronimo
Glory Guys, The
Rough Night in Jericho
Sam Whiskey
Slaughter on Tenth Avenue

LAWRENCE, Diarmuid
Exploits at West Poley

LAWRENCE, Quentin
Man Who Finally Died, The
Secret of Blood Island, The

LAZARUS, Ashley
E'Lollipop
Golden Rendezvous

LEACH, Wilford
Pirates of Penzance

LEACOCK, Philip
Baffled
Innocent Sinners
Kidnappers, The
Riders of the New Forest
Tamahine
Spanish Gardener

LEACOCK, Richard
Chair, The (Co)
Primary (Co)

LEADER, Anton M.
Children of the Damned

LEAL, Orlando
Improper Conduct (Co)

LEAN, David
Blithe Spirit
Bridge on the River Kwai, The
Brief Encounter
Doctor Zhivago
Great Expectations
Lawrence of Arabia
Oliver Twist
Passage to India, A
Ryan's Daughter
Summertime
This Happy Breed

LEAR, Norman
Cold Turkey

LECONTE, Patrice
Hairdresser's Husband, The
Monsieur Hire

LEDERER, Charles
Never Steal Anything Small

LEE, Jack
Captain's Table, The
Robbery Under Arms
Town Like Alice, A

LEE, Rowland V.
Mother Carey's Chickens
Powder Town
Son of Frankenstein
Three Musketeers, The
Toast of New York, The

LEE, Spike
Jungle Fever
Mo' Better Blues
She's Gotta Have It

LEECE, Mary Pat
Bred and Born (Co)

LEEDS, Herbert I.
Bunco Squad

LE GRICE, Malcolm
Blackbird Descending
Emily (Third Party Speculation)
Finnegan's Chin - Temporal
  Economy

LEHMAN, Ernest
Portnoy's Complaint

LEHMANN, Michael
Hudson Hawk

LEHMUSKALLIO, Markku
Raven's Dance

LEIGH, Mike
Bleak Moments
Grown Ups
High Hopes
Life is Sweet

LEISEN, Mitchell
Frenchman's Creek
Girl Most Likely, The
Hands Across the Table
Hold Back the Dawn
Midnight
To Each His Own
Tonight We Sing

LEISER, Erwin
Mein Kampf

LELAND, David
Wish You Were Here

LELOUCH, Claude
Another Man, Another Woman
Bonne Année, La
Loin du Viêt-nam (Ep)
Visions of Eight (Ep)
Vivre pour Vivre

LE MASSON, Yann
Kashima Paradise (Co)

LEMKE, Klaus
Amore
Komischer Heiliger, Ein

LEMMON, Jack
Kotch

LEMONT, John
Konga

LENZI, Umberto
From Hell to Victory (Co)
Samson and the Slave Queen

LEO, Malcolm
This Is Elvis (Co)

LEONARD, Robert Z.
Duchess of Idaho
Everything I Have is Yours
Great Ziegfeld, The
King's Thief, The
Pride and Prejudice
Rich Full Life
Ziegfeld Girl

LEONE, Sergio
Colossus of Rhodes, The
For a Few Dollars More
Good, the Bad and the Ugly, The
Once Upon a Time in America

LERNER, Murray
From Mao to Mozart - Isaac
Stern in China

LEROY, Mervyn
Any Number Can Play
Bad Seed, The
F.B.I. Story, The
Five Star Final
Gold Diggers of 1933
Gold Diggers of 1935
I am a Fugitive from a Chain Gang
Little Caesar
Little Women
Lovely To Look At
Madam Curie
Mister Robert (Co)
One-Piece Bathing Suit, The
Random Harvest
Strange Lady in Town
Waterloo Bridge
Without Reservations

LEROY, Serge
On l'Appelle France
Shattered

LESIEWICZ, Witold
Passenger (Co)

LESTER, Mark L.
Armed and Dangerous
Commando
Firestarter
Stunts

LESTER, Richard
Butch and Sundance: The Early Days
Cuba
Funny Thing Happened on the Way

to the Forum, A
Juggernaut
Knack, The
Mouse on the Moon, The
Ritz, The
Robin and Marian
Royal Flash
Superman II
Superman III

LETERRIER, François
Goodbye Emmanuelle

LETO, Marco
Black Holiday

LETTRICH, Andrzej
Death Comes in the Rain
Twelfth Hour (Co)

LEVANT, Brian
Beethoven
Problem Child 2

LE VIEN, Jack
King's Story, A

LEVIN, Henry
Ambushers, The
Bandit of Sherwood Forest,
  The (Co)
Come Fly With Me
Desperados, The
Genghis Khan
Honeymoon Hotel
If a Man Answers
Jolson Sings Again
Journey to the Centre of the Earth
Lonely Man
Murderers
That Man Bolt (Co)
Where the Boys Are

LEVIN, Sid
Let the Good Times Roll (Co)

LEVINSON, Barry
Avalon
Bugsy
Diner
Good Morning Vietnam
Natural, The
Rain Man
Tin Men
Young Sherlock Holmes and the
  Pyramid of Fear

LEVITOW, Abe
Gay Purr-ee
Phantom Tollbooth, The (Co)

LEVEY, Don
Herostratus

LEVY, Gerry
Bodystealers, The

LEVY, Ralph
Bedtime Story
Do Not Disturb

LEVY, William A.
Slumber Party '57

LEWIN, Albert
Picture of Dorian Gray, A

LEWIN, Ben
Favour, the Watch and the Very
  Big Fish, The
Welcome to Britain

LEWIS, Edward Tim
Serving Two Masters

LEWIS, George, B.
Humanoid, The

LEWIS, Jay
Invasion Quartet

LEWIS, Jerry
Disorderly Orderly, The
Nutty Professor, The
Three on a Couch
Which Way to the Front?

LEWIS, Jonathan
Before Hindsight

LEWIS, Joseph H.
Falcon in San Francisco, The
Lady Without a Passport, A
Retreat Hell

LEWIS, Milo
Egghead's Robot
Troublesome Double, The

LEWIS, Robert
Anything Goes

LEWIS, Robert Michael
Inside Job

LEYTES, Joseph
Valley of Mystery

L'HERBIER, Marcel
Late Mathias Pascal, The

LI Jun
Serfs

LIEBERMAN, Jeff
Blue Sunshine

LIEBERMAN, Robert
Table for Five

LIGHT, Chuck
Lovejoy's Nuclear War (Co)

LILIENTHAL, Peter
Schoolmaster Hofer

LINDBLOM, Gunnel
Summer Paradise

LINDGREN, Lars Magnus
Dear John

LINDQUIST, Jan
They Call Us Misfits (Co)

LINDTBERG, Leopold
Village, The

LING Tzufong
Daughters of China (Co)

LIPSCOMB, James
Blue Water, White Death (Co)

LIPSKY, Oldrich
Man from the First Century, The

LISBERGER, Stephen
Tron

LITTIN, Miguel
Jackal of Nahueltoro, The

LITTLEWOOD, Joan
Sparrows Can't Sing

LITTMAN, Lynne
Testament

LITVAK, Anatole
Anastasia
Battle of Russia, The (Co)
Five Miles to Midnight
Goodbye Again
Journey, The
Lady in the Car with Glasses and
   A Gun, The
Night of the Generals, The

LLOYD, Frank
Blood on the Sun
Mutiny on the Bounty

LO Wei
Back Alley Princess

LOACH, Ken
Big Flame, The
Cathy Come Home
Days of Hope
Hidden Agenda
Kes
Poor Cow
Riff-Raff

LOADER, Jayne
Atomic Café (Co)

LOGAN, Joshua
Ensign Pulver
Paint Your Wagon
South Pacific

LOGAN, Stanley
Falcon's Brother, The

LOMBARDI, Francisco J.
Lion's Den

LOMBARDO, Lou
Russian Roulette

LOMNICKI, Jan
Action by the Arsenal
Toast

LONCRAINE, Richard
Brimstone and Treacle
Missionary, The

LONGINOTTO, Kim
Cross and Passion (Co)
Theatre Girls (Co)

LOPUSHANSKY, Konstantin
Letters From a Dead Man

LORD, Jean-Claude
Doves, The
Visiting Hours

LORRE, Peter
Lost One, The

LOSEY, Joseph
Blind Date
Boom
Boy With Green Hair, The
Criminal, The
Don Giovanni
Go-Between, The
Modesty Blaise
Romantic Englishwoman, The
Secret Ceremony
Servant, The

Sleeping Tiger, The

LOUVISH, Simon
To Live in Freedom

LOWENSTEIN, Richard
Strikebound

LOWENTHAL, John
Trials of Alger Hiss, The

LUBIN, Arthur
Ali Baba and the Forty Thieves
Escapade in Japan
First Travelling Saleslady, The
Francis Joins the W.A.C.S.
Impact
Phantom of the Opera
Star of India

LUBITSCH, Ernst
Design for Living
If I Had a Million (Ep)
Madame Dubarry
Monte Carlo
Ninotchka
Shop Around the Corner, The
To Be or Not to Be
Trouble in Paradise

LUCAS, George
American Graffiti
Star Wars

LUCIDI, Maurizio
Can Be Done Amigo
Last Chance

LUDWIG, Edward
Big Wheel, The
Old Man Rhythm

LUHRMANN, Baz
Strictly Ballroom

LUMET, Sidney
Anderson Tapes, The
Appointment, The
Deadly Affair, The
Deathtrap
Dog Day Afternoon
Equus
Fail Safe
Hill, The
Murder on the Orient Express
Network
Offence, The
Prince of the City
Q & A
Running on Empty
Serpico
Stage Struck
That Kind of Woman
Twelve Angry Men
Verdict, The
Wiz, The

LUSKE, Hamilton
Alice in Wonderland (Co)

LYNCH, David
Blue Velvet
Dune
Elephant Man, The
Wild at Heart

LYNE, Adrian
Fatal Attraction
Flashdance
Foxes
Jacob's Ladder

LYNN, Jonathan
Clue
My Cousin Vinny
Nuns on the Run

LYNN, Robert
Postman's Knock

LYON, Francis D.
Great Locomotive Chase, The
Young and the Brave, The

LYSSY, Rolf
Confrontation: Assassination in
   Davos
Swissmakers, The

●

MAAS, Dick
Lift, The

McBRIDE, Jim
Big Easy, The
Breathless

MacCAIG, Arthur
Patriot Game, The

McCALLUM, John
Nickel Queen

McCANN, Chuck
World of Hans Christian
   Andersen (Co)

McCAREY, Leo
Affair to Remember, An
Going My Way
Once Upon a Honeymoon
Ruggles of Red Gap

McCAREY, Ray
Falcon's Alibi, The
Hot Tip (Co)
Little Orvie
Pack Up Your Troubles (Co)
Passport to Destiny

McCARTHY, Matt
Robin Hood Junior (Co)
Unbroken Arrow, The
Zoo Robbery, The (Co)

McCARTHY, Michael
Operation Amsterdam

McCOWAN, George
Frogs
Magnificent Seven Ride, The
Shadow of the Hawk

MACDONALD, David
Brothers, The
Cairo Road
Christopher Columbus
Good-Time Girl
Moonraker
Petticoat Pirates (Co)

McDONALD, Frank
Gun Smugglers

MacDONALD, Peter
Rambo III

McDONELL, Fergus
Private Information

McDOUGALL, Don
Spiderman - The Dragon's Challenge

McDOUGALL, Ranald
Man on Fire
Subterraneans, The
World, the Flesh and the Devil, The

McELWEE, Ross
Sherman's March

McEVEETY, Bernard
Bears and I, The
Napoleon and Samantha
One Little Indian

McEVEETY, Vincent
Castaway Cowboy, The
Charley and the Angel
Firecreek
Herbie Goes Bananas
Herbie Goes to Monte Carlo
Menace on the Mountain
Million Dollar Duck
Strongest Man in the World, The
Superdad
Treasure of Matacumbe, The

McGRATH, Joseph
Bliss of Mrs. Blossom, The
Digby the Biggest Dog in the World
Rising Damp

McGUANE, Thomas
92 in the Shade

MACH, Josef
Man Is Not Alone, A

MACHULSKI, Juliusz
Va Banque

MACK, Russell
Lonely Wives
Meanest Gal in Town, The

MacKENDRICK, Alexander
Don't Make Waves
High Wind in Jamaica, A
"Maggie", The
Mandy
Man in the White Suit
Whisky Galore

MacKENZIE, John
Cheviot, the Stag and the Black,
  Black Oil, The
Fourth Protocol, The
Honorary Consul, The
Long Good Friday, The
Ruby
Unman, Wittering and Zigo

MacKINNON, Gillies
Conquest of the South Pole

MacKINNON, Stewart
Because I am King
Justine (Co)

McLAGLEN, Andrew V.
Ballad of Josie, The
Bandolero
Cahill
Chisum
Devil's Brigade, The
Dynamite Man from Glory Jail
Hellfighters
Last Hard Men, The
North Sea Hijack
One More Train to Rob
Rare Breed, The
Sahara
Sea Wolves, The
Something Big

Undefeated, The
Way West, The
Wild West, The
Wild Geese, The

McLAUGHLIN, Sheila
Committed (Co)
She Must Be Seeing Things

McLEOD, Norman Z.
Casanova's Big Night
Horse Feathers
If I Had a Million (Ep)
It's a Gift
Let's Dance
Monkey Business
Paleface
Private Wore Skirts, The
Topper

McMILLAN, Ian
Festival of Fools (Co)

McMULLEN, Ken
Ghost Dance
Resistance

McMURRAY, Mary
Assam Garden, The

McNAUGHT, Bob
Grand National Night

McNAUGHTON, Ian
And Now for Something
  Completely Different

McNAUGHTON, John
Henry: Portrait of a Serial Killer

MACOVEC, Milos
Prague: Zero Hour

MacPHERSON, Kenneth
Borderline

MacTAGGART, James
All the Way Up

McTIERNAN, John
Die Hard
Medicine Man
Predator

McWILLIAMS, Donald
Creative Process: Norman
  McLaren, The

MADDEN, Lee
Hell's Angels '69

MADDOW, Ben
Savage Eye, The (Co)

MAGNOLI, Albert
Purple Rain

MAGNUSON, John
Lenny Bruce Performance Film, The

MAGWOOD, Paul
Chandler

MAISCH, Herbert
Friedrich Schiller

MAJEWSKI, Janusz
Epitaph to Barbara Rodziwill

MAKAVEJEV, Dusan
Montenegro
W.R. Mysteries of the Organism

MALICK, Terrence
Badlands
Days of Heaven

MALLE, Louis
Amants, Les
Ascenseur pour l'Echafaud
Atlantic City USA
Au Revoir Les Enfants
Calcutta
Feu Follet, Le
Lift to the Scaffold
Milou En Mai
Pretty Baby
Viva Maria!
Zazie Dans le Métro

MALMUTH, Bruce
Nighthawks

MALONE, Arthur
Plague on Your Children, A (Prod)

MAMET, David
House of Games
Things Change

MAMOULIAN, Rouben
Blood and Sand
Golden Boy
Queen Christina
Silk Stockings

MANAGADZE, Nodar
Warmth of Your Hands (Co)

MANAGADZE, Shota
Crucified Island
Warmth of Your Hands (Co)

MANDEL, Robert
F/X - Murder By Illusion

MANDER, Kay
Kid From Canada, The

MANDOKI, Luis
White Palace

MANDUKE, Joe
Fury on Wheels

MANGOLTE, Babette
Cold Eye
Sky on Location, The
What Maisie Knew

MANKIEWICZ, Francis
Beaux Souvenirs, Les

MANKIEWICZ, Joseph L.
Cleopatra
Honey Pot, The
Quiet American, The
Sleuth
Suddenly Last Summer
There Was a Crooked Man...

MANKIEWICZ, Tom
Dragnet

MANN, Anthony
Bamboo Blonde
Border Incident
Cimarron
Dandy in Aspic, A
Desperate
Devil's Doorway
Far Country, The
Glenn Miller Story, The
Heroes of Telemark, The
Man from Laramie

Naked Spur, The
Reign of Terror
Sing Your Way Home
Tall Target, The
Tin Star
Two O'Clock Courage
Winchester '73

MANN, Daniel
About Mrs. Leslie
Ada
Butterfield 8
For the Love of Ivy
Hot Spell
I'll Cry Tomorrow
Judith
Our Man Flint
Revengers, The
Who's Got the Action?
Willard

MANN, Delbert
All Quiet on the Western Front
Dark at the Top of the Stairs, The
David Copperfield
Fitzwilly Strikes Back
Gathering of Eagles, A
Jane Eyre
Kidnapped
Lover Come Back
Night Crossing
Outsider, The
Pink Jungle, The
Quick Before it Melts
Woman Without a Face

MANN, Michael
Jericho Mile, The
Keep, The
Manhunter
Violent Streets

MARCEL, Terry
Hawk the Slayer
Jane and the Lost City

MARCH, Alex
Amazing Captain Nemo, The
Dangerous Days of Kiowa Jones,
  The

MARGOLIS, Jeff
Richard Pryor Live in Concert

MARIN, Edwin L.
Abilene Town
Christmas Carol, A
Johnny Angel
Lady Luck
Nocturne
Race Street
Show Business
Tall in the Saddle

MARKER, Chris
Battle of the Ten Million, The
Joli Mai, Le
Sans Soleil
Spiral, The (Ep)

MARKLE, Fletcher
Gun Moll
Incredible Journey, The
Man with a Cloak, The

MARKLE, Peter
Youngblood

MARQUAND, Richard
Birth of The Beatles
Eye of the Needle
Jagged Edge

MARSHALL, Frank
Arachnophobia

MARSHALL, Garry
Beaches
Flamingo Kid, The
Frankie & Johnny
Nothing in Common
Overboard
Young Doctors in Love

MARSHALL, George
Blue Dahlia
Boy, Did I Get A Wrong Number!
Company of Cowards!
Cry for Happy
Destry Rides Again
Duel in the Jungle
Gazebo, The
How the West Was Won (Co)
Imitation General
It Started With a Kiss
Mating Game, The
Military Policeman
Money from Home
Never a Dull Moment
Pack up Your Troubles (Co)
Perils of Pauline
Scared Stiff
Sheepman, The
Star Spangled Rhythm
Valley of the Sun

MARSHALL, Penny
Awakenings
Big
Jumpin' Jack Flash

MARSHALL, William
Phantom Planet, The

MARTIN, Charles
Death of a Scoundrel
My Dear Secretary

MARTIN, E.A.
Heart of Texas Ryan

MARTIN, Henry
Big George is Dead
Grove Music

MARTIN, Murray
Keeping Time

MARTINSON, Leslie H.
Fathom
Mrs. Pollifax - Spy

MARTON, Andrew
Around the World Under the Sea
Clarence, the Cross-Eyed Lion
Crack in the World
Gypsy Colt
King Solomon's Mines (Co)
Longest Day, The (Co)
Underwater Warrior
Wild North, The

MASELLI, Francesco
Amore in Citté (Ep)

MASRI, Mai
Women from South Lebanon (Co)

MASSOT, Joe
Song Remains the Same, The (Co)

MASTERS, Quentin
Stud, The

MASTERSON, Peter
Trip to Bountiful, The

MASTROIANNI, Armand
He Knows You're Alone

MATE, Rudolph
Black Shield of Falworth, The
Deep Six, The
D.O.A.
For the First Time
Mississippi Gambler
Rawhide Years
Rough Company
Second Chance
Seven Seas to Calais
Siege at Red River
Three Violent People
Union Station
When Worlds Collide

MATTELART, Armand
Spiral, The (Ep)

MAX - LINDER, Maud
Laugh with Max Linder

MAXWELL, Ronald F.
Little Darlings
Night the Lights Went Out in
  Georgia, The

MAY, Elaine
Ishtar
New Leaf, A

MAY, Joe
House of the Seven Gables

MAY, Nick
Invaders, The

MAYBERRY, Russ
Spaceman and King Arthur, The

MAYLAM, Tony
Cup Glory
Riddle of the Sands, The
Split Second
White Rock

MAYO, Archie
Night after Night
Night in Casablanca, A
Petrified Forest, The
Svengali

MAYOUX, Valerie
Spiral, The (Ep)

MAZURSKY, Paul
Blume in Love
Bob & Carol & Ted & Alice
Down and Out in Beverly Hills
Harry and Tonto
Moscow on the Hudson
Next Stop, Greenwich Village
Scenes from a Mall
Unmarried Woman, An
Willie and Phil

MAZZETTI, Lorenza
Together

MEDAK, Peter
Changeling, The
Krays, The
Zorro the Gay Blade

MEDFORD, Don
November Plan, The
Organisation, The

To Trap a Spy

MEDOWAY, Gary
Heavenly Kid, The

MEDVED, Josef
Twelth Hour (Co)

MEDVEDKIN, Alexander
Happiness

MEEVES, Helmut
Kettledrummer, The (Ep)

MEGAHY, Francis
Great Riviera Bank Raid, The

MEHRJUI, Darioush
Cow, The
Cycle, The

MEINECHE, Annelise
Seventeen

MEISEL, Kurt
Madeleine - Tel 136211

MEKAS, Adolfas
Hallelujah the Hills
Windflowers

MELANCON, André
Bach & Broccoli
Summer of the Colt

MELENDEZ, Bill
Dick Deadeye
Race for Your Life, Charlie Brown
Snoopy Come Home

MELVILLE, Jean-Pierre
Enfants Terribles, Les
Flic, Un

MENDES, Lothar
Flight for Freedom

MENENDEZ, Ramon
Stand and Deliver

MENGES, Chris
World Apart, A

MENZEL, Jiri
Capricious Summer
Crime in a Girl's School (Co)
Those Wonderful Movie Cranks

MENZIES, William Cameron
Invaders from Mars
Whip Hand, The

MEPPIEL, Jacqueline
Spiral, The (Ep)

MERCHANT, Ismail
Courtesans of Bombay

MEREDITH, Burgess
Man on the Eiffel Tower, The

MERRILL, Keith
Windwalker

MERTZ, Arthur
Off the Dole

MESCHKE, Michael
Purgatorio

MESZAROS, Marta
Bye Bye Red Riding Hood

Diary for My Children
Diary for My Loves

METCALF, Andy
Unstable Elements: Atomic
  Stories 1939-1985 (Co)

METZGER, Radley
Cat and the Canary, The

MEYER, Jean
Femmes Savantes, Les
Tartuffe, Le

MEYER, Nicholas
Deceivers, The
Star Trek II - The Wrath of Khan
Star Trek IV: The Undiscovered
  Country
Time after Time

MEYER, Russ
Beyond the Valley of the Dolls
Cherry, Harry and Raquel
Faster, Pussycat! Kill! Kill!
Up
Vixen

MEYERS, Sidney
Quiet One, The
Savage Eye, The (Co)

MICHAEL, George
Drums of Destiny

MICHAELS, Richard
Once Upon a Family

MICHAELYAN, Sergei
Bonus, The

MIHALKA, George
My Bloody Valentine

MIKABERIDZE, Kote
My Grandmother

MIKELS, Ted V.
I Crossed the Colour Line

MIKHALKOV, Nikita
Dark Eyes
Oblomov

**MIKHALKOV -
KONCHALOVSKY, Andrei**
Asya's Happiness
Duet for One
First Teacher, The
Inner Circle
Maria's Lovers
Nest of Gentlefolk, A
Runaway Train
Uncle Vanya

MIKKELSEN, Laila
Little Ida

MILES, Christopher
Time for Loving
Virgin and the Gypsy, The

MILESTONE, Lewis
All Quiet on the Western Front
Arch of Triumph
General Died at Dawn, The
Halls of Montezuma
Lucky Partners
Mutiny on the Bounty
My Life with Caroline
No Minor Vices
Ocean's Eleven

Of Mice and Men
Purple Heart, The
They Who Dare
Widow, The

MILIUS, John
Big Wednesday
Conan the Barbarian
Dillinger
Red Dawn
Wind and the Lion, The

MILLAND, Ray
Panic in the Year Zero!
Safecracker, The

MILLAR, Gavin
Dreamchild

MILLAR, Stuart
Rooster Cogburn
When the Legends Die

MILLER, Claude
Impudent Girl, An
Inquisitor, The
Meilleure Façon de Marcher, La

MILLER, David
Back Street
Hammerhead
Opposite Sex, The

MILLER, George
Mad Max
Mad Max II
Mad Max Beyond Thunderdome
   (Co)
Twilight Zone - The Movie (Ep)
Witches of Eastwick, The

MILLER, George
Man From Snowy River
Neverending Story II: The Next
   Chapter

MILLER, Harvey
Bad Medicine

MILLER, Jason
That Championship Season

MILLER, Jonathan
Take a Girl Like You

MILLER, Michael
Jackson County Jail
National Lampoon's Class
   Reunion

MILLER Robert Ellis
Bachelor Girl Apartment
Baltimore Bullet
Buttercup Chain, The
Girl from Petrovka
Reuben, Reuben
Sweet November

MILLER, Sidney
Tammy and the Millionaire

MILLS, John
Sky West and Crooked

MILLS, Reginald
Tales of Beatrix Potter

MILNER, Dan
Phantom from 10,000 Leagues,
   The

MILONAKOS, Pilas
Emanuelle Queen Bitch

MILTON, Robert
Devotion
Westward Passage

MINER, Steve
Friday the 13th Part 2
Friday the 13th - The Final Chapter

MINER, Worthington
Hat, Coat and Glove
Let's Try Again

MINGAY, David
Rude Boy (Co)

MINNELLI, Vincente
American in Paris, An
Bells Are Ringing, The
Brigadoon
Cobweb, The
Courtship of Eddie's Father, The
Designing Woman
Father of the Bride
Father's Little Dividend
Four Horsemen of the
   Apocalypse, The
Gigi
Goodbye Charlie
Kismet
Lust for Life
Madame Bovary
Meet Me in St. Louis
On a Clear Day You can See
   Forever
Pirate, The
Reluctant Debutante, The
Sandpiper, The
Some Came Running,
Story of Three Loves, The (Co)
Tea and Sympathy
Two Weeks in Another Town
Undercurrent

MITA, Merata
Patu

MITCHELL, Eric
Underground USA

MIZOGUCHI, Kenji
Life of O-Haru, The
Sansho Dayu
Ugetsu Monogatari

MLIKOVSKY, Cestmir
Cucumber Hero, The

MOELLER, Philip
Break of Hearts

MOGUY, Leonide
Action in Arabia

MOIR, Bruce
Mr. Symbol Man (Co)

MOLINARO, Edouard
Cage Aux Folles, La
Cage Aux Folles II, La

MOLLBERG, Rauni
Earth is a Sinful Song

MOLLO, Andrew
It Happened Here (Co)
Winstanley (Co)

MONGER, Chris
Just Like a Woman

Repeater

MONICELLI, Mario
Let's Hope It's a Girl

MONTAGNE, Edward
McHales's Navy
Reluctant Astronaut, The
Tattooed Stranger, The

MONTALDO, Giuliano
Machine Gun McCain

MONTESI, Jorge
Omen IV: The Awakening (Co)

MONTGOMERY, George
From Hell to Borneo

MONTGOMERY, Patrick
Man You Loved to Hate, The

MONTGOMERY, Robert
Lady in the Lake

MOORE, Kieron
Progress of Peoples, The

MOORE, Michael
Fastest Guitar Alive, The

MOORE, Richard
Silent Flute, The

MOORE, Robert
Chapter Two
Cheap Detective, The
Murder by Death

MOORE, Simon
Under Suspicion

MOORHOUSE, Jocelyn
Proof

MORA, Philippe
Brother Can You Spare a Dime?
Swastika

MORAHAN, Christopher
All Neat in Black Stockings
Clockwise

MORLEY, Peter
Kitty - Return to Auschwitz

MORRIS, David Burton
Purple Haze

MORRIS, Errol
Thin Blue Line, The
Vernon, Florida

MORRIS, Howard
Who's Minding the Mint?
With Six You Get Eggroll

MORRISON, Paul
Unstable Elements: Atomic
   Stories 1939-1985 (Co)

MORSE, Hollingsworth
Daughters of Satan

MORTON, Rocky
D.O.A. (Co)

MOWBRAY, Malcolm
Private Function, A

MOXEY, John
Circus of Fear

MOYLE, Alan
Times Square

MUDD, Victoria
Broken Rainbow

MUGGE, Robert
Black Wax

MUIR, Roger
Treasure Island (Co)

MUKDAHSANIT, Yuthana
Tongpan (Co)

MULCAHY, Russell
Highlander

MULLIGAN, Robert
Bloodbrothers
Come September
Great Imposter, The
Love With the Proper Stranger
Rat Race, The
Same Time, Next Year
Spiral Road, The
Summer of '42
To Kill a Mockingbird

MULLOY, Phil
Give Us This Day
In the Forest

MULVEY, Laura
Crystal Gazing (Co)
Riddles of the Sphinx (Co)

MUNK, Andrzej
Eroica
Passenger (Co)

MUNOZ, Susana
Madres - The Mothers of Plaza de
   Mayo, Las (Co)

MURAKAMI, Jimmy T.
Battle Beyond the Stars
When the Wind Blows

MURCH, Walter
Return to Oz

MURNAU, F.W.
Last Laugh, The
Nosferatu
Sunrise

MURPHY, Dudley
Sport Parade, The

MURPHY, Geoff
Freejack
Goodbye Porkpie

MURPHY, Pat
Anne Devlin
Maeve (Co)

MURPHY, Ralph
Panama Flo

MURRAY, Bill
Quick Change (Co)

MURRAY, Russell
Destinations

MUSK, Cecil
Blow Your Own Trumpet

MUSKER, John
Little Mermaid, The (Co)

MUSSER, Charles
Before the Nickelodeon

MUTRUX, Floyd
Aloha Bobby and Rose
American Hot Wax

MWINYIPEMBE, Musindo
Blacks Britannica (Co)

MYCROFT, Walter C.
Banana Ridge

MYER, Clive
Justine (Co)

MYERS, Zion
Sidewalks of New York (Co)

MYERSON, Alan
Police Academy 5: Assignment
  Miami Beach
Steelyard Blues

NADEL, Arthur H.
Clambake
Underground

NAIR, Mira
Mississippi Masala
Salaam Bombay!

NARIZZANO, Silvio
Georgy Girl
Loot
Under Ten Flags (Co)
Why Shoot the Teacher?

NARLIYEV, Hodjakuli
Daughter-in-Law

NAVA, Gregory
Norte, El

NAUMOV, Vladimir
Pavel Korchagin (Co)

NAZARRO, Ray
Hired Gun

NEAL, Peter
Glastonbury Fayre

NEAME, Ronald
Chalk Garden, The
First Monday in October
Foreign Body
Gambit
Hopscotch
Horse's Mouth, The
I Could Go On Singing
Meteor
Million Pound Note
Mister Moses
Odessa File, The
Poseidon Adventure, The
Prime of Miss Jean Brodie,The
Scrooge
Tunes of Glory

NEARS, Colin
Cruel Garden
Restless Eye: Eugene Delacroix
  (1798-1863)

NEEDHAM, Hal
Hooper
Smokey and the Bandit
Smokey and the Bandit Ride Again

NEGULESCO, Jean
Best of Everything, The
Count Your Blessings
Hello-Goodbye
Johnny Belinda
Mask of Dimitrios, The
Pleasure Seekers, The
Scandal at Scourie
Titanic

NEILAN, Marshall
Tanned Legs
Vagabond Lover

NEILL, Roy William
Frankenstein Meets the Wolfman
Sherlock Holmes and the
  Secret Weapon
Woman in Green, The

NEILSON, James
Bon Voyage!
Doctor Syn - Alias the Scarecrow
Flareup
Johnny Shiloh
Legend of Young Dick Turpin, The
Moon Pilot
Moonspinners, The
Return of the Gunfighter
Summer Magic
Where Angels Go... Trouble
  Follows

NEKES, Werner
Kelek
Two-men

NELSON, Gary
Alan Quatermain and the Lost City
  of Gold
Black Hole, The
Freaky Friday
Santee

NELSON, Gene
Harem Holiday
Hootenanny Hoot
Kissin' Cousins
Your Cheatin' Heart

NELSON, Ralph
Charly
Counterpoint
Flight of the Doves
Lilies of the Field
Once a Thief
Soldier Blue
Tick... Tick... Tick...
Wilby Conspiracy, The
Wrath of God, The

NEMEC, Jan
Diamonds of the Night
Martyrs of Love
Party and the Guests, The

NESBITT, Derren
Amorous Milkman, The

NESBITT, Frank
Dulcima

NEUFELD Jr, Sigmund
Conquest of the Earth (Co)

NEUMANN, Kurt
Son of Ali Baba
Watusi

NEUREUTHER, Eric
Bohrer, Der

NEWELL, Mike
Awakening, The
Destiny
Good Father, The
Man in the Iron Mask, The
Silent Voice

NEWFIELD, Sam
Gas House Kids
Lady Confesses, The
Lone Rider in Cheyenne
Lone Rider Rides On
Lone Rider's Texas Justice
Nabonga
Rolling Down the Great Divide
Tiger Fangs

NEWLAND, John
My Lover, My Son
Spy With My Face, The

NEWMAN, Joseph M.
Great Dan Patch, The
Lawbreakers, The
Tarzan the Ape Man
Thunder of Drums, A

NEWMAN, Paul
Effect of Gamma Rays on
  Man-in-the-Moon Marigolds, The
Never Give an Inch
Rachel, Rachel

NIBLO, Fred
Big Gamble
Dangerous Hours
Mark of Zorro, The

NICHOLLS Jr, George
Big Game
Chasing Yesterday
Chatterbox
Finishing School (Co)
Marines Fly High
M'Liss
Return of Peter Grimm, The
Soldier and the Lady, The
Witness Chair, The

NICHOLS, Charles
Charlotte's Web (Co)

NICHOLS, Dudley
Government Girl
Sister Kenny

NICHOLS, Mike
Biloxi Blues
Catch-22
Day of the Dolphin, The
Fortune, The
Heartburn
Postcards from the Edge
Regarding Henry
Who's Afraid of Virginia Woolf?
Working Girl

NICHOLS, Sandra
Maragoli

NICHOLSON, Jack
Goin' South
Two Jakes, The

NICHOLSON, Nick
Treasure Island (Co)

NICOL, Alex
Screaming Skull, The

NIEMENS, Edouard
Angel Dust

NIGH, William
Doomed to Die

NIMOY, Leonard
Good Mother, The
Star Trek III - The Search for Spock
3 Men and a Baby

NOELTE, Rudolf
Castle, The

NOFAL, Emil
Kimberley Jim
Wild Season

NOLBANDOV, Sergei
Ship With Wings

NORMAN, Leslie
Dunkirk
Long, the Short and the Tall, The
Shiralee
Spare the Rod

NORRIS, Aaron
Braddock: Missing in Action III

NORTON, B.W.L.
Baby - Secret of the Lost Legend
More American Graffiti

NOSSECK, Max
Brighton Strangler, The

NOVAK, Ivo
Byzantine Merchant's Treasure
Crime in a Girls' School (Co)

NOYCE, Phillip
Blind Fury
Dead Calm
Patriot Games

NUGENT, Elliott
If I Were Free
My Girl Tisa
Skipper Surprised His Wife,The
Strictly Dynamite
Two Alone

NUNN, Trevor
Lady Jane

NYBY, Christian
Six Gun Law
Thing from Another World, The

NYBY II, Christian
Mission Galactica: The
  Cylon Attack (Co)

OBLOWITZ, Michael
King Blank

O'BRIEN, Jim
Dressmaker, The

O'CONNOLLY, Jim
Crooks and Coronets
Tower of Evil
Valley of Gwangi, The

O'CONNOR, Pat
Cal
Fools of Fortune
January Man, The
Month in the Country, A
Stars and Bars

ODETS, Clifford
None But the Lonely Hearts
Story on Page One, The

O'FERRALL, George More
Three Cases of Murder (Ep)

OGILVIE, George
Max Max Beyond Thunderdome
(Co)

OGURI, Koshei
Muddy River

O'HARA, Gerry
Bitch, The
Blind Man's Buff
Brute, The
Maroc 7
Paganini Strikes Again
Professor Popper's Problems

O'HERLIHY, Michael
Fighting Prince of Donegal,The

OKTEN, Zeki
Herd, The (Co)

OLIANSKY, Joel
Competition, The

OLIVIER, Laurence
Hamlet
Henry V
Richard III
Three Sisters

OLMI, Ermanno
Fidanzati, I
Posto II
Legend of the Holy Drinker,The
Long Live the Lady!

OLSSON, Stellan
Close to the Wind
Sven Klang's Combo

O'MALLEY, David
Guardian of the Wilderness

O'NEIL, Robert
Wonder Woman

OPHULS, Marcel
Clavigo
Sense of Loss, A

OPHULS, Max
Caught
Exile, The
Letter From an Unknown Woman
Ronde, La
Signora di Tutti, La

ORDYNSKI, Vasily
Red Square

ORMROD, Peter
Rachel and the Beelzebub
Bombadiers

O'ROURKE, Dennis
Half Life

ORR, Dianne
SL - 1 (Co)

ORTEGA, Kenny
News Boys

ORTEGA, Pascal
Bad Hats

ORTHEL, Rolf
Shadow of a Doubt

ORTON, Harold
Blinker's Spy Spotter
4D Special Agents
Wreck Raisers

OSHIMA, Nagisa
Diary of a Shinjuku Thief
In the Realm of the Senses
Merry Christmas, Mr. Lawrence

O'SULLIVAN, Thaddeus
December Bride
On a Paving Stone Mounted

OSWALD, Gerd
Agent for H.A.R.M.

OSWALD, Richard
Living Dead, The
Unheimliche Geschichten,
Grausige Nachte

OTHNIN-GERARD, Dominique
Omen IV: The Awakening

OTOMO, Katsuhiro
Akira

OUEDRAOGO, Idrissa
Tilai
Yaaba

OURY, Gerard
Mad Adventures of Rabbi Jacob,
The

OVE, Horace
Baldwin's Nigger
King Carnival
Pressure
Reggae

OWEN, Cliff
Bawdy Adventures of Tom Jones,
The
Magnificent Two, The
No Sex Please - We're British
Off Beat
Ooh! You Are Awful
Steptoe and Son
That Riviera Touch
Vengeance of She, The

OWEN, Don
Ernie Game, The
Nobody Waved Goodbye

OZ, Frank
Dark Crystal, The (Co)
Housesitter
Little Shop of Horrors, The
Muppets Take Manhattan, The
What About Bob?

OZEP, Feodor
Living Corpse, The

OZEROV, Juri
Visions of Eight (Ep)

OZU, Yasujiro
Autumn Afternoon, An
Early Spring
Flavour of Green Tea Over
Rice, The
I Was Born But...
Late Spring
Ohayo
Record of a Tenement

Gentleman, The
Tokyo Story

PABST, G.W.
Dreigroschenoper, Die
Kameradschaft
Pandora's Box
Paracelsus
West Front 1918
White Hell of Pitz Palu (Co)

PAGE, Anthony
Lady Vanishes, The

PAKULA, Alan J.
All the President's Men
Comes A Horseman
Klute
Love and Pain and the Whole
Damn Thing
Parallax View, The
Presumed Innocent
Rollover
Sophie's Choice
Starting Over

PAL, George
Atlantis the Lost Continent
Seven Faces of Dr. Lao
Tom Thumb

PALCY, Euzhan
Dry White Season, A
Rue Cases - Nègres

PALLARDY, Jean-Marie
Hot Acts of Love

PANAMA, Norman
Baited Trap, The
Not With My Wife, You Don't!
Road to Hong Kong
That Certain Feeling (Co)

PANFILOV, Gleb
Vassa

PAOLELLA, Domenico
Guns of the Black Witch
Hate for Hate

PAPOUSEK, Jaroslav
Best Age, The

PARADJANOV, Sergo
Colour of Pomegranates, The

PARIS, Jerry
Never a Dull Moment
Police Academy 2: Their First
Assignment
Police Academy 3: Back in Training

PARKER, Alan
Angel Heart
Birdy
Bugsy Malone
Come See the Paradise
Commitments, The
Fame
Midnight Express
Pink Floyd - The Wall
Shoot the Moon

PARKER, Cary
Girl in the Picture

PARKER, Francine
FTA

PARKER, Jayne
Almost There

PARKS, Gordon
Shaft
Shaft's Big Score
Supercops, The

PARKS Jr, Gordon
Superfly

PARRISH, Robert
Bobo, The
Cry Danger
Doppelganger
Duffy
Fire Down Below
Marseille Contract, The
Saddle the Wind
San Francisco Story, The

PARRY, Gordon
Bond Street
Sailor Beware
Tom Brown's Schooldays
Tread Softly Stranger
Yank in Ermine, A

Parsons, Jack
Blackhill Campaign

PASCAL, Gabriel
Caesar and Cleopatra
Major Barbara

PASOLINI, Pier Paolo
Arabian Nights
Decameron, The
Gospel According to St. Matthew
Oedipus Rex
Theorem

PASSENDORFER, Jerzy
Destination Berlin
Scenes of Battle

PASSER, Ivan
Cutter's Way
Intimate Lighting
Silver Bears

PATEL, Raj
Tangled Web

PATRONI, Griffi Giuseppe
'Tis Pity She's a Whore

PATTREA, Purnendu
Letter from the Wife

PAUL, Byron
Lt. Robinson Crusoe

PAVLOVIC, Vladislav
Marvellous Mum

PEARCE, A. Leslie
Fall Guy, The

PEARCE, Richard
Heartland
No Mercy

PECK, Ron
Strip Jack Naked

PECKINPAH, Sam
Ballad of Cable Hogue
Bring Me the Head of
Alfredo Garcia
Convoy
Cross of Iron

Getaway, The
Guns in the Afternoon
Junior Bonner
Killer Elite, The
Major Dundee
Osterman Weekend, The
Pat Garrett & Billy the Kid
Straw Dogs
Wild Bunch, The

PEERCE, Larry
Goodbye Columbus
One Potato, Two Potato
Two-Minute Warning
Window to the Sky
Wired

PEETERS, Barbara
Monster

PELISSIER, Anthony
History of Mr. Polly, The
Meet Mr. Lucifer

PENN, Arthur
Alice's Restaurant
Bonnie and Clyde
Chase, The
Georgia's Friends
Left Handed Gun, The
Mickey One
Missouri Breaks, The
Night Moves
Visions of Eight (Ep)

PENNEBAKER, D.A.
Chair, The (Co)
Don't Look Back
Monterey Pop
Primary
Town Bloody Hall (Co)

PENNELL, Eagle
Last Night at the Alamo

PENNINGTON, Richards C. M.
Challenge for Robin Hood, A
Dentist on the Job
Ladies Who Do
Sky Pirates

PEREIRA, Miguel
Veronico Cruz

PERIER, Etienne
Bridge to the Sun
Swordsman of Siena

PERKINS, Anthony
Psycho III

PERKINS, Nigel
Justine (Co)

PERRY, Frank
Compromising Positions
Diary of a Mad Housewife
Doc
Hello Again
Man on a Swing
Mommie Dearest
Monsignor
Rancho Deluxe
Swimmer, The

PETERSEN, Wolfgang
Boat, The
Enemy Mine
Neverending Story, The
One or the Other
Shattered

PETIT, Christopher
Flight to Berlin
Radio On
Unsuitable Job for A Woman, An

PETRI, Elio
Investigation of a Citizen Above
    Suspicion

PETRIE, Daniel
Betsy, The
Cat and Mouse
Lifeguard
Main Attraction, The
Neptune Factor, The
Raisin in the Sun
Resurrection

PETRIE Jr, Daniel
Toy Soldiers

PETRONI, Giulio
Death Rides a Horse

PETROV, Vladimir
Peter the Great Part I

PETTY, Cecil
Peregrine Hunters, The

PEVNEY, Joseph
Away all Boats

PEYSER, John
Young Warriors, The

PFLEGHAR, Michael
Visions of Eight (Ep)

PHILPOTT, Richard
Road Movie

PIALAT, Maurice
Enfance Nue, L'
Loulou
Police
To Our Loves

PICHEL, Irving
Before Dawn
Destination Moon
Great Rupert, The
Martin Luther
O.S.S.
Quicksand
They Wont Believe Me

PICKARD, Tom
Birmingham is What I Think With

PIEROTTI, Piero
Pirate and the Slave Girl, The

PIERSON, Frank R.
King of the Gypsies
Looking Glass War, The
Star Is Born, A

PILGER, John
Year Zero - The Silent Death of
    Cambodia

PINKAVA, Josef
Holidays with Minka
Kittens Not Carried

PINTOFF, Ernest
Harvey Middleman, Fireman
Jaguar Lives

PIRES, Gerard
Erotissimo

PIROSH, Robert
Valley of the Kings

PLATT-MILLS, Barney
Bronco Bullfrog
Hero

PLICKA, Karel
Earth Sings, The

PLUMMER, Peter
Junket 89

PO Chih Leong
Ping Pong

PODMANITSKY, Felix von
Nuremberg Trials, The (Prod)

PODSKALSKY, Zdenek
Out of Reach of the Devil

POGOSTIN, S. Lee
Hard Contract

POIRIER, Anne-Claire
Scream from Silence, A

POITIER, Sidney
Buck and the Preacher
Hanky Panky
Let's Do It Again
Piece of the Action, A
Stir Crazy
Warm December, A

POJAR, Bretislav
Big Fish, The

POLAK, Jindrich
Game Without Rules
Voyage to the End of the Universe

POLANSKI, Roman
Chinatown
Cul-de-Sac
Dance of the Vampires
Frantic
Knife in the Water
Macbeth
Pirates
Repulsion
Tenant, The

POLIAKOFF, Stephen
Close My Eyes

POLITI, Edna
Anou Banou or The Daughters of
    Utopia

POLLACK, Barry
Cool Breeze
This Is a Hijack

POLLACK, Sydney
Absence of Malice
Electric Horseman, The
Havana
Jeremiah Johnson
Out of Africa
Scalphunters, The
They Shoot Horses Don't They?
Three Days of the Condor
Tootsie
Way We Were, The

POLLAK, Claire
Cross and Passion (Co)
Theatre Girls (Co)

POLLAK, Kay
Elvis! Elvis!

POLLET, Jean-Daniel
Paris Vu Par (Ep)

POLLOCK, George
Kill or Cure
Murder Ahoy
Murder at the Gallop
Murder Most Foul
Murder She Said
Ten Little Indians
Village of Daughters

POLONSKY, Abraham
Force of Evil

PONTECORVO, Gillo
Battle of Algiers

PONTING, Herbert
Ninety Degrees South

POOL, Lea
Anne Trister

POOLEY, Olaf
Johnstown Monster, The

POOYA, Rafigh
In Defence of the People

POPKIN, Leo
Well, The (Co)

PORTILLO, Lourdes
Madres - The Mothers of Plaza de
    Mayo, Las (Co)

POST, Ted
Beneath the Planet of the Apes
Go Tell the Spartans
Hang 'Em High
Harrad Experiment, The
Magnum Force

POTENZA, Anthony
No Nukes (Co)

POTTER, H.C.
Likely Story, A
Miniver Story, The
Mr. Blanding Builds His Dream
    House
Mister Lucky
Second Chorus
Story of Vernon and Irene Castle,
    The

POTTERTON, Gerald
Heavy Metal

POTTS, Ian
Stranger than Fiction

POUND, Stuart
Ampersand
Codex
Stylus

POWELL, Dick
Enemy Below, The
Split Second
You Can't Run Away From It

POWELL, Michael
Age of Consent
Battle of the River Plate, The (Co)
Black Narcissus (Co)
Boy Who Turned Yellow, The
Canterbury Tale, A (Co)

49th Parallel
Gone to Earth (Co)
I Know Where I'm Going! (Co)
Ill Met by Moonlight (Co)
Life and Death of Colonel
  Blimp, The (Co)
Matter of Life and Death, A (Co)
Peeping Tom
Red Ensign
Red Shoes, The (Co)
Small Back Room, The (Co)
Something Always Happens
They're a Weird Mob

POWELL, Tristram
American Friends

POWER, John
Picture Show Man, The

PRAUNHEIM, Rosa von
Army of Lovers
City of Lost Souls

PREMINGER, Otto
Anatomy of a Murder
Angel Face
Bonjour Tristesse
Bunny Lake Is Missing
Cardinal, The
Carmen Jones
Court-martial of Billy Mitchell, The
Human Factor, The
In Harm's Way
Laura
Rosebud
Such Good Friends

PRESSBURGER, Emeric
Battle of the River Plate, The (Co)
Black Narcissus (Co)
Canterbury Tale, A (Co)
Gone to Earth (Co)
I Know Where I'm Going! (Co)
Ill Met by Moonlight (Co)
Life and Death of Colonel
  Blimp, The (Co)
Matter of Life and Death, A (Co)
Red Shoes, The (Co)
Small Back Room (Co)

PRESSMAN, Michael
Bad News Bears in Breaking
  Training, The
Boulevard Nights
Teenage Mutant Ninja Turtles II: The
  Secret of Ooze

PREVIN, Steve
Born to Sing
Waltz King, The

PROSHKIN, Alexander
Cold Summer of 53, The

PROTAZANOV, Yakov
Aelita

PUDOVKIN, Vsevolod
Deserter, The
End of St Petersburg, The
Harvest
Mother
Storm Over Asia

PUENZO, Luis
Official Version, The
Old Gringo

PYUN, Albert
Sword and the Sorcerer, The

QUESTED, John
Loophole

QUILICI, Folco
Tiko and the Shark

QUINE, Richard
Bell, Book and Candle
Hotel
How to Murder Your Wife
It Happened to Jane
Moonshine War, The
Paris When it Sizzles
Prisoner of Zenda, The
Sex and the Single Girl
Strangers When We Meet

RABAN, William and Marilyn
Black and Silver

RABENALT, Arthur Maria
Arena of Fear
Between Time and Eternity
Grosse Wunschkonzert, Das
Last Waltz, The

RADEMAKERS, Fons
Assault, The

RADFORD, Michael
1984
White Mischief

RADVANYI, Geza
Arzt von Stalingrad, Der
Ihr Verbrechen War Liebe

RAEBURN, Michael
Beyond the Plains Where Man
  Was Born

RAFELSON, Bob
Black Widow
Five Easy Pieces
King of Marvin Gardens
Mountains of the Moon
Stay Hungry

RAFFERTY, Kevin
Atomic Café (Co)
Hurry Tomorrow (Co)

RAFFERTY, Pierce
Atomic Café (Co)

RAFFILL, Stewart
Across the Great Divide
Adventures of the Wilderness Family
Ice Pirates
Mac and Me
Shipwreck
Tender Warrior
When the North Wind Blows

RAFKIN, Alan
Nobody's Perfect
Ride to Hangman's Tree, The
Shakiest Gun in the West
Ski Party

RAIMI, Sam
Crimewave
Evil Dead, The
Evil Dead II

RAINER, Yvonne
Film About A Woman Who...
Kristina Talking Pictures
Lives of Performers
Working Title: Journeys from
  Berlin/1971

RAIZMAN, Yuli
Cavalier of the Gold Star
Communist, The
Private Life
Wife, The

RAKOFF, Alvin
City on Fire
Crossplot
Hoffman
Romeo and Juliet
Say Hello to Yesterday
Treasure of San Teresa, The

RAMIS, Harold
Caddyshack
National Lampoon's Vacation

RANCE, Mark
Death and the Singing Telegram

RANKIN, Arthur
Last Unicorn, The (Co)

RAPPAPORT, Mark
Imposters
Local Color
Scenic Route, The

RAPPENEAU, Jean-Paul
Cyrano de Bergerac
Vie de Château, La

RAPPER, Irving
Adventures of Mark Twain
Forever Female
Marjorie Morningstar
Now Voyager
Rhapsody in Blue

RASH, Steve
Buddy Holly Story, The

RATOFF, Gregory
Intermezzo

RAWLINS, John
Arizona Ranger

RAY, Bernard B.
Buffalo Bill in Tomahawk
  Territory

RAY, Nicholas
Born to be Bad
Flying Leathernecks
James Brothers, The
King of Kings
Lusty Men, The
On Dangerous Ground
Party Girl
They Live by Night
Woman's Secret, A

RAY, Satyajit
Adventures of Goopy and Bagha
Adversary, The
Aparjito
Company Limited
Days and Nights in the Forest
Distant Thunder
Home and the World, The
Mahanagar
Middle Man, The
Monihara

Pather Panchali
Philosopher's Stone
Three Daughters
Two Daughters
World of Apu

RAYMAKER, Herman C.
Adventure Girl
Night Cry

RAYMOND, Jack
Milagro Beanfield War, The
Ordinary People

REED, Carol
Agony and the Ecstasy, The
Follow Me
Key, The
Last Warrior, The
Midshipman Easy
Odd Man Out
Oliver!
Our Man in Havana
Running Man, The
Stars Look Down, The
Third Man, The
True Glory, The (Co)
Way Ahead, The

REED, Luther
Dixiana

REED, Roland D.
House of Secrets, The

REES, Jerry
Too Hot to Handle

REEVE, Geoffrey
Caravan to Vaccares

REEVES, Michael
Witchfinder General

REGNOLI, Pierre
Playgirls and the Vampire

REID, Alastair
Baby Love

REINER, Carl
All of Me
Dead Men Don't Wear Plaid
Enter Laughing
Jerk, The
Oh God!
One and Only, The

REINER, Rob
Misery
Princess Bride, The
Stand by Me
Sure Thing, The
This is Spinal Tap!
When Harry Met Sally...

REINHARDT, Gottfried
Betrayed
Story of Three Loves, The (Co)
Town Without Pity

REINHARDT, Max
Midsummer Night's Dream, A (Co)

REINIGER, Lotte
Adventures of Prince Achmet, The

REINL, Harald
Chariot of the Gods, The

REIS, Irving
Bachelor Knight

Big Street, The
Crack-Up
Falcon Takes Over, The
Footlight Fever
I'm Still Alive
One Crowded Night
Three Husbands
Weekend for Three

REISNER, Allen
All Mine to Give

REISNER, Charles F.
Big Store, The
Lost in a Harem

REISZ, Karel
Dog Soldiers
French Lieutenant's Woman, The
Gambler, The
Isadora
Morgan - A Suitable Case for
   Treatment
Night Must Fall
Sweet Dreams
We are the Lambeth Boys

REITHERMAN, Wolfgang
Hunting Instinct, The
Robin Hood
Sword in the Stone, The

REITMAN, Ivan
Ghostbusters
Ghostbusters II
Kindergarten Cop
Legal Eagles
Meatballs
Stripes
Twins

REITZ, Edgar
Cardillac
Zero Hour

RELPH, Michael
Davy
Desert Mice
Out of the Clouds (Co)
Rockets Galore
Ship that Died of Shame, The (Co)
Square Ring, The (Co)

RENE, Norman
Long Time Companion

RENNIE, Barbara
Sacred Hearts

RENOIR, Jean
Boudu Sauvé des Eaux
Crime de M. Lange, Le
Grande Illusion, La
Marseillaise, La
Règle du Jeu, La
This Land is Mine
Vanishing Corporal, The
Woman on the Beach

RESNAIS, Alain
Last Year in Marienbad
Loin de Viêt-nam (Ep)
Mon Oncle D'Amérique

REVESZ, Gyorgy
Danger on the Danube

REYNOLDS, Burt
End, The
Gator
Sharkey's Machine

REYNOLDS, Kevin
Robin Hood: Prince of Thieves

REYNOLDS, Sheldon
Assignment to Kill

RHONE, Trevor D.
Smile Orange

RICH, David Lowell
Airport '80: The Concorde
Eye of the Cat
Lovely Way to Go, A
Plainsman, The
Rosie
Runaway Train, The
That Man Bolt (Co)
Three Guns for Texas

RICH, John
Boeing Boeing

RICHARDS, Dick
Culpepper Cattle Co, The
Farewell My Lovely
Heat
Man, Woman and Child
March or Die
Rafferty and the Gold Dust Twins

RICHARDSON, Amanda
Carry Greenham Home (Co)

RICHARDSON, Boyce
Cree Hunters of Mistassini (Co)

RICHARDSON, Ralph
Home at Seven

RICHARDSON, Tony
Border, The
Dead Cert
Hamlet
Joseph Andrews
Loneliness of the Long Distance
   Runner, The
Loved One, The
Mademoiselle
Ned Kelly

RICHMOND, Tony
Déjà Vu

RICHTER, Hans
Dreams that Money Can Buy

RIEFENSTAHL, Leni
Blue Light, The

RIGGS, Marlon T.
Tongues Untied

RILLA, Wolf
Bachelor of Hearts
Cairo
Piccadilly Third Stop
Scamp, The
Village of the Damned
Witness in the Dark

RIPPLOH, Frank
Taxi Zum Klo

RISI, Dino
Amore in Citté (Ep)
Priest's Wife, The

RITCHIE, Michael
Bad News Bears
Candidate, The
Divine Madness
Downhill Racer

Fletch
Fletch Lives
Golden Child, The
Island, The
Prime Cut
Semi-Tough
Smile
Wildcats

RITT, Martin
Back Roads
Black Orchid, The
Brotherhood, The
Casey's Shadow
Conrack
Front, The
Great White Hope, The
Hemingway's Adventures of a
   Young Man
Hombre
Long Hot Summer, The
Murphy's Romance
Norma Rae
Nuts
Outrage, The
Pete 'n' Tillie
Sound and the Fury, The

RIVETTE, Jacques
Amour Par Terre, L'
Belle Noiseuse, La (Divertimento)
Céline et Julie Vont en Bateau

ROACH, Hal
Fra Diavolo

ROBBE-GRILLET, Alain
Trans-Europe Express

ROBBIE, Seymour
C.C. and Company

ROBBINS, Matthew
*batteries not included
Dragonslayer
Hot One, The

ROBBINS, Tim
Bob Roberts

ROBERT, Charles E.
Hurry, Charlie, Hurry

ROBERT, Yves
Grand Blond Avec Une Chaussure
   Noire, Le
My Father's Glory
My Mother's Castle

ROBERTS, Alan
Hollywood Blue

ROBERTS, C. Larry
SL-1 (Co)

ROBERTS, Stephen
Ex-Mrs Bradford, The
If I Had a Million (Ep)
Lady Consents, The
Romance in Manhattan
Star of Midnight

ROBERTSON, John S.
Beyond Victory
Dr. Jekyll & Mr. Hyde
Grand Old Girl, The
His Greatest Gamble
Wednesday's Child

ROBINS, John
Best of Benny Hill, The
Love Thy Neighbour

That's Your Funeral

ROBINSON, Bruce
How to Get Ahead in Advertising
Withnail and I

ROBINSON, Debra J.
I Be Done Was Is

ROBINSON, Dick
Brother of the Wind

ROBINSON, Phil Alden
Field of Dreams
Woo Woo Kid, The

ROBISON, Arthur
Warning Shadows

ROBSON, Mark
Bedlam
Bridges at Toko-Ri, The
Earthquake
From the Terrace
Ghost Ship
Inn of the Sixth Happiness, The
Isle of the Dead
Little Hut, The
Lost Command, The
Peyton Place
Prize, The
Roughshod
Seventh Victim, The
Valley of the Dolls
Von Ryan's Express

ROCHA, Glauber
Lion has Seven Heads
Terra em Transe

ROCHANT, Eric
Autobus
World Without Pity

ROCHLIN, Sheldon
Paradise Now

RODDAM, Franc
Aria (Ep)
Bride, The
Lords of Discipline, The
Quadrophenia

ROE, Willy
Confessions of the David Galaxy
   Affair
Playbirds
Queen of the Blues

ROEG, Nicolas
Aria (Ep)
Bad Timing
Castaway
Eureka
Insignificance
Man Who Fell To Earth, The
Track 29

ROEMER, Michael
Plot Against Harry, The

ROGELL, Albert S.
Carnival Boat
Grand Jury
Suicide Fleet
Sweepstakes
Tip Off, The

ROGERS, Charles
Bohemian Girl (Co)

ROGERS, Maclean
Not Wanted on Voyage
Old Mother Riley's Jungle Treasure

ROGOSIN, Lionel
Come Back Africa
On the Bowery

ROGOVOI, Vladimir
Officers

ROHAC, Jan
Thousand Clarinets, A (Co)

ROHMER, Eric
Collectionneuse, La
4 Adventures of Reinette and
   Mirabelle
Full Moon in Paris
Good Marriage, A
Green Ray, The
My Girlfriend's Boyfriend
Paris Vu Par (Ep)
Pauline at the Beach
Tale of Springtime, A

ROLEY, Sutton
Chosen Survivors
How to Steal the World

ROMANEK, Mark
Static

ROMARE, Ingela
Courage to Live

ROMER, Rolf
Hostess

ROMERO, George A.
Night of the Living Dead, The
Monkey Shines

ROMM, Mikhail
Lenin in 1918
Lenin in October

RONAY, Esther
Rapunzel, Let Down Your Hair (Co)

ROPELEWSKI, Tom
Madhouse

ROSE, Les
Title Shot

ROSE, Robina
Jigsaw
Nightshift

ROSEN, Martin
Plague Dogs, The
Watership Down

ROSEN, Phil
Dangerous Corner
Gangs Incorporated
I Killed That Man
Man with Two Lives
Step by Step

ROSENBAUM, Marianne
Peppermint Freedom

ROSENBERG, Max
World of Abbott and Costello (Co)

ROSENBERG, Stuart
April Fools
Brubaker
Drowning Pool, The
Investigation of Murder, An

Love and Bullets
Pope of Greenwich Village, The
Voyage of the Damned
WUSA

ROSENTHAL, Rick
American Dreamer
Bad Boys
Halloween II

ROSHAL, Grigori
Moussorgsky

ROSI, Francesco
Carmen
Christ Stopped at Eboli
Chronicle of a Death Foretold
Hands Over the City
Three Brothers

ROSS, Herbert
California Suite
Dancers
Footloose
Funny Lady
Goodbye Girl, The
Goodbye Mr. Chips
Last of Sheila, The
My Blue Heaven
Owl and the Pussycat, The
Pennies from Heaven
Play It Again Sam
Protocol
Secret of My Success, The
Seven-per-cent Solution, The
Sunshine Boys, The
Turning Point, The

ROSSELLINI, Roberto
Age of Cosimo de Medici, The
Amore, L' (A Human Voice and a
   Miracle)
Augustine of Hippo
Blaise Pascal
Fear
Francis, God's Jester
Germany - Year Zero
Italy: Year One
Machine That Kills, The
Paisa
Prise du Pouvoir par Louis XIV, La
Rome, Open City
Seven Deadly Sins (Ep)
Stromboli
Voyage to Italy

ROSSEN, Robert
All the King's Men
Body and Soul
Hustler, The
Island in the Sun
Lilith

ROSSIF, Frederic
To Die in Madrid

ROSSO, Franco
Babylon
Dread Beat and Blood
Nature of the Beast, The
Sixty Four Day Hero

ROSSON, Richard
Behind the Headlines
Hideaway, The

ROTH, Joe
Coupe de Ville

ROUCH, Jean
Paris Vu Par... (Ep)

ROUSE, Russell
Carnival of Thieves
Fastest Gun Alive, The
House of Numbers
Oscar, The
Thief, The
Thunder in the Sun
Well, The (Co)

ROWAN, David
Tom Phillips

ROWLAND, Roy
Affair With A Stranger
Boys' Ranch
Bugles in the Afternoon
5,000 Fingers of Dr. T, The
Hit the Deck
Killer McCoy
Many Rivers to Cross
Seven Hills of Rome
Slander
Stranger in Town
Viva Las Vegas!

ROZEMA, Patricia
I've Heard the Mermaids Singing

ROZIER, Jacques
Adieu Philippine

RUBBO, Michael
Tommy Trickery and the Stamp
   Traveller
Waiting for Fidel

RUBEN, J. Walter
Ace of Aces
Great Jasper, The
Man of Two Worlds
No Marriage Ties
No Other Woman
Phantom of Crestwood, The
Public Defender, The
Roadhouse Murder, The
Secret Service
Success At Any Price
Where Sinners Meet

RUBEN, Joseph
Sleeping With the Enemy

RUBENS, Percival
Mr. Kingstreet's War

RUDOLPH, Alan
Choose Me
Mortal Thoughts
Remember my Name
Roadie
Trouble in Mind

RUGGLES, Wesley
Are These Our Children?
I'm No Angel
Roar of the Dragon
Street Girl

RUIZ, Raúl
Great Events and Ordinary People
Hypothesis of the Stolen Painting
Penal Colony, The
Suspended Vocation

RUMBELOW, Steven
Faust

RUNZE, Ottokar
Banner, The
Knife in the Back, The
Lord von Barmbeck, Der
Lost Life

Viola and Sebastian (Co)

RUSH, Richard
Freebie and the Bean
Getting Straight
Stunt Man, The

RUSSELL, Chuck
Nightmare on Elm Street 3:
   Dream Warriors

RUSSELL, Ken
Altered States
Aria (Ep)
Billion Dollar Brain
Boy Friend, The
Crimes of Passion
Devils, The
French Dressing
Gothic
Lisztomania
Mahler
Music Lovers, The
Savage Messiah
Tommy
Valentino
Women in Love

RUSSELL, William D.
Best of the Badmen
Bride for Sale

RUTTMANN, Walter J.
Berlin - Symphony of a City

RYAN, Frank
Call Out the Marines (Co)

RYAZANOV, Eldar
Carnival Night, The

RYBKOWSKI, Jan
Peasants

RYCHMAN, Ladislav
Crime in a Girls' School (Co)

RYDELL, Mark
Cinderella Liberty
Cowboys, The
For the Boys
Harry and Walter Go to New York
On Golden Pond
Reivers, The
River, The
Rose, The

RYE, Stellan
Student von Prag, Der (Co)

SADVOSKY, V.
Goal Goal Another Goal

SAGAL, Boris
Antagonists, The
Charge is Murder, The
Crimebusters, The
Girl Happy
Made in Paris
Omega Man, The
Operation Heartbeat
Thousand Plane Raid, The

ST. CLAIR, Mal
Big Noise, The
Bullfighters, The
Dancing Masters, The
Goldie Gets Along
Jitterbugs

SAKS, Gene
Cactus Flower
Odd Couple, The

SALA, Vittorio
Spy in Your Eye

SALE, Richard
Girl Next Door, The
Meet Me After The Show
Ticket to Tomahawk

SALKOW, Sidney
Great Sioux Massacre, The

SALT, Brian
Toto and the Poachers

SALTER, James
Three

SAMPSON, Ed
Fast and Furious (Co)

SAMSONOV, Samson
Journey Through Fire

SANDER, Helke
All-Round Reduced Personality, The

SANDERS, Denis
Elvis That's the Way It Is
One Man's Way

SANDERS-BRAHMS, Helma
Shirin's Wedding

SANDRICH, Jay
Seems Like Old Times

SANDRICH, Mark
Aggie Appleby, Maker of Men
Carefree
Cockeyed Cavaliers
Follow the Fleet
Gay Divorcee, The
Hips, Hips, Hooray!
Shall We Dance?
Top Hat
Woman Rebels, A

SANFORTH, Clifford
Murder by Television

SANG Hu
New Year Sacrifice

SANGSTER, Jimmy
Fear in the Night
Horror of Frankenstein, The
Lust for a Vampire

SANIN, Alexander
Polikushka

SANTELL, Alfred
Breakfast for Two
Having a Wonderful Time
Right to Romance, The

SANTLEY, Joseph
Blonde Cheat
Meet the Missus
She's Got Everything
There Goes the Groom
Walking on Air

SARAFIAN, Richard C.
Fragment of Fear
Gangster Wars
Man in the Wilderness
Man Who Loved Cat Dancing, The

Run Wild, Run Free
Vanishing Point

SARGENT, Joseph
Coast to Coast
Forbin Project, The
Goldengirl
Hell with Heroes, The
Jaws - The Revenge
MacArthur the Rebel General
Nightmares
One Spy Too Many
Spy in the Green Hat, The
Sunshine
Taking of Pelham 123, The
White Lightning

SARNE, Michael
Joanna
Myra Breckinridge

SASDY, Peter
Countess Dracula
Doomwatch
Hands of the Ripper
Nothing But the Night
Taste the Blood of Dracula
Welcome to Blood City

SASLAVSKY, Luis
Way of the Wicked

SAUNDERS, Charles
Hornets' Nest
Man without a Body, The (Co)
Operation Cupid
Strictly Confidential

SAUNDERS, John
'36 to '77 (Co)

SAURA, Carlos
Ay! Carmela
Carmen
Caza, La
Cria Cuervos
Golfos, Los
Love Bewitched, A
Peppermint Frappé

SAVILLE, Philip
Best House in London, The
Fellow Traveller
Oedipus the King

SAVILLE, Victor
Conspirator, The
Iron Duke, The
Kim
Tonight and Every Night

SAYLES, John
Baby It's You
Brother From Another Planet
Lianna
Return of the Secaucus Seven

SAYYAD, Parvis
Mission, The

SCHAEFER, George
Doctors' Wives
Pendulum

SCHAFFNER, Franklin J.
Best Man, The
Boys From Brazil, The
Double Man, The
Island in the Stream
Nicholas and Alexandra
Patton Lust for Glory
Planet of the Apes

Sphinx
Welcome Home
Woman of Summer

SCHATZBERG, Jerry
Honeysuckle Rose
Panic in Needle Park
Scarecrow
Seduction of Joe Tynan, The
Street Smart
Sweet Revenge

SCHEERER, Robert
How to Beat the High Cost of Living
World's Greatest Athlete, The

SCHELLERUP, Henning
Sweet Jesus, Preacher Man

SCHENCK, George
Superbeast

SCHENKEL, Carl
Knight Moves

SCHEPISI, Fred
Barbarosa
Chant of Jimmy Blacksmith, The
Cry in the Dark, A
Plenty
Roxanne
Russia House, The

SCHERTZINGER, Victor
Friends and Lovers
One Night of Love
Strange Justice
Woman Between, The

SCHEUMANN, Gerhard
War of the Mummies (Co)
White Coup, The (Co)

SCHILLER, Greta
Before Stonewall

SCHILLER, Lawrence
American Dreamer (Co)
Executioner's Song, The

SCHILLING, Niklaus
Expelled from Paradise
Nightshade

SCHIRCK, Heinz
Headlines for Murder

SCHLATTER, George
Norman... Is That You?

SCHLESINGER, John
Believers, The
Billy Liar
Black Legend (Co)
Darling
Falcon and the Snowman, The
Far From the Madding Crowd
Honky Tonk Freeway
Kind of Loving, A
Marathon Man
Midnight Cowboy
Pacific Heights
Sunday Bloody Sunday
Visions of Eight (Ep)
Yanks

SCHLONDORFF, Volker
Coup de Grâce, Le
Death of a Salesman
Degree of Murder, A
Handmaid's Tale, The
Kettledrummer, The (Ep)

Lost Honour of Katherina Blum, The
Ruth Halbfass
Strohfeuer
Sudden Fortune of the Poor People
   of Kombach, The
Swann in Love
Young Torless

SCHLOSSBERG, Julian
No Nukes (Co)

SCHMITZ, Oliver
Mapantsula

SCHOEDSACK, Ernest
Blind Adventure
Four Feathers, The
Grass (Co)
King Kong (Co)
Last Days of Pompeii, The
Long Lost Father
Mighty Joe Young
Son of Kong

SCHOLTER, Yvonne
Donna

SCHONFELD, Victor
Animals Film, The (Co)

SCHONGER, Hubert
Little People, The

SCHORM, Ewald
Saddled with Five Girls

SCHOTT, Dale
Care Bears Movie II: A New
   Generation

SCHRADER, Paul
American Gigolo
Blue Collar
Cat People
Comfort of Strangers, The
Hardcore Life, The
Mishima: A Life In Four Chapters

SCHROEDER, Barbet
Reversal of Fortune

SCHROETER, Werner
Death of Maria Malibran

SCHUB, Esther
Fall of the Romanov Dynasty, The

SCHULHOFF, Petr
Fear

SCHULTZ, Carl
Seventh Sign, The
Travelling North

SCHULTZ, Michael
Car Wash
Greased Lightning
Last Dragon, The
Sgt. Pepper's Lonely Hearts Club
   Band

SCHUMACHER, Joel
Cousins
Dying Young
Flatliners
Incredible Shrinking Woman, The
Lost Boys, The
St. Elmo's Fire
Street Fleet

SCHUSTER, Harold
Marine Raiders

So Dear to My Heart

SCHWARZE, Hans Dieter
Abused Love Letters, The
End of a Business Trip, The

SCORER, Mischa
Haunt of Man, The

SCORSESE, Martin
After Hours
Alice Doesn't Live Here Anymore
American Boy: A Profile of Steven
  Prince
Boxcar Bertha
Cape Fear
Color of Money, The
Goodfellas
Last Temptation of Christ, The
Last Waltz, The
New York, New York
New York Stories (Ep)
Raging Bull
Taxi Driver

SCOTT, Cynthia
Company of Strangers, The

SCOTT, James
Chance, History, Art...
Every Picture Tells a Story
'36 to '77 (Co)

SCOTT, Peter Graham
Big Day, The
Breakout
Captain Clegg
Cracksman, The
Father Came Too
Headless Ghost, The
Mister Ten Per Cent
Subterfuge

SCOTT, Ridley
Alien
Black Rain
Blade Runner
Duellists, The
Someone to Watch Over Me
Thelma & Louise

SCOTT, Tony
Beverly Hills Cop II
Days of Thunder
Hunger, The
Last Boy Scout, The
Loving Memory
Top Gun

SEABOURNE, Peter
Escape from the Sea

SEARLE, Francis
Gelignite Gang, The

SEATON, George
Airport
Counterfeit Traitor, The
Country Girl, The
Hook, The
Little Boy Lost
Pleasure of His Company,
  The
Showdown
Teacher's Pet
Thirty Six Hours
What's So Bad About Feeling
  Good?

SEBASTIAN, Fred
Flash and the Firecat

SEDGWICK, Edward
Cameraman, The
Spite Marriage

SEEGER, Peggy
Festival of Fools (Co)

SEGAL, Alex
Joy in the Morning
Ransom, A

SEIDELMAN, Susan
Cookie
Desperately Seeking Susan

SEILER, Lewis
Big Shot, The
Guadalcanal Diary

SEITER, William A.
Allegheny Uprising
Chance at Heaven
Dimples
Diplomaniacs
Fraternally Yours
If I Had a Million (Ep)
In Person
Is My Face Red?
Lady Takes a Chance, A
Life of the Party, The
Peach O' Reno
Professional Sweetheart
Richest Girl in the World, The
Room Service
Sing and Like It
Too Many Cooks
Way Back Home
We're Rich Again
Young Bride
You Were Never Lovelier

SEITZ, Franz
Disorder and Early Suffering

SEITZ, George B.
Andy Hardy's Blonde Trouble
Andy Hardy's Double Life
China Caravan
Midnight Mystery
Wild Horse Mesa

SELANDER, Lesley
Masked Raiders
Mysterious Desperado, The
Pistol Harvest
Raiders
Riders from Tucson
Road Agent

SELLAR, Ian
Venus Peter

SELPIN, Herbert
Titanic (Co)

SELTZER, David
Punchline

SEMBENE, Ousmane
Black Girl
Ceddo
Xala

SEN, Mrinal
Genesis
Outsiders, The

SENFT, Haro
Day With the Wind, A

SEQUENS, Jiri
Windy Mountain

SERIOUS, Yahoo
Young Einstein

SERRADOR, Narciso
House that Screamed, The

SERREAU, Colin
Romuald et Juliette

SEVEN, Johnny
Navajo Run

SEWELL, Vernon
Curse of the Crimson Altar
Ghost Ship
House of the Mystery

SHABAZZ, Menelik
Burning an Illusion
Time and Judgement

SHADE, John
Swap, The

SHAFFER, Deborah
Wobblies, The (Co)

SHAH, Hasan
Rough Cut and Ready Dubbed (Co)

SHAND, Ian
Kadoyng
Mischief

SHANE, Maxwell
Naked Street, The

SHANLEY, John Patrick
Joe Versus the Volcano

SHAPIRO, Ken
Groove Tube, The

SHAPIRO, Owen
Chameleon

SHAPIRO, Sue
Rapunzel, Let Down Your Hair (Co)

SHARALIEV, Borislav
Goodbye Friends

SHARMAN, Jim
Rocky Horror Picture Show, The
Shock Treatment

SHARP, Don
Adventures of Hal 5
Bear Island
Brides of Fu Manchu, The
Callan
Curse of the Fly
Face of Fu Manchu, The
Four Feathers, The
It's All Happening
Jules Verne's Rocket to the Moon
Our Man in Marrakesh
Thirty Nine Steps, The

SHARP, Ian
Music Machine, The
Who Dares Wins

SHARPSTEEN, Ben
Dumbo
Fantasia

SHATNER, William
Star Trek V: The Final Frontier

SHAUGHNESSY, Alfred
6.5 Special

SHAVELSON, Melville
Five Pennies, The
Houseboat
It Started in Naples
Mixed Company
New Kind of Love, A
Yours Mine and Ours

SHAW, Don
Rough Cut and Ready Dubbed (Co)

SHEAR, Barry
Across 110th Street
Billion Dollar Threat
Deadly Trackers
Karate Killers, The

SHELDON, James
Brazen Bell, The
Devil's Children, The

SHELDON, Sidney
Buster Keaton Story, The

SHELTON, Ron
Blaze
White Men Can't Jump

SHEN Chiang
Return of the Dragon

SHENGELAYA, Eldar
Blue Mountains

SHENGELAYA, Georgy
Pirosmani

SHEPARD, Sam
Far North

SHER, Jack
3 Worlds of Gulliver, The

SHERIN, Edwin
Valdez is Coming

SHERIDAN, Jim
Field, The
My Left Foot

SHERMAN, Gary A.
Poltergeist III
Vice Squad

SHERMAN, George
Against All Flags
Bandit of Sherwood Forest, The (Co)
Battle at Apache Pass, The
Big Jake
Count Three and Pray
Daniel Boone - Frontier Trail Rider
Golden Horde
Hell Bent for Leather
Last of the Fast Guns
Treasure of Pancho Villa, The
Vendetta

SHERMAN, Lowell
Bachelor Apartment
High Stakes
Ladies of the Jury
Morning Glory
Royal Bed, The

SHERMAN, Vincent
All Through the Night
Hasty Heart, The
Lone Star
Naked Earth
Pillow to Post
Return of Doctor X, The

SHERWOOD, Bill
Parting Glances

SHIH Hui
Letter with the Feathers

SHINDO, Kaneto
Children of Hiroshima
Kuroneko

SHOLDER, Jack
Renegades

SHONTEFF, Lindsay
Curse of Simba
Devil Doll

SHUI Hua
White Haired Girl (Co)

SHYER, Charles
Baby Boom
Father of the Bride

SIDNEY, George
Anchors Aweigh
Bathing Beauty
Bye Bye Birdie
Cass Timberlane
Eddy Duchin Story, The
Half a Sixpence
Key to the City
Kiss Me Kate
Love in Las Vegas
Pal Joey
Red Danube
Three Musketeers, The
Ticklish Affair, A
Young Bess

SIEGEL, Don
Big Steal, The
Black Windmill, The
Charley Varrick
Coogan's Bluff
Count the Hours
Dirty Harry
Escape from Alcatraz
Flaming Star
Hell is for Heroes
Hound Dog Man
Killers, The
Line Up, The
Madigan
Riot in Cell Block 11
Rough Cut
Shootist, The
Telefon
Two Mules for Sister Sara
Verdict, The

SIGNORELLI, Joe
Easy Money

SILBER, Glen
El Salvador: Another Vietnam (Co)
War at Home, The (Co)

SILBERG, Joel
Breakdance
Rappin'

SILVER, Joan Micklin
Between the Lines
Crossing Delancey
Hester Street
Step Kids

SILVERSTEIN, Elliot
Car, The
Cat Ballou
Man Called Horse, A

SIMMONS, Anthony
Black Joy
On Giant's Shoulders
Optimists of Nine Elms, The
Your Money or Your Wife

SIMON, Frank
Queen, The
Weekend of a Champion

SIMON, S. Sylvan
Mr. Griggs Returns
Abbott and Costello in Hollywood

SINATRA, Frank
None But the Brave

SINCLAIR, Andrew
Breaking of Bumbo, The
Under Milk Wood

SINGLETON, John
Boyz 'N the Hood

SINKEL, Bernhard
Berlinger (Co)
Girl's War, The (Co)

SIODMAK, Robert
Crimson Pirate, The
Cry of the City
Custer of the West
Killers, The
Menschen am Sonntag (Co)
Phantom Lady
Rough and the Smooth, The
Spiral Staircase, The
Suspect, The
Tunnel 28

SIRK, Douglas
All I Desire
All That Heaven Allows
Battle Hymn
Habanera, La
Hitler's Madman
Imitation of Life
Interlude
Magnificent Obsession
Pillars of Society
Schlussakkord
Sign of the Pagan
Sleep My Love
Tarnished Angels, The
Thunder on the Hill
Time to Love and a Time to Die, A
To New Shores
Written on the Wind

SJOBERG, Alf
Frenzy
Miss Julie

SJOMAN, Vilgot
Handful of Love, A
I am Curious - Blue
I am Curious - Yellow
My Sister, My Love
You're Lying

SJOSTROM, Victor
He Who Gets Slapped
Phantom Carriage, The
Scarlet Letter, The

SKALSKY, Stepan
Black Dynasty

SKOLIMOWSKI, Jerzy
Deep End
Depart, Le
Rysopis

Shout, The

SLATE, Lane
Trip to Kill (Co)

SLOANE, Paul
Consolation Marriage
Down to Their Last Yacht
Geronimo
Half Shot at Sunrise
Travelling Husbands

SLOMAN, Edward
Dog of Flanders, A

SMART, Ralph
Bush Christmas

SMIGHT, Jack
Airport '75
Battle of Midway
Damnation Alley
Frankenstein: The True Story
I'd Rather be Rich
Kaleidoscope
Moving Target, The
No Way to Treat a Lady
Secret War of Harry Frigg, The
Strategy of Terror

SMITH, Brian
Man from Hong Kong, The

SMITH, Harry
Heaven and Earth Magic Feature,
The

SMITH, Harry W.
Louisiana Territory

SMITH, John
Shine So Hard (Co)

SMITH, John N.
Sitting in Limbo

SMITH, Mel
Tall Guy, The

SMITH, Peter
Private Enterprise, A
Trouble with 2B
What Next?

SNOAD, Harold
Not Now, Comrade (Co)

SNOW, Michael
Back and Forth (——)
Region Centrale, La

SOBOTA, Miroslav
No Return Ticket (Co)

SODERBERGH, Steven
sex, lies and videotape

SOLAN, Peter
Boxer and Death, The

SOLANAS, Fernando E.
Hour of the Furnaces

SOLAS, Humberto
Lucia

SOLDATI, Mario
Her Favourite Husband

SOLT, Andrew
Imagine John Lennon
This Is Elvis (Co)

SONTAG, Susan
Promised Lands

SPARR, Robert
More Dead than Alive
Swinging Summer, A

SPENCER, Harvey
Aussie Assault

SPENCER, Ronald
'Copter Kids, The
Seal Island
Smokey Joe's Revenge

SPHEERIS, Penelope
Decline of Western Civilization, The
Wayne's World

SPIELBERG, Stephen
Always
Close Encounters of the Third Kind
   (Special Edition)
Color Purple, The
Duel
Empire of the Sun
Hook
Indiana Jones and the Last Crusade
Indiana Jones and the Temple of
   Doom
Jaws
1941
Raiders of the Lost Ark
Sugarland Express
Twilight Zone - The Movie (Ep)

SPOTTISWOODE, Roger
Air America
Best of Times
Deadly Pursuit (Shoot to Kill)
Stop Or My Mom Will Shoot
Terror Train
Under Fire

SPOTTON, John
Memorandum (Co)

SPRINGSTEEN, R.G.
Bullet for a Badman
Showdown
Taggart

SPRY, Robin
One Man

SQUIRE, Anthony
Mr. Selkie

SROUR, Heiny
Leila and the Wolves

STAFFORD, Brendan J.
Men Against the Sun

STAHL, John M.
Imitation of Life
Letter of Introduction
Magnificent Obsession
Only Yesterday
When Tomorrow Comes

STAHL, Ray
Scarlet Spear (Co)

STALLONE, Sylvester
Paradise Alley
Rocky II
Rocky III
Rocky IV
Staying Alive

STANLEY, Paul
Mission Impossible v. The Mob

STARK, Graham
Magnificent 7 Deadly Sins, The

STARRETT, Jack
Cleopatra Jones
Gravy Train, The
Losers, The
Race with the Devil
Strange Vengeance of Rosalie, The

STAUDTE, Wolfgang
Underdog, The
Visit To Alberti

STEANE, Andrew
They Found a Cave

STEIN, Paul L.
Born to Love
Common Law
Poison Pen
Sin Takes a Holiday

STEIN, Peter
Summer Guests

STEINBERG, David
Paternity

STEINHOFF, Hans
Hitlerjunge Quex

STEINMANN, Danny
Friday the 13th - A New Beginning

STEKLY, Karel
Discovery on Fuzzy Hill

STERN, Bert
Jazz on a Summer's Day

STERN, Steven
Devil and Max Devlin, The

STERN, Tom
Trip to Kill (Co)

STERNBERG, Josef von
American Tragedy, An
Blonde Venus
Crime and Punishment
Devil is a Woman, The
Dishonoured
Jet Pilot
Macao
Morocco
Shanghai Express
Thunderbolt

STERNER, Anita
John Everett Millais

STEVENS, George
Alice Adams
Annie Oakley
Bachelor Bait
Damsel in Distress, A
Diary of Anne Frank, The
Gunga Din
I Remember Mama
Kentucky Kernels
Nitwits, The
Only Game in Town, The
Quality Street
Shane
Swing Time
Talk of the Town
Vigil in the Night
Vivacious Lady

STEVENS, Robert
In the Cool of the Day
I Thank a Fool

STEVENSON, Robert
Absent Minded Professor, The
Back Street
Bednobs and Broomsticks
Blackbeard's Ghost
Gnome-mobile, The
Herbie Rides Again
In Search of the Castaways
Island at the Top of the World, The
Jane Eyre
Joan of Paris
Kidnapped
Las Vegas Story, The
Love Bug, The
Mary Poppins
Mickey Mouse Anniversary
  Show (Co)
Misadventures of Merlin Jones, The
Monkey's Uncle, The
My Forbidden Past
Old Yeller
One of Our Dinosaurs Is Missing
Return to Yesterday
Shaggy D.A., The
That Darn' Cat
Walk Softly Stranger
Woman on Pier 13

STEWART, Douglas Day
Thief of Hearts

STEWART, Peter
Gun Code

STEWART, William G.
Father Dear Father

STIGLIANO, Roger
Fun Down There

STILLER, Mauritz
Herr Arnes Pengar
Thomas Graal's Best Film

STILLMAN, Whit
Metropolitan

STOCKL, Ulla
Erika's Passions

STOLOFF, Ben
Don't Turn 'Em Loose
Fight For Your Lady
Radio City Revels
Sea Devils
Super Sleuth
To Beat the Band
Two in the Dark

STONE, Andrew
Cry Terror
Decks Ran Red
Great Waltz, The
Julie
Last Voyage, The
Never Put It in Writing
Password is Courage, The
Ring of Fire
Secret of My Success, The
Song of Norway

STONE, Oliver
JFK
Platoon
Salvador
Talk Radio
Wall Street

STOPPARD, Tom
Rosencrantz & Guildenstern Are
  Dead

STORCH, Wolfgang
Frauen Siedlung

STOUMAN, Louis Clyde
Black Fox, The

STRAUB, Jean-Marie
Chronicle of Anna Magdalena
  Bach, The
Eyes Do Not Want to Close at
  All Times (Co)
Fortini/Cani (Co)
History Lessons (Co)
Not Reconciled
Too Early, Too Late

STRAYER, Frank R.
Murder at Midnight
Vampire Bat, The

STREISAND, Barbra
Prince of Tides
Yentl

STRICK, Joseph
Portrait of the Artist as a Young Man
Savage Eye, The (Co)
Ulysses

STROHEIM, Erich von
Foolish Wives
Greed
Queen Kelly

STROYEVA, Vera
Generation of Conquerors, A
Heart of Russia, The

STUART, Mark
Please Sir

STUART, Mel
If it's Tuesday, This Must Be Belgium
I Love My Wife
One is a Lonely Number

STURGES, John
Backlash
Eagle Has Landed, The
Gunfight at O.K. Corral
Hallelujay Trail, The
Hour of the Gun
Ice Station Zebra
It's a Big Country (Ep)
Joe Kidd
Law and Jake Wade, The
Marooned
McQ
Never So Few
Right Cross
Satan Bug, The
Scarlet Coat, The
Underwater!
Valdez the Halfbreed

STURGES, Preston
Beautiful Blonde from Bashful
  Bend, The
Mad Wednesday
Palm Beach Story, The

STURRIDGE, Charles
Aria (Ep)
Handful of Dust, A
Where Angels Fear to Tread

SUBOTSKY, Milton
World of Abbott and
  Costello (Prod) (Co)

SUCHER, Joel
Free Voice of Labour: The Jewish
  Anarchists (Co)

SUITACEK, Vladimir
Thousand Clarinets, A (Co)

SULLIVAN, Edgar P.
Secret Love Games

SULLIVAN, Fred G.
Cold River

SUMMERS, Jeremy
Crooks in Cloisters
Five Golden Dragons
One Hour to Zero
Petticoat Pirates (Co)
Punch and Judy Man, The
Sammy's Super T-Shirt

SUMMERS, Walter
Battle of the Coronel and
  Falkland Islands, The

SUTHERLAND, Edward
Every Day's a Holiday
Flying Deuces
Having A Wonderful Crime
Mr. Robinson Crusoe
Navy Comes Through, The
Secret of the French Police
Sing Your Worries Away
Sky Devils

SVANKMAJER, Jan
Alice

SWACKHAMER, E.W.
Spiderman

SWAIM, Bob
Balance, La
Masquerade

SWEENEY, Bob
Bristle Face

SWIFT, David
Good Neighbour Sam
Parent Trap, The
Pollyanna
Under the Yum Yum Tree

SYBERBERG, Hans Jurgen
Confessions of Winifred Wagner,
  The
Ludwig: Requiem for a Virgin King

SYDOW, Rolf von
Du Land der Liebe

SYKES, Peter
Committee, The
Demons of the Mind
House in Nightmare Park, The
Steptoe and Son Ride Again
To the Devil a Daughter

SZABO, Istvan
Colonel Redl
Meeting Venus

SZE Tung-San
Sons and Daughter

SZWARC, Jeannot
Bug
Enigma
Jaws 2

Santa Claus - The Movie
Somewhere in Time

TAKAMOTO, Iwao
Charlotte's Web (Co)

TALALEY, Rachel
Freddy's Dead: The Final Nightmare

TANNEN, William
Flashpoint

TANNER, Alain
Jonah Who Will Be 25 in the Year
  2000
Messidor
Salamandre, La

TARKOVSKY, Andrei
Andrei Rublev
Ivan's Childhood
Mirror
Nostalgia
Sacrifice, The
Solaris
Stalker
Steam-Roller & The Violin, The

TASHLIN, Frank
Alphabet Murders, The
Glass Bottom Boat, The
Susan Slept Here
Who's Minding the Store?

TASS, Nadia
Malcolm

TATI, Jacques
Jour de Fête
Mon Oncle
M. Hulot's Holiday
Parade
Playtime

TAUROG, Norman
Adventures of Tom Sawyer
Big City
Birds and the Bees, The
Boys' Town
Bride Goes Wild, The
Bundle of Joy
Caddy, The
California Holiday
Dr. G and the Bikini Machine
Double Trouble
Hold 'Em Jail
If I Had a Million (Ep)
It Happened at the World's Fair
Jumping Jacks
Live a Little, Love a Little
Lucky Boy
Men of Boy's Town
Pardners
Please Believe Me
Sergeant Deadhead
Speedway
Stooge, The
Tickle Me
Toast of New Orleans, The
You're Never Too Young

TAVERNIER, Bertrand
Death Watch
Life and Nothing But
'Round Midnight
Semaine de Vacances, Une
Sunday in the Country
These Foolish Things
Watchmaker of Saint Paul, The

TAVIANI, Paolo and Vittorio
Good Morning Babylon
Night of San Lorenzo, The
Night Sun
Padre Padrone

TAYLOR, Don
Damien Omen II
Dawn Killer
Echoes of a Summer
Escape from the Planet of the
  Apes
Five Man Army, The
Jack of Diamonds
Tom Sawyer

TAYLOR, Judd
Battlefield

TAYLOR, Robert
Heidi's Song

TAYLOR, Sam
Exit Smiling
Nothing But Trouble
Tempest

TCHALENKO, John
Wall of Light

TCHISSOUKOU, Jean-Michel
Chapel, The

TEAGUE, Lewis
Cat's Eye
Cujo
Death Vengeance
Dirty O'Neil - The Love Life of a
  Cop (Co)
Jewel of the Nile, The
Navy Seals

TEMPLE, Julien
Absolute Beginners
Aria (Ep)
Earth Girls Are Easy
Great Rock 'N' Roll Swindle, The

TEMPLETON, George N.
Gift for Heidi

TENNYSON, Pen
Proud Valley, The

TESHIGAHARA, Hiroshi
Summer Soldiers
Woman of the Dunes

TESSARI, Duccio
Better a Widow

TETZLAFF, Ted
Dangerous Profession, A
Fighting Father Dunne
Gambling House
Riff Raff
Son of Sinbad
Time Bomb
White Tower, The
Window, The

TEUBER, Monika
Primel - Kleines Maedchen Zu
  Verleihen

TEWKSBURY, Peter
Doctor, You've Got to be Kidding!
Emil and the Detectives
Stay Away Joe
Sunday in New York
Trouble With Girls, The

THABET, Lofti
That God Should Be on the Side of
  the People is Not Enough (Co)

THEW, Anna
Hilda Was a Goodlooker

THIELE, Rolf
Girl Rosemarie
Kettledrummer, The (Ep)
Tonio Kroger

THOMAS, Anthony
Death of a Princess
Search for Sandra Laing, The
Six Days in Soweto

THOMAS, Gerald
Big Job, The
Bless This House
Carry On Abroad
Carry On Again Doctor
Carry On At Your Convenience
Carry On Behind
Carry On Cabby
Carry On Camping
Carry On Cleo
Carry On Constable
Carry On Cowboy
Carry On Cruising
Carry On Dick
Carry On Doctor
Carry On England
Carry On Emmannuelle
Carry On Girls
Carry On Henry
Carry On Jack
Carry On Loving
Carry On Matron
Carry On Nurse
Carry On Regardless
Carry On Screaming
Carry On Sergeant
Carry On Spying
Carry On Teacher
Carry On up the Jungle
Carry On up the Khyber
Don't Lose Your Head
Duke Wore Jeans, The
Follow that Camel
Iron Maiden, The
Raising the Wind
That's Carry On

THOMAS, Michael
Come Fly With Me II

THOMAS, Ralph
Above Us the Waves
Campbell's Kingdom
Checkpoint
Clouded Yellow
Conspiracy of Hearts
Doctor at Large
Doctor in Clover
Doctor in Distress
Doctor in Love
Doctor in Trouble
High Bright Sun, The
Hot Enough for June
Love Ban, The
Mad About Men
Nobody Runs Forever
No, My Darling Daughter
Pair of Briefs, A
Percy
Percy's Progress
Quest for Love
Some Girls Do
Tale of Two Cities, A
39 Steps, The
Upstairs and Downstairs

Wild and the Willing, The

THOMAS, Ralph L.
Terry Fox Story, The

THOMAS, Robert
Bonne Soupe, La

THOMPSON, J. Lee
Alligator Named Daisy, An
Ambassador, The
Battle for the Planet of the Apes
Cape Fear
Conquest of the Planet of the Apes
Country Dance
Death Wish 4: The Crackdown
Evil that Men Do
Eye of the Devil
Fire Walker
Greek Tycoon, The
Guns of Navarone, The
Huckleberry Finn
Ice Cold in Alex
John Goldfarb, Please Come Home!
King Solomon's Mines
Mackenna's Gold
Most Dangerous Man in the
  World, The
Murphy's Law
No Trees in the Street
Passage, The
Return from the Ashes
St. Ives
Taras Bulba
10 to Midnight
Tiger Bay
Weak and the Wicked, The
What a Way To Go!
White Buffalo, The
Yield to the Night

THORNDIKE, Andrew
German Story, The (Co)
Old New World, The
Russian Miracle (Co)

THORNDIKE, Annelie
German Story, The (Co)
Russian Miracle (Co)

THORPE, Jerry
Company of Killers
Day of the Evil Gun
Venetian Affair, The

THORPE, Richard
All the Brothers Were Valiant
Black Hand, The
Carbine Williams
Challenge to Lassie
Date with Judy, A
Follow the Boys
Honeymoon Machine, The
Horizontal Lieutenant, The
House of the Seven Hawks, The
It's a Big Country (Ep)
Ivanhoe
Knights of the Round Table, The
Man Proof
On an Island With You
Pistolero of Red River, The
Prisoner of Zenda, The
Scorpio Letters, The
Sun Comes Up, The
Tartars, The
Tarzan's Secret Treasure
Ten Thousand Bedrooms
That Funny Feeling
Three Little Words
Twenty Mule Team
Vengeance Valley
White Cargo

THORSEN, Karen
James Baldwin: The Price of a Ticket

TI Chang
Daughters of China (Co)

TILL, Eric
Hot Millions
Improper Channels
Walking Stick, The

TILLMAN, Lynne
Committed (Co)

TIRL, Jiri
Pistol, The

TOBACK, James
Exposed

TOKAR, Norman
Apple Dumpling Gang, The
Big Red
Boatniks, The
Candleshoe
Cat From Outer Space, The
Follow Me Boys
Happiest Millionaire, The
No Deposit No Return
Rascal
Savage Sam
Snowball Express
Suit, The
Those Calloways
Ugly Dachsund, The

TOPPER, Burt
Devil's 8, The

TORNATORE, Giuseppe
Cinema Paradiso
Everybody's Fine

TORS, Ivan
Rhino
Zebra in the Kitchen

TOTTEN, Robert
Wild Country, The

TOURNEUR, Jacques
Appoinment in Honduras
Berlin Express
Cat People
City Under the Sea
Days of Glory
Easy Living
Experiment Perilous
Flame and Arrow, The
Giant of Marathon, The
Great Day in the Morning
Lepoard Man, The
Out of the Past

TOWNE, Robert
Tequila Sunrise

TOYE, Wendy
All for Mary
Raising a Riot
Three Cases of Murder (Ep)
We Joined the Navy

TRAMONT, Jean-Claude
All Night Long

TRAUBERG, Leonid
Cloak, The (Co)
Vyborg Side, The (Co)
Youth of Maxim, The (Co)

TRENCHARD-SMITH, Brian
BMX Bandits

TRENKER, Luis
Knights of the Black Eagle

TRENT, John
Bush Baby

TRESSLER, Georg
Magnificent Rebel, The
Merry Wives of Windsor, The

TREVELYAN, Humphrey
'36 to '77 (Co)

TRIANA, Jorge Ali
Time to Die, A

TRIER, Lars von
Element of Crime

TRINH Minh-Ha
Naked Spaces

TRIVAS, Victor
Head, The

TRNKA, Jiri
Midsummer Night's Dream, A

TROELL, Jan
Emigrants, The
Hurricane
New Land, The

TROTTA, Margarethe von
Friends and Husbands - A
   Labour of Love
German Sisters, The
Rosa Luxemburg
Second Awakening of Christa
   Klages, The
Sisters or the Balance of
   Happiness

TRUENDA, Fernando
Mad Monkey

TRUFFAUT, François
Fahrenheit 451
Femme d'à Côté, La
Jules et Jim
Nuit Américaine, La
Sirène du Mississippi, La
Tirez sur le Pianiste
Wild Child

TRUMAN, Michael
Daylight Robbery
Go to Blazes

TRUMBULL, Douglas
Brainstorm
Silent Running

TRYON, Glenn
Beauty For the Asking
Gridiron Flash
Law West of Tombstone, The
Two in Revolt

TSUCHIMOTO, Noriaki
Minamata

TUCHNER, Michael
Fear is the Key
Likely Lads, The
Trench Coat
Villain
Wilt

TUCHOCK, Wanda
Finishing School (Co)

TUGGLE, Richard
Tightrope

TULLY, Montgomery
Battle Beneath the Earth
Two Wives at One Wedding

TURELL, Saul
Love Goddesses, The (Prod)(Co)

TURNER, Ann
Celia
Point Counterpoint

TURPIE, Jonnie
Out of Order

TUTTLE, Frank
Cry in the Night, A
Hell on Frisco Bay
Island of Lost Women
This Gun for Hire

TYMIENIECKA, Binia
Soviet Art

UDERZO, Alberto
Asterix and Cleopatra (Co)
Asterix the Gaul (Co)

UKAMAU, Group
Banners of the Dawn
Blood of the Condor
Clandestine Nation, The
Get Out of Here
Principal Enemy, The

ULMER, Edgar G.
Beyond the Time Barrier
Black Cat, The
Menschen am Sonntag (Co)

UNDERWOOD, Ron
City Slickers

USTINOV, Peter
Hammersmith is Out
Lady L
Vice Versa

UYS, Jamie
Beautiful People

VADIM, Roger
Barbarella
Pretty Maids all in a Row

VAJDA, Ladislas
Woman with No Name, The

VALDEZ, Luis
Bamba, La

VALERII, Tonino
Reason to Live, A Reason to
   Die, A

VAN AKEREN, Robert
Woman in Flames, A

VANCE, Daniel J.
Trained to Kill

VAN DORMAEL, Jaco
Toto the Hero

VAN DYKE, W.S.
Mala the Magnificent
Marie Antoinette
San Francisco
Stand Up and Fight
Tarzan the Ape Man
Trader Horn

VAN HORN, Buddy
Any Which Way You Can
Dead Pool, The

VAN LIEROP, Robert
People Organised, The

VAN PEEBLES, Mario
New Jack City

VAN SANT, Gus
Drugstore Cowboy
Mala Noche
My Own Private Idaho

VARDA, Agnès
Lions Love
Loin de Viêt-nam (Ep)
Vagabonde

VARNEL, Marcel
Band Waggon
Bell-bottom George
Convict 99
Ghost of St Michael's, The
Let George Do It
Oh, Mr. Porter!
Turned Out Nice Again

VAS, Robert
Orders from Above

VASCONCELLOS, Tete
El Salvador: Another Vietnam (Co)

VASILIEV, Dmitri
Alexander Nevsky (Co)
Secret of Eternal Night

VASILIEV, Sergei
Chapayev
Heroes of Shipka
October Days

VAVRA, Otakar
Against All
First Rescue Party
Krakatit

VEBER, Francis
Three Fugitives

VÉDRÈS, Nicole
Paris 1900

VERBONG, Ben
Girl With the Red Hair

VERHOEVEN, Michael
Bit of Fat, A

VERHOEVEN, Paul
Ewiger Walzer
Heidelberger Romance

VERHOEVEN, Paul
Basic Instinct
Flesh and Blood
Fourth Man, The
Robocop
Survival Run

Total Recall

VERNEUIL, Henri
Guns for San Sebastian
Nightcaller
Sicilian Clan, The
Twenty-Fifth Hour, The

VERTOV, Dziga
Enthusiasm
Man With the Movie Camera
Sixth of the Earth, A
Three Songs of Lenin

VICAS, Victor
Wayward Bus, The

VIDOR, Charles
Cover Girl
Farewell to Arms, A
Gilda
His Family Tree
It's a Big Country (Ep)
Joker is Wild, The
Love Me or Leave Me
Muss 'Em Up
Rhapsody
Song to Remember, A
Song Without End
Strangers All
Tuttles of Tahiti, The

VIDOR, King
Comrade X
Duel in the Sun
Fountainhead, The
Man without a Star
Ruby Gentry
Wine of Youth

VIGNE, Daniel
Return of Martin Guerre, The

VIGO, Jean
A Propos de Nice
Atalante, L'

VILSTRUP, Li
History Book, The (Co)

VIOLA, Al
Mr. Forbush and the Penguins

VISCONTI, Luchino
Damned, The
Death in Venice
Ossessione
Rocco and his Brothers
Senso
White Nights

VITALE, Frank
Montreal Main

VLACIL, Frantisek
Valley of Bees, The

VOGEL, Virgil
Land Unknown
Mole People, The
Sword of Ali Baba, The

VORLICEK, Vaclav
End of an Agent

WACHSMANN, Daniel
Hamsin - Eastern Wind

WADLEIGH, Michael
Wolfen
Woodstock

WAGGNER, George
Drums of the Desert
Wolfman, The

WAJDA, Andrzej
Ashes and Diamonds
Danton
Everything for Sale
Generation
Innocent Sorcerers
Kanal
Land of Promise
Landscape After Battle
Lotna
Love in Germany, A
Man of Iron
Siberian Lady Macbeth
Wedding, The

WALAS, Chris
Fly II, The

WALDRON, Gy
Moonrunners

WALKER, Giles
Last Straw, The
90 Days

WALKER, Hal
Road to Utopia

WALKER, Nancy
Can't Stop the Music

WALKER, Peter
House of Mortal Sin
House of the Long Shadows
Schizo

WALLACE, Richard
Adventure in Baltimore
Bombadier
Bride by Mistake
Fallen Sparrow
Girl, A Guy and a Gob, A
Little Minister, The
Obliging Young Lady
Sinbad the Sailor
Tycoon

WALLACE, Stephen
Blood Oath

WALLACE, Tommy Lee
Fright Night II
Halloween III: Season of the
  Witch

WALSH, Raoul
Blackbeard the Pirate
Distant Drums
Distant Trumpet, A
Gentleman Jim
High Sierra
Hitting a New High
Klondike Annie
Manpower
Naked and the Dead, The
Objective Burma!
O'Rourke of the Royal Mounted
Private's Affair
Pursued
Roaring Twenties, The
Sea Devils, The
Sheriff of Fractured Jaw
Strawberry Blonde
Tall Men, The

They Died With their Boots On
They Drive by Night
Thief of Bagdad, The
What Price Glory
White Heat

WALTERS, Charles
Ask Any Girl
Dangerous When Wet
Don't Go Near the Water
Easter Parade
Glass Slipper, The
High Society
If you Feel Like Singing
Jumbo
Please Don't Eat the Daisies
Spinster, The
Tender Trap, The
Unsinkable Molly Brown, The
Walk Don't Run

WAN Lai-Ming
Uproar in Heaven

WANAMAKER, Sam
Catlow
Executioner, The
File of the Golden Goose, The
Sinbad and the Eye of the Tiger

WANG Pu
White Haired Girl (Co)

WANG, Wayne
Chan is Missing
Dim Sum - A Little Bit of Heart
Eat a Bowl of Tea

WANG Yu
Beach of the War Gods
One-Armed Boxer

WARD, David S.
King Ralph
Major League

WARD, Vincent
Navigator

WARHOL, Andy
Chelsea Girls
Kitchen

WARREN, Charles Marquis
Charro!
Tension at Table Rock

WATERS, John
Hairspray

WATKINS, Peter
Culloden
Privilege
Punishment Park
War Game, The

WATSON, Paul
Block, The (Prod)

WATT, Harry
Fiddlers Three
Overlanders, The
Siege of Pinchgut, The
Target for Tonight
Where No Vultures Fly

WAYNE, John
Green Berets, The (Co)

WEBB, Peter
Give My Regards to Broad Street

WEBB, Robert D.
Glory Brigade, The
Guns of the Timberland
Love Me Tender
Proud Ones, The

WEBER, Lois
Blot, The

WECHTER, David
Midnight Madness (Co)

WEEKS, Stephen
Gawain and the Green Knight
I, Monster
Sword of the Valiant: The Legend of
  Gawain and the Green Giant

WEGENER, Paul
Student von Prag, Der (Co)

WEHAGE, Peter
Mensch Mutter

WEIDENMANN, Alfred
Canaris
Seduction of Julia, The

WEILL, Claudia
Girlfriends

WEIR, Peter
Dead Poet's Society
Gallipoli
Green Card
Last Wave, The
Picnic at Hanging Rock
Plumber, The
Witness
Year of Living Dangerously, The

WEIS, Don
Affairs of Dobie Gillis
Critic's Choice
Did you Hear the One About the
  Travelling Saleslady?
It's a Big Country (Ep)
Just This Once
Looking for Love
Pyjama Party

WEISS, Jiri
Coward, The
New Heroes Will Arise
Play for Life

WELLES, Orson
Chimes at Midnight
Citizen Kane
Immmortal Story, The
Macbeth
Magnificent Ambersons, The
Othello
Stranger, The
Touch of Evil

WELLMAN, William A.
Across the Wide Missouri
Beau Geste
It's a Big Country (Ep)
Magic Town
Nothing Sacred
Pioneer Builders
Public Enemy
Westward the Women
Wings

WENDERS, Wim
Alice in the Cities
American Friend, The
Goalkeeper's Fear of the
  Penalty, The

Hammett
Kings of the Road
Paris, Texas
Wings of Desire

WENDKOS, Paul
Attack on the Iron Coast
Cannon for Cordoba
Gidget Goes Hawaiian
Gidget Goes to Rome
Guns of the Magnificent
 Seven
Hell Boats
Special Delivery

WERKER, Alfred
Gun Point
House of Rothschild, The
Kidnapped
My Pal Wolf
Sealed Cargo

WERNER, Gosta
Victor Sjostrom

WERNER, Peter
No Man's Land

WERTMULLER, Lina
Blood Feud
Night Full of Rain, A
Swept Away

WEST, Roland
Monster, The

WHATHAM, Claude
All Creatures Great and Small
Swallows and Amazons
That'll Be the Day

WHEELER, Anne
Bye Bye Blues
War Story, A

WHELAN, Tim
Bad Man's Territory
Higher and Higher
Seven Days Leave
Step Lively

WHITE, Jules
Sidewalks of New York (Co)

WHORF, Richard
Champagne for Caesar
Hidden Eye, The
Luxury Liner

WHYTE, Michael
Creggan (Co)
Our Business is Fun

WIARD, William
Tom Horn

WICKES, David
Silver Dream Racer
Sweeney

WICKI, Bernhard
Bridge, The
Kettledrummer, The (Ep)
Longest Day, The (Co)
Saboteur Code Name Morituri
Short Weights

WIDERBERG, Bo
Elvira Madigan
Pram, The
Raven's End

WIELAND, Joyce
Raison Avant la Passion, La

WILCOX, Fred M.
Birds and the Bees, The
Forbidden Planet
Master of Lassie
Secret Garden, The

WILCOX, Herbert
Elizabeth of Lady Mead
Irene
Lady is a Square, The
Lady With a Lamp, The
Odette
These Dangerous Years
Trent's Last Case
Wings and the Woman
Yellow Canary, The

WILDE, Cornel
Maracaibo
No Blade of Grass
Shark's Treasure

WILDER, Billy
Apartment, The
Avanti
Double Indemnity
Fedora
Front Page, The
Irma la Douce
Kiss Me Stupid
Lost Weekend, The
Major and the Minor, The
Private Life of Sherlock
 Holmes, The
Sabrina Fair
Seven Year Itch
Some Like It Hot
Witness for the Prosecution

WILDER, Gene
Adventure of Sherlock Holmes'
 Smarter Brother, The
Haunted Honeymoon
Woman In Red
World's Greatest Lover, The

WILDER, W. Lee
Man without a Body, The (Co)

WILDHAGEN, Georg
Marriage of Figaro, The

WILLIAMS, Derek
Hunted in Holland

WILLIAMSON, Judith
Sign is a Fine Investment, A

WILLIS, Jack
Paul Jacobs and the Nuclear
 Gang (Co)

WILSON, Frederick
Camerons, The

WILSON, Hugh
Burglar
Police Academy

WINCER, Simon
D.A.R.Y.L.
Lighthorseman, The
Harley Davidson and the Marlboro
 Man
Phar Lap - Heart of a Nation

WINDUST, Bretaigne
Murder Incorporated

WINER, Lucy
Rate it X (Co)

WINHAM, Francine
Rapunzel, Let Down Your
 Hair (Co)

WINKLER, Irwin
Guilty by Suspicion

WINNER, Michael
Appointment with Death
Big Sleep,The
Chato's Land
Chorus of Disapproval, A
Climb Up the Wall
Death Wish
Death Wish II
Death Wish III
Firepower
Games, The
Hannibal Brooks
I'll Never Forget What's 'is name
Jokers, The
Lawman
Mechanic, The
Nightcomers, The
Play it Cool
Scorpio
Sentinel, The
Stone Killer, The
Won Ton Ton, the Dog Who
 Saved Hollywood

WINSLOW, Susie
All This and World War II

WINSOR, Terry
Party Party

WINSTON, Ron
Don't Just Stand There

WINTER, Donovan
Deadly Females, The

WIONCZEK, Roman
Enigma Secret

WIRTH, Franz Peter
Arme Mann Luther, Der

WISBAR, Frank
Devil Bat's Daughter
Strangler of the Swamp

WISE, Herbert
Julius Caesar
Lovers!

WISE, Robert
Andromeda Strain, The
Audrey Rose
Blood on the Moon
Bodysnatcher, The
Criminal Court
Curse of the Cat People, The (Co)
Day the Earth Stood Still, The
Executive Suite
Haunting, The
Helen of Troy
Hindenburg, The
Lady of Deceit
Mystery in Mexico
Sand Pebbles, The
Set-Up, The
Silent Bell, The
Somebody Up There Likes Me
Sound of Music, The
Star
Star Trek the Motion Picture
This Could Be the Night

Three Secrets
Two for the Seesaw
West Side Story (Co)

WISEMAN, Frederick
Basic Training
Canal Zone
Essene
High School
Hospital
Juvenile Court
Law and Order
Manoeuvre
Meat
Model
Primate
Sinai Field Mission
Welfare

WITNEY, William
Arizona Raiders
I Escaped from Devil's Island
Master of the World

WOHL, Ira
Best Boy

WOLFFHARDT, Rainer
Death Before Dying
Hier Kein Ausgang Nur Ubergang

WOLFSON, P.J.
Boy Slaves

WOLHEIM, Louis
Sin Ship, The

WOLLEN, Peter
Crystal Gazing (Co)
Friendship's Death
Riddles of the Sphinx (Co)

WOLMAN, Dan
Nana

WOOD, Duncan
Bargee, The
Some Will, Some Won't

WOOD, Edward D.
Plan Nine from Outer Space

WOOD, Sam
Command Decision
Day at the Races, A
For Whom the Bell Tolls,
Goodbye Mr. Chips
Heartbeat
Ivy
King's Row
Kitty Foyle
Night at the Opera, A
Stratton Story, The

WOODHEAD, Leslie
Three Days in Szczecin
Year of the Torturer

WOODRUFF, Frank
Cross-Country Romance
Curtain Call
Play Girl
Repent at Leisure
Wildcat Bus

WOODS, Arthur
Radio Parade of 1935

WOOLLEY, Richard
Brothers and Sisters
Illusive Crime
Telling Tales

WORSLEY, Wallace
Hunchback of Notre Dame, The

WORTH, Howard
Raga

WORTH, Jan
Doll's Eye

WREDE, Casper
One Day in the Life of Ivan
  Denisovich
Private Potter
Ransom

WRENN, Trevor
Erotic Inferno

WRIGHT, Ralph
Perri (Co)

WRYE, Donald
Ice Castles

WU Chao-Ti
Girls on Ice

WYBORNY, Klaus
Birth of a Nation

WYETH, Peter
Eugene Atget
12 Views of Kensal House

WYLER, William
Ben Hur
Desperate Hours
Detective Story
Funny Girl
How to Steal a Million
Jezebel

WYNN, Bob
Resurrection of Zachary Wheeler

XIE Yin
Two Stage Sisters

YANAGIMACHI, Mitsuo
Fire Festival

YANCHEV, Vladimir
First Courier, The

YANG Fengliang
Ju Dou (Co)

YARBROUGH, Jean
Devil Bat, The
Humphrey Takes a Chance
Jack and the Beanstalk
Naughty Nineties, The

YARMATOV, Kamil
Soldiers of the Revolution

YATES, Hal
Footlight Varieties

YATES, Peter
Breaking Away
Bullitt
Deep, The
Dresser, The
For Pete's Sake
Friends of Eddie Coyle, The

House on Carroll Street, The
How to Steal a Diamond in 4
  Uneasy Lessons
Janitor, The
John and Mary
Krull
Mother, Jugs and Speed
Murphy's War
One Way Pendulum
Robbery
Summer Holiday
Suspect

YEAWORTH Jr, Irvin S.
Blob, The

YEH Ming
Magic Lotus Lantern, The

YEN, Kung
Two Without Scarves

YORKIN, Bud
Arthur 2: On the Rocks
Divorce American Style
Inspector Clouseau
Never too Late
Start the Revolution Without Me
Thief Who Came to Dinner, The

YOSSELIANI, Otar
Favourites of the Moon

YOUNG, Robert
Vampire Circus
World Is Full of Married Men, The

YOUNG, Robert M.
Ballad of Gregorio Cortez
Rich Kids

YOUNG, Roger
Lassiter

YOUNG, Terence
Amorous Adventures of Moll
  Flanders, The
Cold Sweat
Dr. No
From Russia With Love
Mayerling
Red Beret, The
Red Sun
Sidney Sheldon's Bloodline
They Were Not Divided
Thunderball
Triple Cross
Valley of Eagles
Wait Until Dark

YOUNG, Tony
Port of Escape

YOUNGSON, Robert
Days of Thrills and Laughter
Golden Age of Comedy
Laurel and Hardy's Laughing
  20s
When Comedy Was King

YUAN Muzhi
Street Angel

YUTKEVITCH, Sergei
Man with a Gun
Skanderberg

ZADEK, Peter
Ice Age

ZAGUMMY, Alexander
Without Prejudice

ZAMPI, Mario
Bottoms Up!
Happy Ever After
Laughter in Paradise
Naked Truth, The
Too Many Crooks
Top Secret

ZANUCK, Lili Fini
Rush

ZANUSSI, Krzysztof
Behind the Wall
Camouflage
Catamount Killing, The
Family Life
From a Far Country
Illumination
Night Duty (Co)
Spiral, The
Year of the Quiet Sun, A

ZARKHI, Alex
Member of the Government
  (Co)

ZAVATTINI, Cesare
Amore in Citté (Ep)

ZEBROWSKI, Edward
Night Duty (Co)

ZEFFIRELLI, Franco
Champ, The
Hamlet
Romeo and Juliet
Taming of the Shrew, The
Traviata, La

ZEHETGRUBER, Rudolf
Kafer Auf Extratour, Ein

ZEMAN, Karel
Baron Munchhausen

ZEMECKIS, Robert
Back to the Future
Back to the Future: Part II
Back to the Future: Part III
I Wanna Hold Your Hand
Romancing the Stone
Used Cars
Who Framed Roger Rabbit?

ZEMGANO, I.
Centre Forward (Co)

ZETTERLING, Mai
Visions of Eight (Ep)

ZGURIDI, Alexander
Life in the Arctic

ZHANG Nuanxin
Sacrificed Youth

ZHANG Yimou
Ju Dou (Co)
Raise the Red Lantern
Red Sorghum

ZHILIA, V.
My Daughter

ZHURALEV, V.
Inseparable Friends

ZIDI, Claude
Cop, Le

ZIEFF, Howard
Hollywood Cowboy
House Calls
Main Event, The
My Girl
Private Benjamin
Slither
Unfaithfully Yours

ZIEWER, Christian
Walking Tall

ZINNEMANN, Fred
Act of Violence
Behold a Pale Horse
Day of the Jackal, The
Five Days One Summer
Hatful of Rain, A
Julia
Little Mister Jim
Man For All Seasons, A
Oklahoma!
Sundowners, The

ZINNER, Peter
Salamander, The

ZITO, Joseph
Rosemary's Killer
Invasion USA
Missing In Action

ZUBRYCKI, Tom
Friends and Enemies
Kemira Diary of a Strike

ZUCKER, David
Airplane! (Co)
Naked Gun, The
Naked Gun 2 ½: The Smell of
  Fear, The
Ruthless People (Co)
Top Secret (Co)

ZUCKER, Jerry
Airplane! (Co)
Ghost
Ruthless People (Co)
Top Secret (Co)

ZUNIGA, Frank
Further Adventures of the
  Wilderness Family, The
Golden Seal, The

ZUYLEN, Erik Van
In For Treatment (Co)

ZWEIBACK, Martin
You Can't Have Everything

ZWICK, Edward
About Last Night

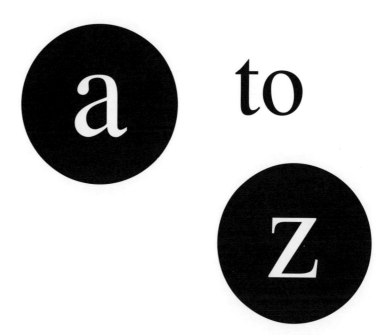

SHORTS

Titles listed in this section run for a total of 49 minutes or less. The content is not restricted to fiction. Unlike the Features Section the titles are listed by Distributor. The reason for this is that the listings are not exhaustive. Titles are listed to demonstrate the nature of the material held by the library. Those distributors without listings have a few words on the material they hold and we recommend contacting them (addresses given at the beginning of the book) in order to receive their own catalogue.

Arts Council
The Arts Council produce and distribute films whose subject matters focus on a variety of Art forms.

BFI Film and Video Distribution
The BFI holds a broad range of material from early silent cinema through to material produced under the BFI Production Board's New Directors scheme.

Canadian High Commission
Canada House distribute films produced in Canada covering both documentary and fiction.

CFL
This library is run by the government's Central Office of Information and holds titles relating to instruction and information on a breadth of topics such as health and industry.

Cinema Action
Cinema Action produce and distribute political titles of Socialist orientation.

Cine Nova
Cine Nova hold a variety of titles which promote and celebrate the role of Women.

Concord Films Council Ltd.
Concord is now the largest 16mm educational film library of its kind in the UK covering documentaries, fiction and animated films on contemporary issues.

Esso
Esso hold titles for educational purposes promoting their research and engineering work.

Filmbank
Filmbank have a vast collection of shorts ranging from UK documentaries all the way through to infamous Hollywood cartoon characters such as Bugs Bunny and Disney Titles. A special range of titles is the Rank Look at Life series. This collection of documentaries can be fascinating to a modern day audience looking back to the period of filming.

Glenbuck
Glenbuck act as a sub-distributor and take bookings for a number of holdings such as Contemporary Film's extensive collection.

Sheila Graber
Sheila Graber distributes her own animated shorts.

Leeds Animation Workshop
Leeds Animation Workshop are a group of women who produce and distribute their own animated films.

London Filmmakers Co-Operative
The Co-Operative produce their own titles but also have an extensive library which includes surrealist and experimental films.

Metro Pictures
Metro Pictures distribute a variety of short films but most focus on politics and are produced internationally by independent film-makers.

The Post Office
The Post Office Library holds classic titles produced under the legendary GPO Film Unit. It continues to house contemporary titles relating to promoting the Post Office's work and philately.

RSPB
The Royal Society for the Protection of Birds hold a number of titles on species of birds and their welfare.

Scottish Central Film Library
The Scottish Central Film Library holds mostly films produced in or relating to Scotland. In addition there are also internationally made titles which have had some form of success in the country.

	COUNTRY OF PRODUCTION	YEAR	DIRECTOR	RUNNING TIME	VERSION	16mm	16mm RENTAL FEE
Alan Bush	GB	1983	Anna Ambrose	64		AC	20.00
Alfred Wallis	GB	1973	Christopher Mason	23		AC	10.00
American: Abstractions Accident (1973)	GB	1973-6	Jules Engel	14		AC	10.00
Shapes & Gestures (1976)							
Train Landscapes (1974-75)							
Wet Paint (1979)							
Anish Kapoor	GB	1984	Geoff Dunlop	14		AC	10.00
Anthony Gross/Hector Hoppin: The Complete Works	GB	1932/36		29	col/bw	AC	15.00
Architecture Of Frank, The	GB	1983	Murray Grigor	15		AC	20.00
Art Of Claude Lorrain, The	GB	1970	Dudley Shaw	25		AC	15.00
Art We Deserve?, The	GB	1979	Jeremy Marre	46		AC	15.00
Avant-Garde of the 20's:							
Le Retour à la Raison	GB	1922	Man Ray	10		AC	15.00
Anaemic Cinema	FR	1926	Marcel Duchamps			AC	15.00
Ballet Mechanique, Le	GB	1924	Fernand Leger/Dudley Murphy			AC	15.00
Barbara Hepworth At The Tate	GB	1968	Bruce Beresford	12		AC	10.00
Basil Bunting	GB	1982	Peter Bell	36		AC	15.00
Being Here And There	GB	1990	Ka Choi	17		AC	10.00
Ben Nicholson	GB	1985	John Read	25		AC	15.00
Bernice Abbot – American Photographer	GB	1989	Erwin Leiser	30		AC	15.00
Bill Woodrow	GB	1984	Geoff Dunlop	17		AC	10.00
Blast	GB	1975	Vorticist Movement	23		AC	10.00
Blue Too	GB	1989	Peter Harvey	35		AC	15.00
Bolden Lad, The	GB	1980	John Tchalenko	35		AC	15.00
Bridget Riley	GB	1979	David Thompson	40		AC	14.00
Bubbles (see Out of the Inkwell)							
Building The Industrial Revolution	GB	1975	Mick Gold	40		AC	15.00
Carved In Ivory	GB	1975	Lord Clark	30		AC	15.00
Case Of Marcel Duchamp, The	GB	1984	David Rowan	98		AC	20.00
Clocks of the Midnight Hours	GB	1989	Simon Reynell	26		AC	15.00
Dance House	GB	1990	Peter Mumford	12x5 2x30		AC	15.00
Dance Umbrella Festival	GB	1988	Klaus Witting			AC	
Dancers	GB	1978	John Chesworth	31		AC	15.00
David Hockney On Modern Art	GB	1981	David Rowan	46		AC	15.00
De Kooning at Work	GB	1980	Erwin Leiser	35		AC	15.00
Dinosaurs In The Playground	GB	1978	Claire Calder-Marshall	38		AC	15.00
Duane Michals (1939-1997)	GB	1978	Ed Howard/Theodore Haimes	14	col/bw	AC	10.00
Edward Allington	GB	1984	Geoff Dunlop	16		AC	10.00
Edward Burra	GB	1973	Peter K. Smith	31		AC	12.00
Edward Hopper	GB	1981	Roll Peck	47		AC	15.00
Egg Dances	GB	1990	Pete Anderson	49		AC	15.00
Elizabeth Maconchy	GB	1985	Margaret Williams	48		AC	15.00
Employing The Image	GB	1989	Amanda Holiday	17		AC	15.00
England, Home and Beauty	GB	1976	Christopher Mason	38		AC	15.00
Eternal Day Of Michel, The	GB	1981	Brothers Quaij & Keith Griffiths	30		AC	15.00
Europe After The Rain	GB	1978	Mick Gold	88		AC	20.00
Exit No Exit	GB	1988	Paminder Vir/Sallie Estep	26		AC	15.00
Eye of the Heart, The	GB	1978	Paintings of Cecil Collins	48		AC	14.00
Fall, The	GB	1990	Darshan Singh Bhuller			AC	
Fathers Of Pop	GB	1979	Julian Cooper	47		AC	15.00
Five Women Painters:	GB	1893-1932	Jane Jackson	5x26		AC	
Carrington: Dora Carrington	GB	1890-1956	Jane Jackson			AC	
Fast and Furious: The Life and Times of Nina	GB	1877-1970	Jane Jackson			AC	
Laura Knight	GB	1893-1981	Jane Jackson			AC	
Flesh And Blood	GB	1990	Margaret Williams	17		AC	10.00
Four Artists	GB	1988	Michael Blackwood	45		AC	15.00
Francis Bacon	GB	1963	David Thompson	11		AC	10.00

	COUNTRY OF PRODUCTION	YEAR	DIRECTOR	RUNNING TIME	VERSION	16mm	16mm RENTAL FEE
Frank Auerbach	GB	1978	Tony Cash	18		AC	10.00
Frankenthaler – Towards a New Climate	GB	1978	Perry Miller Adato	30		AC	15.00
Freefall: Gaby Agis	GB	1988	Bob Bentley	26		AC	15.00
Frida Kahlo & Tina Modotti	GB	1982	Laura Mulvey	30		AC	15.00
Giacometti	GB	1965	Michael Gill	14		AC	10.00
Great Ice Cream Robbery	GB	1971	James Scott (Oldenberg)	35		AC	15.00
Great Noises That Fill the Air	GB	1989	Simon Reynell	26		AC	15.00
Grove Carnival	GB	1981	Henry Martin/Steve Shaw	18		AC	9.00
Hand Of Adam, The	GB	1975	Murray Grigor	33		AC	15.00
Henri Gaudier Brzeska	GB	1968	Arthur Cantrill	30		AC	15.00
Henry Moore and Landscape			Bill Nelson	26		AC	15.00
Henry Moore At The Tate	GB	1970	Walter Lassally	14		AC	10.00
Hogarth	GB	1977	Edward Bennett	25		AC	15.00
Hokusai: An Animated Sketchbook	GB	1978	Tony White	5.5		AC	10.00
How Does It Feel?	GB	1976	Mick Csaky	60		AC	20.00
Howard Hodgkin	GB	1982	Judy Marle	37		AC	15.00
I Build My Time	GB	1976	Kurt Schwitter	30		AC	15.00
Imperial City	GB	1980	David Rowan	45		AC	15.00
Jack B Yeats	GB	1981	Thaddeus O'Sullivan	34		AC	15.00
Jazz Dance	GB	1990	Yossi Bal	34		AC	15.00
Jeff Keen Films	GB	1983	Margaret Williams	32		AC	15.00
John Sell Cotman	GB	19B2	Ann Turner	29		AC	9.00
Joseph Wright of Derby	GB	1990	Catherine Collis	25		AC	15.00
Julian Opie	GB	1984	Geoff Dunlop	19		AC	10.00
Kathe Kollowitz	GB	1981	Ron Orders/Norbert Bunge	44		AC	15.00
Keith Vaughan	GB	1984	John Bulmer	29		AC	15.00
Kinetics: The Record of an Exhibition	GB	1972	Slade School of Fine Art	20		AC	15.00
Kites	GB	1980	Simon Heaven	28		AC	15.00
Landscape From A Dream	GB	1978	Tristram Powell	30		AC	15.00
Lautrec	GB	1974	Geof f Dunbar	7		AC	10.00
Le Bohemian Noir Et Le	GB	1990	V. Amani Naphtali	25		AC	15.00
Lee Krasner – The Long View	GB	197B	Barbara Rose	30		AC	15.00
Lichtenstein In London	GB	1968	Bruce Beresford	20		AC	10.00
Like As The Lute	GB	1979	Brian Eastman	37		AC	15.00
Linear Rhythm	GB	1990	Rosa Fong	24		AC	10.00
Locale	GB	1979	Charles Atlas/Merce Cunningham	30		AC	15.00
Love In A Cold Climate	GB	1990	Kwesi Owusu	33		AC	15.00
Machines for the Suppression of Time	GB	1980	Douglas Lowdnes	40		AC	15.00
Magritte: The False Mirror	GB	1970	David Sylvester	25		AC	15.00
Malevich Suprematism	GB	1970	David Sylvester	9		AC	10.00
Mantegna	GB	1973	Dudley Shaw	14		AC	10.00
Margaret Tait: Film-maker	GB	1983	Margaret Williams	35		AC	15.00
Mary Ellen Bute films: Mood Contrasts Colour Rhapsody	GB	1954-58	U.S. Experimental	11		AC	15.00
Master Photographers:	GB	1982		35		AC	15.00
Alfred Eisenstadt	GB	1982		35		AC	15.00
Bill Brandt	GB	1982		35		AC	15.00
Andreas Feiniger	GB	1982		35		AC	15.00
Jacques-Henri Lartigue	GB	1982		35		AC	15.00
André Keresz	GB	1982		35		AC	15.00
Ansel Adams	GB	1982		35		AC	15.00
Matisse: A Sort of Paradise	GB	1969	Lawrence Gowing/John Jones	30		AC	15.00
Memory Pictures	GB	1989	Pratibha Parmar	25		AC	15.00
Messages from Bhupen Khakhar	GB	1983	Judy Marle	37		AC	15.00
Michael Snow	GB	1982	Keith Griffiths	31		AC	15.00
Monet in London	GB	1974	David Thompson	18		AC	10.00
Moving Stills	GB	1989	Renny Barlett	10x5		AC	10.00
Music in Progress	GB	1978	Charles Mapleston	44		AC	15.00
Nativity, The	GB	1966	Dudley Shaw Ashton	28		AC	15.00

	COUNTRY OF PRODUCTION	YEAR	DIRECTOR	RUNNING TIME	VERSION	16mm	16mm RENTAL FEE
Never Again: DV8 Physical Theatre	GB	1989	Bob Bentley	26		AC	15.00
No Problem (Ken Campbell)	GB	1981	Ian Johnson	30		AC	15.00
Normal Vision: Malcolm LeGrice	GB	1983	Margaret Williams	27		AC	15.00
Odeon Cavalcade	GB	1973	Barry Clayton	35		AC	15.00
One Foot in Eden	GB	1973	Barrie Gavin	49		AC	15.00
One Is A Long Memoried Woman	GB	1990	Frances-Anne Solomon	49		AC	15.00
Our Business Is Fun	GB	1975	Michael Whyte	60		AC	20.00
Painting Chicago	GB	1982	Judy Marle	38		AC	15.00
Pantomine Dame, The	GB	1982	Elizabeth Wood	47		AC	15.00
Part Of The Struggle	GB	1985	Norbert Bunge	36		AC	15.00
Pastorale	GB	1982	David Hutt	42		AC	15.00
Performance Art Film	GB	1975		33		AC	15.00
Phantom Captain Appears	GB	1978	Ian Johnson	42		AC	15.00
Phillip King: Sculptor	GB	1974	Peter Day/Anthony Parker	20		AC	10.00
Photomontage Today	GB	1982	Chris Rodrigues	35		AC	15.00
Picasso the Sculptor	GB	1968	Sir Roland Penrose	27		AC	15.00
Playing the Environment Game	GB	1973	Mick Gold	30		AC	15.00
Polishing Black Diamonds	GB	1989	Susannah Lopez	21		AC	10.00
Pottery Ladies	GB	1985	Jenny Wilkes	4x26		AC	10.00
Poussin	GB	1968	Dudley Shaw	21		AC	10.00
Pre-Raphaelite Revolt, The	GB	1967	David Thompson	30		AC	15.00
Public Places	GB	1982	Howard Silver	17		AC	10.00
Punch and Judy: Tragical Comedy or Comical Tragedy	GB	1980	Keith Griffiths	47		AC	15.00
Rembrandt's Three Crosses	GB	1969	Dudley Shaw Ashton	15		AC	10.00
Return Journey	GB	1981	Ian Potts	45		AC	15.00
Richard Hamilton	GB	1969	James Scott	25		AC	15.00
Robert Motherwell	GB	1978	Michael Blackwood	28		AC	15.00
Rolanda Polonsky Sculptor	GB	1971	Rolanda Polonsky	10		AC	10.00
Rubens and England	GB	1974	Richard Bigham	15		AC	10.00
Rumanian Brancusi	GB	1976	Sean Hudson	26		AC	15.00
Saint Adolf II	GB	1971	Rosebrook Productions	20		AC	15.00
Sam Sherry	GB	1980	John Tchalenko	16		AC	10.00
Sam Smith: Genuine England	GB	1976	Dudley Shaw Ashton	18		AC	10.00
Schiele in Prison	GB	1980	Mick Gold	48		AC	15.00
Secret World Odilon Redon, The	GB	1973	Stephen Cross	30		AC	15.00
Silvershine	GB	1988	Yugesh Walia	26		AC	15.00
Slade Women	GB	1980	Tony Cash	48		AC	15.00
Somewhere Over the Rainbow	GB	1981	Robert Natkin	45		AC	20.00
Spiral Cage, The	GB	1990	Paul Anderson	25		AC	15.00
Steel n' Skin	GB	1979	Steve Shaw	36		AC	15.00
Stones & Flies	GB	1988	Philip Haas	38		AC	15.00
Susan Hiller	GB	1980	Christopher Swayne	17		AC	10.00
Third Front, The	GB	1978	Peter Wyeth	35		AC	15.00
Threading Time	GB	1990	Rashpal Dhaliwal	15		AC	10.00
Tony Cragg	GB	1984	Geoff Dunlop	13		AC	10.00
Turner	GB	1966	David Thompson	28		AC	15.00
Two Falling Too Far	GB	1991	Margaret Williams	17	bw	AC	10.00
Ubu	GB	1978	Goeff Dunbar	20		AC	10.00
Utterance : The Music Of Nusrat Fateh Ali Khan	GB	1990	Pervaiz Khan	22		AC	10.00
Walking Away With The Music	GB	1988	Shafeeq Vellani	30		AC	15.00
Way and Its Power, The	GB	1976	Jeremy Marre	45		AC	15.00
Woodman	GB	1979	Peter Francis	35		AC	15.00
Word Of Mouth	GB	1990	John Gwyn/Tom Pickard	10x25		AC	15.00
World Of Gilbert & George, The	GB	1981	Gilbert & George	69		AC	20.00

Art Eye

	COUNTRY OF PRODUCTION	YEAR	DIRECTOR	RUNNING TIME	VERSION	16mm	16mm RENTAL FEE
Broken Skin	GB	1991	Anna Campion	11		Art Eye	30.00
En Rachachant	FR	1990	Jean-Marie Straub/Daniéle Huillet	10	est	Art Eye	50.00
Every Revolution Is A Throw Of Dice	FR	1977	Jean-Marie Straub	11	est	Art Eye	20.00
Final	FR	1989	Irene Jouannet	14		Art Eye	20.00
I'm Hungry, I'm Cold	FR	1984	Chantel Akerman	12	est	Art Eye	25.00
Introduction To Arnold Schoenberg's Accompaniment To A Cinematographic Scene	W.GER/ IT	1972	Jean-Marie Straub	15	est	Art Eye	20.00
Karin's Face	SWE	1985	Ingmar Bergman	14		Art Eye	25.00
Kinopravda							
No 21	USSR	1925		17	st		25.00
No 22	USSR	1925			st		25.00
Letter To Freddy Buache	FR	1981	Jean-Luc Godard	11	est	Art Eye	25.00
Machorka-Muff	W.GER	1962	Jean-Marie Straub	17	est	Art Eye	20.00
Not Reconciled	W.GER	1965	Jean-Marie Straub	52		Art Eye	35.00
The Bridgroom, The Comedienne & The Pimp	DE	1970	Jean-Marie Straub	23	est	Art Eye	20.00
Zero De Conduite	FR	1990	Jean-Marie Straub	45	est	Art Eye	35.00

BD

	COUNTRY OF PRODUCTION	YEAR	DIRECTOR	RUNNING TIME	VERSION	16mm	16mm RENTAL FEE
Pagoda	GB	1982	Sadek Moghadas	28		BD	15.00
Perfect Mistress, The	GB	1981	Anthony Harrild	60		BD	40.00
Speleogenesis	GB	1980	Sid Perou/Lindsay Dodd	22		BD	20.00
Red Galaxy Films:							
Interzone	GB	1983	Phil Day	23		BD	
Idiot, The	GB	1983	Rob Goldie	15		BD	
Reptile House	GB	1983	Andy Hibbert	24		BD	
End of the Reel	GB	1983	Tony Combes	19		BD	20.00

	COUNTRY OF PRODUCTION	YEAR	DIRECTOR	RUNNING TIME	VERSION	16mm	16mm RENTAL FEE
Adventures of Flutterguy,The	GB	1976	Donald Holwill	20	col	BFI	6
Abel Gance, Yesterday and Tomorrow	FK	1963	Nelly Kaplan	28	eng	BFI	9
Act of God – Lightning	GB	1981	Peter Greenaway	26	col	BFI	15
Advance Democracy	GB	1983	Ralph Bond	18	bw	BFI	8
Adventurer, The	USA	1917	Charles Chaplin	30	st	BFI	9
After Peterloo	GB	1981	Peter Wyeth	28	bw	BFI	15
Ai-Ye (Mankind)	USA	1949	Ian Hugo	24	col	BFI	10
Aldermaston Pottery	GB	1965	M. Darlow/T.Searle	20	bw	BFI	6
Alfalfa	GB	1987	Richard Kwietnowski	9	col	BFI	10
All Aboard	USA	1917	Harold Lloyd	12	bw	BFI	6
Allen Ginsberg and Lawerence Beat	USA	1966	Ferlinghetti Bores in Action	29	bw	BFI	8
Alone with the Monsters	GB	1958	Nazil Nour	20	bw	BFI	30
Alphabet, The	USA	1968	David Lynch	4	col	BFI	8
Alternative Fringe	GB	1991	Candy Guard	3	col	BFI	10
American Tourists	GB	1957	Segment from 'This Week'	5	bw	BFI	6
Amy!	GB	1980	Laura Mulvey/Peter Wollen	34	col	BFI	20
And So To Work	GB	1936	Richard Massingham	19	bw	BFI	6
Animated Genesis	GB	1959	Peter Foldes/Joan Foldes	22	col	BFI	6
Animated Motion (Parts 1-5)	CAN	1976	Norman McLaren/Grant Munro	42	col	BFI	15
Animation for Live Action	GB	1978	Vera Neubauer	25	col/bw	BFI	15.5
Another Fine Mess	USA	193U	Laurel and Hardy	29	bw	BFI	10
Appetit D'Oiseau	FR	1965	Peter Foldes	13	col	BFI	7.5
Architectural Millinery	USA	1954	Sidney Peterson	7	bw	BFI	10
Around Perception	CAN	1969	Pierre Hebert	17	col	BFI	6
Asparagus	USA	1979	Susan Pitt	18	col	BFI	10
At Land	USA	1944	Maya Deren	14	bw	BFI	6
Atomic Dangers	GB	1966	Tim Hewat	25	col	BFI	10
Au Fou!	JAP	1966	Yoji Kuri	9	col	BFI	8
Autumn Spectrum (see Hy Hirsch programme)	USA	1958	Hy Hirsch	11	col	BFI	8
Babylon	GB	1985	Peter Lord/David Sproxton	15	col	BFI	15
Ballad of Reading Gaol, The	GB	1988	Richard Kwietnowski	12	col	BFI	15
Ballad of the Top Hat	HOLL	1936	Max de Haas	30	bw	BFI	8
Banquet	POL	1975	Zofia Oraczewska	10	col	BFI	10
Barney Oldfield's Race for Life	USA	1914	Mack Sennett	15	bw/st	BFI	6
Before and After the Monsoon	GB	1982	Michael Grigsby	35	col	BFI	12.5
Begone Dull Care	CAN	1949	Norman McLaren	8	col	BFI	6
Behind the Screen	USA	1916	Charles Chaplin	30	bw/st	BFI	9
Bells of Atlantis	USA	1952	Ian Hugo	10	col	BFI	6
Bewitched Matches	USA	1913	Emile Cohl	5	bw/st	BFI	6
Big Bill Broonzy	USA	c1940	Four Songs	9	bw/st	BFI	8
Big Business	USA	1929	Laurel and Hardy	20	bw/st	BFI	8
Big Snit,The	CAN	1985	Richard Condie	10	col	BFI	8
Black and White	USSR	1932	Leanid Amalrik/Ivan Ivanov-Vano	8	bw/est	BFI	7.5
Black Mood	GB	1970	World in Action	25	col	BFI	10
Blacktop	USA	1952	Charles and Riay Eames	11	col	BFI	6
Bluebeard's Last Wife	GB	1966	John Stoddard	17	col	BFI	6
Boccioni's Bike	USA	1981	Skip Battaglia	8.5	col	BFI	8
Body Beautiful	GB	1990	Joanna Quinn	6	col	BFI	15
Boggie-Doodle	USA	1940	Norman McLaren	4	col	BFI	6
Bonzoby	GB	1925	George E. Studdy	4	bw/st	BFI	6
Boogie-Doodle	USA	1940	Norman McLaren	4	col	BFI	6
Boot's Beeston Factory	GB	1935	Boots Commercial	6	bw	BFI	6
Breakfast on the Grass	USSR	1988	Pritt Pjarn	25	col/est	BFI	15
Bride and Groom	GB	1956	John Daborn	10	col	BFI	6
Broochpin and the Sinful Clasp	GB	1989	Joanne Woodward	20	col	BFI	25
Cabinet of Doctor Caligari, The	GER	1919	Robert Wiene – EXTRACT	48	sd	BFI	25
Cabinet of Jan Svankmajer, The	GB	1984	Brothers Quay	14	col	BFI	10
Cadet Rousselle	CAN	1947	George Dunning	8	col	BFI	6

	COUNTRY OF PRODUCTION	YEAR	DIRECTOR	RUNNING TIME	VERSION	16mm	16mm RENTAL FEE
Camera Makes Whoopee	GB	1935	Norman McLaren	15	bw/st	BFI	20
Carmen	GER	1933	Lotte Reiniger	10	bw/st	BFI	6
Carnival	GB	1985	Susan Young	8	col	BFI	7.5
Cartier-Bresson	GB	1964	BBC 'Monitor' Segment	12	bw	BFI	6
Certificate of Poverty (October)	SEN	1980	Moussa Bathily	30	col/est	BFI	15
Chalk Mark, The	GB	1989	Bernard Rudden	22	col	BFI	20
Champion, The	USA	1915	Charles Chaplin	30	bw/st	BFI	10
Charge and Countercharge	USA	1968	Emile D'Antonio on McCarthy	43	bw	BFI	15
Chef, The	USA	1919	Harold Lloyd	12	bw/st	BFI	6
Chiefs	USA	1969	Richard Leacock	18	col	BFI	10
Children at School	GB	1937	Basil Wright (prod Grierson)	23	bw	BFI	8
Christmas Play, The	GB	1959	Hazel Swift	23	col	BFI	6
City, The	USA	1939	Ralph Steiner/Willard Van Dyke	44	bw	BFI	10
Class, The	GB	1963	'Monitor' Film by John Schlesinger	46	bw	BFI	10
Coal Face	GB	1935	Alberto Cavalcanti (prod Grierson)	11	bw	BFI	6
Collapse of the Tacoma Narrows Suspension Bridge, The	USA	1940		3	bw/st	BFI	6
Colloque de Chiens	FK	1977	Raul Ruiz	21	col/eng	BFI	10
Colour Box	GB	1935	Len Lye	3.5	col	BFI	6
Colour Capers	GB	1957	Frank Holland	4	col	BFI	6
Comic Story, The	GB	1981	Russell J. Brooke	8	col	BFI	8
Communications Primer	USA	1954	Ray and Charles Eames	22	col	BFI	10
Conquest of the Pole	FR	1912	Georges Méliès	23	bw/st	BFI	8
Coping With Cupid	GB	1991	Viviane Albertine	19	col	BFI	20
County Hospital	USA	1932	Laurel and Hardy	18	bw	BFI	6
Cours du Soir	FR	1967	Nicolas Ribowski	29		BFI	10
Crack of the Whip	GB	1969	World in Action	25	bw	BFI	10
Creature Comforts	GB	1989	Nick Park	5	col	BFI	10
Criminal Tango	FR	1985	Solveig von Kleist	5	col	BFI	8
Cumberland Story, The	GB	1947	Humphrey Jennings	39	bw	BFI	10
Cure, The	USA	1917	Charles Chaplin	30	bw/st	BFI	10
Cybernetic 5.3	USA	1971	John Stehura	7	col	BFI	6
D.G. Phalke 1870-1944, Pioneer of Indian Cinema	IND	1967		20	bw	BFI	6
Dance of the Colours	GER	1938	Hans Fischinger	5	col	BFI	6
Dance Squares	CAN	1962	Rene Jodoin/Trevor Fletcher	4	col	BFI	6
Day in the Life ot a Coalminer, A	GB	1910	Early Documentary	10	bw/st	BFI	6
Daybreak Express	USA	1953	D. A. Pennebaker	6	col	BFI	6
Dear Phone	GB	1977	Peter Greenaway	17	col	BFI	8
Decision, The	GB	1981	Vera Neubauer	33	col	BFI	18
Deckie Learner	GB	1965	Michael Grigsby	40	bw	BFI	10
Degrees of Blindness	GB	1988	Cerith Wyn Evans	19	col	BFI	20
Delivery Man	USA	1982	Emily Hubley	8	col	BFI	12
Delivery Man, The	USA	1982	Emily Hubley	8	col	BFI	12
Demeny Programme 1896, The	FK	1896	Pioneer Film-making	16	bw/st	BFI	6
Demonstration, The	GB	1968	World in Action	25	bw	BFI	10
Desist Film	USA	1959	Stan Brakhage	7	bw	BFI	6
Diana's Hair Ego	USA	1990	Ellen Spiro	29	col	BFI	25
Diary tor Timothy, A	GB	1945	Humphrey Jennings	39	bw	BFI	9
Dim Little Island	GB	1949	Humphrey Jennings	11	bw	BFI	6
Dimensions of Dialogue	CZ	1982	Jan Svankmajer	13	col	BFI	10
Do Detectives Think?	USA	1927	Laurel and Hardy	30	bw/st	BFI	10
Dog and Cat	USSR	1955	L. Atamanov	18	col/est	BFI	8
Don Shayn	CZ	1970	Jan Svankmajer	30	col	BFI	20
Dots and Loops	USA	1940	Norman McLaren	5	col	BFI	6
Double Whoopee	USA	1929	Laurel and Hardy	30	bw/st	BFI	10
Down to the Cellar	CZ	1983	Jan Svankmajer	15	col	BFI	10
Drama Among the Puppets	FR	1908	Emile Cohl	3	bw/st	BFI	6
Drawing That Walk	GB	1938	Comp: Marie Seton/K.H. Frank	34	bw	BFI	10
Drawings That Walk and Talk 1906-1933	GB	1938	Development of Animation	34	bw	BFI	10

	COUNTRY OF PRODUCTION	YEAR	DIRECTOR	RUNNING TIME	VERSION	16mm	16mm RENTAL FEE
Dreamland Express	GB	1982	David Anderson	14	col	BFI	10
Dry Hands	GB	1964	Ian Clark	6		BFI	6
Eames Lounge Chair	USA	1956	Charles and Ray Eames	3	bw	BFI	6
Early Actualities 1899-1905			Early Newsreels	12	bw/st	BFI	6
Early Animation		1903-10		32.5	bw	BFI	15
EARLY ANIMATION COMPILATION *	GB/USA			10	33 mins	BFI	15
Early Bird	GB	1983	Peter Lord/David Sproxton	5	col	BFI	10
Early Disney: Animation 3	USA	1933/4	David Hand/Burton Gillett	29	bw	BFI	8
Early Disney: Animation 2	USA	1931/32	Burton Gillett	29	bw	BFI	8
Early Disney: Animation I	USA	1924/29	Walt Disney	22	bw	BFI	8
Early Edison shorts 1893-1901	USA		Includes First Film Advertising	16	bw/st	BFI	6
Early Sound Films1896-1926	USA			17	bw/st	BFI	10
Early Trick Films 1895-1912	USA			17	bw/st	BFI	6
Easy Street	USA	1917	Charles Chaplin	29	bw/st	BFI	8
Eaux d'artifice	USA	1953	Kenneth Anger	13	col	BFI	20
Eclipse of the Sun Virgin	USA	1967	George Kuchar	12	col	BFI	12
Edwardian Showman's Collection, An	GB		Titles from 1910	17	bw	BFI	6
Edwin S. Porter, The Films of	GB	1903-7	Edwin S. Porter	37	bw	BFI	10
Ein Brudermord	GB	1981	Brothers Quay	5	col	BFI	7.5
Emergence of Eunice	USA	1981	Emily Hubley	6	col	BFI	10
Enough to Eat	GB	1936	Edgar Anstey	20	bw	BFI	6
Entr'acte	FR	1924	René Clair	23	bw/st	BFI	10
Epitaph for a Young Man	GB	1966	Denis Mitchell	25	bw	BFI	10
Eros Ersosion	GB	1990	Anna Thew	42	col	BFI	30
Every Day Except Christmas	GB	1957	Lindsay Anderson	40	bw	BFI	10
Everybody's All Actor, Shakespeare Said	GB	1971	Barney Platts-Mills	28	col	BFI	10
Exploits of Elaine, The	USA	1914	Leonard Wharton	33	st	BFI	9
Fairy of the Phone	GB	1936	William Coldstream/Basil Wright	12	bw	BFI	6
Fall of the House of Usher	USA	1928	Watson/Weber	16	st	BFI	6
Fatty Issues	GB	1990	Candy Guard	5	col	BFI	10
Feet of Song	GB	1989	Erica Russell	5	col	BFI	10
Felix Hollywood	USA	1927	Pat Sullivan	8	bw/st	BFI	6
Felix in Hollywood	USA	1927	Feline Animation	11	st	BFI	6
Felix Makes a Move	USA	1924	Pat Sullivan	7	bw/st	BFI	6
Felix Makes a Movie	USA	1924	More Feline Animation	11	st	BFI	6
Felix Wins and Loses	USA	1926	Pat Sullivan	6	bw/st	BFI	6
Fiddle-De-Dee	CAN	1947	Norman McLaren	4	col	BFI	6
Films of Georges Méliès 1896-1908	FR		Three Different Selections	3x12	st	BFI	6
Finishing Touch, The	USA	1928	Laurel and Hardy	25	st	BFI	9
Fire!	GB	1901	Early Brighton Film-making	6	st	BFI	5
Fireworks	USA	1953	Kenneth Anger	13	col	BFI	20
Fischer Quintuplets, The	USA	1963	Marvin Schlenker/Richard Leacock/Joyce Copra	29/26	bw	BFI	15
Flames of Passion	GB	1989	Richard Kwietnioski	19	bw	BFI	20
Flat, The	CZ	1968	Jan Svankmajer	13	bw	BFI	8
Floating	GB	1991	Richard Heslop	40	col	BFI	30
Four Short Films	GB	1903-7	Edwin S. Porter	20	bw	BFI	10
Frisco Honeymoon Films	USA	1926	Mack Sennett	14	st	BFI	6
From Soup to Nuts	USA	1928	Laurel and Hardy	30	st	BFI	9
Frozen Music	GB	1983	Michael Eaton	23	col	BFI	20
Full Circle	GB	1971	Tim Wood	12	col	BFI	6
Fun Factory, The	USA	1959	Doc on Mac Sennett	25	bw	BFI	9
Gay Shoe Clerk, The (See 4 Short Films)							
Generation Gap	GB	1973	Peter Hickling/Bob Godfrey	10	col	BFI	6
Gentlemen in Room Six, The	USA	1951	Alexander Hammid	11	bw	BFI	6
Georges Méliès	FR	1953	Georges Franju	30	eng	BFI	9
Geti-Tey-Fishing in Senegal	SEN	1980	Samba Felix N'Diaye	41	col	BFI	20
Ghosts Before Breakfast	W.GER	1928	Hans Richter	9	st	BFI	6
Girls Night Out	GB	1987	Joanna Quinn	10	col	BFI	10

	COUNTRY OF PRODUCTION	YEAR	DIRECTOR	RUNNING TIME	VERSION	16mm	16mm RENTAL FEE
Globe of Delights	GB	1971	Deanna Wisbey	13	col	BFI	6
Godard 1980	GB	1980	Interview in English	18	col	BFI	12
Gondola Eye, The	USA	1963	Ian Hugo	16	col	BFI	8
Goodnight Nurse	USA	1929	Lupino Lant	30	st	BFI	6
Grandmother, The	GB	1970	David Lynch	35	col	BFI	20
Great Train Robbery, The	USA	1903	Edwin S. Porter	12	st	BFI	6
Guernica	FR	1950	Alain Resnais/Robert Hessens	12	st	BFI	6
H is for House	GB	1973/78	Peter Greenaway	9	col	BFI	6
Hans Richter Programme	GER	1921/28	Hans Richter	9/12	bw/st	BFI	8
Happy in the Morning	GB	1938	Alberto Cavalcanti	12	bw	BFI	6
Happy Mother's Day, A	USA	1963	Marvin Schlenker/Richard Leacock/Joyce Copra	29/26	bw	BFI	15
Happy Mother's Day, A (See Fischer Quintuplets, The)							
Harlequin	GER	1931	Lotte Reiniger	23	bw	BFI	6
Harmfulness of Tobacco, The	GB	1991	Nick Hamm	28	col	BFI	25
Head Rag Hop	GB	1970	Peter Turner	3	col	BFI	6
Hearts of Age	USA	1934	Orson Welles	5	st	BFI	6
Hell Unlimited	GB	1936	Norman McLaren/Helen Biggar	20	st	BFI	7.5
History of Nothing	GB	1963	Eduardo Paolozzi	14	bw	BFI	6
Hog Wild	USA	1930	Laurel and Hardy	20	bw	BFI	9
Hold Me While I'm Naked	USA	1966	George Kuchar	15	col	BFI	12.5
Hole, The	USA	1962	John Hubley	15	col	BFI	6
Holy Psychic	GB	1989	Phil Hendy	15	col	BFI	30
Hoppity Pop	CAN	1946	Norman McLaren	3	Col	BFI	6
Hor's D'Oeuvre	CAN	1960	Colin Low	8	bw	BFI	6
Hotel des Invalides	FK	1951	Georges Franju	23	est	BFI	6
Hotel E	EST	1991	Pritt Pjarn	28	col	BFI	30
House	USA	1955	Charles and Ray Eames	15	bw	BFI	6
Housing Problems	GB	1935	Edgar Anstey	15	bw	BFI	6
Humerous Phases of Funny Faces	CAN	1906	J. Stuart Blackton	2.5	bw	BFI	3.5
I, An Actress	USA	1977	George Kuchar	9	bw	BFI	10
Ident	GB	1989	Richard Goleszowski	5	col	BFI	10
Images Pour Debussy	FR	1952	Jean Mitry	11	bw	BFI	6
In the Night	W.GER	1931	Walter Ruttman	7	bw	BFI	6
Inauguration of the Pleasure Dome	USA	1954	Kenneth Anger	37	col	BFI	25
Industrial Britain	GB	1931	Robert Flaherty	22	bw	BFI	9
Information Machine, The	USA	1957	Charles and Ray Eames	10	col	BFI	6
Intervals	GB	1969	Peter Greenaway	6	col	BFI	6
Introduction to Feedback	USA	1960	Charles and Ray Eames	11	bw	BFI	6
Invisible City	GB	1991	Mark Jay	18	col	BFI	30
J. S. Bach Fantasia	CZ	1960	Jan Svankmajer	5	bw	BFI	10
Jabberwocky	CZ	1971	Jan Svankmajer	14	col	BFI	10
James Broughton Programme	USA	1951	James Broughton	37	bw	BFI	15
Janacek: Intimate Excursions	GB	1983	Brothers Quay	27	col	BFI	10
Jazz of Lights	USA	1954	Ian Hugo	16	col	BFI	9
Jeff Keen Trilogy	GB	1968	Jeff Keen	10	bw/col	BFI	10
Jeux des Anges	FK	1964	Walerian Borowczyk	12	col	BFI	6
John Gilpin's Ride to York	GB	1908	Cecil Hepworth	6	st	BFI	5
John Grierson at the National Film Theatre	GB	1959	Grierson on British Documentary	13	bw	BFI	6
John Huston: Face to Face	GB	1963	John Freeman Interviews Huston	30	bw	BFI	9
King Coal	SWITZ	1948	Jules Pinschewer	3	col	BFI	6
King's Stamp, The	GB	1935	William Coldstream	20	col	BFI	6
Kiss, The	USA	1896	John Rice	1	st	BFI	6
Kustom Kar Kommandos	USA	1965	Kenneth Anger	3	col	BFI	7
L'ecole des Facteurs	FR	1947	Jacques Tati	15	bw	BFI	10
L'idee	FR	1934	Berthold Bartosch	27	bw	BFI	10
Lady Lazarus	GB	1991	Sandra Lahire	25	bw/col	BFI	30
Lambert and Co	USA	1964	D. A. Pennebaker/Robert Van Dyke	14	bw	BFI	8
Last Trick, The	CZ	1964	Jan Svankmajer	12	col	BFI	10

	COUNTRY OF PRODUCTION	YEAR	DIRECTOR	RUNNING TIME	VERSION	16mm	16mm RENTAL FEE
Late Edition	GB	1983	Peter Lord/David Sproxton	5	col	BFI	10
Leave 'em Laughing	USA	1928	Leo McCarey	30	st	BFI	9
Legend of Bo Diddley	USA	1966	Gary Sherman	16		BFI	6
Len Lye Programme	GB	1933/41	Len Lye	6	bw/col	BFI	6
Leonardo's Diary	CZ	1972	Jan Svankmajer	12	col	BFI	10
Life and Death of 9413 Hollywood Extra, The	USA	1928	Robert Florey/Slavko Vorkapich	15	st	BFI	6
Life and Times of John Huston Esq, The	GB	1967	Robert Graef	45	bw	BFI	10
Life of an American Cowboy, The	USA	1902	Edwin S. Porter	16	st	BFI	12
Lines Horizontal	CAN	1962	Norman McLaren	6	col	BFI	6
Lines Vertical	CAN	1960	Norman McLaren	6	col	BFI	6
Listen to Britain	GB	1942	Humphrey Jennings/Stewart McAllister	20	bw	BFI	10
Little Phantasy on a Nineteenth Century Painting, A	CAN	1946	Norman McLaren	4	bw	BFI	6
Lives of Firecrackers	CAN	1979	Sandy Moore	11	col	BFI	6
London Can Take It	GB	1940	Humphrey Jennings/Harry Watt	10	bw	BFI	6
London to Brighton in Four Minutes	GB	1952	BBC	4		BFI	6
Looking for Langston	GB	1988	Isaac Julien	45		BFI	30
Loony Tom	USA	1951	James Broughton	10		BFI	6
Loop	CAN	1977	Anna Fodorova	10	col	BFI	6
Lotte Eisner in Germany	USA	1980	S. Mark Horowitz	34	eng	BFI	12
Lucifer Rising	USA	1981	Kenneth Anger	28		BFI	35
Lumière Programme 1895	FK	1895	First Public Film Show in Britain	8		BFI	5
Luxo Jr.	USA	1986	John Lasseter/Bill Reeves	2	col	BFI	6
Make Me Psychic	USA	1978	Sally Cruikshank	8	col	BFI	7.5
Manipulation	GB	1991	Daniel Greaves	7	col	BFI	10
Marching the Colours	CAN	1942	Guy Glover	3	col	BFI	6
Marcus Lycinius	IT	1910	Early Italian Spectacular	18	st	BFI	6
Martington Crescent Interantional World Cup	GB	1984	Martin Funnell	5	col	BFI	10
Mascot, The	FR	1933	Ladislas Starevitch	18	bw	BFI	6
Mass	GB	1976	Asa Sjostrom	15	bw	BFI	6
Mathematician, The	GB	1976	Stan Hayward	3.5	col	BFI	3.5
Mathematics Peepshow	USA	1961	Charles & Ray Eames	11	col	BFI	10
Meat	GB	1990	Aleksandra Lech	26		BFI	30
Mediation on Violence	USA	1948	Maya Deren	15	st	BFI	6
Meet Bela Lugosi and Oliver Hardy	USA	1952	Two Short Interviews	8		BFI	6
La Merle	CAN	1958	Norman McLaren	5	col	BFI	6
Meshes of the Afternoon	USA	1943	Maya Deren	13	st	BFI	6
Mick Jagger	GB	1967	TV Clip	25		BFI	9
Militants, The	GB	1967	World in Action	25		BFI	9
Miracle, The	GB	1976	Jack Daniel	13	col	BFI	6
Miss Queencake	GB	1991	Amanda Holiday	24		BFI	30
Models	GB	1964	World in Action	25		BFI	9
Momma Don't Allow	GB	1956	Karel Reisz/Tony Richardson	22		BFI	
Mongreloid, The	USA	1978	George Kuchar	9		BFI	10
Moods of the Sea	USA	1942	Slavko Vorkapich	10		BFI	6
Mor Vran	FR	1931	Jean Epstein	26		BFI	9
More of Harvey Spencer Blair	USA	1960	US TV Comedy Show	27		BFI	9
Mosaic	CAN	1965	Norman McLaren	6	col	BFI	6
Mother's Day	USA	1948	James Broughton	22		BFI	9
Musical Poster	GB	1941	Len Lye	2	col	BFI	7.5
Mutiny Ain't Nice	USA	1938	Dave Fleischer	7	bw	BFI	6
Muybridge Revisited	GB	1987	Michael Snow	5	col	BFI	10
My Baby Just Cares For Me	GB	1987	Peter Lord	3	col	BFI	10
My Childhood	GB	1972	Bill Douglas	46		BFI	25
N or NW	GB	1937	Len Lye	8	bw	BFI	8
Navajo Films	USA	1966	Seven Films by Navajo	9-22		BFI	5-6
Neighbours	CAN	1952	Norman McLaren	8		BFI	6
Never Come Morning	GB	1989	Tim Burke	13	bw	BFI	30
Never Weaken	USA	1921	Harold Lloyd	28	st	BFI	9

	COUNTRY OF PRODUCTION	YEAR	DIRECTOR	RUNNING TIME	VERSION	16mm	16mm RENTAL FEE
New Earth	HOLL	1934	Joris Ivens	23		BFI	9
Next	GB	1989	Barry Purves	5	col	BFI	10
Night on the Bare Mountain	FR	1934	Alexandre Alexeieff/Claire Parker	6	bw	BFI	6
Night Visitors	GB	1989	Richard Ollive	6	col	BFI	15
Nightclub	GB	1983	Jonathan Hodgson	6	col	BFI	8
No Surrender	GB	1969	World in Action	26		BFI	9
Off-On	USA	1968	Scott Bartlett	10		BFI	6
Oh What a Knight	HOLL	1982	Paul Driessen	4	col	BFI	5
On Land at Sea and in the Air	HOLL	1980	Paul Driessen	10	col	BFI	8
On Probation	GB	1983	Peter Lord/David Sproxton	5	col	BFI	10
Once Upon a Time	POL	1957	Jan Lenica/Walerian Borowczyk	9	bw	BFI	6
One of Many	USSR	1927	N. Khodateyev	16	(24 fps)/bw	BFI	8
				21	(18 fps)/bw	BFI	8
Organchik	USSR	1934	N. Khodatayev	21	bw	BFI	8
Origins of the Motion Picture 1889-97	USA	1955	Precursors of theCinema	21		BFI	6
Ossuary, The	CZ	1970	Jan Svankmajer	10	bw/est	BFI	10
Otto Messmer and Felix the Cat	USA	1977	John Canemaker	25	col/bw	BFI	8
Pacific 231	FR	1949	Jean Mitry	10		BFI	6
Pagan Rhapsody	USA	1970	George Kuchar	23		BFI	15
Palmy Days	GB	1983	Peter Lord	5	col	BFI	10
Papageno	GER	1935	Lotte Reiniger	12	bw	BFI	6
Parade, The	USA	1952	Charles & Ray Eames	20	bw	BFI	6
PATHE – Colour Programme	FR	1911-13			col	BFI	8
Pedicure, The	FK	1914	Max Linder	14	st	BFI	6
Pen Point Percussion	CAN	1951	Norman McLaren	12	col	BFI	6
Permutations	USA	1968	Computer Animation	19		BFI	6
Permutations and Experiments in Motion Graphics	CAN	1968	John Whitney	19	col	BFI	8
Peter Sellers	GB	1965	TV Interview	21		BFI	9
Pett and Pott	GB	1934	Alberto Cavalcanti	33		BFI	9
Phantasy, A	CAN	1952	Norman McLaren	8	col	BFI	6
Le Phonographe	CAN	1969	Walerian Borowczyk	6	col	BFI	6
Photographer, The	USA	1947	Willard Van Dyke	27		BFI	9
Pit and the Pendulum and Hope, The	CZ	1983	Jan Svankmajer	15	bw	BFI	12.5
Play of the Waves, The	SWITZ	1955	Jules Pinschewer	5	col	BFI	12.5
Pleasure Garden, The	GB	1953	James Broughton	38		BFI	9
Plow that Broke the Plains, The	USA	1936	Pare Lorentz	28		BFI	9
La Poulette Grise	CAN	1947	Norman McLaren	6	col	BFI	6
Private Life of a Cat, The	USA	1948	Alexander Hammid	23		BFI	5.5
Private Life of Oliver VIII, The	USA	1934	Laurel and Hardy	28		BFI	9
Private Secretary	USA	1956	US TV Playlet	28		BFI	6
Public Voice	DE	1989	Leif Marcusson	11		BFI	15
Puce Moment	USA	1949	Kenneth Anger	6		BFI	12
Pullman Bride, The	USA	1916	Mack Sennett	26	st	BFI	6
Punch and Judy (The Lychgate)	CZ	1966	Jan Svankmajer	10	col	BFI	10
Putting on the Ritz	GB	1974	Antoinette Starkiewicz	4	col	BFI	6
Quartet	USSR	1947	Alexander Ivanov	10	col/est	BFI	7.5
Quasi at the Quadkadero	USA	1975	Sally Cruikshank	10	col	BFI	6
Quiet Week in the House, A	CZ	1969	Jan Svankmajer	10	col/eng	BFI	10
Rabbit's Moon	USA	1956	Kenneth Anger	16		BFI	10
Rain	HOLL	1929	Joris Ivens	19	st	BFI	6
Rapid Eye Movements	USA	1977	Jeff Carpenter	13	col	BFI	10
Rauschenberg	USA	1966	US Artist in Mid-Career	30		BFI	6
Reason to Live, A	USA	1976	George Kuchar	26	bw	BFI	20
Red Skelton Show, The	USA	1960	O. Henry Adaptation	27		BFI	6
Remembering Winsor McCay	USA	1976	John Canemaker	20	col	BFI	10
Rescued by Rover	GB	1905	Cecil Hepworth	8	st	BFI	5
Rhythmus 21	W.GER	1921	Hans Richter	3	st	BFI	5
Ritual in Transfigured Time	USA	1946	Maya Deren	16	st	BFI	6

	COUNTRY OF PRODUCTION	YEAR	DIRECTOR	RUNNING TIME	VERSION	16mm	16mm RENTAL FEE
River, The	USA	1938	Pare Lorentz	30		BFI	9
Roadways	GB	1937	Stuart Legg/William Coldstream	16		BFI	6
Robert Breer Programme	USA	1956/58	Robert Breer	15	col	BFI	7.5
Rope Dancer	W.GER	1986	Raimund Krumme	10	col	BFI	10
Rosalie	FR	1966	Walerian Borowczyk	15	bw	BFI	6
Rosebud	GB	1991	Cheryl Farthing	14		BFI	30
Rythmetic	CAN	1956	Norman McLaren	9	col	BFI	6
Sales Pitch	CAN	1983	Peter Lord/David Sproxton	5	col	BFI	10
Sally Cruikshank Programme	USA	1971-80	Sally Cruikshank	14	col	BFI	8
Salvation Guaranteed	GB	1989	Karen Ingham	21	col	BFI	30
Sang des Bêtes, Le	FR	1949	Georges Franju	20		BFI	9
Saving of Bill Blewitt, The	GB	1936	Harry Watt	25		BFI	9
Scorpio Rising	USA	1963	Kenneth Anger	28		BFI	30
Seashell and the Clergyman, The	FR	1928	Germaine Dulac	44	st	BFI	12
Second Class Mail	GB	1984	Michael Snow	4	col	BFI	7.5
See it Now	USA	1954		38		BFI	9
Selection of Early Films 1895-1913				45	st	BFI	8
Serenal	CAN	1959	Norman McLaren	4	col	BFI	6
Serpent, The	USA	1971	Scott Bartlett	15		BFI	6
Seven Up	GB	1964	Michael Apted	40		BFI	12
Short and Suite	CAN	1959	Norman McLaren	4	col	BFI	6
Short Fuse	USA	1991	Warren Sonbert	37	col	BFI	30
Short Vision, A	GB	1956	Joan & Peter Foldes	6	col	BFI	6
Sigmund Freud's Dora	USA	1979		38		BFI	16.5
Silvikrin Ballet	GB	1954	Dopey Shampoo Ad	3		BFI	5
Skating Rink, The	USSR	1927	N.D. Bartram/Yuri Zhelyabuzhsky	6	(24 fps)/bw	BFI	6
				8	(18 fps)/bw	BFI	6
Skullduggery	USA	1962	Stan Van Der Beek	5		BFI	5
Skyscraper	USA	1958	Willard Van Dyke/Shirley Clarke	20		BFI	9
Sleeping Beauty	FR	1934	Alexandre Alexeieff	4	col	BFI	6
Soigne Ton Gauche	FR	1936	Rene Clement	12	bw	BFI	10
Song of Ceylon	GB	1935	Basil Wright	40		BFI	12
Song of the People	GB	1945	Maxwell Munden	30		BFI	9
Song of the Prairies	CZ	1949	Jiri Trnka	21	col	BFI	8
South Sea Sweetheart	GB	1938	George Pal	8	col	BFI	6
Spare Time	GB	1939	Humphrey Jennings	18		BFI	6
Spotting a Cow	HOLL	1983	Paul Driessen	7	col/eng	BFI	8
St Louis Blues	USA	1929	Bessie Smith	16		BFI	6
Stain, The	GB	1991	Marjut Rimminen/Christine Roche	11	col	BFI	10
Stars and Stripes	USA	1939	Norman McLaren	3	col	BFI	6
Stills	DE	1979	Leif Marcusson	10	col	BFI	10
Story of a Writer	USA	1964	US TV Doc on Ray Bradbury	24		BFI	9
Stravinsky – the Paris Years	GB	1983	Brothers Quay	27	col	BFI	10
Street of Crocodiles	GB	1986	Brothers Quay	20	bw/col	BFI	15
Sunday in September	GB	1961	World in Action	25		BFI	9
Surface Tension	GB	1986	Simon Pummell	25	col	BFI	10
Tale of Tales	CAN	1980	Yuri Norstein	29	col/est	BFI	20
TANGO	POL	1983	Zbigniew Rybczynski	10	col	BFI	8
Teddy at the Throttle	USA	1916	Mack Sennett	27	st	BFI	6
Television Commercials	Gli	1962	Lux, Scotties, Duhonnet, Guards	4		BFI	5
They Travel by Air	GB	1948	Richard Massingham	18		BFI	6
Thicker Than Water	USA	1935	Laurel and Hardy	20		BFI	6
Third Avenue E1	USA	1956		11		BFI	5
Thirteen Cantos of Hell	GB	1955	Peter King	17	bw	BFI	6
This Little Broom	CAN	1985	Brothers Quay	11	col	BFI	10
Three Knights, The	GB	1982	Mark Baker	12	col	BFI	8
Through the Magiscope	USA	1969	Ian Hugo	10		BFI	6
Thursday's Children	GB	1954	Lindsay Anderson/Guy Breton	22		BFI	5

BFI

	COUNTRY OF PRODUCTION	YEAR	DIRECTOR	RUNNING TIME	VERSION	16mm	16mm RENTAL FEE
Time Is	GB	1964	Don Levy	30		BFI	9
Today and Tomorrow	GB	1937	Ralph Bond/Ruby Grierson	19		BFI	6
Today We Live	GB	1937	Ralph Bond/Ruby Grierson	24		BFI	7.5
Tonespor	DE	1983	Leif Marcusson	8	col	BFI	10
Towed in a Hole	USA	1933	George Marshall	20		BFI	6
Town, The	USA	1943	Josef von Sternberg	11		BFI	6
Toxic	GB	1990	Andrew McEwan	9	col	BFI	15
Trade Tattoo	GB	1936	Len Lye	5		BFI	5
Trick Films	FR	1904			bw/col	BFI	
Twice a Man	USA	1963	Gregory Markopoulos	40		BFI	15
Two Bag	CAN	1952	Norman McLaren	3	bw	BFI	6
Universe	CAN	1960	Roman Kroitor/Colin Low	28	bw	BFI	10
Unusual Match, An	USSR	1955	M. Paschenko	20	col/est	BFI	10
UPA Commercials	USA	1957	TV Ads by UPA	11		BFI	5
Valley Town	USA	1940	Willard Van Dyke	28		BFI	9
Van Gogh	FR	1948	Alain Kesnais	16		BFI	6
Vertical Features Remake	GB	1978	Peter Greenaway	45		BFI	22
Virile Games	CZ	1988	Jan Svankmajer	14	col	BFI	15
Wadi	IS	1981	Amos Gitai	45	est	BFI	20
Walk Through H, A	GB	1978	Peter Greenaway	41		BFI	20
Walker, The	GB	1973	Stephen Weatherill	8	col	BFI	6
Wavelength	USA	1967	Michael Snow	45		BFI	30
Weak and Wide Astray	GB	1991	Tom Paine	19	col	BFI	30
What Ho! She Bumps	GB	1937	George Pal	8	col	BFI	6
Why Man Creates	USA	1968	Saul Bass	25	col	BFI	8
Wild Night In El Reno	USA	1977	George Kuchar	6		BFI	10
Window on Canada: Norman McLaren's Subjects	CAN	1959		30	bw	BFI	8
Windows	CAN	1972	John Gibbons	4	bw	BFI	5
Wishful Thinking	GB	1990	Candy Guard	5		BFI	
Yantra	USA	1960	James Whitney	8	col	BFI	6
You Be Mother	GB	1990	Sarah Pucill	7	bw	BFI	10
Zygosis	GB	1990	Gavin Hodge	27	col	BFI	30

CA

Title	Country of Production	Year	Director	Running Time	Version	16mm	16mm Rental Fee
Arise Ye Workers	GB	1973	cinema action	25		CA	20
Fighting the Bill	GB	1970	cinema action	35		CA	15
Hands off Student Unions	GB	1972	cinema action	33		CA	20
Miners Film, The	GB	1974/5	cinema action	49		CA	20
Not a Penny on the Rent	GB	1968	cinema action	22		CA	20
Season's Change, The	GB	1968	cinema action	42		CA	20
Squatters	GB	1969	cinema action	18		CA	20
UCS 1	GB	1971	cinema action	23		CA	20

CHC

Title	Country of Production	Year	Director	Running Time	Version	16mm	16mm Rental Fee
Alouette	CAN	1944	Norman McLaren	3	bw	CHC	Free
Animated Motion Frame By Frame (5 Parts)	CAN	1976-78	Norman McLaren	42		CHC	Free
Around is Around	CAN	1959	Norman McLaren	10		CHC	Free
Ballet Adagio	CAN	1971	Norman McLaren	10		CHC	Free
C'est L'aviron	CAN	1944	Norman McLaren	3	bw	CHC	Free
Camera Makes Whoopee	CAN	1935	Norman McLaren	15		CHC	Free
Chairy Tale, A	CAN	1957	Norman McLaren	10	bw	CHC	Free
Dollar Dance	CAN	1943	Norman McLaren	5.5		CHC	Free
Dots	CAN	1949	Norman McLaren	2.5		CHC	Free
Fiddle de Dee	CAN	1947	Norman McLaren	3.5		CHC	Free

	COUNTRY OF PRODUCTION	YEAR	DIRECTOR	RUNNING TIME	VERSION	16mm	16mm RENTAL FEE
After the Game	USA	1979	Donna Grey	19		CN	20.00
And What Does Your Mother Do? (Y Su Mama Que Hace?)	COL	1981	Cine-Mujer	10		CN	20.00
Animation for Live Action	GB	1978	Vera Neubauer	25		CN	25.00
Apartments	AUSTR	1977	Megan McMurchy	10		CN	20.00
Arranged Marriage, The	GB	1986	Jazvinder Phull	5		CN	15.00
Arrows	GB	1984	Sandra Lahire	15		CN	20.00
Back Inside Herself	USA	1984	Saundra Sharp	4.5	bw	CN	20.00
Binding Love	GB	1985	Karen Ingham	29	bw	CN	25.00
Bread And Dripping	AUSTR	1982	Women's Film Collective	20		CN	20.00
Can't You Take a Joke?	AUSTR	1989	Viki Dun	26	bw	CN	25.00
Carmen Carrascal	COL	1982	Cine-Mujer	30		CN	25.00
Choosing Children	USA	1984	Debra Chasnoff	45		CN	35.00
Clotheslines	USA	1982	Roberta Cantow	33		CN	25.00
Coalmining Women	USA	1982	Elizabeth Barrett	40		CN	25.00
Cold Draft, A	GB	1989	Lis Rhodes	30		CN	25.00
Comedy in Six Unnatural Parts	USA	1975	Jan Oxenburg	25		CN	25.00
Daniella & Nicole	GB	1984	El Glinoer	26		CN	20.00
Death of A Father – A Conspiracy of Silence, The	GB	1986	Jane Harris	29		CN	25.00
Edge	GB	1986	Sandra Lahire	7		CN	10.00
Epic Poem, An	GB	1982	Lezli-Ann Barrett	30		CN	25.00
First Communion	GB	1986	Martine Thoquenne	13		CN	20.00
Focii	GB	1975	Jeanette Iljon	6	st	CN	15.00
For Good	GB	1979	Christine Booth	45		CN	10.00
Four Women	USA	1978	Julie Dash	7		CN	20.00
Free Show	GB	1979	Jayne Parker	16	bw	CN	15.00
G	GB	1979	Susan Stein	6	bw	CN	10.00
Gently Down The Stream	USA	1981	Su Friedrich	14	st/bw	CN	20.00
Goose Or Common	GB	1985	Lis Rhodes	1		CN	5.00
Greenham Granny	GB	1986	Caroline Goldie	42		CN	25.00
Hairpiece: A Film For Nappy Headed People	USA	1982	Ayoka Chenzira	10		CN	20.00
Hands Off (Blijk van m'n Lijf)	NETH	1984	Monique Renault	18	est	CN	20.00
Hey Mack	GB	1982	Tina Keane	15		CN	15.00
Hidden Wisdom	GB	1988	Patricia Diaz	11	bw	CN	20.00
Home Movie	USA	1975	Jan Oxenburg	12		CN	20.00
Homes For The People	GB	1945	Kay Mander	30	bw	CN	20.00
House Divided, A	USA	1913	Alice Guy	13	st/bw	CN	20.00
I Cat	GB	1980	Jayne Parker	10		CN	15.00
I Dish	GB	1982	Jayne Parker	16		CN	15.00
I Substitute	GB	1985	Harriet McKern	13		CN	15.00
I'm In Heaven	GB	1989	Jill Daniels	28		CN	20.00
I'm Not A Feminist, But...	GB	1985/6	Marjut Rimminen	7		CN	15.00
Illusions	GB	1982	Julie Dash	34	bw	CN	25.00
In Lands Where Serpents Speak	GB	1986	Janni Perton	13		CN	20.00
In Nomine Domine (In the Name of the Lord)	NETH	1982	Monique Renault/Vruchtboom	4	est	CN	10.00
Inside Job	GB	1984	Maya Brandt	6		CN	15.00
Intrusions	GB	1976	Caroline Sheldon	32		CN	20.00
Ironing	USA	1979	Lynne Conroy	15		CN	15.00
Ironing To Greenham	GB	1985	Lis Rhodes/Joanna Davis	1		CN	5.00
Judgement Day	GB	1989	Victoria Mapplebeck	12	bw	CN	15.00
Keeper of Accounts	GB	1987	Lily Markiewicz	14	sep/mag	CN	15.00
Killing Us Softly – Advertising's Image Of Women	USA	1979	Jean Kilbourne	30		CN	30.00
Light Reading	GB	1978	Lis Rhodes	20	bw	CN	25.00
Lucy	GER	1984	Verena Rudolph	47	bw	CN	25.00
Made In China	USA	1985	Lisa Hsia	30		CN	25.00
Maidens	AUSTR	1978	Jeni Thornley	33		CN	20.00
Mantra	GB	1976	Jeanette Iljon	5	bw	CN	10.00
Mark Of Lilith, The	GB	1986	Bruna Fionda	32		CN	25.00
Meditation on Violence	USA	1945	Maya Deren	13	bw	CN	15.00

	COUNTRY OF PRODUCTION	YEAR	DIRECTOR	RUNNING TIME	VERSION	16mm	16mm RENTAL FEE
CN							
Meshes Of the Afternoon	USA	1943	Maya Deren	14	bw	CN	25.00
Much Madness	GB	1985	Lis Rhodes/Joanna Davis	1		CN	5.00
Mum's The Word	AUSTR	1982	Carole Kostanich	23		CN	20.00
Mysteries	GB	1982	Judith Higginbottom	6		CN	10.00
Nice Coloured Girls	AUSTR	1987	Tracy Moffatt	18		CN	25.00
No.8 Bus	GB	1985	Lis Rhodes/Joanna Davis	1		CN	5.00
Now	USA	1976	Babette Mangolte	10		CN	10.00
Often During the Day	GB	1979	Joanna Davis	16		CN	25.00
Pecking Order, The	GB	1989	Vicky Smith	5		CN	15.00
Petal for a Paragraph	GB	1985	Lis Rhodes/Joanna Davis	1		CN	5.00
Photographic Exhibits		1984	Clair Barwell	20		CN	20.00
Pictures On Pink Paper	GB	1982	Lis Rhodes	35		CN	25.00
Pink Patterns	GB	1985	Lis Rhodes/Joanna Davis/4 Corners	1		CN	5.00
Plutonium Blonde	GB	1987	Sandra Lahire	15		CN	25.00
Pornography	GB	1985	Lis Rhodes/Joanna Davis	1		CN	5.00
Positions Of Power	GB	1983	Jacky Garstin/Delyse Hawkins	35		CN	20.00
Rabbit On The Moon	AUSTR	1987	Monica Pellizzari	13	est	CN	25.00
Rape Culture	USA	1983	M Lazarus/R Wunderlich	35		CN	25.00
Reassemblage	USA	1982	Trinh Minh-ha	40		CN	45.00
Red Skirts on Clydeside	GB	1983	Sheffield Film Co-op	40		CN	25.00
Ritual in Transfigured Time	USA	1946	Maya Deren	14	bw	CN	15.00
Rituals Of Memory	GB	1977	Pat Murphy	15	bw	CN	20.00
Rootless Cosmopolitans	GB	1990	Ruth Novaczek	20		CN	25.00
Seashell And The Clergyman (La Coquille et le Clergymanman), The	FR	1927	Germaine Dulac	30	bw/st	CN	25.00
Separate Skin	USA	1987	Dierdre Fishel	26		CN	20.00
Serious Undertakings	AUSTR	1983	Helen Grace/Erika Addis	28		CN	25.00
Serpent River	GB	1989	Sandra Lahire	30		CN	30.00
17 Rooms (Or What Lesbians Do In Bed)	GB	1985	Caroline Sheldon	10		CN	20.00
Shadow Of A Journey	GB	1980	Tina Keane	20		CN	20.00
Shadow Panic	AUSTR	1989	Margot Nash	25		CN	25.00
She Said	GB	1982	Susan Stein	30		CN	20.00
Shubh-Vivah		1984	Nina Sabnani	5		CN	15.00
Smiling Madame Beudet (La Sourianr Mme Beudet), The	FR	1922	Germaine Dulac	35	st/bw	CN	25.00
Song Of Air, A	AUSTR	1987	Merilee Bennett	26		CN	25.00
Suspense	USA	1913	Lois Weber	13	st/bw	CN	20.00
Swing Song	GB	1985	Lis Rhodes/Joanna Davis	1		CN	5.00
Terminals	GB	1986	Sandra Lahire	15		CN	20.00
That's Entertainment/TheConjuror's Assistant	GB	1979	Jeanette Iljon	35	bw	CN	15.00
The Dancing Silhouttes	GB	1983	Felicity Field	27		CN	30.00
The Decision	GB	1981	Vera Neubauer	33		CN	25.00
There? Where?	USA	1979	Babette Mangolte	9		CN	10.00
Three Short Episodes	GB	1980	Rachel Finkelstein	10		CN	10.00
Tiger Lily	GB	1985	Lis Rhodes/Joanna Davis	1		CN	5.00
Tiger's Milk — Women of Nicaragua, The	GB	1987	Fiona Macintosh/4 Corners	30		CN	25.00
To Be a Woman	GB	1951	Jill Craigie	18	bw	CN	20.00
To Be Silent Is The Most Painful Part	GB	1985	Cheryl Edwards	6		CN	15.00
To Grips with the Grit	GB	1984-85	El Glinoer	20	bw	CN	20.00
Uranuim Hex	GB	1987	Sandra Lahire	11		CN	15.00
Waking Up to Rape	USA	1985	Meri Weingarten	35		CN	25.00
Watch That Lift!	GB	1986	Martine Lumbroso	13		CN	15.00
White Room, The	GB	1983	El Glinoer	20	bw	CN	20.00
White Words	GB	1985	Lis Rhodes/Joanna Davis	1		CN	5.00
Windscale	GB	1985	Lis Rhodes/Joanna Davis	1		CN	5.00
Wish You Were Here (The Dog Beneath the Skin)	GB	1976	Jeanette Iljon	6	st	CN	5.00
Women of the Rhondda	GB	1972	Esther Ronay	20		CN	25.00
Words And Wealth	GB	1985	Lis Rhodes/Joanna Davis	1		CN	5.00
Wrestling	GB	1980	Gabrielle Brown	20		CN	20.00

Films on Offer

	COUNTRY OF PRODUCTION	YEAR	DIRECTOR	RUNNING TIME	VERSION	16mm	16mm RENTAL FEE
'A'	POL	1966	Jan Lenica	9		GB	5
Abbott & Costello Shorts	USA			20		GB	15
Abyss	FR	1974	Gilbert Dassonville	17		GB	7.50
Acropolis of Athens	GR	1961	Robert Manthoulis	20		GB	7.50
Acupuncture Anaesthesia	CHI	1972	Shanghai Scientific	49		GB	10
Adolescense	FR	1968	Vladimir Forgency Old and Young Ballet Dancers	22	est	GB	10
Adventures in Perception	HOLL	1971	Han Van Gelder Escher Drawings	21		GB	7.50
Aladdin and the Magic Lamp	GB		Lotte Reiniger	12		GB	5
Alberto Giacometti	SWITZ	1970	Peter Munger/Ernst Sheideggcr	29		GB	10
Album	CZ	1981	Evzen Plitek	7		GB	7.50
Alf, Bill and Fred	GB	1964	Bob Godfrey	7		GB	5
All Saints Day – Poland	POL	1970	John Minchinton	13		GB	7.50
Allo, Allo	RUM	1963	Popescu Gopo	10		GB	10
Almost Everyone Does	GB	1972	Youth Drug Abuse	14		GB	7.50
Alpha Omega	IT	1962	Bruno Bozzetto	7		GB	5
Amelia and the Angel	GB	1958	Ken Russell	30		GB	10
Among The Pelicans	RUM	1962	Ion Bostan	16		GB	10
Amsterdam	HOLL	1965	Herman van der Horst	20		GB	7.50
Andy Wharhol & His Clan	W.GER	1970		46		GB	15
Animal War, Animal Peace	USA	1968	Hugh Falkus	29		GB	10
Appalachian Spring	USA	1968	Peter Glushanok	31		GB	10
Aquarelle	FR	1965	Dominique de Louche	9		GB	5
Aquarium	BULG	1973	Zdenka Doitcheva	12		GB	10
Araby	POL	1963	Zbigniew Raplewski	12		GB	5
Arctic Journey	GB	1969	Richard Gayer	22		GB	10
Arrivals	GB	1983	Mari Peacock	20		GB	18
Artist's Proof	GB	1956	John Gibson	25		GB	10
As A Matter of Fact	AUSTR	1979		28		GB	18
Astronautes, Les	FR	1959	Walerian Borowczyk	12		GB	7.50
Awake from Mourning	GB	1982	Chris Austin	50		GB	25
Award for Mr Rossi, An	IT	1960	Bruno Bozzetto	10		GB	5
Axe and the Lamp	GB	1964	John Halas	7		GB	5
Bach to Bach	USA	1967	Paul Leaf	6		GB	5
Balablok	CAN	1972	Bretislav Pojar	7		GB	5
Banished from Paradise	BULG	1968	Todor Dinov	8		GB	5
Barefoot Doctors of Rural China	USA	1975	Liane Li	48		GB	20
Battle for Guadalcanal	USA			30		GB	15
Beachhead to Berlin	USA			20		GB	10
Bead Game	CAN	1977	Ishu Patel	5		GB	5
Beara	EIR	1979	Paddy Carey	17		GB	7.50
Bezhin Meadow	USSR	1967	Sergei Yutkevitch	31	est/eng	GB	15
Big Clubs, The	W.GER	1974	Joachim Kreck	49	eng	GB	20
Binding Love	GB	1986		30		GB	18
Bird's Life	CZ	1973	Adolf Born	9		GB	5
Bitter Wages	GB	1984	Audrey Droisen	37		GB	25
Black Pudding	GB	1969	Nancy Edell	5		GB	5
Blood Ties	AUSTR	1989	Jane Stevenson	35		GB	20
Bluebottles	GB	1928	Ivor Montagu	32	st	GB	7.50
Blues According to Lightnin' Hopkins	USA	1968	Les Blank	9		GB	15
Booom	UN	1980	Bretislav Pojar	11		GB	7.50
Bow Bells	GB	1950	Anthony Simmons	15		GB	7.50
Brancusi Retrospective	USA	1970	Paul Falkenberg/Hans Namuth	23		GB	10
Brendan Behan's Dublin	EIRE	1966	Norman Cohen	29		GB	18
Bridges of China	CHI	1966		10		GB	5
Broadway by Light	USA	1957	William Klein	10		GB	5
Broken English	GB	1979	Derek Jarman	14		GB	15
Building for Books	EIR	1958	J.H. Mendoza	22		GB	25
Buster Keaton Comedies:							

GB	COUNTRY OF PRODUCTION	YEAR	DIRECTOR	RUNNING TIME	VERSION	16mm	16mm RENTAL FEE
Chemist, The	1936	USA	Al Christie	20		GB	10
Ditto	1937	USA	Charles Lamont	20		GB	10
Jailbait	1937	USA	Charles Lamont	20		GB	10
Love Nest on Wheels	1936	USA	Raymond Kane	20		GB	10
Mixed Magic	1937	USA	Charles Lamont	20		GB	10
Butterfly Ball	GB	1974	Lee Mishkin	4		GB	5
Call of Love	BULG	1973	Konstantin Grogorov	12		GB	5
Carmen	W.GER	1933	Lotte Reiniger satire	10		GB	5
Catapult	AUST	1976	Andrew Vial	9		GB	5
Charles Chaplin Comedies:							
Adventurer, The	USA	1917	Charles Chaplin	10	sd	GB	10
Night in the Show, A	USA	1915	Charles Chaplin	27	sd	GB	10
Shanghaied	USA	1915	Charles Chaplin	27		GB	10
Chess Fever	USSR	1926	Vsevolod Pudovkin	20	est	GB	7.50
Chien Andalou, Un	FR	1929	Luis Buñuel	17		GB	20
Child's Christmas in Wales	USA	1961	Dylan Thomas Story	26		GB	10
Child's Voice, A	EIR	1978	Kieran Hickey	30		GB	10
Children's Film Packs (Nos 1-10)	USA		Various	31-37		GB	10
Chinese Acrobats (Parts 1-7)	CHI	1973		11-20		GB	5
Chris Barber's Jazz Band	GB	1956	Giorgio Gormelsky	20		GB	10
Christmas For Sale	GB	1984	Iain McCall	7		GB	10
Chulas Fronteras	USA	1976	Les Blank	58		GB	20
Circus	GB	1985	Ann Barefoot	5		GB	10
City of Mud	CZ	1963		7		GB	5
Clayman	CZ	1972	Jan Zahradnik	3		GB	5
Code of the West	USA	1947	William Berke	57		GB	15
Colour of Man	USA	1955	Robert Carl Cohen	10		GB	5
Come On	AUSTR	1978	Elizabeth Mcrae	8.5		GB	10
Come on, Danger!	USA	1932	Robert Hill	54		GB	15
Conspiracy	USA	1939	Lew Landers	59		GB	20
Cow on the Frontier	YUGO	1970	Dragutin Vanak	9		GB	5
Cradle of Genius	EIR	1959	Paul Rotha	31		GB	10
Creative Artists of India	IND	1963	B.D. Garga	13		GB	7.50
Criticus	YUGO	1962	Aleksandar Marks	9		GB	5
Crossing the Great Sagrada	GB	1924	Adrian Brunel	15	st	GB	10
Cry of Jazz	USA	1959	Edward Bland	33		GB	10
Curley	USA	1947	Bernard Carr	53		GB	15
Curtain Call	USA	1952	Jean Oser	10		GB	10
Cut it Out	GB	1925	Adrian Brunel	19	st	GB	7.50
Cyclone	CB	1964	Santiago Alvarez	22		GB	7.50
Daisy, The	BULG	1965	Todor Dinov	6		GB	5
Dancer's World, A	USA	1957	Peter Glushansk	30		GB	10
Daumier — Eye-Witness of an Epoch	HOLL	1973	Nico Crama	11		GB	7.50
David	GB	1951	Paul Dickson	40		GB	15
David and Goliath	USA	1973	Mal Couch	15		GB	15
Day, The	GB	1960	Peter Finch	27		GB	10
Daydreams	GB	1929	Ivor Montagu	34		GB	10
Death Coast	SWE	1974	Per Gunnar Evander/Ake Kimbre	35		GB	10
Death: How Can You Live It?	USA	1972		19		GB	15
Del Mero Corazon	USA	1979	Les Blank	20		GB	10
Dermis Probe	GB	1965	Richard Williams	5		GB	5
Disney Studio	USA	1940		26		GB	15
Doomed to Win	USA		James Gleason	18		GB	10
Drip, The	EIR	1985	Trish McAdam	14		GB	12
Dry Wood	USA	1973	Les Blank	37		GB	15
Dwightiana	USA	1959	Maria Menken	12		GB	7.50
Early Talking Pictures (2 Vols)				12		GB	10
Edgar Kennedy Comedies	USA	1930s/	65 programmes	x20		GB	10

GB	COUNTRY OF PRODUCTION	YEAR	DIRECTOR		RUNNING TIME	VERSION	16mm	16mm RENTAL FEE
1848	FR		Victoria Mercanton		40	eng	GB	7.50
1895 How the Movies Move	FIN	1974	Aito Makinen		18	eng	GB	7.50
Eight Minutes to Midnight	USA	1980	Mary Benjamin		30		GB	30
Eight or Nine in the Morning	GB	1972	Felix Greene		25		GB	10
Eisenstein — A Survey	GB		John Lane		20		GB	7.50
Elsa	FIN	1982			5		GB	10
Entombed Warriors	AUSTR	1984	Bob Kingsbury		47		GB	15
Everyday Occurence	YUGO		Vatroslav Mimica		10		GB	5
Extinct World of Gloves	CEZCH	1983	Jiri Barta		15		GB	15
Eyes Do Not Want to Close At All Times	GER	1969					GB	20
Faithful Departed	EIR	1967	Kieran Hickey		10		GB	5
Feast of the Damned	YUGO	1959	Dusan Makavejev		8		GB	5
Femme Fleur, La	FR	1965	Jan Lenica		13		GB	7.50
Fifty Fighting Years	GB	1973	Roland Bisohff/Stanley Forman		34		GB	10
Filmfinders Comedy Collection			Collection assembled by Philip Jenkinson		x30		GB	15
Filming Nature's Mysteries	USA	1977			20		GB	15
First Twenty Years					x30		GB	15
Flaming Gold	USA	1934	Ralph Ince		54		GB	15
Flatland	USA	1965	Eric Martin		12		GB	10
Flicker Flashback (30 vols)	USA	1943			10		GB	10
Follow You, Follow Me	GB	1979	Roger Lambert		35		GB	15
Frailty Thy Name is Woman	FR	1968	Nadine Trintignant		25	est	GB	10
Freedom Railway	GB	1974	Felix Greene		45		GB	20
Friendship First, Competition Second	GB	1972	Felix Greene		25		GB	10
Funny Valentine	GB	1979	Maya Brandt		2.5		GB	5
Galathea	W.GER	1936	Lotte Reiniger		12		GB	5
Geography of the Body	USA	1947	Willard Maas		7		GB	5
Gerard Manley Hopkins	GB	1972	Peter Francis Browne		30		GB	10
Glass	HOLL	1958	Bert Haanstra		11		GB	5
Glassworks	GB	1978	Murray Martin		20		GB	15
Glory to Felix Tournachon 19th Century Photographer	FR	1967	A. Martin/M. Boschet		20		GB	7.50
God Respects Us When We Work, But Loves Us When We Dance	USA	1967/8	Les Blank		20		GB	15
God's Island	USA	1980	Ramuna Macdonald		10		GB	7.50
Good Cause Wimmin	GB	1983	Penney Florence		20		GB	18
Grand Canyon	USA	1958	James Algar		29		GB	20
Grant North	GB	1969	Jack Hazan		16		GB	7.50
Grasshopper and the Ant, The	GB	1955	Lotte Reiniger		10		GB	5
Great Treasure House, A	GB	1972	Felix Greene		25		GB	10
Greece of Christian Greeks	GB	1972	Kostas Chronopoulos		43		GB	15
Greek Sculpture	GB	1958	Basil Wright/Michael Ayrton		24		GB	10
Hand of Adam	GB	1975	Murray Grigor		33		GB	10
Hang Up	CZ	1981	J. Doubrava/A. Born M. Macowek		12		GB	15
Hangman, The	USA	1964	Paul Julian/Les Goldman		11		GB	5
Hanoi, Tuesday 13th	CB	1967	Santiago Alvarez		38		GB	10
Hat, The	USA	1964	John Hubley		16		GB	7.50
He Restoreth My Soul	USA	1981	Mel White		28		GB	15
Heart is Burning, The	SWE	1967	Ralph Lundsten		1		GB	10
Heart of Spain	USA	1948	H. Klein/G. Karpaki		20		GB	7.50
Heart, Sweet Heart	USSR	1972	WHO animation		10		GB	5
Helen, Queen of the Nautch Girls	IND	1972	Anthony Korner		30		GB	10
Here Comes the Bride	GB	1982	Frances Bowyer		30		GB	18
Hetty King — Performer	GB	1970	David Robinson		30		GB	30
High Fidelity	GB	1976	Antoinette Starkiewicz		4		GB	5
History of Animation	USA	1976	Disney		21		GB	15
History of Science Fiction	USA	1971	Isaac Asimov		26		GB	10
History of The WASA	SWE	1982	Anders Wahlgren		25		GB	10
Histria, Heraclea and Swans	RUM	1969	Ion Bostan		12		GB	10
Hole, The	BULG	1967	Olenka Doycheva		8		GB	5

GB	COUNTRY OF PRODUCTION	YEAR	DIRECTOR	RUNNING TIME	VERSION	16mm	16mm RENTAL FEE
Homage to Rodin	FR		Marc de Gastyne	19		GB	7.50
Home	USA	1974	John C. Stevens	28		GB	10
Homo Sapiens	RUM	1959	Popescu Gopo Animation	10		GB	5
Horse, The	POL	1967	Witold Giersz	7		GB	5
How the Myth was Made	GB	1978	George C. Stoney Making of 'Man of Aran'	59		GB	20
How to Hunt a Mammoth	CZ	1982	Ludvik Kadlecek	11.5		GB	15
How to Marry a Princess	RUM	1959	Popescu Gopo	30		GB	15
Hunger	CAN	1973	Peter Foldes	12		GB	7.50
I Think They Call Him John	GB	1964	John Krish	28		GB	10
I Want to be Famous	GB	1975	Roger Lambert	40		GB	15
I'm a Man	USA	1969	Peter Rosen	20		GB	7.50
Images pour Bach	FR	1970	Jean Jabely	7		GB	5
Images pour Debussy	FR	1952	Jean Mitry	9		GB	5
Immortal Land, The	GB	1959	Basil Wright	40		GB	25
In a Box	CAN	1967	Eliot Noyes Jr	4		GB	5
Incident at Hawk's Hill	USA	1979	Disney	29		GB	20
Incomplete	BULG	1967		8		GB	5
Indian Fantasy	FR	1938/56	Anthony Gross/Hector Hoppin	18		GB	7.50
Indoor Games Near Newbury	GB	1976	Chris Clough	5		GB	5
Interviews with My Lai Veterans	USA	1970	Joseph Strick	22		GB	10
Invention of Photography	FR	1967	Andre Martin	22		GB	10
Ireland, Land of Beauty	EIR	1964		15		GB	10
Iron Trees will Blossom	GB		Felix Greene	14		GB	10
It's Not Your Imagination	CAN	1980		20		GB	18
Jealousy	BULG	1963	Todor Dinov	8		GB	5
Jetee, La	FR	1964	Chris Marker	29		GB	10
Jim Dine	USA	1970	Christian & Michael Blackwood	30		GB	10
Johnny	W.GER	1968	Richard Scheinpflug	14		GB	7.50
Johnny Yes No	GB	1981	Peter Care	22		GB	15
Josef Kilian	CZ	1964	Pavel Juracek/Jan Schmidt	40	est	GB	15
Jury of Her Peers, A	USA	1980	Sally Heckell	30		GB	15
Kaleidoscope	CZ	1969		10		GB	5
Katutura	SWITZ	1972	Ulrich Schweizer	37		GB	10
L.S. Lowry	GB	1973	Philip Thomson	17		GB	7.50
Labyrinth	POL	1963	Jan Lenica	15		GB	7.50
Land Without Bread	SP	1932	Luis Buñuel	29	est	GB	10
Larry Rivers	GB	1970	Christian & Michael Blackwood	30		GB	10
Last Respects	GB	1981	Mole Hill	6		GB	10
Laurel and Hardy Comedies:	1927-						
Call of the Cuckoo	1932	USA	Clyde Bruckman	18		GB	10
Flying Elephants		USA	Frank Butler	19	sd	GB	10
From Soup to Nuts		USA	Edgar Kennedy	18		GB	10
Laurel and Hardy Murder Case		USA	James Parrott	30		GB	10
Scram		USA	Ray McCarey	20		GB	10
Second Hundred Years, The		USA	Fred Guiol	19	sd	GB	10
Should Married Men Go Home?		USA	James Parrott	20		GB	10
Wrong Again		USA	Leo McCarey	20		GB	10
Law of the Jungle	USA	1942	Jean Yarbrough	57		GB	20
LBJ	CB	1968	Santiago Alvarez	18		GB	7.50
Lead Dress	AUSTR	1984		9		GB	10
Legion of the Lawless	USA	1939	David Howard	59		GB	15
Leon Errol Comedies	USA	1094's	1940's 47 programmes	x20		GB	10 each
Leonardo Da Vinci: First Man of the Renaissance	USA			10		GB	10
Let My People Go	GB	1961	John Krish	18		GB	7.50
Life's Laboratory	BULG	1973	Luben Tsolov	10		GB	10
Linda Beyond The Expected		1978	Audrey Summerhill	11		GB	12
Linoprints	GB	1958	Antony West	20	est	GB	10
Lion's Holiday, A	USSR	1964	Fedor Khitrouk	20	est	GB	10

	COUNTRY OF PRODUCTION	YEAR	DIRECTOR	RUNNING TIME	VERSION	16mm	16mm RENTAL FEE
Little Chimney Sweep	GB	1936	Lotte Reiniger	10		GB	5
Little Umbrella	CZ	1957	Bretislav Pojar	16		GB	7.50
Long Shadows of the Plantation	HOLL	1979	Janne Giese	30		GB	18
Looking at Playgroups	GB	1970	Oscar Marzaroli	29		GB	10
Loons Necklace, The	CAN	1948	Budge Crawley	10		GB	5
Lotte Reiniger's Art	GB	1970	Animator at work	12		GB	5
Love and Film	YUGO	1961	Ivor Vrbanci	11		GB	5
Love and the Zeppelin	CZ	1956	Jan Brdecka	8		GB	7.50
Love and the Zeppelin	CZ	1956	Jan Brdecka	8		GB	10
Lvan Susanin	USSR		Soviet opera ext	27		GB	10
Mackintosh	GB	1968	Murray Grigor	30		GB	10
Magic Horse, The	GB		Lotte Reiniger	10		GB	10
Magic of Disneyland	USA			21		GB	15
Magic of Disneyworld	USA			30		GB	20
Magic Pillow	USA	1980	Lyn Gerry	12		GB	15
Mahatma & the Mad Boy	USA	1972	Ismail Merchant	26		GB	10
Making of 'Ruddigore'	GB	1966	Halas & Batchelor	9	bw	GB	10
Many Moons	GB	1975	R. Ingle/E. Money	13		GB	7.50
Marcel Proust	FR	1962	Jacques Letellier	21		GB	7.50
March to Aldermaston	GB	1958	Lindsay Anderson et al	35		GB	10
Marion's Story	GB	1976	Nicci Crowther	10		GB	10
Marx for Beginners	GB	1978	Bob Godfrey	7		GB	5
Masque of the Red Death	YUGO	1969	Pavao Stalter/Branko Ranitovic	10		GB	5
Meeting the Man — James Baldwin	GB	1970	Terence Dixon	26		GB	15
Men in Silence	GB	1964	John Halas	6		GB	5
Metamorphosis of Mr Samsa	CAN	1977	Caroline Leaf	10		GB	5
Methods	HUNG	1969	Judit Vas	22	est	GB	10
Mid Air	GB	1986	Vera Neubauer	20		GB	20
Mists for Time	EIR	1968	Patrick Carey	26		GB	15
Mole and the Rocket	CZ	1971	Zdenek Miler	9		GB	5
Mole and the Umbrella	CZ	1971	Zdenek Miler	9		GB	5
Monsieur Tête	POL	1959	Jan Lenica	13		GB	5
More than a Million Years	GB	1976	Political Prisoners in Indonesia	27		GB	10
Mr Rossi Buys a Car	IT	1966	Bruno Bozzetto	11		GB	5
Mr Rossi Goes Camping	IT	1970	Bruno Bozzetto	12		GB	5
Mr Rossi Goes Skiing	IT	1963	Bruno Bozzetto	12		GB	5
Mr Rossi on Photo Safari	IT	1971	Bruno Bozzetto	9		GB	5
Mr Rossi on the Beach	IT	1963	Bruno Bozzetto	12		GB	5
Music Academy	GB	1965	John Halas	10		GB	10
Music from Oil Drums	USA	1956	Pete Seeger	14		GB	7.50
National Gallery	USA		Washington Gallery	9		GB	10
National Gallery: A PrivateView (12 parts)				12x26		GB	15
New Directions in Science Fiction	USA		James Gunn	20		GB	10
Night Journey	USA	1961	Alexander Hammid	29		GB	10
No Other Woman	USA	1933	J. Walter Ruben	58		GB	15
Notre Dame — Cathédrale de Paris	FR	1967	Georges Franju	18	sc	GB	7.50
Now	CB	1964	Santiago Alvarez	6		GB	5
Nuit et Brouillard	FR	1955	Alain Resnais	28	est	GB	10
Number One	W.GER	1973	Joachim Kreck	10		GB	5.00
Oh My Darling	HOLL	1978	Borge Ring	7		GB	5
Oisin	EIR	1970	Patrick Carey	17		GB	7.50
On a Tightrope	CZ	1973	Jan Zahridnik	8		GB	5
On the Twelfth Day	GB	1955	Wendy Toye	22		GB	10
Once a Crocodile Always a Crocodile	USSR	1971	Alvar Serebrinkov	10		GB	5
One Eyed Men are Kings	FK	1974	Michel Leroy	15		GB	10
One Nation, Many People	GB	1972	Felix Greene	25		GB	10
One of the Missing	GB	1967/9	Anthony Scott	26		GB	10
One, Two, Three	GB	1975	Sue Crockford	32		GB	5

	COUNTRY OF PRODUCTION	YEAR	DIRECTOR	RUNNING TIME	VERSION	16mm	16mm RENTAL FEE
Only Logical Way, The	GB	1971	Tim Hohenboken	27		GB	15
Open Window	HOLL		EEC Landscapes	17		GB	7.50
Opera	IT	1970	Bruno Bozzetto	10		GB	5
Owl Who Married a Goose	CAN	1974	Caroline Leaf	8		GB	5
Pan	HOLL	1961	Herman van der Horst	23		GB	10
Papageno	W.GER	1935	Lotte Reiniger	11		GB	5
Parched Land, The	GB	1978	Kieron Moore	48		GB	15
Paris la Nuit	FK	1955	Jacques Baratier	23		GB	7.50
Partie de Campagne, Une	FR	1937	Jean Renoir	40	est	GB	20
Passing the Message	HOLL	1981	Cliff Bestall/Michael Gavshon	47		GB	15
Pearson Island	AUSTR	1971	Douglas Steen	15		GB	10
Peking Symphony Orchestra	USA	1965	Felix Greene	20		GB	7.50
Penny Whistle Boys	GB	1963	Kenneth Law	14		GB	7.50
Peoples Army	GB	1972	Felix Greene	25		GB	10
Peoples' Communes	GB	1972	Felix Greene	25		GB	10
Peoples' March for Jobs	GB	1981	ACT Films	33		GB	15
Personal History of the Australian Surf, A	AUSTR	1981	Michael Blakemore	52		GB	20
Photographic Exhibits	GB	1984	Clair Barwell	20		GB	15 each
Picasso			Selection of Picasso's works	20		GB	15
Piscina, La	IT	1976	Bruno Bozzetto	7		GB	10
Plaza (On the Beach)	POL	1964	Edward Sturtis	8		GB	5
Poets Against the Bomb	GB	1981	Francis Fuchs	30		GB	20
Potters at Work	CAN	1976	Marty Gross	29		GB	15
Potters of Hebron	IS	1976	Robert Haber	40		GB	25
Premièr Nuit, La	FR	1957	Georges Franju	20		GB	7.50
Prince Igor	USSR		Borodin opera ext	37		GB	10
Propos de Nice, A	FR	1930	Jean Vigo	26	st	GB	10
Proud to be British	GB	1972	Nick Broomfield	28		GB	10
Pull My Daisy	USA	1958	Robert Frank/Alfred Leslie	27		GB	10
Punkin	USA	1972	Maurice Kahmi/Vanessa Lee	15		GB	7.50
Puss in Boots	GB	1953	Lotte Reiniger	10		GB	10
Q Ships	GB	1928	Geoffrey Barkas	38		GB	20
Quick Money	USA	1937	Edward Killy	59		GB	15
Real Lies	GB	1981	Audrey Summerhill	45		GB	30
Reality of Karel Appel	NETH	1961	Jan Vrijam	12		GB	10
Red Stain, The	CZ	1962	Zdenek Miler animation	14		GB	7.50
Refugees	IND	1971		14		GB	10
Reggae	GB	1970	Horace Ove	59	mag	GB	25
Rembrandt, Painter of Man	HOLL	1957	Bert Haanstra	20		GB	7.50
Requiem for 500,000	POL	1965	J. Bossak/W. Kazmierczar	25		GB	10
Return Engagement	USA	1935	Ford Sterling	20		GB	10
Ritual – Collective Psyche of Japan	CAN	1979	Kalle Lasn	29		GB	15
RKO Collection	USA		33 programmes of silent screen comedy and drama	33x10		GB	10
Rodin – The Burghers of Calais	USA	1969	Robin Jones/Robert Kwetsky/Bernard Stone	17		GB	10
Romantic Versus Classic Art	GB	1973	13 episodes writtten and presented by Lord Kenneth Clark	27-50		GB	20
Russian Classics (Study Extracts)				10		GB	10
Sandcastle, The	CAN	1977	Co Hodeman	12		GB	7.50
Scarabus	BEL	1971	Gerald Frydman	20		GB	15
Science Fiction Films	USA	1972	James Gunn	28		GB	10
Sculptor's Landscape	GB	1958	John Read	28		GB	15
Sea Dream	CAN	1980	Ellen Besen/Bill Speers	6		GB	5
Seat, The	POL	1969	Daniel Szczechura	7		GB	5
Secrets of the Paintings	RUM	1961		20		GB	7.50
Self Health	USA	1974	Catherine Allen	23		GB	18
Self Reliance	GB	1972	Felix Greene	25		GB	10
Selling of the Female Image	AUSTR	1977	Carole Kostanich	9		GB	15

GB

	COUNTRY OF PRODUCTION	YEAR	DIRECTOR	RUNNING TIME	VERSION	16mm	16mm RENTAL FEE
Seven Arts	RUM	1958	Popescu Gopo	11		GB	5
Seven Deadly Sins	USA	1961	Arthur Klein	20		GB	7.50
SF Editor at Work, An	USA		John W. Campbell	26		GB	10
Shadow of Hiroshima	JAP	1956	H. Teshigawa	25		GB	10
Sheila	GB	1971	Jeffrey Schwartz	15		GB	7.50
Shine So Hard/La Vie Lounge	GB	1981	John Smith	33		GB	25
Short History	RUM	1956	Popescu Gopo	8		GB	10
Silent Pioneers				42		GB	25
Singing Lesson, The	POL	1967	Lindsay Anderson	20	est	GB	7.50
Size Ten	AUSTR	1979		18		GB	18
Sleeping Beauty	GB		Lotte Reiniger	10		GB	5
Small Change	GB	1986		10		GB	15
Smile Please	GB	1981	Maya Brandt	4		GB	5
Snow White and Rose Red	GB		Lotte Reiniger	10		GB	10
So, This Is Jolly Good	GB	1925	Adrian Brunel	16		GB	10
Soho	GB	1980	Jan Mathews	20		GB	18
Song of the Prairie	CZ	1949	Jiri Trnka	21		GB	7.50
Sosua	USA	1981	Harriet Taub/ Harry Kafka	30		GB	20
Soufriere, La	W.GER	1976	Werner Herzog	30	eng	GB	15
Soup Run	GB	1974	Guy Magar	11		GB	5
Spaceplace	USA		Account of 1969 Apollo moonflight	10		GB	15
Spectre de la Danse	FR	1960	Dominique Delouche	20	sc	GB	7.50
Spend it All	USA	1971	Les Blank	41		GB	15
Stan's Gold Rush	USA		Hal Roach	11		GB	5
Star of Bethlehem	W.GER	1921	Lotte Reiniger	20	bw	GB	5
Starlet	BULG	1965	Radka Bukvarova	8		GB	5
Stolen Heart	GB	1934	Lotte Reiniger	10		GB	5
Stranger Left No Card	GB	1952	Wendy Toye	22		GB	7.50
Street, The	CAN	1976	Caroline Leaf	10		GB	5
Struggle of the Species	BULG	1973	Konstantin Kostov	10		GB	5
Substitute	YUGO	1961	Dusan Vukotic	9		GB	5
Sun's Gonna Shine, The	USA	1968	Les Blank	10		GB	7.50
Sunburst	CAN	1970		5		GB	5
Sunday by the Sea	GB	1953	Anthony Simmons	14		GB	7.50
Sunny Tribe	USSR	1945	Bee's life-cycle	21		GB	7.50
Sweet Sounds	USA	1976	Richard Robbins	28		GB	10
Symmetry	USA	1967	Phillip Stapp ext	11		GB	5
Symphonie Mecanique	FR	1956	Jean Mitry	13		GB	7.50
Taking A Part	GB	1979	Jan Worth	45		GB	30
Taris	FR	1931	Jean Vigo	11		GB	5
Taught To Be Girls	GB	1979	Melanie Chait	15		GB	12
Tex Beneke & the Glen Miller Orchestra				17		GB	10
Theatre Laboratorium	POL	1964	Michael Elster	20	est	GB	7.50
Then the Rains	IND	1969	Ramesh Gupta	13		GB	7.50
Three Wishes	GB		Lotte Reiniger	10		GB	5
Thriller	GB	1979	Sally Potter	40		GB	25
Thumbelina	GB		Lotte Reiniger	10		GB	10
Time Piece	USA	1965	Jim Henson	7		GB	5
To Russia With Elton	GB	1979	Dick Clement	40		GB	22
Token Gesture	CAN	1978	Micheline Lanctot	8.5		GB	10
Toot, Whistle, Plunk and Boom	USA	1953	C. August Nicholls/ Ward Kimball	10		GB	15
Touchwood	AUSTR	1981	Gillian Armstrong	34		GB	20
Towers, The	USA	1954	William Hale	20		GB	7.50
Training Future Players of China's Classical Theatre	CHI	1957		30		GB	10
Travelling Painters of Russia	USSR	1972	Lyudmila Lazareva	27.5	eng	GB	15
True Story of the Civil War	USA	1957	Louis Stouman	33		GB	10
Tsiamelo: A Place of Goodness	GB	1983	Ellen Kuzwayo/Blanche Tsimataima	56		GB	20
Turning Point, The	S.AFK	1971	Lionel Friedberg	25		GB	10

	COUNTRY OF PRODUCTION	YEAR	DIRECTOR	RUNNING TIME	VERSION	16mm	16mm RENTAL FEE
GB							
Two in Love	USSR	1965	Mikhail Bogin	37	est/sc	GB	10
Under the Eagle's Wing	RUM	1963	Ion Bostan	17	eng	GB	7.50
Unknown Eiffel	USA	1974	Joan Laskoff	28		GB	15
Up is Down	USA	1970	Millie Goldsholl	6		GB	5
Veronika 4 Rose	GB	1983		48		GB	30
Vincent Van Gogh	HOLL	1953	Jan Hulsker	26		GB	10
Visual Variations of Noguchi	USA	1954	Maria Menken	5		GB	5
Voyage of Mr Q	FR/USA	1961	Don Wolfe	19		GB	7.50
Waiting for Alan	GB	1983	Richard Woolley	45		GB	25
Wajda on the Set	POL	1968	J. Ziarnik	17	est	GB	7.50
Watching Looking	GB	1980	Caroline Sheldon	20		GB	18
We Aim To Please	AUSTR	1977	Margot Nash	13		GB	12
We All Have Our Reasons	USA	1984	Frances Reid	30		GB	18
We Will Not Be Beaten	USA	1978	Mary Tiseo	35		GB	25
Werner Herzog Eats His Shoe	USA	1980	Les Blank	20		GB	15
What's A Nice Girl Like You Doing In A Place LikeThis?	USA	1963	Martin Scorsese	9		GB	15
When I'm Rich	GB	1977	Derek Phillips	5		GB	5
Who Cares	GB	1969	Nick Broomfield	18		GB	7.50
Wholly Communion	GB	1965	Peter Whitehead	30		GB	10
Women of the World	USA	1975	Faith Hubley	11		GB	10
Women Against the Bill	GB	1972	Esther Ronay	20		GB	7.50
Women of the World	USA	1975	Faith Hubley	11		GB	5
Wrestling Game	GB	1962	Gerry Levy	34		GB	10
You Have Struck a Rock!	USA	1981	Deborah May	28		GB	20
Zero de Conduite	FR	1933	Jean Vigo	40	est/fr	GB	35
Zoo	HOLL	1962	Bert Haanstra	12		GB	5

F Wales

Title	Country of Production	Year	Director	Running Time	Version	16mm	16mm Rental Fee
Century City	GB	1988	Chapter Animation	12		F Wales	6
Eyeballs Against The Windscreen	GB	1986	Dane Gould	30		F Wales	18
The Joke Works	GB	1991	Jeremy Bubb/Graham Jones	35		F Wales	18
Zombie UB40	GB	1988	Christine Wilks	12		F Wales	18

LAW

Title	Country of Production	Year	Director	Running Time	Version	16mm	16mm Rental Fee
Alice in Wasteland	GB	1991	LAW	12		LAW	10
Council Matters	GB	1984	LAW	10		LAW	10
Crops and Robbers	GB	1986	LAW	15		LAW	10
Give Us A Smile	GB	1983	LAW	12.5		LAW	10
Home and Dry?	GB	1987	LAW	8		LAW	10
Matter of Interest, A	GB	1990	LAW	13		LAW	10
Out to Lunch	GB	1989	LAW	12		LAW	10
Pretend You'll Survive	GB	1981	LAW	9		LAW	10
Risky Business	GB	1980	LAW	15		LAW	10
Who Needs Nurseries? We Do!	GB	1978	LAW	11		LAW	10

	COUNTRY OF PRODUCTION	YEAR	DIRECTOR	RUNNING TIME	VERSION	16mm	16mm RENTAL FEE
A & B in Ontario	CAN	1984	JoyceWieland	17		LFMC	14.45
A Capriccio		1991	Trofimova Lisa	20		LFMC	17.00
<A> Film	GB	1974	David Crosswaite	10		LFMC	10.00
A la Mode	USA	1958	Stan Vanderbeek	5		LFMC	10.00
A-B-C-D-E-F=1-36	POL	1974	Ryszard Wasko	8		LFMC	10.00
A.I.D.S.C.R.E.A.M.	USA	1990	Jerry Tartaglia	6		LFMC	10.00
Ab Ovo Usque Ad Mala	GB		Julian Woropay	3		LFMC	10.00
Aber Bach	GB	1976	Richard Welsby	5		LFMC	10.00
About Butter	FIN	1987	S. J. Van Ingen	10		LFMC	10.00
Absence	USA	1976	Stan Brakhage	10		LFMC	10.00
Abstractions:Jude GertrudeStein Film	POL	1974	William Moritz	2		LFMC	10.00
Academic Still Life	GB	1977	Malcolm LeGrice	6		LFMC	10.00
Accretion	GB	1973	John Du Cane	7		LFMC	10.00
Across the Field of Vision	GB	1982	Lucy Pantelli	10		LFMC	10.00
Act	CAN		Sandra Meigs			LFMC	10.00
Act II	USA	1980	Owen Shapiro	22		LFMC	18.70
Act of Seeing With One's Eyes	USA	1971	Stan Brakhage	30	st	LFMC	25.50
Act of Seeing With One's Own Eyes, The Aftermath	USA	1981	Stan Brakhage	11		LFMC	10.00
Action at a Distance	GB	1980	Peter Gidal	35		LFMC	29.75
Acts of Superimposition: Interior & Vanishing Point	GB	1975-76	David Parsons	17		LFMC	14.45
Acumen	GB	1991	Andrew Kotting	20		LFMC	17.00
Adebar	AUST	1957-8	Peter Kubelka	1		LFMC	10.00
Adebar & Schwechater	AUST	1957-58	Peter Kubelka	3		LFMC	10.00
Advent Matter			Stephen Hurrell	10		LFMC	10.00
Adventures of a Good Citizen, The	POL	1937	F./S. Themerson	10		LFMC	10.00
Adventures of the Exquisite Corpse (Kodak Ghost Poems)	GB	1970	Andrew Noren	45		LFMC	38.25
Adventurous But Luckless Life of William Parmagino	W. GER	1968	Klaus Wyborny	20		LFMC	17.00
Adynata	USA	1987	Thornton, Leslie	30		LFMC	25.50
Aerial	GB	1974	Margaret Tait	4		LFMC	10.00
Aesthetic Quality, An	USA	1967	Vaughan Obern	4		LFMC	10.00
After Lumiere	GB	1974	Malcolm LeGrice	16		LFMC	13.60
After the Colours			Seip Mattyn	5		LFMC	10.00
After the Music	GB	1979	Nick Collins	7		LFMC	10.00
Aftermath	USA	1981	Stan Brakhage	11	st	LFMC	10.00
Agnus Die Kinder Synapse	USA	1991	Stan Brakhage			LFMC	10.00
Air	GB		Marilyn Halford	6		LFMC	10.00
Airplane Glue I Love You	USA	1970	LesterHoward	20		LFMC	17.00
Airs	USA	1976	Stan Brakhage	25		LFMC	21.25
Alaska	W.GER	1968	O Dore	18		LFMC	15.30
Albacore	USA		Stan Brakhage			LFMC	
All My Life	USA	1966	Bruce Bailli	3		LFMC	10.00
Altergraphies	FR	1982	Frederique Devaux	10		LFMC	10.00
America is Waiting	USA	1981	Bruce Conner	4		LFMC	10.00
Amicothek	W.GER		Irm Sommer	14		LFMC	11.90
Anagram	GB	1981	Nicky Hamlyn	40		LFMC	34.00
Analytical Studies II: Un-Framed Lines	USA	1971-76	Paul Sharits	30		LFMC	25.50
Anamnesis 1/2/3	HOLL	1969	Fran Zwartjes	18		LFMC	15.30
Andante Mia Mon Troppo	HOLL	1988	Barbara Meter	6		LFMC	10.00
Anemometer	GB	1974	Chris Welsby	10		LFMC	10.00
Angel	USA	1957	Joseph Cornell	3	st	LFMC	10.00
Angles of Incidence	GB	1973	William Raban	12	st	LFMC	10.20
Angular Momentum	GB	1973	Bill Brand	20		LFMC	17.00
Animated Films	GB	1986	Agnes Hay	15		LFMC	12.75
Animated Picture Show		1972	Russell Adams	3	bw	LFMC	10.00
Anju	GB	1970	Annabel Nicolson	15	st	LFMC	12.75
Another Window (Variations)	GB	1987	George Saxon	20		LFMC	17.00
Anticipation of the Night	USA	1958	Stan Brakhage	43	sd/18fps	LFMC	36.55
Apertures	GB	1977	John Woodman	5	st	LFMC	10.00

	COUNTRY OF PRODUCTION	YEAR	DIRECTOR	RUNNING TIME	VERSION	16mm	16mm RENTAL FEE
Aphasia: Caught in the Act	CAN	1987	Sandra Meigs	4		LFMC	10.00
Approach	GB	1975	David Parsons	10		LFMC	10.00
Apropos of San Francisco	USA	1968	Charles Levine	4		LFMC	10.00
Arabic One	USA	1980	Stan Brakhage	3		LFMC	10.00
Arabic Two	USA	1980	Stan Brakhage	4		LFMC	10.00
Arbitrary Limits	GB	1982	Mike Dunford	30		LFMC	25.50
Archway Road Movie Newsreel One – the Buildup	GB	1982	Richard Philpott	25	mag	LFMC	21.50
Arctic Desire	USA	1975	Bruce Wood	7		LFMC	10.00
Arnulf Rainer	AUST	1960	Peter Kubelka	7		LFMC	10.00
Arran	GB	1974	Jane Clark	20		LFMC	17.00
Art Schmart	GB		Marek Budzynski	7		LFMC	10.00
Artificial Light	USA	1969	Hollis Frampton	25		LFMC	21.50
Arts Vietnam			Sacha Ivanovitch	28		LFMC	23.80
Associations	GB	1975	John Smith	7		LFMC	10.00
At the Academy	GB	1974	Guy Sherwin	5		LFMC	10.00
Atlantic Waves	GB	1986	Tom Scott	10		LFMC	10.00
Attermire	GB	1977	Renny Croft			LFMC	
Au Revoir Renee	GB	1989	Tony Fletcher	15		LFMC	12.75
Aus der Ferne – The Memo Book	GER	1988-9	Mueller Matthias	28		LFMC	23.80
Automaton Film	GB	1981	Jo Comino	25		LFMC	21.25
Autumn Feast, The	USA	1968	Piero Heliczer	14	st	LFMC	11.90
Autumn Scenes	GBF	1979	William Raban	25		LFMC	21.50
Autumn Spectrum	USA	1958	Hy Hirsch	8		LFMC	10.00
Aviary, The	USA	1955	Joseph Cornell	5		LFMC	10.00
Award Presentation to Andy Warhol	USA	1983	Jonas Mekas	13		LFMC	11.05
Axiomatic Granularity	USA	1979	Paul Sharits	20		LFMC	17.00
Az Iz	USA	1983	Betzy Bromberg	37		LFMC	31.45
Babylon Series 1	USA	1989	Stan Brakhage	6		LFMC	10.00
Babylon Series 2	USA	1990	Stan Brakhage	5		LFMC	10.00
Babylon Series 3	USA	1990	Stan Brakhage	6		LFMC	10.00
Back in Bedford	AUSTR	1976	John Dunkley-Smith	23		LFMC	19.55
Bahlsen Pan, The	W.GER	1983	H. Kober/J. Dobele	5		LFMC	10.00
Ballade des Amants Maudits, Le	BEL	1971	Roland Lethem	12		LFMC	10.20
Ballet Mecanique	GB	1983	Leger Fernand/Murphy Dudley	16		LFMC	13.60
Barely White	GB	1985	Emina Kurtagic	3		LFMC	10.00
Barn Rushes			Larry Gottheim	35		LFMC	29.75
Bathers, The I: Les Baigneurs	GB	1986	Michael Maziere	6		LFMC	10.00
Bathers, The II: Swimmer	GB	1987	Michael Maziere	7		LFMC	10.00
Beach, The	GB	1978	Phillip Hoffman	2	st	LFMC	4.00
Bedroom	GB	1971	Peter Gidal	30		LFMC	25.50
Begin Now – What Will Be	GB	1976	Owen Shapiro	22		LFMC	18.70
Behind Closed Doors	GB	1985	Anna Thew	14		LFMC	11.90
Bent Time	USA	1984	Barbara Hammer	22		LFMC	18.70
Berkeley Bath Brothel			Dandy Daley	30		LFMC	25.50
Berlin Horse	GB	1970	Malcolm LeGrice	8		LFMC	10.00
Berlin, Meine Augen	GB	1982	Anna Thew	18		LFMC	15.30
Bessie Smith	USA	1969	Charles Levine	13		LFMC	11.05
Between	GER	1988	Claudia Schillenger	10		LFMC	10.00
Between the Frames	GB	1976	Sarah Child	5		LFMC	10.00
Beverly Hills Flop	GB	1985	Richard Philpott	9		LFMC	10.00
Big Parade	GB		Steve Farrer	15		LFMC	12.75
Bird	AUST	1972	Edwin Moses	2		LFMC	10.00
Bird Xerox	GB		Nick Gordon Smith	8		LFMC	10.00
Birth of Venus & Frabjous Day	USA	1968	Norman Rubington	13		LFMC	11.05
Black & White Film			Helmut Nickels	36		LFMC	30.60
Black Tower, The	GB	1987	John Smith	24		LFMC	20.40
Blackness	GB		Ken McMullen	10		LFMC	10.00
Blind Stepping	GB	1975	Terence Ellis	12	st	LFMC	10.20

	COUNTRY OF PRODUCTION	YEAR	DIRECTOR	RUNNING TIME	VERSION	16mm	16mm RENTAL FEE
Blonde Cobra	USA	1959-63	Ken Jacobs	28		LFMC	23.80
Blood Sky			Michael Maziere	3		LFMC	3.00
Blue Bathroom	GB	1979	John Smith	28		LFMC	23.80
Blue Moses	USA	1964	Stan Brakhage	11		LFMC	10.00
Blue Movie	CAN	1970	David Rimmer	6	st	LFMC	10.00
Blue Rich and Fertile	GB	1988	Jonathan Dronsfield	2		LFMC	10.00
Blue's Transit	GER	1988	Barbara Thiel	8		LFMC	10.00
Blurt	GB	1983	Anna Thew	30		LFMC	25.50
Blurt Roll 2	GB	1986-87	Anna Thew	5		LFMC	10.00
Body Politic	USA	1988	Betzy Bromberg	39		LFMC	33.15
Body Press			Dan Graham	11		LFMC	10.00
Body Ritual	USA	1968	Robert Dvorak	3		LFMC	10.00
Body Work	GB	1980	Anne Parisio	14		LFMC	11.90
Bonded Dissolution			David Hykes	9		LFMC	10.00
Boobs Alot	AUSTR	1967	Aggy Read	3		LFMC	10.00
Boot Film	USA	1967	Roger Ackling	8		LFMC	10.00
Boys/Life	USA	1991	Roth Phillip B.	15		LFMC	12.75
Breakfast	GB	1972-76	Michael Snow	17		LFMC	14.45
Breathdeath	USA	1964	Stan Van Der Beek	10		LFMC	10.00
Brick Wall Film			Jane Tingle	3		LFMC	10.00
Bridge	GB	1980	John Woodman	10		LFMC	10.00
Bridge of Heaven, The	USA	1977	Bruce Wood	33		LFMC	28.50
Bridges		1986	Theo Wright	10		LFMC	10.00
Broadwalk	GB	1972	William Raban	12		LFMC	10.20
Bruce Nauman Story, The	USA		Shelby Kennedy	11		LFMC	10.00
Brute Charm	USA	1989	Emily Breer	25		LFMC	25.50
Buffalo One, Buffalo Two	USA		Colleen Sullivan	14		LFMC	11.90
Burial Path	USA	1978	Stan Brakhage	10		LFMC	10.00
C'Mon Babe (Danke	USA	1978	Sharon Sandusky	11		LFMC	10.00
C/O/N/S/T/R/U/C/T	GB	1974	Peter Gidal	26	st	LFMC	30.60
Cable Car Melody			Charles Wright	26		LFMC	22.10
Calling Hearts Film			Stephen Hurrell	10		LFMC	10.00
Calling Mr. Smith	GB	1943	F./S. Themerson	10		LFMC	10.00
Camera Piece for Sunlight and 45 Fingers Clouds			Jenny Okun	9		LFMC	10.00
Canal	CA		Richard Kerr	22		LFMC	18.70
Candidates, The	USA	1968	Robert Preston	3		LFMC	10.00
Cans	GB	1975	Ian Kerr	3		LFMC	10.00
Canterbury Trucking	GB	1975	Terence Ellis	5		LFMC	10.00
Capitalism Schmaitalism		1983	Brian Sharpe	3		LFMC	10.00
Carn Ingli Common	GB		Tim Cawkwell	4		LFMC	10.00
Carousel	GB	1986	Noski Deville	5		LFMC	10.00
Cartoon Theatre of Dr. Gaz, The	GB	1977-79	Jeff Keen	12		LFMC	10.20
Castle One (The Light Bulb Film)	GB	1966	Malcolm LeGrice	20		LFMC	17.00
Castro Street	USA	1967	Bruce Bailli	10		LFMC	10.00
Caswallon Trilogy	USA		Stan Brakhage	10		LFMC	10.00
Cat and the Woman — A Cautionary Tale, The	GB	1987	Jayne Parker	3		LFMC	10.00
Cat Perturbations			Roger Hammond	10		LFMC	10.00
Cave Aperture	GB	1978	Renny Croft	6		LFMC	10.00
Celestial Navigation	GB	1980	John Smith	9	mag	LFMC	10.00
Cezanne's Eye	GB	1990	Michael Maziere	30		LFMC	25.50
Cezanne's Eye II	GB	1991	Michael Maziere	25		LFMC	21.50
Chameleon	GB	1990	Tanya Syed	5		LFMC	10.00
Chamnan	USA	1990	Lawrence F Brose	14	bw	LFMC	11.90
Champ Provencal	GB	1979	Rose Lowder	9	st	LFMC	10.00
Change With the Wind	GB	1979	Fredlund Lynne	12	mag	LFMC	10.20
Chap Who Thinks a Spade's a Spade, The	GB	1979	Peter Samson	15		LFMC	12.75
Children of Synanon Face (B)			Howard Lester	15		LFMC	12.75
Choral Fantasy			Gary Popovich	29		LFMC	24.65

	COUNTRY OF PRODUCTION	YEAR	DIRECTOR	RUNNING TIME	VERSION	16mm	16mm RENTAL FEE
Christ Mass Sex Dance	USA	1991	Stan Brakhage	5		LFMC	10.00
Christ or Feathers	GB	1976	Will Milne	24		LFMC	20.40
Christmas Tree	GB	1970	Jan Greenlagh	5		LFMC	10.00
Chumlum	USA	1964	Ron Rice	26		LFMC	22.10
Ciao Bella	USA	1978	Betzy Bromberg	13		LFMC	11.05
Ciao Ciao			Anarno Vergine	6		LFMC	10.00
Cibernetic 5.3	USA	1961-65	John Stethura	8		LFMC	10.00
Cigarettes and TV			William Keddell	18		LFMC	15.30
Cinetracts	FR	1968	Godard et al	20		LFMC	17.00
Circle Line			Maggie Warwick	12		LFMC	10.20
Circles of Confusion	USA	1974	Bill Brand	15		LFMC	12.75
Circus Girls	USA	1971	Walter Gutman	28		LFMC	23.80
Circus Riders	USA	1979	Martha Haslanger	17		LFMC	14.45
City	GB		William English	17		LFMC	14.45
City Streaming	USA	1990	Stan Brakhage	25		LFMC	21.25
Cityscape			Paul Botham	8		LFMC	10.00
Clap	GB	1980	John Devine	6		LFMC	10.00
Claw Your Eye	USA	1989	James Carmen	6	bw	LFMC	10.00
Clear Cut	GB	1979	Michael Maziere	18		LFMC	15.30
Clenched Fist, The			David Botsford	12		LFMC	10.20
Clockwise (Accept No Substitutes)	GB		Roger Hammond	6		LFMC	10.00
Close to Home	GB	1985	Nina Danino	28		LFMC	23.80
Closer Outside	CAN	1980	Vincent Grenier	10	st	LFMC	10.00
Clothed in Muscle-A Dance of the Body	USA	1983	Walter Gutman	45		LFMC	38.25
Clouds	GB	1969	Peter Gidal	10		LFMC	10.00
Clouds	GB	1975	Jenny Okun	3		LFMC	
Coast View with Aneas and Cumaeon Parables	GB	1981	Tim Cawkwell	17		LFMC	14.45
Coastal Calls	GB	1982	Rob Gawthrop	12		LFMC	10.20
Cold Draft, A	GB	1978	Lis Rhodes	30		LFMC	25.50
Colour Flight	GB	1939	Len Lye	4		LFMC	10.00
Colour Poems	GB	1974	Margaret Tait	12		LFMC	10.20
Colour Prejudice	GB	1977	John Devine	12		LFMC	10.20
Colour Sound Frames	USA	1979	Paul Sharits	27		LFMC	22.95
Colour Work	GB	1981	Michael Maziere	18		LFMC	15.30
Colours of the Time	GB	1972	William Raban	4	st	LFMC	10.00
Come Closer	USA	1968	Hy Hirsch	5		LFMC	10.00
Commercial Break	GB	1980	Chris Garratt	3		LFMC	
Concentration	GB	1974-5	Terence Ellis	16	st	LFMC	13.60
Condition of Illusion	GB	1975	Peter Gidal	30	st	LFMC	25.50
Confession	USA		Stan Brakhage	25		LFMC	21.25
Conical Solid	USA	1974	Anthony McCall	10	st	LFMC	10.00
Conjurer's Assistant (That's Entertainment)	GB	1978	Jeanette Lijon	35		LFMC	29.75
Continuum	USA	1986	Dominic Angerame	15		LFMC	12.75
Contract	GB	1989	William English	10	bw/st	LFMC	10.00
Corridor	USA	1970	Lawder Standish	22		LFMC	18.70
Corrigan Having Recovered	GB	1979	Tim Bruce	26		LFMC	22.10
Cosmos	USA	1970	Jordon Belson	6		LFMC	10.00
Couleur de la Forme, La	USA	1968	Hy Hirsch	5		LFMC	10.00
Coulesurs Mecaniques	FR	1983	Rose Lowder	16		LFMC	13.60
Counting 1 to 100 or X	JAP	1972	Taka Limura	12		LFMC	10.20
Covert Action	USA	1986	Abigail Child	10		LFMC	10.00
Cow's Drama, The	GB	1983-84	Paul Bush	38		LFMC	32.30
Creation	USA	1979	Stan Brakhage	17		LFMC	14.45
Crofton Rd. SE5	GB/GER	1989	Gockell Gerd	5		LFMC	10.00
Cross	GB	1974	John Du Cane	60		LFMC	51.00
Crossing the Bering Strait	USA		Tina Wasserman	8		LFMC	10.00
Cup and the Lip, The	USA	1986	Warren Sonbert	20		LFMC	17.00
Cup of Tea: A Film, A	GB	1979	Tim Bruce	23		LFMC	19.55

	COUNTRY OF PRODUCTION	YEAR	DIRECTOR	RUNNING TIME	VERSION	16mm	16mm RENTAL FEE
Cupidon	GB	1985	Lois Davis	3		LFMC	10.00
Cursivits	FR	1982	Michel Amarger	10		LFMC	10.00
Daily I Am Awakened	W.GER	1983	Christine Markgraf	12		LFMC	10.20
Dam	GB	1988	William English	3		LFMC	10.00
Damned if You Don't	USA	1987	Su Friedrich	42		LFMC	42.00
Dance of the Body, A	USA	1981	Walter Gutman	45		LFMC	38.25
Dance Party in the Kingdom of Lilliput	JAP	1970	Taka Limura	14		LFMC	11.90
Dance, The	CAN	1979	David Rimmer	5		LFMC	10.00
Dark Leader	GB	1990	David Leister	4	bw	LFMC	10.00
Davonzutragen (Carry Away The Bought)			Kiefer Urs	25		LFMC	21.50
Dawn and Dusk	GB	1977	John Woodman	9	st	LFMC	10.00
Dawn Chorus	GB	1987	John Tappenden	5		LFMC	10.00
Daybreak and Whiteye	USA	1979	Stan Brakhage	8		LFMC	10.00
Dead Pigeon	GB	1987	Richard Philpott	40		LFMC	34.00
Dead, The	USA	1979	Stan Brakhage	11		LFMC	10.00
Death and the Singing Telegram	USA	1983	Mark Rance	114		LFMC	50.00
Debt Begins at 20	USA	1980	Stephanie Beroes	40		LFMC	34.00
Decodings	USA	1988	Michael Wallin	15		LFMC	18.75
Deconstruction Sight	USA	1990	Dominic Angerame	13	bw	LFMC	11.05
Deep Space	GB	1973	Mike Dunford	10		LFMC	10.00
Defense d'Afficer	FR	1968	Hy Hirsch	7		LFMC	10.00
Delicacies of Moltern Horror Synapse, The	USA		Stan Brakhage	10		LFMC	10.00
Demonstration Movie No. I	USA	1968	Ron Finne	4		LFMC	10.00
Denials	GB	1985	Peter Gidal	30		LFMC	25.50
Deptford Creek	GB		Nick Collins	13		LFMC	11.05
Depth of Field	GB	1973	Annabel Nicolson	10		LFMC	10.00
Depth of Filmed	GB	1973	Annabel Nicolson	6		LFMC	10.00
Der Job	GER	1988	Ruth Becht	6		LFMC	10.00
Derby Film — Winter 1982 + Untitled 1973-36	GB		Terence Ellis	20		LFMC	17.00
Dernier Chant d'Amour de Marilyn, Le	BEL		Roland Lethem	3		LFMC	10.00
Desert	USA		Stan Brakhage	15		LFMC	12.75
Design in Motion			Herbert Kowser	3		LFMC	10.00
Desire Drives Her Car	CAN	1988-89	Kathleen Maitland-Carter	9		LFMC	10.00
Destroying Angels	GB	1986	Carl Johnson	17		LFMC	14.45
Developing Pictures	GB	1982	Tony Bloor	2		LFMC	10.00
Diagonal Symphony	USA	1921-24	Viking Eggeling	7	st	LFMC	10.00
Diary Item	GB	1978	Martin Hearne	12		LFMC	10.20
Dimension of Noise (Modern Art)			Garry Gipps	35		LFMC	29.75
Dining Room	GB	1990	William English	21	bw/st	LFMC	17.85
Diploteratology	USA	1967	Owen Land (formerly George Landlow)	7		LFMC	10.00
Dirt Bath Sequence	FR		Piero Heliczer	15		LFMC	12.75
Discreet Call of Nature, The	GB	1985	Joanna Woodward	8		LFMC	10.00
Discussion, The	GB		Ken McMullen	12		LFMC	10.20
Distancing	GB	1979	Rob Gawthrop	15		LFMC	12.75
Distinguishing Marks	GB	1974	Terence Ellis	5	bw	LFMC	10.00
Diverse Motions	GB	1984	Tim Cawkwell	7		LFMC	10.00
Divided Room			Julian Roberts	13		LFMC	11.05
Divinations	USA	1964	Storm De Hirsch	6		LFMC	10.00
Divine Miracle	USA	1972	Diana Krumins	9		LFMC	10.00
Doctor's Dream, The	USA	1978	Ken Jacobs	25		LFMC	21.50
Documentary of Beuy's Work in London (March 1972)	GB	1972	Ken McMullen	9		LFMC	10.00
Dog Star Man: Prelude	USA		Stan Brakhage	25		LFMC	21.25
Dolly Cake	CAN	1976	Mike Jones	20		LFMC	17.00
Domestic Sanitation — Reel 1	GB	1976	Helen Chadwick	15		LFMC	12.75
Domestic Sanitation — Reel 2	GB	1976	Helen Chadwick	15		LFMC	12.75
Dominion	USA	1974	Stan Brakhage	4	st	LFMC	10.00
Doorway	USA	1970	Larry Gottheim	7	st	LFMC	10.00
Dorothy Parker's The Waltz	CAN	1985	Shereen Jerrett	8		LFMC	10.00

LFMC	COUNTRY OF PRODUCTION	YEAR	DIRECTOR	RUNNING TIME	VERSION	16mm	16mm RENTAL FEE
DP	CAN	1983	Peter Dudar	17		LFMC	14.45
Drawing Distinctions	GB	1981	Lucy Pantelli	13	mag	LFMC	11.05
Dream, NYC,	USA	1977	Stan Brakhage	25		LFMC	21.25
Dreamscape		1987	Marek Budzynski	12		LFMC	10.20
Dresden Dynamo	GB	1971-72	Lis Rhodes	5		LFMC	10.00
Drift			Renny Croft	16		LFMC	13.60
Dripping Water	CAN	1969	JoyceWieland	10		LFMC	10.00
Duet	GB	1983	Roger Hewins	3		LFMC	10.00
Duet Voor Cello en Film	NETH	1985	Fredereike Jochems	26		LFMC	22.10
Dula	GB	1984	Renny Bartlett	25		LFMC	21.25
Dulux	GB	1981	Roger Hammond	5		LFMC	10.00
Duo Concertantes	USA	1962-64	Larry Jordon	9		LFMC	10.00
Duplicity I	USA	1978	Stan Brakhage	20		LFMC	17.00
Duplicity II	USA	1978	Stan Brakhage	20		LFMC	17.00
Durga	GB	1985	Alia Syed	23		LFMC	19.55
Early Abstractions 1&3	GB	1939/1942	Harry Smith	4		LFMC	10.00
Early Abstractions 7	GB		Harry Smith	6		LFMC	10.00
East Coast	GB	1982	Martin Sercombe	11		LFMC	10.00
Easy Out & Down Wind	USA	1971-73	Pat O'Neill	23		LFMC	19.55
ecce homo	USA	1989	Jerry Tartaglia	7	10.00	LFMC	19.55
Echoes of Silence (Reel 2 only)	DEN	1965	Peter Emanuel Goldman	30		LFMC	25.50
Eclipse: Still Life No. 3	CAN	1980	Robert Rayher	2		LFMC	10.00
Eclipsed	CAN	1985	Robert Rayher	8	bw	LFMC	10.00
Edge Forces	USA	1976	Bruce Wood	11	st	LFMC	10.00
Eiapopeia	W.GER	1983	Klaus Weller	1		LFMC	10.00
Eiffel Trifle	GB	1972	Paul Botham	8		LFMC	10.00
Eight Fifty-Five	AUSTR		John Dunkley-Smith	21		LFMC	17.85
8mm Notes on 16mm	GB	1971	Peter Gidal	40		LFMC	34.00
Ela Fly Butterphant & Runner + Untitled		1975	Skelton Marlys	12		LFMC	10.20
Electric Collage for Dance	USA	1969	Stan Van Der Beek	10	st	LFMC	10.00
Electric Palace	GB	1985	Simon Margetts	8		LFMC	10.00
Element	USA	1973	Amy Greenfield	12		LFMC	10.20
Emanations	GB		John Du Cane	60		LFMC	51.00
Emily	GB		Tony Fletcher	10		LFMC	10.00
End, The	GB	1986	Patrick Keiller	18		LFMC	15.30
Endangered	USA	1988	Barbara Hammer	18		LFMC	15.30
English for Today	W.GER	1983	Schmelzdahin	2		LFMC	10.00
Enjeux	FR	1984	Yann Beauvais	6		LFMC	10.00
Epileptic Seizure Comparison	USA	1986	Paul Sharits	30		LFMC	25.50
Epilogue	GB	1979	Peter Gidal	8		LFMC	10.00
Epilogue to Oobieland Part 5	USA	1974	Walter Ungerer	40 secs		LFMC	10.00
Episodic Generation	USA	1978	Paul Sharits	30		LFMC	25.50
Erlanger Programme, The	GB	1972	Roger Hammond	25		LFMC	21.25
Erota/Afini	GB	1973	Mike Leggett	25		LFMC	21.50
Eureka	CAN	1980	Robert Rayher	5		LFMC	10.00
Euripides' Movies	GB	1987	Gad Hollander	13		LFMC	11.05
European Diaries	USA	1966	Mead Taylor	44		LFMC	37.40
Evening's Young, The	USA	1981	Ralph Records	4		LFMC	10.00
Excelsior – Reifen	USA	1983	Walter Ruttman	3		LFMC	10.00
Excercises	W.GER	1983	Oehme Anke	9		LFMC	10.00
Excerpts From the Russian Revolution	USA	1973	Ken Jacobs	22	3D	LFMC	18.70
Exit Right	GB	1976	Chris Garratt	5		LFMC	10.00
Experiment in Meditation, An	USA	1970	Storm De Hirsch	18		LFMC	15.30
Experimental Rhythms	CAN	1976	Peter Lipskis	20		LFMC	17.00
Eye and the Ear, The	GB	1944-45	F./S. Themerson	10		LFMC	10.00
Eye Myth	USA	1972	Stan Brakhage	9 secs		LFMC	10.00
Face (A)	JAP	1976	Taka Limura	20		LFMC	17.00
Faces of Faces	W.GER		Robert Hout	6		LFMC	10.00

	COUNTRY OF PRODUCTION	YEAR	DIRECTOR	RUNNING TIME	VERSION	16mm	16mm RENTAL FEE
Facts in the Case of M. Valdemar, The	USA	1976	Janis Crystal Lipzin	12		LFMC	10.20
Faded Wallpaper	GB	1988	Tina Keane	20		LFMC	17.00
Faintings	BEL	1989	Hinant Guy Marc	7		LFMC	10.00
Faith Triumphant	GB	1989	David Leister	3		LFMC	10.00
Fall of the House of Usher	GB	1981	David Finch	30	mag	LFMC	25.50
Fast Religion	GB		Marek Budzynski	22		LFMC	18.70
Fat Film		1989	Mike Hoolboom	4		LFMC	10.00
Father Movie	USA	1980	Ball Gordon	10		LFMC	10.00
Fattendre	GB	1978	Will Milne	12		LFMC	10.20
Faust 3: Candida Albacors	USA		Stan Brakhage	25		LFMC	21.25
Faust Film: An Opera: Part 1	USA		Stan Brakhage	43		LFMC	36.55
Faust IV	USA	1989	Stan Brakhage	37		LFMC	31.45
Faust's Other: An Idyll	USA		Stan Brakhage	43		LFMC	36.55
Fauve		1990	Donna Cameron	11	st	LFMC	10.00
Fee Sanguinaire, Le	BEL	1968	Roland Lethem	27		LFMC	22.95
Felder 9.6	GER	1989	Thomas Mank	10	bw	LFMC	10.00
Fez	GB	1971-72	Annabel Nicolson	3		LFMC	10.00
Field Film No. 2	GB	1977	Terence Ellis	12		LFMC	10.20
Field Film No. 3 (The Dutch Hostage Movie)	GB	1977	Terence Ellis	30		LFMC	25.50
Field of Women	GB	1991	Diana Mavroleon	22		LFMC	18.70
Fil(m)age	FR	1985	M Amarger/F.Devaux	3		LFMC	10.00
Film About Ski Slopes	GB		Karen Smith	20		LFMC	17.00
Film Exercises 4 & 5	USA		John Whitney & Bernie O'Regan	5		LFMC	10.00
Film for Judy, A			Bernie O'Regan	15		LFMC	12.75
Film Form	USA	1969	Stan Van Der Beek	10		LFMC	10.00
Film Formed			Alan Brooks	20/40		LFMC	variable
Film in Which There Appears...	USA		Owen Land (formerly George Landlow)	5		LFMC	10.00
Film No. 1	GB	1972	David Crosswaite	10		LFMC	10.00
Film of Their 1973 Spring Tour	USA	1974	Owen Land (formerly George Landlow)	12		LFMC	10.20
Film Print	GB	1973-74	Peter Gidal	40		LFMC	34.00
Film Sound	GB	1984	Andrew Moss	15		LFMC	12.75
Film Strips I	JAP	1967	Taka Limura	11	st	LFMC	10.00
Film Strips II	JAP	1970	Taka Limura	12		LFMC	10.20
Film That Rises to the Surface of Clarified Butter	USA	1968	Owen Land (formerly George Landlow)	10		LFMC	10.00
Film, A	GB	1977	Abraham Krespin	14		LFMC	11.90
Films for Music for Film Everbest, Vigil	USA	1990	Lawrence F Brose	8		LFMC	10.00
Filmusic 1	GB	1978	Chris Garratt	20		LFMC	17.00
Filmusic 2	GB	1978	Chris Garratt	10		LFMC	10.00
Finishes	USA	1981	Peter Beckman	13		LFMC	11.50
Fire of Waters	USA	1965	Stan Brakhage	7		LFMC	10.00
First Comes Love	USA	1990	Su Friedrich	21	bw	LFMC	17.85
First Film	GB	1974	Richard Welsby	3	st	LFMC	10.00
First Memory	GB	1981	Nina Danino	20		LFMC	17.00
First Vampires, The	GB	1983	Brian Cleaver	5		LFMC	10.00
Fish Variations	GB	1982	Tim Cawkwell	9		LFMC	10.00
Five Bar Gate	GB	1976	David Parsons	9		LFMC	10.00
Flak	GB	1970	Graeme Ewens	10		LFMC	10.00
Flash Frames	GB	1980	Alan Renton	11		LFMC	10.00
Flashing Flesh and Bones 1&2		1987	Maeve Woods	48		LFMC	21.60
Flavia	GB	1972-73	Annabel Nicolson	6		LFMC	10.00
Flesh Tones	USA	1969	Walter Chappell	10		LFMC	10.00
Flexipede, The	GB	1969	Tony Pritchett	2		LFMC	10.00
Flicker, The	USA	1966	Tony/Beverly Conrad	30	tape sd	LFMC	25.50
Flora Faddy Furry Dance Day, The	GB	1989	Richard Philpott	10		LFMC	10.00
Fluxus Anthology	USA	1966	Fluxus Group	46		LFMC	39.10
Flying Truck, The	GB	1987	David Finch	15		LFMC	12.75
Focal Lengths	GB	1978	David Parsons	10		LFMC	10.00
Focus	GB	1971	Peter Gidal	7		LFMC	10.00

LFMC

	COUNTRY OF PRODUCTION	YEAR	DIRECTOR	RUNNING TIME	VERSION	16mm	16mm RENTAL FEE
Fog Line	USA	1970	Larry Gottheim	12	st	LFMC	10.20
Footsteps	GB		Marilyn Halford	6		LFMC	10.00
For Godard Fans Only	SWITZ	1981	Toni Streiff	5		LFMC	10.00
Forest Bay	GB	1973	Chris Welsby	5		LFMC	10.00
Forgotten Fictions	GB	1986	David Finch	19		LFMC	16.15
Fortuna	USA	1969	Woody Garvey	7		LFMC	10.00
Four Relations of Movement & Timestream Cigarette		1972	G. Bechtold	10		LFMC	10.00
Four Sound Films	W.GER	1974-75	Helmut Nickels	10		LFMC	10.00
4th Wall	GB	1978	Peter Gidal	45		LFMC	38.25
Frames	GB	1985	Brian Cleaver	13		LFMC	11.05
Frames	GB	1971-72	Annabel Nicolson	6		LFMC	10.00
Frames & Cages and Speeches	USA	1979	Martha Haslanger	13	st	LFMC	11.05
Frank Stein			Ivan Zulueta	3		LFMC	10.00
Free Radicals	NZ	1979	Len Lye	4		LFMC	10.00
Free Show	GB	1979	Jayne Parker	16		LFMC	13.60
Freud Jung Split, The	CAN		Jonathon Pollard	10		LFMC	10.00
Friday	USA	1967	Obern Vaughan	6		LFMC	10.00
Friday Fred	GB	1980	Mike Leggett	15	mag	LFMC	12.75
From Sunset to Sunrise			Dan Graham	6		LFMC	10.00
From the Exterior	NETH		Barbara Meter	8		LFMC	10.00
Frozen Flashes	W.GER	1982	O Dore	29		LFMC	24.65
Frozen Flight	USA	1977	Bruce Wood	32		LFMC	27.20
Fudge Sunday	USA		Robert Dvorak	2		LFMC	10.00
Funf Film	W.GER		Peter Rohr	8		LFMC	10.00
Furies	USA	1984	Sarah Petty	3		LFMC	10.00
Fuses	USA	1965-68	Carolee Schneemann	25		LFMC	21.50
Fuzz Against Junk	USA	1968	Norman Rubington	15		LFMC	12.75
Gadflies	USA	1976	Stan Brakhage	14		LFMC	11.90
Gallery	USA	1971	Ken Rudolf	6		LFMC	10.00
Game II	GB	1982-83	Richard Philpott	8		LFMC	10.00
Garden of Earthly Delights, The	USA	1981	Stan Brakhage	2.5	col/st	LFMC	10.00
Gate Seventy Eight (Carnival)	GB	1978-79	Jaffer Mohammed	7		LFMC	10.00
Gentlemen	GB	1988	David Farringdon	15		LFMC	12.75
Gently Down the Stream	USA	1981	Su Friedrich	15	bw/st	LFMC	12.75
Georgia	USA	1970	Ball Gordon	4		LFMC	10.00
Gertrug Number One	W.GER	1971	Nekes Werner	12		LFMC	10.20
Ghost of the Borie, The	GB	1984	Emina Kurtagic	12		LFMC	10.20
Ghost Stories	GB	1983	Nicky Hamlyn	30		LFMC	25.50
Girl Chewing Gum, The	GB	1976	John Smith	12	mag	LFMC	10.20
Gladstone Played	NZ	1976	William Keddell	18		LFMC	15.30
Glory Boys?	GB	1983	Vanda Carter	4		LFMC	10.00
Goethe and the S.S. Girls			Brian Sharpe	40		LFMC	34.00
Gottinger Vision, Die	BE	1988	Volker Schonwart	7		LFMC	10.00
Graded Grains and Rhythmic Excercises	GB	1980	Peter Samson	12		LFMC	10.20
Grandfather's Footsteps	GB	1983	Anne Rees-Mogg	33		LFMC	28.05
Grass	GB		Paul Bush	11		LFMC	10.00
Graz, The	GB		Jeff Keen	5		LFMC	10.00
Great Sadness of Zohara, The	USA	1983	Nina Menkes	40		LFMC	40.00
Green Cut Gate	USA	1970	Fred Drummond	16	st	LFMC	13.60
Green Kiss	W.GER	1983	Josef Stohr	2		LFMC	10.00
Green, The	EIR		Kilroy Kiernan	10		LFMC	10.00
Guesswork	GB	1979	Nicky Hamlyn	11	mag	LFMC	10.00
Guide	GB	1984	Jim Forster	25		LFMC	21.50
Guilt	GB	1988	Peter Gidal	40		LFMC	34.00
Gulls and Buoys	USA	1973	Robert Breer	8		LFMC	10.00
Hackney Marshes	GB	1977	John Smith	15		LFMC	12.75
Hall	GB	1968-69	Peter Gidal	10		LFMC	10.00
Hamer Barker – Portrait of a Lancashire Farmer	GB	1985	C. Clemence/J. Cole	20		LFMC	17.00

	COUNTRY OF PRODUCTION	YEAR	DIRECTOR	RUNNING TIME	VERSION	16mm	16mm RENTAL FEE
Hands	USA	1971	Karen Johnson	3		LFMC	10.00
Harmony	GB		Jo Comino	6		LFMC	10.00
He Was Born, He Suffered, He Died	USA	1974	Stan Brakhage	7	st	LFMC	10.00
Headgear	GB	1991	David Leister	6	bw	LFMC	10.00
Heads	GB	1969	Peter Gidal	35	st	LFMC	29.75
Heads for the Talebearer	GB		George Saxon	10		LFMC	10.00
Heart of Gold	GB		David Finch	11		LFMC	10.00
Hell Spit Flexion	USA		Stan Brakhage	1		LFMC	10.00
Hello Skinny	USA	1979	Ralph Records	3		LFMC	10.00
Hergebrachtes	GB		Kiefer Urs	25		LFMC	21.50
Herz (Heart)	W.GER	1985	Regine Steenbock	7		LFMC	10.00
Hide and Seek	EIR	1990	Orlagh Mulcahy	7		LFMC	10.00
Hide and Seek	GB	1987	Moira Sweeney	16		LFMC	13.60
High Key	IT	1985	Andrea Garofalo	7		LFMC	10.00
High Stepping	GB	1970	Roger Hammond	13		LFMC	11.05
Highway	GB	1976-79	Jaffer Mohammed	6		LFMC	10.00
His Romantic Movement	CAN	1985	Richard Kerr	18		LFMC	15.30
Historical Perspective, An	GB	1975	Terence Ellis	5	st	LFMC	10.00
History of Motion in Motion	USA	1966	Stan Van Der Beek	10		LFMC	10.00
Hochhaus	W.GER	1987	Thomas Mank	7		LFMC	10.00
Home Movie	W.GER	1974	Roger Arguile	23		LFMC	19.55
Home Movies			Danny Seymour	20		LFMC	17.00
Home Movies Reel 1	GB	1970-77	Jarman Derek	10		LFMC	15.00
Home Movies Reel 2	GB	1975-76	Jarman Derek	10		LFMC	15.00
Horizon	GB	1982	Fionna Wire	15		LFMC	12.75
Horseman, The Woman and the Moth, The	USA	1968	Stan Brakhage	20	st	LFMC	17.00
House Light	GB	1980-81	Joanna Millet	11		LFMC	10.00
House that Jack Built, The	GB		Goerge Saxon	7		LFMC	10.00
Hoy	GB	1984	Christopher Newby	15		LFMC	12.75
Hugh MacDiarmid: A Portrait	GB	1964	Margaret Tait	9		LFMC	10.00
Humpback Angel, The	GB		Joanna Woodward	15		LFMC	12.75
I Cat	GB	1980	Jayne Parker	10		LFMC	10.00
I Dish	GB	1990	Jayne Parker	16		LFMC	13.60
I Never Get Home	CAN	1990	Ken Berry	2		LFMC	10.00
I Scream Screen Dream	USA		Alan Brooks	4		LFMC	10.00
I Seek	GB	1985	Julia Harrington	16		LFMC	13.60
Illusive Crime	GB	1976	Richard Woolley	33		LFMC	28.05
Image Moment	GB	1984-85	Michael Maziere	30		LFMC	25.50
Imaginary	GB	1988	Moira Sweeney	7		LFMC	10.00
Impromptu	FR	1989	Rose Lowder	8		LFMC	10.00
Improvisations for Shawn, Tape Treatment and Projection	GB	1985	Rob Gawthrop	20		LFMC	17.00
In Flight	GB		Marilyn Halford	12		LFMC	10.20
In Motion	GB	1981	Martin Sercombe	11		LFMC	10.00
In Narcissus' Pool	EIR	1988	Meredith Monk	12		LFMC	
In Quest for Meat Joy	USA	1969	Carolee Schneemann	17		LFMC	14.45
Incontinence	USA	1978	Manuel De Landa	18		LFMC	15.30
Inferential Current	USA	1979	Paul Sharits	8		LFMC	10.00
Inflorescence	USA	1971	John Gruenberger	7		LFMC	10.00
Inside	GB	1982	El Glinoer	8		LFMC	10.00
Inside and Outside	GB	1975	Richard Woolley	30		LFMC	25.50
Inside Out	GB	1978	Nicky Hamlyn	38		LFMC	32.30
Int/Ext	GB	1976	Steve Farrer	6		LFMC	10.00
Interieur Interiors (To A.K.)	USA	1978	Vincent Grenier	15		LFMC	12.75
Interim	USA	1953	Stan Brakhage	25		LFMC	21.25
Interlude	GB	1989	David Leister	12	bw	LFMC	10.20
Invisible Space	GB	1982	El Glinoer	6		LFMC	10.00
Invocation	GB	1985	Lesley Keen	5		LFMC	10.00
Iro (Colours)	JAP	1979	Taka Limura	11		LFMC	10.00

LFMC

	COUNTRY OF PRODUCTION	YEAR	DIRECTOR	RUNNING TIME	VERSION	16mm	16mm RENTAL FEE
Is That It? Scene 1 (Images of Young People)	GB	1986	Thust Will	21		LFMC	11.90
Is That It? Scene 2 (Images of School)	GB	1986	Will Thust	11		LFMC	10.00
Is That It? Scene 3 (Images of War)	GB	1986	Will Thust	15		LFMC	12.75
Is That It? Scene 4 (Images of the East End)	GB	1986	Will Thust	12		LFMC	10.20
Is That It? Scene 5 (Images of Fear)	GB	1986	Will Thust	10		LFMC	10.00
Is That It? Scene 6 (Images of Control)	GB	1986	Will Thust	21		LFMC	17.85
Island Design	USA	1976	Bruce Wood	7		LFMC	10.00
It's a Mixed-Up World	CAN	1982	Peter Lipskis	8		LFMC	10.00
Itch, Scratch, Itch Cycle, The	USA	1977	Manuel De Landa	8		LFMC	10.00
Jalostitlan and Encarnacion	CAN	1984	Phillip Hoffman	6		LFMC	10.00
Japsen	Switz	1987	Mathis Muda/Rist Pippilotti/Rist P	12		LFMC	10.20
Jesus: The Film	W.GER	1986	Michael Brynntrup	125		LFMC	56.25
Jim and Ernie	CAN	1984	Phillip Craig	27	bw	LFMC	22.95
Jinx	USA	1981	Ralph Records	3		LFMC	10.00
Journey, The	GB	1975	Ian Breakwell	30		LFMC	25.50
Journeys	GB	1981-82	Nick Collins	5		LFMC	10.00
K	GB	1989	Jayne Parker	13	bw	LFMC	11.05
Kaleidoscope	NZ	1935	Len Lye	4		LFMC	10.00
Kali-Film	GER	1989	Wilhelm/Birgit Hein	90		LFMC	45.00
Kaskara	W.GER	1974	O Dore	20		LFMC	17.00
Keeper of Accounts	GB	1987	Lily R Markiewicz	20		LFMC	17.00
Kinestasis 60	USA	1970	Charles Braverman	4		LFMC	10.00
King Was In His Counting House, The	GB	1980	Kennedy C/Maguire R.	18		LFMC	15.30
Kino Da!	USA	1981	Henry Hills	2	bw	LFMC	10.00
Kiss, The	GB	1985	Annabel Hands	3		LFMC	10.00
Kitchen Door In Semi Moonlight	GB	1986	Julie Osborne	27		LFMC	22.95
Kitchener-Berlin	CAN	1990	Phillip Hoffman	34		LFMC	28.90
Klipperty Klopp	GB	1986	Andrew Kotting	12		LFMC	10.20
Kniephofstrasse	GB	1973-74	Richard Woolley	25		LFMC	21.50
Kopenhagen 1930	GB	1977	Peter Gidal	40		LFMC	34.00
Kugelkopf (An Ode to IBM)	AUST	1987	Mattuschka Mara	6	bw	LFMC	10.00
Kyudo	GB	1980	Grayson Simon	6		LFMC	10.00
L'Ange Frenetique	GB	1985	Maggie Jailler	5		LFMC	10.00
Lapis	USA	1965	James Whitney	9	st	LFMC	10.00
Lawale	W.GER	1969	O Dore	42		LFMC	35.70
Leading Light	GB	1975	John Smith	11	st	LFMC	10.00
Legend of Big Sur	USA	1969	Walter Chappell	15		LFMC	12.75
Legend for Fountains	USA	1957-70	Joseph Cornell	17	st	LFMC	14.45
Lemon	USA	1969	Hollis Frampton	7	st	LFMC	10.00
Length of Time, A	GB	1970	Anne Rees-Mogg	23		LFMC	19.55
Lens Tissue	GB	1973	Mike Dunford	5		LFMC	10.00
Lensless	GB	1971	John Du Cane	5		LFMC	10.00
Letter to a Long Lost Friend	CAN	1980	Robert Rayher	8		LFMC	10.00
Letter to D.H. in Paris	USA	1968	David Brooks	4		LFMC	10.00
Levels	GB	1980	Alan Renton	6	mag	LFMC	10.00
Liberation	USA	1967	Henry Polonsky		20	LFMC	17.00
Light Movements	GB	1977	John Woodman	11		LFMC	10.00
Light Reading	GB	1979	Lis Rhodes	20		LFMC	17.00
Light Sleep	GB	1981	John Smith	6		LFMC	10.00
Light Support	GB		George Saxon	10		LFMC	10.00
Line	USA	1966-67	T Anderson/Brodwick	11		LFMC	10.00
Line 1,2,3,A	JAP	1972	Taka Limura	17		LFMC	14.45
Line Describing a Cone	USA	1973	Anthony McCall	30		LFMC	25.50
Lion's Tale, A	USA	1968	Walter Ungerer	13		LFMC	11.05
Little Dog for Roger	USA	1968	Malcolm LeGrice	13		LFMC	11.05
Little Fable, A	USA	1978	Robert Pike	4		LFMC	10.00
Little Stabs at Happiness	USA	1963	Ken Jacobs	18		LFMC	15.30
Littlehamptons	GB	1974-80	Rob Gawthrop	33		LFMC	28.05

	COUNTRY OF PRODUCTION	YEAR	DIRECTOR	RUNNING TIME	VERSION	16mm	16mm RENTAL FEE
Living Memory	GB	1980	Anne Rees-Mogg	39		LFMC	33.15
Lizard Mosaic	USA	1960	Karen Johnson	3		LFMC	10.00
LMNO	USA	1978	Robert Breer	10		LFMC	10.00
Logically Speaking	GB		Laura Smith-Hastings	28		LFMC	23.80
London Suite (Getting Sucked In)	GB	1990	Vivienne Dick	28		LFMC	23.80
London-Capewrath-London	GB	1978	Jenny Okun	10		LFMC	10.00
Long Eyes of Earth	USA	1990	Lawrence F Brose	10	bw	LFMC	10.00
Looking Into and Out of a Winter Diary	GB	1985	Nick Collins	9		LFMC	10.00
Looks Familiar	GB	1989	Kayla Parker	3	bw	LFMC	10.00
Loop	GB	1970	Peter Gidal	8		LFMC	10.00
Loose String	GB	1982	El Glinoer	6		LFMC	10.00
Loud Visual Noises	USA		Stan Brakhage	3		LFMC	10.00
Love	JAP	1963	Taka Limura	12	sd	LFMC	20.00
Love ('Ai')	JAP	1963	Taka Limura	12		LFMC	10.20
Love Love Love	GB	1967	Michael Nyman	5		LFMC	10.00
Lovelies and Dowdies	GB		Ken McMullen	30		LFMC	25.50
Lovemaking I	USA	1968	Stan Brakhage	5	st	LFMC	10.00
Lovemaking II	USA	1968	Stan Brakhage	10	st	LFMC	10.00
Luck Is the Residue of Desire	CAN	1982	Richard Kerr	20		LFMC	17.00
MA: Space/Time in the Garden of Ryoan-Ji	JAP	1989	Taka Limura	16		LFMC	
Macbeth a Tragedy & Welcome Adieu	GB	1983	Anne Rees-Mogg	6		LFMC	10.00
Machine of Eden	USA	1979	Stan Brakhage	12		LFMC	10.20
Mad Metropolis	GB	1979	A Soma. (Formerly J. Apps)	15		LFMC	12.75
Magdalena Viraga	USA	1985	Nina Menkes	90		LFMC	50.00
Magic Act, A	GB	1984	David Leister	12		LFMC	10.20
Maja Replicate	GB	1971	Fred Drummond	15		LFMC	12.75
Man and His Dog, 69, & Recreation	USA	1968	Robert Breer	10		LFMC	10.00
Man in the Dark Sedan	USA	1980	Ralph Records	5		LFMC	10.00
Man with a Movie Camera	GB	1973	David Crosswaite	8		LFMC	10.00
Man You Love to Hate, The	W.GER	1984	Leschig Gregor	6		LFMC	10.00
Manifest Der Finster Spinsters	GER	1987	Joritz Cathy/Hahne Marille	5		LFMC	10.00
Mankinda	USA	1957	Stan Van Der Beek	10		LFMC	10.00
Marasmus	USA	1981	Betzy Bromberg	24		LFMC	20.40
Marie-Edith	GB	1981	Penn Valerie	8		LFMC	10.00
Marilyn Times Five	USA	1974	Bruce Conner	13		LFMC	11.05
Market	GB	1971-72	Annabel Nicolson	3		LFMC	10.00
Married Life	GB	1982	Jones V./Andrews C	15		LFMC	12.75
Married Print	GB	1982	Rob Gawthrop	6		LFMC	10.00
Marvo Movie	GB	1967	Jeff Keen	5		LFMC	10.00
Mary Quant Mask of Death, The	GB	1982	Masuak Greg	11		LFMC	10.00
Masquerade	USA	1981	Larry Jordan	5		LFMC	10.00
Mass for the Dakota Sioux	USA	1964	Bruce Bailli	24		LFMC	20.40
Matter of Boabab — with One Growth, The	USA	1966-70	Pola Chapelle	2		LFMC	10.00
Mayhem	USA	1986	Abigail Child	20		LFMC	17.00
Meat of Other Times	GB	1983	Will Milne	30		LFMC	25.50
Meatdaze	GB	1971	Jeff Keen	10		LFMC	10.00
Mechanical Flight	GB	1985	Joy Elliot	5		LFMC	10.00
Meditation	USA	1972	Jordon Belson	10		LFMC	10.00
Meg			D./M. Riollano	8		LFMC	10.00
Melting	USA	1970	Thom Anderson	6		LFMC	10.00
Memories of King Richard	FR		John Felton	10		LFMC	10.00
Mercy	USA	1989	Abigail Child	10		LFMC	10.00
Mesa Verde	USA		Stan Brakhage			LFMC	
Mesopotamiam Background, The	GB	1977	Will Milne	15		LFMC	12.75
Message From Budapest	GB	1988	Michael Maziere	15		LFMC	12.75
Messages Messages			Michael Wiese	28		LFMC	23.80
Messiah in the Shadow of Death, The	GB	1985	Richard Philpott	10		LFMC	10.00
Metacta 361	USSR	1985/5	Gleb/Igor Alenikov	20		LFMC	17.00

LFMC	COUNTRY OF PRODUCTION	YEAR	DIRECTOR	RUNNING TIME	VERSION	16mm	16mm RENTAL FEE
Migration	CAN	1969	David Rimmer	12		LFMC	10.20
Mile End Purgatorio	GB	1991	Guy Sherwin	1		LFMC	10.00
Mill Film	GB	1971-72	Annabel Nicolson	2		LFMC	10.00
Miller and the Sweep, The	GB	1985	Joanna Millett	6		LFMC	10.00
Mills Lawn School	FR		John Felton	10		LFMC	10.00
Mirror Films	GB		Steve Farrer	16		LFMC	13.60
Misconceptions	GB	1981-82	Peter Milner	10		LFMC	10.00
Missing, The	GB	1980	Jo Comino	6		LFMC	10.00
MM-FF	GB	1977	Richard Beard	8		LFMC	10.00
Mnemosyne	GB	1985	Gad Hollander	16		LFMC	13.60
Mobile Statics	USA	1969	Helmut Schultz	6		LFMC	10.00
Moirage	USA	1966-88	Stan Van Der Beek	10		LFMC	10.00
Molten Shadow	USA	1976	Bruce Wood	8		LFMC	10.00
Moment	USA	1972	Bill Brand	25		LFMC	21.25
Mona Lisa	GB	1983	Roger Hewins	2		LFMC	10.00
Money	USA	1985	Henry Hills	15		LFMC	12.75
Mongoloid	USA	1978	Bruce Conner	4		LFMC	10.00
Monkey's Birthday	GB	1975	David Larcher	35		LFMC	29.75
Moon Time	USA	1989	James Browne	7		LFMC	10.00
Moonlight Sonata	USA	1979	Larry Jordan	5		LFMC	10.00
Moral Judge	GB	1987	Gina Gables Czarnecki	4		LFMC	10.00
Mosaik im Vertauen	AUST	1955	Peter Kubelka	17		LFMC	14.45
Mothfight	GB	1985	Vanda Carter	8		LFMC	10.00
Mothlight	USA	1964	Stan Brakhage	4		LFMC	10.00
Motion Picture	GB	1980	Lucy Pantelli	12		LFMC	10.20
Motorcycle/Pylon	GB	1987	Michael Denton	3		LFMC	10.00
Mourning Garden Blackbird	GB	1984	Anna Thew	7		LFMC	10.00
Movie No. 1	GB		Peter Gidal	5		LFMC	10.00
Movie Set Theory, A Universe of Discourse	USA	1975-76	Gordon Dana	21		LFMC	17.85
Movie, A	USA	1966	Bruce Conner	12		LFMC	10.20
Moving Studies in Black and White	GB	1979	Marilyn Halford	25		LFMC	21.25
Murder Psalm	USA	1981	Stan Brakhage	17		LFMC	14.45
Musical '79	GB	1979	Rob Gawthrop	15		LFMC	12.75
Mute Women	GB	1989	Dan Reed	8		LFMC	15.30
Muybridge Film	GB	1975	Anne Rees-Mogg	5		LFMC	10.00
My Film	GB		Adrian Munsey	15		LFMC	12.75
My First Gay Film?	GB	1982	Steve Farrer	12		LFMC	10.20
Myths and Legends	GB	1987	Wilkie Pier	7		LFMC	7.00
N.O.T.H.I.N.G.	USA	1968	Paul Sharits	36		LFMC	30.60
Nature Boy	GB	1990	David Leister	14	bw	LFMC	11.90
Neo Classic		1971	Robert Morris	14		LFMC	11.90
Neon Diver	GB	1990	Tina Keane	18		LFMC	15.30
Net & Glaze of Cathexis	USA		Stan Brakhage			LFMC	
New Improved Institutional Quality	USA	1976	Owen Land (formerly George Landlow)	5		LFMC	10.00
New Sketches	GB	1978	Marilyn Halford	30		LFMC	25.50
New York	GB	1978	Margy Kinmonth	6		LFMC	10.00
New York Eye and Ear Control	CAN	1964	Michael Snow	34		LFMC	28.90
New York, This Is The History Of	USA	1988	Jem Cohen	20		LFMC	17.00
Newsreel: Jonas in the Brig	USA	1973	Storm De Hirsch	5	st	LFMC	10.00
Nightlight	GB	1976	Rob Gawthrop	6		LFMC	10.00
Nightlights	GB	1986	Joy Elliot	9		LFMC	10.00
Nine Jokes	GB	1971	Ian Breakwell	13	st	LFMC	11.05
1970	USA	1970	Robert Breer	5		LFMC	10.00
1933	CAN	1967	JoyceWieland	5		LFMC	10.00
Nine Variations on a Dance Theme	USA	1968	Harris Hilary	11		LFMC	10.00
Nitsch	AUS	1969	Ed/Irm Sommer	14		LFMC	11.90
No Lawns in Hyderabad	GB	1976-79	Jaffer Mohammed	10		LFMC	10.00
No Sir Orison	USA	1975	Owen Land (formerly George Landlow)	2		LFMC	10.00

	COUNTRY OF PRODUCTION	YEAR	DIRECTOR	RUNNING TIME	VERSION	16mm	16mm RENTAL FEE
No. 5 Reversal	CAN	1989	Josephine Massarella	10		LFMC	10.00
Norwood	GB	1983	Patrick Keiller	26		LFMC	22.10
Nose, The	USA	1970	Howard Lester	38		LFMC	32.30
Nosegay, A	GB	1986	Maggie Jailler	17		LFMC	14.45
Nostalgia	USA	1971	Hollis Frampton	36		LFMC	30.60
Not Available in Case of Emergency	W.GER	1985	Funke/Monika Stern	15		LFMC	12.75
Not to See Again	GB	1966	Nicky Hamlyn	13	mag	LFMC	11.05
Notebook	USA	1962	Marie Menken	10		LFMC	10.00
Notes on a Line	GB	1987	David Leister	12	bw	LFMC	10.20
Notes on the Circus	USA	1970	Jonas Mekas	13		LFMC	11.05
Nothing is Something	USA	1966	Anne Rees-Mogg	9	st	LFMC	10.00
Now	GB		Iijon Jeanette	7		LFMC	10.00
Nuclear Family	GB	1990	Kayla Parker	5	bw	LFMC	10.00
Nymphlight	USA	1979	Joseph Cornell	8		LFMC	10.00
'O'	GB	1990	Nick Gordon Smith	10		LFMC	10.00
Observing Enemy Movements (A)	USA	1980-81	David Rodowick	10		LFMC	10.00
Observing Enemy Movements (B)	USA	1980-81	David Rodowick	10		LFMC	10.00
Occassion			Fred Marshall	10		LFMC	10.00
Ocean Wave	GB	1983	Steve Farrer	12		LFMC	10.20
Odd Bod With Bugle	EIR		Kilroy Kiernan	5		LFMC	10.00
Oh Death How Nourishing You Are	W.GER	1979	Margaret Raspe	15		LFMC	12.75
Oh Dem Watermelons	USA	1965	Robert Nelson	12		LFMC	10.20
Old Harry Rocks	GB	1978	Rob Gawthrop	6		LFMC	10.00
On Edge & Mark Twain & Cutting Corners	GB	1974	Terence Ellis	12	st	LFMC	10.20
On the Day	GB	1979	Martin Hearne	15	st	LFMC	12.75
On the Marriage Broker Joke...	USA	1980	Owen Land (formerly George Landlow)	17		LFMC	14.45
On the Pond	CAN	1978	Phillip Hoffman	9		LFMC	10.00
One	GB		N. Burton & A. Kennedy	12		LFMC	10.20
One	GB	1968	Anne Rees-Mogg	20		LFMC	17.00
One Frame Duration	JAP	1977	Taka Iimura	12		LFMC	10.20
One Minute Movies	USA	1980	Ralph Records	5		LFMC	10.00
One Nation Under TV	USA	1985	Ruth Peyser	2		LFMC	10.00
One Second in Montreal	CAN	1969	Michael Snow	25	st	LFMC	21.50
1 to 60 Seconds	JAP	1973	Taka Iimura	30		LFMC	25.50
One Woman Waiting	CAN		Masserella Josephine	9		LFMC	10.00
Operation	GB	1978	Rob Gawthrop	9		LFMC	10.00
Optic Nerve	USA	1985	Barbara Hammer	16		LFMC	13.60
Opus One Plus			Herbert Kowser	2		LFMC	10.00
Ora	GB	1980	A Soma. (Formerly J. Apps)	13	st	LFMC	11.05
Orange	USA	1960	Karen Johnson	3		LFMC	10.00
Orpheus and Eurydice	USA	1984	Lesley Keen	6		LFMC	10.00
Other Reckless Things	USA	1984	Janis Crystal Lipzin	20		LFMC	17.00
Our Lady of the Sphere	USA	1969	Larry Jordan	10		LFMC	10.00
Overflow Solutions	GB	1981	Tony Fisher	15		LFMC	12.75
Oyinbo Pepper	GB	1986	Enahoro Carole	20		LFMC	17.00
Painting 1/2 (2 Screen)	GB	1986	Michael Maziere	3		LFMC	10.00
Panels for the Walls of the World	USA	1967	Stan Van Der Beek	8		LFMC	10.00
Panorama	GB	1968	Simon Hartog	3		LFMC	10.00
Parables			Frances Earnshaw	12		LFMC	10.20
Parallax III	GB	1977	Richard Welsby	3	st	LFMC	10.00
Parcelle	FR	1979	Rose Lowder	2		LFMC	10.00
Park Film	GB	1972	Chris Welsby	7	st	LFMC	10.00
Part 1 and 2/78	NETH	1978	John Devine	8		LFMC	10.00
Part Time Virgin	GB	1972	Mike Dunford	35	mag	LFMC	29.75
Particles in Space	NZ	1979	Len Lye	4		LFMC	10.00
Pasht	USA	1979	Stan Brakhage	6		LFMC	10.00
Passage	GB	1982-83	Nick Collins	13		LFMC	11.05
Passages	GB	1986	William English	24		LFMC	20.40

LFMC

	COUNTRY OF PRODUCTION	YEAR	DIRECTOR	RUNNING TIME	VERSION	16mm	16mm RENTAL FEE
Passing Through & Torn Formations	CAN	1988	Phillip Hoffman	14		LFMC	11.90
Past Possessed	GB	1984	Steve Farrer	20		LFMC	17.00
Pastel Pussies	USA		Judith Wardell	3		LFMC	10.00
Pastorale	USA	1965	Stan Van Der Beek	10		LFMC	10.00
Patacake Patacake Baker's Man	W.GER	1979	Margaret Raspe	20		LFMC	17.00
Path Ways	GB	1991	Llias Pantos	8	bw	LFMC	10.00
Pavement The	GB	1988	Diana Mavroleon	15		LFMC	12.75
Peaches and Cream	USA	1970	Charles Levine	5		LFMC	10.00
Pecking Order, The	GB	1989	Smith Vicky	5		LFMC	10.00
Perfect Film	USA	1986	Ken Jacobs	22	bw	LFMC	18.70
Perforce	IT	1968	G. Barucello	15		LFMC	12.75
Perils	USA		Abigail Child	5		LFMC	10.00
Periodic Variations in an Elastic Medium	USA	1973-76	Janis Crystal Lipzin	16		LFMC	13.60
Persisting	GB	1978	Ian Kerr	9		LFMC	10.00
Pestilent City	USA	1968	Peter Emanuel Goldman	15		LFMC	12.75
Petit Mal	USA	1977	Betzy Bromberg	18		LFMC	15.30
Peyote Queen	USA	1965	Storm De Hirsch	8		LFMC	10.00
Pfaueninsel (Auf der)	AUST	1971	Kurt Kren	1		LFMC	10.00
Pharaoh's Parachute, The	GB	1982	Peter Samson	30	mag	LFMC	25.50
Phoenix Farm	GB	1980	Claire Barwell	10		LFMC	10.00
Phone/Film Portraits	1985	USA	Dominic Angerame	6		LFMC	10.00
Photo Film	GB	1967	Fred Drummond	10	st	LFMC	10.00
Photo/graph/film	GB	1973	Peter Gidal	5	st	LFMC	10.00
Photoplay	GB		Lucy Pantelli	40		LFMC	34.00
Picture Planes	GB	1977	David Parsons	15		LFMC	12.75
Picture Planes 2	GB	1979	David Parsons	20		LFMC	17.00
Pictures on Pink Paper	GB	1982	Lis Rhodes	35		LFMC	29.75
Piece Mandala/End War	USA	1966	Paul Sharits	5		LFMC	10.00
Piece Touche	AUST	1989	Martin Arnold	16		LFMC	13.60
Pieces	GB	1971	Ken McMullen	7		LFMC	10.00
Place Between Our Bodies, The	USA	1976	Michael Wallin	33		LFMC	25.00
Place Mattes	USA	1987	Barbara Hammer	18		LFMC	15.30
Place of Work	GB	1976	Margaret Tait	31		LFMC	26.35
Place on the Hill	GB	1979	Rob Gawthrop	6		LFMC	10.00
Play Mountain Place	USA	1971	Trevor Black	30		LFMC	25.50
Plumbline	USA	1968-72	Carolee Schneemann	15		LFMC	12.75
Plutonium Blonde	GB	1986	Sandra Lahire	15		LFMC	12.75
Poemfield No. 3	USA	1967	Stan Van Der Beek	6		LFMC	10.00
Poet of a Half Past Three, The	GB	1981	Joanna Woodward	11		LFMC	10.00
Pointillist Dance	GB	1988	David Leister	14	bw	LFMC	11.90
Points of View	USA	1979	Joanna Kiernan	19		LFMC	16.15
Polkafox	W.GER	1982	Kober H ./Dobele J.	4		LFMC	10.00
Pool, The	GB	1991	Jayne Parker	10	bw	LFMC	10.00
Poontang Trilogy	USA	1966	Ben Van Meter	8		LFMC	10.00
Portrait Subject Object	GB		Peter Gidal	10		LFMC	10.00
Post Office Tower Retowered	GB	1977-78	Ian Kerr	variable		LFMC	negot.
Pour Faire un Bon Voyage			Ahmet Kut	20		LFMC	17.00
Preferisco Danzare	IT	1985	Stefano Bortolussi	10		LFMC	10.00
Preservation& Steaming & Incline	GB	1976-82	Rob Gawthrop	24		LFMC	20.40
Primitive	GB	1982	Brian Cleaver	3		LFMC	10.00
Problem Being, The	GB	1979	Christine Felce	20		LFMC	17.00
Project I and II	GB	1981	Rob Gawthrop	12		LFMC	10.20
Projected Film	GB		Frances Earnshaw	12		LFMC	10.20
Propaganda	GB	1973	Richard Woolley	9		LFMC	10.00
Prothalamion	USA	1978	Ball Gordon	4		LFMC	10.00
Psychedelic Storm		1967	Keith Griffith	5		LFMC	10.00
Putney Reach	GB	1975	Renny Croft	12		LFMC	10.20
?O, Zool (The Making of a Fiction Film)	CAN	1988	Phillip Hoffman	26		LFMC	22.10

LFMC	COUNTRY OF PRODUCTION	YEAR	DIRECTOR	RUNNING TIME	VERSION	16mm	16mm RENTAL FEE
Ralph Records Compilation	USA		Ralph Records	34		LFMC	28.90
Ransom Note	USA		Howard Lester	2		LFMC	10.00
Rat Life and Diet in North America	USA	1968	Joyce Wieland	16		LFMC	13.60
Rate of Change	USA	1968	Bill Brand	18		LFMC	15.30
Raw Nerves	USA	1979	Manuel De Landa	20		LFMC	17.00
Ray Gun Virus	USA	1978	Stephanie Beroes	14		LFMC	11.90
Real as a Dream	GB	1986-87	Steve Farrer	20		LFMC	17.00
Real Time	GB	1974	Anne Rees-Mogg	32		LFMC	27.20
Recital	USA	1978	Stephanie Beroes	20		LFMC	17.00
Recreation	USA	1985	Robert Breer	5		LFMC	10.00
Red Car, The	CAN	1985	Peter Lipskis	4		LFMC	10.00
Red Sea, The	GB	1992	Michael Maziere	25		LFMC	21.50
Reflections	GB	1972	William Pye	17		LFMC	14.45
Reflections on Black	USA	1958	Stan Brakhage	12		LFMC	10.20
Reflections on My Shadow	GB	1982	John Woodman	30		LFMC	25.50
Reichstag Fire Part One	GB	1976	N.Burton/A.Kennedy	12		LFMC	10.20
Reign of the Vampire	GB	1970	Malcolm LeGrice	15		LFMC	12.75
Reindeer Slaughter at Lake Krutvattner	SWE		Louis O'Konor	6		LFMC	10.00
Relations	GB	1974	John Du Cane	45		LFMC	38.25
Reliable Witness	GB	1981	Roger Hammond	12		LFMC	10.20
Remedial Reading Comprehension	GB	1970	Owen Land (formerly George Landlow)	5		LFMC	10.00
Repertory	GB	1973	Ian Breakwell	9		LFMC	10.00
Report	USA	1965	Bruce Conner	13		LFMC	11.05
Retour d'un Repere	FR	1979	Rose Lowder	20		LFMC	17.00
Revelation	USA		Gordon Ball	4		LFMC	10.00
Rhythm	NZ	1957	Len Lye	1		LFMC	10.00
Riddle of Lumen, The	USA	1972	Stan Brakhage	15		LFMC	12.75
Rime of the Ancient Mariner, The	USA	1977	Larry Jordan	42		LFMC	35.70
Rinecar	NETH	1984	Claudia Kolgen	8		LFMC	10.00
Road Ended at the Beach, The	CAN	1983	Phillip Hoffman	33		LFMC	28.05
Robot Bee	GB		Steve Farrer	10		LFMC	10.00
Rocking and Rolling	GB	1978	Bob Fearns	14		LFMC	11.90
Roman Numerals I	USA		Stan Brakhage	8	st	LFMC	10.00
Roman Numerals II	USA	1979	Stan Brakhage	8	st	LFMC	10.00
Roman Numerals III	USA	1979	Stan Brakhage	3	st	LFMC	10.00
Roman Numerals IV	USA	1980	Stan Brakhage	3	st	LFMC	10.00
Roman Numerals V	USA	1980	Stan Brakhage	3	st	LFMC	10.00
Roman Numerals VI	USA	1979	Stan Brakhage	11	st	LFMC	10.00
Roman Numerals VII	USA		Stan Brakhage	5	st	LFMC	10.00
Romantic Italy	GB	1975	Chris Garratt	8		LFMC	10.00
Roman Numerals IX	USA	1980	Stan Brakhage	3		LFMC	10.00
Room	CAN		Vincent Grenier	5		LFMC	10.00
Room Double Take	GB	1967	Peter Gidal	10		LFMC	10.00
Room to Move	GB	1971	Ken McMullen	12		LFMC	10.20
Rose Hobart	USA	1939	Joseph Cornell	19		LFMC	16.15
Roslyn Romance (Is It Really True?)	USA	1977	Bruce Bailli	17		LFMC	14.45
Rotor	GB	1980	John Tappenden	S11	10.00	LFMC	5.00
Route 66	GB		Mike Dunford	20		LFMC	17.00
Rubber Cement	USA	1975	Robert Breer	10		LFMC	10.00
Rubblewomen/Trummerfraun	CAN	1985	Bak Gamma	15		LFMC	12.75
Rue des Teinturiers	FR	1979	Rose Lowder	33	st	LFMC	28.05
Running Dog	USA	1982	David Rodowick	3		LFMC	10.00
Runs Good	USA	1970	Pat O'Neill	15		LFMC	12.75
Rush de Rouch, Les	GB	1984	Emina Kurtagic	9		LFMC	10.00
Russian Revolution (excerpts from)			Ken Jacobs	22		LFMC	18.70
RX Recipe	GB		Jayne Parker	12		LFMC	10.50
Ryoanji	USA	1990	Lawrence F Brose	20		LFMC	17.00
S:tream:S:S:ection:	USA	1968-71	Paul Sharits	42		LFMC	35.70

	COUNTRY OF PRODUCTION	YEAR	DIRECTOR	RUNNING TIME	VERSION	16mm	16mm RENTAL FEE
Sad Movies	NETH		Wim Vanderlinden	17		LFMC	14.45
Sadist Beats the Unquestionably Innocent, The	W.GER	1979	Margaret Raspe	6		LFMC	10.00
Safehouse	GB	1984	Kenneth Henwood	20		LFMC	17.00
Sailboat	CAN	1967	JoyceWieland	5		LFMC	10.00
Sailor Trailer & the Trinking Laughter of Little Girls	GB	1984	Anna Thew	8		LFMC	10.00
Salon of '83	GB	1983	Steve Farrer	10		LFMC	10.00
Same	GB	1980	Will Milne	12	mag	LFMC	10.20
Sanday	GB	1987	Nick Collins	16		LFMC	13.60
Satrika	W.GER	1984	Bettina Bayerl	3		LFMC	10.00
Saugus Series	USA	1974	Pat O'Neill	17		LFMC	14.45
Scaling	CAN		Mike Hoolboom	5		LFMC	10.00
Scenes de la Vie Francaise: La Ciotat	FR	1986	Rose Lowder	26		LFMC	22.10
Scenes de la Vie Francaise: Paris	FR	1986	Rose Lowder	3		LFMC	10.00
Scenes from Under Childhood	USA	1967	Stan Brakhage	25		LFMC	21.25
Schweineschnitzel	W.GER	1971	Margaret Raspe	8		LFMC	10.00
Science Friction	USA	1959	StanVanderbeek	10		LFMC	10.00
Scratch No. 2	GB	1973	Mike Dunford	12		LFMC	10.20
Seashore	GB	1971	David Rimmer	11	st	LFMC	10.00
Seated Figures	CAN	1990	Michael Snow	40		LFMC	34.00
Secret Cinema	USA	1966	Paul Bartel	28		LFMC	23.80
Secret Garden, The	USA	1987	Phil Solomon	20		LFMC	17.00
Secret Monkeys	GB	1980	Peter Knight	12	mag	LFMC	10.20
Sedate, The	GB	1982	Jim Forster	17		LFMC	14.45
Seeboden Summer	GB	1981	Tony Fletcher	25		LFMC	21.50
Seeing and Not Seeing	JAP	1972	Taka Limura	6		LFMC	10.00
Selbstbewegung des Frautomaten, Die	W.GER		Margaret Raspe	12		LFMC	10.20
Self Heal	GB	1987	Andrew Kotting	35		LFMC	29.75
Self Portrait	GB	1978	Emina Kurtagic	7		LFMC	10.00
Self Portrait (Collins)	GB	1983	Nick Collins	4		LFMC	10.00
Seminar Das	W.GER	1967	Nekes Werner	32		LFMC	27.20
Sense of Movement	GB	1979	Lucy Pantelli	10		LFMC	10.00
Senseless	USA	1962	Ron Rice	28		LFMC	28.30
Sentence, The	GB	1978	Claire Creswell	10		LFMC	10.00
Sentimental Journey	GB	1978	Michael Maziere	7		LFMC	10.00
Sentimental Journey	USA	1977	Anne Rees-Mogg	30		LFMC	25.50
Separate Incidents	GB	1981	Alan Renton	18		LFMC	15.30
Sermons and Sacred	USA	1989	Lynn Sachs	29		LFMC	24.65
Serpent River	GB	1989	Sandra Lahire	30		LFMC	25.50
Seven Days	GB	1974	ChrisWelsby	20		LFMC	17.00
7P	GB	1978	John Smith	7		LFMC	10.00
7362	USA	1965-67	Pat O'Neill	6		LFMC	10.00
Sexe Engrage, Le	BEL	1970	Roland Lethem	16		LFMC	13.60
Sexual Meditations	USA	1979	Stan Brakhage	23		LFMC	19.55
Sexual Meditations: Hotel	USA	1972	Stan Brakhage	5.5		LFMC	10.00
Sexual Meditations: Office Suite	USA	1972	Stan Brakhage	5		LFMC	10.00
Sexual Meditations: Open Field	USA	1973	Stan Brakhage	6		LFMC	10.00
Sexual Meditations: Room With A View	USA	1971	Stan Brakhage	3		LFMC	10.00
Sforzinda	GB	1977	Tim Cawkwell	13		LFMC	11.05
Shadowman	GB	1991	Phillip Sanderson	12		LFMC	10.20
Shadows of the For Real	GB		David Johnson	3		LFMC	10.00
Shadrac	USA	1985	Sarah Petty	3		LFMC	10.00
Shaman: A Tapestry of Sorcerers	USA	1970	Storm De Hirsch	12		LFMC	10.20
Shapes	GB	1970	Annabel Nicolson	7	st	LFMC	10.00
Shawn, Tape Treatment	GB		Rob Gawthrop	20		LFMC	17.00
She Was Good Looking – Her, She Had A Nice Face			Angie Smith	37		LFMC	31.45
Sheep	GB	1970	Mike Leggett	3	st	LFMC	
Sheepman and the Sheared: Part 1&2	GB	1970-75	Mike Leggett	13	st	LFMC	11.05
Sheet	GB	1970	Ian Breakwell/Ian Leggat	21	mag	LFMC	17.85

	COUNTRY OF PRODUCTION	YEAR	DIRECTOR	RUNNING TIME	VERSION	16mm	16mm RENTAL FEE
Shepherds Bush	GB	1970	Mike Leggett	20		LFMC	17.00
Shift	AUSTR	1980	Michael Clark	30		LFMC	25.50
Short Ends & Commercial Break	GB	1977	Chris Garratt	7		LFMC	10.00
Short Film Series (A)	GB	1976-80	Guy Sherwin	23		LFMC	19.55
Short Film Series (B)	GB	1976-80	Guy Sherwin	21		LFMC	17.85
Short Films of 1974	USA	1975	Stan Brakhage	20		LFMC	17.00
Short Films of 1975	USA	1975	Stan Brakhage	43		LFMC	36.55
Shower & Loop	GB	1968	Fred Drummond	12	st	LFMC	10.20
Showerproof	GB	1968	Fred Drummond	10		LFMC	10.00
Shutter	JAP	1979	Taka Limura	25		LFMC	21.50
Si See Sunni	USA	1970	Charles Levine	5		LFMC	10.00
Side Seat Paintings	GB		Michael Snow	20		LFMC	17.00
Sidewinders Delta	USA	1976	Pat O'Neill	17		LFMC	14.45
Sightseeing	W.GER	1979	Hering Rainer	1		LFMC	10.00
Sign	GB	1974	John Du Cane	45		LFMC	38.25
Silent Film	GB	1982	Michael Maziere	15		LFMC	12.75
Silent Partner	GB	1977	Peter Gidal	35		LFMC	29.75
Silent Search	GB	1981	El Glinoer	18		LFMC	15.30
Silk Screen Films	GB	1974-75	Steve Farrer	15	mag	LFMC	12.75
Silver Street	GB	1974	Nicky Hamlyn	4		LFMC	10.00
Silver Surfer	GB	1972	Mike Dunford	15		LFMC	12.75
Sincerity I	USA	1973	Stan Brakhage	25		LFMC	21.25
Sincerity II	USA	1975	Stan Brakhage	35		LFMC	29.75
Sincerity III	USA	1978	Stan Brakhage	40		LFMC	34.00
Sink or Swim	USA	1990	Su Friedrich	48	bw	LFMC	40.80
Sirius Remembered	USA	1959	Stan Brakhage	12	st	LFMC	10.20
Sitting	USA	1977	Ball Gordon	2		LFMC	10.00
Siva	USA	1989	Charles Levine	2		LFMC	10.00
Six Little Pieces on Film	W.GER	1978	Klaus Wyborny	35		LFMC	29.75
69	USA	1979	Irving Denys	8		LFMC	10.00
Sketches	USA	1976	Stan Brakhage	12		LFMC	10.20
Sky Hills Sheep Water Grass	GB	1985	Paul Bush	7		LFMC	10.00
Sky Light	GB	1988	Chris Welsby	26		LFMC	22.10
Skylight	GB	1984	Michael Maziere	3		LFMC	10.00
Slamming Door	GB	1970	Roger Hammond	8		LFMC	10.00
Slides	GB	1971	Annabel Nicolson	20	st	LFMC	17.00
Slip	GB	1973	Mike Dunford	5		LFMC	10.00
Slow Glass	GB	1991	John Smith	40		LFMC	34.00
Slow Grain	GB	1973	David Parsons	10		LFMC	10.00
Sluice	USA	1979	Stan Brakhage	6		LFMC	10.00
Smoke	GB	1985-87	David Leister	8		LFMC	10.00
Snap Shots		1972	Russell Adams	4		LFMC	10.00
Snig	GB	1982	Jayne Parker	6		LFMC	10.00
So Is This	CAN	1982	Michael Snow	43		LFMC	36.55
Something is Happening	GB	1984	Jones V./Andrews C	15		LFMC	12.75
Somewhere Between Jalostitlan and Encarnation		1984	Phillip Hoffman	6		LFMC	10.00
Son Are You Down There?	GB	1984	Carl Johnson	12		LFMC	10.20
Song About Happiness	GB	1988	Franco Bosisio	17		LFMC	14.45
Songs for Swinging Larvae	USA	1981	Ralph Records	6		LFMC	10.00
Soothing the Bruise	USA	1980	Betzy Bromberg	21		LFMC	17.85
Souffrances d'un Oeuf Meutri, Les	USA	1967	Roland Lethem	19		LFMC	16.15
Soul in a White Room	GB	1967	Simon Hartog	3		LFMC	10.00
Space for Message	GB	1979	M. Browett	30		LFMC	25.50
Spaced	GB	1971-72	Annabel Nicolson			LFMC	10.00
Spanish Banks	GB	1972	Annabel Nicolson	3		LFMC	10.00
Speak	GB	1964	John Latham	11		LFMC	10.00
Spectacular Anonymity Film	GB	1976	George.E.Saxon	10	mag	LFMC	10.00
Spherical Space	USA	1976	Stan Van Der Beek	4	mag	LFMC	10.00

	COUNTRY OF PRODUCTION	YEAR	DIRECTOR	RUNNING TIME	VERSION	16mm	16mm RENTAL FEE
Spider	USA	1979	John Woodman	11		LFMC	10.00
Spiral	USA	1987	Emily Breer	12		LFMC	
Split Decision	USA	1979	Bill Brand	16		LFMC	13.60
Sporting Life, The	GB		Jim Divers	6		LFMC	10.00
Sprocket Holes		1973	Stephen Morrow	11		LFMC	10.00
Square Inch Field	CAN	1968	David Rimmer	11		LFMC	10.00
SSS	USA	1988	Henry Hills	5		LFMC	10.00
St. Therese Part 2			Piero Heliczer	13		LFMC	11.05
Stabat Mater	GB	1990	Nina Danino	8		LFMC	10.00
Stadt in Flammen	CH	1984	Dahlin Schmelz	6		LFMC	10.00
Standard Time	CAN	1967	Michael Snow	8		LFMC	10.00
Star Garden	USA	1974	Stan Brakhage	22	st	LFMC	18.70
Starlight	USA		Bob Fulton	5		LFMC	10.00
Still Andy	GB		Peter Gidal	3		LFMC	10.00
Still Life	GB	1976	Jenny Okun	6		LFMC	10.00
Still Life with Pear	USA		Mike Dunford	12		LFMC	10.20
Stonebridge Park	GB	1981	Patrick Keiller	21		LFMC	17.85
Stones Off Holland	GB	1988	Richard Philpott	8.5		LFMC	10.00
Storm	GB	1980	John Tappenden	11		LFMC	10.00
Straight and Narrow	USA	1970	Tony/Beverly Conrad	10		LFMC	10.00
Streamline	GB	1976	Chris Welsby	8		LFMC	10.00
Structural Studies	USA	1974	Hein Wilhelm/Hein Birgit	40		LFMC	34.00
Structured Walks	GB	1975	Renny Croft	6		LFMC	10.00
Study 16	USA	1990	Lawrence F Brose	1	bw	LFMC	10.00
Subway	GB	1973	David Parsons	10		LFMC	10.00
Summer Diary	GB	1976-77	John Smith	30		LFMC	25.50
Supports	GB	1978	Rob Gawthrop	6		LFMC	10.00
Surfacing on the Thames	CAN	1970	David Rimmer	8	st	LFMC	10.00
Surrounded Islands	GB	1983	Stephen Javor	32		LFMC	27.20
Susan at the Hayward	GB	1975	Annabel Nicolson	3		LFMC	10.00
Swamp	GB	1985	Simon Casel/Lou Marx	20		LFMC	
Swan	GB	1987	Alia Syed	4		LFMC	10.00
Sweet Structure	GB	1972-75	David Parsons	9		LFMC	10.00
Swimmer	GB	1987	Michael Maziere	6		LFMC	10.00
Swiss Army Knife with Rats and Pigeons	USA		Robert Breer	6		LFMC	10.00
Swollen Moo	GB	1985	Lois Davis	3		LFMC	10.00
Sync Sound	GB	1973	Mike Dunford	10		LFMC	10.00
Sync Sound	JAP	1973	Taka Limura	12		LFMC	10.20
T.G. Psychic Rally in Heaven	GB	1981	Derek Jarman	8		LFMC	12.00
T.O.U.C.H.I.N.G.	USA	1969	Paul Sharits	12		LFMC	10.20
Tailpiece	GB	1976	Margaret Tait	10		LFMC	10.00
Tails	USA	1976	Paul Sharits	4		LFMC	10.00
Taking a Line for a Walk	GB	1983	Lesley Keen	11		LFMC	10.00
Tal Farlow	NZ	1980	Len Lye	1		LFMC	10.00
tale part told, A	GB	1991	Turner Sarah	4		LFMC	10.00
Talk			Julian Roberts	13		LFMC	11.50
Talla	GB	1967-68	Malcolm LeGrice	20	st	LFMC	10.00
Tantra 1	CAN		Gordon Payne	6		LFMC	10.00
Taped Sessions	USA	1982	Owen Shapiro	36		LFMC	30.60
Tattooed Man, The	USA	1970	Storm De Hirsch	35		LFMC	29.75
Tautology			Mike Dunford	5		LFMC	10.00
Tea for Two			Al Wong	5		LFMC	10.00
Telling and Showing			Christine Felce	45		LFMC	38.25
Ten Cents a Dance (Parralax)	CAN	1985	Onodera Midix	30		LFMC	25.50
Ten Commandments of Love, The	GB	1979	Cordelia Swann	3		LFMC	10.00
Ten Drawings	GB	1976	Steve Farrer	20		LFMC	17.00
Ten Green Bottles			Marilyn Halford	6		LFMC	10.00
Ten Shots	GB	1973	Richard Woolley	10		LFMC	10.00

	COUNTRY OF PRODUCTION	YEAR	DIRECTOR	RUNNING TIME	VERSION	16mm	16mm RENTAL FEE
Tender Kisses	GB	1972	Mike Leggett	15		LFMC	12.75
Terrible Mother, The	USA	1984	Walter Ungerer	24		LFMC	20.40
Thank You Jesus for the Eternal Present	USA	1973	Owen Land (formerly George Landlow)	5		LFMC	10.00
That Has Been	GB	1984	Nicky Hamlyn	38		LFMC	32.30
That Stage	AUSTR	1990	Houston Steven	33		LFMC	28.05
That's All	GB	1968	Simon Hartog	11		LFMC	10.00
Thatch of Night, The	USA	1990	Stan Brakhage	10	st	LFMC	10.00
The Adjournment			J.L. Blumenfeld/J Wollodarsky	5		LFMC	10.00
Thin Blue Lines	GB	1982	Susan Young	6		LFMC	10.00
Things Being What They Are	GB	1988	Janni Perton	4		LFMC	10.00
Third Reich and Roll	USA	1978	Ralph Records	5		LFMC	10.00
Third Time Never Finishes	USA	1981	Peter Beckman	13	mag	LFMC	11.05
Thirty Sound Situations	POL	1975	Wasko Ryszard	10		LFMC	10.00
Three Mirrors			Diana Mavroleon	23		LFMC	19.55
Three Paces	GB	1989	Alia Syed	12		LFMC	10.20
Three Short Episodes	GB	1980	Rachel Finkelstein	10		LFMC	10.00
Threshold	GB	1972	Malcolm LeGrice	10		LFMC	10.00
Tics	GB	1986	Brian Sharpe	15		LFMC	12.75
Tides	GB	1982	Amy Greenfield	12		LFMC	10.20
Time and Motion Study	GB		Malcolm LeGrice	15		LFMC	12.75
Time of the Locust	USA	1967	Peter Gessner	12		LFMC	10.20
Time Over Again	GB	1991	Lucy Pantelli	23	bw	LFMC	19.55
Timed 1,2,3	JAP	1972	Taka Limura	9		LFMC	10.00
Timelength 1,2,3,4	JAP	1972	Taka Limura	12		LFMC	10.20
Timepiece	GB	1986	David Leister	3	bw	LFMC	10.00
To Eat or Not to Eat	GB		El Glinoer	6		LFMC	10.00
To Grips with the Grit	GB	1984	El Glinoer	20		LFMC	17.00
To See the Fram and Not to See the Frame	JAP		Taka Limura	12		LFMC	10.20
To the Dairy	GB	1975	Annabel Nicolson	3		LFMC	10.00
Tomorrow and Tomorrow – Let Them Swing	W.GER	1974	Margaret Raspe	20		LFMC	17.00
Top Dog Rules O.K.			J. Marcus/C. Powell	15		LFMC	12.75
Torbay Sole	GB	1986	Pauline Wakeham	5		LFMC	10.00
Touch Tone Phone Film	USA	1972	Bill Brand	6		LFMC	10.00
Tournesols, Les	FR	1982	Rose Lowder	3		LFMC	10.00
Traces	NETH	1990	Barbara Meter	16		LFMC	13.60
Track	GB	1980	Martin Sercombe	7		LFMC	10.00
Tracking Cycles	GB	1975	Ron Haselden	12	st	LFMC	10.20
Tractor	USSR	1987	Gleb/Igor Alenikov	12	bw	LFMC	10.20
Tragi-Comedy of Marriage, The	USA	1968	Robert Pike	8		LFMC	10.00
Train Fixation	AUSTR	1977	John Dunkley-Smith	10		LFMC	10.00
Trains of Thought	CAN	1983	Marin Lorne	10		LFMC	10.00
Transitions	CAN	1982	Sternberg Barbara	10		LFMC	10.00
Transmogrification	GB	1980	Anne Rees-Mogg	7	st	LFMC	10.00
Transylvania 1917	GB	1985	Peter Dudar	29		LFMC	24.65
Trapline	GB	1977	Ellie Epp	15		LFMC	12.75
Travelling Circle	GB	1982	El Glinoer	18		LFMC	15.30
Tree	GB	1972	Mike Dunford	9	st	LFMC	4.50
Treefall	CAN	1973	David Rimmer	5		LFMC	10.00
Trees	USA	1960	Kurt Kren	5		LFMC	10.00
Trial Balloons	USA	1983	Robert Breer	5		LFMC	10.00
Triangular	USA		Stan Brakhage	9		LFMC	10.00
Trilogy	GB		Jeff Keen	10		LFMC	10.00
Trio	USA	1976	Stan Brakhage	7		LFMC	10.00
Troilus & Cressida	GB	1982	David Finch	11		LFMC	10.00
True Love	GB	1972	Mike Dunford	9	mag	LFMC	10.00
Tryptichon	GER	1987	Thomas Mank	11	bw	LFMC	10.00
Tung	USA	1966	Bruce Bailli	3	st	LFMC	10.00
Tusalava	NZ	1929	Len Lye	9		LFMC	10.00

	COUNTRY OF PRODUCTION	YEAR	DIRECTOR	RUNNING TIME	VERSION	16mm	16mm RENTAL FEE
Tuxedo Theatre, The	USA	1968	Warren Sonbert	21	st	LFMC	17.85
Twenty-Four Frames per Second	JAP	1975-78	Taka Limura	12		LFMC	10.20
2	W.GER	1975	Helmut Nickels	7		LFMC	10.00
Two Children Threatened By A Nightingale	GB	1986	Joanna Woodward	5		LFMC	10.00
Two Houses	GB	1977-80	Kosmian-Ledward E.	41		LFMC	34.85
2 Mins 46 Sec 16 Frames	JAP	1972	Taka Limura	9		LFMC	10.00
Two Space	US	1984	Larry Cuba	8		LFMC	10.00
Types	GB	1975	John Du Cane	18	st	LFMC	15.30
TZ	USA		Robert Breer	8		LFMC	10.00
Ubi Est Terram Ooobiae (Part 2)	USA		Walter Ungerer	5		LFMC	10.00
Un Chant d'Amour	FR	1950	Jean Genet	23		LFMC	19.55
Uncertainty	GB	1987	Nicky Hamlyn	24		LFMC	20.40
Unconscious London Strata	USA	1979-82	Stan Brakhage	20		LFMC	17.00
Und Sie	W.GER	1967	Hein Wilhelm/Hein Birgit	11		LFMC	10.00
Underground Movie			Tim Bruce	12		LFMC	10.20
Underground, The	GB	1983	Richard Philpott	6		LFMC	10.00
Unfolding	GB	1989	Alia Syed	14		LFMC	11.90
Unknown Woman	GB	1991	Kayla Parker	9		LFMC	10.00
Unreachable Homeless	W.GER	1978	Klaus Wyborny	25	st	LFMC	21.25
Unsere Afrikareise	AUST	1966	Peter Kubelka	12		LFMC	10.20
Unspoken	GB	1987	Michael Maziere	9		LFMC	10.00
Untitled	GB	1979	Peter Gidal	8		LFMC	10.00
Untitled	GB		Nicky Hamlyn	8		LFMC	10.00
Untitled	GB	1980	Michael Maziere	18		LFMC	15.30
Untitled (1975)	W.GER	1975	Helmut Nickels	9		LFMC	10.00
Untitled (1976/77)	W.GER	1976-77	Helmut Nickels	4		LFMC	10.00
Untitled (1981)	W.GER	1981	Helmut Nickels	10		LFMC	10.00
Untitled (Arakelian)			Francine Arakelian	5		LFMC	10.00
Untitled (Broadgate)	GB		William English	8		LFMC	10.00
Untitled IV, 5	W.GER		Helmut Nickels	11		LFMC	10.00
Upstairs, Inside	CAN	1984-5	Kathleen Maitland-Carter	7		LFMC	10.00
Uranium Hex	GB	1987	Sandra Lahire	11		LFMC	10.00
Urban Fire			Carl Brown	15		LFMC	12.75
Urban Peasants	USA	1976	Ken Jacobs	40		LFMC	34.00
Us Down by the Riverside	USA	1966	Jud Yalkut	3		LFMC	10.00
Vache Qui Rumine, La	FR	1970	George Rey	3	st	LFMC	10.00
Vacuum			Michael Denton	4		LFMC	10.00
Valentin de las Sierras	USA	1967	Bruce Baillie	10		LFMC	10.00
Valley Fever	USA	1975	Stephanie Beroes	25		LFMC	21.25
Valse Triste	USA	1978	Bruce Conner	5		LFMC	10.00
Valtos	GB	1987	Patrick Keiller	11		LFMC	10.00
Vampire de la Cinematheque, Le	BEL	1971	Roland Lethem	16		LFMC	13.60
Variant	GB	1973	John Du Cane	14		LFMC	11.90
Verifica Incerta, La	IT	1967	Gianfranco Barucello	45		LFMC	38.25
Versailles	GB	1976	Chris Garratt	11		LFMC	10.00
View	GB	1970	William Raban	4	mag	LFMC	10.00
View from Reardon	GB	1980	Tim Bruce	16		LFMC	13.60
Views from Ilford Hill	USA	1982-83	Joanna Millet	11		LFMC	10.00
Visible Compendium, The	USA	1991	Larry Jordan	17		LFMC	20.00
Visible Inventory 6: Motel Dissolve	USA	1978	Janis Crystal Lipzin	15		LFMC	12.75
Vision		1984	Colin Brady	3		LFMC	10.00
Vision in Meditation 2: Mesa Verda	USA	1989	Stan Brakhage	20	st	LFMC	17.00
Vision in Meditation 4: D.H. Lawrence	USA	1990	Stan Brakhage	20	st	LFMC	17.00
Vision of the Fire Tree	USA	1991	Stan Brakhage	5	st	LFMC	10.00
Visions in Meditation 3: Plato's Cave	USA		Stan Brakhage	20		LFMC	17.00
Visions of a City	USA	1957-78	Larry Jordan	8		LFMC	10.00
Visit	GB	1976	Tim Bruce	10		LFMC	10.00
Visitor's London			Monika Fabig	12		LFMC	10.20

	COUNTRY OF PRODUCTION	YEAR	DIRECTOR	RUNNING TIME	VERSION	16mm	16mm RENTAL FEE
Vistasound	GB	1977-81	Mike Leggett	45		LFMC	38.25
Voyeuristic Tendencies	USA	1984	Dominic Angerame	20		LFMC	17.00
W Hole	GB	1972	Mike Leggett	8	mag	LFMC	10.00
Waiting			Kosmian-Ledward E.	5		LFMC	10.00
Walk	GB	1990	Christian Anstice	8		LFMC	10.00
Wall Support	GB	1977	George Saxon	10	mag	LFMC	10.00
War Songs	USA	1990	Lawrence F Brose	12	bw	LFMC	10.20
Washington Cat	USA		Robert Bundy	5		LFMC	10.00
Water Colour	GB	1982	Joanna Millet	9		LFMC	10.00
Water Colours	GB	1982	Mike Collier	20		LFMC	17.00
Waterfall	USA	1980	David Hilton	28		LFMC	23.80
Waterway	GB	1976	Richard Welsby	5	st	LFMC	10.00
Waterworx	CA	1985	Rick Hancox	6		LFMC	10.00
Wavelength	USA	1966-67	Michael Snow	45		LFMC	38.25
Waves			Obern Vaughan	3		LFMC	10.00
Waves and Graves	GB	1984-91	David Leister	14	bw	LFMC	11.90
Way to the Shadow Garden, The	USA	1955	Stan Brakhage	12		LFMC	10.20
We Shall March Again	USA	1965	Lenny Lipton	10		LFMC	10.00
Wende	NETH	1985	Claudia Kolgen	8		LFMC	10.00
Western American Impressions	CA	1985	Peter Lipskis	20		LFMC	17.00
Western Gothic, The			Sandra Meigs	5		LFMC	10.00
Western History	USA	1971	Stan Brakhage	8		LFMC	10.00
Wet Decks	GB	1986	Will Milne	20		LFMC	17.00
What Just for Me?	USA	1979	Deborah Lowensberg	24		LFMC	20.40
What Mozart Saw on Mulberry Street, The	USA	1955	Joseph Cornell	11		LFMC	10.00
What People Do	GB	1981	Andrew McKay	22		LFMC	18.70
What's Wrong With This Picture?	USA	1972	Owen Land (formerly George Landlow)	5		LFMC	10.00
Whitchurch Down (Duration)	GB	1972	Malcolm LeGrice	8		LFMC	10.00
White Calligraphy	JAP	1967	Taka Limura	12		LFMC	10.20
White Dust	GB	1984	Jeff Keen	16		LFMC	13.60
Who Do You Think You Are?	USA	1987	Mary Filippo	10	bw	LFMC	10.00
Who Needs Full Colour When Real Life is So Black and White	GB	1984	Annabel Hands	30		LFMC	25.50
Wide Angle Saxon	USA	1974	Owen Land (formerly George Landlow)	22		LFMC	18.70
Wife, The	GB	1981	Brenda Horsman	12		LFMC	10.20
Wind up Working in a Gas Station	GB	1976-79	Jaffer Mohammed	6		LFMC	10.00
Wind-Up	USA	1985	David Leister	12		LFMC	10.20
Window	USA	1976	Stan Brakhage	11		LFMC	10.00
Window Water Baby	USA	1959	Stan Brakhage	12	st	LFMC	10.20
Winter	USA	1964-66	David Brooks	6		LFMC	10.00
Winter Epitaph for Michael Furey	CAN	1967	W. Wees	6		LFMC	10.00
Witches Cradle Out-takes	USA	1943	Maya Deren	10		LFMC	10.00
Woman, A			Kosmian-Ledward E.	11		LFMC	10.00
Women of Morocco			Victor Musgrave	10		LFMC	10.00
Wonder Ring, The	USA	1955	Stan Brakhage	6		LFMC	10.00
Word Movie	USA	1966	Paul Sharits	4		LFMC	10.00
Word, The	GB	1979	A Soma. (Formerly J. Apps)	9		LFMC	10.00
Work in London (March 1972)			Ken McMullen			LFMC	
Work in Progress Teil A	W.GER	1967-70	Hein Wilhelm/Hein Birgit	46	mag	LFMC	39.10
Works for a Diarama			Steve Farrer	12		LFMC	10.20
Works in the Field	USA	1978	Bill Brand	45		LFMC	38.25
World			Jordon Belson	10		LFMC	10.00
World in Focus	CAN	1976	Vincent Grenier	20	st	LFMC	17.00
World Turned Upside	GB	1985	Peter Milner	10		LFMC	10.00
X	CAN	1976	Vincent Grenier	9	st	LFMC	6.50
X Requests	CAN	1976	Andrew Fisher/Michael Newman	15		LFMC	12.75
Yelling Fire	CAN	1980	Robert Rayher	5		LFMC	10.00
Yes No Maybe Not	GB	1967	Malcolm LeGrice	8		LFMC	10.00
Ying Yang			Marilyn Halford	5		LFMC	10.00

LFMC

	COUNTRY OF PRODUCTION	YEAR	DIRECTOR	RUNNING TIME	VERSION	16mm	16mm RENTAL FEE
You Take Care Now	CAN	1990	Ann Marie Fleming	10		LFMC	10.00
Young Girl in Blue, The	GB	1978-79	Penny Webb	19		LFMC	16.15
Yyaa	POL	1973	Bruszewski Wojciech	5		LFMC	10.00
Zalongos	GB	1989	Sophia Phoca	8	bw	LFMC	10.00
Zeitaufnahmen			Kurt Kren	3		LFMC	10.00
Zeno's Arrow			Sarah Child	5		LFMC	10.00
Zoom Lapse	GB	1980	John Du Cane	15		LFMC	12.75

Mainline

	COUNTRY OF PRODUCTION	YEAR	DIRECTOR	RUNNING TIME	VERSION	16mm	16mm RENTAL FEE
Broken English – 3 songs by Marianne Faithful	GB	1979	Derek Jarman	14		Mainline	15.00
London Calling/	GB	1980	Don Letts/Mick Calvert	15		Mainline	30.00
Pop Group,The/	GB	1979	Don Letts/Mick Calvert	12		Mainline	30.00
Slits, The	GB	1979	Don Letts/Mick Calvert	24		Mainline	30.00

MP

	COUNTRY OF PRODUCTION	YEAR	DIRECTOR	RUNNING TIME	VERSION	16mm	16mm RENTAL FEE
A Turnip Head's Guide to Alan Parker	GB	1987	Arthur Ellis	8		MP	17.25
Blood Ah Goh Run	GB	1982	Kuumba Black Arts	20		MP	23.00
Borom Sarret (The Cartdriver)	SEN	1964	Ousmane Sembene	20	est	MP	23.00
Chircales (The Brickmakers)	COL	1972	Marta Rodriguez/George Silva	42	bw	MP	23.00
Chuck Norris – The Man, His Music	GB	1987	Arthur Ellis	15		MP	17.25
Controlling Interest	USA	1977	California Newsreel	45		MP	28.75
Don't Eat Today or Tomorrow	NETH	1985	Rob Hof	41		MP	34.50
El Salvador: In the Name of Democracy	EL SAL/USA	1983-84	Salvadorian Film Institute	29		MP	23.00
For the First Time	CB	1967	Octavio Cortazar	12	bw	MP	15.00
Girl She is 100%, The	JAP	1983	Yamakowa Naoto	11	bw/est	MP	12.25
In the Skies Wild Noise	GUY/USA	1983	Lewanne Jones	28		MP	23.00
It Aint Half Racist Mum	GB	1978	Campaign Against Racism In the Media (CARM)	30		MP	23.00
Malcolm X – Struggle for Freedom	USA	1965	John Taylor/Lebert Bethune	25		MP	23.00
No Place to Hide	USA	1982	Tom Johnson/Lance Bird	30		MP	28.75
Operacion La	USA	1982	Anna-Maria Garcia	39		MP	28.75
Real Thing, The	USA	1984	Peter Schnall	36		MP	34.50
Starting From Nina – the Politics of Education	CAN	1978	Development Education Centre Canada	30		MP	23.00
Step Forward Youth	GB	1977	Menelik Shabazz	30		MP	23.00
TAAW	SEN	1979	Ousmane Sembene	26	est	MP	27.60
Union Maids	USA	1975	Julia Klein/Jim Reichert	45	bw	MP	25.30
Violation	AUSTR	1980	Beth McRae	27		MP	23.00
With Babies and Banners	USA	1978	Lorraine Grey Women's Labour History Film Project	45		MP	27.60
Women in Arms	NIC/USA	1980	Victoria Shultz	30		MP	23.00
You Have Struck a Rock	USA	1981	Deborah May	28		MP	23.00

SCFL

	COUNTRY OF PRODUCTION	YEAR	DIRECTOR	RUNNING TIME	VERSION	16mm	16mm RENTAL FEE
Band Concert	USA	1935	Wilfred Jackson	9		SCFL	7.74
Critic, The	USA		Ernest Pintoff Cartoon	4		SCFL	2.50
Dear Green Place	GB	1967	Michael Pavett/Oscar Marzroli	15		SCFL	8
Donegals, The	GB	1977	Mike Alexander	27		SCFL	5
Emperor's New Armour, The	USA	1970	R.O. Blechman	6		SCFL	3.50
Field of Honor	USA	1974	Robert Zemeckis	14		SCFL	5.25
Fog	USA	1972		9		SCFL	3.50
Goodbye Uncle	GB	1980	Norman Pollock	44		SCFL	14

SG	COUNTRY OF PRODUCTION	YEAR	DIRECTOR	RUNNING TIME	VERSION	16mm	16mm RENTAL FEE
Art Horses	GB	1985	Sheila Graber	3		SG	11
Be a Good Neighbour	GB		Sheila Graber	5		SG	11
Beginning of the Armadillos	GB	1981	Sheila Graber	10		SG	11
Bio and Bones	GB	1986	Sheila Graber	10		SG	11
Boy and the Cat	GB	1975	Sheila Graber	10		SG	11
Boy and the Song	GB	1976	Sheila Graber	5		SG	11
Cat and the Tune	GB	1977	Sheila Graber	4		SG	11
Christmas Round the World	GB	1978	Sheila Graber	5		SG	11
Dance Macabre	GB	1982	Sheila Graber	5		SG	11
Evolution	GB	1979	Sheila Graber	4		SG	11
Expressionism	GB	1980	Sheila Graber	5		SG	11
Face to Face	GB	1980	Sheila Graber	4		SG	11
Four Views of Landscape	GB	1976	Sheila Graber	4		SG	11
Gilbert & Sullivan-Mod.Major Gen and When I Went to the Bar	GB	1975	Sheila Graber	7		SG	11
Heidi's Horse	GB	1987	Sheila Graber	17		SG	11
Henry Moore	GB	1982	Sheila Graber	6		SG	11
How the Camel got his Hump	GB	1981	Sheila Graber	10		SG	11
How the Leopard got his Spots	GB	1981	Sheila Graber	10		SG	11
How the Rhino Got his Skin	GB	1981	Sheila Graber	10		SG	11
How the Whale got his Throat	GB	1981	Sheila Graber	10		SG	11
Howway the Lasses	GB	1977	Sheila Graber	3		SG	11
Inside Look North	GB	1977	Sheila Graber	4		SG	11
Lady of Shallott	GB	1976	Sheila Graber	5		SG	11
Larn Yersel' Geordie	GB	1979	Sheila Graber	10		SG	11
Leonardo da Vinci	GB	1982	Sheila Graber	4		SG	11
Marking Time	GB	1978	Sheila Graber	4		SG	11
Michelangelo	GB	1975	Sheila Graber	4		SG	11
Mondrian	GB	1978	Sheila Graber	3		SG	11
Moving On	GB	1976	Sheila Graber	4		SG	11
My River Tyne	GB	1986	Sheila Graber	10		SG	11
New Year Round the World	GB	1986	Sheila Graber	10		SG	11
Phil the Fluter's Ball	GB	1977	Sheila Graber	5		SG	11
Sing-Song of Old Man Kangaroo	GB	1981	Sheila Graber	10		SG	11
The Butterfly that Stamped	GB	1981	Sheila Graber	10		SG	11
The Cat that Walked Alone	GB	1981	Sheila Graber	15		SG	11
The Crab that Played with the Sea	GB	1981	Sheila Graber	10		SG	11
The Elephant's Child	GB	1981	Sheila Graber	11		SG	11
The Face in Art	GB	1982	Sheila Graber	5		SG	11
Toys will be Toys	GB	1989	Sheila Graber	5		SG	11
Twelve Days of Christmas	GB	1975	Sheila Graber	5		SG	11
William Blake	GB	1978	Sheila Graber	5		SG	11

WFA

	COUNTRY OF PRODUCTION	YEAR	DIRECTOR	RUNNING TIME	VERSION	16mm	16mm RENTAL FEE
Abortion Film, The	USA	1977	Cambridgeport Film Corp	22		WFA	7.70
Agrindus Way, The	GB	1973	War On Want	24		WFA	12.20
Away With All Pests	USA	1972	Blue Bus [Prod Co]	27		WFA	23.00
Blow Hard	CAN	1979	National Film Board	9		WFA	6.00
Bottle Babies	GER	1975	Peter Krieg	28		WFA	14.00
Chaplin Extracts	USA		Charles Chaplin	40		WFA	5.00
Cock Crows AT Midnight	CHI	1965	China Film Corp	15		WFA	6.00
Controlling Interests	USA	1977	Larry Adleman	45		WFA	21.00
Day Of The Land	PAL/LEB	1978	Samed [Prod Co]	40		WFA	23.40
Doctor Ma Hai Teh	GB	1979	Felix Greene	40		WFA	12.00
Dread Beat An' Blood	GB	1978	Franco Rosso	45		WFA	22.00
Easy Pill To Swallow, An	CAN	1979	Robert Lang	28		WFA	14.00
Eritrea '79 [The Strategic Withdrawal]	ERI	1979	EPLF Cine Prod Unit	20		WFA	12.20
Guatemala – After The Earthquake	GB	1976	David Elstein	30		WFA	12.20
History Book, The (nine chapters)	DEN	1974	J. Hastrup	15		WFA	
I Am Somebody	USA	1970	Madelyn Anderson	28		WFA	15.00
In The Bank	USA	1915	Charles Chaplin	10		WFA	5.00
Into The Mouths Of Babes	USA	1978	Ken Sable	30		WFA	14.40
Key, The	PAL	1976	Ghaleb Chaath	30		WFA	17.80
Last Grave At Dimbaza	GB	1974	Nana Mahano-Morena Films	55		WFA	24.00
Misery Au Borinage	BEL	1933	Joris Ivens	26		WFA	20.00
New Technology: Whose Progress?	GB	1980	Education Media	35		WFA	21.00
No Act Of God	CAN	1977	National Film Board	30		WFA	12.20
Nursing: The Politics Of Caring	USA	1977	Joan Finch/Timothy Sawyer	22		WFA	14.00
Protected	AUST	1976	Alessandro Cavadini	56		WFA	14.40
Rent Collection Courtyard	GER	1973	Peter Krieg	12		WFA	6.60
Rhodesia: The Other Side	NETH	1977	Roeland Kerbosch	22		WFA	12.20
Sisters Of The Grassland	CHI	1973	China Nat Film Corp	45		WFA	16.60
Smoking: A Double Standard	GB	1978	Mike Gillard	30		WFA	12.20
Taking Our Bodies Back	USA	1977	Margaret Lazurus	33		WFA	14.40
Tea Machine, The	GB	1980	John Crumpton	20		WFA	10.50
Tilt	CAN	1972	Don Arioli	19		WFA	6.60
Tomorrow's Epidemic	UN	1980	Freidrich Puhl	15		WFA	12.20
We've Always Done It This Way	GB	1978	Alan Bell	50		WFA	23.40
Who Will Be Sentenced Now?	CAN	1978	Boyce Richardson/David Newman	29		WFA	12.20
Women & Revolution in Eritrea	GER	1981	Gordian Troller/C. Defferge	40		WFA	21.00
You Hide Me	GB	1972	Kwate Nee Owoo	25		WFA	10.00

X Scarlett Street.

View for the Bridge.

The Detective.   Std only.

X The Sweet Smell of Success ← Dott Cum
   the Lady Vanishes. (Vincent Price).

The Anniversary.
The phantom tollbooth.
Cape Fear.

✓ The Big Heat.   (Lee marvin).
         (Fritz Lang?).
Hang my Gallows high
or   Out of the Best.   (Mitchum).
      Raising Arizona £50
→ Parralax View. Std.

✓ Hang em high

   Our Man in Hawaii ←
✓ Night of the iguana. Std.
   the Long hot summer. Std. ✓
   man in the white suit Std. ✓